T0331831

Multiple Sensorial Media Advances and Applications:

New Developments in MulSeMedia

George Ghinea
Brunel University, UK

Frederic Andres
CVCE, Luxembourg & NII, Japan

Stephen Gulliver
University of Reading, UK

Senior Editorial Director:	Kristin Klinger
Director of Book Publications:	Julia Mosemann
Editorial Director:	Lindsay Johnston
Acquisitions Editor:	Erika Carter
Development Editor:	Michael Killian
Production Editor:	Sean Woznicki
Typesetters:	Mike Brehm, Jennifer Romachak
Print Coordinator:	Jamie Snavely
Cover Design:	Nick Newcomer

Published in the United States of America by
Information Science Reference (an imprint of IGI Global)
701 E. Chocolate Avenue
Hershey PA 17033
Tel: 717-533-8845
Fax: 717-533-8661
E-mail: cust@igi-global.com
Web site: http://www.igi-global.com

Library of Congress Cataloging-in-Publication Data

Multiple sensorial media advances and applications: new developments in MulSeMedia / George Ghinea, Frederic Andres, and Stephen Gulliver, editors.
    p. cm.
  Includes bibliographical references and index.
  Summary: "This book provides a comprehensive compilation of knowledge covering state-of-the-art developments and research, as well as current innovative activities in Multiple Sensorial Media and its importance in media design"--Provided by publisher.
  ISBN 978-1-60960-821-7 (hardcover) -- ISBN 978-1-60960-822-4 (ebook) -- ISBN 978-1-60960-823-1 (print & perpetual access) 1. Multimedia systems. 2. Senses and sensation. I. Ghinea, George, 1970- II. Andres, Frederic, 1962- III. Gulliver, Stephen.
  QA76.575.M858 2012
  006.7--dc23
                        2011024049

British Cataloguing in Publication Data
A Cataloguing in Publication record for this book is available from the British Library.

All work contributed to this book is new, previously-unpublished material. The views expressed in this book are those of the authors, but not necessarily of the publisher.

List of Reviewers

Tacha Serif
Oluwakemi Ademoye
Fotis Spyridonis
Roberto Fraile
Daniel Garcia
Tor-morten Gronli
Fernando Ferri
Rajkumar Kannan
Jarle Hansen
Amit Sheth
Sethuraman Panchanathan

Table of Contents

Section 3
MulSeMedia Interfaces

Section 4
MulSeMedia Applications

Detailed Table of Contents

Section 1
Multiple Senses and Consideration of Presence

Alberto Gallace, University of Milano-Bicocca, Italy
Mary K. Ngo, University of Oxford, UK
John Sulaitis, Bunnyfoot Ltd, Harwell, UK
Charles Spence, University of Oxford, UK

Research that has been conducted to date has convincingly shown that increasing the number of senses stimulated in a Virtual Reality (VR) simulator can dramatically enhance a user's sense of presence, their enjoyment, and even their memory for the encounter/experience. In this chapter, the authors highlight some of the most exciting potential applications associated with MulSeMedia while in a simulated environment. They then review the key technical challenges associated with stimulating multiple senses in a VR setting, focusing on the particular problems associated with the stimulation of the senses of touch, smell, and taste. Finally, they discuss how the findings provided by the extant research in the cognitive neurosciences might help to overcome, at least in part, some of the cognitive and technological limitations affecting the development of multisensory VR systems.

Helen Farley, University of Southern Queensland, Australia
Caroline Steel, University of Queensland, Australia

Immersion has been defined as the 'the subjective impression that one is participating in a comprehensive, realistic experience', and is seen as a necessary condition for 'presence'. This chapter will look at those characteristics of the MulSeMedia experience which facilitate immersion in three-dimensional virtual environments including Multi-user Virtual Environments (MUVEs) such as Second Life, Massively Multiplayer Online Role-playing games (MMORPGs) such as World of Warcraft, and various three-dimensional simulations.

Section 2
Individual Difference, Perception and Culture

Chapter 3

Markos Kyritsis, Brunel University, UK
Stephen Gulliver, University of Reading, UK

Learning the spatial layout of an environment is essential in application domains including military and emergency personnel training. Training each and every member of staff, however, within a real-world space cannot practically be achieved, especially if the space is under-development or potentially unsafe. The aim of this chapter is to demonstrate how individual difference factors can significantly impact upon training requirements when acquiring spatial knowledge from a virtual environment. Focusing on dimensions such as gender, orientation skill, cognitive style, system knowledge, and environmental knowledge, the authors show how individual user differences significantly influence the training time required to ensure effective virtual environment spatial knowledge acquisition.

Chapter 4

Simon Hayhoe, London School of Economics, UK

This chapter describes an investigation into the premise that blind programmers and web-developers can create modern Graphical User Interfaces through perceptions of MulSeMedia, and whether perceptual culture has a role in this understanding. Its purpose it to: 1) investigate whether the understanding of computer interfaces is related to perceptual culture as well as perceptual ability; 2) investigate whether it is possible for a person who has never seen to understand visual concepts in informational technology through non-visual senses and memories; and 3) provoke questions as to the nature of computer interfaces, and whether they can ever be regarded as MulSeMedia style interfaces.

Chapter 5

Maria Chiara Caschera, Istituto di Ricerche sulla Popolazione e le Politiche Sociali, Italy
Arianna D'Ulizia, Istituto di Ricerche sulla Popolazione e le Politiche Sociali, Italy
Fernando Ferri, Istituto di Ricerche sulla Popolazione e le Politiche Sociali, Italy
Patrizia Grifoni, Istituto di Ricerche sulla Popolazione e le Politiche Sociali, Italy

There is a growing research activity that explores how to consider cultural issues during the design of multimodal interaction systems. This chapter is focused on such a challenging topic, proposing a grammatical approach representing multicultural issues in multimodal languages. The approach is based on a grammar, that is able to produce a set of structured sentences, composed of gestural, vocal, audio, graphical symbols, and so on, along with the meaning that these symbols have in the different cultures.

This chapter describes an interaction technique wherein web pages are parsed so as to automatically generate a corresponding 3D virtual environment with haptic feedback. The automatically created 3D scene is composed of "hapgets" (haptically-enhanced widgets), which are three dimensional widgets providing a behavior that is analogous to the behavior of the original HTML components but are also enhanced with haptic feedback. Moreover, for each 2D map included in a web page a corresponding multimodal (haptic-aural) map is automatically generated. The proposed interaction technique enables the haptic navigation through the internet as well as the haptic exploration of conventional 2D maps for the visually impaired users.

Chapter 7

Olfaction is now becoming available in MulSeMedia because of recent progress of an olfactory display. One of the important functions of the olfactory display is to blend multiple of odor components to create a variety of odors. The authors have developed an olfactory display to blend up to 32 odor components using solenoid valves. High -speed switching of a solenoid valve enables us to blend many odors instantaneously at any recipe even if the solenoid valve has only two states such as ON and OFF. Since it is compact and is easy to use, it has been so far used to demonstrate a movie, an animation and a game with scents, and this chapter presents these endeavours.

In a field of application of VR technologies, lots of multi-sensory entertainments have been developed. Researchers have been trying not only to develop the haptic, tactile, olfactory, and taste displays individually, but also to represent subtle sensations with combinations of multiple displays. In this chapter, the authors introduce three entertainment applications which utilize multi-sensory stimulation for representing and improving the reality of virtual worlds. (1) Haptic Canvas: An entertainment system with dilatant fluid based haptic device, (2) Fragra: An entertainment system with a hand-mounted olfaction display, and (3) Invisible: An entertainment system that reproduce presence of virtual creatures by indirect information.

Chapter 9

Tom A. F. Anderson, Flinders University of South Australia, Australia

Zhi-Hong Chen, National Central University, Taiwan

Yean-Fu Wen, National Chiayi University, Taiwan

Marissa Milne, Flinders University of South Australia, Australia

Adham Atyabi, Flinders University of South Australia, Australia

Kenneth Treharne, Flinders University of South Australia, Australia

Takeshi Matsumoto, Flinders University of South Australia, Australia

Xi-Bin Jia, Beijing University of Technology, China P.R.C

Martin Luerssen, Flinders University of South Australia, Australia

Trent Lewis, Flinders University of South Australia, Australia

Richard Leibbrandt, Flinders University of South Australia, Australia

David M. W. Powers, Flinders University of South Australia, Australia

The Thinking Head is an embodied conversational agent that be used in intelligent tutoring systems as the representation of a teacher and tutor for one-on-one computer learning and teaching. Although there are many applications that benefit from an embodied conversational agent and there has been a push in the research community towards improving embodied conversational agents, the authors' main area of research lies in the creation of applications for second language learning. They have explored speech synthesis and speech recognition to permit users to interact with computer systems with their voices. To facilitate language learning through conversation, they have incorporated these auditory capabilities into the Thinking Head; additionally, the authors seek to create a bridge between the virtual and physical worlds through physical manipulation, achieved primarily through visual input recognition with affordable devices such as webcams.

Chapter 10

George Ghinea, Brunel University, UK

Oluwakemi Ademoye, Brunel University, UK

In MulSeMedia, together with the auditory and visual senses, it is envisaged that the olfactory will increasingly be employed, especially so with the increase in computing processing abilities and in the sophistication of olfactory devices employed. It is not surprising, however, that there are still many unanswered questions in the use of olfaction in MulSeMedia. Accordingly in this chapter the authors present the results of an empirical study which explored one such question, namely does the correct association of scent and content enhance the user experience of multimedia applications?')

Virtual reality applications and immersive environments provide an ideal test bed for the integration of multiple sensory cues. This is due to the goal of VR simulation environments to copy reality as good as possible and this again is due to the nature of human users who are relating their reactions and behavior on the evaluation of several sensory cues. Therefore, the integration of multimedia sensory cues is considered as an integral objective of any virtual reality application to allow addressing multiple sensors for human users. This chapter describes an immersive bicycle simulator called FIVISquare. Sensory feedback from skin, muscles, and joints are integrated within this virtual reality visualization environment. By doing this it allows for simulating otherwise dangerous traffic situations in a controlled laboratory environment.

Chapter 12

In this chapter, the authors mainly focus on combining the primary and collateral modalities of the information resource in an intelligent and effective way in order to provide better multimodal information understanding, classification, labelling and retrieval. Image and text are the two modalities we mainly talk about here. A novel framework for semantic-based collaterally cued image labelling had been proposed and implemented, aiming to automatically assign linguistic keywords to regions of interest in an image.

Chapter 13

The study described in this chapter analyzes social and conceptual evolutions of digital media and proposes an interactive mixed-space media model which communicates the information contents and enhances the user experience between interactive space of physical objects and online virtual space. Its feedback gives information through user performance among its MulSeMedia interfaces. The research widens previous research publications, and precisely gives a definition of a fuzzy logic cognitive and emotional perception level to the metaplastic multimedia model. It augments the interaction quality within its conceptual media space through an action-making loop and gives as a result new contents of information within its metaplastic metaspace configurations.

Preface

INTRODUCTION

The term 'multimedia' is often used, however formal definitions for 'multimedia' vary significantly. In the fields of art and education, multimedia is the act of 'using more than one medium of expression or communication' (oxford dictionary online). In the domain of computing it is the 'incorporating of audio and video, especially interactively' (oxford dictionary online). The problem is that, as well as conflicting, such definitions provide limited distinction from traditional methods of information dissemination.

Multimedia involves the issues of media and content, and relates to the uses of a combination of different content forms, yet it unclear how 'multimedia', a term coined in 1966 by Bob Goldsteinn, is really distinct from many other communication methods. Traditional communication methods, such as theatre, a lecture or even an open debate, involve the use of multiple forms of communication, e.g. inclusion of music, drama, speech, text, demonstration and non-verbal expression, etc. Some claim that 'multimedia' is distinct as it is does not relate to traditional forms of printed or hand-produced material, yet most modern newspapers include text and still images; which taken literally is also the use of multiple content forms. It may be argued that multimedia must be multimodal, i.e. include multiple communication modes, however this argument is hard to justify when multiple content forms (e.g. video and text) can be contained in the single file and will be perceived using the same user senses.

The confliction in definitions raises the concerning question: What value does limited sensory multimedia provide? This overly dismissing question is clearly without value, since the research under the banner of 'multimedia' has brought significant progress and development. In the creative industries 'multimedia' development has supported the creation of new art-forms, the instant dissemination of news and social comment, art and media. Digital video technologies now monopolies the dissemination of television and have changed the future of video and film distribution and business models. In the area of commerce 'multimedia' has supported globalization, customer interaction, work-practises via increase use of remote, and pervasive working. In education, 'multimedia' has supported the visualization and teaching of multidimensional teaching material, the development of remote computer-based training, which increases both the flexibility of and accessibility of educational structures. 'multimedia' interfaces are common place, and have been introduced into all areas of our lives - from the latest smart phone in your pocket to the self checkout in your local supermarket. The increasing dependence on online and automated services means that the business of the future will depend significantly on user interaction via computer-based interactive and 'multimedia' systems. Although it is clear that multimedia has provided considerable benefits to man-kind, the common range of sensory interaction with users is surprisingly limited.

Human senses are the physiological capacities that provide an input for perception. Traditionally humans were defined as having five senses (i.e. sight, hearing, taste, smell and touch), however increased research in the field of perception has increased this list to include senses, such as balance, acceleration, temperature, pain, proprioception, etc. In 1955 Morton Heilig wrote a paper entitled 'The Cinema of the Future', in which he detailed his vision of multi-sensory theatre. In 1962 he built a prototype of his vision, dubbed sensorama, which was able to display wide-angled stereoscopic 3D images, provide body tilting, supply stereo sound, and also provide users with wind and aroma feedback during the film. Heilig was unable to obtain financial backing, so work with Sensorama was halted. Multimedia applications and research has subsequently primarily focused on two human senses, i.e. audio and visual sense. This consistent reliance on visual and audio mediums has removed investment and interest from the complex interplay between physical senses and has limited multiple sensory research to a limited range of high cost research domains.

Interestingly, advances in computational and device technologies, combined with the commercial success and acceptance of 3D and haptic media presentation devices (e.g. 3D cinema and the Nintendo Wii), has increased commercial interest in engaging additional senses within the multimedia experience. This integration is leading to a paradigm shift away from traditionally defined 'multimedia' systems towards more interactive MulSeMedia system – multiple sensory media's. Many would define MulSeMedia systems as 'muli-modal' systems, however this is not fair. Not all multimodal systems are by definition multi-sensory, yet MulSeMedia must be multimodal by definition.

MulSeMedia is, therefore, a new term which recognizes that traditional multimedia or multimodal applications need to be thought of in a new light in the 21st century. One might even argue that for the vast majority of cases, the term 'multimedia' is, in actual fact, a misnomer, since only two-types of media (video and audio) are actually used. So, in this case, *bi-media* might actually be a more accurate reflection of the situation. A similar comment could apply to multi-modal applications, as most employ a binary combination of visual, audio or haptic modalities; again *bi-modal* is probably more suited in these cases.

We are, of course, interested in MulSeMedia, and, with the publication of this book, wish to highlight the variety of work that is done in the area. We believe we have exciting, high quality contributions from a wide variety of researchers involved in the area – MulSeMedia is happening in all corners of the world, and it is happening now.

BOOK STRUCTURE

This book is structured into four key areas which: 1. introduce to the need and benefits of multisensory systems; 2. expands upon the importance of multisensory systems when interacting with a range of individuals, giving specific consideration to individual differences, physical perception and user culture; 3. introduces research concerning haptic and olfactory MulSeMedia interfaces; 4. investigates a range of practical MulSeMedia applications, i.e. entertainment, education, research, semantic interpretation and media modeling. The structure of sections and book chapters is defined below:

1. Multiple senses and consideration of presence.
    - Chapter 1 - Multisensory Presence in Virtual Reality: Possibilities & Limitations.
    - Chapter 2 - Multiple Sensorial Media and Presence in 3D Environments.

2. Individual difference, perception and culture.
   ◦ Chapter 3 - Appreciating Individual Differences: Exposure time requirements in Virtual Space.
   ◦ Chapter 4 - Non-Visual Programming, Perceptual Culture and MulSeMedia: Case studies.
   ◦ Chapter 5 - Multiculturality and Multimodal Languages.
3. MulSeMedia interfaces
   ◦ Chapter 6 - Haptic rendering of HTML components and 2D maps included in web pages.
   ◦ Chapter 7 - Olfactory Display Using Solenoid Valves and Fluid Dynamics Simulation.
4. MulSeMedia applications
   ◦ VR: Chapter 8 - Entertainment Media Arts with Multi-Sensory Interaction.
   ◦ Education: Chapter 9 - Thinking Head MulSeMedia – A Storytelling Environment for Embodied Language Learning.
   ◦ Research: Chapter 10 - User Perception of Media Content Association in Olfaction-Enhanced Multimedia
   ◦ Research: Chapter 11 - Multimedia Sensory Cue Processing in the FIVIS Simulation Environment.
   ◦ Semantics: Chapter 12 - Cross-modal Semantic-associative Labelling, Indexing and Retrieval of Multimodal Data.
   ◦ Modelling: Chapter 13 - The MultiPlasticity of New Media.

1. Multiple Senses and Consideration of Presence

It is essential that the reader understands the reasons for our pushing for development of MulSeMedia technologies. MulSeMedia provides an endless potential for user immersion, an essential element of presence, which is critical in the user's perception of enjoyment and memory. The first section in this book, introduces the reader to the critical need to include multiple senses in media design, i.e. development of MulSeMedia systems, when trying to obtain user presence.

Human perception, as described in the introduction, is inherently multisensory; involving visual, auditory, tactile, olfactory, gustatory, nociceptive (i.e., painful) etc. With this multisensory bombardment it is unsurprising that the vast majority of life's most enjoyable experiences involve the stimulation of several senses simultaneously, e.g. sight and touch, sound and smell, etc. A virtual rose may seem visually appealing, however it is little substitute to the emotional, and olfactory impact of a full bunch of flowers. The true multisensory nature of life has been considered by a small number of people, mostly in the amusement industry, with the majority of computer and virtual reality (VR) applications only considering, including and/or stimulation only one, or at most two, senses. Typically vision (sight), audition (sound), and, on occasion, haptics (touch) have been included in developed of interactive environments, yet focus on this sense does not reflect the real interplay of multisensory inputs from the real world. The research that has been conducted to date has clearly shown that increasing the number of senses stimulated in a VR simulator will dramatically enhance a user's sense of immersion, and therefore the development of user presence. Immersion is defined as the subjective impression that one is participating in a comprehensive, realistic experience and is seen as a necessary condition for the creation of 'presence', which is a psychologically emergent property of immersion and is directly related to user enjoyment and influences memory formation during the encounter/experience. Research shows that greater quantity of sensory information provided by the virtual environment relates to a higher the sense of presence, and that as more sensory modalities are stimulated, presence is also similarly increased. It can therefore be expected, that MulSeMedia, engaging a range of senses, enhances presence and subsequently enjoyment and/or user information assimilation.

Given that the MulSeMedia technology has recently gained increasing levels of commercial success, due to improved functionality and reduced costs associated with VR systems, the likelyhood is that truly multisensory VR should be with us soon.

It is important to note that there are both theoretical and practical limitations to the stimulation of certain senses in VR. This is well demonstrated by Heilig's 1962 *Sensorama* experience, which showed the huge potential of multisensory systems, however ran out of funding due to limited appreciation of commercial application.

Chapter 1, entitled "Multisensory Presence in Virtual Reality: Possibilities and Limitations" by Alberto Gallace, Mary K. Ngo, John Sulaitis, and Charles Spence, highlights some of the most exciting potential applications associated with engaging more of a user's senses in a simulated environment. They review the key technical challenges associated with stimulating multiple senses within a VR setting and focus on the particular problems associated with the stimulation of traditional MulSeMedia senses (i.e. touch, smell, and taste). Gallace et al. highlight the problems associated with the limited bandwidth of human sensory perception and the psychological costs associated with users having to divide their attention between multiple sensory modalities simultaneously; a negative implication of information overload. Finally, Gallace et al. discuss how the findings provided by the extant research in the field of cognitive neurosciences might help to overcome some of the cognitive and technological limitations affecting the development of multisensory VR systems.

Chapter 2, entitled "Multiple Sensorial Media and Presence in 3D Environments" by Helen Farley and Caroline Steel, looks at the characteristics of the MulSeMedia experience that facilitate user immersion within three-dimensional virtual environments; including discussion of Multi-user Virtual Environments (MUVEs), such as Second Life, and Massively Multiplayer Online Role-playing games (MMORPGs), such as World of Warcraft. Evidence, extracted from extensive literature pertaining to gaming and/or work surrounding user interfaces enabling haptic feedback, tactile precision and engaging other sensory modalities, states that though there are multiple factors that impede and facilitate immersion, it is clear that the practical ability to interact with and engage multiple senses is one of the key factors. Farley and Steel begin chapter 2 by unravelling the relationship between 'immersion', with a special emphasis on 'sensory immersion', and 'presence' in relation to MulSeMedia systems. In addition, they looks at the nature of the sensory stimulation provided by MulSeMedia systems in relation to the amount of immersion that it engenders and the value that is provides; e.g. a sound that is directional will have a positive effect on immersion and sensory feedback that is not conflicting will further enhance the immersive experience. Farley and Steel conclude by discussing some of the challenges that MulSeMedia systems will face in order to develop on the considerable promises.

2. Individual Difference, Perception and Culture

MulSeMedia relates to any multi-sensory interactive user experience, which is commonly defined as requiring a combination of at least one continuous (i.e. sound and video) and one discrete (i.e. text, images) medium. MulSeMedia facilitates an infotainment duality, which means that it not only is able to transfer information to a user, but is also provides the user with a subjective experience (relating to preferences, self-assessment, satisfaction and / or enjoyment). Ability to understand the MulSeMedia content, and perception of enjoyment from this content, is ultimately dependent on user perception, pre-knowledge and individual differences.

There has been an abundance of research dealing with how perceptual (i.e. physical and cultural), pre-knowledge (i.e. education and experience), and individual user differences (i.e. physical and cognitive) impact our perception and use of computer-based technologies. It has long been one of the central tenets of our research philosophy that 'multimedia' should to be user-centric, allowing personalised interaction as a result of an understanding of user needs. MulSeMedia technology, unsurprisingly, is not an exception; but more than ever requires user focus to manage the interplay of sensual. If user individual characteristics are not taken into account in the development of MulSeMedia systems and applications, and if their perception of media quality (i.e. the user experience) is ignored, then we run the risk of designing niche MulSeMedia applications, which although intrinsically novel and alluring, lack a wider user appeal. The second section in this book introduces the reader to the need to consider user differences in the development, use and perception of MulSeMedia systems. Physical ability, cognitive style, age, gender, culture, systems experience, pre-knowledge, etc. all play an essential part in how the user perceives MulSeMedia and must be understood to ensure relevant perception of content.

Accordingly in chapter 3, entitled "Appreciating Individual Differences: Exposure time requirements in Virtual Space" by Markos Kyritsis and Stephen Gulliver, looks at the experience of learning the spatial layout of environments. Although focusing on single media perception, the research focuses on the impact of gender, orientation skill, cognitive style, system knowledge, and environmental knowledge when users are learning a virtual space. The chapter makes a strong case for including individual user differences in the development of MulSeMedia, as the results of their research show that user characteristics significantly influence the training time required to ensure effective virtual environment spatial knowledge acquisition.

MulSeMedia holds considerable potential to people with physical or learning limitations. By managing provision of information away from limited sensory inputs (e.g. audio captions for dyslexic users interacting with heavy text media), MulSeMedia allows users to gain assistive help that allows easier user interaction. Although allowing access, the interplay and reliance on more sense also risks the loss of information. In chapter 4, entitled "Non-Visual Programming, Perceptual Culture and MulSeMedia: Case studies of five blind computer programmers" by Simon Hayhoe, describes an investigation into the premise that blind programmers and web-developers can create modern Graphical User Interfaces (GUIs) through perceptions of MulSeMedia, and whether perceptual culture has a role in this understanding. Since MulSeMedia is inherently multi-modal, it comes as no surprise that research has been undertaken that addresses the use of MulSeMedia for people who have limited sensory perception in one (or more) senses. To this end, Hayhoe explores whether MulSeMedia can inform accessible interface design and explores the boundaries of accessing computer interfaces in a MulSeMedia manner (in this particular case, through non-visual perceptions and memories). The chapter shows that programmers who had been introduced to, and educated using a range of visual, audio and / or tactile devices, could adapt to produce code with GUIs, but programmers who were educated using only tactile and audio devices preferred to shun visual references in their work.

The perception of MulSeMedia is critical to it ultimate acceptance, however people in different countries, cultures, using different languages and semiotic perceptual structures will ultimately understand information differently. To consider the impact of cultural aspects we have included chapter 5, entitled "Multiculturality and Multimodal Languages" by Maria Chiara Caschera, Arianna D'Ulizia, Fernando

Ferri and Patrizia Grifoni, which recognises that the way in which people communicate changes according to their culture. This chapter focuses on this challenging MulSeMedia topic, and proposes a grammatical approach for the representation of multicultural issues in multimodal languages. The approach is based on a grammar that is able to produce a set of structured sentences, composed of gestural, vocal, audio, graphical symbols, along with the meaning that these symbols have in the different cultures.

3. MulSeMedia Interfaces

In the field of computing, the interface refers to a point of interaction between the information components, and includes the consideration of development of relevant hardware and software technologies. The inclusion of multiple-sensory input has been shown to be essential to increased user immersion and presence. Moreover, experience and interaction ability with the sensory interface has been shown as an individual difference that impacts user experience. It is therefore essential that MulSeMedia interaction is considered in this book. Section three of this book relates to research concerning proposed use of Haptic (touch) and Olfactory (smell) interfaces.

Haptic technology, or haptics, is a tactile feedback technology that takes advantage of the user's sense of touch. By applying forced feedback, vibrations and/or motion to interaction hardware the user get a physical feeling of virtual object presence. Haptics has been applied in fields including Virtual Reality, Medicine and Robotics, allowing for the sensation of touch; which is especially useful to those who rely on this due to their remote location (e.g. a bomb disposal team), or because of physical limitation (e.g. blind or partially sighted).

Chapter 6, entitled "Haptic rendering of HTML components and 2D maps included in web pages" by Nikolaos Kaklanis, Konstantinos Moustakas and Dimitrios Tzovaras, describes an interaction technique where web pages are automatically parsed, in order to generate a corresponding 3D virtual environment with haptic feedback. A web page rendering engine was developed, to automatically create 3D scenes that are composed of "hapgets" (haptically-enhanced widgets); three dimensional widgets that provide semantic behaviour analogous to that of the original HTML components, but that is enhanced with haptic feedback. For example, 2D maps included in the original web page are represented by a corresponding multimodal (haptic-aural) map, automatically generated from the original. The proposed interaction technique enables the user to experience a haptic navigation through the internet, as well as the haptic exploration of conventional 2D online maps; a consider benefit for visually impaired users. This interface technology offers great potential for visually impaired users, and demonstrates how individual and physical difference can be supported via access to information that is currently totally inaccessible using the existing assistive technologies.

The olfactory system is the sensory system used for olfaction, i.e. the sense of smell. The sense of smell is linked directly to the central hemisphere of the brain; uncontrollably linking sensation of certain smells to memory and emotion. Despite regular attempts to incorporate smell in virtual reality simulations, olfactory interfaces and systems are limited. Olfaction technologies, due to recent progress of in olfactory displays, are becoming available and therefore inclusion in Multiple Sensorial Media is fast becoming a practically commercially desirable possibility. Interestingly, one of the important functions of the olfactory display is to blend multiple of odor components to create a variety of odours.

Chapter 7, entitled "Olfactory Display Using Solenoid Valves and Fluid Dynamics Simulation" by Takamichi Nakamoto, Hiroshi Ishida and Haruka Matsukura, describes a developed olfactory display to blend up to 32 odour components using solenoid valves. High-speed switching of a solenoid valve enables the efficient blending of a range of instantaneously odours, even if the solenoid valve has only two states such as ON and OFF. Since the developed system is compact and is easy to use, it has been so far used to scent a movie, an animation and a game. At present the multisensory media content developer must manually adjust the concentration sequence, since the concentration varies from place to place. Nakamoto et al. discuss how manually determined concentration sequences are not accurate and, therefore it takes much time to make the plausible concentration sequence manually. Since the spread of odour in spatial domain is very complicated, the isotropic diffusion from the odour source is not valid. Since the simulated odour distribution resembles the distribution actually measured in the real room, a CFD simulation enabled Nakamoto et al. to reproduce the spatial variation in the odour intensity that the user would experience in the real world. In this chapter, most users successfully perceived the intended change in the odour intensity when they watched the scented movie; where they approached an odour source hindered by an obstacle.

4. MulSeMedia Applications

The editors have defined a number of important application areas where consideration of MulSeMedia systems holds considerable potential. Although far from comprehensive, the following list shows areas where MulSeMedia applications are practically being developed: context-aware systems, adaptive and personalized media delivery, distributed communication and use in risk environments, sensory integration, cognitive retraining, virtual reality immersion, enhanced media, quality of service and quality of perception considerations, emotional interaction and consideration, user emotional modelling, e-learning and education and interactive e-commerce. In the fourth and final section of our text we highlight a number of application areas, i.e. areas where use of multisensory systems are practically impacting user experience. Although this section covers five short chapters, these application areas show just a short glance of the potential that MulSeMedia system hold.

Entertainment

The entertainment industries have always been very interested in the area of MulSeMedia, however device availability and cost has historically restricted common acceptance. With the rare exception of specialist entertainment systems at arcades, or at purpose build theatres, MulSeMedia entertainment was limited to use of visual and audio media. With the introduction of home surround sound, the WII, the fit-board and the iphone, interactive visual, audio and haptic devices have become commercially available, thus fuelling consumer desire for MulSeMedia interactive entertainment. Compounded by the push and the standardisation of 3D television, and the ubiquitous introduction of touch screen technologies, entertainment is seen by the editors as a driving force in the development of new MulSeMedia technologies.

In Chapter 8, Masataka Imura and Shunsuke Yoshimoto address the topic of MulSeMedia-based entertainment. Recognising the allure of combining different sensorial experiences in the realm of entertainment, the authors introduce and discuss the use of three MulSeMedia applications for representing and improving the reality of virtual user worlds: (1) Haptic Canvas: An entertainment system with dilatant fluid based haptic device; (2) Fragra: An entertainment system with a hand-mounted olfaction display and; (3) Invisible: An entertainment system that represents existence of virtual creatures by indirect information.

Education

Use of 'multimedia' technology in schools has been widely researched. Results are often mixed in focus, highlighting the benefit of sensory enforcement, yet also stressing concerns about attention divide and reduced student focus. Despite concerns, however, multimedia systems have facilitated computer-based training, which increases both the flexibility of and accessibility of many to educational structures. MulSeMedia systems offer an extension of interactive and sensory training that is only recently available to all.

Chapter 9, entitled "Thinking Head MulSeMedia – A Storytelling Environment for Embodied Language Learning" broadly focuses on the uses of MulSeMedia in Education. Recognising that traditional tutoring systems using only one or at most two modalities opens up new possibilities to be potentially exploited by MulSeMedia application and content designers alike, the chapter authors (Tom A. F. Anderson, Zhi-Hong Chen, Yean-Fu Wen, Marissa Milne, Adham Atyabi, Kenneth Treharne, Takeshi Matsumoto, Xi-Bin Jia, Martin Luerssen, Trent Lewis, Richard Leibbrandt and David M. W. Powers) present the reader with *Thinking Head*. This is a conversational agent that plays the role of a tutor/teacher in an individual learning environment employing multi-sensorial interaction.

Based on previous work done by Tom Anderson, which explored the use of speech synthesis/recognition as an added interaction modality, the authors introduce these within the Thinking Head. Moreover, they attempt to bridge the virtual-physical divide through physical manipulation achieved via visual input recognition. It is noteworthy to remark that the authors achieve this by employing an inherently affordable and widely available device – a webcam. Whilst the webcam is not traditionally thought of as a MulSeMedia device, the work described in the chapter shows that any single-media, single-modality device can automatically become a MulSeMedia input if employed in a multi-sensorial context. The world of MulSeMedia devices is therefore much larger than one would think at first sight (or smell, or touch,…).

Research

Current Virtual Reality (VR) and Augmented Reality (AR) environments have advanced visual and audio outputs, but the use of smell is either very limited or completely absent. Adding olfactory stimulation to current virtual environments will greatly enhance the sense of presence, or 'realness' of the environment – or will it? The first recorded attempt of combining artificially generated smell with audiovisual occurred in 1906; when the audience of the Rose Bowl football game were sprayed with the scent of roses. In 1943, Hans Laube released selected odours at specific times and durations, which led to the development of a 35 minute 'smell-o-drama' movie called Mein Traum in which 35 different odours were released to accompany the drama presentation. Despite continued efforts to introduce smell into MulSeMedia entertainment experiences, limited research has been done concerning the actual perceptual benefit.

Chapter 10, entitled "User Perception of Media Content Association in Olfaction-Enhanced Multimedia", by Gheorghita Ghinea and Oluwakemi Adeoye empirically asks the question - does the correct association of scent and content enhance the user experience of multimedia applications? Ghinea and Adeoye present the results of an empirical study that varied olfactory media content association by combining video excerpts with semantically related and unrelated scents, and subsequently measured the impact that this variation had on participants' perception of the olfaction-enhanced multimedia experience. Results show a significant difference in opinions in respect of the ability of olfactory media to heighten the sense of reality. Interestingly, the use of unrelated scents was not found to significantly affect the degree to which participants found the olfactory media annoying.

In chapter 11, entitled "Multimedia Sensory Cue Processing in the FIVIS Simulation Environment", the authors (Rainer Herpers, David Scherfgen, Michael Kutz, Jens Bongartz, Ulrich Hartmann, Oliver Schulzyk, Sandra Boronas, Timur Saitov, Holger Steiner and Dietmar Reinert) expand details relating to the research being carried out in the FIVIS project. In the FIVIS project, at the Bonn-Rhein-Sieg University of Applied Sciences in Sankt Augustin Germany, an immersive bicycle simulator has been developed. It allows researchers to simulate dangerous traffic situations within a safe controlled laboratory environment. The system has been successfully used for road safety education of school children, as well as to conduct multimedia perception research experiments. The MulSeMedia simulator features a bicycle equipped with steering and pedaling sensors, an electrical motor brake, a panoramic back-projection-based visualization system, optical tracking cameras and an optional motion platform. The FIVIS simulation system has proven to be extensible (due to the use of the Python scripting language and XML) and is well suited for perceptual and stress related research. The visualization system's projection screens occupy a high percentage of the rider's visual field, which, together with the adapted 3D rendering process, contributes to a high degree of immersion.

Semantics and Modelling

Semantics is the study of meaning. Modelling is the act of representing something. Both are essential to ensure relevant capture of MulSeMedia content, and context relevant user perception. To look at some of the applications domains relating to media semantics and modelling we have included two chapters that look at the capture and representation of media content.

Chapter 12, entitled "Cross-modal Semantic-associative Labelling, Indexing and Retrieval of Multimodal Data" by Meng Zhu and Atta Badii, looks at how digitalised media and information is typically represented using different modalities, and then subsequently distributed through relevant sensory channels. The use and interaction of such a huge amount of data is therefore highly dependent on the effective and efficient cross-modal labelling, indexing and retrieval of information in real-time. Zhu and Badii focus on the combining of the primary and collateral modalities of information resources in an intelligent and effective way; in order to provide better media understanding, classification, labelling and retrieval. Image and text are the two modalities use by the Authors, however application is possible to a wider range of media forms. A novel framework for semantic-based collaterally cued image labelling is proposed by the authors and subsequently implemented that automatically assigns linguistic keywords to regions of interest in an image. A visual vocabulary was constructed based on manually labelled image segments and the Authors use Euclidean distance and Gaussian distribution to map the low-level region-based image features to the high-level visual concepts defined in the visual vocabulary. Both the collateral content and context knowledge were extracted from the collateral textual modality to bias the mapping process. A semantic-based high-level image feature vector model was constructed based on the labelling results, and the performance of image retrieval using this feature vector model appears to outperform both content-based and text-based approaches in terms of its capability for combining both perceptual and conceptual similarity of the image content.

Chapter 13, entitled "The MultiPlasticity of New Media" by Gianluca Mura, looks at the problem of modelling interactive MulSeMedia systems. Interactive systems engineering is an interdisciplinary field that normally involves interdevelopment communication from experts in computer and systems engineering, interaction design, software development, aesthetic, ethnography, psychology and usability. Accordingly, MulSeMedia interactive systems, involving the consideration of complex user needs, demands suitable conceptual and multisensorial media definition model. This study analyzes social and conceptual evolutions of digital media and proposes an interactive mixed-space media model, which communicates the media contents effectively in order to enhance the user experience between interactive space of physical objects and online virtual space. Feedback from the interactive mixed-space media model provides information concerning user performance when using a range of multisensorial interfaces. The research widens previous research findings, and gives the reader a specific definition of the cognitive and emotional perception using a metaplastic multimedia model. The chapter describes how the interaction quality within its conceptual media space, through an action-making loop, facilitates the creation of new information content within its metaplastic metaspace configurations.

CONCLUSION

We are delighted and excited, in equal measure, to have edited this first book on MulSeMedia – multiple sensorial media. We have had quality contributions from a range of researchers and practitioners. We hope its readers share our feelings and enjoy the book.

George Ghinea
Brunel University, UK

Frederic Andres
CVCE, Luxembourg & NII, Japan

Stephen Gulliver
University of Reading, UK

September 2010

Section 1
Multiple Senses and Consideration of Presence

Chapter 1

Multisensory Presence in Virtual Reality:
Possibilities & Limitations

Alberto Gallace
University of Milano-Bicocca, Italy

Mary K. Ngo
University of Oxford, UK

John Sulaitis
Bunnyfoot Ltd, UK

Charles Spence
University of Oxford, UK

ABSTRACT

Perception in the real world is inherently multisensory, often involving visual, auditory, tactile, olfactory, gustatory, and, on occasion, nociceptive (i.e., painful) stimulation. In fact, the vast majority of life's most enjoyable experiences involve the stimulation of several senses simultaneously. Outside of the entertainment industry, however, the majority of virtual reality (VR) applications thus far have involved the stimulation of only one, or at most two, senses, typically vision, audition, and, on occasion, touch/ haptics. That said, the research that has been conducted to date has convincingly shown that increasing the number of senses stimulated in a VR simulator can dramatically enhance a user's 'sense of presence', their enjoyment, and even their memory for the encounter/experience. What is more, given that the technology has been improving rapidly, and the costs associated with VR systems are continuing to come down, it seems increasingly likely that truly multisensory VR should be with us soon (albeit 50 years after Heilig, 1962, originally introduced Sensorama). However, it is important to note that there are both theoretical and practical limitations to the stimulation of certain senses in VR. In this chapter, after having defined the concept of 'neurally-inspired VR', we highlight some of the most exciting potential applications associated with engaging more of a user's senses while in a simulated environment. We then review the key technical challenges associated with stimulating multiple senses in a VR setting. We focus on the particular problems associated with the stimulation of the senses of touch, smell, and taste.

DOI: 10.4018/978-1-60960-821-7.ch001

We also highlight the problems associated with the limited bandwidth of human sensory perception and the psychological costs associated with users having to divide their attention between multiple sensory modalities simultaneously. Finally, we discuss how the findings provided by the extant research in the cognitive neurosciences might help to overcome, at least in part, some of the cognitive and technological limitations affecting the development of multisensory VR systems.

If the virtual reality apparatus, as you called it, was wired to all of your senses and controlled them completely, would you be able to tell the difference between the virtual world and the real world?

What is real? How do you define real? If you're talking about your senses, what you feel, taste, smell, or see, then all you're talking about are electrical signals interpreted by your brain.

From 'The Matrix' (1999)

INTRODUCTION

One of the main aims of virtual reality (VR) is to make people feel 'real' what is actually not really there. However, just as the above quotation suggests (see also Haden, 2005), the very question to be addressed here is what is 'real'? In our culture, we take for granted the fact that the physical world is real and continues to exist regardless of whether we observe it or not. However, from a psychological standpoint, feelings and sensations are only real for a given observer (they do not, in themselves, exist); That is, perceptual 'facts' only exist within our minds/brains. Electrochemical signals are processed by our brains and this results in percepts that might, or then again just might not, have a counterpart in the external world (note that perceptual illusions constitute just one well-known example of 'a perceptual reality' that does not correspond to an actual external stimulus; e.g., Gregory, 1966, 1967). On the basis of such considerations, it soon

becomes clear that in order for VR simulators to effectively create environments that "feel real", they should try to reproduce the same neuronal activation as that generated by external stimuli. This is an important point because it suggests that the aim of VR is not necessarily to seek the closest correspondence possible between the qualities of real and virtual objects, but rather between the neural activation that is generated by real objects and events and that generated by virtual objects and events. Consequently, VR should be based, to a far greater extent than many people realize, on what we know about the ways in which our brains process incoming sensory signals (i.e., an approach that can be defined as 'neurally-inspired' VR). In this chapter, we focus on the relationship between the development of VR systems and one key attribute of the way in which information is processed by the human brain: Namely, the integration of signals generated by different sensory systems that leads to the construction of the multisensory perceptual experience of objects and events in the external world.

VR has come a long way over the last few decades (Laurel, 1995). However, the majority of research has been devoted to enhancing the quality/resolution of VR in just one sensory modality, namely vision (e.g., Burdea & Coiffet, 1994). It is, however, important to note that we perceive with all of our senses, and not just with our eyes (no matter whether we are aware of it or not). Audition, touch, taste, and smell (just to cite a few of the many senses; see Durie, 2005) all contribute to our everyday multisensory experiences (see Calvert, Spence, & Stein, 2004, for a review). Indeed, it has been argued that the majority of life's most enjoyable experiences are inherently multisensory (e.g., Spence, 2002). Think only of a great meal. The food must not only look good. The smell, temperature, taste, and even the sound (yes, the sound; see Zampini & Spence, 2004) need to be appropriate as well in order to create a truly memorable dining experience (though note that striking incongruity can also be memorable). Actually, even if we are not fully aware of it, our brains likely judge 'all' experiences in terms of a perceptual 'whole' (what is known as multisensory Gestalt; e.g., Gallace & Spence, in press; Spence, Sanabria, & Soto-Faraco, 2007) rather than on the basis of a single channel of information.

Try watching a movie sitting on your sofa, standing in a crowded waiting room, or at the cinema. Would you find the same visual stimulation equally enjoyable, emotionally-charged, and attention-capturing in all three situations? We believe not. This example therefore helps to illustrate two key points. First, that we evaluate most of our experiences on the basis of a combination of information from several different senses (even if we are not necessarily aware of it all of the time). This evaluation is also based on certain qualities of the 'background' stimulation rather than solely on aspects of the foreground, and/or attended stimuli. Second, the example also illustrates the important role played by kinaesthetic signals, which provide information about the posture and movement of our bodies, in our explicit evaluations of a given experience (even of a stimulus one might think of as being purely visual; e.g., see Taylor & McCloskey, 1991). That is, all of these incoming sensory signals, together with our current internal and emotional states, enter the neural computations that lead to our final perceptual experience of a certain stimulus.

Since our brains integrate signals from multiple information sources, it becomes obvious that in order to be truly effective, VR must be based on multisensory rather than unisensory stimulation. This point becomes all the more important when

one considers the fact that multisensory integration (and, more generally, perception) appears to be based on the principles of Bayesian decision theory incorporating Maximum-Likelihood Estimation (MLE; e.g., Deneve & Pouget, 2004; Ernst & Banks, 2002; Ernst & Bülthoff, 2004; see also Knill & Richards, 1996). One of the key points of the application of this mathematical approach to human perception is that the importance of each sensory modality for our behavior varies widely according to the context (e.g., we rely more on touch and audition at night than during the day). More specifically, according to the MLE account of perception, it is the overall level of variance associated with each sense that plays a key role in determining which sensory input will dominate our perception. It is thought that a general statistical principle, which tends to minimize the variance associated with the final multisensory perceptual estimate, determines the degree to which one sensory modality (or cue) will 'dominate' our perception over another modality estimate (or cue). Why should this be relevant to the development of multisensory VR systems? Well, according to the MLE account, we do not always need to present a huge amount of information in every sensory modality in order for a multisensory virtual display to be effective (i.e., to give rise to the 'neural signature' associated with a seemingly richly-rendered multisensory perceptual event or object).

Due to the fact that the importance of each sensory signal in the final multisensory perceptual estimate is determined by the context, even a partially degraded signal might, under the appropriate conditions, be sufficient to elicit a particular percept. Given the actual limitations of display technologies, especially for stimulating the non-visual senses, the possibility of reducing the actual amount of information that needs to be presented in order to elicit the same percept certainly constitutes a very promising idea. (Incidentally one might note that the very same principle constitutes the very core of the television invention. It works because of our limitations in temporal processing of light sources!) For example, it is now well-known that auditory signals tend to be mislocalized toward the position of concurrently-presented visual signals (this is known as the 'ventriloquism' effect; Alais & Burr, 2004; Howard & Templeton, 1966). What is more, the extent of this mislocalization can be accurately predicted using MLE. In terms of VR environments, this suggests that even a limited number of sources of auditory information can be sufficient to perceive stimuli as arising from multiple different positions of the visual field (at least when the events that need to be presented are audio-visual; see also Driver, 1996). That is, complex auditory displays might not be necessary under all conditions in order to create realistic audiovisual VR.

Even certain aspects of gustatory perception might be tackled in VR environments by means of the principles of sensory dominance and multisensory integration. Coloring a food or drink item, for example, has been found to significantly affect its perceived taste, smell, and flavour qualities (e.g., Morrot, Brochet, & Dubourdieu, 2001; see Spence, Levitan, Shankar, & Zampini, 2010, for a recent review). Therefore, it might well be possible that a relatively wide range of gustatory, olfactory, and flavour percepts can be elicited using nothing more than a relatively small number of tastants and olfactants providing that any concurrently-presented visual information (that has been shown to dominate in this particular context) is used appropriately. A similar line of thinking can also be adopted for those oral-somatosensory and tactile aspects that contribute to our evaluation (enjoyment) of food. That is, it has been reported that modulating the tactile characteristics of a cup can result in a change of a person's judgments regarding the liquid that is held within (see Spence & Gallace, 2011, for a review). And, as we will see later,

auditory cues can be used to modulate a food's textural properties (Zampini & Spence, 2004; Spence, 2011a). It soon becomes clear, therefore, that exploiting the results that are nowadays being provided by the psychological and neuroscientific literature on the rich multisensory interactions among the human senses might provide effective guidelines with which to reduce the overall amount of information that is needed in order to reproduce a certain multisensory percept in a VR environment.

Multisensory Presence

As anyone knows who has experienced unisensory visual VR, it simply does not deliver the high degree of presence (defined as the feeling of being in the place/situation that is being simulated; Bangay & Preston, 1998; Schuemie, van der Straaten, Krijn, & van der Mast, 2001; Slater & Wilbur, 1997) that one might wish for (e.g., Barfield & Weghorst, 1993). What is more, these days, simply increasing the specifications (i.e., by enhancing the screen resolution or refresh rate) of a visual display tends to deliver only an incremental enhancement in the sense of presence and/or satisfaction on the part of the user of the VR system (see Barfield & Hendrix, 1995; Dinh, Walker, Hodges, Song, & Kobayashi, 1999; Hendrix & Barfield, 1996). As a consequence, VR researchers are increasingly coming to the realization that they need to look elsewhere in order to enhance the multisensory sense of presence that they can achieve through their VR simulations.

Great progress has certainly been made in auditory VR over the past decade or two. In fact, virtual auditory displays now constitute a central part of many VR applications (e.g., Hendrix & Barfield, 1996; Martin, McAnally, & Senova, 2001). There has also been a growing interest in the development of haptic/tactile VR (e.g., Burdea, 1996; Iwata, 2008). Researchers have also turned their attention to question the opportunities inherent in terms of enhancing the sense of presence afforded by the introduction of virtual olfactory displays (see Barfield & Danas, 1996; Cater, 1992; Jones, Bowers, Washburn, Cortes, & Satya, 2004), and/or even, on occasion, by stimulating a user's taste-buds (see Hoffman, Hollander, Schroder, Rousseau, & Furness, 1998; see also Hashimoto, Inami, & Kajimoto, 2008; Hashimoto Nagaya, Kojima, Miyajima, Ohtaki, Yamamoto, et al., 2007).

The trend, then, has recently been toward stimulating more of a user's senses in order to enhance the multisensory sense of presence. That said, most commercially-available VR systems do not, as yet, include tactile/force-feedback, smell (olfaction), or taste (gustatory) stimulation (see Figure 1). However, we believe that even using virtual stimuli that constitute an imperfect reproduction of real stimuli might prove effective in terms of enhancing a user's sense of presence, at least when all of the sensory stimuli presented in a given context are 'congruent' (that is, when they all contribute to give rise to a certain percept).

Having described the state-of-the-art, and the future direction in the development of multisensory VR devices, we will now highlight the relative importance of each of the human senses in terms of creating a 'well-blended' multisensory VR environment. Then, we analyze the relevance of the latest empirical evidence provided by the study of body ownership and of its role in enhancing the sense of presence (and the sense of 'owning' a virtual body or avatar) in multisensory VR. Finally, we describe some of the key technological and cognitive problems that are associated with the use of multisensory displays, and we try to provide possible solutions to at least some of these important (and current) issues.

MULTISENSORY VR ENVIRONMENTS: PAST, PRESENT AND FUTURE

"If we're going to step through the window into another world, why not go the whole way?" Morton Heilig (1962)

The origin of multisensory VR simulators can be dated back to 1962, when Morton Heilig patented the Sensorama Simulator (see Figure 2). This invention, which was created well before the massive increase in computing power and availability of computers that took place in the 1980s, is widely recognized as constituting the first truly multisensory simulator. As Heilig described it at the time: *"The present invention, generally, relates to simulator apparatus, and more particularly, to apparatus to stimulate the senses of an individual to simulate an actual experience realistically."* This device consisted of a machine in which the user was presented with 3D images, smells, stereo sound, wind, and vibrations. A few films were made especially for Sensorama. In one of these, the user was able to experience a motorcycle ride through Brooklyn. The sense of presence was enhanced by blowing wind through the user's hair (see also below), by presenting the sounds and smells of the city, and by simulating bumps in the road by means of a vibrating chair. Although this invention was never a commercial success, and never attracted sufficient funding for further development, the principles behind its creation are the very same as those that are currently animating the development of many of the multisensory VR systems today.

We have come a long way in the half-century since the invention of Sensorama, and multisensory VR systems have now been tested in a large number of contexts. In fact, the number of activities that can benefit from relatively simple

Figure 1. A) Number of studies published related to unimodal visual as compared to bimodal (visuo-tactile) VR systems across the years. B) Number of studies published divided by their main subject area. Terms searched for unimodal visual: vision or visual, and virtual reality. Terms searched for bimodal visuotactile: vision or visual, and virtual reality and touch or haptic. The research was performed on the content of the abstracts. Research performed the 20th March 2010 on 28 databases, including: Biotechnology and Bioengineering Abstracts, Biological Sciences, Environmental Engineering Abstracts, Health and Safety Science Abstract, Medline, Psychinfo.

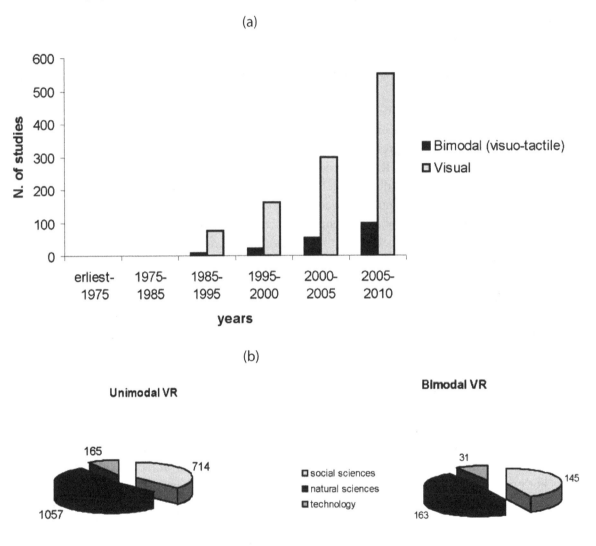

multisensory simulators are most likely endless: Everything from training people to operate (either literally or metaphorically) in dangerous situations (e.g., Heilig, 1962; Vlahos, 2006; Washburn & Jones, 2004; Washburn, Jones, Satya, Bowers, & Cortes, 2003) through to mak-ing educational experiences more engaging and memorable (e.g., Onyesolu, 2009); and from enhancing the on-line shopping (see Spence & Gallace, in press, for a review) to differentiating the entertainment experience, be it in video games, while watching television, or at the cin-

Figure 2. Sketch (on the left) and picture (on the right) of the Sensorama Simulator patented by M. L. Heilig (1962). This invention is widely credited as being the first simulator designed to stimulate multiple senses (see text for details). [Figure reproduced from Heilig (1962, Figure 5), Patent 3,050,870.]

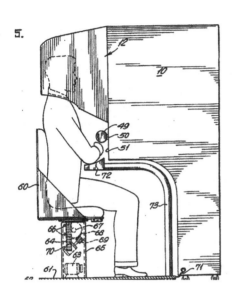 

ema/opera (e.g., Heilig, 1992; Robinett, 1992; Washburn & Jones, 2004).

There has also been a great deal of interest in the use of VR in a variety of clinical applications (e.g., Rothbaum, Hodges, Kooper, Opdyke, Williford, & North, 1995). For example, one interesting recent use of VR has been to try and help treat people with various anxiety-related conditions, such as social phobia and claustrophobia (Strickland, Hodges, North, & Hegworst, 1997). The evidence that is now available on this topic already shows that VR can be used to help desensitize people to their fear of heights (e.g., Rothbaum et al., 1995), and similarly to treat people suffering from arachnophobia (e.g., Carlin, Hoffman, & Weghorst, 1997). We believe that, in all of these cases, the addition of extra modalities of sensory stimulation might offer important advantages, for example in terms of reducing the duration and increasing the effectiveness of clinical treatments. VR applications have also been used to distract patients involved in painful clinical procedures, such as wound care (e.g., involving

bandage change, wound cleaning, etc.) for burns victims (Esselman, Thombs, Magyar-Russell, & Fauerbach, 2006). Similarly, VR has been adopted to treat those amputees who experience chronic pain. Specifically, virtually re-creating an arm (either by simply using a mirror projection of the healthy arm or by means of more sophisticated VR systems; e.g., Murray, Patchick, Pettifer, Caillette, & Howard, 2006; Murray, Pettifer, Howard, Patchick, Caillette, Kulkarni, & Bamford, 2007) can be used to alleviate the pain that these patients normally experience (and that they localize in the position where their amputated limb once was; see Moseley, Gallace, & Spence, 2008, in press, for a review; see also the section on projecting sensations to virtual bodies).

The growing trend toward using multisensory VR systems in order to present information to human users also seems to be supported by the empirical findings suggesting that (just as demonstrated in real situations) the more senses you engage, the more immersive the user's experience and the better his/her performance will be.

For example, it has been shown that increasing the number of modalities of sensory input in a virtual environment can lead to an increase in a user's memory for the objects placed within it (e.g., Dinh et al., 1999). Similarly, the visualization of complex data sets can also be facilitated by adding haptic stimulation/manipulation to a visual display (e.g., Brooks, Ming, Batter, & Kilpatrick, 1990; Yannier, Basdogan, Tasiran, & Sen, 2008). Even mobile phones have now started to adopt multisensory VR technologies (involving combined visual and haptic feedback) in order to simulate the pressure of a real button (see Lee & Spence, 2008). Laboratory-based research has now shown that stimulating multiple senses can provide significant advantages in terms of the usability and accessibility of these devices (Lee & Spence, 2009).

It is worth noting that, under certain conditions, mixing real and virtual objects might provide the most viable solution to the problem of increasing the realism of a certain situation, given the current limits on display technology. One example of the application of this concept comes from a series of experiments reported by Hoffman and his colleagues (1998). They investigated the advantages of using real objects within multisensory VR displays in order to try and enhance a user's sense of presence. In one of these experiments, the participants either saw, or both saw and touched, objects in a virtual world ('Kitchen World'). In particular, participants picked up a virtual plate either by picking up a real plate or by pulling the trigger button of a 3-D mouse. Allowing participants to feel the physical properties of a real plate resulted in them generating expectations concerning the properties of other virtual objects within the virtual environment. In essence, the real touch condition led to the perception that other objects in the virtual environment would feel similarly real and that those objects would also retain their real, physical properties (e.g., texture and weight). Hoffman et al.'s results therefore show that being able to physically touch a real object can make the virtual objects in a scene, not to mention the virtual experience (VE) as a whole, more realistic.

In a different experiment, Hoffman et al. (1998) went on to compare a condition in which the participants were allowed to physically bite into a virtual candy bar in an immersive VR environment to a condition in which they had to imagine biting into a virtual candy bar instead (i.e., the candy bar was only presented visually in VR). Unsurprisingly, the former condition gave rise to a significantly increased sense of presence when compared to performance in the latter condition. In the experiments summarized in this section, the mixing of real objects with virtual objects within multisensory (i.e., bimodal) VR systems enhanced the user's sense of presence, at least when congruent information is presented from real and mediated sources.

It is worth noting here that one of the main problems with many studies testing the effect of multisensory stimulation within VR environments is to differentiate any relevant perceptual effect from a (far less interesting) response bias interpretation. That is, there is a danger that the addition of a supplementary sensory modality to a display might only affect the participants' explicit response to a given stimulus but not his/her actual experience. In other words, the participants might change their response to an auditory stimulus when another visual stimulus happens to be presented, but only because they start to respond to the qualities of the visual stimulus rather than to the auditory stimulus itself. Moreover, people might rate a certain situation as being more engaging than another simply because they are aware of the fact that more sensory stimuli are present and that the experimenter is likely to be investigating this very aspect of the test situation. That is, people's explicit responses are often affected by the experimenter's expectancy regarding a participant's response (see Orne, 1962).

One possible solution to this problem is to rely less on questionnaire procedures and more on perceptual, neural, and physiological measures of perception/performance (e.g., Meehan, Insko, Whitton& Brooks, 2001; Slater, 2002; see also Slater, 2004, for a discussion on this point). That is, asking a user about their perceived sense of presence within a given environment may be of little use, while measuring the time of response to certain aspects of the setting, or analysing his/her physiological reactions (e.g., changes in heart rate, skin conductance, blood pressure, body temperature, etc.), might be more informative and, crucially, less subject to response bias and experimenter expectancy effects.

The Future of Multisensory VR Devices

One recent attempt to develop an effective multisensory VR system comes from the collaboration between the Universities of York and Warwick in the United Kingdom. The researchers at these institutions are developing what they describe as a 'Virtual Cocoon' (see http://www.science-daily.com/releases/2009/03/090304091227.htm; downloaded 19/03/2010). This system features a high-definition high dynamic screen, which allows the researchers concerned to represent more accurately the wide range of light intensity levels that one can find in real scenes (e.g., from direct sunlight to faint starlight). Additionally, it features a device that, it is claimed, can release smells from directly under the wearer's nose, another device to spray flavours directly into the wearer's mouth, a fan and heater that can create different tactile conditions of heat and humidity on the wearer's face, and surround-sound speakers capable of recreating ambient noise/soundscapes.

Unfortunately, however, the 'Virtual Cocoon' currently only exists as a prototype and we imagine that it will take many years before it will be publically available to the users of VR, if, that is, progress ever gets that far. Moreover, in our opinion, there are some seemingly important limitations with the system (such as the lack of oral-somatosensory textural information associated with the presentation of real foods/flavours; see also the following section) that need to be considered before a device such as this can be considered as offering a potentially truly multisensory experience to its user. Nevertheless, the 'Virtual Cocoon' does seem to offer an intriguing platform from which to develop an effective VR system that is truly multisensory in the future: That said, one should always be sceptical given the number of devices that have been suggested over the years to possess great 'potential' but which have never actually made it to the marketplace. Moreover, different devices might be more or less successful as a function of their given target users. In the gaming industry, for example, something small, portable, and economical might offer the most appealing solution, whereas other industries might not be satisfied by these attributes alone. The company 'VirtuSphere' has recently developed a unique VR sphere made of ABS plastic and polycarbonate which allows a user to walk, jump, and even run while wearing special wireless VR glasses (http://thefutureofthings.com/pod/199/virtual-reality-real-pain.html; downloaded 19/03/2010). Currently, the VirtuSphere weighs somewhere in the region of 200-220 kg, stands 2.6-3.0 m high, and costs an estimated 50,000-100,000 US Dollars! Although designed for multiple applications, such as military simulations and gaming, one cannot help but wonder how many people will have the space and money to place such a cumbersome device in their own homes. Physical size, number of sensory modalities stimulated (and their combinations), and the cost of implementation, therefore, are all likely to determine the results of any commercial competition regarding which is the best multisensory VR system.

MULTISENSORY SYMPHONY: THE ROLE OF EACH SENSE/INSTRUMENT

The enhancement of the sense of presence resulting from the engagement of two or more of a user's senses can be dramatic. This can, for example, be compared to the difference that one experiences when listening to a given piece of music played by a single instrument versus listening to the same piece when played by the entire orchestra. An important point to bear in mind here is that the technology involved in multisensory VR need not be expensive or necessarily even exceedingly sophisticated. For example, for the state-of-the-art driving simulator at the Max Planck centre for Biological Cybernetics in Tübingen, Germany, the researchers have invested large sums of money in extremely high quality visual (and auditory) simulation. However, they soon became aware that the virtual driving experience was failing to deliver a real sense of presence, the kind that one might hope for following the investment of so much money in one's equipment! The solution, when it came, was very simple: They just mounted two plastic battery operated hand-held fans, one on either side of the participant (one is reminded here of Heilig's, 1962, original Sensorama, which utilized a very similar solution). Trial-and-error soon revealed that blowing air onto the participant's face when the simulated vehicle started to move dramatically increased the user's sense of presence. Of course, this example of the benefits of adding tactile stimulation to an audiovisual simulator is nothing if not anecdotal. However, just as we have seen in the previous section of this chapter, there is now a growing body of empirical data to show that the more senses you engage in any kind of multisensory simulation, the more engaging (and memorable) the overall experience will be (e.g., Dinh et al., 1999; Hoffman et al., 1998; Washburn et al., 2003).

One important issue to be considered here relates to finding the correct/most appropriate role for each sense within a given multisensory VR environment. That is, just as in a symphony, not all of the instruments should necessarily be played at the same volume, and not all of them are equally important for rendering a given piece of music. It is the harmonious blend of their sounds that contributes to making the piece of music enjoyable for the listener. The question to be answered here then becomes one of how important each of the senses (or particular combination of senses) is within a multisensory VR environment, and when should one sense be considered as being more important than the others for the user's overall multisensory experience?

Vision

When thinking about engaging multiple senses, it is common to think about whether they should be weighted equally, or whether instead more resources (be they financial, technical, or in terms of bandwidth) should be given over to stimulating those senses where participants direct the majority of their attentional resources. In this regard, it is interesting to note that most researchers tend to believe that vision is the dominant sense (e.g., Sivak, 1996). One of the claims that one often hears is that people tend to direct their attention preferentially toward the visual modality (e.g., Heilig, 1992; Posner, Nissen, & Klein, 1976). So, for example, Heilig has argued that sight monopolizes human attention. He has even provided seemingly exact percentages regarding the extent to which each of our senses captures attention (see Figure 3). The empirical evidence has, however, provided only partial support for his claims. That is, researchers now seem to agree on the fact that, consistent with the MLE theory (e.g., Deneve & Pouget, 2004; Ernst & Banks, 2002; Ernst & Bülthoff, 2004), the role of each sense in the multisensory perception of a given object, say, actually depends on the specific conditions of the object's presentation (or on the response that should be provided). For example, vision might dominate over touch when size, orientation, and more generally, spatial and macrogeometric aspects of the object need to be evaluated. By contrast touch/haptics might be of greater use when microgeometric properties, pliability, and the temperature of the object are concerned (see Spence & Gallace, 2007, 2008, for reviews). Moreover, it should be noted that the degree of integration among different sensory modalities might vary with the age of the user (e.g., see Gori, Del Viva, Sandini, & Burr, 2008, for evidence showing that young children do not integrate optimally in terms of MLE).

That said, VR engineers nevertheless do need to make informed decisions about how much of their resources should be devoted to the development of enhancing the stimulation delivered to each of a user's senses. How, then, should one come to an informed decision on this score? There are several possible metrics that offer themselves up for consideration here: One idea would be to use information concerning the 'bit-rate' of each sensory modality (i.e., measured in terms of the quantity and quality, of information that a given sensory system can analyze, as expressed in bits; that is, if human can perceive a total of 16 different stimuli within a given sensory modality they can process 4 bits of information; e.g., Desor & Beauchamp, 1974; Miller, 1956; Questler, 1956; Zimmerman, 1989). Researchers who have attempted to quantify the bit rate of the various senses have come up with the following figures (see Table 1). On the basis of this data, it would appear, once again, that vision wins out the competition against the other senses (i.e., in terms of having the widest bandwidth). It is, however, worth noting that the technological limitations that affected the presentation of tactile stimuli in many previous studies might have disadvantaged this particular sensory modality in these computations (thus perhaps requiring a new and more reliable measure of the bandwidth of each sense).

Given the increasing interest in cognitive neuroscience, and the decline of the computer metaphor for the human mind, an alternative means of deciding how much of one's resources need to be devoted to each sense emerges from a consideration of the amount of the neocortex (the

Figure 3. Setup used by Petkova and Ehrsson (2008) in their simulation of out of the body experiences

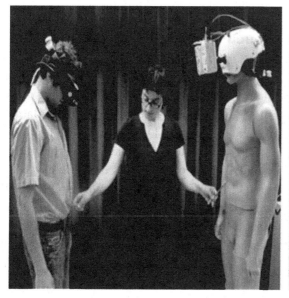
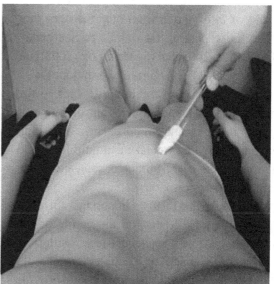

Table 1. Table summarizing the number of sensors, number of afferents, information transmission rates/channel capacity (from Zimmerman, 1989), % of attentional capture (from Heilig, 1992) and % of neocortex (Felleman & van Essen, 1991) relative to each sensory modality. See main text for the limitations affecting the interpretations of these data.

Sensory system	N. of sensors	N. of afferents	Channel capacity (bits/s)	Psychophysical channel capacity (bits/s)	% Attentional capture	% Neocortex
Vision	$2*10^8$	$2*10^6$	10^7	40	70%	55%
Audition	$3*10^4$	$2*10^4$	10^5	30	20%	3.4%
Touch	10^7	10^6	10^6	5	4%	11.5%
Taste	$3*10^7$	10^3	10^3	1(?)	1%	0.5%
Smell	$7*10^7$	10^5	10^5	1(?)	5%	n.a.

phylogenetically more recent part of our brain) that is given over to the processing of each sense. Felleman and van Essen (1991) conducted what is, perhaps, the most authoritative review of this topic (albeit on the brain of the macaque!). According to the data, they argued that 55% of the neocortex is devoted in some way to the processing of visual stimuli, 7.9% to the processing of motor stimuli, 11.5% to touch, 3.4% to hearing and 0.5% to taste (see Table 1). Even in this case, however, one should consider the fact that the occipital cortex (an area of the brain that until a few years ago was considered to be involved only in the processing of visual aspects of stimuli) has recently been found to be implicated in the processing of information from other sensory modalities as well (e.g., Ghazanfar & Schroeder, 2006; Sathian 2005; Schroeder & Foxe 2005; Sur & Leamey 2001). (It is further worth noting also that even the 0.5% of the brain devoted to the sense of taste can take complete control over your behavior under certain circumstances – just think what happens when you take a mouthful of food that tastes unexpectedly bitter, or sour, and hence might be off, or poisonous).

Now while the relative importance of each sense is likely to depend on the nature of the simulation that one is engaged in (e.g., battlefield vs. restaurant scenario, for example; Bardot et al., 1992; Vlahos, 2006), these figures at least provide

an objective measure that one can debate. It is certainly true that all statistics are consistent with the claim that vision is dominant in terms of the amount of neocortex devoted to it (Felleman & van Essen, 1991; see also Sereno, Dale, Reppas, Kwong, Belliveau, Brady, et al., 1995), in terms of information theory (Questler, 1956; Zimmerman, 1989), and, seemingly, in terms of researchers' intuitions (e.g., Heilig, 1992; Posner et al., 1976; Sivak, 1996). On the other hand, given that we already have highly impressive VR in the visual modality, spending on technology to stimulate the other senses is likely to give rise to dramatic improvements if only people can be convinced to acquire the relevant equipment.

Touch/Haptics

Touch is the first of our senses to develop, and it provides us with our most fundamental means of contact with the external world (e.g., Barnett, 1972; Gottlieb, 1971). The skin, with its 18,000 square centimeters of surface area (constituting about 16-18% of an adult's body weight; Montagu, 1971), also constitutes the largest of our sense organs (e.g., Field, 2001; Montagu, 1971). Tactile receptors inform us about the status of our body by direct contact. That is, the information that is provided by the skin does not necessarily need to be converted into hypotheses regarding the distal world (Gregory, 1967). It is no coincidence that touch has always been considered 'the' sense that allows us to discern between what is real and what is not (see Berkeley, 1732) and the sense that cannot be fooled. That is, the tactile information provided by the skin is, by default, considered 'real' and we often come to touch whenever there is a doubt of regarding how 'genuine' is a given sensory signal. Moreover, it has even been claimed that '*No other sense can arouse you like touch...* ' (Field, 2001, p. 57). On the basis of such considerations, it would seem that touch is certainly the sense that offers the greatest potential for future development within a multisensory VR environment (despite the fact that its large sensory surface makes touch one of the hardest senses to stimulate convincingly; see Iwata, 2008, for a review). Certain researchers have even gone so far as to argue that touch makes us feel that our experiences are real, and that exploiting this sensory modality is likely to be 'the Holy Grail' of VR.

VR devices in which tactile contact is not provided, or where it is simply 'substituted' by, say, visual or auditory information regarding the contact between our body and the environment (such as impact sounds), often fail to elicit a convincing sense of presence. This is likely due to the fact that people are simply more used to interacting with objects using their hands rather than their voices or a mouse, say. It is also worth considering here that, from a phylogenetic point of view, the use of our hands preceded the use of language by our ancestors (e.g., De Thomas, 1971; MacDaniel & Andersen, 1998). Similarly, over the course of ontogenesis, we learned to interact successfully with objects long before we mastered the ability to communicate using language (e.g., Bernhardt, 1987; Gottlieb, 1971). Therefore, nothing seems to provide the same level of intuitiveness as touch does whenever an interaction with objects is required (see also Ho, Reed, & Spence, 2007).

Recent studies have shown that visuo-haptic interfaces (in particular, remote manipulation devices; see Gallace, Tan, & Spence, 2007) can be used to support even complex long-distance interactions such as those involved in clinical operations by a surgeon in one country on a patient in another (e.g., Marescaux, Leroy, Gagner, Rubino, Mutter, Vix, et al., 2001; Tavakoli & Howe, 2008). Interestingly, most of the VR systems that have been developed to date, have tried to replicate tactile sensations at one of the body surface's most sensitive locations, the fingertips (see Iwata, 2008, for a recent review of the range of haptic stimulation devices that are currently available). However, the aim of a fully immersive multisensory VR system should be to present information across the entire body surface (or at least over a substantially greater surface area than that currently stimulated by the Phantom and similar force-feedback devices). The goal of achieving full-body virtual touch (Iwata, 2008) might be less challenging than expected (see Dennett, 1991, for one philospher's pessimistic early view of the possibility of virtual tactile stimulation). This is because scientific research has shown that; 1) tactile receptive fields are larger on certain areas of the body (e.g., the back) than others (Weinstein, 1968), therefore a smaller number of stimulators can be used on those parts of the body that have a lower sensitivity in order to simulate the presence of a given stimulus; and 2) people do not appear to be aware that multiple stimuli are being presented on their skin (regardless of whether they are presented on the fingertips or on the rest of the body surface) whenever more than three stimuli are concurrently presented (e.g., Gallace, Tan, & Spence, 2006, 2008; see also Gallace & Spence, 2008, for a discussion of the limitations that affect tactile information processing). This is likely due to the fact that when multiple stimuli are presented, we simply can't (at least without a great deal of practice) attend to more than two or three of them at any given moment. Moreover, it is also possible that, under certain conditions of stimulus presentation, the available information is automatically organized into patterns and/or perceptually 'completed' (Gallace & Spence, 2009, in press). That is, when more than two fingers are concurrently stimulated we might feel more like having an object in our hand, rather than feeling separate sensations on each finger (see Gallace & Spence, in press; O'Regan, 1992).

Therefore, it might be possible that stimulating only a limited number of body positions would result in the perception of more complex perceptual patterns even without the need to provide more complete (and resource-consuming) high-resolution stimulation across the entire body surface (cf. Dennett, 1991). This factor might be even more relevant when any lack of tactile stimulation happens to be compensated for by the presence of consistent information from other sensory modalities. Moreover, these observations also suggest that, given the limited number of stimuli that people can perceive when presented at the same time, VR should provide only that information that is strictly relevant to the task at hand. That is, we do not always feel the presence of the clothing on our skin or of the chair in which we are sitting (at least if we do not concentrate on these aspects of our tactile milieu; see Holmes & Spence, 2006, for a review). Therefore, providing this additional information within a complex virtual scenario would likely be of scarce use, and even deleterious in terms of bandwidth. Similarly, we are generally fully aware of changes in the available information (given the fact that 'transients' automatically capture attention), but not necessarily of those parts of a scene that remain the same (e.g., Gallace Tan, & Spence, 2006b; Levin & Simons, 1997). Once again, these considerations from the extant cognitive and neuroscientific research on human information processing suggest that, within a virtual environment, only a small percentage of the information (for example, that concerning the transients) is really necessary to be rendered in high definition in order to elicit a given percept.

Beside the advantages of adding tactile contact to human-machine/object VR interactions, the situations in which multisensory VR is likely to benefit the most from the addition of tactile stimulation are certainly those where human-to-human interactions (i.e., contact) need to be simulated. We now know that interpersonal tactile stimulation can have a profound effect on people's social behaviors. Touch can modulate people's tendencies to comply with requests, affect attitudes toward specific services, create bonds between couples or groups, strengthen romantic relationships; and even enhance the likelihood of behaving morally (Crusco & Wetzel, 1984; Erceau & Guéguen, 2007; Morhenn, Park, Piper, & Zak, 2008; see Gallace & Spence, 2010, for a review), regardless of whether or not the tactile contact itself can be remembered explicitly. These effects are likely attributable to a number of different factors. For example, the fact that tactile contact facilitates the release of oxytocin (Henricson, Berglund, Määttä, Ekman, & Segesten, 2008), and that certain tactile fibers (i.e., 'C afferents'; Löken, Wessberg, Morrison, McGlone, & Olausson, 2009; Vallbo, Olsson, Westberg, & Clark, 1984) seem to be connected with those brain areas that are responsible for evaluating the hedonic aspects of stimuli are only two of these reasons. As far as this point is concerned, it seems like we are still far from implementing interpersonal tactile contact into multisensory VR.

Most of the economic efforts that have been directed toward adding interpersonal tactile contact to virtual interactions seem to have come from the pornography industry (note that similar considerations also apply to the development of virtual scent displays; Digiscents Inc., personal communication – 'the smell of latex, anyone?'). In fact, the sex business is certainly the one with the greatest interest in developing immersive VR systems that can effectively simulate human-to-human and human-to-virtual avatar intimate (i.e., sexual) interactions (e.g., Lynn, 2004; see also Nelson, 1974, for the first mention of the concept of 'teledildonics'). Beyond the pornography industry, however, research on the development of tactile feedback for interpersonal virtual interactions seems to be moving at a relatively slow pace. As it turns out, one of the major criticisms of 'collaborative virtual environments' has been precisely that they lack emotional warmth and nonverbal intimacy (e.g., Mehrabian, 1967; Sproull & Kiesler, 1986; see also Gallace & Spence, 2010).

One interesting attempt to investigate the role of touch in social VR interaction has come from a series of studies reported by Basdogan, Ho, Slater, and Srinivasan (1998). They asked their participants to use haptic devices, which allowed them to feel one another's digital avatars, while performing a collaborative task. The results demonstrated that adding virtual interpersonal touch to a visual interaction improved the participants' performance on a spatial task as well as increasing their subjective ratings of "togetherness" (see also Sallnas, Rassmus-Grohn, & Sjostrom, 2000). Some mobile applications are now using haptic technology to simulate social touch. Researchers from the Kajimoto Laboratory in Japan recently created an application/interface for the iPhone that simulates two people, in distant physical locations, tickling each other's palms (see youtube.com/watch?v=MeOnbdaQmtU&feature= player_embedded; downloaded 09/06/2011). Unfortunately, however, the majority of attempts to add social touch to VR interactions appear to be limited to very early stages of development and, more often than not, never seem to progress beyond the stage of good 'ideas' (perhaps because there is too much of a reliance on questionnaire measures as a source of data).

Recently, Spence and Gallace (2010) posed the question of whether virtual touch could ever provide the same benefits of real touch (for example, in terms of oxytocin release, a hormone related to human and animal bonding behaviour)? Very little evidence has been provided so far on this topic. Moreover, one of the few studies to have

directly addressed this question failed to demonstrate significant results. Specifically, Haans, IJsselsteijn, Graus, and Salminen (2008) investigated whether or not virtual touch could be used to elicit the 'Midas touch effect' (i.e., the increased compliance with a request that is seen whenever it is accompanied by tactile contact; see Gallace & Spence, 2010, for a review). Their results showed that this effect does not appear to occur when people are touched by a haptic device, even one designed to simulate mediated social touch. Note, though, that in Haans and colleagues' study, the 'social' component of the tactile stimulation was more cognitive than perceptual. That is, the participants received vibrations via an arm strap and were told that these stimuli were deliberately initiated by a confederate. No actual efforts were made in this study to simulate a real social stimulus (i.e., touch). Therefore, one might wonder if different results could have been obtained had different conditions of stimulus presentation been used (e.g., using visuo-tactile virtual stimulations that more closely mimic certain aspects of actual social touch).

We believe, though, that negative results such as those reported by Haans and colleagues (2008) need to be evaluated in light of the lack of knowledge that we currently have concerning the cognitive and neural correlates of processing the more social aspects of tactile information (see Gallace & Spence, 2010). For example, we know that certain aspects of tactile social interactions seem to be mediated by neural fibres (C afferents) that respond particularly vigorously to the slow stroking of the skin, but relatively poorly to rapid deformations of the skin surface (e.g., Bessou, Burgess, Perl, & Taylor, 1971; Iggo, 1977; see also Olausson et al., 2008). However, we do not know whether a stimulus can be interpreted as 'social' as a function of any visual, auditory, and/or olfactory information that happens to be presented at the same time. That is, will seeing a hand that strokes your arm, but critically only stimulates a small number of tactile receptors on your skin still be interpreted as a 'stroke'? This is certainly one important issue for the future development of multisensory VR systems. In fact, simulating the perception of the tactile aspects of a stroke or caress (cf. Hertenstein, Keltner, App, Bulleit, & Jaskolka, 2006, for the report that people can correctly identify emotions from the experience of being touched by a stranger on their arm) might be less resource-demanding and technologically challenging under conditions of 'congruent' multisensory stimulus presentation as compared to conditions where only the tactile modality is stimulated.

Smell

Olfaction, being a rather primitive sense (at least from a phylogenetic point of view), is critical to everyday life. It tells us to leave a burning building (at least if we are not asleep; Cain, & Turk, 1985), or whether a given food is rotten or potentially poisonous (see Robinett, 1992). Often, we rely on our sense of smell in order to decide whether or not it is safe to engage further with a given stimulus. Olfactory cues are also used in mate selection (Spence, 2002) and certain smells have been found to be effective in terms of eliciting pleasant moods and feelings (e.g., Spence, 2003). Given that olfactory information is relatively simple to deliver and that a number of smell delivery systems have been designed in the last few years (e.g., Davide, Holmberg, & Lundström, 2001; Yanagida, Kawato, Noma, & Tetsutani, 2004; see Table 2), it is surprising that so few studies have been conducted on the potentials of adding this form of stimulation to multisensory VR environments.

In one of the few papers published in this area, Vlahos (2006) reported that the addition of a scent collar to standard VR equipment (e.g., goggles offering a stereoscopic view, headphones providing binaural sounds, and movement sensors) can help to create immersive multisensory environments in which soldiers can be prepared for just the kinds of situations that they may subsequently encounter in a war zone. That is, soldiers on

Table 2. Selection of recently developed devices designed to artificially deliver smell and their known limitations

Device	Producer	Description	Known Problems
iSmell	Digiscents company	-A device connected to USB or serial PC ports consisting of pots of oils infused with different scents (128 primary odors) -Designed to emit a smell when a user visits a specific web site or open an email	-The claim that they could generate any smell from a combination of a few basic smells, remains unproven (Washburn & Jones, 2004) -The company ceased trading in 2001 before a fully functional version of iSmell hit the marketplace
Aromajet	aromajet.com	Smell device for VR games and medical applications	Small number of odours presented
ScentKiosk Scent Dispenser	ScentAir Technologies	A smell delivery system where users can create custom scents	Limited to the presentation of 3 scents
Scent collar	anthrotronix.com and the Institute of Creative Technologies	-Collar that fit around a users neck, which holds four scent cartridges -The release of scents by the collars can be controlled by a wireless interface (Morie et al., 2003)	Small number of odours presented

the ground often find themselves in an unknown area under circumstances that are unfamiliar and often highly stressful. The unusual smells produced by exploding bombs and mines, burning trucks and buildings, and decaying corpses may overwhelm the newly-deployed soldiers and may interfere with the completion of their mission. However, olfactory cues can also provide information that may be vital for a soldier's survival: Burning wires may, for example, indicate an electrical problem in an aircraft, while the smell of a cigarette could signal the presence of the enemy. Trainee doctors can also benefit from the presence of odours in VR environments in order to identify certain pathologies (cf. Keller, Kouzes, Kangas, & Hashem, 1995; Willis, Church, Guest, et al., 2004). It would be of great importance in the future to put these intuitions on the possible advantages of using smell in VR under scrupulous testing, using both psychophysical and electrophysiological measures.

Certainly, the delivery of olfactory stimuli has its own technical, as well as perceptual, problems. Gilbert (2008), in his review of the early history of attempts to introduce fragrances/odours to the cinema setting; see above) during the mid 20th Century, noted that technical problems severely limited the use of this kind of device and compromised any expectations regarding its success. Part of the problem here was that it was difficult to clear the air after having delivered the odours. The available technology has certainly improved greatly since the first versions of Odorama, AromaRama, and Smell-O-Vision were introduced, and personalized seat-mounted delivery is now used in certain cinemas. In particular, by delivering odours directly to the nostrils, far less odorant has to be dispensed and hence it is much easier to clear the air in time for the next delivery of a scent. Considering the fact that the reliable presentation of odours in VR environments is now a very real possibility, the question to be answered becomes one of: what precisely is the purpose of delivering an odour in a VR environment? Is it to set (or

modify) the user's mood, is it to enhance the ambience (or atmosphere), or is it to provide congruent olfactory stimulation regarding the piece of fruit that the VR user has just picked up? One should also consider the fact that the delivery of odour as compared to the presentation of other stimuli is slower. These considerations alone would seem to set the limits of the VR situations that might benefit from the addition of odours. Moreover, it is worth noting that in order to be effective a VR system where smells are presented needs to use replaceable odorants. Consequently, people will need to buy a variable number of replacement odorant cartridges from time to time. The question to be answered here then becomes: Will the perceived benefit coming from the addition of smell to a VR system be sufficient to make people willing to frequently pay for it? This is a matter that, if not taken seriously enough, might very well jeopardize the possible success of any smell delivery system for virtual environments.

Interestingly, there are now a large number of empirical studies that suggest that the stimulation of the sense of smell might offer important advantages to multisensory VR situations. For example, it has been shown that the release of certain smells (be they presented at a sub- or supra-threshold level) will make subjects rate the people they see on a computer screen as being more attractive than they otherwise would (e.g., Demattè, Österbauer, & Spence, 2007; Li, Moallem, Paller, & Gottfried, 2007; see also Williams & Bargh, 2008, for the effect of the warmth of a cup held in the hand on the perception of interpersonal warmth). That is, the evaluation of the visual qualities of a stimulus can be significantly affected by the concurrent presentation of a certain smell (see also Baron, 1997). How can such findings be made relevant to VR simulations? The main point here is the more accurate and precise become the reproduction of details regarding highly complex visual stimuli such as faces and bodies, the more bandwidth and computational power is required for stimulus rendering and movement. Therefore, anything that can (with a low cost in terms of the bandwidth) be used to make virtual stimuli more 'beautiful', more attractive, and more 'real' is certainly of great help in terms of enhancing both the user's sense of presence and his/her enjoyment.

There are numerous potential uses for olfactory VR: For example, olfactory stimuli might be used to put the users of VR equipment into a certain state of alertness (e.g., think of the smell of coffee; Ho & Spence, 2006; Kole, Snel, & Lorist, 1998), to improve their athletic and/or cognitive performance (e.g., Chen, Katdare, & Lucas, 2006; Raudenbush, Corley, & Eppich, 2001), or else to relax them, say, when VR is being used to help alleviate the pain of dressing burns victims – i.e., think of the smell of lavender; see Atanassova-Shopova, & Boycheva, 1973; Lehrner, Eckersberger, Walla, Pötsch, & Deecke, 2000; Spence, 2002, 2003). It is important to note at this point that people do not necessarily have to be aware of the odour in order for it to affect their behaviour/perception. In fact, sometimes subliminally-presented odours appear to work more effectively because people are simply not aware of their presence (see Li et al., 2006).

Finally, it is worth noting that failing to provide olfaction in VR settings might also have deleterious effects on the user's sense of presence in those conditions in which virtual interactions do not occur in 'smell-proof' environments. That is, if the presentation of smell is not controlled, it is possible that other environmental smells might interfere with the user's perception of a given situation. Think about the consequences of perceiving smells from the cafeteria while experiencing a seaside holiday situation for a user's sense of presence!

Pheromones

While pheromones have had a mixed reception in the scientific literature over the years (e.g., Meredith, 2001), the evidence now convincingly supports their role in modulating at least certain aspects of human behaviours (Bensafi, 2004; Jacob, Kinnunen, Metz, Cooper, & McClintock, 2001; Jacob & McClintock, 2000; McClintock, 1971; Stern & McClintock, 1998). While the control of a person's ovulation using pheromonal cues is unlikely to have a wide application in VR, it should be noted that people can detect another's emotional state using pheromonal cues. This opens up the possibility of releasing the smell of fear in VR or military simulations (e.g., Ackerl, Atzmueller, & Grammer, 2002; Cain, & Turk, 1985 ; Zhou & Chen, 2008). One can only imagine how much more immersive the experience of being in the dungeon with Lara Croft could be made with the release of a little 'smell of fear' mixed with that stale dungeon odour (and what about delivering the 'smell of blood' while playing the video game Resident Evil?).

A recent neuroimaging study has shown that certain areas of the brain involved in the processing of social (e.g., the right fusiform cortex) and pleasant aspects of the stimuli (the right orbitofrontal cortex) as well as areas related to sexual motivation (e.g., the right hypothalamus) respond to airborne natural human sexual sweat (Zhou & Chen, 2008). This finding provides clear neuroscience evidence that socio-emotional meanings, including those that are of a more sexual nature, can be conveyed via human sweat. This important result is certainly relevant to any discussion of the possible advantages of the introduction of pheromonal cues to VR environments. In particular, this class of stimuli, even if consciously undetected, might affect the functioning of certain brain areas (such as those responsible for our perception of pleasure). Pheromones, then, might be adopted together with other sensory stimuli in order to target certain brain areas and so enhance the qualities of a given virtual environment. Unfortunately, research on how different sources of information interact to enhance the activity of certain brain areas still lack development for combinations of senses that also contain pheromonal information. Moreover, a more practical problem here is that it is unclear whether or not pheromones can be synthesized for mass production just like other odorants (note indeed that using human sweat is unlikely to be a viable solution to this problem).

Pain

Of all of our senses, pain is certainly the one that is more directly related to our well-being. In fact, pain can be defined as an unpleasant sensory and emotional experience that minimizes immediate harm by motivating escape (e.g., Auvray, Myin, & Spence, 2010; Darwin, 1872). Failing to promptly react to painful stimuli typically has disastrous consequences for the integrity of the body. It is pain, indeed, that informs us about possible damage to our bodily tissues and there is nothing like pain to urge us to organize our responses to external stimuli. That pain is highly adaptive in our everyday lives is beyond dispute, but what about the need for simulating pain within a multisensory VR environment? Do we really need to virtually reproduce painful sensations? We believe that the answer is 'yes', at least under certain conditions. For instance, VR settings might be used in the future to control external devices, such as mechanical body armor or even robots, and whenever the integrity of these devices is at risk pain might offer the best option to inform the user to engage in more appropriate protective behaviors (though see Auvray et al., 2010). It is worth noting that pain might be useful to help simulate those conditions in which high levels of stress are expected (such as that of a doctor operating in extreme conditions during a natural disaster, say). The training of soldiers is only one among the many situations in which adding pain to multisensory VR might offer an important advantage.

Pain in all of the above-mentioned situations might be substituted (e.g., just as in most of the currently available videogames) by visual or auditory signals, but will they be just as effective (given that nothing is as effective as pain in cap-

turing our attention; see Spence, Bentley, Phillips, McGlone, & Jones, 2002)? Evidence from the study of patients affected by leprosy would seem to suggest that this might not be the case. These patients experience, in their leprous member, an absence of feelings of pain that often results in self-generated damage. Interestingly, back in 1969, Brand and Ebner developed a prosthetic system that could substitute pain by means of pressure stimulators attached to an intact part of the body (see also Brand & Yancey, 1993). Their results showed that these devices were of little use for the patients concerned. In particular, given that the new stimuli did not force the patient to react to them, just as a really painful stimuli does, it turned out that they were soon largely ignored.

Interestingly, there have already been attempts to add pain to virtual interactions. In particular, an arm-wrestling system that delivers electric shock to the loser has been designed and tested by researchers. In fact, it appears that the gaming industry is finally showing increasing interest in the development of multisensory VR environments in which pain can also be delivered. That is, it seems like gamers might enjoy the added realism provided by feeling shots, stabs, slams, and hits dealt to their on-screen characters/avatars in war videogames for example; (http://us.i1.yimg. com/videogames.yahoo.com/feature/special-vest-lets-players-feel-video-game-blows/534921; downloaded 19/03/2010).

Interoceptive Signals

Signals originating from the external world are not the only information processed by our brains. That is, our internal organs continuously provide information regarding our body and its current status. In certain situations we can feel our heart beating faster or our lungs pumping more air than usual (see Craig, 2002, for a review). Interestingly, it has been demonstrated that our physiological state can affect the cognitive evaluations of emotional stimuli and vice versa (see Damasio, 1994, for an extensive review of this topic). Reproducing (or rather inducing) physiological states that are compatible with the situations that one wants to virtually re-create is certainly something that may contribute to the realism of multisensory VR experiences. Although one possibility in this sense is to use drugs that can change the pattern of activation of certain organs (although usually in a highly nonspecific way; e.g., Fraguas, Marci, Fava, Iosifescua, Bankier, Loh, & Dougherty, 2007), a more viable (and safer) option might be to use biofeedback. Biofeedback can be used to provide information regarding the functioning of our organs, even under conditions where we are generally unaware of such stimuli. That is, visual, tactile, and auditory stimuli can all be used to reproduce or, at the very least, provide a feedback signal concerning information that is related to our emotional reactions to certain stimuli (e.g., our heartbeat, our rate of breathing, our sweating, our blood pressure, even our salivation, etc.; see Spence, 2011b).

How, then, might biofeedback be used to enhance the sense of presence within a multisensory environment? This might be achieved, for example, by providing altered biofeedback to simulate a certain physiological reaction (e.g., fear) to the users of multisensory VR. Indeed, it has already been shown that tactile and auditory information regarding one person's heartbeat can be used to change another person's heartbeat. That is, presenting, either tactually or auditorily, an accelerated heartbeat results in an acceleration of the heartbeat of the person who happens to be listening to, or feeling, it (see Bason & Cellar, 1972; Gray, Harrison, Wiens, & Critchley, 2007; Standley, 1991; Västfjäll, 2006; see also Vallns, 1966). Gallace and Spence recently asked the participant in one of their experiments to sit in a dimly-illuminated room where a heartbeat sound was presented over an external loudspeaker. They found that the acoustically-presented frequency of the heartbeat affected their participants' physiological arousal measured by means of the skin

conductance response (i.e., a 110bpm heartbeat sound increased the participants' skin conductance as compared to a 60bpm heartbeat sound or no sound). Following on from such observations, it becomes clear that one might attempt to increase the realism of a certain multisensory situation by presenting biofeedback that is consistent with the situation that is being simulated. That is, understanding how inputs from our different exteroceptive senses interact with physiological (i.e., interoceptive) signals in order to give rise in our brain to complex emotional reactions is certainly something that will help the development of fully immersive multisensory VR environments.

PROJECTING SENSATIONS TO VIRTUAL BODIES (TOUCH, PAIN)

"Josh's Avatar opens his eyes, and looks around with amazed awareness. He blinks, the strange hues of the alien vision flooding his brain. He moves awkwardly, sitting up. He takes a deep breath and smells the air. His nostrils flare with the flood of new alien smells. He looks at his hand, staring at it, working the fingers. He looks down and stares at his body, he touches it with one hand. Feels the skin. Smooth. Warm" (From 'Avatar' 2010)

The last few years have seen a rapid growth of interest in the study of the cognitive and neural correlates of 'body representation'. Importantly, it has been shown that by using certain behavioral procedures, people can start to perceive that a rubber hand is an actual part of their body (e.g., Slater, Pérez Marcos, Ehrsson, & Sanchez-Vives, 2009; see Makin, Holmes, & Ehrsson, 2008, for a review). Even more interestingly, people can feel that their body is actually positioned in the location of a distant mannequin if the visual information that they get comes from a camera placed on the mannequin's head (Aspell, Lenggenhager, & Blanke, 2009; Petkova & Ehrsson, 2008). Sometimes, they even report taking ownership of the mannequin's body! It is relevant to note here that, by itself, visual information is insufficient to induce this illusion. That is, people need to see the mannequin's body being touched, but also, critically, to feel at exactly the same time that their own body is being touched in the same position. These recent discoveries then open up intriguing perspectives on the field of VR systems development. That is, the experience of 'becoming' a humanoid robot in tele-robotics/tele-surgery and the feeling of 'owning' a simulated body in VR environments would probably enhance user control, realism, and the feeling of presence.

What, then, are the potential problems related to these new approaches to human VR multi-sensory interface design? The first relates to the psychological consequences of owning a different body or even simply controlling a robotic arm. For example, Petkova and Ehrsson (2008), after having elicited the illusion that people 'owned' the body of a mannequin (by stimulating the abdomen of the mannequin at the same time as that of the participant), threatened the abdomen of the mannequin with a knife. They observed an increase in their participants' physiological stress levels. That is, under the appropriate conditions, threatening an external object led to similar (albeit reduced) physiological responses to those obtained by threatening the participants' real body (see Moseley, Gallace & Spence, 2011, for a recent review). Clearly, one might wonder what the consequences of this increase in physiological stress every time an external tactile interface or robotic arm is used would be.

Another interesting consideration related to the physiological consequences of perceiving an external object as part of one's own body comes from a recent study by Moseley, Olthof, Venema, Don, Wijers, Gallace, and Spence (2008). In that study, the researchers elicited the illusion that an artificial rubber arm was part of the participant's own body (i.e., they induced the rubber arm illusion in their participants). Interestingly they noted that

the skin temperature of the participant's own arm (placed in the same part of space as the artificial arm) decreased. That is, the thermoregulation of a given body-part was altered whenever participants started to feel sensations as arising from an artificial arm. What then happens to thermoregulation and, more generally, to people's vital physiological functions when they start to take ownership of virtual bodies and robotic arms? And what are the longer-term psychological and emotional responses and/or consequences of this? Do different people, for example, 'accept' more or less easily the presence of a tactile interface on their body (till they feel it as an actual part of their body) or rather reject it as an extraneous constraint (which sometimes occurs in the case of transplanted limbs; e.g., Hu, Lu, Zhang, Wu, Nie, Zhu, et al., 2006)? And does this depend on the demographic (e.g., age or cultural level) or psychological (e.g., see the 'need for touch' index; Peck & Childers, 2003; see Spence & Gallace, in press, for a recent review) parameters? Moreover, one might wonder whether or not VR interfaces requiring a person to take control of a body will be too cognitively or emotionally challenging for the rapidly growing older population. Indeed, it should be noted that these devices will, sooner or later, target this section of the population, given their potentially important contribution to the understanding of sensory loss caused by aging and the often-reported complaints of the older population regarding a lack of tactile stimulation in their life (see Lee, Poliakoff, & Spence, 2009). These concerns are likely to provide further constraints on, and motivation for, the development of VR interfaces in the years to come.

The findings of the neuroscientific literature on the theme of body ownership are certainly suggestive of important advantages in using visuo-tactile interfaces to elicit ownership of virtual bodies or avatars. Moreover, these studies are also important in terms of the possibilities that they raise about how to study the effectiveness of virtual stimuli in eliciting these kinds of experiences. For example, in one interesting study, Schaefer, Heinze, & Rotte (2009) used an artificial hand that appeared, visually, to be connected to the participants' own body in order to give the impression that they had a supernumerary third arm. The researchers reported that activation in the somatosensory cortex was modulated by the perceived presence of the supernumerary limb (i.e., the cortical representation of the thumb shifted to a more medial and superior position). Moreover, this modulation of cortical activity was found to be predictive of the strength of the feeling that the third arm actually belonged to the participant. This finding raises the possibility of using neuroimaging techniques to test the effectiveness of virtual devices in eliciting the sense of ownership of a virtual body/avatar. Another, even simpler, possibility suggested by the previously mentioned study by Moseley and his colleagues (2008) is to measure the temperature of real body parts after the use of virtual prosthesis.

There have been a number of fascinating high-profile studies recently that have used VR to create out-of-body experiences. Critically, these crossmodal effects (or illusions), which are very dramatic, cannot be induced solely by stimulating the eyes (or for that matter the ears), but instead require that tactile stimulation is simultaneously delivered to the observer's body and to the body that the participant in these studies sees through their goggles (e.g., Ehrsson, 2007; Lenggenhager, Tadi, Metzinger, & Blanke, 2007; Slater, Perez-Marcos, Ehrsson, & Sanchez-Vivez, 2009). Note here that all of these advances in creating the sensation of 'owning' virtual bodies would not have been possible without the insight provided by neurocognitive research. That is, researchers in this field of study have highlighted the specific constraints that affect these phenomena. For example, they have shown that synchronization between seeing a rubber hand being touched and feeling tactile stimuli in the corresponding part of their body is an important factor for inducing an illusion of body ownership (e.g., Armel &

Ramachandran, 2003). That is, scientific research concerning how information regarding our body is integrated in the brain to provide a 'sense of self' is vitally important to determining both the limits and potentiality of creating fully-functional virtual bodies or avatars. Certainly, there are still a number of questions that researchers need to address in the near future, such as to what extent we can project our sensations to virtual bodies? Can painful and proprioceptive sensations also be projected to an external avatar?

TECHNICAL AND COGNITIVE PROBLEMS IN MULTISENSORY VR

VR systems cannot simulate reality perfectly. In fact, VR requires the use of computer hardware and software to create artificial environments that 'feel' real and that elicit a sense of 'presence' in the user. Two of the main goals of a VR system are: 1) To create a *realistic* perception, and 2) To create a virtual environment that can be felt/perceived in *real-time*. While the development and progress of VR systems that can effectively accomplish these goals has been exponential over the last few decades, there are still a number of technical limitations related to the equipment used to create VR. It is important to recognize that there are also cognitive limitations related to how, and how much, humans perceive artificial/virtual objects/elements.

Low-resolution, pixelated images can certainly detract from the realism of objects presented in VR. It comes as no surprise, therefore, that much of the focus in terms of improving VR in recent years has been on increasing the resolution of visual VR elements (e.g., Burdea & Coiffet, 1994). High-fidelity VR simulators, however, require a great deal of processing power, typically resulting in system failures, hangs, and glitches, not to mention heavy and expensive machinery. Moreover, it is important to ask whether or not high-fidelity simulators can really help people perform (i.e., efficiently accomplish specific tasks/goals) in VR environments?

Robertson, Czerwinski, Larson, Robbins, Thiel, and van Dantzich (1998) demonstrated that the retrieval of information and items contained in a virtual interface could be improved by displaying the items in 3-D rather than 2-D. In a subsequent study, however, Cockburn and McKenzie (2002) suggested that presenting information in 3-D actually hindered rather than enhanced performance as compared to a 2-D condition. They tested participants' retrieval of items in physical and virtual 2-D, 2½-D (see Marr, 1983), and 3-D environments and observed that the participants were not only slower to do so in both the physical and virtual 3-D as compared to the 2-D environments, but the participants also felt that the 3-D environments were more cluttered and confusing. Given that participants' performance was worse even in the physical 3-D environment (relative to the physical 2-D environment), not just the virtual environments, this seems to reflect a problem associated with the human processing of visual information, rather than a problem with the VR system itself. One of the reasons 3-D displays sometimes give rise to worse performance than 2-D displays may be because 3-D displays require more visual processing resources to analyze the stimuli. The assumption underlying the use of 3-D imagery in VR is that, relative to 2-D imagery, it provides an additional dimension (i.e., depth) in which information can be viewed and processed, and thus, should aid in tasks requiring spatial memory. However, the additional dimension may require additional processing that might ultimately lead to less efficient performance. Thus, Wickens, Olmos, Chudy, and Davenport's (1997) conclusion that *"whether the benefits of 3-D displays outweigh their costs turns out to be a complex issue, depending upon the particular 3-D rendering chosen, the nature of the task, and the structure of the information to be displayed"* (p. 2) seems appropriate here.

Understanding human vision and implementing this understanding into the design of VR can not only enhance the VR experience (i.e., improve the "presence" of the human in VR) but it can, in turn, free-up the technical processing power needed to create such high-fidelity, visual simulators and allow for the shift of focus to the development of other sensory modalities in VR. For example, in human vision, objects presented in foveal view (i.e., at the center or gaze) are sharp (permitting optimal visual acuity), whereas objects presented in the periphery tend to be blurred Based on the understanding of this fundamental aspect of visual perception/processing, some VR researchers have already begun implementing this into the development of simulators that only render high-fidelity outputs (i.e., visual scenes) to where the user's attention is focused (i.e., where saccades are directed), while degrading the resolution of peripheral objects. Such gaze-contingent displays help to reduce the overall processing power required to generate visual VR, given that the entire visual scene no longer needs to be rendered in such high-definition (Baudisch, DeCarlo, Duchowski, & Geisler, 2003). Moreover, this revised rendition of visual VR also simulates human vision more realistically.

Understanding the limitations and capabilities of visual perception will dramatically help advance the progress of VR simulation. Exactly the same considerations apply to the other sensory modalities. For example, the existence of robust crossmodal links in spatial attention, discovered recently by cognitive neuroscientists (e.g., Spence & Driver, 2004), means that people are likely to attend auditorily wherever they happen to be attending visually. Thus, understanding these aspects of human sensory perception, and, in particular, the spatial links in attention between the senses is necessary for developing VR systems that can effectively create a sense of multisensory presence for the user.

One of the major limitations in VR technology relates to the operation of VR in 'real-time'. This can be due to the fact that either the computer isn't relaying the information provided in VR fast enough, or we are not processing the relayed information fast enough. Moreover, the synchrony of the component sensory inputs used to make up a given percept in VR is vital to producing VR that feels 'real'. Imagine a badly dubbed movie. Research has shown that people can tolerate a lag between visual and auditory speech information of up to 100 ms (see Vatakis & Spence, 2010, for a review). Beyond this, the asynchrony of the visual and auditory information can be not only distracting, but it can also break the user from the realism of the experience (e.g., an actor speaking). Moreover, an incorrect latency in tracking a movement can even make the user/operator feel sick. The temporal resolution of VR systems is also crucial in biofeedback (Baram & Miller, 2006). If the timing of the feedback is off, people do not benefit from the biofeedback provided in VR. For example, patients with multiple sclerosis have been shown to exhibit significant improvements in their ability to walk only when using immediate VR visual feedback cues. While the temporal resolution of both the multiple sources of sensory stimulation and the relay of this information to the user are important to the enjoyment of VEs, its importance is made even clearer when considering its role in facilitating distributed or remote VR operations such as tele-surgery and potentially dangerous military operations. For example, where a doctor performs surgery on a patient in a remote location, mere milliseconds of lag-time, between what the doctor does in the VR environment and the real-time output on the patient, can be severely detrimental to the outcome of the task at hand. In this case, any delay can mean the difference between life and death (see Marescaux et al., 2001).

Another relevant technical problem related to the development of VR systems is related to the fact that the functioning of any mechanical device (such as actuators within a force-feedback system) is always associated with the presence of friction (e.g., Colgate, Stanley, & Brown, 1995). Note that friction is not always present in real-life situations. Indeed, our bodies move through air and are generally not connected to any external mechanical system. However, within a VR environment, an operator might perceive the presence of an external device, rather than concentrating on the actual stimulation provided, because of the presence of this mechanical limitation. Attempts to remove this problem have concentrated on the use of magnetic levitation systems (e.g., Berkelman, & Dzadovsky, 2009; Berkelman & Hollis, 1997). That is, the forces within systems such as these are not mechanically produced but determined by the strength of oriented magnetic fields. Although this kind of device offers interesting possibilities they are, at the moment at least, confined to the simulation of objects/textures that can be explored using a hand-held device (see for example the Maglev 200, by Butterfly Haptics). The possibility of immersing the whole body within an array of complex magnetic field generators that are able to provide force feedback to any part of the body would seem, at the moment, to remain in the realms of science-fiction.

Specific Problems Related to the Stimulation of Touch, Taste, and Olfaction

Tactile/haptic input is primarily delivered through the use of devices such as the Phantom force feedback device (e.g., Iwata, 2008; Trantakis, Bootz, Strauss, Nowatius, Lindner, et al., 2003). The price of these devices has dropped dramatically in recent years. However, even when two of these are used, they only give the opportunity for the control and stimulation of the finger and thumb (e.g., as in the simulation of precision grip; Ernst & Banks, 2002). That is, they cannot be used to simulate the presence of an object in the hand of the user, say. Moreover, this device is not immune to problems related to friction and degrees of freedom. Finally, the user must limit the movements of all of those parts of the body that are not in contact with the device in order to use it properly (e.g., one cannot even open his arms while using it).

As compared to tactile stimulation, the delivery of olfactory stimulation is somewhat easier. In fact, the receptor surface for this sense is relatively small when compared to that of the tactile modality. Moreover, humans cannot accurately localize smells. Therefore we can easily attribute olfactory stimuli to different positions in space (i.e., a sort of olfactory 'ventriloquism'), as a function of concurrently-presented visual, auditory or tactile information (i.e., there is no need to worry about directional stimulators in order to simulate the presence of a given odour coming from a given stimulus). However, the problem here, as noted by the developers of the old smell-enhanced cinema (see Gilbert, 2008), is that while you can deliver an odour relatively easily it may take time to remove it. As Vlahos (2006) acknowledges when talking about the use of scent in cinema: *"The filmmakers were stymied by technological challenges – securing believable scents, dispersing them at the right times, and changing odours without overlap"* (Vlahos p. 76). A few attempts to develop effective devices for presenting olfactory stimuli have been presented by a number of researchers in the last few years (e.g., Washburn, Jones, Satya, & Bowers, 2003; Yanagida, Kawato, Noma, & Tetsutani, 2004; see also **Table 2**). Unfortunately, however, so far it is still unclear how accurately these devices can reproduce smells, and perhaps more importantly, just how many different smells these systems can present. Although systems that can deliver fragrances (e.g., Dematte et al., 2006; Kole et al., 1998) are now becoming relatively cheap, another challenge to be faced seems to be the ability to deliver as wide a range of scents

as one might want (given that people seem to be able to recognize about 10,000 different scents; see Gilbert, 2008).

In summary, the main obstacle to the presentation of olfactory stimuli in multisensory VR settings is not fundamentally related to technical limitations but the limited know-how about how quickly a fragrance from a distal source should diffuse, how intense it should be, and how long it should linger in order to be accurately and effectively perceived. Perhaps the best use for olfaction is not for rapid event-related simulations (e.g., making a person smell each of the objects that they happen to pick up in a virtual market or supermarket, say), but rather for scene/mood setting (e.g., providing the smell of the damp dungeon in a Laura Croft video game) as well as eliciting certain emotional states/alertness (see above).

What about the stimulation of the sense of taste? Despite the fact that there is certainly scope to simulate food textures using auditory and tactile cues (Hashimoto et al., 2007, 2008), there is currently no system that can deliver anything more advanced than simple tastants via tubes placed in a person's mouth. In fact, there is no way to simulate oral texture, the feel of an ice cream melting in one's mouth, say. We now know that auditory cues can be used to enhance the textural attributes of foods (e.g., Zampini & Spence, 2004). However, with no simulated taste and/or oral-somatosensory texture system in sight (if you'll excuse the visual metaphor) the optimal solution for those applications where the simulation of taste and/or flavour is needed may well be to provide real food, and engage the user in mixed real and virtual encounters (see above). An exciting possibility with regards to the simulation of food texture comes from research by Hashimoto et al. (2007, 2008) in Japan. They have been able to simulate a number of foods using a virtual straw. The user of their device sucks the virtual food (a food of their choice depicted on a place-mat) and the straw gives the sounds and vibrations associated with eating that food. The authors claimed that the impression of food texture is realistic, despite the fact that no food stimuli were actually presented. Should this device be combined with appropriate olfactory stimulation, the promise is of a rather realistic virtual eating experience.

Cognitive Problems

So far in this review, we have highlighted some of the key potentials and pitfalls associated with VR applications. While increasing the number of senses that are stimulated in a VR application can enhance the sense of presence, these benefits have to be weighed against the potential costs associated with stimulating more of an interface user's senses. One of the key problems here relates to the delays, and hence synchronization, that can be inherent in each form of sensory stimulation (see also Richard et al., 1996). Indeed, we have already seen how a similar problem affected the early development of scent-enhanced cinema (Gilbert, 2008). A second problem relates to the fact that humans have only limited attentional resources, and hence the more senses that are stimulated, and the more senses that a user has to monitor, the fewer attentional resources will be available for each sensory modality (see Spence & Driver, 1997).

Miller (1956) suggested that each of our senses has a processing limit of 7 (+2) bits of information. Loftin (2003) took this suggestion, and proposed that the addition of each extra sense might allow people to circumvent this human information-processing limit. The claim was that we might be able to process an additional 7 (+2) information bits for each additional sensory modality that was utilized (e.g., in a VR display). It should, though, be noted that Miller also suggests that: *"The point seems to be that, as we add more variables to the display, we increase the total capacity, but we decrease the accuracy for any particular variable. In other words, we can make relatively crude judgments of several things simultaneously."*

Here, Miller seems to be pointing to the fact that attentional resources are not distinct (or separate) for each modality, but are, to some extent, shared (see Lavie, 2005; Spence & Driver, 1997). As a consequence, the more sensory modalities that are stimulated in a VR application, the more a user's attention has to be divided between their senses (Spence & Driver, 1997). It is important to note that this position is diametrically opposed to the workload models that are popular in traditional human factors research (see Hancock, Oran-Gilad, & Szalma, 2007; Wickens, 1980, 1984, 2008).

The key point to note is that under most conditions there will be a trade-off between the number of senses that are stimulated simultaneously, and the amount of attentional resources available for the processing of the stimuli presented in each modality. That is, having to monitor for olfactory stimuli will impair visual speeded performance (Spence, Kettenman, Kobal, & McGlone, 2000). This is not to say that smell should not be used, but rather that one needs to be aware that stimulating an extra sense, if that requires users to monitor another sense, may not come without some cost to performance. One solution here is to present environments in which all sensory modalities presented work together in synergy (i.e., to provide redundant information), rather than competing for attentional or processing resources. That is, all sensory stimuli presented within a given VR environment should contribute to reproduce the neural activity that is generated by an actual stimulus/event.

CONCLUSION

Perception is inherently multisensory. Indeed, the majority of life's most enjoyable experiences (if not all of them) stimulate several senses at the same time. The evidence reviewed in this chapter has shown that increasing the number of senses stimulated in a VR environment can increase the sense of presence, the user's enjoyment, and even their memory for the encounter (e.g., Dinh et al., 1999). The possibility of developing multisensory VR systems is now close at hand given that technology is improving and the costs of these non-visual VR systems are declining rapidly. We have seen that the one sense that shows the most immediate promise in terms of being utilized is olfaction. We have also shown that touch is the sense where more research resources need to be directed given the importance of this sensory modality in generating judgments of 'reality' from the users and the very large receptor surface involved.

That said, this chapter has highlighted the fact that there are still both theoretical and practical limitations on the virtual stimulation of our senses. In particular, we have seen that there are limitations that are very specific for each of our sensory modalities (e.g., related to the problem of friction for touch/haptics or to the cleaning of the air after an olfactory stimulus has been delivered). There are, of course, also other problems that apply to all of the senses, or else are associated with presenting multiple sensory stimuli in different modalities at the same time (e.g., those related to multisensory synchronization). We believe that certain of these limitations will probably affect this field of research for many years to come. However, here we also suggest that exploiting the knowledge that we have concerning how our brains integrate information from multiple senses is key to the development of effective and technologically sustainable VR systems. That is, we believe that understanding the neurocognitive bases of our behaviour is certainly something that cannot be avoided if one's aim is to reproduce realistic percepts. For example, knowledge regarding how the brain processes pleasant stimuli can be used to target, by means of different sources of sensory information, those very neural mechanisms. Pleasure, in this case, might be obtained even with physically impoverished stimuli, but using a blend of sensory stimuli perfectly designed to hit their target (i.e., increasing the brain activity of

those areas of the brain, such as the orbitofrontal cortex, responsible for the feeling of pleasure).

The same line of reasoning highlighted above also applies to every other aspect of our sensory experiences. In particular, exploiting the mechanisms of sensory dominance might help to overcome both the technological and cognitive problems associated with creating immersive VR settings. That is, the take home message of this chapter is that VR, in order to be effective (given the technical and cognitive limitations discussed here), should be based on brain mechanisms rather than on the attempt to reproduce the characteristics of physical stimuli (an approach that we named 'neurally-inspired VR'). Research on the mechanisms of multisensory perception is certainly the field that promises the largest opportunities in this direction. In particular, we suggest here that the development of VR systems would benefit from a better understanding of the Bayesian decision principles governing our perception (in both unisensory and multisensory contexts). That is, knowing what sensory modality dominates over the others in a given situation, or under certain conditions of stimulus presentation, will limit the amount of information that needs to be reproduced in a virtual environment in order to give rise to a certain percept. What is more, the notion of superadditivity (i.e., the idea that individually weakly-effective sensory cues may sum to give rise to an effect that is much larger than the sum of the parts; Stein & Meredith, 1998; Stein & Stanford, 2008) is also one that is worth pursuing in the domain of multisensory VR.

REFERENCES

Ackerl, K., Atzmueller, M., & Grammer, K. (2002). The scent of fear. *Neuroendocrinology Letters, 23*, 79–84.

Alais, D., & Burr, D. (2004). The ventriloquist effect results from near-optimal bimodal integration. *Current Biology, 14,* 257–262.

Armel, K. C., & Ramachandran, V. S. (2003). Projecting sensations to external objects: Evidence from skin conductance response. *Proceedings. Biological Sciences, 270,* 1499–1506. doi:10.1098/rspb.2003.2364

Aspell, J. E., Lenggenhager, B., & Blanke, O. (2009). Keeping in touch with one's self: Multisensory mechanisms of self-consciousness. *PLoS ONE, 4*(8), e6488. doi:10.1371/journal.pone.0006488

Atanassova-Shopova, K. S., & Boycheva, I. (1973). On certain neurotropic effects of lavender essential oil. *Bulletin of the Institute of Physiology, XV,* 149–156.

Auvray, M., Myin, E., & Spence, C. (2010). The sensory-discriminative and affective-motivational processing of pain. *Neuroscience and Biobehavioral Reviews, 34,* 214–223. doi:10.1016/j.neubiorev.2008.07.008

Bangay, S., & Preston, L. (1998). An investigation into factors influencing immersion in interactive virtual environments. *Studies in Health Technology and Informatics, 58,* 43–51.

Baram, Y., & Miller, A. (2006). Virtual reality cues for improvement of gait in patients with multiple sclerosis. *Neurology, 66,* 178–181. doi:10.1212/01.wnl.0000194255.82542.6b

Bardot, I., Bochereau, L., Bourgine, P., Heyd, B., Hossenlopp, J., Martin, N., et al. (1992). Cuisiner artificial: Un automate pour la formulation sensorielle de produits alimentaires [Artificial oven: A robot for synthesizing the smells of food]. *Proceedings of the Interface to Real and Virtual Worlds Conference,* 451-461.

Barfield, W., & Danas, E. (1996). Comments on the use of olfactory displays for virtual environments. *Presence (Cambridge, Mass.), 5,* 109–121.

Barfield, W., & Weghorst, S. (1993). The sense of presence within virtual environments: A conceptual framework. In Salvendy, G., & Smith, M. (Eds.), *Human computer interaction: Hardware and software interfaces* (pp. 699–704). Amsterdam: Elsevier.

Barnett, K. (1972). A theoretical construct of the concepts of touch as they relate to nursing. *Nursing Research, 21,* 102–110.

Baron, R. A. (1997). Of cookies, coffee, and kindness: Pleasant odors and the tendency to help strangers in a shopping mall. *Aroma-Chology Review, 6,* 3–11.

Bason, P. T., & Cellar, B. G. (1972). Control of the heart rate by external stimuli. *Nature, 4,* 279–280. doi:10.1038/238279a0

Bensafi, M. (2004). Sniffing human sex-steroid derived compounds modulates mood, memory and autonomic nervous system function in specific behavioral contexts. *Behavioural Brain Research, 152,* 11–22.

Berkeley, G. (1732). *An essay towards a new theory of vision* (4th Ed.). http://psychclassics.yorku.ca/ Berkeley/vision.htm

Berkelman, P., & Dzadovsky, M. (2009). Extending the motion ranges of magnetic levitation for haptic interaction. World Haptics 2009 - *Third Joint EuroHaptics conference and Symposium on Haptic Interfaces for Virtual Environment and Teleoperator Systems,* 2009 (pp. 517-522).

Berkelman, P. J., & Hollis, R. L. (1997). Dynamic performance of a hemispherical magnetic levitation haptic interface device. In *SPIE International Symposium on Intelligent Systems and Intelligent Manufacturing, SPIE Proc. Vol. 3602,* Greensburgh PA, September 1997.

Bernhardt, J. (1987). Sensory capabilities of the fetus. *MCN. The American Journal of Maternal Child Nursing, 12,* 44–46. doi:10.1097/00005721-198701000-00014

Bessou, P., Burgess, P. R., Perl, E. R., & Taylor, C. B. (1971). Dynamic properties of mechanoreceptors with unmyelinated (C) fibers. *Journal of Neurophysiology, 34,* 116–131.

Brand, P., & Ebner, M. A. (1969). Pressure sensitive devices for denervated hands and feet: A preliminary communication. *Journal of Bone and Joint Surgery, 51,* 109–116.

Brand, P., & Yancey, P. (1993). *Pain: The gift nobody wants.* New York: Harper Collins.

Brooks, F. P. Jr, Ming, O.-Y., Batter, J. J., & Kilpatrick, P. J. (1990). Project GROPE: Haptic displays for scientific visualization. *Computer Graphics, 24,* 177–185. doi:10.1145/97880.97899

Burdea, G., & Coiffet, P. (1994). *Virtual reality technology.* New York: Wiley.

Burdea, G. C. (1996). *Force and touch feedback for virtual reality.* New York: John Wiley & Sons.

Cain, W. S., & Turk, A. (1985). Smell of danger: An analysis of LP-gas odorization. *American Industrial Hygiene Association Journal, 46,* 115–126. doi:10.1080/15298668591394527

Calvert, G. A., Spence, C., & Stein, B. E. (Eds.). (2004). *The handbook of multisensory processes.* Cambridge, MA: MIT Press.

Carlin, A. S., Hoffman, H. G., & Weghorst, S. (1997). Virtual reality and tactile augmentation in the treatment of spider phobia: A case report. *Behaviour Research and Therapy, 35,* 153–158. doi:10.1016/S0005-7967(96)00085-X

Cater, J. P. (1992). The noses have it! *Presence (Cambridge, Mass.), 1,* 493–494.

Chen, D., Katdare, A., & Lucas, N. (2006). Chemosignals of fear enhance cognitive performance in humans. *Chemical Senses, 31,* 415–423. doi:10.1093/chemse/bjj046

Cockburn, A., & McKenzie, B. (2002). Evaluating the effectiveness of spatial memory in 2D and 3D physical and virtual environments. *CHI 2002, April 20-25.* Minneapolis, Minnesota, USA.

Colgate, J., Stanley, M., & Brown, J. (1995). Issues in the haptic display of tool use. *International Conference on Intelligent Robots and Systems,* Pittsburgh, August 1995.

Craig, A. D. (2002). How do you feel? Interoception: The sense of the physiological condition of the body. *Nature Reviews. Neuroscience, 3,* 655–666.

Crusco, A. H., & Wetzel, C. G. (1984). The Midas touch: The effects of interpersonal touch on restaurant tipping. *Personality and Social Psychology Bulletin, 10,* 512–517. doi:10.1177/0146167284104003

Damasio, A. R. (1994). *Descartes' error: Emotion, reason, and the human brain.* New York: Putnam Publishing.

Darwin, C. (1872). *The expression of the emotions in man and animals.* London: Murray. doi:10.1037/10001-000

Davide, F., Holmberg, M., & Lundström, I. (2001). Virtual olfactory interfaces: Electronic noses and olfactory displays. In *Communications through virtual technology: Identity community and technology in the internet age* (pp. 193–220). Amsterdam: IOS Press.

De Thomas, M. T. (1971). Touch power and the screen of loneliness. *Perspectives in Psychiatric Care, 9,* 112–118. doi:10.1111/j.1744-6163.1971.tb01082.x

Demattè, M. L., Österbauer, R., & Spence, C. (2007). Olfactory cues modulate judgments of facial attractiveness. *Chemical Senses*, *32*, 603–610. doi:10.1093/chemse/bjm030

Deneve, S., & Pouget, A. (2004). Bayesian multisensory integration and cross-modal spatial links. *Journal of Physiology, Paris*, *98*, 249–258. doi:10.1016/j.jphysparis.2004.03.011

Dennett, D. C. (1991). *Consciousness explained*. Boston: Little & Brown.

Desor, J., & Beauchamp, G. (1974). The human capacity to transmit olfactory information. *Perception & Psychophysics*, *16*, 551–556. doi:10.3758/BF03198586

Dinh, H. Q., Walker, N., Hodges, L. F., Song, C., & Kobayashi, A. (1999). Evaluating the importance of multi-sensory input on memory and the sense of presence in virtual environments. *Proceedings of IEEE Virtual Reality Conference 1999*, Houston, TX, 13-17 March (pp. 222-228).

Driver, J. (1996). Enhancement of selective listening by illusory mislocation of speech sounds due to lip-reading. *Nature*, *381*, 66–68. doi:10.1038/381066a0

Durie, B. (2005). Future sense. *New Scientist*, *2484*, 33–36.

Ehrsson, H. H. (2007). The experimental induction of out-of-body experiences. *Science*, *317*, 1048. doi:10.1126/science.1142175

Erceau, D., & Guéguen, N. (2007). Tactile contact and evaluation of the toucher. *The Journal of Social Psychology*, *147*, 441–444. doi:10.3200/SOCP.147.4.441-444

Ernst, M. O., & Banks, M. S. (2002). Humans integrate visual and haptic information in a statistically optimal fashion. *Nature*, *415*, 429–433. doi:10.1038/415429a

Ernst, M. O., & Bülthoff, H. H. (2004). Merging the senses into a robust percept. *Trends in Cognitive Sciences*, *8*, 162–169. doi:10.1016/j.tics.2004.02.002

Esselman, P. C., Thombs, B. D., Magyar-Russell, G., & Fauerbach, J. A. (2006). Burn rehabilitation: State of the science. *American Journal of Physical Medicine & Rehabilitation*, *85*, 383–413. doi:10.1097/01.phm.0000202095.51037.a3

Felleman, D. J., & Van Essen, D. C. (1991). Distributed hierarchical processing in primate cerebral cortex. *Cerebral Cortex*, *1*, 1–47. doi:10.1093/cercor/1.1.1-a

Field, T. (2001). *Touch*. Cambridge, MA: MIT Press.

Fraguas, R., Marci, C., Fava, M., Iosifescua, D. V., Bankier, B., Loh, R., & Dougherty, D. D. (2007). Autonomic reactivity to induced emotion as potential predictor of response to antidepressant treatment. *Psychiatry Research*, *151*, 169–172. doi:10.1016/j.psychres.2006.08.008

Gallace, A., & Spence, C. (2008). The cognitive and neural correlates of "tactile consciousness": A multisensory perspective. *Consciousness and Cognition*, *17*, 370–407. doi:10.1016/j.concog.2007.01.005

Gallace, A., & Spence, C. (2009). The cognitive and neural correlates of tactile memory. *Psychological Bulletin*, *135*, 380–406. doi:10.1037/a0015325

Gallace, A., & Spence, C. (2010). The science of interpersonal touch: An overview. *Neuroscience and Biobehavioral Reviews*, *34*, 246–259. doi:10.1016/j.neubiorev.2008.10.004

Gallace, A., & Spence, C. (in press). Do Gestalt grouping principles influence tactile perception? *Psychological Bulletin*.

Gallace, A., Tan, H. Z., & Spence, C. (2006a). Numerosity judgments in tactile perception. *Perception*, *35*, 247–266. doi:10.1068/p5380

Gallace, A., Tan, H. Z., & Spence, C. (2006b). The failure to detect tactile change: A tactile analogue of visual change blindness. *Psychonomic Bulletin & Review*, *13*, 300–303. doi:10.3758/BF03193847

Gallace, A., Tan, H. Z., & Spence, C. (2007). The body surface as a communication system: The state of art after 50 years of research. *Presence (Cambridge, Mass.)*, *16*, 655–676. doi:10.1162/pres.16.6.655

Gallace, A., Tan, H. Z., & Spence, C. (2008). Can tactile stimuli be subitized? An unresolved controversy within the literature on numerosity judgments. *Perception*, *37*, 782–800. doi:10.1068/p5767

Ghazanfar, A. A., & Schroeder, C. E. (2006). Is neocortex essentially multisensory? *Trends in Cognitive Sciences*, *10*, 278–285. doi:10.1016/j.tics.2006.04.008

Gilbert, A. (2008). *What the nose knows: The science of scent in everyday life*. New York: Crown Publishers.

Gori, M., Del Viva, M., Sandini, G., & Burr, D. C. (2008). Young children do not integrate visual and haptic form information. *Current Biology*, *18*, 694–698. doi:10.1016/j.cub.2008.04.036

Gottlieb, G. (1971). Ontogenesis of sensory function in birds and mammals. In E. Tobach, L. R., Aronson, & E. F. Shaw (Eds.), *The biopsychology of development* (pp. 67-128). New York: Academic Press.

Gray, M. A., Harrison, N. A., Wiens, S., & Critchley, H. D. (2007). Modulation of emotional appraisal by false physiological feedback during fMRI. *PLoS ONE*, *2*(6), e546. doi:10.1371/journal.pone.0000546

Gregory, R. L. (1966). *Eye and brain: The psychology of seeing*. New York: McGraw-Hill.

Gregory, R. L. (1967). Origin of eyes and brains. *Nature*, *213*, 369–372. doi:10.1038/213369a0

Haans, A., IJsselsteijn, W. A., Graus, M. P., & Salminen, J. A. (2008). The virtual Midas touch: Helping behavior after a mediated social touch. In *Extended Abstracts of CHI 2008* (pp. 3507–3512). New York: ACM Press.

Haden, R. (2005). Taste in an age of convenience. In Korsmeyer, C. (Ed.), *The taste culture reader: Experiencing food and drink* (pp. 344–358). Oxford: Berg.

Hancock, P. A., Oron-Gilad, T., & Szalma, J. L. (2007). Elaborations of the multiple-resource theory of attention. In Kramer, A. F., Wiegmann, D. A., & Kirlik, A. (Eds.), *Attention: From theory to practice* (pp. 45–56). Oxford: Oxford University Press.

Hashimoto, Y., Inami, M., & Kajimoto, H. (2008). Straw-like user interface (II): A new method of presenting auditory sensations for a more natural experience. In M. Ferre (Ed.), *Eurohaptics 2008, LNCS, 5024*, 484-493. Berlin: Springer-Verlag.

Hashimoto, Y., Nagaya, N., Kojima, M., Miyajima, S., Ohtaki, J., & Yamamoto, A. (2007). Straw-like user interface: Virtual experience of the sensation of drinking using a straw. [Los Alamitos, CA: IEEE Computer Society.]. *Proceedings World Haptics*, *2007*, 557–558.

Heilig, M. (1962). *Sensorama stimulator*. U.S. Patent #3,050,870.

Heilig, M. L. (1992). El cine del futuro: The cinema of the future. *Presence (Cambridge, Mass.)*, *1*, 279–294.

Hendrix, C., & Barfield, W. (1996). The sense of presence with auditory virtual environments. *Presence (Cambridge, Mass.)*, *5*, 290–301.

Henricson, M., Berglund, A.-L., Määttä, S., Ekman, R., & Segesten, K. (2008). The outcome of tactile touch on oxytocin in intensive care patients: A randomised controlled trial. *Journal of Clinical Nursing, 17*, 2624–2633. doi:10.1111/j.1365-2702.2008.02324.x

Hertenstein, M. J., Keltner, D., App, B., Bulleit, B. A., & Jaskolka, A. R. (2006). Touch communicates distinct emotions. *Emotion (Washington, D.C.), 6*, 528–533. doi:10.1037/1528-3542.6.3.528

Ho, C., Reed, N. J., & Spence, C. (2006). Assessing the effectiveness of "intuitive" vibrotactile warning signals in preventing front-to-rear-end collisions in a driving simulator. *Accident; Analysis and Prevention, 38*, 989–997. doi:10.1016/j.aap.2006.04.002

Ho, C., & Spence, C. (2005). Olfactory facilitation of dual-task performance. *Neuroscience Letters, 389*, 35–40. doi:10.1016/j.neulet.2005.07.003

Hoffman, H. G., Hollander, A., Schroder, K., Rousseau, S., & Furness, T. I. (1998). Physically touching and tasting virtual objects enhances the realism of virtual experiences. *Journal of Virtual Reality, 3*, 226–234. doi:10.1007/BF01408703

Holmes, N. P., & Spence, C. (2006). Beyond the body schema: Visual, prosthetic, and technological contributions to bodily perception and awareness. In Knoblich, G., Thornton, I. M., Grosjean, M., & Shiffrar, M. (Eds.), *Human body perception from the inside out* (pp. 15–64). Oxford: Oxford University Press.

Howard, I. P., & Templeton, W. B. (1966). *Human spatial orientation*. New York: Wiley.

Hu, W., Lu, J., Zhang, L., Wu, W., Nie, H., & Zhu, Y. (2006). A preliminary report of penile transplantation. *European Urology, 51*, 1146–1147.

Iggo, A. (1977). Cutaneous and subcutaneous sense organs. *British Medical Bulletin, 33*, 97–102.

Iwata, H. (2008). Design issues in haptic devices. In Lin, M. C., & Otaduy, M. A. (Eds.), *Haptic rendering: Foundations, algorithms, and applications* (pp. 53–66). Wellesley, MA: AK Peters. doi:10.1201/b10636-5

Jacob, S., Kinnunen, L. H., Metz, J., Cooper, M., & McClintock, M. K. (2001). Sustained human chemosignal unconsciously alters brain function. *Neuroreport, 12*, 2391–2394. doi:10.1097/00001756-200108080-00021

Jacob, S., & McClintock, M. K. (2000). Psychological state and mood effects of steroidal chemosignals in women and men. *Hormones and Behavior, 37*, 57–78. doi:10.1006/hbeh.1999.1559

Jones, L. M. Bowers, C. A., Washburn, D., Cortes, A., & Satya, R. V. (2004). The effect of olfaction on immersion into virtual environments. In *Human performance, situation awareness and automation: Issues and considerations for the 21st century* (pp. 282-285). Lawrence Erlbaum Associates.

Keller, P., Kouzes, R., Kangas, L., & Hashem, S. (1995). Transmission of olfactory information in telemedicine. In K. Morgan, R. Satava, H. Sieburg, R. Matteus, & J. Christensen (Eds.), *Interactive technology and the new paradigm for healthcare* (pp. 168-172). Amsterdam: IOS.

Knill, D. C., & Richards, W. (1996). *Perception as Bayesian inference*. Cambridge, MA: Cambridge University Press.

Kole, A., Snel, J., & Lorist, M. M. (1998). Caffeine, morning-evening type and coffee odour: Attention, memory search and visual event related potentials. In Snel, J., & Lorist, M. M. (Eds.), *Nicotine, caffeine and social drinking: Behaviour and brain function* (pp. 201–214). Amsterdam: Harwood Academic.

Laurel, B. (1995). Virtual reality. *Scientific American, 273*(3), 90.

Lavie, N. (2005). Distracted and confused?: Selective attention under load. *Trends in Cognitive Sciences, 9,* 75–82. doi:10.1016/j.tics.2004.12.004

Lee, J.-H., Poliakoff, E., & Spence, C. (2009). The effect of multimodal feedback presented via a touch screen on the performance of older adults. In M. E. Altinsoy, U. Jekosch, & S. Brewster (Eds.), *Lecture Notes in Computer Science (LNCS), 5763,* 128-135.

Lee, J.-H., & Spence, C. (2008). Assessing the benefits of multimodal feedback on dual-task performance under demanding conditions. In *Proceedings of the 22nd British Computer Society Human-Computer Interaction Group Annual Conference* (pp. 185-192). Liverpool John Moores University, UK, 1-5 September 2008. British Computer Society.

Lee, J.-H., & Spence, C. (2009). Feeling what you hear: Task-irrelevant sounds modulates tactile perception delivered via a touch screen. *Journal of Multisensory User Interfaces, 2,* 145–156. doi:10.1007/s12193-009-0014-8

Lehrner, J., Eckersberger, C., Walla, P., Pötsch, G., & Deecke, L. (2000). Ambient odor of orange in a dental office reduces anxiety and improves mood in female patients. *Physiology & Behavior, 71,* 83–86. doi:10.1016/S0031-9384(00)00308-5

Lenggenhager, B., Tadi, T., Metzinger, T., & Blanke, O. (2007). Video ergo sum: Manipulating bodily self-consciousness. *Science, 317,* 1096–1099. doi:10.1126/science.1143439

Levin, D. T., & Simons, D. J. (1997). Failure to detect changes to attended objects in motion pictures. *Psychonomic Bulletin & Review, 4,* 501–506. doi:10.3758/BF03214339

Li, W., Moallem, I., Paller, K. A., & Gottfried, J. A. (2007). Subliminal smells can guide social preferences. *Psychological Science, 18,* 1044–1049. doi:10.1111/j.1467-9280.2007.02023.x

Loftin, R. B. (2003). Multisensory perception: Beyond the visual in visualization. *Computing in Science & Engineering, 5*(4), 56–58. doi:10.1109/MCISE.2003.1208644

Löken, L. S., Wessberg, J., Morrison, I., McGlone, F., & Olausson, H. (2009). Coding of pleasant touch by unmyelinated afferents in humans. *Nature Neuroscience, 12,* 547–548. doi:10.1038/nn.2312

Lynn, R. (2004). Ins and outs of teledildonics. *Wired.* September 24, 2004. Downloaded 20-03-2010.

Makin, T. R., Holmes, N. P., & Ehrsson, H. H. (2008). On the other hand: Dummy hands and peripersonal space. *Behavioural Brain Research, 191,* 1–10. doi:10.1016/j.bbr.2008.02.041

Marescaux, J., Leroy, J., Gagner, M., Rubino, F., Mutter, D., & Vix, M. (2001). Transatlantic robot-assisted telesurgery. *Nature, 413,* 379–380. doi:10.1038/35096636

Martin, R. L., McAnally, K. I., & Senova, M. A. (2001). Free-field equivalent localization of virtual audio. *Journal of the Audio Engineering Society. Audio Engineering Society, 49,* 14–22.

McClintock, M. K. (1971). Menstrual synchrony and suppression. *Nature, 229,* 244–245. doi:10.1038/229244a0

Meehan, M., Insko, B., Whitton, M., & Brooks, F. (2001). *Objective measures of presence in virtual environments,* Presence 2001, 4th International Workshop, May 21-23, http://www.temple.edu/presence2001 /conf-format&schd.htm, paper can be found on http:/ /www. cs. unc.edu/-meehan/presence2000 /MeehanPresence2000.htm

Mehrabian, A. (1967). Attitudes inferred from nonimmediacy of verbal communication. *Journal of Verbal Learning and Verbal Behavior, 6,* 294–295. doi:10.1016/S0022-5371(67)80113-0

Meredith, M. (2001). Human vomeronasal organ function: A critical review of best and worst cases. *Chemical Senses*, *26*, 433–445. doi:10.1093/chemse/26.4.433

Miller, G. A. (1956). The magical number seven, plus or minus two: Some limits on our capacity for processing information. *Psychological Review*, *63*, 81–97. doi:10.1037/h0043158

Montagu, A. (1971). *Touching: The human significance of the skin*. New York: Columbia University Press.

Morhenn, V. B., Park, J. W., Piper, E., & Zak, P. J. (2008). Monetary sacrifice among strangers is mediated by endogenous oxytocin release after physical contact. *Evolution and Human Behavior*, *29*, 375–383. doi:10.1016/j.evolhumbehav.2008.04.004

Morie, J. F., Iyer, K., Valanejad, K., Sadek, R., Miraglia, D., Milam, D., et al. (2003). *Sensory design for virtual environments*. SIGGRAPH 2003 Sketch, July, 2003; www.ict.usc.edu/publications/SensDesign4VE.pdf

Morrot, G., Brochet, F., & Dubourdieu, D. (2001). The color of odors. *Brain and Language*, *79*, 309–320. doi:10.1006/brln.2001.2493

Moseley, G. L., Gallace, A., & Spence, C. (2008). Is mirror therapy all it is cracked up to be? Current evidence and future directions. *Pain*, *138*, 7–10. doi:10.1016/j.pain.2008.06.026

Moseley, G. L., Gallace, A., & Spence, C. (in press). Bodily illusion in health and disease: physiological and clinical perspectives and the concept of a cortical body matrix. *Neuroscience and Biobehavioral Reviews*.

Moseley, G. L., Olthof, N., Venema, A., Don, S., Wijers, M., Gallace, A., & Spence, C. (2008). Psychologically induced cooling of a specific body part caused by the illusory ownership of an artificial counterpart. *Proceedings of the National Academy of Sciences of the United States of America*, *105*, 13168–13172. doi:10.1073/pnas.0803768105

Murray, C. D., Patchick, E., Pettifer, S., Caillette, F., & Howard, T. (2006). Immersive virtual reality as a rehabilitative technology for phantom limb experience. *Cyberpsychology & Behavior*, *9*, 167–170. doi:10.1089/cpb.2006.9.167

Murray, C. D., Pettifer, S., Howard, T., Patchick, E., Caillette, F., Kulkarni, J., & Bamford, C. (2007). The treatment of phantom limb pain using immersive virtual reality: Three case studies. *Disability and Rehabilitation*, *29*, 1465–1469. doi:10.1080/09638280601107385

Nelson, T. (1974). *Computer lib/dream machines*. Self-published.

O'Regan, J. K. (1992). Solving the "real" mysteries of visual perception: The world as an outside memory. *Canadian Journal of Psychology*, *46*, 461–488. doi:10.1037/h0084327

Olausson, H. (2008). Functional role of unmyelinated tactile afferents in human hairy skin: Sympathetic response and perceptual localization. *Experimental Brain Research*, *184*, 135–140. doi:10.1007/s00221-007-1175-x

Onyesolu, M. O. (2009). Virtual reality laboratories: An ideal solution to the problems facing laboratory setup and management. In *Proceedings of the World Congress on Engineering and Computer Science*. San Francisco, CA, USA, 20-22 October, 2009.

Orne, M. T. (1962). On the social psychology of the psychological experiment: With particular reference to demand characteristics and their implications. *The American Psychologist, 17,* 776–783. doi:10.1037/h0043424

Peck, J., & Childers, T. L. (2003a). Individual differences in haptic information processing: The "Need for Touch" scale. *The Journal of Consumer Research, 30,* 430–442. doi:10.1086/378619

Petkova, V. I., & Ehrsson, H. H. (2008). If I were you: Perceptual illusion of body swapping. *PLoS ONE, 3*(12), e3832. doi:10.1371/journal. pone.0003832

Posner, M. I., Nissen, M. J., & Klein, R. M. (1976). Visual dominance: An information-processing account of its origins and significance. *Psychological Review, 83,* 157–171. doi:10.1037/0033-295X.83.2.157

Questler, H. (1956). Studies of human channel capacity. In Cherry, C. (Ed.), *Information theory: Papers read at a symposium on 'information theory' held at the Royal Institution, London, September 12th to 16th 1955* (pp. 361–371). London: Butterworths Scientific Publications.

Raudenbush, B., Corley, N., & Eppich, W. (2001). Enhancing athletic performance through the administration of peppermint odor. *Journal of Sport & Exercise Psychology, 23,* 156–160.

Robertson, G. G., Czerwinski, M., Larson, K., Robbins, D., Thiel, D., & Van Dantzich, M. (1998). Data mountain: using spatial memory for document management. *Proceedings of UIST '98, 11th Annual Symposium on User Interface Software and Technology, 153,* 162.

Robinett, W. (1992). Comments on "A nose gesture interface device: Extending virtual realities". *Presence (Cumbridge, Mass.), 1,* 493.

Rothbaum, B. O., Hodges, L. F., Kooper, R., Opdyke, D., Williford, J., & North, M. M. (1995). Effectiveness of virtual reality graded exposure in the treatment of acrophobia. *The American Journal of Psychiatry, 152,* 626–628.

Sallnas, E., Rassmus-Grohn, K., & Sjostrom, C. (2000). *Supporting presence in collaborative environments by haptic force feedback. ACM Transactions on Computer-Human Interaction (TOCHI).* New York: ACM Press.

Sathian, K. (2005). Visual cortical activity during tactile perception in the sighted and the visually deprived. *Developmental Psychobiology, 46,* 279–286. doi:10.1002/dev.20056

Schaefer, M., Heinze, H.-J., & Rotte, M. (2009). My third arm: Shifts in topography of the somatosensory homunculus predict feeling of an artificial supernumerary arm. *Human Brain Mapping, 30,* 1413–1420. doi:10.1002/hbm.20609

Schroeder, C. E., & Foxe, J. (2005). Multisensory contributions to low-level, "unisensory" processing. *Current Opinion in Neurobiology, 15,* 454–458. doi:10.1016/j.conb.2005.06.008

Schuemie, M. J., van der Straaten, P., Krijin, M., & Mast, C. (2001). Research on presence in virtual reality: A survey. *Journal of Cyber Psychology and Behavior, 4*(2), 183–202.

Sereno, M. I., Dale, A. M., Reppas, J. B., Kwong, K. K., Belliveau, J. W., & Brady, T. J. (1995). Borders of multiple visual areas in humans revealed by functional magnetic resonance imaging. *Science, 268,* 889–893. doi:10.1126/science.7754376

Sivak, M. (1996). The information that drivers use: Is it indeed 90% visual? *Perception, 25,* 1081–1089. doi:10.1068/p251081

Slater, M. (2002). Presence and the sixth sense. *Presence (Cambridge, Mass.), 11,* 435–439. doi:10.1162/105474602760204327

Slater, M. (2004). How colourful was your day? Why questionnaires cannot assess presence in virtual environments. *Presence (Cambridge, Mass.)*, *13*, 484–493. doi:10.1162/1054746041944849

Slater, M., Perez-Marcos, D., Ehrsson, H. H., & Sanchez-Vives, M. V. (2009). Inducing illusory ownership of a virtual body. *Frontiers in Neuroscience*, *3*(2), 214–220. doi:10.3389/neuro.01.029.2009

Slater, M., & Wilbur, S. (1997). A framework for immersive virtual environments (FIVE): Speculations on the role of presence in virtual environments. *Presence (Cambridge, Mass.)*, *6*, 603–616.

Spence, C. (2002). *The ICI report on the secret of the senses*. London: The Communication Group.

Spence, C. (2003). A new multisensory approach to health and well-being. *Essence*, *2*, 16–22.

Spence, C. (2011a). Sound design: How understanding the brain of the consumer can enhance auditory and multisensory product/brand development. In K. Bronner, R. Hirt, & C. Ringe (Eds.), *Audio Branding Congress Proceedings 2010* (pp. 35-49). Baden-Baden, Germany: Nomos Verlag.

Spence, C. (2011b). Mouth-watering: The influence of environmental and cognitive factors on salivation and gustatory/flavour perception. *Journal of Texture Studies*, *42*, 157–171. doi:10.1111/j.1745-4603.2011.00299.x

Spence, C., Bentley, D. E., Phillips, N., McGlone, F. P., & Jones, A. K. P. (2002). Selective attention to pain: A psychophysical investigation. *Experimental Brain Research*, *145*, 395–402. doi:10.1007/s00221-002-1133-6

Spence, C., & Driver, J. (1997). Cross-modal links in attention between audition, vision, and touch: Implications for interface design. *International Journal of Cognitive Ergonomics*, *1*, 351–373.

Spence, C., & Driver, J. (Eds.). (2004). *Crossmodal space and crossmodal attention*. Oxford, UK: Oxford University Press.

Spence, C., & Gallace, A. (2007). Recent developments in the study of tactile attention. *Canadian Journal of Experimental Psychology*, *61*, 196–207. doi:10.1037/cjep2007021

Spence, C., & Gallace, A. (2008). Making sense of touch. In Chatterjee, H. (Ed.), *Touch in museums: Policy and practice in object handling* (pp. 21–40). Oxford: Berg Publications.

Spence, C., & Gallace, A. (2011). Multisensory design: Reaching out to touch the consumer. *Psychology and Marketing*, *28*, 267–308. doi:10.1002/mar.20392

Spence, C., & Ho, C. (2008). Crossmodal information processing in driving. In C. Castro & L. Hartley (Eds.), *Human factors of visual performance in driving* (pp. 187-200). Boca Raton, Fl: CRC Press.

Spence, C., Kettenmann, B., Kobal, G., & McGlone, F. P. (2000). Selective attention to the chemosensory modality. *Perception & Psychophysics*, *62*, 1265–1271. doi:10.3758/BF03212128

Spence, C., Levitan, C., Shankar, M. U., & Zampini, M. (2010). Does food color influence taste and flavor perception in humans? *Chemosensory Perception*, *3*, 68–84. doi:10.1007/s12078-010-9067-z

Spence, C., Sanabria, D., & Soto-Faraco, S. (2007). Intersensory Gestalten and crossmodal scene perception. In Noguchi, K. (Ed.), *Psychology of beauty and Kansei: New horizons of Gestalt perception* (pp. 519–579). Tokyo: Fuzanbo International.

Sproull, L., & Kiesler, S. B. (1986). Reducing social context cues: Electronic mail in organizational communication. *Management Science*, *32*, 1492–1512. doi:10.1287/mnsc.32.11.1492

Standley, J. M. (1991). The effect of vibrotactile and auditory stimuli on perception of comfort, heart rate, and peripheral finger temperature. *Journal of Music Therapy, 28*, 120–134.

Stein, B. E., & Meredith, M. A. (1993). *The merging of the senses.* Cambridge, MA: MIT Press.

Stein, B. E., & Stanford, T. R. (2008). Multisensory integration: Current issues from the perspective of the single neuron. *Nature Reviews. Neuroscience, 9*, 255–267. doi:10.1038/nrn2331

Steingarten, J. (2002). *It must've been something I ate.* New York: Knopf.

Stern, K., & McClintock, M. K. (1998). Regulation of ovulation by human pheromones. *Nature, 392*, 177–179. doi:10.1038/32408

Strickland, D., Hodges, L., North, M., & Weghorst, S. (1997). Overcoming phobias by virtual reality exposure. *Communications of the ACM, 40*, 34–39. doi:10.1145/257874.257881

Sur, M., & Leamey, C. A. (2001). Development and plasticity of cortical areas and networks. *Nature Reviews. Neuroscience, 2*, 251–262. doi:10.1038/35067562

Tavakoli, M., & Howe, R. D. (2008). Haptic implications of tool flexibility in surgical tele-operation (pp. 377-378). *2008 Symposium on Haptic Interfaces for Virtual Environment and Teleoperator Systems.*

Taylor, J. L., & McCloskey, D. I. (1991). Illusions of head and visual target displacement induced by vibration of neck muscles. *Brain, 114*, 755–759. doi:10.1093/brain/114.2.755

Trantakis, C., Bootz, F., Strauss, G., Nowatius, E., Lindner, D., & Cakmak, H. (2003). Virtual endoscopy with force feedback – a new system for neurosurgical training. *International Congress Series, 1256*, 782–787. doi:10.1016/S0531-5131(03)00292-9

Vallbo, A. B., Olsson, K. A., Westberg, K.-G., & Clark, F. J. (1984). Microstimulation of single tactile afferents from the human hand: Sensory attributes related to unit type and properties of receptive fields. *Brain, 107*, 727–749. doi:10.1093/brain/107.3.727

Vallns, S. (1966). Cognitive effects of false heart-rate feedback. *Journal of Personality and Social Psychology, 4*, 400–408. doi:10.1037/h0023791

Västfjäll, D. (2006). *Affecting emotional experience with auditory-vibrotactile heartbeat false feedback.* Poster presented at the 7th Annual Meeting of the International Multisensory Research Forum. Trinity College, Dublin, 18-21 June.

Vatakis, A., & Spence, C. (2010). Audiovisual temporal integration for complex speech, object-action, animal call, and musical stimuli. In Naumer, M. J., & Kaiser, J. (Eds.), *Multisensory object perception in the primate brain* (pp. 95–121). New York: Springer. doi:10.1007/978-1-4419-5615-6_7

Vlahos, J. (2006). The smell of war. *Polar Science, 8*, 72–95.

Washburn, D., & Jones, L. M. (2004). Could olfactory displays improve data visualization? *Computing in Science & Engineering, 6*(6), 80–83. doi:10.1109/MCSE.2004.66

Washburn, D. A., Jones, L. M., Satya, R. V., Bowers, C. A., & Cortes, A. (2003). Olfactory use in virtual environment training. *Modeling & Simulation Magazine, 2*(3), 19–25.

Weinstein, S. (1968). Intensive and extensive aspects of tactile sensitivity as a function of body part, sex, and laterality. In Kenshalo, D. R. (Ed.), *The skin senses* (pp. 195–222). Springfield, Ill.: Thomas.

Wickens, C. D. (1980). The structure of attentional resources. In Nickerson, R. S. (Ed.), *Attention and performance* (*Vol. 8*, pp. 239–257). Hillsdale, NJ: Erlbaum.

Wickens, C. D. (1984). Processing resources in attention. In Parasuraman, R., & Davies, D. R. (Eds.), *Varieties of attention* (pp. 63–102). San Diego, CA: Academic Press.

Wickens, C. D. (2008). Multiple resources and mental workload. *Human Factors, 50*, 449–454. doi:10.1518/001872008X288394

Wickens, C. D., Olmos, O., Chudy, A., & Davenport, C. (1997). *Aviation display support for situation awareness. University of Illinois Institute of Aviation Technical Report (ARL-97-10/ LOGICON-97-2)*. Savoy, IL: Aviation Research Laboratory.

Williams, L. E., & Bargh, J. A. (2008). Experiencing physical warmth promotes interpersonal warmth. *Science, 322*, 606–607. doi:10.1126/ science.1162548

Willis, C. M., Church, S. M., & Guest, C. M. (2004). Olfactory detection of human bladder cancer by dogs: Proof of principle study. *British Medical Journal, 329*, 712–715. doi:10.1136/ bmj.329.7468.712

Yanagida, Y., Kawato, S., Noma, H., & Tetsutani, N. (2004). Personal olfactory display with nose tracking. *Proceedings of IEEE Virtual Reality Conference* (pp. 43-50). IEEE CS Press.

Yannier, N., Basdogan, C., Tasiran, S., & Sen, O. L. (2008). Using haptics to convey cause-and-effect relations in climate visualization. *IEEE Transactions on Haptics, 1*, 130–141. doi:10.1109/ TOH.2008.16

Zampini, M., & Spence, C. (2004). The role of auditory cues in modulating the perceived crispness and staleness of potato chips. *Journal of Sensory Science, 19*, 347–363. doi:10.1111/j.1745-459x.2004.080403.x

Zhou, W., & Chen, D. (2008). Encoding human sexual chemosensory cues in the orbitofrontal and fusiform cortices. *The Journal of Neuroscience, 28*, 14416–14421. doi:10.1523/JNEURO-SCI.3148-08.2008

Zimmerman, M. (1989). The nervous system in the context of information theory. In R. F. Schmidt & G. Thews, *Human physiology* (2nd complete Ed.) (pp. 166-173). Berlin: Springer-Verlag.

Chapter 2
Multiple Sensorial Media and Presence in 3D Environments

Helen Farley
University of Southern Queensland, Australia

Caroline Steel
University of Queensland, Australia

ABSTRACT

Immersion has been defined as the 'the subjective impression that one is participating in a comprehensive, realistic experience' (Witmer & Singer, 1998), and is seen as a necessary condition for 'presence'. This chapter will look at those characteristics of the MulSeMedia experience which facilitate immersion in three-dimensional virtual environments including Multi-User Virtual Environments (MUVEs) such as Second Life, Massively Multiplayer Online Role-Playing Games (MMORPGs) such as World of Warcraft, and various three-dimensional simulations.

Though there are multiple factors that impede or facilitate immersion, one of the key factors is the ability to engage multiple senses. Chris Dede (2009) has described this as 'sensory immersion'. An environment that produces a greater sense of sensory immersion, will produce a greater feeling of presence (Witmer & Singer, 1998: p. 228); a psychologically emergent property of immersion (Zhu, Xiang, & Hu, 2007: p. 265). It has been shown that the more sensory information provided by the virtual environment, the higher the sense of presence (Franceschi, Lee, & Hinds, 2008: p. 6) and that as more sensory modalities are stimulated presence is similarly increased (Steuer, 1992). It can therefore be expected, that MulSeMedia, engaging a range of senses, should enhance presence. Evidence can be extracted from the extensive literature pertaining to gaming and presence, and the work surrounding user interfaces enabling haptic feedback, tactile precision and engaging other sensory modalities.

This chapter will begin by unraveling the relationship between 'immersion', with a special emphasis on 'sensory immersion', and 'presence' in relation to MulSeMedia. In addition, it will look at the nature of the sensory stimulation provided by MulSeMedia in relation to the amount of immersion it engenders. For example, sound that is directional will have a positive effect on immersion and sensory feedback that is not conflicting will further enhance the immersive experience.

DOI: 10.4018/978-1-60960-821-7.ch002

INTRODUCTION

For educators, the appeal of virtual environments is enormous. The diversity of educational contexts provides an assortment of experiences that accommodate a range of learning styles. Neil Fleming identified four types of learning styles: (a) visual; (b) auditory; (c) reading/writing; and (d) kinesthetic, tactile, or exploratory, resulting in the acronym VARK (Fleming & Baume, 2006: p. 6; Bonk & Zhang, 2006: p. 250). Beyond recognizing that these learning styles exist, learners born after the mid-1970s expect that learning will be responsive to their preferred style (Bonk & Zhang, 2006: p. 250). Kinesthetic learners are frequently insufficiently catered for and authentic movement in 3D worlds may help to meet this need. Kinesthetic learning activities compel students to move, sometimes requiring significant exertion (Begel, Garcia, & Wolfman, 2004: pp. 183-184). This exploits what Jean Piaget called 'sensori-motor learning,' in which physical activity transforms into representative mental symbols (Piaget, 1999: pp. 37-38). The increasing importance of hands-on learning has already been glimpsed in the rising prevalence of realistic and complex simulations, interactive scenarios and commutative news stories (Bonk & Zhang, 2006: p. 251). Given the diversity of students attending university, it seems prudent to seek out an environment where all learning styles can be accommodated.

There are many educators responsive to these needs, endeavoring to give their students the most authentic learning experiences possible. What better way to train an architect than to let him or her design and construct a building; walk around in it when completed and then go back and correct any deficiencies or experiment with alternatives? A prospective surgeon will learn best by performing surgery on a patient that cannot die and a student of history will appreciate and more fully understand historical events if for just an hour or two they could take on a role and wander around a battleground or participate in a significant legal trial. Participation could decrease reaction times, improve hand-eye coordination and raise learners' self-esteem (Lawrence, 1986: p. 52; Pearson & Bailey, 2007: p. 1). For some disciplines, the educational affordances of a virtual environment such as Second Life are obvious (Salmon, 2009: p. 529). These environments are so appealing to students and educators because the senses are artificially stimulated to evoke emotional responses, introduce new ideas and entertain in new and exciting ways. These computer-mediated environments provide sensory information including visual, audio and haptic information so that a multi-modal understanding of the environment can be constructed (Butler & Neave, 2008: p. 140). The simple presentation of information is arguably not as valid as engaging students in interacting with that information as becomes possible in an immersive virtual environment (Tashner, Riedl, & Bronack, 2005).

There is evidence to suggest that the game technology employed in many virtual environments may improve learner motivation and engagement via immersion (Fassbender & Richards, 2008: p. 1). Engaged students who are responsible for their own learning through an active approach tend to experience a deeper level of learning compared to those who are merely passive recipients of information. Problem-solving, authentic learning experiences, virtual learning, online collaboration and other active methods, will usurp more conventional didactic approaches to learning. Further, Curtis Bonk and Ke Zang (2006) also flag a greater emphasis on reflection for students to 'internalize and expand upon their learning pursuits' (Bonk & Zhang, 2006; Sanders & McKeown, 2008: p. 51) and this can be readily facilitated through interaction in and with an immersive virtual environment.

PRESENCE AND IMMERSION

When something is perceived by the human brain – whether it actually exists in the world or on a screen in a virtual environment – it is inclined to act as if it were real. Edward Castranova posits that this is because for the vast majority of human evolution, virtual objects did not exist and hence there was no evolutionary necessity to develop the ability to distinguish between the real and the virtual. In fact, it takes significant additional effort for the brain to keep reminding itself that something is not real (Castranova, 2001: pp. 27-28). This can be evidenced by the heightened physiological responses measured during challenging episodes simulated during immersion in virtual environments which are contrived to mimic those responses arising in the real world (for example see Moore, Wiederhold, Wiederhold, & Riva, 2002). As virtual environments become more sophisticated and lifelike, it becomes yet more difficult for the brain to distinguish between what is real and what is virtual, particularly if that environment and the emotions it engenders are pleasant (Castranova, 2001: pp. 27-28). This is an important realization; if simulations in virtual worlds are sufficiently immersive and realistic and that realism can be augmented by the stimulation of multiple senses, then the motivation for distinguishing virtual from real is sufficiently low that for all intents and purposes, learners *are* actually engaged in practicing authentic physical skills with corresponding application in the 'real' world. The learners can be said to be fully *immersed*.

When speaking of virtual environments, Chris Dede defines immersion as: 'the subjective impression that one is participating in a comprehensive, realistic experience' (C. Dede, 2009: p. 66); it is a psychological state characterized by a user perceiving his or herself to be enveloped by, part of, and interacting with an environment able to afford a continuous stream of stimuli and experiences. Further he breaks immersion into three subcategories, namely: actional, symbolic

and sensory immersion. Dede describes actional immersion as empowering the participant to instigate actions not possible in the real world that have novel, intriguing consequences. In turn, symbolic immersion involves triggering powerful semantic associations via the content of a virtual environment. And finally – and most relevant to this discussion of MulSeMedia – sensory immersion involves manipulating the human senses in order to create the feeling that one is located in a different physical space to the space where the body is actually physically located. This requires the participant to feel that he or she is actually in the environment as opposed to looking through a window into the virtual world (C. Dede, 1995: p. 50). Various technologies – particularly those exploiting MulSeMedia – facilitate sensory immersion, thereby locating the experience in three-dimensional space. These technologies provide visual stimulation, stereoscopic sound and haptic feedback, applying vibrations and forces to the participant (C. Dede, 2009: p. 66).

In any virtual environment, presence – that feeling of actually 'being there' – is dependent on both involvement and immersion. Involvement relies on focusing attention on a consistent set of stimuli and immersion depends on perceiving oneself as a part of the flow of stimuli; the dynamic stream of available sensory inputs and events that interact with the observer's activities and in turn respond to them. Users that are fully immersed sense that they are interacting directly – rather than remotely – with the environment and perceive they are part of that environment (Witmer & Singer, 1998: p. 227; Stanney & Salvendy, 1998: p. 156). An environment imparting a greater sense of immersion will produce elevated levels of presence (Witmer & Singer, 1998: p. 228).

There are many factors that influence the degree of immersion and presence. Though the specific focus of this chapter is MulSeMedia, it is important to recognize that factors other than those derived from the range of human senses are important in achieving immersion and in fact, it has been widely acknowledged that they are not reliant on total photo- and audio-realism within the virtual environment (McMahan, 2003: p. 68). These factors include the visual representations of avatars (Nowak & Biocca, 2004); isolation from the physical environment; using one's natural mode of movement and control (Stanney & Salvendy, 1998: p. 156); the ability to interact with the environment and with other autonomous actors (Mel Slater, Usoh, & Steed, 1994: p. 131); decreased lag time between user action and environment reaction (M. Slater & Usoh, 1994: p. 126; Zhu, et al., 2007: p. 265); the participant's experience using a virtual environment (Vinayaga-moorthy, Brogni, Gillies, Slater, & Steed, 2004: p. 149); the motivation of the learner (J. Robertson, de Quincey, Stapleford, & Wiggins, 1998: p. 2); behavioral realism (Blascovich, et al., 2002: pp. 111-112); the level of skill of the users and the technical difficulties encountered (Aldrich, 2009: p. 89; Jones, 2005: p. 421); among many others which are well-represented in the extensive literature pertaining to both immersion and presence.

In order to achieve sensory immersion, the human brain has to blend input from several sensory modalities in a continuous and dynamic fashion. Even so, each sensory system is widely believed to operate independently though research has shown this sensory independence is illusory (Biocca & Choi, 2001: p. 249). In reality, the interaction of the various sensory systems generates cross-modal effects, such that large amounts of information perceived by one sense may be selectively disregarded when competing with data from more dominant sensory inputs (Chalmers & Zányi, 2009: p. 9). Put simply, when confronted with multimodal stimuli, humans are unable to attend to all of them at one. Those stimuli considered to be 'not pressing' are at least temporarily disregarded (Chalmers, Debattista, Mastroropoulou, & dos Santos, 2007: p. 2). Even so, the number of sensory systems stimulated appropriately has been found to increase immersion and presence (Stanney & Salvendy, 1998: p: 163; Slater, et al., 1994: p. 130;

Richard, Tijou, Richard, & Ferrier, 2006: 208). But their relation to one another beyond simple additive measure remains undetermined (Morie, et al., 2003: p. 1). Traditional virtual reality systems fail to stimulate all of the sensory systems and even those senses that are stimulated only receive a restricted experience (Chalmers & Zányi, 2009: p. 9). What would seem more desirable is that all of the sensory systems be *selectively* stimulated such that there would be no noticeable deficit in the overall amount of stimulation that is received via the various sensory systems. No matter what the source or nature of the sensory stimulus, immersion is best achieved if there is no indication that the stimulus is produced by an artificial device or via a display (Mel Slater, et al., 1994: p. 131).

Significant to this discussion of immersion, presence and multi-sensorial media is the notion of *vividness*. Jonathan Steuer defines vividness as '… the representational richness of a meditated environment as defined by its formal features; that is, the way in which an environment presents information to the senses.' He goes on to remark that vividness is entirely a characteristic of the technology and is therefore, stimulus-driven (Steuer, 1992: p. 80). Multiple factors contribute to vividness. These include sensory breadth and sensory depth. The former refers to the number of sensory dimensions presented simultaneously, and the latter to the resolution within each of these perceptual channels (Steuer, 1992: p. 80; Schuemie, Van der Straaten, Krijn, & Van der Mast, 2001: 194). Traditional media such as television and print are generally lacking in sensory breadth, being entirely reliant on sight and sound (Steuer, 1992: p. 81). Sensory depth is dependent on the amount of data encoded and the data bandwidth of the transmission channel. This can be expressed in terms of 'quality'. When we are operating in the real world, sensory depth is taken for granted in that our senses are always operating at maximum bandwidth. This assumption can't be made in virtual environments. Sensory depth is limited by the technologies employed (Steuer, 1992: p. 83;

Biocca & Choi, 2001: p. 248). Within each sensory channel, many sensory cues may not be supported or may be inconsistent (Biocca & Choi, 2001: p. 248). Finally, it is worth noting that virtual reality – that notional feeling of presence in a virtual environment – actually resides in an individual's consciousness, so that the particular contribution of sensory input to the emersion of presence will vary significantly between individuals (Steuer, 1992: p. 80; (Washburn & Jones, 2004: p. 80).

THE SENSORY SYSTEMS

Traditionally, five sensory systems have been described: the proprioceptive system (the basic orienting system that is responsible for maintaining mechanical equilibrium); the haptic system responsible for the sensation of touch and skin sensations; the auditory system; the taste-smell system; and the visual system. There is a certain amount of redundancy in the combined functioning of these systems. For example, several systems may supply data to reinforce the perception of one event. This does have certain advantages in that it reduces the likelihood of alternative explanations for the same set of stimuli (Steuer, 1992: p. 81-82; Biocca & Choi, 2001: p. 249; Sun, Campos, & Chan, 2004: p. 248; Dede, Salzman, Loftin, & Sprague, 1999). This is where MulSeMedia becomes important; perception can be reinforced by the provision of information from multiple senses leading to a greater sense of immersion. Conversely, in a virtual environment, if information garnered from visual cues is contradicted by information from other sources, immersion and consequently, the feeling of presence is compromised. For example, if a user is looking at a forest on a computer screen or virtual reality goggles but the sounds and smells are consistent with being in a computer laboratory, then the user will not feel as if he or she is actually in a forest: immersion and hence, presence, is compromised (Zybura & Eskeland, 1999; Biocca & Choi, 2001: p. 248;

Sadowski & Stanney, 2002: 795). This section deals with the stimulation of the individual sensory systems and the factors affecting immersion within each.

Proprioception

A person's sense of the position and orientation of his or her body and its several parts is called *proprioception* (Mine, 1997: p. 5; M. Slater & Usoh, 1994: p. 126; Blade & Padgett, 2002: p. 22) and is infrequently stimulated even in the most sophisticated MulSeMedia applications. Proprioception includes both vestibular sensing as well as kinesthetic feedback from muscles, tendons and joints and provides cues to the velocity and acceleration of oneself. If a person moves without visual cues, he or she can still usually tell where they are due to proprioceptive feedback. This process is called *path integration* or *dead reckoning* (Klatzky, Loomis, Beall, Chance, & Golledge, 1998: p. 293; Bakker, et al., 1999: p. 37; Ruddle & Péruch, 2004: p. 301; Sun, et al., 2004: p. 246). A good sense of orientation is needed in a virtual environment if it is to be effectively used for applications such as training and design evaluation. Ordinary geographical orientation relies on visual as well as proprioceptive feedback to a person moving through the world. However, navigation around a virtual environment generally relies on an interface that lacks proprioceptive feedback (Bakker, Werkhoven, & Passenier, 1999: p. 36).

The consequence of proprioceptive input is the formation of an unconscious mental model of the body and its dynamics. In order for immersion to occur, this mental model must match the displayed sensory information concerning the virtual body or avatar (M. Slater & Usoh, 1994: p. 126). If the match between proprioception and sensory data about the corresponding dynamics of the body is high, then the person in the virtual world is likely to identify with their avatar, leading to a heightened sense of presence (M. Slater & Usoh, 1994): p. 130. Even so, studies using simple imagined and movements confirm that the rotational aspect of proprioceptive information is more significant than the translational component for spatial judgments. Experimentally this becomes explicit when looking at the effects of head-mounted displays as compared to the use of treadmills as sources of proprioceptive information. The HMD which allows for physical rotation brings greater navigational benefit. Though clearly having some impact on immersion and presence, and on the completion of navigational tasks in virtual environments, the research into the influence of the various components of proprioceptive feedback are conflicting and inconclusive (Ruddle & Péruch, 2004).

What is known is that proprioceptive cues facilitate more accurate predictions of both distance and direction travelled when visual cues are absent or obscured in virtual environments. Proprioceptive feedback is provided when interfaces such as treadmills are used as opposed to joysticks which supply no such cues (Darken, Cockayne, & Carmein, 1997; Darken, Allard, & Achille, 1998; Klatzky, et al., 1998: p. 297). A virtual treadmill was developed using software that mapped characteristic head movements when walking on the spot to simulate walking in the virtual environment. Users walking with the virtual treadmill reported a higher sense of presence and could complete tasks more accurately within the environment. The virtual treadmill was also adapted to simulate climbing ladders or stairs for applications such as firefighting training simulations (M. Slater & Usoh, 1994: pp. 138-140). Hiroo Iwata and Takashi Fujii developed an alternative input device for achieving the same end. The user is restricted to one position by a waist-high hoop while making walking movements on a low-friction surface providing kinesthetic feedback. The position of both feet is tracked to control movement through the virtual environment (Bakker, et al., 1999: p. 37; Iwata & Fujii, 1996). More imaginative solutions that have been developed include a unicycle-like pedaling device (Darken, et al., 1997: p. 214) and a harness with roller skates (Iwata & Fujii,

1996: pp. 60-61) but these represent but a very attempts at utilizing proprioceptive feedback in virtual environments. The effect of proprioceptive feedback on immersion and presence is clearly an under-researched and under-theorized area that needs to be addressed if the development of effective MulSeMedia is to progress.

Skin-Mediated Sensory Systems

Apart from sound and sight, touch would be the next most common sense exploited in computer-human interfaces (Kaye, 2004: p. 50). Haptic feedback – associated with touch - is that information that is typically derived from the skin and often refers to that information derived from active touch and manual exploration (Blade & Padgett, 2002: p. 20). Historically, some movies have sought to incorporate haptic sensations into the experience in order to facilitate immersion and presence. Filmgoers who went to screenings of *Earthquake* (1974) and *The Tingler* (1959) experienced haptic sensations through vibrating devices attached to theatre seats (Steuer, 1992: p. 82; Castle, 1959). In virtual environments, the provision of haptic feedback further enhances the immersive experience, leading to heightened believability through interaction with three-dimensional objects (Butler & Neave, 2008). In learning, the use of haptic devices provides an opportunity to mentally store the tactual image of an object along with its visual image (Katz & Krueger, 1989). The lack of haptic feedback limits precision and exacerbates fatigue because of the lack of surfaces to rest or lean on. Even though this is an area of intensive research, there is not yet an effective haptic device that does not restrict the mobility of the user (Mine, 1995: p. 1; Mine, Brooks, & Sequin, 1997: p. 19; Mine, 1997: p. 4).

Research into the effects of haptic sensations and immersion has primarily been restricted to the sensation of touch or force-feedback in the hands. Though routinely neglected, other cutaneous senses are also worthy of attention. These would include light touch, deep pressure, vibration, pain and temperature (Blade & Padgett, 2002: p. 18). Fans, heaters and air-conditioners could all provide heightened virtual experiences but have not been evaluated in any significant way (Dinh, Walker, Song, Kobayashi, & Hodges, 1999: p. 223). To enable successful medical and surgical simulations in a virtual environment, there would need to be haptic feedback to create a degree of realism not present in standard interfaces (Hayward, et al., 2004). Haptic clues provide information about weight, surface structure, size, flexibility and shape (Luursema, Verwey, Kommers, & Annema, 2008).

When applied to controllers, haptics involves the development of software algorithms that synthesize computer generated forces to be experienced by the user for perception and manipulation of virtual objects through touch (Basdogan & Srinivasan, 2002). Information about the resistance of an object is conveyed to the learner by giving active resistance to certain motions of the user. This mechanism is referred to as 'force feedback' (Bergamesco, Frisoli, & Barbagli, 2002). The ability to have programmable mechanical properties facilitates a bidirectional exchange of energy, and therefore information, between the user and the virtual environment (Hayward, Astley, Cruz-Hernandez, Grant, & Robles-De-La-Torre, 2004). The utilization of haptics has been adopted across numerous disciplines including neuroscience, biomechanics, robot design and control, psychophysics, mathematical modeling and simulation (Richard, et al., 2006: p. 208). This technology has been extensively used in medicine where it is used for surgical simulation, telemedicine, interfaces for blind people and rehabilitation of patients with neurological disorders (Basdogan & Srinivasan, 2002; Richard, et al., 2006: p. 209). Haptics also incorporates the idea of kinesthesia (or proprioception) as the ability to perceive the position of one's body, movement and weight. The term 'haptic channel' collectively designates the sensory and motor components of haptics as the hand, by way of example, perceives the world

while acting upon it. Tactile and kinesthetic channels work in conjunction to provide the means to perceive and act on the environment (Hayward, et al., 2004).

Haptic Interfaces (HI) are robotic systems which allow users to interact with virtual objects using the sense of touch via the use of force feedback (Bergamesco, et al., 2002). The Phantom Omni by Sensable Technologies is an example of a commercialized Haptic Interface (Butler & Neave, 2008). The 3D environment or virtual object is viewed on a screen as the user interacts with it. The main limitation of the Phantom Omni, apart from the high cost, is the restrictive range of movement and the provision of feedback for only one point of contact (Butler & Neave, 2008). There are several variants of the Phantom Omni, but generally a stylus is grasped or the user's finger slides into a thimble so that he or she can have the experience of running a finger over the surface of an object (Hayward, et al., 2004). The type of haptic feedback this device utilizes is known as 'point interaction' and allows for six degrees of freedom. A variation of this device which has been used for virtual sculpting is the 'Sensable Phantom Haptic Pen'. The pen also has six degrees of freedom, which is sufficient to give the location and orientation of an object in space (Creighton & Ho-Stuart, 2004). Even so, users report that they would prefer to be able to move around a virtual object, rather than being confined to a single spot (Butler & Neave, 2008). In addition, it is a single user device and its high cost makes it inaccessible for most classroom contexts. Less expensive options are available, such as the Logitech Force 3D Pro but these devices do not have the fidelity or low-level control access needed for many educational simulations (Grow, Verner, & Okamura, 2007). Another alternative would be the force feedback joystick. Though this has fewer degrees of freedom than the Phantom Haptic Pen, it is widely available and is already familiar to many computer users (Butler & Neave, 2008). By way of contrast, the

Museum of Pure Form is a funded project to enable users to virtually touch fragile and valuable sculptures through a specially designed haptic Interface and virtual projection system. The HI takes the form of an exoskeleton that fits over the upper arm, providing force feedback with a separate haptic interface for the fingers (PERCO, 2002). The visitor to the museum is able to see the art pieces but is actually interacting with a digital representation of that piece. The haptic feedback is such that to the user it will feel like he or she is moving a hand along the surface of the sculpture (Bergamesco, et al., 2002).

The Virtual Reality Glove is another interface controller that utilizes haptic technology. In order to detect hand movements, a strain-gauge sensor or flex sensor measures the physical position of the fingers and micro-actuators provide force feedback. A positioning device measures the 3D coordinates of the glove in space. Unfortunately, the prohibitively high cost of the device, due to its complicated construction and expensive components, mean that it has had little application in educational contexts. In addition, the response time tends to be slow, (Lin, 2009) undermining its potential as a controller for authentic 3D movement in a virtual environment. Some, like Goldmeier (2009b) categorise these gloves, along with six other virtual reality technology innovations, as failed attempts in recent times (Goldmeier, 2009a). A controller that holds more promise in this context currently is the Nintendo Wiimote that comes with the Nintendo Wii console. Haptic feedback is simulated via the onboard vibration-producing motor (Brindza & Szweda, 2008). The Wiimote is the device with the most potential for educational use due to its low cost, adaptability and its popularity as a gaming controller. For example, it is expected that the Wiimote will soon be used for interacting with the MUVE, Second Life to provide many exciting possibilities (Boulos, Hetherington, & Wheeler, 2007; Sreedharan, Zurita, & Plimmer, 2007).

String-based haptic interfaces are composed of actuators that are linked together or linked to a manipulation tool. These interfaces are fixed-based, suitable for large workspaces, and are not intrusive. In addition they are light, safe and relatively inexpensive. Conversely, they are also very complex, can be difficult to set up and can be difficult to control (Richard, et al., 2006: p. 209). An example of such a device is the SPIDAR-H (space interface device for artificial reality – human-scale) which provides haptic sensation to both hands and exhibits various aspects force feedback associated with contact, weight, and inertia of objects. Force feedback on both hands is provided by eight motors placed in the corners of a cube surrounding the user. Each hand is attached to three strings, in turn attached to three motors. The motors adjust the tension and length of each string, thereby generating appropriate force for each hand. The user looks through the string interface to a stereoscopic image of the virtual environment on the wall of the cube (Richard, et al., 2006: p. 214). This interface has not been widely adopted.

Haptic feedback may not be the only advantage conferred by haptic devices; it may become possible to record haptic interactions if some sort of recording device is installed either in the computer generating the virtual environment or the haptic controller. The concept of playing back haptic stimuli to the user may have some useful applications. For example, a user with access to a desktop haptic device may touch and feel the prerecorded textures of a car seat that is advertised by a car company over the Internet. Possibly, preprogrammed haptic devices could be used to rehabilitate patients with neurological damage by displaying pre-recorded haptic trajectories in order to improve their motor-control skills. Alternatively, elite athletes could train virtually and then examine their virtual performances. For example, a runner could examine if the foot hit the ground in a balanced manner or examine motional postures (Basdogan & Srinivasan, 2002).

There are still other areas that haptics could address. One of the most disconcerting aspects of virtual environments is the ability to pass through objects in a way not possible in the non-virtual environment. Passive haptics, whereby passive physical objects are incorporated into virtual environments to physically simulate the virtual objects, may help to provide a more realistic experience and thereby increase presence. A study conducted by Brent Insko demonstrated that the inclusion of passive physical objects into the environment did increase the feeling of presence and significantly increased spatial knowledge transfer. The real value in adding passive haptics can be seen in training in environments with impaired visibility where participants would be unable to rely on visual cues (Insko, 2001). Again, this is an area in need of further research and development.

Auditory System

Much research has been done on the various relationships between the aspects of visual representation and immersion in virtual environments. This intense effort has not been replicated in regards to the significance of the aural landscape to immersion in virtual worlds. Audio design has frequently been neglected and regarded as the 'poor relative' of graphics, irrespective of the considerable body of evidence that points to its potential to facilitate presence. This trend is in part due to the technological limitations of computational capacity at the time, leading to an almost complete surrender of audio performance for the sake of heightened graphics which is computationally expensive (Duridanov & Simoff, 2007). Poor audio fidelity has no counterpart in the real world. The background hum or hiss of amplifiers has no correlate in nature, particularly coming from a single source. Many media designers believe that the experience of immersion begins with audio and go to great lengths to remove audible hums and maintain the dynamic range of the original sounds. Reeves and Nass conducted an experiment whereby viewers were exposed to videos with sound of high fidelity and low fidelity. The results amply demonstrated that audio fidelity was far more significant than visual fidelity and the authors suggested that designers of multimedia should focus their attention on audio design at the expense of visual fidelity (Reeves & Nass, 2002: pp. 208-210; Davis, et al., 1999: pp. 1200-1201).

Auditory cues can be used to enhance the feeling of presence in a virtual environment without the requirement for significantly elevated computational power, especially when required for other systems (Dinh, et al., 1999: p. 223; Davis, Scott, Pair, Hodges, & Oliverio, 1999: p. 1197). These cues take three forms: live speech, Foley sounds and ambient sounds. The first is obvious and is most significant in creating social presence. Foley sounds are those sounds triggered by the environment and contribute to perceptual presence; an example would be the sound of surf crashing on a beach. Ambient sounds are the ones most likely to affect the emotional state of the user and would include background music (J. Robertson, et al., 1998: 4). The human ability to differentiate different sounds results from our ability to detect differences in amplitude and frequency, in addition to differences in arrival time and intensity in the signal between the two ears (Steuer, 1992: p. 83).

Surprisingly, the addition of audio cues to a virtual environment also enhances the subjective 3D static visual quality of the display without any changes being made to that display. In an experiment conducted by Elizabeth Davis and her colleagues, participants who entered into a virtual environment with the addition of auditory cues reported that the proportions and 3D perspective of visual objects appeared more correct, that the depth and volume of virtual spaces appeared more realistic, that the field of view was more natural and in general, the virtual environment seemed more real with the addition of ambient sounds (Davis, et al., 1999: p. 1200). Auditory cues generally are included in most applications exploiting MulSeMedia but rarely attract the sort of attention that visual fidelity does. This is changing with the release of inexpensive speakers, amplifiers and headphones that are frequently packaged with home computer systems.

Olfaction and Gustation

Smell or olfaction is rarely used in human-computer interaction. There are numerous very good reasons for this being the case: it is technically challenging to issue scents on demand; it is difficult to create smells that reflect what they are supposed to represent; and there are significant issues relating to research focus and direction (Kaye, 2004: p. 50; Zybura & Eskeland, 1999). Further, it is only appropriate for ambience or in 'calm' settings where a scent can come to the user's attention and drift from it again. Though users quickly become accustomed to an ambient smell; a change in aroma rouses attention though it cannot convey fast action (Kaye, 2004: pp. 50, 52).

The use of aromas to facilitate immersion has a long and colorful history. In the 1950s, cinema owners were concerned about the tendency for people to stay at home watching television, rather than going to the movies. Various technologies were developed to enhance the cinema experience including vibrating seats, 3D glasses and scent technologies. The travel documentary *Behind the Great Wall* was released using 'Aromarama' which funneled scent through the cinema's air-conditioning system (Kaye, 2004: p. 54; Bonzi, 1959). Shortly after, the 1960 film, *Scent of Mystery* starring Elizabeth Taylor, attracted widespread media attention, not because of its plot but because it was the first (and only) film to use Smell-O-Vision. Scents were automatically released at set times during the movie. Unfortunately, the equipment malfunctioned causing the scents to be released at the wrong times; and the movie was a flop (Cardiff, 1960). Two decades later, filmgoers attending screenings of the John Waters' comedy movie *Polyester* experienced 'Odorama' whereby they were given scratch and sniff cards

and were instructed to scratch the card at appropriate times during the movie (Steuer, 1992: p. 82; Waters, 1981). Olfaction was also used in what can arguably be described at the first attempt at creating a comprehensive MulSeMedia. Morton Heiling developed 'Sensorama' which was an immersive, virtual reality motorbike game that utilized the sense of smell. Nine fans simulated the feeling of wind on the rider's face, a vibrating seat reflected the sensation of riding over different, and the scents were produced to simulate a rider passing a pizza restaurant or flower garden. Unfortunately, the system was never developed commercially (Kaye, 2004: p. 54; Dinh, et al., 1999: p. 222; Fisher, 1991). Another interesting example of the use of scent in virtual reality is the virtual firefighting training developed by John Cater at the Deep Immersion Virtual Environment Laboratory at the Southwest Research Institute. The project resulted in the creation of a backpack mounted firefighter training device which delivered any of eight scents through the oxygen mask that makes up part of the usual firefighting kit (Zybura & Eskeland, 1999; Washburn & Jones, 2004: p. 80; Richard, et al., 2006: p. 212).

There is little doubt that using olfactory cues in virtual environments could facilitate performance in some instances, especially those that specifically require recognition or recall (Sadowski & Stanney, 2002: p. 795). The human olfactory system utilizes the sensation of odors for detection, recognition, discrimination and differentiation or scaling (Barfield & Danas, 1996; Richard, et al., 2006: p. 208). Interestingly, it has many direct connections to the area of the brain where emotions are regulated; namely the limbic system. Evidence suggests that odors can be effective in manipulating mood while also increasing vigilance, decreasing stress, and improving recall and retention of learned materials. The powerful influences of the olfactory system can be manipulated by incorporating odors into a virtual environment to produce a more realistic experience, thereby increasing levels of presence and enhancing performance on some tasks (Sadowski & Stanney, 2002: p. 797; Richard, et al., 2006: p. 211).

The human nose contains about 1000 different types of receptor, each attuned to a different chemical bond which affords a scent its characteristic smell. Because of the complexity of the sensory system associated with smell, it is extremely difficult to accurately reproduce smells on demand. Consequently, there is no rigorous, systematic, and reproducible classification for smells (Kaye, 2004: p. 50; Richard, et al., 2006: p. 210). These days inkjet technologies show the most promise for developing on-demand scents for human-computer interfaces such as with gaming (Kaye, 2004: p. 54). AromaJet.com have developed the Pinoke system, an aroma-generating system which is worn around a user's neck or is mounted next to the gaming monitor or screen. Aromas are delivered at appropriate times when triggered by software. A replaceable cartridge stores the scent until used (AromaJet, 2000; Washburn & Jones, 2004: p. 81; Richard, et al., 2006: p. 213).

Immersion is often compromised due to the inadvertent supply of inappropriate olfactory cues. Every environment has an ambient smell and on the vast majority of occasions, will not be consistent with the visual cues seen in a virtual environment. This is conflated by the huge individual variations in sensitivity both to differing olfactory stimuli but also to changes in concentration of the same scent. As a general rule, the sense of smell becomes less sensitive as an individual ages with the peak sensitivity achieved during that individual's fourth decade (Zybura & Eskeland, 1999). Zybura and Eskeland identified five areas for future research in olfaction and virtual reality. These are position tracking to ensure coordinated release of scents when moving past the appropriate area in a virtual environment; scent storage and delivery; appropriate concentration and duration regulation taking into account individual differences in sensitivity; and scent production - an ideal interface will be able to produce any smell from a limited number of available chemicals, much like colors are mixed in a printer (Zybura & Eskeland, 1999).

Even though olfaction is rarely incorporated into MulSeMedia to facilitate immersion, gustation is yet more neglected; very little research has been conducted on the value of gustatory or 'taste' feedback on immersion and presence. Significantly, about seventy-five percent of taste is contributed by our sense of smell which is why olfaction and gestation are frequently considered together (Chalmers & Zányi, 2009: p. 13). Taste as perceived by the tongue, can be measured using a biological membrane sensor. The sensor measures the levels of the five basic tastes, namely sweet, sour, bitter, salty and 'unami' (the fifth basic taste created by glutamate). Any taste can be synthesized from the five elements of taste (Iwata, Yano, Uemura, & Moriya, 2003: p. 1).

One study conducted by Hoffman and colleagues demonstrated that gustatory feedback increased participants' sense of realism in a virtual environment (Hoffman, Hollander, Schroder, Rousseau, & Furness III, 1998). It should be noted, however, that the participants did actually take a bite from a real chocolate bar – even though they could only see it virtually - so that in addition to gustatory feedback there were also significant haptic clues associated with chewing on an actual foodstuff. A more recent attempt was made by Iwata and colleagues in 2003, whereby a haptic interface mimicked the taste, sound and feeling of chewing food. An interface placed in the mouth recreated the force of the food, a bone vibration microphone generated the sound of biting, while the actual taste was recreated with chemicals delivered via a micro injector (Iwata, et al., 2003; Chalmers & Zányi, 2009: 13). Due to the relative complexity of generating gustatory feedback, the desirability of accompanying haptic cues in the mouth, and issues surrounding hygiene the routine incorporation of gustatory feedback in MulSeMedia applications seems a long way off. It may be necessary that such a development will not occur until a pressing need surfaces, perhaps in relation to training for tasting or detecting toxic or illegal chemical markers for example.

Visual System

Most of the research on the influence of sensory input on immersion and hence, presence has focused on visual parameters including the degree of visual detail, field of view (FOV), stereopscopic versus bioptic viewing, the effect of head tracking and the level of visual realism (Duridanov & Simoff, 2007). Interestingly, the research has not always revealed information that would align with 'common sense'. For example, contrary to what might be expected, Byron Reeves and Clifford Nass found no significant difference in levels of immersion when participants were shown scenes in high fidelity or poor fidelity (Reeves & Nass, 2002: pp. 204-206); and from an evolutionary standpoint this makes perfect sense. We are frequently viewing the world in less than optimal conditions; a heavy winter fog may make the drive to work challenging or it might be difficult to spot the dog in the park if you've left his walk too late in the day. We frequently have to function with sub-optimal visual cues.

Intuitively, one would assume that the greater the level of virtual realism, the greater the sense of presence and this time the literature has borne this out. Pictorial realism based on the connectedness, continuity, consistency, and meaningfulness of the perceptual stimuli presented to participants contributes to the emergence of presence. The feeling of depth was that characteristic of the visual stimuli that contributed most to the feeling of presence (Stanney & Salvendy, 1998: p. 162). Another important component of visual input is its response to movement and interaction. For example, the accurate rendering of shadows and reflections in response to the movements of a user's avatar will lead to a greater sense of presence (M. Slater & Usoh, 1994: p. 135). However, visual realism comes at the cost of increased

computational cost which in itself can lead to a decreased frame rate and a resultant decreased sense of presence (Dinh, et al., 1999: p. 222). In addition, it is beyond the capabilities of existing technology to represent all the varied richness and subtleties of the real world (Vinayagamoorthy, et al., 2004: p. 148; Bakker, et al., 1999: p. 38).

Again, following our intuition we would assume that the size of a display would play a significant part in the formula for immersion and presence. And again, the literature bears this out; the larger the screen, the more of the visual display is in peripheral vision, i.e. the boundary between the display and the real physical environment is farther away from the centre of vision, making the boundary less noticeable. Reeves and Nass compared arousal and recall in a two groups of people: one group viewed several scenes on a 22-inch screen and another viewed the same scenes on a 90-inch screen. They found that the larger the screen, the more aroused the viewers were. Further, the participants were tested for recall a week later with the viewers having used the larger screen having significantly better recall (Reeves & Nass, 2002: p. 195-198). The evolutionary reason for this may not be too difficult to fathom. To navigate our way around the real world; we make significant use of our peripheral vision. In the absence of very large screens, most experiences in virtual environments is mediated through desktop virtual systems, whereby the user can see through the eyes or position of an avatar on the screen – in Second Life the default position is behind the avatar's head – but the experience is not three-dimensional (Blade & Padgett, 2002: p. 18). Desktop displays do not enable the use of peripheral vision in virtual environments. George Robertson and his colleagues suggested that *peripheral lenses* could perhaps be used simulate peripheral vision and thereby more closely simulate real world vision; these lenses are panels on either side of the main display. They represent viewpoints that originate at the same point as the main view, but which are pointed out to either side. Though anecdotally this seemed to enhance certain navigational tasks, this result did not hold up under formal research (G. Robertson, Czerwinski, & van Dantzich, 1997: pp. 15-16). These findings are closely related to Field of View, referring to the number of degrees in the visual field. A person generally has two eyes and consequently an overlapping 140-degree FOV. A FOV that exceeds sixty to ninety degrees may give rise to a greater sense of immersion (Blade & Padgett, 2002): p. 19). Obviously, the FOV will be much higher in a CAVE (Cave Automatic Virtual Environment) – consisting of three walls on which stereoscopic images are displayed – than on a desktop system, generating a correspondingly higher sense of presence (Lee, et al., 2007: p. 275; Schuemie, et al., 2001: p. 194).

On a different tack, vivid mental imagery of the virtual environment is a critical factor in immersion (Schlosser, 2003: p. 185). James Cameron's movie *Avatar* is the embodiment of this approach. Though heavily reliant on the technology that produced the 3D experience in that movie, the designers of the visual experience put an extraordinary amount of effort into making every scene and every component of every scene, photorealistic such that every audience member would feel completely immersed in the movie's main setting, the exquisite and dangerous, Pandora (Fitzpatrick, 2009: p. 12). Interestingly, as the Na'vi the blue-skinned humanoids that populate the planet, move through their bioluminescent environment, plants and shrubs light up as they are touched. This exploits the phenomenon known as cross-modal sensory integration, whereby one dimension of a sensory stimulus – in this case visual input – is mapped to another stimulus; in this example to the sense of touch. Though the movie cannot provide direct haptic stimulus, it does so indirectly by the alignment of visual stimuli to haptic events (Biocca & Choi, 2001: pp. 249-251).

Though beautifully drawn and envisioned, *Avatar* is most significant for its exploitation of stereopsis using special cinematography and purpose-built glasses to facilitate immersion. Stereopsis is defined as the binocular vision of images with different views for each eye to distinguish depth (Blade & Padgett, 2002: p. 24). Generally speaking, users of 3D immersive systems that utilize stereoscopic imagery with a head-mounted display report a greater sense of immersion than those using ordinary two-dimensional desktop displays (see Gutiérrez, et al., 2007: p. 156). Allowing students of anatomy to change the perspective shown by rotating a virtual object, helps them to develop visuo-spatial representations (Luursema, Verwey, Kommers, Geelkerken, & Vos, 2006). This ability to conceptualise 3D shapes is enhanced by the use of haptic technology, making it easier to learn about objects that ordinarily could not be touched or walked around because of substantial risks in real-life settings (Dettori, et al., 2003).

On the down side, one of the significant factors that may detract from the quality of visual input is the delay in update of visual data after the user has moved while wearing a head-mounted display. This can also be an issue when using a stereoscopic spatially immersive display. This tendency is also exacerbated because of the necessity for a small degree of aniso-accommodation (unequal focus across both eyes) that such a system requires, resulting in a disturbance in subsequent binocular disturbance known as 'binocular dysphoria'. This can also be experienced with desktop stereoscopic displays and has even been identified subsequent to viewing 3D movies at the cinema such as *Avatar* (Stanney & Salvendy, 1998: p. 142; Cameron, 2009). The brain uses at least ten cues for depth perception. Movies shown in 3D and most other technologies used to generate the illusion of depth rely on only one: parallax error. The brain must actively suppress its response to the other cues. This suppression does not necessarily end with the conclusion of the 3D experience but may persist for hours or days. There is some speculation that with consistent exposure on a daily or near daily basis, the 'binocular dysphoria' may become permanent; a warning worth heeding for those considering the purchase of a 3D television or developing MulSeMedia intended for prolonged and regular use (Pesce, 2010).

THE CHALLENGE AND PROMISE OF MULSEMEDIA

With the rapid development of technology and advances in computational power, MulSeMedia is increasing in sophistication with different sensory modalities being incorporated in order to facilitate immersion and hence, presence. Scott Jochim, creator and co-owner of Custom Theatre Solutions claims to 'engineer experiences' using olfactory, haptic, auditory and visual cues. His company sells hardware which can be used at home using motion codes that are accessible via the internet to accompany DVDs (Parks, 2006). Visual information can be delivered in 3D via head-mounted displays or screens, all sound is bi-aural so that the soundscape changes as the individual moves around the room, there's a fully-integrated fragrance system and a wave chamber audio feedback system located at the base of each seat (Jochim, 2006). In a more experimental setting, the VIREPSE (virtual reality platform for simulation and experimentation) multi-modal virtual environment has been created for use in an educational context, making use of visual, auditory, haptic and olfactory feedback. The haptic feedback is supplied through the string-based SPIDAR-H supplying feedback to both hands and cues associated with weight, contact and inertia of objects. Stereoscopic images are projected onto a large rear screen and olfactory information is delivered via the Osmooze piezo-electric scent-delivery system (Meulenkamp, n.d.; Richard, et al., 2006: pp. 214-215). The system was developed to allow students to immerse themselves in the abstract concept of the Bohr atomic model, i.e. the quantization of the energy levels which students traditionally find difficult to understand (Richard, et al., 2006: p. 216). The use of immersive sound,

haptic feedback, stereoscopic vision, olfactory cues and the ability for students to directly interact with the electrons increased both the cognitive and sensori-motor performance of the students through facilitating immersion and hence, presence in this simulation (Richard, et al., 2006): p. 221.

Though the promise of MulSeMedia is considerable, so are the challenges. Designers of new MulSeMedia will have to deal with numerous issues including parallelism of actions, action sequencing of synchronization, the amalgamation of information gathered from differing input devices, as well as the combination or separation of information (fission mechanism) to be directed to different devices (Navarre, et al., 2005: pp. 170-171). The rendering of MulSeMedia requires sophisticated and powerful computational needs for accurate rendering of data and reduced lag time, factors indirectly influencing immersion (Chalmers, Debattista, & Ramic-Brkic, 2009: p. 1101).

The complexities of supplying accurate sensory feedback and facilitating immersion have been examined in-depth in this chapter. Enhancing immersion and facilitating presence using MulSeMedia is far more complex than just arousing more sensory systems. Immersion does not increase proportionally with each additional sense stirred. Though generally speaking, the more senses stimulated the better, just how those systems interact with each other is far less certain. For example, as already discussed, hi-fidelity sound can enhance visual perceptions of the virtual environment and taste is largely a consequence of smell.

With any given virtual scene, to accurately recreate realism in any one of the sensory systems requires computational power, techniques and knowledge not yet available. Instead, researchers and designers need to develop a thorough understanding of the factors that facilitate immersion and more subtly probe that mysterious connection between immersion and presence. To avoid redundancy – while recognizing that some remains desirable - limitations on human perception need to be exploited. For example, for anyone in the operating in the real world, cross modal effects can render large amounts of sensory data useless; ignored in the presence of data from other stronger senses (Chalmers, et al., 2009: p. 1102). This redundancy can be exploited so that only sensory information that will be actually noticed would be supplied, with a corresponding decrease in computational power. The challenge remains in knowing exactly what data can be eliminated and which is crucial to maintaining immersion and the feeling of 'being there', i.e. presence. Finally, sensory data are not the only contributing factors to immersion and presence. MulSeMedia needs to exploit some of those other factors that are equally significant including the level of interactivity, motivation and intent of the user, and appropriate task design.

REFERENCES

Aldrich, C. (2009). *Learning Online with Games, Simulations, and Virtual Worlds: Strategies for Online Instruction.* San Francisco: Jossey-Bass.

Arangarasan, R., & Gadh, R. (2000, 10-13 September). *Geometric modeling and collaborative design in a multi-modal multi-sensory virtual environment.* Paper presented at the DETC'00 ASME Design Engineering Technical Conference, Baltimore, Maryland.

AromaJet. (2000). AromJet.com Retrieved 3 March, 2010, from http://www.aromajet.com

Bakker, N. H., Werkhoven, P. J., & Passenier, P. O. (1999). The Effects of Proprioceptive and Visual Feedback on Geographical Orientation in Virtual Environments. *Presence (Cambridge, Mass.), 8*(1), 36–53. doi:10.1162/105474699566035

Barfield, W., & Danas, E. (1996). Comments on the use of olfactory displays for virtual environments. *Presence (Cambridge, Mass.), 5*(1), 109–121.

Basdogan, C., & Srinivasan, M. A. (2002). Haptic rendering in virtual environments. In Stanney, K. M. (Ed.), *Handbook of virtual environments: design, implementation, and applications* (pp. 117–134). Mahwah: Lawrence Erlbaum Associates.

Begel, A., Garcia, D. D., & Wolfman, S. A. (2004). Kinesthetic Learning in the Classroom. *ACM SIGSCE Bulletin, 36*(1), 183–184. doi:10.1145/1028174.971367

Bergamesco, M., Frisoli, A., & Barbagli, F. (2002). *Haptics technologies and cultural heritage application.* Paper presented at the Computer Animation Conference.

Biocca, F., & Choi, J. K. Y. (2001). Visual Touch in Virtual Environments: An Exploratory Study of Presence, Multimodal Interfaces, and Cross-Modal Sensory Illusions. *Presence (Cambridge, Mass.), 10*(3), 247–265. doi:10.1162/105474601300343595

Blade, R. A., & Padgett, M. L. (2002). Virtual Environments Standards and Terminology. In Stanney, K. M. (Ed.), *Handbook of Virtual Environments: Design, Implementation, and Applications* (pp. 15–27). New Jersey: Erlbaum Associates.

Blascovich, J., Loomis, J. M., Beall, A. C., Swinth, K. R., Hoyt, C. L., & Bailenson, J. N. (2002). Immersive Virtual Environment Technology as a Methodological Tool for Social Psychology. *Psychological Inquiry, 13*(2), 103–124. doi:10.1207/S15327965PLI1302_01

Bonk, C. J., & Zhang, K. (2006). Introducing the R2D2 Model: Online Learning for the Diverse Learners of the World. *Distance Education, 27*(2), 249–264. doi:10.1080/01587910600789670

Bonzi, L. (1959). *Writer.* USA: Behind the Great Wall.

Boulos, M. N. K., Hetherington, L., & Wheeler, S. (2007). Second Life: an overview of the potential of 3-D virtual worlds in medical and health education. *Health Information and Libraries Journal, 24*(4), 233–245. doi:10.1111/j.1471-1842.2007.00733.x

Brindza, J., & Szweda, J. (2008). *Wiimote interactions for freshman engineering education.* Notre Dame, Indiana: NetScale Laboratory.

Butler, M., & Neave, P. (2008). *Object appreciation through haptic interaction.* Paper presented at the *Hello! Where are you in the landscape of educational technology? Proceedings ascilite Melbourne 2008.* from http://www.ascilite.org.au/conferences/melbourne08/procs/butler-m.pdf

Cameron, J. (Writer) (2009). Avatar [Film]. In J. Cameron & J. Landau (Producer). USA: 20th Century Fox.

Cardiff, J. (Writer) (1960). Scent of Mystery [Film]. In M. Todd, Jr (Producer). USA.

Castle, W. (Writer) (1959). The Tingler [Film]. USA: Columbia Pictures.

Castranova, E. (2001). *Virtual Worlds: A First-Hand Account of Market and Society on the Cyberian Frontier.* Center for Economic Studies & Ifo Institute for Economic Research.

Chalmers, A., Debattista, K., Mastroropoulou, G., & dos Santos, L. P. (2007). There-Reality: Selective Rendering in High Fidelity Virtual Environments. *The International Journal of Virtual Reality, 6*(1), 1–10.

Chalmers, A., Debattista, K., & Ramic-Brkic, B. (2009). Towards high-fidelity multi-sensory virtual environments. *The Visual Computer, 25*(12), 1101–1108. doi:10.1007/s00371-009-0389-2

Chalmers, A., & Zányi, E. (2009). *Real Virtuality: emerging technology for virtually recreating reality* (pp. 1–20). BECTA.

Creighton, I., & Ho-Stuart, C. (2004). *A sense of touch in online sculpting.* Paper presented at the 2nd international conference on Computer graphics and interactive techniques in Australasia and South East Asia Singapore.

Darken, R. P., Allard, T., & Achille, L. B. (1998). Spatial Orientation and Wayfinding in Large-Scale Virtual Spaces: An Introduction. *Presence (Cambridge, Mass.), 7*(2), 101–107. doi:10.1162/105474698565604

Darken, R. P., Cockayne, W. R., & Carmein, D. (1997). *The Omni-Directional Treadmill: A Locomotion Devic for Virtual Worlds.* Paper presented at the UIST '97, Banff, Canada.

Davis, E. T., Scott, K., Pair, J., Hodges, L. F., & Oliverio, J. (1999). *Can audio enhance visual perception and performance in a virtual environment.* Paper presented at the Human Factors and Ergonomics Society 43rd Annual Meeting

Dede, C. (1995). The Evolution of Constructivist Learning Environments: Immersion in Distributed, Virtual Worlds. *Educational Technology, 35*(5), 46–52.

Dede, C. (2009). Immersive Interfaces for Engagement and Learning. *Science, 323*(5910), 66–69. doi:10.1126/science.1167311

Dede, C., Salzman, M. C., Loftin, R. B., & Sprague, D. (1999). Multisensory Immersion as a Modeling Environment for Learning Complex Scientific Concepts. In Roberts, N., & Feurzeig, W. (Eds.), *Modeling and Simulation in science and mathematics education.* New York: Springer.

Dettori, A., Avizzano, C. A., Marcheschi, S., Angerilli, M., Bergamasco, M., Loscos, C., et al. (2003). *Art Touch with CREATE haptic interface.* Paper presented at the ICAR 2003: The 11th International Conference on Advanced Robotics.

Dinh, H. Q., Walker, N., Song, C., Kobayashi, A., & Hodges, L. F. (1999). *Evaluating the importance of multi-sensory input on memory and sense of presence in virtual environments.* Paper presented at the IEEE Virtual Reality Conference, Houston, Texas.

Duridanov, L., & Simoff, S. (2007). 'Inner Listening' as a Basic Principle for Developing Immersive Virtual Worlds. *Online - Heidelberg Journal of Religions on the Internet, 2*(3).

Fassbender, E., & Richards, D. (2008). *Using a Dance Pad to Navigate through the Virtual Heritage Environment of Macquarie Lighthouse, Sydney Virtual Systems and Multimedia* (pp. 1–12). Berlin: Springer.

Fisher, S. S. (1991). Virtual Environments, Personal Simulation & Telepresence. In Helsel, S., & Roth, J. (Eds.), *Virtual Reality: Theory, Practice and Promise*. Westport: Meckler Publishing.

Fitzpatrick, L. (2009). *The Art of Avatar*. New York: Abrams.

Fleming, N., & Baume, D. (2006). Learning Styles Again: VARKing up the Right Tree! *Educational Developments, 7*(4), 4–7.

Franceschi, K. G., Lee, R. M., & Hinds, D. (2008). *Engaging E-Learning in Virtual Worlds: Supporting Group Collaboration*. Paper presented at the 41st Hawaii International Conference on System Sciences.

Goldmeier, S. (2009a). Virtual Worlds: Seven failed virtual reality technologies.

Goldmeier, S. (2009b). Virtual Worlds: Seven failed virtual reality technologies, from http://io9.com/5280347/7-failed-virtual-reality-technologies

Grow, D. I., Verner, L. N., & Okamura, A. M. (2007). *Educational haptics*. Paper presented at the The AAI 2007 Spring Symposia - Robots and Robot Venues.

Gutiérrez, F., Pierce, J., Vergara, V. M., Coulter, R., Saland, L., Caudell, T. P., et al. (2007). The Effect of Degree of Immersion upon Learning Performance in Virtual Reality Simulations for Medical Education. In J. D. Westwood, R. S. Haluck, H. M. Hoffman, G. T. Mogel, R. Phillips, R. A. Robb & K. G. Vosburgh (Eds.), *Medicine Meets Virtual Reality 15: in vivo, in vitro, in silico: Designing the Next in Medicine* (Vol. 125, pp. 155-160). 2007: IOS Press.

Hayward, V., Astley, O. R., Cruz-Hernandez, M., Grant, D., & Robles-De-La-Torre, G. (2004). Haptic interfaces and devices. *Sensor Review, 24*, 16-29.

Hoffman, H. G., Hollander, A., Schroder, K., Rousseau, S., & Furness, T. III. (1998). Physically Touching and Tasting Virtual Objects Enhances the Realism of Virtual Experiences. *Virtual Reality (Waltham Cross)*, (3): 226–234. doi:10.1007/BF01408703

Insko, B. E. (2001). *Passive Haptics Significantly Enhances Virtual Environments*. Chapel Hill: University of North Carolina.

Iwata, H., & Fujii, T. (1996). *Virtual perambulator: A novel interface device for locomotion in virtual environment*. Paper presented at the Virtual Reality Annual International Symposium (VRAIS 96).

Iwata, H., Yano, H., Uemura, T., & Moriya, T. (2003). *Food Simulator*. Paper presented at the International Conference on Artificial Reality and Telexistence 2003.

Jochim, S. (2006). CTS: A Motion Company Retrieved 2 March, 2010, from http://customtheatersolutions.biz

Jones, C. (2005). Who are you? Theorising from the Experience of Working Through an Avatar. *E-learning, 2*(4), 414–425. doi:10.2304/elea.2005.2.4.414

Katz, D., & Krueger, L. E. (1989). *The world of touch*. Hillsdale, NJ: L. Erlbaum Associates.

Kaye, J. J. (2004). Making Scents: aromatic output for HCI. *Interaction, 11*(1), 48–61. doi:10.1145/962342.964333

Klatzky, R. L., Loomis, J. M., Beall, A. C., Chance, S. S., & Golledge, R. G. (1998). Spatial updating of self-position and orientation during real, imagined, and virtual locomotion. *Psychological Science, 9*(4), 293–298. doi:10.1111/1467-9280.00058

Lawrence, G. H. (1986). Using computers for treatment of psychological problems. *Computers in Human Behavior, 2*(2), 43–62. doi:10.1016/0747-5632(86)90021-X

Lee, C. H., & Liu, A. Del_Castillo, S., Bowyer, M., Alverson, D. C., Muniz, G., et al. (2007). Towards an Immersive Virtual Environment for Medical Team Training. In J. D. Westwood, R. S. Haluck, H. M. Hoffman, G. T. Mogel, R. Phillips, R. A. Robb & K. G. Vosburgh (Eds.), *Medicine Meets Virtual Reality 15: in vivo, in vitro, in silico: Designing the Next in Medicine* (Vol. 125, pp. 274-279). Amsterdam: IOS Press.

Lin, M.-Y. (2009). United States Patent No. FreshPatents.com: USPTO.

Loomis, J. M., Fujita, N., Da Silva, J., & Fukusima, S. S. (1992). Visual Space Perception and Visually Directed Action. *Journal of Experimental Psychology. Human Perception and Performance, 18*(4), 906–921. doi:10.1037/0096-1523.18.4.906

Luursema, J.-M., Verwey, W. B., Kommers, P. A. M., & Annema, J.-H. (2008). The role of stereopsis in virtual anatomical learning. *Interacting with Computers, 20*(4-5), 455–460. doi:10.1016/j.intcom.2008.04.003

Luursema, J.-M., Verwey, W. B., Kommers, P. A. M., Geelkerken, R. H., & Vos, H. J. (2006). Optimizing conditions for computer-assisted anatomical learning. *Interacting with Computers, 18,* 1123–1138. doi:10.1016/j.intcom.2006.01.005

McMahan, A. (2003). Immersion, Engagement, and Presence: A Method for Analyzing 3-D Video games. In Wolf, M. J. P., & Perron, B. (Eds.), *The Video Game Theory Reader* (pp. 67–86). New York: Routledge.

Meulenkamp, W. (n.d.). Osmooze Perfume Distribution Solution Retrieved 3 March, 2010, from http://www.osmooze.com

Mine, M. R. (1995). *Virtual Environment Interaction Techniques*. Chapel Hill: University of North Carolina.

Mine, M. R. (1997). *Exploiting Proprioception in Virtual-Environment Interaction*. Chapel Hill: University of North Carolina.

Mine, M. R., Brooks, F. P., Jr., & Sequin, C. H. (1997). *Moving objects in space: exploiting proprioception in virtual-environment interaction.* Paper presented at the 24th Annual International Conference on Computer Graphics and Interactive Techniques, Los Angeles.

Moore, K., Wiederhold, B. K., Wiederhold, M. D., & Riva, G. (2002). Panic and Agoraphobia in a Virtual World. *Cyberpsychology & Behavior, 5*(3), 197–202. doi:10.1089/109493102760147178

Morie, J. F., Iyer, K., Valanejad, K., Sadek, R., Miraglia, D., Milam, D., et al. (2003). *Sensory Design for Virtual Environments*. Paper presented at the International Conference on Computer Graphics and Interactive Techniques ACM SIGGRAPH 2003 Sketches & Applications

Navarre, D., Palanque, P., Bastide, R., Schyn, A., Winckler, M., Nedel, L. P., et al. (2005). *A Formal Description of Multimodal Interaction Techniques for Immersive Virtual Reality Applications*. Paper presented at the Tenth IFIP TC13 International Conference on Human-Computer Interaction.

Nowak, K. L., & Biocca, F. (2004). The Effect of the Agency and Anthropomorphism on Users' Sense of Telepresence, Copresence, and Social Presence in Virtual Environments. *Presence (Cambridge, Mass.)*, *12*(5), 481–494. doi:10.1162/105474603322761289

Parks, J. R. (2006, September). Hold on to your CTS. *A2Z Magazine, September*.

Pearson, E., & Bailey, C. (2007). *Evaluating the potential of the Nintendo Wii to support disabled students in education*. Paper presented at the ICT: providing choices for learners and learning. ascilite. from http://www.ascilite.org.au/ conferences/ singapore07/procs/ pearson-poster.pdf

PERCO. (2002). The Museum of Pure Form Retrieved 6th June, 2009, from http://www.pureform.org

Pesce, M. (2010, 21 February). Keep doing that and you'll go blind. Weblog posted to http://www.abc.net.au/unleashed/ stories/s2813511.htm.

Piaget, J. (1999). The Stages of the Intellectual Development of the Child. In Slater, A., & Muir, D. (Eds.), *The Blackwell Reader in Developmental Psychology* (pp. 35–42). Oxford: Blackwell Publishing.

Reeves, B., & Nass, C. (2002). *The Media Equation: How People Treat Computers, Television, and New Media Like Real People and Places*. Stanford: CSLI Publications.

Richard, E., Tijou, A., Richard, P., & Ferrier, J.-L. (2006). Multi-modal virtual environments for education with haptic and olfactory feedback. *Virtual Reality (Waltham Cross)*, *10*(3/4), 207–225. doi:10.1007/s10055-006-0040-8

Robertson, G., Czerwinski, M., & van Dantzich, M. (1997). *Immersion in Desktop Virtual Reality*. Paper presented at the 10th annual ACM symposium on User interface software and technology Banff, Alberta.

Robertson, J., de Quincey, A., Stapleford, T., & Wiggins, G. (1998). *Real-Time Music Generation for a Virtual Environment*. Paper presented at the ECAI98 workshop on AI/Alife and Entertainment.

Ruddle, R. A., & Péruch, P. (2004). Effects of proprioceptive feedback and environmental characteristics on spatial learning in virtual environments. *International Journal of Human-Computer Studies*, *60*, 299–326. doi:10.1016/j.ijhcs.2003.10.001

Sadowski, W., & Stanney, K. (2002). Presence in Virtual Environments. In Stanney, K. M. (Ed.), *Handbook of Virtual Environments: Design, implementation, and applications* (pp. 791–806). Mahwah: Lawrence Erlbaum Associates Publishers.

Salmon, G. (2009). The future for (second) life and learning. *British Journal of Educational Technology*, *40*(3), 526–538. doi:10.1111/j.1467-8535.2009.00967.x

Sanders, R. L., & McKeown, L. (2008). Promoting Reflection through Action Learning in a 3D Virtual World. *International Journal of Social Sciences*, *2*(1), 50–55.

Schlosser, A. E. (2003). Experiencing Products in the Virtual World: The Role of Goal and Imagery in Influencing Attitudes versus Purchase Intentions. *The Journal of Consumer Research*, *30*(2), 184–198. doi:10.1086/376807

Schuemie, M. J., Van der Straaten, P., Krijn, M., & Van der Mast, C. A. P. G. (2001). Research on Presence in Virtual Reality: A Survey. *Cyberpsychology & Behavior, 4*(2), 183–201. doi:10.1089/109493101300117884

Slater, M., & Usoh, M. (1994). Body-Centred Interaction in Virtual Environments. In Thalmann, N. M., & Thalmann, D. (Eds.), *Artificial Life and Virtual Reality* (pp. 125–147). John Wiley and Sons.

Slater, M., Usoh, M., & Steed, A. (1994). Depth of Presence in Immersive Virtual Environments. *Presence (Cambridge, Mass.), 3*(2), 130–144.

Sreedharan, S., Zurita, E. S., & Plimmer, B. (2007). *3D Input for 3D Worlds*. Paper presented at the OzCHI Conference.

Stanney, K., & Salvendy, G. (1998). Aftereffects and Sense of Presence in Virtual Environments: Formulation of a Research and Development Agenda. *International Journal of Human-Computer Interaction, 10*(2), 135–187. doi:10.1207/s15327590ijhc1002_3

Steuer, J. (1992). Defining virtual reality: dimensions determining telepresence. *The Journal of Communication, 42*(4), 73–93. doi:10.1111/j.1460-2466.1992.tb00812.x

Sun, H.-J., Campos, J. L., & Chan, G. S. W. (2004). Multisensory integration in the estimation of relative path length. *Experimental Brain Research, 154*(2), 246–254. doi:10.1007/s00221-003-1652-9

Tashner, J. H., Riedl, R. E., & Bronack, S. C. (2005, January 2005). *Virtual Worlds: Further Development of Web-Based Teaching.* Paper presented at the Hawaii International Conference on Education, Honolulu, Hawaii.

Vinayagamoorthy, V., Brogni, A., Gillies, M., Slater, M., & Steed, A. (2004). *An investigation of presence response across variations in visual realism.* Paper presented at the 7th Annual International Presence Workshop.

Washburn, D. A., & Jones, L. M. (2004). Could olfactory displays improve data visualization? *Computing in Science & Engineering, 6*(6), 80–83. doi:10.1109/MCSE.2004.66

Waters, J. (Writer) (1981). Polyester [Film]. USA: New Line Cinema.

Witmer, B. G., & Singer, M. J. (1998). Measuring Presence in Virtual Environments: A Presence Questionnaire. *Presence (Cambridge, Mass.), 7*(3), 225–240. doi:10.1162/105474698565686

Zhu, Q., Xiang, K., & Hu, S. (2007). *Design an Immersive Interactive Museum in Second Life.* Paper presented at the Second Workshop on Digital Media and its Application in Museum & Heritage.

Zybura, M., & Eskeland, G. A. (1999). *Olfaction for Virtual Reality.* University of Washington.

Section 2
Individual Difference, Perception and Culture

60

Chapter 3
Appreciating Individual Differences:
Exposure Time Requirements in Virtual Space

Markos Kyritsis
Brunel University, UK

Stephen Gulliver
University of Reading, UK

ABSTRACT

Learning the spatial layout of an environment is essential in application domains including military and emergency personnel training. Training each and every member of staff, however, within a real-world space cannot practically be achieved, especially if the space is under-development or potentially unsafe. The aim of this chapter is to demonstrate how individual difference factors can significantly impact upon training requirements when acquiring spatial knowledge from a virtual environment. Although experimental setup is not MulSeMedia, the impact of appreciating individual differences is of direct relevance to MulSeMedia technologies. This chapter shows how individual differences impact information assimilation; showing that user information assimilation, and therefore feedback, must be personalised for individual needs. The chapter looks at the importance of: gender, orientation skill, cognitive style, system knowledge, and environmental knowledge – showing how individual user differences significantly influence the training time required to ensure effective virtual environment spatial knowledge acquisition (SKA). We introduce the problem of contradicting literature in the area of SKA, and discuss how the amount of exposure time given to a person during VE training is responsible for the feasibility of SKA.

DOI: 10.4018/978-1-60960-821-7.ch003

INTRODUCTION

Learning Virtual Space

The ability to 'learn' the environment before engaging in navigation is an area of interest for a variety of application domains (Egsegian et al., 1993, Foreman et al, 2003). Traditionally spatial training is accomplished by providing users with maps and briefings of an environment. These methods, however, only provide topological knowledge of the environment, which whilst being more flexible, pays little attention to the details of routes and landmarks (Thorndyke, 1980; Golledge, 1991). Procedural learning has a distinct advantage as can be seen in the experiments of Thorndyke and Hayes-Roth (1982); where participants with procedural knowledge of an environment estimated route distances significantly better than participants who had acquired just topological knowledge. Navigation therefore appears to rely heavily on previously acquired visual information, e.g. the process of re-orientation during navigation in a previously visited environments (Montello, 2005), which relies on previously seen "visual references" in order to adjust bearings during navigation. Maps and other traditional navigational equipment cannot provide this level of supporting information. VE training promises to provide procedural knowledge through exploration, and has caught the attention of a variety of researchers all attempting to determine whether virtual training is more efficient than training through more traditional methods (Witmer et al., 1995; Goerger et al., 1998; Waller et al., 1998; Foreman et al., 2003).

Learning in virtual environments relies on the ability of users to develop an understanding of space by creating a cognitive map of the environment (Asthmeir et al., 1993; Cobb and d'Cruz, 1994; Silverman and Spiker, 1997; Clark and Wong, 2000; Riva and Gamberini, 2000). Cognitive maps are mental representations of space that people develop in order to acquire an understanding of space, both virtual and real, through either procedural knowledge or survey knowledge (Thorndyke, 1980; Golledge, 1991; Witmer et al., 1995; Goerger et al., 1998). When learning in a procedural manner, cognitive maps are created through the act of navigation (Montello, 2005). Navigation itself is made up of two separate and very distinct processes. The first of these processes is locomotion, which is the movement of a person within an environment. The second process is way-finding, which is the planning of routes that a person undergoes when trying to get to a specific destination (Montello, 2005). It is understood that during self-directed locomotion (where the person is actively moving about in the environment solving problems - such as avoiding obstacles), there is a tendency to acquire more spatial knowledge (Feldman and Acredolo, 1979). Virtual environment training provides self-directed locomotion without the possibility of a dangerous life-threatening situation, making it very suitable for emergency and military training.

Interestingly, research concerning spatial knowledge acquisition through VEs, provides a variety of contradicting results. The findings, although conflicting, appear to be subject to a key influencing factor, 'required exposure time' (Witmer et al., 1996; Darken and Banker, 1998; Waller et al., 1998; Goerger et al., 1998; and Darken and Peterson, 2001). This factor is the exposure time that a user will spend learning the environment in order to achieve spatial knowledge acquisition.

The Impact Of Training Time

Witmer et al. (1996), Wilson et al. (1996), Waller et al. (1998), and Foreman et al. (2003) all conducted experiments in order to conclude whether spatial knowledge acquisition can be acquired from a VE representation of the real world. These experiments involved a group of participants navigating through virtual space and acquiring spatial knowledge, and then comparing the results to a group that learned the environment through conventional methods such as maps or photographs. These experiments concluded that a VE can be more beneficial than traditional training. However, this is only the case if a long exposure time is given to the users.

Darken and Banker (1998) reported that experts perform better using conventional methods such as maps, while Goerger et al. (1998) reported that all participants had a greater success using conventional methods. Goerger et al. (1998) acknowledge, that with longer exposure times, virtual reality training may in fact be more beneficial, however, this is hard to determine since the exposure times that a user spent in each experiment differed. Waller et al (1998) allowed for two minutes, Darken and Banker allowed for a set 60 minute exposure, and Goerger et al. (1998) allowed for a set 30 minute exposure, yet they referred to this as a short exposure time. It was, therefore unclear how much exposure time is deemed as required, and if in fact various environmental attributes and individual user differences can affect the required exposure time.

In an attempt to clarify this situation, Darken et al. (1999) and Koh et al. (1999) discussed why spatial knowledge acquisition research delivers contradictory results. They both made the argument that individual user differences are an extremely important factor in the development of cognitive maps, and that a one-size-fits all situation may not be possible when determining required exposure time. Darken et al. (1999) also examined how cognitive and biological differences affect a series of cognitive processes, which are critical to navigation. They stated that previous knowledge, aptitude, orientation ability, strategy, perceptual motoric and memorial knowledge, all influenced the navigational skill of the user. According to Koh et al. (1999) and Waller et al. (2001) there is a need to identify these individual differences and to understand how they affect performance when acquiring spatial knowledge. Therefore, we proceed by identifying and discussing commonly

defined individual differences of users that affect navigation skills, and therefore the exposure time required to acquire spatial knowledge from a VE. Understanding how these individual differences affect navigational skill will help VE trainers understand the required exposure times necessary for a specific user to acquire spatial knowledge from a particular environment. Since people are different, a one-size fits all approach to training time does not seem logical.

Individual Differences Impacting User Navigation

Individual differences have been considered for many years in Visuospatial research, which considers a very broad spectrum of research of understanding concerning images, space and spatial knowledge acquisition (Hegarty and Waller, 2005). This chapter considers the key individual user differences: gender, experience / knowledge, orientation skill, age, and cognitive styles. As suggested by Darken et al. (1999), each of these human attributes influence the navigational skills of the user when they navigate in a novel environment.

Gender Issues in Navigation

There is evidence that gender plays a significant role in acquiring spatial knowledge from a VE. Waller et al. (1998) showed that females were particularly disorientated in a virtual maze, since they reported large bearing errors when drawing a retrospective maze map. Although women's ability is more constrained when learning spatial characteristics of a virtual environment, their difficulty when navigating in the maze may be constrained by strategy rather than ability. Both Sandstrome et al. (1998) and Moffat et al. (1998) have provided explanations as to why male users navigate better in a maze. One of the deficiencies of a maze is that it relies heavily on geometrical navigation, rather than the use of landmark cues. Sandstrome et al. (1998) concluded that women rely heavily on the use of object landmarks for navigation, where men seem to use both structural landmarks and object landmarks.

The difficulty that women may face when navigating through an environment with limited landmarks, suggests that the required exposure time required by women to acquire the spatial information is increased when environments lack well placed object landmarks. Accordingly, women have problems navigating environments that are complex by nature (such as a maze), however this does not mean that for other types of environments their navigation skills will suffer, or that if given enough exposure time their knowledge of the environment will not equal that of the men. This theory is backed by Vila et al. (2002), who indicate that as exposure time in the environment increases, the navigational differences between the genders decreases.

Aptitude and Spatial Orientation Skills

The most discussed individual user difference, in the area of spatial knowledge acquisition, is orientation skill. Most experiments testing for spatial knowledge acquisition attempt to keep orientation skill consistent amongst participants (Witmer et al., 1996; Goerger et al., 1998; and Waller et al., 1998). It is obvious that research considers spatial orientation skills as being a very influential attribute during a variety of areas involving human-computer interaction, such as browsing and other visual tasks (Gomez et al., 1986; Vicente et al., 1987; Stanney and Salvendy, 1995), however controlling the variation of orientation skill limits the appreciation of its impact. There is strong evidence that individuals have different orientation abilities, which are determined by biological factors (Smith and Millner, 1981; Maguire et al., 1996; Maguire et al., 1999; Maguire et al., 2000). Research points to the hippocampus area, which is placed in the centre of the brain, as being responsible for providing spatial memory. To measure spatial and spatial orientation, vari-

ous spatial visualisation and orientation tests that can determine a person's orientation skill, such as the Guilford-Zimmerman orientation survey (Guilford and Zimmerman, 1948). Other tests exist (such as spatial memory, and spatial scanning tests), but spatial orientation tests are thought to be more successful in determining a user's ability to acquire spatial knowledge (Waller, 2001).

Although the orientation skill of a user is often thought to be the most critical individual difference, due to variable control there is actually no proof, to the best of our knowledge, that it has the most impact on the required exposure time. This will be considered in more detail in this chapter.

Cognitive Styles

The concept of people adopting different strategies in order to solve problems and make decisions was first presented by Allport (1937) who presented cognitive styles as a person's preferred way of perceiving, remembering, thinking and problem solving. Since then research has looked into cognitive styles, and has referred to them as persistent strategies adapted by individuals when faced with problem solving tasks (Robertson, 1985). In more detail, cognitive styles affect perceiving, remembering, organising, processing, thinking and problem solving (Liu and Ginther, 1999).

Many different learning strategies are consistently adopted by a user in order to solve a problem. Messick (1976) identified as many as 19 different cognitive styles, and Smith (1984) identified 17. Schmeck (1988) grouped them using two distinctly different, but general, learning styles. The first is a more holist learning style, which is referred to as field-dependent and seems to emerge from activity in the right hemisphere of the brain. The second is a more analytical learning style that is referred to as field-independent and seems to emerge from activity in the left hemisphere of the brain.

Field-dependent people are more passive when learning (Witkin et al.,1977), and prefer to learn information by focusing on the information as a whole - rather than breaking it down. Field-independent users are more active when learning new information and prefer to acquire information in a serial fashion by breaking it down (Pask, 1979). Goodenough (1976) and Witkin et al. (1977) stated that field-independent people sample more relevant cues to solve a problem, whilst field-dependent people sample more irrelevant cues to the current problem. In terms of landmarks, which are considered cues for navigation, field-independent users will benefit more from informative landmarks. This is also seen in research concerning 'hypermedia navigation' (Chen and Macredie, 2001), which indicates that field-dependent users were more efficient when they had to take a more holistic strategy, and navigate using a map of the overall system. In this research field-independent users benefited more from an analytical strategy, which included a depth-search of the entire system (Ford and Chen, 2001).

Knowledge and Experience of Environment and IT System

Knowledge concerning the system, whether it is a desktop computer that allows for mouse and keyboard input, or if it an immersive device, can have a limiting effect due to an overload of mental tasks. This overload is described by Booth et al. (2000) and is explained to be a limitation to attention due to unfamiliar controls and interfaces. According to Booth et al (2000) this occurs mainly because there is an attention dividing of tasks, which are required to navigate and perceive the information seen on the screen. More effort is required to understand and interact with the interface, therefore not enough attention is given to creating cognitive maps of the environment. In compensation, a longer exposure time is required.

More effort is also required if an environment is novel (i.e. if the user has never navigated through this type of architectural structure). In Human

Computer Interaction, the difference during navigation between experts VS novices is critical for interface design (Dix et al., 1993; Eberts, 1994). Kuipers (1975), Brewer (2000) and Mania et al. (2005) explain how experience with a certain type of environment gives rise to certain structures in human knowledge memory. These structures are called schemas and are formed in human memory due to past experiences (Pelagatti. al. 2009). Schemas consist of perceptual information and language comprehension, and are invoked when interacting with new information. The required exposure time to learn an environment depends on memory performance, which is in turn influenced by Schemas, which are affected by the consistency of items in the environment, i.e. whether an item is likely to exist in such an environment (Brewer and Nakamura, 1984). Another theory is called the inconsistency effect and argues that inconsistent items positively influence memory (Lampinen et al., 2001). It is clear that schemas are highly relevant to landmark information and that a person with strong past experiences navigating through a certain type of environment will be more able to recognise key landmarks, and therefore create a cognitive map faster than a similar person with no experience navigating within such an environment.

Knowledge of the environment was considered to be a variable in the experiment of Darken and Banker (1998), who only selected experienced mountaineers for their experiment. Darken and Banker (1998) reported, however, that the advanced mountaineers did not benefit from the 60 minute exposure time in the VE, yet did benefit from using a map. Interestingly, they did not, to the best of our knowledge, test user orientation skills. Instead, Darken and Banker (1998) used participants that have a large experience with navigating through real wilderness using cues and maps. This does not mean, however, that these participants were experienced with the VE system, or had a high aptitude and orientation skill.

Summary

It is clear from literature that individual differences, i.e. the physical and pre-knowledge/experience of individuals, appear to significant impact the required exposure time when learning the spatial layout of a virtual space. It is important, however, to understand this impact more specifically. Accordingly, the following section expands upon experimentation to understand the impact of differences in more detail.

EXPERIMENTATION

To control our experimental participants we: i) begin by selecting a large number of participants; ii) run pre-tests to control the impact as a result of confounding user individual differences; iii) placed participants into groups according to their individual differences; iv) developed a range of controlled virtual spaces for experimentation; v) had participants undertake controlled experiments. The following text aims to expand these stages.

Outlining Experimental Pre-Tests

Since our research focuses on discovering the importance of five specific individual user differences (i.e. gender, orientation skill, cognitive style, system knowledge, and environmental knowledge), five different pre-test difference filters were required. The following presents how participants were placed into appropriate participant groups by using pre-testing to minimise experimental variation between individual difference groups.

Gender - The most appropriate method of determining gender was through the use of a pre-test questionnaire, as used by Waller et al. (1998).

Orientation Skill - As with previous research in the domain of spatial knowledge acquisition, our work follows the standard test for determining participant orientation - the Guilford-Zimmerman orientation survey. This test comprises of various pictures of a boat along with multiple choice answers (see Figure 1). Each picture is split into two. The boat in the lower image is at a different position and / or angle from the top image. The users must imagine the direction in which the boat moved. Direction and angle are represented by a series of dots and dashes, as seen in Figure 1 (Guilford, Zimmerman,1948). The user must determine and select an answer. After scoring, participants are segmented into those with a relative high and low aptitude. Although the authors initially highlighted considerable concerns relating to the dot-dash feedback process, this was independently validated (Kyritsis and Gulliver, 2009), and demonstrated that the traditional GZ test works well for categorisation of user Orientation skills.

Cognitive Style - Many identified strategies are adopted by users in order to solve problems. Messick (1976) identified as many as 19 different approaches, yet Schmeck (1988) grouped them to form two distinct styles. The first is a more holist learning style, referred to as field-dependent and seems to emerge from activity in the right hemisphere of the brain. The second referred to as field-independent, is a more analytical style and seems to emerge from activity in the left hemisphere of the brain. This seems to relate to the learning styles of holistic strategy versus the serialistic strategy as proposed by Messick (1994). Field-dependent people are more passive when learning information, they prefer to learn information by focusing on the information as a whole, rather than breaking it down. Field-independent users are more active when learning new information and prefer to acquire information in a serial fashion by breaking it down. The implication that this has on navigation can be seen in previous research on 'hypermedia navigation'.

Chen et al. (2005) compared a variety of tools to determine the cognitive styles of their participants. They found that the best test was the Cognitive Styles Analysis (CSA) test by Riding (1991). An alternative test that was considered, named the

Figure 1. Questions in the GZ test

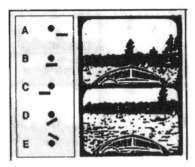   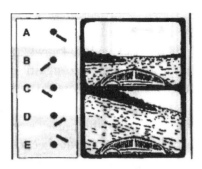

a) The boat has moved left and down, so the correct answer is C

b) The boat has moved to the left and downwards, and has rotated anticlockwise, therefore B is the correct answer

Group Embedded Figures Test proposed by Witkin et al. (1971), has several problems since levels of field dependence are inferred from poor field independence performance (Ford & Chen, 2001).

System Knowledge - Participant system knowledge was controlled through the use of both a questionnaire, and a mouse dexterity test. The questionnaire asked participants to declare how much they used a computer. A simple dexterity test was developed to measure the time it took a participant to click a box that appeared in a random corner of the screen. Twenty clicks were measured in total, and the total time was calculated. Participants that declared low system knowledge in the questionnaire took on average twice the time to click on the boxes as participants that stated that they were experts in using a computer.

Environmental Knowledge - Environmental knowledge is the only individual user difference being considered that can be experimentally altered. Environmental knowledge implies that a participant has experience navigating in a particular environment type; therefore by allowing a group of participants some "training" time before the experimental process begins, an increase environmental knowledge can be established. We selected a group of participants who were

identical in nature to the control, and allowed them to navigate for five minutes in each of the environment types, in advance of the experiment, to give an increased environmental knowledge. A similar technique was used for the VR long-immersive group Waller et al. (1998).

The pre-tests were used to filter 100 original participants down to just 48, which were then used in our experiment. Six groups were used, each consisting of 8 people with characteristics as defined in Table 1. These six groups are: the control experimental group (male, holist participants with high system and orientation scores and low environmental knowledge – defined by the general nature of participants); the gender group (female participants – all other groups contained only male participants); the cognitive group (analytical – all other groups contained holist participants); those with low systems knowledge – all others were tested as having high system knowledge; those with high environmental knowledge – all others were not given the additional time within each environment; and those with low orientation skills – all others were tested as relatively high using the Gilford Zimmerman test.

Table 1. Participant Groups

	Gender		Cognitive		Orientation		Environmental Knowledge		System Knowledge	
	M	F	A	H	L	H	L	H	L	H
Control	✓			✓		✓	✓			✓
Gender		✓		✓		✓	✓			✓
Cognitive Style	✓		✓			✓	✓			✓
Orientation Skill	✓			✓	✓		✓			✓
Environmental Knowledge	✓			✓		✓		✓		✓
System Knowledge	✓			✓		✓	✓		✓	

(M – Male; F – Female; A – Analytic; H – Holist; L – Low; H – High)

Developing Appropriate Virtual Environments

A desktop based maze environment, similar to the one developed by Waller et al. (1998) was created and used in our experiments. The environment was non-immersive and simplified to reduce the change of confounding experimental variables. The reason for using a maze environment was again to simplify perceptual input, since it has been theorized that people remember most angles as a right angles during the development of cognitive maps (Gillner and Mallot 1998). In order to investigate the impact of individual differences across a range of environments, four controlled environments were developed to consider significant variation of specific environmental factors. Table 2 displays information about the environments that were developed.

The following text shows how environmental factors were implemented in our experiment:

Size - no formal definition exists as to what a large scaled environment is; as opposed to a small scaled one. Accordingly, we had to distinguish between a large and a small size environment. We reasoned that a space of approximately 75m x 75m should be used to represent the 'small' size category, as this can contain a single building floor-plan. A larger size 150m x 150m should represent the 'larger' size category, which could (if required) contain multiple locations.

Spatial Layout Complexity (SLC) - SLC relates to the number of objects, such as walls that obstruct the sight of a user from various reference points such as visible landmarks. A common and simple way used in literature of altering the complexity seems to be the use of walls to obstruct the user's vision in a virtual maze (Marsh and Smith 2001). Our work also used this approach as it allows fast VE development and consistent experimentation (see Figures 2 and Figure 3).

Table 2. Table of environments incorporated in the experimental process

Environment Type	Informative Object Landmarks	Size	Complexity
Control	High	Small	Low
Large Size	High	Large	Low
Complex Layout	High	Small	High
Low landmark	Low	Small	Low

Figure 2. a) and b) shows view in the VE respectively before and after object placement

a)

b)

Landmark information -Stankiewicz and Kalia (2004) present how landmark information is comprised of visibility and consistency, as well as how descriptive it is to the user. Altering these values renders a landmark more or less useable and can have a negative impact on learning - especially if the landmark moves to another location. There is some uncertainty as to what can be considered as a landmark, however Stankiewicz and Kalia (2004) argue that there are in fact two types of landmarks; structural and object. Structural landmarks are things such as T-Junctions, dead ends and other informative structures. Object landmarks are objects such as trees and paintings that do not determine the environmental geometry but are instead simple objects that can be used as navigational aides. The way of ensuring that useable landmarks are present in the environment is presented by Vinson (1999), who provides information on how to add landmarks and make

Figure 3. Control environment: a) two obstructions per horizontal row (with 8 rows) b) 16 unique landmarks

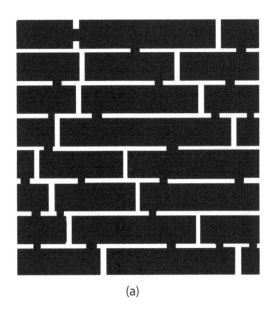

(a)

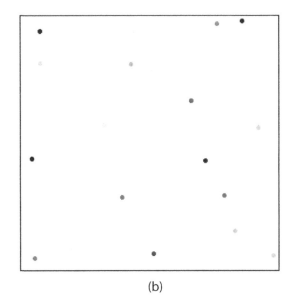

(b)

navigation less complex. Therefore the landmark information was controlled by the amount of unique object landmarks available during navigation. All virtual environments were populated with a variety of landmarks that serve as an navigational aids for the testing phase. In our work, a low landmark count is defined as four unique landmarks in the whole map, a large count is that of sixteen unique landmarks (see Figure 2 (b)).

EXPERIMENTAL PROCESS

Once all participants were categorised, and environments were defined and created, experiments started. Four identical personal desktop computers were used; each set-up with one of the defined environments (as described in Table 2). Participants in each group were separated into four subgroups with two participants from each group, and each subgroup was assigned a different experimental order, which was implemented to avoid experimental order effects. Each participant was asked to move around the virtual space. Once each participant felt that they had 'learned' the layout of the environment, a paper map was handed to the participant. To judge whether the participant had 'learned' the space' we used a method defined in the experiments undertaken by Waller et al. (1998). In order to demonstrate that spatial knowledge was acquired, the participants had to point to the location of landmarks on the paper map. If the participant pointed to a space within the quad sector of the correct corridor (see Figure 3), they were said to have demonstrated that they had 'learned' the position of the landmark. If they failed, the participant resumed navigation.

A log was kept of participant actions, including the amount of time they stopped, as well as their total time.

Each group navigated in all four environments:

- Control environment (see Figure 3) – all other environments differ from the control in just one way. The control environment is small, has two obstructions per row, and is populated with 16 unique object landmarks.
- The large environment is four times the size of the control environment.
- The complex environment has four, instead of two, obstructions (walls) per row.
- The low landmark environments has four instead of sixteen unique landmarks.

RESULTS

In this section we look at the results from the six experimental participant groups (as described in Table 1.

Understanding the Control

The control group is the benchmark participant group, which enables the impact of factors to be statistically compared. The results of the control group are summarised in Table 3.

The results of the control group show the relative impact of different environments on the required exposure time. We ran separate univariate analysis of variance with respectively size, complexity and low-landmark as the independent variable and time as the dependant variable. All the environmental factors significantly impact

Table 3. Results of the control group

	Large Size	Complex Environment	Low Landmark Environment	Control Environment
Time Taken (mins) to acquire spatial knowledge from the environment	0:22:14	0:15:06	0:14:24	0:11:52

exposure time (size - F(1,1) = 395.913, P<0.01; complexity - F(1,1) = 18.717, P<0.01}; and low landmark - F(1,1) = 19.093, P<0.01). Accordingly, it is critically justified that environmental factors must be considered to ensure correct exposure time. In this chapter, however, the impact of VR environment will only be mentioned if significantly interacting with user differences.

Significance of Gender

Both Bryden and Tapley (1977) and Petersen and Linn (1985) implied that females were less capable at orientation than males in a VE. Waller et al. (1998), found that females are particularly disorientated in a virtual maze, with large bearing errors, and have difficulties in drawing the maze that they just navigated through. Moffat et al (1998) reported that males learn a virtual maze faster than females, while Crook et al (1993) suggest that males learn a topographical map faster than females.

The gender group in our experiments had similar results in all pre-tests to the control group; so the only difference was in respect to gender (females). The results of the gender group can be seen in Table 4. To compare between the gender group and the control group we used separate independent sample T-Test for each environment, allowing us to determine whether the gender significantly impacted required exposure time from different environments.

For the control, large size and complex environments there was no significance difference. For the low landmark environment, however, a considerable significance occured (Mean Difference 0:06:07; Std Err 0:00:37, p < 0.001). This implies that women take much longer in low landmark environments to acquire spatial knowledge than men. This finding supports the results of Sandstrome et al. (1998), who concluded that women rely heavily on the use of object landmarks for navigation; more than men who seem to use both geometrical and spatial structures and landmarks for navigation and development of cognitive maps.

Results indicate that gender only significantly impacts required exposure time in an environment with low frequency of unique landmarks. Interestingly, unlike the within relationship for the control group there was a significant difference between time taken to acquire information from the complex and low landmark environments. Our experiment therefore concludes that women performed just as well as men when it comes to acquiring spatial knowledge in all types of environments, with the exception of environments with low landmark frequency. This finding raises a concern that women must be provided sufficient landmarks in a virtual environments or female navigation and acquisition of spatial information will be negatively impacted when compared to men with a similar user profile.

Significance of Cognitive Style

An important question, concerning cognitive styles, is whether field-independent users would have better scores in a landmark-rich environment than field-dependent users. We initially hypothesized that field-independent users would acquire spatial knowledge faster than field-dependent users, due to their tendency to learn faster in a less-procedural way (such as that of traditional

Table 4. Results (H:M:S) and statistical significance of gender (gender vs control group)

	Large Size	Complex	Low Landmark	Control
Time taken by the gender group	0:23:19	0:16:04	0:20:31	0:13:05
Time taken by the control group	0:22:14	0:15:06	0:14:24	0:11:52

maps). The cognitive-style group was identical to the control, except that participants had a analytical cognitive style. The time results of the cognitive style group can be seen in Table 5. To compare between the cognitive group and the control group we used a separate independent sample T-Test for each environment. This allowed us to determine whether the cognitive style of the user (analytical / holistic), significantly impacted the time taken to acquire information from different environments.

No significant difference occurred in the control environment, however for the large size environment a significance did occur between analytical and holistic users, with holist users taking significantly less time than analytical (Mean Difference 0:05:19; Std Err 0:00:30, p < 0.001). For the complex environment, this test showed a significance difference between analytical and holistic users, with analytical users taking significantly less time to acquire information from the complex environment (Mean Difference 0:02:32; Std Err 0:00:47, p = 0.006). For the low landmark environment, no significant difference was measured, which implies that the number of landmarks does not significantly impact the results of people with different cognitive styles.

Holist users (the control group) seemingly required less time to learn the relative visual references, since they focus on information within the environment as a whole. When placed in a larger environment, holist users more quickly acquired spatial knowledge, when compared to analytic users; as learning the interaction of landmarks in the visual field took less time than the specific placement of disparate and distributed objects. Siegel and White (1975), states that people first learn landmarks, then learn routes, and only then create a cognitive map of the area. If analytic users take more initial time to analyze the difference between specific object landmarks, results imply that additional exposure time should be allocated to field independent individuals to allow them to develop an understanding of specific objects in large size environments.

For the complex environment, our test showed a significant difference between analytical and holistic users; with analytical users taking significantly less time to acquire information from the complex environment. As previously stated, field-dependent people are more passive when learning information, and therefore prefer to learn by focusing on information as a whole, rather than breaking it down (Pask 1979). Moreover, Goodenough (1976) and Witkin et al. (1977) state that field-independent (analytic) users sample more relevant cues, such as signs pointing in relative directions. Increasing the complexity of an environment reduces the number of objects in the current field of view, and therefore reduces the ability of the holist user to determine the relative visual relationships between landmarks. This increases the time required for field-independent users to learn an environment "as a whole". A complex environment layout instead supports procedural learning of specific objects, and therefore aids analytic users; who "breakdown" information to facilitate the development of a cognitive map. It would be interesting to look at this issue further, to help provide a better understanding of how cognitive style limits specific users when undertaking virtual environment training (e.g. training military personnel).

Table 5. Results (H:M:S) and statistical significance of cognitive styles

	Large Size	**Complex**	**Low Landmark**	**Control**
Time taken by the cognitive styles group	0:27:44	0:12:34	0:15:14	0:12:46
Time taken by the control group	0:22:14	0:15:06	0:14:24	0:11:52

Significance of Orientation Skill

Perhaps the most discussed individual difference relating to navigation is orientation skill (OS). The OS group in this research differed to the control group, as they had low scores in the Guilford Zimmerman orientation survey. To compare between the low orientation group and the control group (see Table 6). We did a separate independent sample T-Test for each environment, which allowed us to determine whether the orientation skill of the user significantly impacts the time taken to acquire information from different environments.

Results showed a significant difference between those with high and low orientation skills, when navigating in all environment types. In fact, orientation skill appears to be the user individual difference that most impacts spatial knowledge acquisition. Someone with a low OS is therefore "doomed" to suffer with navigation. Individuals can enhance their OS score over significant durations through pro-longed training; however this process will take a very long time and would not be practically feasible when acquiring spatial knowledge from a VE.

Significance of Environmental Knowledge

Environmental knowledge relates to knowledge and experience that a participant has within a specific environment type. Research suggests that a user may find a novel environment more difficult to navigate. The time taken for the high environmental knowledge group can be seen in Table 7. To compare between the high environmental knowledge group and the control group we did separate independent sample T-Test for each environment. This allows us to determine whether high environmental knowledge significantly impacts the time taken to acquire spatial information from different environments.

Results showed a significant difference between those with high and low levels of environmental knowledge for all environments. It is interesting that even though the experience time was only short, users showed a significant decrease in the overall time taken to acquire spatial knowledge. The result suggests that navigators with experience in a certain type of environment have the competitive advantage over novices, and supports the notion that "experienced" navigators carry knowledge of navigating through a certain type of environment to various environments made up of similar factors. Additional research

Table 6. Results and statistical significance of orientation skills

	Large Size	Complex	Low Landmark	Control
Time Taken by the OS group	0:28:09	0:20:06	0:20:21	0:17:33
Time taken by the control group	0:22:14	0:15:06	0:14:24	0:11:52

Table 7. Results and statistical significance of environmental knowledge

	Large Size	Complex	Low Landmark	Control
Time taken by Environmental knowledge group	0:18:57	0:11:25	0:10:42	0:08:07
Time taken by the control group	0:22:14	0:15:06	0:14:24	0:11:52

is required to determine whether variation in MulSeMedia senses (i.e. due to experience to sensory limitations) impacts the users' ability to interact.

Significance of System Knowledge

Level of system knowledge can have a significant effect on learning. Pass et al. (2003) stated that different interaction methods impose different cognitive loads onto the user. If a new or complex system is needed as part of a task, the users' ability to complete the task may be constrained by not having enough available working memory (Cooper, 2004); since it is theorised that working memory is extremely limited in capacity and duration. As the complexity of cognitive elements increases, so does the amount of required working memory (Chandler and Sweller, 1996). Since a user with low system knowledge is also learning the system, whilst undertaking the task, this increases cognitive load. Accordingly, low system knowledge can result in mental overload via a process called 'attention divide' (Booth et al. 2000); where a user's attention is split between learning how to use the computer and solving the task at hand. The 'system knowledge' group was made up of participants who had little or no knowledge of computers. These participants had the lowest scores on the mouse dexterity test, which was created to test a participants' ability with the input devices. The time taken for the 'system knowledge' group to acquire spatial knowledge from the different environments is displayed clearly in Table 8. To compare between the low system knowledge group and the control group we did separate independent sample T-Test for each

environment. This allows us to determine whether a low level of system knowledge significantly impacts the time taken to acquire information from different environments.

Results showed that a significant difference between those with high and low level of system knowledge for all environments. Accordingly, we have shown that system knowledge, the most easily trainable skill, significantly impacts the required exposure time for all environments.

The results from the 'system knowledge' group strongly support the findings of Booth et al. (2000). Participants with low level of system knowledge required significantly longer exposure times in all environments, when compared to the control group. The implication of this result on navigation training is that people with less experience of a particular computer system or device interface style will have a significant disadvantage when learning the spatial layout of the VE; when compared to those people with previous experience of the system of interface. Accordingly, those with lower experience of the system and interface require more exposure time, or additional system training. As the complexity of MulSeMedia technology increases, this factor must be considered to ensure user knowledge of technology systems.

Summary

This section has presented results that show that certain individual differences impact the exposure time required to effectively acquire information from virtual space. In summary results show that:

Table 8. Results and statistical significance of system knowledge

	Large Size	Complex	Low Landmark	Control
Time taken by the low system knowledge group	0:28:28	0:20:21	0:20:09	0:15:45
Time taken by the control group	0:22:14	0:15:06	0:14:24	0:11:52

- Gender: (i.e. women) require significantly more exposure time when navigating in a low landmark environment.
- Orientation skill: (i.e. those with low OS score) need significantly more exposure time in all types of environments.
- Cognitive style: If a user is analytic, exposure time is significantly negatively affected in large environments, yet significantly positively affected in complex environments. If a user is holistic, exposure time is significantly positively affected in large environments, yet significantly negatively affected in complex environments.
- Environmental Knowledge: (i.e. those with environment pre-knowledge) require less exposure time in all environments.
- System knowledge: (i.e. those with low system knowledge) require more exposure time in all environments.

CONCLUSION AND REVIEW OF IMPLICATIONS

Virtual mapping, modeling and use in training is of growing importance. It offers significant potential in the effective training of staff, especially in developing or unsafe space, however a one-size fits all approach cannot be justified. As virtual training receive increased acceptance, and as additional MulSeMedia technologies increase the complexity of interacting information assimilation, it is critical that personalization of VR content is considered to minimize the impact of individual user differences.

This chapter has contributed towards a better understanding of how individual differences impact exposure time required to acquire spatial knowledge; and has yielded the following results:

- Overall, orientation skill is the most influential skill, in terms of the mean total time taken throughout the environments, yet this skill is difficult to train.
- System knowledge seems to be the second most important skill, and is fortunately easy to train, as it is a matter of getting accustomed to the training interface.
- Environmental knowledge is also important throughout, in all environments, experts will have an advantage over novices. Fortunately, research suggests that this skill can be trained over time.
- Females have a serious disadvantage when it comes to learning from environments that are low in the number of unique landmarks. Whether this can change after training, is something that could be looked at in future work. Theoretically, however, a female with high environmental knowledge, and high system knowledge, could out-perform a male with low environmental and system knowledge.
- Field-independent users will acquire spatial knowledge faster from a complex environment; however field-dependent users have the advantage in large environments. These learning styles are formed through life, and it is unlikely that a learning style will change through training.

Significant legal, political and ethical implications exist for any organizations or governments who do not supply appropriate training to staff that later leads to injury or death. As exposure of untrained staff is inappropriate, use of personalized MulSeMedia training technologies offers considerable opportunities for removing training safety concerns. This chapter, has shown clearly that user individual differences impact spatial knowledge acquisition in simple systems. A one-size fits all approach to training significantly risk user safety when placed within the real-world space. Additional research is required in this field to increase our understanding of the impact of multimodal and mulsimedia interaction.

User individual differences also seemingly impact factors including: perceived level of immersion, impacting level of presence; and multimodal information assimilation, which will impact the level of different information types being assimilated by users; however additional research is required. MulSeMedia virtual space provides a significant opportunity for those who require additional periods of training, however personalized user requirements must be considered if effective information transfer, and effective immersion, is to be achieved in future.

REFERENCES

Allport, G. W. (1937). *Personality: A psychological interpretation*. New York: Holt & Co.

Asthmeir, P., Feiger, W., & Muller, S. (1993). Virtual design: a generic VR system for industrial applications. *Computer Graphics, 17*, 671–677. doi:10.1016/0097-8493(93)90116-Q

Aubrey, J. B., & Dobbs, A. R. (1990). Age and sex differences in the mental realignment of maps. *Experimental Aging Research, 16*(3), 133–139. doi:10.1080/07340669008251540

Booth K. Fisher B. Page S. Ware C. & Widen S. (2000). *Wayfinding in a virtual environment*. Graphics Interface.

Brewer, W. F. (2000). *Bartlett's concept of the schema and its impact on theories of knowledge representation in contemporary cognitive psychology*. In Saito (Ed.), Bartlett, culture and cognition, 69-89, Psychology Press

Brewer, W. F., & Nakamura, G. V. (1984). *The nature and functions of schemas*. Handbook of social cognition, 1, 119-160.

Bryden, S. M., & Tapley, M. P. (1977). An investigation of sex differences in spatial ability: mental rotation of three-dimensional objects. *Canadian Journal of Psychology, 31*(3), 122–130. doi:10.1037/h0081655

Chandler P., & Sweller J. (1996) *Cognitive Load While Learning to Use a Computer Program*. Applied Cognitive Psychology.

Chen, S. Y., & Macredie, R. D. (2001). Cognitive styles and hypermedia navigation: Development of a learning model. *Journal of the American Society for Information Science and Technology, 53*(1), 315. doi:10.1002/1532-2890(2000)9999:9999<::AID-ASI1074>3.0.CO;2-2

Chen, S. Y., Magoulas, G. D., & Dimakopoulos, D. (2005). A Flexible Interface Design for Web Directories to Accommodate Different Cognitive Styles. *Journal of the American Society for Information Science and Technology, 56*(1), 70–83. doi:10.1002/asi.20103

Clark, S. A., & Wong, B. L. W. (2000). *QTVR Support for Teaching Operative Procedures in Dentistry*. People and Computer XIV. Usability or Else! Proceedings of HCL 2000, London.

Cobb S.U.G. & D'Cruz, M. D. (1994). *First UK national survey on industrial application of virtual reality*. VR News, 3.

Cohen, R., & Schuepfer, T. (1980). The representation of landmarks and routes. *Child Development, 51*, 1065–1071. doi:10.2307/1129545

Cooper. G. (2004). *Research into Cognitive Load*. Theory and Instructional Design at UNSW.

Crook, T. H., Young, J. R., & Larrabee, G. J. (1993). The influence of age, gender and cues on computer-simulated topographic memory. *Developmental Neuropsychology*, *9*, 41–53. doi:10.1080/87565649309540543

Darken, R. P., Allard, T., & Achille, L. B. (1999). Spatial Orientation and Wayfinding in Large Scale Virtual Spaces II. *Presence (Cambridge, Mass.)*, *8*(6).

Darken, R. P., & Banker, W. P. (1998). Navigating in Natural Environments: A Virtual Environment Training Transfer Study. *Proceedings of VRAIS*, *98*, 12–19.

Darken, R. P., & Peterson, B. (2001). *Spatial Orientation, Wayfinding, and Representation. Handbook of Virtual Environment Technology* (Stanney, K., Ed.).

Darken, R. P., & Sibert, J. L. (1996). Wayfinding strategies and behaviours in large virtual worlds. *Proceedings of ACM CHI96*, 142-149.

Darroch, I., Goodman, J., Brewster, S., & Gray, P. (2005) The Effect of Age and Font Size on Reading Text on Handheld Computers. In *Proceedings of IFIP INTERACT05: Human-Computer Interaction* pp. 253-266.

Dix, A., Finlay, J., Abowd, G., & Beale, R. (1993). *Human computer interaction*. New York: Prentice Hall.

Eberts, R. E. (1994). *User interface design*. Englewood Cliffs, NJ: Prentice Hall.

Egsegian, R., Pittman, K., Farmer, K., & Zobel, R. (1993). Practical applications of virtual reality to firefighter training. In *Proceedings of the 1993 Simulations Multiconference on the International Emergency Management and Engineering Conference* (pp. 155–160). San Diego, CA: Society of Computer Simulation

Feldman, A., & Acredolo, L. P. (1979). The effect of active versus passive exploration on memory for spatial location in children. *Child Development*, *50*, 698–704. doi:10.2307/1128935

Ford, N., & Chen, S. Y. (2001). Matching/mismatching revisited: An empirical study of learning and teaching styles. *British Journal of Educational Technology*, *32*(1), 5–22. doi:10.1111/1467-8535.00173

Foreman, N., Stanton, D., Wilson, P., & Duffy, H. (2003). Spatial Knowledge of a Real School Environment Acquired From Virtual or Physical Models by Able Bodied Children and Children With Physical Disabilities. *Journal of Experimental Psychology*, *9*(2), 67–74.

Gallistel, C. R. (1990). *The organisation of learning. Cambridge M.A.* The MIT Press.

Gillner, S., & Mallot, H. A. (1998). Navigation and acquisition of spatial knowledge in a virtual maze. *Journal of Cognitive Neuroscience*, *10*, 445–463. doi:10.1162/089892998562861

Goerger, S. Darken R. Boyd M. Gagnon T. Liles S. Sullivan J. & Lawson J.P (1998).Spatial Knowledge Acquisition from Maps and Virtual Environments in Complex Architectural Spaces. In *Proceedings of the 16th Applied Behavioral Sciences Symposium*, 2223, April, U.S. Air Force Academy. Colorado Springs, 610.

Golledge, R. G., Dougherty, V., & Bell, S. (1995). Acquiring Spatial Knowledge: Survey versus Route Based Knowledge. *Unfamiliar Environments Reginald Annals of the Association of American Geographers*, *85*(1), 13158.

Gomez, L. M. Egan D.E. & Bowers C. (1986). Learning to use a text editor: Some learner characteristics that predict success. *HumanComputer Interaction*, *2*, 1–23.

Goodenough, D. (1976). The role of individual differences in field dependence as a factor in learning and memory. *Psychological Bulletin, 83*, 675–694. doi:10.1037/0033-2909.83.4.675

Guilford, J. P., & Zimmerman, W. S. (1948). The Guilford Zimmerman Aptitude Survey. *The Journal of Applied Psychology, 32*, 24–34. doi:10.1037/h0063610

Hasher, L., & Zacks, R. T. (1979). Automatic and effortful processes in memory. *Journal of Experimental Psychology, 108*, 356–388.

Hegarty, M., & Waller, D. (2004). A dissociation between mental rotation and perspective-taking spatial abilities. *Intelligence, 32*, 175–191. doi:10.1016/j.intell.2003.12.001

Hunt, E. & Waller, D. (1999). *Orientation and wayfinding: A review*. ONR Technical Report.

Kirasic, K. C. (2000). Age differences in adults' spatial abilities, learning environmental layout, and wayfinding behavior. *Spatial Cognition and Computation, 2*, 117–134. doi:10.1023/A:1011445624332

Koh, G., Wiegand, T. E., Garnett, R., Durlach, N., & Cunningham, B. S. (1999). Use of Virtual Environments for Acquiring Configurational Knowledge about Specific RealWorld Spaces. *Preliminary Experiment, 8*(6), 632–656.

Kuipers, B. J. (1975). A frame for frames: Representing knowledge for recognition. In Bobrow, D. G., & Collins, A. (Eds.), *Representation and understanding: Studies in cognitive science*. New York: Academic Press.

Kyritsis M., Gulliver S., (2009). *Guilford Zimmerman Orientation Survey: A Validation*, ICICS 2009.

Lampincn, J., Copeland, S., & Neuschatz, J. (2001). Recollections of things schematic: rooms schemas revisited. *Cognition, 27*, 1211–1222.

Liu, Y., & Ginther, D. (1999). Cognitive Styles and Distance Education. *Online Journal of Distance Learning Administration, 2*(3).

Maguire, E. A., Burgess, N., & O'Keefe, J. (1999). Human spatial navigation: cognitive maps, sexual dimorphism, and neural substrates. *Current Opinion in Neurobiology, 9*, 171–177. doi:10.1016/S0959-4388(99)80023-3

Maguire, E. A., Frackowiak, R. S. J., & Frith, C. D. (1996). Recalling Routes around London: Activation of the Right Hippocampus in Taxi Drivers. *The Journal of Neuroscience, 17*(18), 7103–7110.

Maguire, E. A., Gadian, D. G., & Johnsrude, I. S. Good C.D. Ashburner, J. Frackowiak R.S.J., & Frith C.D. (2000). Navigationrelated structural change in the hippocampi of taxi drivers. *Proceedings of the national academy of science* (USA), 97(8)

Mania K. Robinson A. & Brandt K.R. (2005). The effect of memory schemas on object recognition in virtual environments. *Presence: Teleoperators and Virtual Environments archive, 14*(5), 606 – 615

Marsh, T. Smith S. (2001). *Guiding user navigation in virtual environments using awareness of virtual off-screen space*. User Guidance in Virtual Environments: Proceedings of the Workshop on Guiding Users through Interactive Experiences-Usability Centered Design and Evaluation of Virtual 3D Environments. Volker Paelke, Sabine Volbracht(Editors). pg 149-154, Shaker Verlag, Aachen, Germany

Mathews, M. H. (1992). *Making Sense of Place: Children's Understanding of Large Scale Environments*. Hertfordshire, England: Harvester Wheatsheaf.

Messick, S. (1976). *Individuality in learning*. San Francisco: Jossey-Bass.

Messick, S. (1994). The Matter of Style: Manifestations of Personality in Cognition. Learning, and Teaching. *Educational Psychologist*, *29*(3), 121–136. doi:10.1207/s15326985ep2903_2

Moffat, S. D., Hampson, E., & Hatzipantelis, M. (1998). Navigation in a "virtual" maze: sex differences and correlation with psychometric measures of spatial ability in humans. *Evolution and Human Behavior*, *19*, 73–78. doi:10.1016/S1090-5138(97)00104-9

Montello, D. R. (2005) Navigation. In P. Shah & A. Miyake (Eds.), *The Cambridge Handbook of Visuospatial Thinking*. Cambridge University Press, 257-294.

Pask, G. (1979). *Final report of S.S.R.C. Research programme HR 2708*. Richmond (Surrey): System Research Ltd.

Pass, F., & Renkl A. Sweller, J. (2003). Cognitive Load Theory and Instructional Design: Recent Developments. *Educational Psychologist*, *38*(1), 1–4. doi:10.1207/S15326985EP3801_1

Pelagatti, G., Negri, M., Belussi, A., & Migliorini, S. (2009). From the conceptual design of spatial constraints to their implementation in real systems. In *Proceedings of the 17th ACM SIGSPATIAL international Conference on Advances in Geographic information Systems* (Seattle, Washington, November 04 - 06, 2009). GIS '09. ACM, New York, NY, 448-451.

Petersen, A. C., & Linn, M. A. (1985). Emergence and characterization of sex differences in spatial ability. *Child Development*, *56*, 1479–1498. doi:10.2307/1130467

Pine, D. S., Grun, J., Maguire, E. A., Burgess, N., Zarahn, E., & Koda, V. (2002). Neurodevelopmental Aspects of Spatial Navigation: A Virtual Reality fMRI Study. *NeuroImage*, *15*, 396–406. doi:10.1006/nimg.2001.0988

Riding, R. J. (1991). *Cognitive styles analysis*. Birmingham, UK: Learning and Training Technology.

Riding, R. J., & Grimley, M. (1999). Cognitive Style, Gender and Learning from Multi- media. *British Journal of Educational Technology*, *30*(1), 43–56. doi:10.1111/1467-8535.00089

Riva, G., & Gambrini, L. (2000). Virtual reality in telemedicine. *Telemedicine Journal*, *6*, 327–340. doi:10.1089/153056200750040183

Robertson, I. T. (1985). Human information processing strategies and style. *Behaviour & Information Technology*, *4*(1), 19–29. doi:10.1080/01449298508901784

Salthouse, T., Donald, K., & Saults, S. (1990). Age, Self Assessed Health Status and Cognition. *Journal of Gerontology*, *45*(4), 156–160.

Sandstrome, N. J., Kaufman, J., & Huettel, S. A. (1998). Males and females use different distal cues in a virtual environment navigation task. *Brain Research. Cognitive Brain Research*, *6*, 351–360. doi:10.1016/S0926-6410(98)00002-0

Schmeck R.R (1988). Learning strategies and learning styles Plenum Press.

Siegel, A. W., & White, S. H. (1975). The Development of Spatial Representation of Large- Scale Environments. In Reese, H. W. (Ed.), *Advances in Child Development and Behavior*. New York: Academic Press.

Silverman, D. R., & Spiker, V. A. (1997), *Ancient wisdom—future technology. Proceedings of the Human Factor and Ergonomics Society*, 41st Annual Meeting Albuquerque, New Mexico.

Smith, M. L., & Milner, B. (1981). The role of the right hippocampus in the recall of spatial location. *Neuropsychologia*, *19*, 781–793. doi:10.1016/0028-3932(81)90090-7

Smith, R. M. (1984). *Learning how to learn*. Milton Keynes: Open University.

Stankiewicz, B. J., & Kalia, A. (2004). Acquisition and Retention of Structural versus Object Landmark Knowledge When Navigating through a Large-Scale Space. *Journal of Experimental Psychology. Human Perception and Performance, 33*(2), 378–390. doi:10.1037/0096-1523.33.2.378

Stanney, K. M., & Salvendy, G. (1995). Information visualization; assisting low spatial individuals with information access tasks through the use of visual mediators. *Ergonomics, 38*(6), 1184–1198. doi:10.1080/00140139508925181

Thorndyke, P. (1980). *Performance models for spatial and locational cognition (R2676ONR).* Washington, D.C.: The Rand Corporation.

Thorndyke, P., & Hayes-Roth, B. (1982). Differences in spatial knowledge acquired from maps and navigation. *Cognitive Psychology, 14,* 560–589. doi:10.1016/0010-0285(82)90019-6

Vicente, K. J., Hayes, B. C., & Williges, R. C. (1987). Assaying and isolating individual differences in searching a hierarchical file system. *Human Factors, 29*(3), 349–359.

Vila, J. Beccue B. Anandikar S. (2002). The Gender Factor in Virtual Reality Navigation and Wayfinding. *Proceedings of the 36th Hawaii International Conference on System Sciences* (HICSS'03).

Vinson, N. G. (1999) *Design Guidelines for Landmarks to Support Navigation in Virtual Environments.* Proceedings of CHI '99, Pittsburgh, PA.

Waller, D., Hunt, E., & Knapp, D. (1998). The transfer of spatial knowledge in virtual environment training. *Presence (Cambridge, Mass.), 7,* 129–143. doi:10.1162/105474698565631

Waller, D., Knapp, D., & Hunt, E. (2001). Spatial Representations of Virtual Mazes: The Role of Visual Fidelity and Individual Differences. Human Factors. *The Journal of the Human Factors and Ergonomics Society, 43*(1), 147–158. doi:10.1518/001872001775992561

Wilkniss, S. M., Jones, M., Korel, D., Gold, P., & Manning, C. (1997). Agerelated differences in an ecologically based study of route learning. *Psychology and Aging, 12*(2), 372–375. doi:10.1037/0882-7974.12.2.372

Wilson, P. N., Foreman, N., & Tlauka, M. (1997). Transfer of spatial information from a virtual to a real environment. *Human Factors, 39*(4), 526–531. doi:10.1518/001872097778667988

Witkin, H. A. Oltman P.K. Raskin E. & Karp S.A. (1971). *A manual for the group embedded figures test.* Palo Alto, CA: Consulting Psychologists Press.

Witkin, H. A., Moore, C. A., Goodenough, D. R., & Cox, P. W. (1977). Field dependent and field independent cognitive styles and their educational implications. *Review of Educational Research, 47,* 1–64.

Witmer B.G. Bailey J.H. & Knerr B.W. (1995), *Training Dismounted Soldiers in Virtual Environments: Route Learning and Transfer.* U.S. Army Research Institute for the Behavioral and Social Sciences

Witmer, B. G., Bailey, J. H., Knerr, B. W., & Parsons, K. C. (1996). Virtual spaces and real world places: transfer of route knowledge. *International Journal of Human-Computer Studies, 45*(4), 413–428. doi:10.1006/ijhc.1996.0060

Chapter 4

Non–Visual Programming, Perceptual Culture and MulSeMedia:
Case Studies of Five Blind Computer Programmers

Simon Hayhoe
London School of Economics, UK

ABSTRACT

This chapter describes an investigation into the premise that blind programmers and web-developers can create modern Graphical User Interfaces (GUI) through perceptions of MulSeMedia, and whether perceptual culture has a role in this understanding. Its purpose it to: 1) investigate whether the understanding of computer interfaces is related to perceptual culture as well as perceptual ability; 2) investigate whether it is possible for a person who has never seen to understand visual concepts in informational technology through non-visual senses and memories; and 3) provoke questions as to the nature of computer interfaces, and whether they can ever be regarded as MulSeMedia style interfaces. Beyond this, it proposes to: 1) inform accessible MulSeMedia interface design; and 2) investigate the boundaries of accessing computer interfaces through non-visual perceptions and memories.

In order to address these aims and objectives, this chapter discusses the following two research questions: 1) Is the perceptual culture of a blind person as important as physical level of blindness in being able to understand, work with, learn how to use or create and program Graphical User Inerfaces (GUIs)? 2) Can a cultural model of understanding blindness in part explain the difficulties in adapting Windows MulSeMedia applications for blind people?

The study found that programmers who had been introduced to, and educated using a range of visual, audio and / or tactile devices, whether early or late blind, could adapt to produce code with GUIs, but programmers who were educated using only tactile and audio devices preferred to shun visual references in their work.

DOI: 10.4018/978-1-60960-821-7.ch004

INTRODUCTION

It can be said that blind people have been using MulSeMedia for over three centuries. Since the development of pin-prick data sets in the early eighteenth century by the blind Cambridge mathematician Sanderson (Democodus 1774) and the evolution of embossed reading codes by Braille and Moon (Paulson 1987), technology has facilitated an interface for blind people beyond the standard elements of vision and sound. Indeed, it has only been in the latter quarter of the twentieth century that such technologies were usurped by the informal *everyman's* language of Windows, Icons, Menus and Pointers (WIMPs) and pseudo three-dimensional geometry, and that touch interfaces became outdated in information technology.

As Steve Alexander (1998) argued in a magazine article in 1998, "Blind programmers could compete quite nicely in the IT workplace when the mainframe was king. But today, as graphically oriented Windows tool kits displace the text-based mainframe development, blind programmers are facing an uncertain future." As the twentieth century drew to a close this not only made the use of information technologies more difficult to interpret by blind people, it also precluded blind programmers from developing computer applications in these new environments and thus participating in the development of information technologies and computer interfaces. As these technologies became more important in our modern cultures, it was believed that this also meant that people with disabilities of sight became more socially marginalised in business and communications, particularly as the world entered an era of rapid growth in the use of web technologies.

It was as a result of these assumptions that the author developed a research study that investigated the experiences of blind programmers and web developers[1], their educational backgrounds and the affects of this education on their ability to understand modern computer interfaces. The research began as a pilot study in late 2006, using data collected through questionnaires and interviews. The case studies described below then evolved from a post-pilot study analysis and was followed up by data collections over the course of the following two years. The aims of this study were: 1) to examine whether Steve Alexander's statement is valid; 2) to inform the teaching methodologies of IT and computing; and 3) to inform future accessible software development of MulSeMedia style interfaces for blind and visually impaired users. The objectives of this study were thus: 1) to inform a greater understanding of how blind and visually impaired computer users comprehend creating computer programs and two-dimensional interfaces used in the design of computer programs and web-pages; and 2) to inform greater access and equality for blind and visually impaired computer users in the work place and in their domestic use of technology.

What now follows in this introduction is a discussion of the context of this research. Firstly, The Author investigates traditional approaches of technologists to accessible hardware, software and educational methodologies; and secondly, The Author discusses alternative models provided by social researchers and authors in the related fields of the education of computing, technology and the visual arts.

Perceptual Approaches to MulSeMedia Software and Education

Since the early 1990s MulSeMedia technologies have been responsible for new forms of accessible software for blind and visually impaired people. Enterprises such as JAWS screen readers have enabled limited non-visual access to Windows and internet surfing (Parente 2004); Tactile Interactive Multimedia (TIMs) has provided haptic access to interactive MulSeMedia, such as tactile computer games (Achambault & Burger 2000); SmartBo MulSeMedia has made houses more accessible (Elger & Furugen 1998); digitised libraries and on-line catalogues have provided far greater access to information and literature (Lee 2005); *robotic* interfaces have aided non-visual access to email accounts (Estivill-Castro & Seymon 2007); MulSeMedia navigational systems have aided geographical mobility (Gustafson-Pearce, Billett & Cecelja 2007); and MulSeMedia software has been designed that automatically translates Braille into text from printed documents, and vice versa (Sullivan 2009). However, almost all such developments have been implemented by sighted programmers and developers, and little is known about their impact on blind and visually impaired users.

As many of these advances in accessible technology were implemented, it was assumed by the IT journalist Alexander (1998) and the academic author Siegfried (2002) that modern computer interfaces, and in particular visual programming languages, became less accessible to blind and partially sighted users. This assumption was based on the premise that blind users cannot perceive the layout used in Graphical User Interfaces (GUIs), such as Windows, Mac and Linux operating systems, or the symbols devised for Windows, Icons, Menus and Pointers (WIMPs). If this assumption was to prove true, then it not only limited the career prospects of those blind people who wanted to enter IT and computing professions, it also limited the opportunities for blind people who wished to develop accessible software or actively contribute to a large proportion of contemporary society.

In the field of education, several initiatives were undertaken that were based on this assumption, which aimed to alleviate the problems caused by a lack of visual perception and an assumed lack of knowledge of visual symbols. In particular, literature identified methods of adapting programming languages and teaching methods for blind programmers that scripted graphical concepts, allowing access to programming courses in visual languages at university level (Gildea 1970, Vaspori & Arato 1994, Riccobono 2004). There have also been a number of evaluations of individual

pieces of software used to overcome assumed difficulties encountered in the use of GUIs and visually based tests for programmers (Bax 1982, Siegfried 2006, Franqueiro & Siegfried 2006). However, no psychological evaluations have been conducted into the non-visual programming of these 2D visual concepts, or the creative process of programmers who are blind or visually impaired. In this literature, there is also little differentiation between late and early blind students, those with different forms of visual impairment or those who had different educational experiences.

What The Author now discusses are psychological and cultural approaches that assess the use of technology.

Beyond the Perceptual Approach to Accessible Software and Education

There is a body of research that casts doubt on assumptions such as those made by Alexander (1998) and Siegfried (2002), and which further criticises the traditional perceptual approach to judging blindness (Hayhoe 2008). In particular, literature has provided first-hand case studies of successful programmers who lost their sight later in life, adapted to their blindness and successfully trained as computer programmers in mainstream environments, using only the standard adaptive technologies used by less skilled computer users (Kotian 2008, Filpus 2008). In addition, authors working from an educational rather than a technological perspective find that cultural and educational backgrounds, and differences in forms of visual impairment also play a large part in the ability of blind and visually impaired students to adapt to the use of accessible software. In particular, Gallagher, Connolly and Lyne (2005) found that blind people over the age of 35 preferred a range of different teaching methods when approaching IT and computing education, either in mainstream settings or specially adapted courses. These preferences, it is argued, favoured their social and cultural backgrounds as well as their level of blindness. Hence, they argue, it is more important that the education and training of older students should remain flexible and independent, and based on circumstances as well as the level of visual impairment or blindness in older learners.

Similarly, Bocconi et.al. (2007), Douglas (2002) and Jones (2004) find that although a great deal of technology is useful in classroom settings, the software used in both mainstream and special schooling does not account for the diversity of the blind and visually impaired community. As a result, they also find that there are many anomalies in existing accessible technologies that do not take into account the extreme range of blind and visually impaired people's understanding and use of touch and vision, and therefore the individual perceptual culture of the blind or visually impaired person. Thus no context seems to be given in this software, nor can it be, to different life experiences.

Research on the relationship between blindness and 2D art also offer a more complex picture than that provided by technologists. In particular, previous psychological studies of the 2D perception and drawings of people who are totally blind from birth (Kennedy 1983, 1993, 1997, Kennedy & Merkas 2000, Zimler & Keenan 1983, Heller 2000, Eriksson 1998, Katz 1946) show that blind people can understand visual concepts in design and art through touch - including solely 2D representations such as perspective - and can develop an advanced abstract understanding of visual symbols and metaphors. The understanding of these principles, however, does not appear to have been applied to the design of MulSeMedia interfaces.

Furthermore, cultural and historical studies of blindness and art education (Hayhoe 1995, 2000a, 2002, 2003, 2008a, Löwenfeld 1959, Löwenfeld & Munz 1934, Harris 1979) also show that cultural beliefs about levels of perception and blindness, often based on separate cultural phenomena, have restricted the education of blind students and reinforced the social myth that blind people are incapable of perceiving, creating or working with 2D images or concepts. Consequently, in

interviews and observations with blind adults and children, it was also discovered that these beliefs tended to guide students' attitudes and approaches to the visual arts, and in many instances guided their ability to create and perceive art (Hayhoe 2008b).

Similarly, Hayhoe has also established that English students who were educated in traditional special schools before the 1981 Education Act - which was a milestone in providing disabled students access to mainstream education in England and Wales (Hayhoe 2008a) - tended to avoid learning or working with certain elements of the visual arts, whereas those with similar levels of blindness but who had good experiences of art in mainstream schools or attended special schools after the early 1980s tended to learn, work with and produce 2D art more readily (Hayhoe 2008b).

Given that the designs of GUIs are based on symbols and metaphors, such as icons displaying hard disks and wastepaper baskets, the question must therefore be raised: Can this cultural and historical approach of understanding the experiences of blindness explain the difficulties in adapting technologies for blind people? Moreover, given this ambiguity in the consideration of understanding the elements of GUIs, is the educational and cultural background of a blind person as important as level of blindness in being able to understand, work with, learn how to use or create and program GUIs?

A discussion of these questions was applied to the research, which is now presented in the following three sections, with each section presented under numbered headings and each sub-section written under numbered sub-headings. The first section presents the theoretical framework and the data collection methodology used in the implementation of the study. The second section presents five case studies of programmers. In this section, each case study is assigned to a different cultural type, identified after an initial reading of the data. These are: Early Blind (Pre Inclusive Education), Late Blind (Mainstream Education) and Early Blind (Post Inclusive Education). The third section of this paper concludes the findings of section two by addressing the research questions.

THE DEVELOPMENT OF THE RESEARCH STUDY

At the beginning of the project it was decided to adapt the previous historical and cultural approach to research employed in the study of visual art and blindness (Hayhoe 2000a, 2008b), in order to analyse different attitudes towards understanding, working with and creating software that employed GUIs. This approach primarily involved the qualitative investigation of the past lives of successful students and practitioners who were blind, their cultural and educational backgrounds and an exploration of how they adapted their work to suit their blindness. These factors were previously found to demonstrate how attitudes towards their blindness affected their learning and understanding, whether they believed they were physically capable of conducting complex visual tasks and whether they were more influenced by their beliefs than their non-visual perceptions (Hayhoe 2008b). Accordingly, it was decided to collect research data by surveying experienced English speaking programmers who were registered blind and then examining their creative understanding of visual elements of computing, initially through a questionnaire and then through a series of interviews with programmers who were registered blind. This allowed the development of a series of case studies.

In order to sharpen the focus of the case studies, it was decided to distil the research's aims and objectives into a set of five open ended discussion topics to be employed in the questionnaire and interviews. These were: 1) What problems are encountered in programming? 2) How do blind programmers conceptualize their programs? 3) How do blind programmers design computer interfaces that can be used by both blind and sighted users,

particularly those with Graphical User Interfaces (GUIs)? 4) Are programmers who are born blind or become blind early in life culturally different from programmers who become blind later in life? 5) What do blind programmers understand by visual programming concepts, such as Windows, Icons, Menus and Pointers (WIMPS), the concept of a two-dimensional interface, such as a form, and resizing windows and objects on a form?

In accordance with the chosen research approach (Hayhoe 2000a, 2008b) it was also decided to separate factors affecting the previous personal histories of blindness into three different categories of life experiences based on prior memories, and then again according to three different categories of blindness, based on a set of five factors identified by the educational psychologist Lowenfeld (1981). These factors were:

1) Degree of sight retained 2) Cause of blindness 3) Age at onset of blindness 4) Kind of onset of blindness 5) Present eye condition and eye care. (Lowenfeld 1981, pp. 83)

Similar to Lowenfeld, the study of blindness and visual art discovered that adults who were born blind would approach art tasks in a different manner to students who had become blind later in life and still had very strong visual memories. In addition, students who had residual vision would rely more on their remaining sight, despite its diminishment, than their tactile senses. However, in case studies of adults and children on which the research model was based (Hayhoe 2000a, 2008b) it was also discovered that perceptual culture – whether the students were blind from an early age or whether they became blind later in life – made a marked impact on their approach to learning. Even their social and cultural beliefs about themselves, such as their social habits, who they became friends with and the way they saw themselves socially, were often affected by this perceptual culture. As a result, it was decided to adapt Lowenfeld's original categories in order to investigate three cultural groups of programmer according to classifications of memory and current visual perception. These were as follows. CLASSIFICATIONS OF MEMORY: 1) No Visual Memory - Blind from birth or very early blind, 0-4 years. 2) Assimilated Blindness - Blind from mid to late childhood, 4-18 years, educated in older schools for the blind, primarily non-visual. 3) Visual Memory - Blind in adulthood, 18+ years. CLASSIFICATIONS OF BLINDNESS: 1) Total Blindness - No light perception. 2) Minimal Light Perception - Some light perception, but little enough to be usable. 3) Distorted Vision - Light perception, highly distorted but still registered blind; e.g. achromatism, photophobia, tunnel vision or no central vision.

After identifying these categories of blindness it was decided to concentrate on the development of a data collection methodology. A discussion of this, along with the difficulties faced and the solutions designed to overcome these difficulties is now discussed below.

Data Collection Methodology

In both phases of the research it was decided to send out questionnaires that employed open questions eliciting lengthy responses, such as those described in many previous qualitative studies involving small communities of participants (Denzin & Lincoln 2005, Robson 2002, Griffin 1985). These questionnaires were later to be followed by interviews of those who responded, in order to provide protracted answers to the issues raised in the questionnaires. This model of data collection was again based on the previous studies of art students and teachers in schools for the blind (Hayhoe 2008b) and, like this previous study, The Author was again flexible with the people who said that they wished to only participate in interviews or who only wanted to fill in questionnaires.

The questionnaires themselves were designed around the five main research questions, listed at the top of this section, each of which was broken into sub-sections, and all of the participants were

sent the document even if they only wished to involve themselves in the interviews – some quite reasonably felt that they could not afford the time for both elements of the study, and so it was felt that the research questions could be handled in detail in a single interview. At the beginning of the questionnaire, The Author provided information to those participating in the research, using a model devised from a previous study of blind adult students (Hayhoe & Rajab 2000). This was a page and a half of A4 paper describing my own background and the purpose of the research, in order to gain the understanding of all of the participants in the research. In this section of the questionnaire, The Author also described the aims, objectives and methods employed in the research, which was in line with previous models of informed consent used in research on special educational needs (De Laine 2000) and was also in line with the ethical standards devised for previous researches in the same field (Hayhoe 2000b, Hayhoe & Rajab 2000). The two main points from this model included complete anonymity for people who provided personal opinions or details of their lives and the spurning of visual recording media, such as video tapes or photography, to communicate with or provide feedback to early totally blind participants.

After designing the questionnaires, The Author identified programmers who were willing to participate in the research. After initial contact with schools and institutes for the blind and a review of the literature, it was decided to make an appeal for participants internationally, through radio and newsletter requests in the UK, and through messages to several email groups in Europe and North America. After receiving a number of responses from this initial appeal, The Author contacted volunteers with the questionnaires and arranged for interviews if these were also requested.

There were problems encountered with this research process, however. These are now discussed below, along with the strategies that were used to overcome them.

Problems Encountered with the Data Collection Methods

Many of the problems that The Author encountered with these data collection methods were centred on my role as a full time school teacher, the little time available for the research and the anonymity of the computer programmers. However, five particular problems seemed to reoccur and tested the implementation of the research more than any other. The first problem that The Author encountered was that there were only a small number of programmers who were registered blind, and these programmers were not members of a single organisation. Unlike school or college based research, this was particularly problematical as there was no central point through which The Author could remain in contact with the participants. Similarly, the second problem that The Author encountered was requesting time from busy professionals, particularly those in different time zones, and also the time demands of my own position as a school teacher. The third problem was that there was little time available to conduct research within the tight timescale set by The Author. The fourth problem was that the unique, high-profile participants involved in these case studies were too identifiable, and thus the goal of total anonymity became a particular problem. The fifth problem was that of the ambiguity of the language used in computing disciplines, and in the different types of language used by programmers who had their own sub-specialism, such as telecommunications or website development.

In order to overcome these problems The Author adopted four strategies during the implementation and analysis of this study. Firstly, it was decided to conduct more in-depth case studies, expanding the questions and broadening the interviews in order to overcome the problem caused by the small number of programmers. Secondly, The Author lengthened the fieldwork to a maximum of two years and assured the participants that interviews would only be conducted during weekends. Although this left more time between each interview than was initially anticipated, and also meant that there was a longer lag time for retrieving the written interviews; it also meant that only the correct and most relevant participants were included in the research.

Thirdly, anonymity was strengthened during the study by avoiding company or website information for each programmer. It was also decided not to publish the code that The Author was sent to illustrate programming techniques and strategies, as this often gave away the programmer's industrial or commercial connections, and also often included the identities of the programmers within their descriptions. In addition, during the descriptions of the programmers The Author also made their commercial fields' titles as vague as possible, such as web-development or networking, rather than providing more specific information about their specialist fields. Fourthly, The Author employed general, non-language specific terminology where-ever possible in the questionnaires and the interviews, and consciously did not to refer to product names - although it became impossible to eliminate all of these.

What now follows is a discussion of the analysis of this interview and questionnaire data. It begins with a short discussion of the refinement of the data into a manageable series of case studies, and is then followed by a description of five case studies in their categories, followed by an analysis of each category.

CASE STUDIES

Twelve programmers from the UK, Australia, US and Holland (Netherlands) requested questionnaires after my initial appeals for participants. Of these, ten participated in the research, two from the US and Holland, one from Australia and five from the UK. After gathering the data from both questionnaires and interviews The Author analysed the differences between the nationalities, different memory categories and different perceptual levels according to the categories The Author laid out in the section above. After this analysis, three initial points became clear – although it has to be acknowledged that these findings were regarded as purely tentative, as the demographic group surveyed was small. Firstly, there appeared to be no significant differences between programmers according to their nationality, if age, level of blindness and age at which the programmers became blind was taken into account. Secondly, there was a significant difference between the younger and older programmers, even taking into account the level of blindness and the age at which they became blind. Thirdly, there was a significant difference between those who attended older special schools and those who attended mainstream schools, even taking into account the level of blindness, nationality and the age at which they became blind.

Consequently, it was decided to further refine the case studies into three generic categories ac-cording to period and type of education. However, it became apparent that it would be easier only to re-analyse and describe the British programmers, as they were all educated in the same system, making it easier to compare like for like – it was not until the 1981 Education Act that British disabled students were legally included in mainstream education, despite the controversy this caused (Hayhoe 2005, 2008a). This provided five case studies split into three definite categories: 1) Early Blind (Pre 1981): these programmers attended older special schools for the blind, which tended not to teach the breadth of curricula expected in a mainstream school; 2) Late Blind: these programmers all attended mainstream schools; 3) Early Blind (Post 1981): this programmer attended mainstream school.

These five case studies are now described briefly in Table 1. This is then followed by the description of the first case study.

Table 1. An initial analysis of the five case studies in their three categories of analysis

	Early Blind (Pre 1981)		Late Blind		Early Blind (Post 1981)
	Case Study 1	Case Study 2	Case Study 3	Case Study 4	Case Study 5
Age	45	57	50	33	26
Gender	Male	Male	Male	Female	Male
Category of Blindness & Memory	Totally Blind & Non Visual Memory	Totally Blind & Assimilated Blindness	Distorted Vision & Visual Memory	Totally Blind & Visual Memory	Minimal Light Perception & Assimilated Blindness
School Education	School for the Blind	School for the Blind	Mainstream Schools	Mainstream Schools	Mainstream Schools
Highest Educational Level	Higher Education	Higher Education	Higher Education	Higher Education	Higher Education
Job / Position	Programming	Website Developer	Software Development	Director	Software Engineer
Years Programming	28	36	36	Approx 20+ Years	9
Programming Language(s)	(Cobol, C, Pascal, Fortran & Basic)	Non-Visual (Assembly Language, HTML script)	Mixed (Perl, HTML, SQL, PHP)	Mixed (E.g. HTML, PHP, Java, XML, CSS)	Mixed (E.g. MMC, C++, Java, Visual Basic, XML)

Early Blind (Pre 1981) Programmers

Case Study 1: Fernando

The first case study participant The Author called Fernando. He was a 45 year old man who became completely blind very early in life – before the age of five – and worked as a professional computer programmer. In his early years, he attended schools for the blind and then took a university degree. In terms of his computing education, Fernando learnt programming in his latter years at school through Braille tape applications:

We used a small corner of a computer owned by a company called Metal Box - don't know what sort. Basic was the language. It was a wonderful experience. We just used text editors, and ran what we wrote through a Basic interpreter - I don't think it was compiled. (Fernando Research Notes, 2007)

In terms of his language and life experiences, Fernando was considered to have a distinct non-visual culture in his later life; he told me that he used Braille, preferred non-visual concepts in computing and felt he did not want to use visual interfaces – such as WIMPs. He relied heavily on accessible technology and socialised with other blind people on a regular basis. This working perceptual culture was reflected in his earlier programming where he used a teleprinter, and interpreted windows through:

BD3 [a Braille paper tape printer for output], next was a teletypewriter and asking someone to read the print out. (Fernando Research Notes, 2007)

Using Braille generated by his computer was something that Fernando had experienced since his early schooling and he stated that he always used a Braille output device as an interface for reading, and also for providing feedback. After this, he managed to develop his software with Braille output devices in professional settings. In addition, he also gained feedback from audio output devices, although these appeared to play a secondary role to his Brailled feedback:

The first was a "window manager" to control the movement between individual connections to mainframes, on which I mostly programmed or ran applications or used text editors. Each "window" was like a screen of characters--lines of 80 or 132 and 24 or more lines. The second was to a PC through JAWS to run more admin type stuff and access the Internet and Intranet. (Fernando Research Notes, 2007)

In terms of developing or programming his own GUIs, Fernando reported that he did not use or attempt to imagine them whilst he was programming, and indeed tried to avoid any use of them during his career – Fernando appeared to avoid referring to them wherever possible, and treated the notion that he could work with them with sarcasm:

I'm not sure that I have ever met one (Fernando Research Notes, 2007)

In terms of his strategies for programming, Fernando mostly used problem solving methods which were akin to logical mathematics. He would often work through several lines of text at a time, often in sequence, and developed elements of programming, such as loops, through marking appropriate sections of code. This meant that he had to rely a great deal on his memory whilst working – he told me that he held logical problems in his mind, often for long periods at a time:

My main work… is problem solving, so it is more along the lines of tearing programs up while still trying to keep them reproducing a problem." (Fernando Research Notes, 2007)

Finally, in terms of accessing web information, Fernando told me that he surfed the Internet using a text reader. However, largely because of the complex webpage interfaces he encountered, he found that this was not an enjoyable experience, and he seemed to want to avoid his current use:

At work, about 10 years ago, with a PC using JAWS. Oh, it was horrible - still not a lot better. (Fernando Research Notes, 2007)

Case Study 2: Steve

The second case study participant The Author called Steve. He was a completely blind 57 year old man who worked as a website developer. He told me he had residual vision until 14 years old, but after this age had lost his remaining sight over a number of years. In terms of his schooling, he had attended older schools for the blind and then university, where he gained his degree. This latter education was his first experience of mainstream education. Steve was considered to have a fairly strong non-visual culture, and identified himself as a blind person, relied heavily on Braille applications and reading, referred very little to visual concepts when he was describing his experiences, and also relied very heavily on accessible technology applications, such as Braille and audio output devices, as well as the usual accessible programs.

In terms of his programming career, Steve began learning to write code at university in 1972. His early programs were written in Assembly Language, which he told me he found complex at first, but it was a language that he became increasingly comfortable with as his academic career developed; although he also said that he developed a reliance on sighted people to provide feedback for his code on a regular basis:

My first computer program was written at university 1972. The experience was quite interesting and had all the usual frustrations of surmounting the operating system before getting down to

the logic (or otherwise) of the program. I used a Teletype and had sighted people reading for me (Steve Research Notes, 2007)

Steve also found that he relied on Teletype and Braille readers and writers a great deal when he began working as a computer programmer. In addition, he also relied on keyboard and audio interfaces to work through code and as an interface for his everyday ICT usage. Since further developments in technology, however, he found that he was increasingly relying on screen reading software packages, such as JAWS, to work with his computer:

I currently use JAWS with Braille and speech. I have used Teletype / Optacon, I briefly used the Clarke and Smith Braille Link, which I rejected. The TSI VersaBraille, then IB80 Braille display. (Steve Research Notes, 2007)

Steve told me that his new career was coding websites for a living, something he had done for several years during the fieldwork. Relatively speaking, he felt that this step in his career had been an adaptation from his original programming tasks, as it was largely based on his dislike of more visual languages. He found that, despite the visual nature of website interfaces, web languages such as HTML allowed him to continue using raw code, rather than designing visual interfaces or having to imagine visual languages, which he appeared to regard with distaste. In terms of accessing the Internet, he first surfed the web and email over twelve years ago again using JAWS and Braille applications:

I was connected to the Internet whilst working for XXXXXXX [a well known communications' company] in 1996, though I didn't actively access the Web until 2000, when I established my own computer at home...

I was one of few who insisted on sticking to Assembly languages before giving up programming in the early 1990's... I write web pages, in basic HTML. As I've already said, I'm an information provider, not a web techie. I don't do Java and visualise the information I'm presenting. The structure of the information informs the structure of the page. Nothing else makes sense to me." (Steve Research Notes, 2007)

In terms of his programming methodology, Steve told me that he particularly relied on structure and disciplined methods when scripting web pages, although memorisation of the different elements of the script, the location of the code and indenting also informed his structure of scripting:

I don't impose style or other limitations, leaving users to present our information in a way that best suits them. By providing concise, structured text, we achieve a high level of accessibility and usability for the vast majority of readers. (Steve Research Notes, 2007)

Findings: Early Blind (Pre-1981)

In the case studies of both Fernando and Steve, six significant themes arise over and over again in their notes. Firstly, both of these programmers largely rejected the use of GUIs and continued programming with outdated programming interfaces – although Steve had some early residual visual memory he still remained wary of GUIs. Secondly, even when they accessed GUIs, they referred to them as non graphical interfaces and were disparaging about the idea that they were graphical. Thirdly, they both constantly refer to using purely text based languages to design their interfaces, even when they had some form of design element. Steve in particular emphasised that his design was driven by text alone. Fourthly, both programmers relied heavily on Braille scripting for both reading and communicating their code. Even when they had access to fast audio output,

they felt more comfortable relating to Braille text. Fifthly, perhaps as a result of the previous point, both programmers found that their methods relied strongly on the memorisation of lines of code. And finally, as a consequence of the need for memorisation, their method of coding was very disciplined and evolved to rely on a rigid system in the presentation of its language.

What now follows are two case studies of programmers who became blind later in life.

Late Blind (Pre 1981) Programmers

Case Study 3: Jamie

The third case study participant, which The Author named Jamie, was a late blind 50 year old man who still had a small amount of very distorted sight, a fact he attempted to emphasise during the data collection. His professional role was as the developer / programmer for an on-line service. As a child he attended mainstream schools and then university, and he lost his sight when he was in his late 30s. Culturally, he still considered himself to be of a visual culture. His language referred to a great deal of visual concepts, and he only used adaptive technology to enlarge his screen's interface. In his questionnaire and interview answers there were also many references to GUIs, and he seemed to be comfortable discussing their design and use. He also never mentioned using Braille. During the data collection, it was also noted that Jamie did not appear to socialise or work with a large number of other people who were blind.

In terms of his schooling, Jamie learnt programming visually through his school at the age of fourteen, which was in the early 1970s. During this period there were no visual languages and so he scripted raw code using old fashioned second generation programming languages. These were favoured by a maths teacher of his, he remembers, who made him enthusiastic about the need for computing. At the time he also had access to a local mainframe which allowed him to write programs throughout his school career, a facility which he took full advantage of:

The maths teacher at school was keen on computers and we had a "computer club" where we learnt FORTRAN, punched cards, sent them to be processed at County Hall, and received the printed output next week. (Jamie Research Notes, 2007)

In his earliest commercial projects, Jamie used text based systems and interfaces, particularly text based operating systems. He then moved on to a combination of text and GUI systems, a combination he still felt most comfortable with. In terms of the modern GUIs he used for programming websites, Jamie stated that he did not bother using tools and programs that he found difficult to imagine or use. In particular, he could not use animation packages. However, Jamie still used many other elements of GUIs:

I design web pages and can see the interface. However, I disregard elements I cannot use myself such as Flash – I like things to be very plain and simple. (Jamie Research Notes, 2007)

At the time of the research, Jamie told me that he was increasingly coming into contact with visual database languages through his job, such as Perl, PHP and SQL. These were used to develop the workings of an on-line library system that he managed. These languages relied heavily on GUIs for searching and inputting data, which was a factor he did not appear at all concerned with. In addition, he told me that he had little problem accessing websites by using GUI interfaces – although again he said that he preferred to keep these interfaces visually simple, particularly when he surfed the internet using an adapted standard browser:

Perl 5.8 and SQL, together with DOS commands for server-side work, with HTML and PHP 5 on the Web. Currently providing an e-Library of electronic texts via the Web, and trying to automate

this as much as possible e.g. wrote a program that accepts input from a bar-code reader (ISBN number), verifies it, and gets book metadata off Internet sites to update database…

I've used Lynx (a DOS based text browser) but usually use Internet Explorer for day to day Internet work." (Jamie Research Notes, 2007)

Case Study 4: Rachel

The third case study participant The Author named Rachel. She was a 34 year old woman who became completely blind at 26 years of age as a result of diabetic retinopathy. When she first participated in this study she was working as a web-developer and coder, but just before a second interview she was given a directorship of a web development company. As a child Rachel attended mainstream schools, and then entered a higher education institution where she studied for a first degree in drama. After completing her degree she worked as a programmer, and lost her sight shortly afterwards. More recently, Rachel started taking a part-time second degree, studying computer science via distance education with the Open University, UK.

Rachel still considered herself to be part of a sighted culture, through language, her social ties – she lived with a sighted man and said that her friends were almost all sighted – and through her use of technology, which was generally only supplemented by accessible hardware and software. In addition, Rachel did not read Braille and found that this was not a problem in her field of work. In general, she used audio output devices to access computer interfaces.

In terms of her earliest experiences of computing, Rachel told me that she learnt to program before the age of ten. At this age she used her father's computer, which had a text (command) based interface. These experiences were enjoyable, although the programs were also relatively straightforward to write, as she simply copied them from magazines that were widely available at the time. Following these earliest programming experiences, Rachel continued using text only and then standard GUI systems for accessing and programming a series of home and educational computers; she also used similar systems when she became a professional. She has also done so since becoming blind:

I rely entirely on the keyboard to interact with the screen reader and / or OS. For the most part it is an approach I'm capable of and comfortable with. There are inevitable frustrations, but these are born from other people's inability to develop software that will support my goals, rather than my inability to do so with the right tools and skills (Rachel Research Notes, 2007)

In terms of her career, Rachel said that she worked almost entirely with GUI operating systems. However, her use of these was based almost wholly on the visual re-collection of interfaces she had used before becoming blind. For instance, the last operating system that she remembered seeing was Windows' Millennium Edition. Consequently, although she later used Windows' XP and Vista operating systems using a JAWS screen reader - all of which she only became familiar with after she lost her sight - she found that she had to imagine this interface as if it had the same aesthetic appearance as Millennium Edition.

Rachel created websites by using a combination of visual and script based languages, such as Java, HTML, XML and PHP. During the data collection The Author noted that she had no objection to using either type of language; although, because she was more used to producing programs with scripted languages from a very young age, she appeared to feel more comfortable working in this way in more recent projects. Rachel also said that she had no problem designing GUIs, and imagined those that she programmed for others using her visual memory. In particular, she said that she

made great use of visual metaphors, such as 2D buttons, when imagining these web interfaces, often providing facilities on her websites that allowed users to adjust settings that were visual in nature, such as background colour:

I do code web pages and have done so since before I lost my sight. I have a very good visual recollection of a typical browser interface. Internet Explorer is particularly clear and although Mozilla Firefox hadn't come into being when I lost my sight, they follow very similar visual parameters... I can write XML, XHTML/HTML, CSS, Java and a little PHP. I have my own website (xxxx.co.uk), which is XHTML/CSS/PHP based. I'm just starting to develop a web application in Java, which is to be a recipe archive site. (Rachel Research Notes, 2007)

In her use of animated objects, such as Java menus, Rachel also appeared to be able to create forms of animation that she had never encountered when she was sighted, even those that were out of the range of her JAWS screen reader. For instance, in her notes she told me that although Java applets were inaccessible using JAWS, she could imagine their visual appearance as she developed them. This aspect of her work is illustrated in the excerpts from her notes below:

I also know enough about current development techniques for accessible Flash to be aware of how it works in the present. Applets I don't have a visual recollection of, but I've coded them from time to time during my current studies. Applets are more or less completely inaccessible with a screen reader, but from a development perspective I know their capacity and capability (Rachel Research Notes 2007)

Findings: Late Blind (Pre 1981)

In Jamie and Rachel's case studies, four issues relating to the relationship between their previous sighted culture and current working practices stood out more than any others; these made their experiences appear to contrast with those of Steve and Fernando. The first issue raised was that both programmers, despite their advanced forms of blindness, were very keen to design GUIs for sighted as well as blind and visually impaired users, and had a strong preference for the interfaces they used when they were sighted as they did so. The second and related issue was that both programmers, generally speaking, could also imagine new GUIs designed after they had lost their sight, as long as they bore some similarity to those they had used before they lost their sight. Although Jamie told me that he had an issue with animated software such as Flash, which used a form of animation he found inaccessible, he seemed comfortable with languages that used static graphics even-though they had only been developed after he lost his sight.

The third issue that The Author noted was that neither Jamie nor Rachel referred to their use of Braille during the data collection, nor appeared to have any knowledge of it. Neither did they refer to any form of touch experiences in their understanding of their codes or scripting of programs, and still preferred to use mainstream courses and systems adapted to their needs. Rachel in particular, despite her total blindness, was happy to work with mainstream materials during her Open University computer science course. The fourth issue was that both programmers often appeared to refer to visual references whilst reading the text on screen through key strokes and their JAWS software, and were very comfortable referring to the interfaces as GUIs as they did so.

What now follows is the case study of my final participant, who was early blind but schooled after the 1981 Education Act.

Early Blind (Post 1981) Programmer

Case Study 5: Sami

The fifth case study participant The Author named Sami. He was a 26 year old man, who was very early blind and had never had usable vision. During his childhood he had attended mainstream schools, where he had been given help with accessible technology, later on he won a place at university where he studied for a degree. In terms of his earliest computing experiences, Sami was first given access to computer applications during his primary classes and was used to all forms of educational application from a very early age:

I've had no useful vision all my life... My first experience of a computer was a BBC at primary school. It was mostly used to teach typing and Braille. It had a very old external speech synthesiser. I was eight or nine and it was a good experience. Generally it was mostly educational software used. (Sami Research Notes, 2007)

Sami learnt to program a computer during his upper school years, where he took a GNVQ in computing - a national vocational qualification that he used to gain his place at university. His first programming language at this time was a wholly text, or scripted, language. During these initial experiences he used command prompts, audio interfaces and later screen readers to interact with the computer. However, despite the non-visual nature of these early programming classes, Sami felt comfortable programming graphic interfaces. The following is his illustration of these earliest experiences:

My first real introduction to a proper programming language was at college. I was 17 and studying for a GNVQ in computing. One of the modules was programming in Pascal. Before this I'd done a bit of DOS batch script programming, but when I first got the hang of Pascal I found something just clicked and I've been into programming ever since. We used a DOS IDE called turbo Pascal. This was using a DOS screen reader called HAL. I wrote all sorts of applications with very simple GUIs. (Sami Research Notes, 2007)

In terms of surfing the web, Sami told me that he accessed the Internet using a JAWS screen reader. In addition, he also told me that he was happy to use this screen reader to translate elements of GUIs - including buttons, menus, menu bars, tool bars, scroll bars, icons, balloons, tool tips, edit controls, list and combo boxes, and so forth; and that he had no aversion to either interpreting or re-creating these elements in his own software design. In this way he wanted to create interfaces that would appeal to sighted as well as blind and visually impaired users:

Screen readers I use have the ability to simulate mouse movement and control from keyboard; and this is normally the last resort to try to access inaccessible applications… As everything now uses a GUI of some kind it is impossible to use a computer without encountering the complexity of the GUI (Sami Research Notes, 2007)

Finally, in common with many of the other early blind programmers who participated in this study, Sami also found that he had to take a fairly disciplined approach to writing his code. However, he did not feel that he had to use any special methods other than those used by sighted programmers, which he was taught whilst learning to program. In particular, during the data collection he mentioned that he used code indentation and standardised layout techniques whilst programming, which maximised the clarity of his script for quality control within his company:

I can tell you that I use code indentation and code layout techniques and have never had a problem getting any of my interfaces I've put together past

our MMI [Multimedia Interface] people. (Well no more than any of the people I work with). (Sami Research Notes, 2007)

Findings: Early Blind (Post 1981)

Sami's case study was perhaps the most revealing of all of the five. Although he had lived his whole life without sight, he had been educated in mainstream schools and had access to the same curricula as many of his sighted peers. Furthermore, he had also been able to access GUIs at a very young age. Subsequently, four issues in particular appeared to illustrate that this educational and cultural background influenced his programming style as much, if not more, than his early blindness. Firstly, perhaps because of his early familiarity with such interfaces, Sami appeared to be very comfortable using what he knew were graphical interfaces in both his programming environments and his everyday leisure use, even though he relied wholly on screen readers as interfaces. Secondly, he talked about his use of WIMPs using visual references – although when he did discuss these he only described them as abstract concepts, as objects to be navigated using his screen reader. Thirdly, despite never having had usable vision, he felt comfortable incorporating GUIs into his program designs, and would make every effort to make his programs accessible to sighted and blind users alike.

This paper now concludes the findings of all five case studies by addressing my original research questions.

CONCLUSION

In the first section of this chapter The Author introduced a cultural model of analysing blindness and programming, which was based on an earlier model of researching blindness, visual arts and culture (Hayhoe 2000a, 2008b). In this early research, it was found that factors such as educational and cultural background influenced the willingness of blind people to create and study individual aspects of 2D art as much as, if not more so, than how blind they were or whether they had visual memories or not. After describing this previous study, The Author introduced two research questions with which to test this cultural model in this research investigation. In this conclusion, The Author now addresses these two research questions:

Is the educational and cultural background of a blind person as important as physical level of blindness in being able to understand, work with, learn how to use or create and program GUIs?

Based on the evidence of these case studies, there is evidence that this can be true. The five programmers found it easier to use and design GUIs when they had previously had visual memories and when the user had a degree of sight rather than being totally blind, even when the elements of the GUIs they used or programmed were released after the programmer lost his or her sight. For instance, Rachel was able to imagine and create GUIs using elements she had never visually experienced, such as Java applets, using her recollection of previous interfaces. In addition, Jamie was adept at designing and surfing GUIs; although he had difficulty working with Flash, with which he did not feel comfortable.

There is also evidence from these case studies that suggests perceptual and educational culture had a significant influence on these programmers' willingness and ability to work with graphic symbols and icons, particularly WIMPs, than their type of memory and level of blindness alone would indicate. For instance, Sami, who had never had usable vision, was far more willing to use WIMPs and other forms of GUI than Steve, who until the age of fourteen had some usable sight. However, Steve had no exposure to visual metaphors, such as icons or symbols, used in these interfaces during his earliest education,

whereas Sami had. Thus it would appear that in terms of perceptual culture, Sami was almost as familiar and comfortable with visual culture as the late blind programmers were, and much more so than the two early blind programmers who were educated in schools for the blind.

Can a cultural model of understanding blindness in part explain the difficulties in adapting Windows MulSeMedia technologies for blind people?

As stated previously, the evidence derived from the case studies suggests that the five programmers' experiences of computing were at least in part caused by generational and educational factors, and not just physical ability. Furthermore, similar to the answer to the previous research question, perceptual culture appeared to be as important to the approach and ability of these programmers. Hence, questions must now be asked as to whether the traditional, wholly perceptual model previously promulgated by a number of technologists who have written about software and education for blind people is valid in all contexts and social settings. Thus, more research is certainly needed into this aspect of educational and computing theory, and in the development of MulSeMedia software.

More importantly if, as technologists, we are to provide effective solutions to overcome the problems of making software accessible, we must also appreciate that blind people have the intellectual and creative faculties that allow them to understand and design software using elements of MulSeMedia in order to interpret 2D graphical elements, and also to learn about them. This means that broader attitudes, as well as education and software, must change and students must be introduced to a full range of interfaces and inclusive educational experiences from as early an age as possible.

REFERENCES

Alexander S (1998) Blind Programmers Face An Uncertain Future. ComputerWorld.

Bax D D (July 1982) Computer Programmer Aptitude Test for the Totally Blind. Journal of Rehabilitation 48/3/pp. 65-68

Bocconi, S., Dini, S., Ferlino, L., Martinoli, C., & Ott, M. (2007). ICT educational tools and visually impaired students: Different answers to different accessibility needs. In Stephanidis, C. (Ed.), *Universal access in human computer interaction: Applications and services* (pp. 491–500). Heidelberg: Springer. doi:10.1007/978-3-540-73283-9_55

De Laine, M. (2000). *Fieldwork, Participation and Practice: Ethics and dilemmas in qualitative research*. London: Sage.

Denzin, N. K., & Lincoln, Y. S. (Eds.). (2005). *The SAGE Handbook of Qualitative Research*. Thousand Oaks, California: Sage.

Douglas G (2002) ICT, Education and Visual Impairment. British Journal of Educational Technology 32/3/pp. 353-364

Elger, G., & Furugren, B. (1998) SmartBo: An ICT and computer-based demonstration home for disabled people. Paper presented at TIDE 98 Conference, Tokyo, Japan, August 1998

Eriksson, Y. (1998). Tactile Pictures: Pictorial Representations for the Blind 1784-1940. Göteborg: Göteborg University Press

Estivill-Castro V & Seymon S (2007) Mobile Robots for an E-mail Interface for People Who are Blind. In Bredenfeld, A., Jacoff, A., Noda, I., & Takahashi, Y. (Eds.), *RoboCup 2006: Robot Soccer World Cup X* (pp. 338–346). Heidelberg: Springer.

Filpus, P. (2008) Computer Programmer and Analyst. Downloaded from http://www.afb.org/Section.asp? SectionID=7&TopicID=267&SubTopicID=83&DocumentID=3179, on the 12th December 2008)

Franqueiro, K. G., & Siegfried, R. M. (2006) Designing a Scripting Language to Help the Blind Program Visually. Proceedings of the 8th International ACM SIGACCESS Conference on Computers and Accessibility, Portland, Oregon, October 2006

Gallagher, B., Connolly, N., & Lyne, S. (2005) Equal Access to Technology Training (EATT): Improving computer literacy of people with vision impairments aged over 35. International Congress Series Vol. 1282 / pp. 846-850

Gildea, R A J. (1970) Guidelines for Training Blind Computer Programmers. New Outlook for the Blind 64/9/pp. 297-300

Griffin, C. (1985). Qualitative Methods and Cultural Analysis: Young women and the transition from school to un/employment. In Burgess, R. (Ed.), *Field methods in the study of education*. London: Falmer Press.

Gustafson-Pearce O, Billett E & Cecelja F (2007) Comparison Between Audio and Tactile systems for Delivering Simple Navigational Information to Visually Impaired Pedestrians. British Journal of Visual Impairment 25/3/ pp.255-265

Harris, R. W. (1979) Aesthetic Development of Visually Impaired Children: A Curriculum Model for Grades Kindergarten Thru Six. Unpublished Ed.D. thesis, Indiana University, Bloomington.

Hayhoe, S. (1995) The Art Education of Blind Adults. Unpublished MEd by research thesis, Leicester University, British Isles

Hayhoe, S. (2000a) The Effects of Late Arts Education on Adults with Early Visual Disabilities. Educational Research & Evaluation 6/3/ pp. 229-249

Hayhoe, S. (2000b) The Cultural Subjectivity of Research Ethics. Paper presented at the 6th Discussion Group Conference, Keele University, British Isles, November 2000

Hayhoe, S. (2002) The Experience of Children with Visual Impairments in Visual Arts Education. Paper presented at the International Conference on the Politics of Childhood, Hull University, 10th September 2002

Hayhoe, S. (2003). The Development of the Research of the Psychology of Visual Impairment in the Visual Arts. In Axel, E., & Levent, N. (Eds.), *Art Beyond Sight* (pp. 84–95). New York: The American Foundation for the Blind.

Hayhoe, S. (2005) An Examination of Social and Cultural Factors Affecting Art Education in English Schools for the Blind. Unpublished doctoral thesis, Birmingham University, England

Hayhoe, S. (2008a). *God, Money & Politics: English attitudes to blindness and touch, from Enlightenment to integration*. Charlotte, North Carolina: Information Age Publishing.

Hayhoe, S. (2008b). *Arts, Culture and Blindness: Studies of blind students in the visual arts*. Youngstown, New York: Teneo Press.

Hayhoe, S., & Rajab, A. (2000) Ethical Considerations of Conducting Ethnographic Research in Visually Impaired Communities. Paper presented at The European Conference on Educational Research 2000, Edinburgh University, September 2000

Heller, M. A. (2000). *Touch, Representation and Blindness*. Oxford: Oxford University Press.

Jones R (2004) Comparison of the Use of the Internet by Partially-Sighted and Blind Pupils Placed in a Special School Environment. British Journal of Visual Impairment 22/2/pp. 55-58

Katz, D. (1946). *How Do Blind People Draw?* Stockholm: Stockholm Kooperitava Bokfoerlag.

Kennedy, J. (1993). *Drawing and the Blind*. New Haven, Connecticut: Yale University Press.

Kennedy, J. M. (1983) What Can We Learn About Pictures from the Blind? American Scientist 71/ pp. 19-26

Kennedy, J. M. (1997) How the Blind Draw. Scientific American, 276/1/pp. 60-65

Kennedy, J. M., & Merkas, C. (2000) Depictions of Motion Devised by a Blind Person. Psychonomic Bulletin and Review 7/pp. 700-706

Kotian, H. P. (2008) India's First Blind Computer Programmer. Downloaded from http://www.esight.org/view.cfm?id=0&room=n&x=65, on the 12th December 2008)

Lee, Y. S. (2005). The Impact of ICT on Library Services for the Visually Impaired. In Fox, E. A., Neuhold, E., Premsmit, P., & Wuwongse, V. (Eds.), *Digital Libraries: Implementing strategies and sharing experiences* (pp. 44–51). Heidelberg: Springer. doi:10.1007/11599517_6

Lowenfeld, B. (1981) Effects of Blindness on the Cognitive Functioning of Children. In Berthold Lowenfeld on Blindness and Blind People: Selected papers. New York: American Federation for the Blind

Löwenfeld, V. (1959). *The Nature of Creative Activity*. London: Routledge and Kegan Paul.

Löwenfeld, V., & Munz, L. (1934). *Sculpture for the Blind*. Vienna: R M Rohrer.

Parente, P. (2004) Audio Enriched Links: Web page previews for blind users. Proceedings of the 6th international ACM SIGACCESS conference on Computers and accessibility 2004, Atlanta, GA, USA October 2004 pp. 2-8

Paulson, W. R. (1987). *Enlightenment, Romanticism and the Blind in France*. Princeton, NJ: Princeton University Press.

Riccobono M A (2004) A Brighter Future for Blind Children. Braille Monitor, February 2004

Robson, C. (2002). *Real World Research: A resource for social scientists and practioner-researchers*. Oxford: Blackwell Publishing.

Siegfried, R. M. (2002) A Scripting Language to Help the Blind Program Visually. ACM SIGPLAN Notices 37/2/ pp. 53 – 56

Siegfried, R. M. (2006) Visual Programming and the Blind. ACM CIGCSE Bulletin 38/1/pp. 275-278

Sullivan J (2009) Braille Becomes Electric: The trials and triumphs of Braille translation software. Journal of Visual Impairment & Blindness. 103/7/ pp. 389-391

Vaspori, T., & Arato, A. (1994) Ten Years of Computer Use by Visually Impaired People in Hungary. Information Technology & Disabilities 1/3/---. Downloaded from http://people.rit.edu/easi/itd / itdv01n3/arato.htm on the 12th December 2008

Wong, F., Nagarajan, R., & Yaacob, S. (2003) Application of Stereovision in a Navigation Aid for Blind People. Proceedings of the 2003 Joint Conference on Information, Communications and Signal Processing 2003, and the Fourth Pacific Rim Conference on Multimedia

Zimler J and Keenan J M (1983) Imagery in the Congenitally Blind: How Visual are Visual Images? Journal of Experimental Psychology: Learning, Memory, and Cognition. 9 / p. 269-282.

ENDNOTE

[1]   Where this paper refers to programmers, it refers to both programmers and web developers.

Chapter 5
Multiculturality and Multimodal Languages

Maria Chiara Caschera
Istituto di Ricerche sulla Popolazione e le Politiche Sociali, Italy

Arianna D'Ulizia
Istituto di Ricerche sulla Popolazione e le Politiche Sociali, Italy

Fernando Ferri
Istituto di Ricerche sulla Popolazione e le Politiche Sociali, Italy

Patrizia Grifoni
Istituto di Ricerche sulla Popolazione e le Politiche Sociali, Italy

ABSTRACT

The way by which people communicate each other changes in the different cultures due to the different communicative expectations and depending on their cultural backgrounds. The development of the Internet has caused an increasing use of computer systems by people from different cultures, highlighting the need for interaction systems that adapt the interaction according to the cultural background of the user. This is one of the reasons of the growing research activity that explores how to consider cultural issues during the design of multimodal interaction systems. This chapter is focused on such a challenging topic, proposing a grammatical approach representing multicultural issues in multimodal languages. The approach is based on a grammar, that is able to produce a set of structured sentences, composed of gestural, vocal, audio, graphical symbols, and so on, along with the meaning that these symbols have in the different cultures. This work provides a contribution to the area of MulSeMedia research, as it deals with the integration of input produced by multiple human senses and acquired through multiple sensorial media.

DOI: 10.4018/978-1-60960-821-7.ch005

INTRODUCTION

The dialog among different cultures, the differences and diversities emerging in the present multicultural society give rise to communication issues. The way by which people communicate each other changes between different cultures (Foley, 1995) due to the different communicative expectations and depending on their cultural backgrounds. The multicultural society impacts on communication and therefore it gives birth to a multiplicity of verbal and non-verbal interactions.

The subjective cultural attributes, which characterize similarities and differences within and between user groups with different cultural models, need to be considered in HCI design process (Alostath, 2006) (Alostath & Wright, 2005). However, the HCI design does not often consider any cultural model (Barber & Badre, 1998), or it adopts cultural models that are not designed in according to the interpretation design based on culture (Smith et al., 2004). In the last years HCI studies have been focused on cross-cultural development often based on some consideration of cultural cognitive models. In particular, Stivers et al. (2007) provide the study of language acquisition and conceptual development, and the study of the relation of speech production and comprehension to other kinds of behaviour in a cultural context. In (Ein-Dor & Segev, 1990) cultural differences in end-user computing collecting data from end users in the USA and Israel have been investigated. This study has analysed the effect of national environments on four features: organization, structure, procedure, and behaviour. All seems underline the growing need to consider cultural issues during the design of Human Computer Interaction (HCI), and in particular, of multimodal interaction systems. This implies that culturally different user groups have to be considered during the design of interaction systems. Several studies have been focused on the design of interfaces for specific target cultures, and this activity is not

able to produce an appropriate result in term of a system to be shared among users from different cultures (Bourges-Waldegg. & Scrivener, 1998). Furthermore, this challenge has been faced defining guidelines and generalizations that are often not sensitive to the actual context of a system because they are described by a bounded set of variables of the target cultural system, without taking account of the continuous interactions between cultures and their evolutions. However, Gustavsson (1999) has analysed an approach for designing in multimodal systems a context that can be shared by culturally diverse user groups because it can be used as a basis for the design.

In this chapter, the influence of cultural differences in human-human and human-machine communication is investigated. We start from a review of the basic notions about multimodal systems in human-computer interaction (HCI). We have investigated several research studies for understanding how culture has influenced the design of usable computer systems. Afterwards, we have analysed the existing literature on anthropological linguistics for identifying the major linguistic distinctions and peculiarities in different languages linked to the different cultures. This analysis is oriented toward the definition of a multimodal language. This language is based on a grammar, that is able to produce a set of structured sentences, composed of gestural, vocal, audio, graphical symbols, and so on, along with the meaning that these symbols have in the different cultures.

Consistently with the recent advances of old multimedia towards the use of multiple sensorial media (MulSeMedia), this work provides a contribution to the area of MulSeMedia research, as it introduces a new grammatical approach representing multicultural issues in multimodal languages. The proposed approach is general enough to be applicable for whatever modalities and in whichever culture.

MULTIMODALITY IN HCI

Globalisation processes and the wide development and pervasiveness of the Internet have increased the number of computer systems and personal devices intended to be used by people from different countries and cultures. The wide use of these systems in every day life implies the need to consider different communicative users expectations and their cultural backgrounds. Therefore, model of cultures have a great impact on the design of the interaction systems.

Multimodal Interaction has emerged as the future paradigm of HCI. This fact is gathered also by the increasingly application of the multimodal paradigm to computer interfaces making computer behaviour closer to human communication.

The purpose of this chapter is to explore the main features of multimodal interaction in order to understand how they can suit multicultural diverse users' group and to describe methods and approaches for defining a multimodal multicultural language.

This section provides a description of the main features of multimodal system, which are the base for the analysis of multimodal interaction in a multicultural perspective given in the next section (see Section titled "Culture and languages").

A multimodal system is an hw/sw system that allows to receive, to interpret and to process input and generating as output two or more interactive modalities according with an integrated and a coordinated way. Communication among people is often multimodal and, it is obtained combining different modalities. Multimodal interfaces allow several modalities of communication to be harmoniously integrated, making the system communication characteristics more and more similar to the human communication approach (Caschera et al., 2007). Multimodal interfaces provide the user with multiple interaction paradigms through different types of communication input. Data fusion is one of the main problems in human-computer interaction, where each datum is generated through a distinct interaction mode. Furthermore, the management of these multiple processes includes synchronization and selection of the predominant mode. Consequently, an important issue in multimodal interaction is the integration and synchronization of several modalities in a single system. In literature two approaches are often used:

- signal fusion
- information fusion at the semantic level.

The first approach is preferred for matching and synchronizing modalities as speech and labial movement. The semantic fusion is used for modalities that differ in a temporal scale. In this approach, time is very important because chunks of information with different modalities are considered, and integrated if they are temporally close. The integration can be carried out using an intermediate approach between the signal integration and the semantic fusion.

The relation among modal components can be classified as follows (Bellik, 2001):

- Active - when two events, produced by two different devices, cannot be completely and correctly interpreted without ambiguities if one of the two events is unknown;
- Passive - when an event produced by a given device cannot be completely and correctly interpreted without ambiguities if the state of the other devices is unknown.

The input synchronization of a multimodal system can be defined as:

- Sequential - if the interpretation of the interactive step depends on one mode and the modalities can be considered one by one;
- Time-independent Synchronized - if the interpretation of the interactive step depends on two or more modalities and the modes are simultaneous;

- Time-dependent Synchronized - if the interpretation of the interactive step depends on two or more modalities and the semantic dependence of the modalities has a close temporal relationship.

There are several levels of synchronization (W3C):

- Event-level - if the inputs of one mode are received as events and immediately propagated to another mode;
- Field-level - if the inputs of one mode are propagated to another mode after a user has changed the input field or the interaction with a field is terminated;
- Form-level - if the inputs of one mode are propagated to another mode after a particular point of the interaction has been achieved;
- Session-level - if the inputs of one mode are propagated to another mode after an explicit changeover of mode.

The semantic fusion of modal input occurs in two steps: 1) the first matches the modalities to obtain a low level interpretation module, by grouping the input events in multimodal events; 2) the second transfers the multimodal inputs to the high level interpretation module, in order to obtain the meaning of their events. This high level interpretation defines the type of actions that will be triggered by the user and the used parameters. These parameterised actions are passed to the application dialog manager to start their execution.

There is an emerging need for integration among the various input modalities, through signal integration and semantic fusion, and an additional need to disambiguate the various input modalities and coordinate output modalities, to enable the user to have a range of integrated, coordinated interaction modalities.

Martin (Martin, 1997) proposed a theoretical framework for studying and designing multimodal systems based on a classification of six basic types of cooperation between modalities:

- Complementarity: different chunks of information composing the same command are transmitted over more than one mode;
- Equivalence: a chunk of information may be transmitted using more than one mode;
- Redundancy: the same chunk of information is transmitted using more than one mode;
- Transfer: a chunk of information produced by one mode is analysed by another mode;
- Concurrency: independent chunks of information are transmitted using different modalities and overlap in time;
- Specialization: a specific chunk of information is always transmitted using the same mode.

In Literature (Benoit & Others, 2000), several proposals have been advanced for integrating different modalities.

The synchronization level depends on the temporal granularity of the multimodal interaction. Diverse modalities can be combined, using several levels of synchronization according to the expected temporal granularity. In literature there are several approaches to represent the events of multimodal inputs:

- Typed Feature Structures (Cohen & Others, 1997; Johnston & Others, 1997): in this approach, multimodal inputs can be transformed into typed feature structures that represent the semantics attributed to the various modalities. These feature structures are combined by unification (Quickset).

- Syntactic representation (Faure & Julia, 1993): the input multimodal events are represented as a triplet {verb, object, location}. This representation is sufficient for input in the form of speech with deictic references, but it is not clear how this approach can be extended to deal with several modal events.

- Melting pots (Nigay & Coutaz, 1995): a melting pot encapsulates types of structural parts of a multimodal event. The content of a structural part is a time-stamped piece of information. The melting-pots are constructed by events in elementary inputs with different mechanisms of fusion: micro-temporal, macro-temporal and contextual fusion.

- Micro-temporal fusion combines two information units produced concurrently or very close to one another. Macro-temporal fusion combines sequential or temporally close information units, when these units are complementary. Contextual fusion combines information units according to semantic constraints.

- Partial Action Frame (Vo & Wood, 1996; Vo & Waibel, 1997; Vo, 1998): the input of each mode is separately interpreted and then analysed and transformed into a semantic frame containing slots that specify the control parameters. Information in the partial action frames can be incomplete or ambiguous. Each sequence of grouped input events has a score based on their mutual information.

Semantic fusion is not further defined by the characteristics of the events because the above approaches can be used indifferently. For example, speech and pen fusion can be achieved by both Typed Feature Structures and Partial Action Frame. In literature, events for fusing gesture and speech have been represented by Typed Feature Structures or Syntactic Representation. The Melt-

ing Pots approach can be used to fuse speech, keyboard and mouse.

When information conveyed by different modalities are fused, the system has to define the correct interpretation of them. Therefore an important unit for building multimodal systems is the interpretation process. The interpretation of user input is strictly connected with different features, such as available interaction modalities, conversation focus, and interaction context. A correct interpretation can be reached by simultaneously considering semantic, temporal and contextual constraints. For example in multimodal system based on video and audio inputs (Harper & Shriberg, 2004) the interpretation defines a multimodal corpus of digital and temporally synchronized video and audio recordings of human monologues and dialogues.

In the literature, three main different approaches to the fusion process have been proposed, according to the main architectural levels (recognition and decision) at which the fusion of the input signals can be performed: recognition-based, decision-based, and hybrid multi-level fusion. The recognition-based fusion consists in merging the outcomes of each modal recognizer by using integration mechanisms, such as, for example, statistical integration techniques, agent theory, hidden Markov models, artificial neural networks, etc. The decision manager, therefore, processes the integrated sentence and provides its most probable interpretation. The decision-based fusion does not mean merging the features of each recognized input, but directly the semantic information that are extracted from the specific decision managers by using specific dialogue-driven fusion procedures to yield the complete interpretation. In the hybrid multi-level fusion, the integration of input modalities is distributed among the recognition and decision levels. The hybrid multi-level fusion includes the grammar-based fusion strategy, in which the different unimodal inputs are integrated into a unique multimodal input (which we refer also as multimodal sentence) by using the multimodal grammar specification. Subsequently, the dialogue parser applies the grammar rules to interpret the multimodal input. A more extensive discussion about multimodal input fusion strategies can be found in (D'Ulizia, 2009).

A comparison of these approaches (Manchón et al., 2006) showed that the grammar-based paradigm is more coherent with the human-human communication paradigm in which the dialogue is seen as a unique and multimodal communication act. Moreover, the grammar-based strategy is the most natural, if compared with the pre-existing approaches, as it activates the cognitive dynamics that generally reduces the cognitive load and, thus, increases the amount of attention on content.

The most extensively applied class of grammars in natural language processing is the class of context-free grammars (CFGs). However, in order to use CFGs for multimodal language processing, it is necessary to overcome the two main deficiencies of this grammatical formalism, i.e. the lack of constructs both for representing input symbols from different modalities and for modeling semantic and temporal aspects of input symbols. In this attempt, a Multimodal Attribute Grammar (MAG) has been introduced (D'Ulizia et al., 2010), which has a set of attributes (associated with each distinct symbol in the grammar) necessary for managing the multimodal properties of a sentence. This set is composed of four attributes, containing information about the current value (concept) of the symbol, the modality (speech, handwriting, gesture, sketch), the syntactic role (noun phrase, verb phrase, determiner, verb, noun, adjective, preposition, deictic, conjunction), and the modality cooperation (complementary, redundant) with other symbols of the sentence.

The features of multimodal system, analysed in this section, need to be considered in combination with the concept of multiculturality in order to design a multimodal interaction paradigm, which should suit multicultural diverse users' group. For this reason the next section investigate the concept of culture from a HCI perspective.

THE CONCEPT OF CULTURE IN HCI

Many definitions of culture were given in the literature, ranging from a social to a more communication-oriented point-of-view. Following a social-oriented point-of-view, Hofstede (2001) argued that

Culture is the collective programming of the mind that distinguishes the members of one group or category of people from another.

Moreover, Borgman (1986) said that

Culture includes race and ethnicity as well as other variables and is manifested in customary behaviours, assumptions and values, patterns of thinking and communication style.

On the contrary, Bodker and Pederson (1991) and Ford and Kotzé (2005) gave a definition of culture mainly focussed on the way communication takes place. Precisely, Bodker and Pederson (1991) argued that:

Culture is conceptualised as a system of meaning that underlies routine and behaviour in everyday working life.

Finally, Ford and Kotzé (2005) defined culture as:

The patterns of thinking, feeling and acting that influence the way in which people communicate amongst themselves and with computers.

All the above authors provide a conceptual definition of culture, which can not be used effectively by the human-computer interaction community due to the high theoretical level and the lack of practical and concrete aspects related to the interaction with computational machines. This fact has also been highlighted by Hall (2001), which argued that "the difficulty is that these characterizations are descriptive and nor prescriptive, they cannot be used deductively".

Therefore, in the last few years many researchers, starting from the awareness that culture influences the way in which people interact each other, have investigated how culture also influences the way in which people interact with computers. Many studies have been oriented towards the understanding of how cultural differences can be taken into account in the design of usable computer systems. These studies deeply investigated the concept of "culturability", firstly introduced by Barber and Badre (1998) and referred to the combination of culture and usability in the design of human-computer interfaces. Starting from the analysis of the main differences (linguistic, non-verbal, etc.) between cultures, these studies focused on the development of cultural models and guidelines for assisting HCI designers in the creation of multicultural/cross-cultural user interfaces.

A classification of cultural models in web interface design, introduced by Fitzgerald (2004), groups existing cultural models into two classes: cultural dimension (n-factor) models, and cultural marker models.

Cultural dimension models attempt to characterize different cultures on the basis of a number of cultural variables or factors. For instance, Hall (1990) proposed a four-factor model that measures cultural differences in terms of speed of messages, context, space and time. Hofstede (1991) identified five cultural variables for distinguishing among different cultures, that are power distance, uncertainty avoidance, masculinity vs. femininity, individualism vs. collectivism, and time orientation. Trompenaars (1993) presented a cultural model based on the following seven factors: universalism vs. particularism, individualism vs. collectivism, neutral vs. emotional, specific vs. diffuse, achievement vs. ascription, attitudes to time, and attitudes to the environment.

Cultural marker models differentiate cultures on the basis of the signs or symbols, called cultural markers, which are prevalent within a particular cultural group. The first example of cultural marker model was developed by Barber and Badre (1998), which identified the cultural markers into the following interface design elements: colour, spatial organization, fonts, shapes, icons, metaphors, geography, language, flags, sounds, motion, preferences for text vs. graphics, directionality of how language is written (left vs. right), help features and navigation tools. Smith et al. (2004) proposed a cultural model that relies on a smaller number of cultural markers, which are colours, colour combinations, banner adverts, trust signs, use of metaphor, language cues and navigation controls.

In addition to the studies outlined above and devoted to provide cultural models for improving the design of human-computer interfaces, further research studies have focused on providing cross-cultural HCI design approaches. Bourges-Waldegg and Scrivener (1998) proposed a cross-cultural HCI design approach, called Meaning in Mediated Action (MMA). The authors, starting from an analysis on several people with culturally diverse backgrounds for understanding culturally determined usability problems, led to the result that the root of cultural differences in HCI design stays in the divergence between the target meaning and the interpreted meaning of the interface representations (i.e. elements of the interface that have meaning). According to the authors, two persons from different cultures may understand a representation in the same way (giving it the same meaning) if they share the same context. The MMA approach aims at determining shared contexts that can be used as a base to design representations of the interface. A more recent approach, proposed by Shen et al. (2006), adopted a Culture-Centred Design (CCD) perspective. The method consists of four iterative design phases, as shown in Figure 1. The first is the selection and analysis of the target user and her/his cultural conditions. Afterwards, a sketched design (not influenced by styles, trends and cultural references) is carried out. The third phase is the testing and evaluation of user experience with a first working demonstration of the interface. Finally, the design implementation is carried out, which adjusts the interface elements according to the results of the evaluation.

All previous works deeply investigated the use of cultural metaphors for designing web and graphical user interfaces. Our work takes a different perspective since it explores how cultural metaphors can be applied in the design of multimodal interfaces. We start from an analysis of the cultural differences in human communication language (verbal and nonverbal communication) for extending the concept of multimodal grammar, introduced in the Section titled "Multimodality in HCI", for embedding cultural factors in the definition of multimodal languages.

CULTURE AND LANGUAGES

Culture is of fundamental importance in human-human communication. The human ability to correctly generate signals and interpret symbols strongly depends on the cultural background.

Human beings convey meanings not only through verbal (or linguistic) communication but also through various forms of nonverbal communication, such as body language, gesture, facial expressions, touch, eye movements, pictures, graphics, sound, and writing. Both these kinds of human communication are culturally conditioned.

Verbal Communication and Culture

Starting from verbal communication, cultural differences arise when the cultural conventions of the interlocutors are widely different because they use different languages to communicate. In this case, the communication can break down for a twofold reason. The first reason is the different

Figure 1. The Culture-Centred Design approach by Shen et al. (2006)

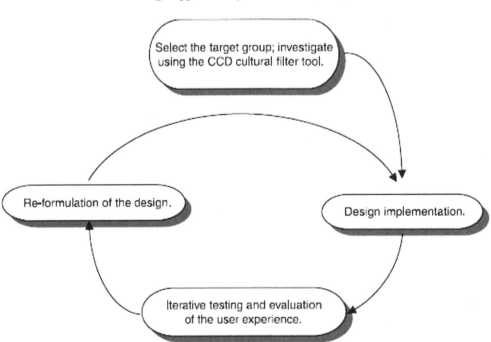

way in which interlocutors encode messages. Any human language relies on five kinds of rules for encoding messages:

- Phonological rules, which refers to the procedures for combining phonemes, i.e. basic sound units of a word (e.g. [k], [sh], etc.). Each language has got a set of phonemes, e.g. the English language has 45 phonemes, while other languages span between 18 and 85. Native speakers produce words starting from the sounds of the language. However, apart the phonological rules of a language, each person speaks with an accent that characterizes his/her tone of voice and inflection. Moreover, also members of a subculture can be identified having accents.

- Morphological rules, which allow combining different sounds into a meaningful word or part of word (e.g. *"un"*, *"com-er"*, etc.). An example of cultural difference in morphological rules stays in the formulation of verb tense. For instance, in English and many other European languages, for expressing an action that is in progress, a suffix is used (e.g. *"is go-ing"*), while in some African language a prefix is used (e.g. *"go"="law"*, *"is going"="n-law"*).

- Syntactic rules, which deal with how words are sequenced together. These rules are reflective of the cultural notion of causality and order. For instance, in English explicit subject pronouns are used (e.g. *"I* come with *you* this afternoon"), while in Chinese subject pronouns are not imperatively used. Syntactic rules of a language denote reasoning patterns within a culture.

- Semantic rules, which concern the meaning of words. Even if an utterance is syntactically correct, there is no assurance that it provides coherent information. Meanings of specific words and phrases are consensually established by people of a cultural

community. Two levels of meaning exist: denotative and connotative. The former refers to the dictionary definition of a term, while the latter concerns the informal grasp that is relatively subjective and personal.

- Pragmatic rules, which consider the use of language according to the context. Pragmatics groups all the context-dependent information in communication. Indeed, the study of the different meanings that can convey a single sentence uttered in different contexts. Pragmatics reflects the cultural expectations of how, when, where, and with whom certain expressions are preferred or prohibited.

The second reason that can lead to the communication breakdown is the different way used for decoding messages. Cultures influences decoding process through ethnocentrism, cultural filters, emotions, value judgments, stereotypes and expectations. At semantic level, intercultural misunderstandings arise when we decode the literal meanings of the words but not the connotative meanings of the messages.

Nonverbal Communication and Culture

Nonverbal human-human communication accompanies verbal communication in most communicative situations, and in most cultures. Many anthropologists distinguish four kinds of nonverbal communication: kinesics, haptics, chronemics, and proxemics.

Kinesics refers to the study of body language. Specifically, it includes the study of gesture, facial expressions, and eye contact.

Gestures, which are distinctive in a specific environment, are known as *emblematic*. These gestures are culturally specified due to the fact that one single gesture may differ in interpretation from culture to culture (Efron, 1941; Ekman & Friesen, 1969). An example is given by the American "V-for-victory" gesture can be made either with the palm or the back of the hand towards the listener. On the other hand, In Britain a 'V' gesture made with the back of the hand towards the listener is inappropriate in polite society. In the interface design, another type of gesture that has been the subject of some study community is the *prepositional gesture* (Hinrichs & Polanyi, 1986). For example, to point at a chair and then pointing at another spot and saying "move that over there". In this case, the gestures interaction with speech is more like the interaction of one grammatical constituent with another than the interaction of one communicative channel with another; in fact, the demonstrative "this" may be seen as a place holder for the syntactic role of the accompanying gesture. These kinds of gestures can be particularly relevant in certain types of task-oriented talk (Bolt, 1987). More common gestures are of four types:

- **Iconic gestures.** They consist of the action or event that are being described. For example, one speaker at the Computer Vision Workshop was describing to his neighbour a technique that his lab was employing. He said *"and we use a wide field cam to [do the body]'"*, *while holding both hands open and bent at the wrists with his fingers pointed towards his body, and the hands sweeping up and down. His gesture shows us the wide field cam "doing the body", and takes the perspective of somebody whose body is "being done"*. Alternatively, he might have put both hands up to his eyes, pantomiming holding a camera, and playing the part of the viewer rather than the viewed (Cassell, 1998). Iconic gestures identify the way in which an action is performed, even if this information is not given in accompanying speech.
- **Metaphoric gestures.** They can be defined as representational, and the concept they refer has no physical form, but it comes

from a common metaphor. An example of this gesture is: "the meeting went on and on" accompanied by a hand indicating rolling motion (Cassell, 1998).

- **Deictic spatialize.** They are discourse entities that have a physical existence, or non-physical discourse entities. An example of this gesture is to point left and then right while saying "well, Sara was looking at the chair across the table". Deictic gestures can be pointed by index fingers and by the whole hand in order to represent entities or ideas or events in space.
- **Beat gestures.** They are movements that do not change in form with the content of the accompanying speech. They have pragmatic function, and they occur with comments on one's own linguistic contribution, speech repairs and reported speech. An example is given in (Cassell, 1998): "she talked first, I mean second" accompanied by a hand flicking down and then up. This kind of gesture is an evaluative or orienting comment.

Facial expressions usually communicate a mood or capture a sentiment, such as surprise, fear, disgust, anger, happiness and sadness. These emotions are expressed in similar ways by people around the world. However, several cultural differences arise in the way people show emotions. For instance, in most cultures men are expected to control their emotions, especially fear, while women are expected to show their emotion more freely. In China and Japan, moreover, a facial expression that would be recognized around the world as conveying happiness may actually express anger or mask sadness, both of which are unacceptable to show overtly. Therefore, although some facial expressions may be similar across cultures, their interpretations remain culture-specific. It is important to understand the cultural context of the user in order to interpret emotions expressed in cross-cultural interactions.

Eye contact can indicate interest, attention, and involvement. In Western culture, eye contact is interpreted as attentiveness and honesty; "look people in the eye" when talking is considered a polite behaviour. On the contrary, in Hispanic, Asian, Middle Eastern, and Native American cultures, eye contact is thought to be disrespectful or rude, and lack of eye contact does not mean that a person is not paying attention.

- *Haptics* refers to the study of touching. Communication touches include kisses, handshakes, pats, and brushes. The meaning conveyed by touch is highly dependent from the culture. Some anthropologists classify cultures as high or low contact according to which senses they use more. For instance, American culture is low contact because there is less touching than the Arabian culture, which is considered high contact.

- *Chronemics* concerns the study of time usage in nonverbal communication. Time perceptions can be expressed through punctuality, willingness to wait, speed of speech or even the amount of time people are willing to listen. According to chronemics, the timing and frequency of any action within an interaction contribute to the process of non-verbal communication. Time perception differs in various cultures. For instance, Americans are constrained by time and try to control it, therefore they are expected to arrive to meetings on time. In China, people do not feel constrained by time, however, being late to meetings means a face-loss.

- *Proxemics* pertains to the perception of physical spaces. According to proxemics, the physical distance between two people can be correlated to the relationship they share be it personal or social. Crossing cultures, a very different use of space for

conversations and negotiations is encountered. For instance, North Americans tend to prefer a large amount of space, perhaps because they are surrounded by it in their homes and countryside. On the contrary, Europeans and Arabs tend to stand more closely with each other when talking, and are accustomed to smaller personal spaces.

DEFINITION OF A MULTIMODAL MULTICULTURAL LANGUAGE

A multimodal interaction system, which aims at the adaptation of the interaction to the user, can not avoid considering cultural factors during interaction. What is needed is an approach that allows incorporating cultural knowledge into multimodal interaction systems. This section proposes a solution to this challenge.

In Section "Multimodality in HCI", we have introduced the grammar-based strategy as a fusion technique for integrating input coming from different modalities into a meaningful sentence. The Multimodal Attribute Grammar (MAG) introduced by D'Ulizia et al. (2010) does not deal explicitly with the cultural background of the user. Starting from the multimodal interaction system based on the MAG, used to generate multimodal languages, this chapter proposes constructs that are necessary for adapting the interaction language to the cultural background of the user.

This is the motivation that led us to extend the MAG towards a multicultural MAG, which is able to represent the cultural differences, discussed in the previous section, into the grammar notation.

The MAG notation may be informally defined as a context-free grammar (CFG) that allows multimodal input modelling using a set of attributes (associated with each distinct symbol - terminal and non-terminal - of the grammar), assignment of attribute values, evaluation rules, and conditions. In particular, the MAG is composed of three elements, as described in D'Ulizia et al. (2010):

1. a CFG with a set of *terminal elements*, a set of non-terminal elements, a set of production rules and a start symbol (or axiom);
2. a collection of attributes of the non-terminal and terminal elements;
3. a collection of semantic functions (or rules) to compute the values of the attributes.

The existing attributes are the following:

*   the *val* attribute, which expresses the current value (concept) of the terminal element,
*   the *mod* attribute, which represents the modality,
*   the *synrole* attribute, which conveys information about the syntactic role, and
*   the *coop* attribute, which expresses the modality cooperation with other terminal elements.

Moreover, the *terminal elements* of the MAG are defined in Caschera et al. (2008) as a 5-tuple that contains the values of the four attributes associated with each terminal element, along with the representation used for the element.

In order to consider the subjective cultural attributes characterising user groups of different cultural models, the attributes of terminal symbols in the Multimodal Attribute Grammar needs to be enhanced. Starting from the definition of *terminal element* in (Caschera et al., 2008), information about the cultural aspects of the users groups has been integrated, and terminal elements depending on cultural background are defined as follows:

Definition 1. *A terminal element E^i is a 6-pla* $(E^i_{mod}, E^i_{repr}, E^i_{time}, E^i_{role}, E^i_{concept}, E^i_{culture})$, *with:*

* $E^i_{mod:}$ *that defines the modality used to create the element E^i*
* E^i_{repr}: *that defines the representation of the element E_i in the specific modality,*
* E^i_{time}: *that defines the temporal interval connected with the element E_i,*

* E^i_{role}: *the syntactic role that the element E_i plays in the Multimodal Sentence,*
* $E^i_{concept}$: *that specifies of the concept name referred to the conceptual structure of the context,*
* $E^i_{culture}$: *that specifies the cultural background of the user that is interacting.*

Terminal symbols in the Multimodal Attribute Grammar are the building units of the Multimodal Language according to the production rules of the grammar (Caschera et al., 2007b). These rules have been dived in: rules that refer to the construction of the *syntax of the grammar* P^g; rules about the *context* P^c; and *temporal rules* P^t.

The set of *production rules* P is:

$$P = \{P^g, P^c, P^t\}$$

Rules of the syntax of the grammar Pg are defined as the production rules of the natural language (Caschera et al., 2007b). Context rules define what is true in the context of interaction and they allow deducing which is the context of interaction.

Finally *temporal rules* impose constraints on temporal intervals of elements. These rules establish how to take into account elements whose temporal intervals are contained in a defined temporal slot (Caschera et al., 2007a).

The cultural issues are embodied in the rules about the context. In fact, these rules address cultural interaction features of different target user groups, and the interaction domain. In detail, the *context* P^c can be divided in: rules about the interaction features of user groups considering their cultural background (P^c_i); and rules about the domain (P^c_d) that describe the domain knowledge and the discourse context knowledge.

To clarify the use of the grammatical approach described above a simple example is presented below.

Example 1. Suppose that the user interacts with a system through a multimodal dialogue interface that supports gesture, voice, sketch and handwriting modalities. In this scenario, suppose that the user makes a gesture with the tip of the thumb and the tip of a finger meeting to create a ring. This gesture has different meanings according to the culture in which it is performed. Indeed, in American culture it means "OK", in Japanese culture it means "money", in French culture it means "zero or worthless", and in Tunisian culture it means "I'll kill you".

In order to represent the various acceptations of this gesture, the terminal element that represents this gesture is characterized by the following n-ple:

- in American culture:
  - E^i_{mod} = (gesture)
  - E^i_{repr} = ("")
  - E^i_{time} = (5, 6)
  - E^i_{role} = (nn)
  - $E^i_{concept}$ =(ok)
  - $E^i_{culture}$ =(American)
- in Japanese culture:
  - E^i_{mod} = (gesture)
  - E^i_{repr} = ("")
  - E^i_{time} = (5, 6)
  - E^i_{role} = (nn)
  - $E^i_{concept}$ =(money)
  - $E^i_{culture}$ =(Japanese)
- in French culture:
  - E^i_{mod} = (gesture)
  - E^i_{repr} = ("")
  - E^i_{time} = (5, 6)
  - E^i_{role} = (nn)
  - $E^i_{concept}$ =(zero)
  - $E^i_{culture}$ =(French)
- in Tunisian culture:
  - E^i_{mod} = (gesture)
  - E^i_{repr} = ("")
  - E^i_{time} = (5, 6)
  - E^i_{role} = (vb)
  - $E^i_{concept}$ =(kill)
  - $E^i_{culture}$ =(Tunisian)

This example underlines that the same representation of a terminal element can refer to different concepts considering the cultural background of the target user.

CONCLUSION

To address the necessity to consider the multicultural issues during the interaction process, this chapter has analysed the main features of the multimodal interaction systems and the relationships between culture and interaction languages.

The multimodal interaction has been examined underlining information and time features to consider during the interaction process. The analysis has been finalized to evaluate how information and time features can suit multicultural target users, and how methods and approaches can be used to define a multicultural grammar.

The definition of this grammar has required the analysis of the concept of culture considering the interaction process between human beings and computers. The study has been also focused on verbal and nonverbal communication investigating them according to cultural differences and the main linguistic distinctions in different cultural contexts.

This evaluation, combined with the analysis of multimodal features from a cultural perspective, has supported the definition of Multimodal Attribute Grammar supporting multicultural communication and interaction.

As a future work, starting from the result of the research described, we are identifying different groups of users, from different cultures sharing the same working environment, and we are identifying differences in the synchronization processes between the different modalities according to the different cultures, and how the multiculturality influences and evolves each cultural communication process.

REFERENCES

W3C (2003) NOTE 8 January 2003, "Multimodal Interaction Requirements", http://www.w3.org/TR/2003/ NOTE-mmi-reqs-20030108/.

Alostath, J. (2006). "Culture-Centred Design: Integrating Culture into Human-Computer Interaction," Doctoral Thesis, The University of York, UK.

Alostath, J., & Wright, P. (2005). "Integrating Cultural Models into Human-Interaction Design," Conference on Information Technology in Asia (CITA2005), Kuching, Sarawak, Malaysia.

Barber, W., & Badre, A. N. (1998). Culturability: The merging of culture and usability. In 4th Conference on Human Factors and the Web: Baskin, Ridge, New Jersey.

Bellik, Y. (2001). "Technical Requirements for a Successful Multimodal Interaction", International Workshop on Information Presentation and Natural Multimodal Dialogue, Verona, Italy.

Benoit, C., Martin, J. C., Pelachaud, C., Schomaker, L., & Suhm, B. (2000). "Audio-Visual and Multimodal Speech Systems". Handbook of Standards and Resources for Spoken Language Systems - Supplement Volume. D. Gibbon (Ed.). 1-95.

Bodker, K., & Pederson, J. (1991). Workplace cultures: Looking at artifacts, symbols, and practices. In: Greenbaum, J., Kyng. M. (eds): Design at work: Cooperative Design of Computer Systems. Lawrence Erlbaum, Hillsdale, NJ.

Bolt, R. A. (1980). Put-that-there: voice and gesture at the graphics interface. *Computer Graphics, 14*(3), 262–270. doi:10.1145/965105.807503

Borgman, C. L. (1986). The User's Mental Model of an Information Retrieval System: an Experiment on a Prototype Online Catalog. *International Journal of Man-Machine Studies, 24*, 47–64. doi:10.1016/S0020-7373(86)80039-6

Bourges-Waldegg, P., & Scrivener, S. A. R. (1998). Meaning, the central issue in cross-cultural HCI design. *Interacting with Computers, 9*(3), 287–309. doi:10.1016/S0953-5438(97)00032-5

Caschera M. C., Ferri F., Grifoni P. (2007): Multimodal interaction systems: information and time features, International Journal of Web and Grid Services (IJWGS), Vol. 3 - Issue 1, pp 82-99.

Caschera, M. C., Ferri, F., & Grifoni, P. (2007b). An Approach for Managing Ambiguities in Multimodal Interaction. OTM 2007 Ws, Part I, LNCS 4805. *Springer-Verlag Berlin Heidelberg, 2007*, 387–397.

Caschera, M. C., Ferri, F., & Grifoni, P. (2008). Ambiguity detection in multimodal systems. Proceedings of the working conference on Advanced visual interfaces. Pp.331-334.

Cassell, J. (1998). *A Framework for Gesture Generation and Interpretation, Computer Vision in Human Machine Interaction* (Cipolla, R., & Pentlan, A., Eds.). New York, USA: Cambridge University Press.

Cohen, P. R., Johnston, M., McGee, D., Oviatt, S., Pittman, J., Smith, I., et al. (1997). "QuickSet: Multimodal interaction for distributed applications". Fifth ACM International Multimedia Conference, ACM Press/Addison-Wesley 31-40.

D'Ulizia, A. (2009). *Exploring Multimodal Input Fusion Strategies. In the Handbook of Research on Multimodal Human Computer Interaction and Pervasive Services: Evolutionary Techniques for Improving Accessibility* (pp. 34–57). IGI Publishing.

D'Ulizia A., Ferri F., Grifoni P. (2010). Generating Multimodal Grammars for Multimodal Dialogue Processing. *IEEE Transactions on Systems, Man, and Cybernetics - Part A: Systems and Humans.* (in press, forthcoming in the Volume 40, Issue 4, July 2010).

Del Galdo, E. (1990). Internationalization and translation: some guidelines for the design of human-computer interfaces. In Factors, E. A. I. H., & Series, E. (Eds.), *Designing User interfaces For international Use, J. Nielsen* (*Vol. 13*, pp. 1–10). Essex: Elsevier Science Publishers Ltd.

Efron, D. (1941). *Gesture and environment*. New York: King's Crown Press.

Ein-Dor, P., & Segev, E. (1990). End-user computing: A crosscultural study. Proc. of the Twenty-Third Annual Hawaii International Conference on System Sciences 1990, Vol. 4, IEEE, 240-250.

Ekman, P., & Friesen, W. (1969). The repertoire of nonverbal behavioral categories -- origins, usage, and coding. *Semiotica, 1*, 49–98.

Faure, C., & Julia, L. (1993). "Interaction homme-machine par la parole et le geste pour l'édition de Documents: TAPAGE". International Conference on Interfaces to Real and Virtual Worlds, 171-180.

Fitzgerald, W. (2004). Models for cross cultural communications for cross-cultural website design. NRC/ERB-1108. April 6, 2004. 11 pages. NRC Publication Number: NRC 46563.

Foley, W. (1995). *Anthropological Linguistics*. Blackwell Publishers Ltd.

Ford, G., & Kotzé, P. (2005). Designing usable interfaces with cultural dimensions. In Costabile, M. F., & Paternó, F. (Eds.), *Lecture Notes in Computer Science LNCS 3585, Human-Computer Interaction - INTERACT 2005* (pp. 713–726). Berlin: Springer.

Gustavsson, M. (1999). *Designing a multimodal system for a culturally diverse user group*. www.ida.liu.se/~ssomc/ papers/Gustavsson.pdf

Hall, E., & Hall, M. R. (1990). *Understanding Cultural Differences*. Yarmouth, Maine: Intercultural Press.

Harper, M. P., & Shriberg, E. (2004). Multimodal model integration for sentence unit detection. *ICMI, 2004*, 121–128. doi:10.1145/1027933.1027955

Hinrichs, E., & Polanyi, L. (1986). Pointing the way: A unified treatment of referential gesture in interactive contexts. In A. Farley, P. Farley & K.E. McCullough (Eds.), Proceedings of the Parasession of the Chicago Linguistics Society Annual Meetings (Pragmatics and Grammatical Theory). Chicago: Chicago Linguistics Society.

Hofstede, G. (1991). *Cultures and Organizations: Software of the Mind*. New York, New York: McGraw-Hill.

Hofstede, G. (2001). *Culture's consequences II: Comparing values, behaviors, institutions & organizations across nations*. Beverly Hills, CA: Sage.

Johnston, M., Cohen, P. R., McGee, D., Oviatt, S. H., Pittman, J. A., & Smith, I. (1997). "Unification-based multimodal integration". 35th Annual Meeting of the Association for Computational Linguistics, Madrid, Spain, 281-288.

Manchón, P., Pérez, G., & Amores, G. (2006). *Multimodal Fusion: A New Hybrid Strategy for Dialogue Systems*. In Proceedings of Eighth International Conference on Multimodal Interfaces (ICMI 2006), Banff, Alberta, Canada. ACM: New York, pp. 357-363.

Martin, J. C. (1997) "Toward Intelligent Cooperation Between Modalities: The Example of a System Enabling Multimodal Interaction with a Map". Proceedings of International Joint Conference on Artificial Intelligence (IJCAI'97) Workshop on "Intelligent Multimodal Systems." Nagoya, Japan.

Niederhoffer, K. G., & Pennebaker, J. W. (2002). Linguistic style matching in social interaction. *Journal of Language and Social Psychology, 21*, 337–360. doi:10.1177/026192702237953

Nigay, L., & Coutaz, J. (1995). "A generic platform for addressing the multimodal challenge". International Conference on Computer-Human Interaction, ACM Press, 98-105.

Shen, S., Woolley, M., & Prior, S. (2006, July). Towards culture-centred design. *Interacting with Computers, 18*(Issue 4), 820–852. doi:10.1016/j. intcom.2005.11.014

Smith, A., Dunckley, L., French, T., Minocha, S., & Chang, Y. (2004). A process model for developing usable cross-cultural websites. *Interacting with Computers, 16*(1), 69–91. doi:10.1016/j. intcom.2003.11.005

Stivers, T. Enfield, N.J. Levinson, S.C. (2007). Person reference in interaction: Linguistic, cultural and social perspectives. Language, culture and cognition. Publisher: Cambridge: Cambridge University Press. pp.1-20.

Trompenaars, F. (1993). *Riding the Waves of Culture: Understanding the Cultural Diversity in Business*. London: Nicholas Brealey.

Vo, M. T., & Waibel, A. (1997). "Modeling and interpreting multimodal inputs: A semantic integration Approach". Technical Report CMU-CS-97-192, Carnegie Mellon University.

Vo, M. T., & Wood, C. (1996). "Building an application framework for speech and pen input integration in multimodal learning interfaces". International Conference on Acoustics, Speech and Signal Processing, IEEE Computer Society, 3545-3548.

Section 3
MulSeMedia Interfaces

Chapter 6

Haptic Rendering of HTML Components and 2D Maps Included in Web Pages

Nikolaos Kaklanis
University of Surrey, UK & Informatics and Telematics Institute, Greece

Konstantinos Moustakas
Informatics and Telematics Institute, Greece

Dimitrios Tsovaras
Informatics and Telematics Institute, Greece

ABSTRACT

This chapter describes an interaction technique wherein web pages are parsed so as to automatically generate a corresponding 3D virtual environment with haptic feedback. The automatically created 3D scene is composed of "hapgets" (haptically-enhanced widgets), which are three dimensional widgets providing a behavior that is analogous to the behavior of the original HTML components but are also enhanced with haptic feedback. Moreover, for each 2D map included in a web page a corresponding multimodal (haptic-aural) map is automatically generated. The proposed interaction technique enables the haptic navigation through the internet as well as the haptic exploration of conventional 2D maps for the visually impaired users. A rendering engine of web pages that was developed according to the proposed interaction technique is also presented.

INTRODUCTION

The Internet is without question the greatest existing collection of resources. The use of the Web is spreading rapidly in most areas of society and daily life. In many countries, the Web is increasingly used for government information and services, education and training, commerce, news, workplace interaction, civic participation, health care, recreation, entertainment, and more. In some cases, the Web is also replacing traditional resources, like books, newspapers, etc.

The Internet provides an opportunity for unprecedented access to information for people with disabilities. Many accessibility barriers to print, audio, and visual media can be much more

DOI: 10.4018/978-1-60960-821-7.ch006

easily overcome through web technologies. For example, when the primary way to get certain bibliographic information was to go to a library and read it on paper, there were significant barriers for many people with disabilities, such as getting to the library, physically getting the resource, and reading the resource. When that same information is also available on the Web in an accessible format, it is significantly easier for many people to access the information. In some cases, the Web allows people with disabilities to do things that were nearly impossible without it. The Web is also an opportunity for unprecedented interaction, enabling people with disabilities to more actively participate in society. Therefore, it must be fully accessible, in order to provide equal access and equal opportunities to people with disabilities.

Despite technological advances aimed at making the Internet accessible and easy to use, the World Wide Web is not wide open for many people. People with disabilities and especially visually impaired users often meet huge obstacles in accessing the internet as the visual is the predominant channel in web navigation. While the most formidable task today may be presenting information in a manner that meets the accessibility needs of people using screen readers, the overarching issue is making everything on the Internet usable by the widest audience possible.

Numerous studies have shown current web accessibility to be less than optimal (Gerber & Kirchner, 2001; Lazar et al., 2007; Mcmullin, 2002). Despite significant advances in assistive technologies, blind and visually impaired Internet users continue to encounter barriers when accessing web content (Gerber & Kirchner, 2001; Sinks & King, 1998; Web Content Accessibility Guidelines 2.0). Navigation through a web page or through a series of web pages can be a difficult process due to the lack of feedback received (Murphy et al., 2008). Screen reading technologies synthesise the main body of text available on each page, outputting a linear rather than spatial representation of information on a page. On web pages containing a large amount of information, task completion time can increase due to additional complexity. This can lead to a greater chance of mistakes and slips (Brajnik, 2004). Petrie et al. (1997) found that moving backwards and forwards through pages, reaching the top of the current node, and looking for a quick method of moving to the home node present significant challenges to users. In the MultiReader report (2001), some visually impaired Internet users were found to close the browser and then re-launch, rather than using the navigation buttons provided. Moving through a sequence of pages such as a flight booking process, can also prove to be complex for users. Problems can be attributed to the visually oriented presentation of information via the computer interface, and restrictions imposed by assistive devices. The text contained in Web pages can be presented via a screen reader, but without the meta-information provided by the layout, pages can be hard to navigate, and the required information can be difficult to find. The values contained in the cells of a table can be read by a screen reader, but the lack of spatial layout means that the relationships between them can quickly become unintelligible. Information contained in graphs, images or models is almost impossible to convey via speech alone. Even when a verbal description of the data can be generated, it is unlikely to capture the rich information contained in the visual presentation.

Accessibility barriers also exist for the visually impaired users as far as it concerns the exploration of maps found on the web. Maps are widely used by people for their travel planning and navigation, even for local and short trips. Free on-line map services, such as Google Maps, OpenStreetMap and MapQuest, make instant access to geographical information easily available. Unfortunately, visually impaired users are partially or completely deprived of such benefits. Even if they may make use of textual descriptions of the directions given by the map services, using text-to-Braille/speech software, an instant and direct access to the map image itself is still unavailable (Wang et al., 2009). Although there are some techniques helping tactile specialists in converting a map image into a tactile format, the procedures involved are typically time-consuming and labor intensive, thus preventing visually impaired users from accessing the map image in real-time and independently of others.

Haptic feedback is a very promising technology to improve virtual world access for people with visual impairment as it provides the means to indicate the presence of objects and boundaries. While the sighted often fail to recognize the importance of their non-visual senses, the visually impaired must make full use of them.

The goal of the proposed framework is primarily to present an innovative interaction technique that allows haptic navigation through the internet for the visually impaired users as well as the haptic exploration of the conventional 2D maps found on the web. A rendering engine of web pages that was developed according to the proposed interaction technique is also presented. Haptic navigation enables free movement within the 3D scene and no sequence is imposed. Consequently, the time required to switch from one screen object to another object may be reduced at the price of a haptic exploration of the scene. Additionally, haptic interaction allows blind users to perceive the structure of the web page as well as provide access to the conventional 2D maps found on the web.

EXISTING ASSISTIVE TECHNOLOGIES FOR THE VISUALLY IMPAIRED

Some of the assistive devices for the visually impaired include alternative keyboards and pointing devices, speech recognition, eye tracking, Braille displays, and screen readers. Screen readers are the most popular assistive technology utilized by users with visual impairments. Because Braille literacy rates are low, speech output is the most common assistive technology for users with visual impairment (Yu et al., 2002). Additionally, other assistive devices for the blind, such as tactile displays, are prohibitively expensive. Screen readers are software packages that, working with computer speakers, read what is displayed on the computer screen out loud, in computer-synthesized speech. Two of the most popular screen readers are JAWS and Window-Eyes. There are also simple versions of screen readers built into some operating systems.

There has been a number of attempts to enhance screen readers. For instance, a math markup language was created to help users of screen readers better understand math formulas (Karshmer & Gillian, 2005). Although this is very helpful for a small subset of blind users, this is not widely used. Another tool, called BrookesTalk, is an integrated screen reader and Web browser tool (Yu et al., 2002). BrookesTalk is independent of visual browsers and also independent of text to speech software applications as it uses Microsoft speech technology. It includes the functionality of a standard Web browser for the blind. However, the main aim is to provide a search and orientation tool for blind users in the form of a virtual toolbar of functions that will provide different synopses of a Web page to help the user decide whether it will be useful to them or not (Zajicek et al., 1999).

Most blind users do type into a keyboard, as they have the keyboard layout memorized and do not need to see the keyboard to use it. Therefore, it is the output, not the input, that is most challenging for blind users (Lazar et al., 2007). Although the use of screen readers is common, visually impaired users can navigate through a web page only when its design follows the guidelines provided by widely known web accessibility standards (e.g. WCAG 2.0).

HAPTIC TECHNOLOGIES

Haptic technology is often used to represent complex graphic-based information. The term "haptic" commonly refers to the sense of touch. More specifically, the haptic sense consists of cutaneous touch and kinesthetic touch (Kim, 2010; Sallnas et al., 2000; Smith, 1997). Cutaneous touch is related to the sensations felt on surface features and tactile perception, which is conveyed via the skin. On the other hand, kinesthetic touch is part of the haptic sensations that involve muscles and tendons, which enable people to recognize the movements of limbs. The sense of haptic is influenced by both the cutaneous touch and the kinesthetic touch (Kim, 2010).

Haptic technology is relatively new, but is widely used across a variety of domains, including the automotive, cellular phone, and entertainment industries; education, training, and rehabilitation; controls and assistive technology development, and medical science; and the scientific study of touch (Hayward et al., 2004). Additionally, haptic technology is embedded in mobile phones to enhance user experience. As of September 2008, over 25 million mobile phones featuring haptic technology were sold worldwide, with 7 million sold in the second quarter of 2008 alone (Ayala, 2008).

Currently, haptics are widely used in different types of applications (Butler & Neave, 2008). Grow et al. (2007) discuss the use of haptics as a means to educate. They propose the use of haptics to present the quantity of force of a ball on another planet, for example. They also briefly mention the use of haptics in museums. Hayward et al. (2004) propose that haptics could be utilized to illustrate physical phenomena, maths and anatomy. They also note that haptics have already been utilized in driving, flying, surgery and other professional simulations.

The study of haptics within the Information Technology community has recently been excited by the commercial availability of haptics devices.

There are many types of haptic devices available on the market, each allowing various degrees of freedom and each allowing force feedback to be produced. The defining deferential of these devices, compared to other devices which are only able to 'read' the users movement, is that they are able to provide feedback in the form of force (Butler & Neave, 2008). The device provides resistance to the user's movement and through this he/she is able to touch a virtual object. Asano et al. (2005) refer to it as a position input and force output device. This bidirectionality is, according to Hayward et al. (2004), the most distinguishing feature of haptic devices. They also comment that it is less complex to read the movement from the user than it is to produce the necessary experiences to guide user senses into recognising a virtual object.

Haptic interaction between the user and the interface or the device has many advantages as it is an intuitive and natural way of communication. Touch is the only sense that enables people to modify and manipulate things in the world (Minogue & Jones, 2006). Moreover, touch is superior to other senses in terms of the perception of certain properties (e.g., textures, compliance, elasticity, viscosity) (Minogue & Jones, 2006). According to brain plasticity theory, human beings have the capability to compensate for their handicaps through the reorganization of brain structure, which often results in enhanced capabilities in the remaining modalities, such as haptic perception (Kim, 2010). The sensory modality of touch in people with visual impairment becomes more enhanced than it is in sighted people.

Older adults with low vision can also be a target user group for haptic technology. Older adults' everyday lives are considerably influenced by haptics (Baccini et al., 2006, Urbano et al., 2005). Examples of haptic technology applications for the elderly include omni-directional mobile wheelchairs with a haptic joystick (Urbano et al., 2005), intelligent walkers with a haptic handle bar (Shim et al., 2005), and vibrating insoles for balance improvement (Priplata et al., 2009).

CHALLENGES IN HAPTIC INTERACTION

Haptic feedback offers an alternative way of presenting information to visually disabled users. Translating a visual model to a haptic model that can be accessed via touch preserves important properties of the data, including its spatial layout. However, a direct mapping is not a complete solution, as the limited 'point-contact' nature of current haptic technology makes successful haptic interaction and object's identification very difficult in the absence of visual stimuli (Jay et al., 2008).

With current haptic technology, interacting with 3D models in the absence of visual cues is not easy. A haptic model, which the user can touch and explore, appears to be a straightforward way of communicating the layout of the data, as the visual representation can be directly translated to the haptic model. Such a model preserves information about the connectivity and structure of the data, which may be difficult to convey using audio alone. Unfortunately, the point contact nature of the device (users normally interact with the virtual world using a single 'pen' probe or stylus) makes haptic interaction a very difficult task when no other information channel is used (e.g. audio).

As Sjostrom reports: 'For a blind person, locating an object with a point probe can be as hard as finding a needle in a haystack' (Sjostrom, 2001). Faconti et al. (2000) conducted an experiment examining how people interpret haptic versions of visual illusions, such as the Necker Cube. The results of the experiment showed that free and unconstrained interaction proved unfeasible (Faconti et al., 2000). If users were placed at a starting point on the relevant object (they were unable to find it without help), they could explore and recognize nearby parts of it, but they were unable to 'jump' from one object to another, thus missing considerable amount of information.

Some other studies report that even after locating an object, maintaining contact with it can be difficult, as the stylus has a tendency to fall off, particularly when the object is convex (Colwell et al., 1998; Sjostrom, 2001). Colwell et al. (1998) noticed that users which are not familiar with haptic interaction, can easily be lost in the virtual environment as they often lose contact with an object they are trying to explore.

The aforementioned problems result when haptic interaction within the virtual environment is completely unconstrained. To aid haptic data exploration for the visually impaired users, it seems appropriate to provide some sort of guidance to users, at least until they are familiar with the data, or confident in the task (Colwell et al., 1998). Sjostrom suggests the use of a virtual 'magnet' to pull users towards haptic items on a virtual desktop that would otherwise be hard to find (Sjostrom, 2001). Other studies have shown that advantage can be gained when the haptic modality is used in conjunction with the auditory channel (Yu et al., 2002). A multi-modal assistive interface could reduce the barriers that are faced by the blind and partially sighted community.

RELATED WORK

Numerous researchers have tried to apply haptic technology to help visually impaired users to understand graphic-based concepts (Brewster, 2002; Liffick, 2003; Plimmer, 2008; Sjostrom et al., 2003). Plimmer et al. (2008) studied the haptic-based educational software called McSig. Educators of students with visual impairment reported that McSig was helpful to students in understanding geometric principles. A force-feedback mouse was devised in the context of the Moose project (Liffick, 2003) to represent graphical interfaces such as windows, icons, and checkboxes, as well as spatial maps, to help students with blindness understand line graphs. Many information technology professionals and researchers have devised haptic-embedded applications including, for example, a haptic-embedded Internet browser (Rotard et al., 2008), games (Roth et al., 2000), maps (Harder & Michel, 2002; Lahav & Mioduser, 2008), a handheld device (Hoggan et al., 2008), and E-trade (Proctor & Vu, 2005). Carneiro et al. (2004) empirically explored the use of touch-based interfaces by visually impaired users. The survey showed that participants' error ratio was significantly reduced and their performances were enhanced, as well.

Related research on the use of haptic devices by visually impaired people includes identification of textures and object shape (Sjotrom & Rassmus-Grohn, 1999), mathematical learning environments and the exploration of mathematical graphs (Yu et al., 2001; Karshmer & Bledsoe, 2002), the exploration of geography maps using audio and tactile feedback (Paciello, 2000), and the construction of cognitive maps (Sanchez & Lumbreras, 1999; Semwal & Evans-Kamp, 2000). Yoshihiro Kawai and Fumiaki Tomita (1996) have presented an interactive tactile display system that is able to support blind people in recognizing 3D objects. Test recognition of geometrical and VRML objects, mathematical surfaces and traffic environment exploration are reported by Magnusson et al. (2002). Kurze et al. (1997, 1999) have done some work in the recognition of three-dimensional objects by blind people. In (Avizzano et al., 2003; Iglesias et al., 2004) authors presented the GRAB system, a new haptic device provided with a set of utilities and applications that allow blind persons to explore a 3D world through touch in conjunction with audio feedback.

Lahav and Mioduser in (2000) created a multi-sensory virtual environment enabling blind people to learn how to explore real life spaces (e.g. public buildings, school or work place). The user interface of their proposed virtual environment consists of a real rooms and objects simulation where users can navigate using a force feedback joystick.

Tzovaras et al. (2004) presented a more interactive and extensible haptic virtual reality system. The proposed method offers several advantages to blind users as compared with previous techniques: providing the ability to use virtual training environments with large workspace, supporting a rather natural interaction using the CyberGrasp haptic device.

There have been many research efforts dedicated to the assistance of the web navigation of the visual impaired. Haptic technologies that allow the presence of elements of HTML in virtual environments using force-feedback (Asakawa et al., 2002) and pin representations (O'Malley & Hughes, 2003) were developed. Hardwick et al. (Hardwick et al., 1998) proposed to use haptic devices to perceive the 3D images of internet pages, represented in the VRML way. Auditory and haptic environments were used by Asakawa et al. (2002) in order to present structured information, as groups of elements. The haptic representation was also used by Rotard et al. (2008), in order to represent information that does not contain text (eg tables, frames, colours and pictures) giving thus the possibility to the blind users of perceiving the visual representation of each web page. Roth & Pun (2003) developed an audio-haptic tool that enables blind users to explore digital pictures using the hearing and feeling modalities. Some similar studies (Morris & Joshi, 2003; Nikolakis et al., 2005) focus in the recognition of borders of each picture, showed that when the visual information is combined with haptic information, the recognition process becomes very effective. Nikolakis et al. (2005) developed an application that accepts as input an HTML page and creates the corresponding haptic representation. O'Malley & Hughes (2003) developed a tool that allows web designers to associate haptic information with 3D content based on VRML.

The need to improve the general usability of interactive maps is widely recognised (Nivala et al., 2003; Nivala et al., 2008, Nivala et al., 2007). Map users desire increasingly intelligent systems that are aware of the context, adaptive and flexible for different types of users, and adaptive to the usage situation and the devices on which maps are presented (Nivala & Sarjakoski, 2003; Sarjakoski & Nivala, 2005). Information contained in maps needs to be simplified and personalized to the specific usage situation (Sarjakoski & Sarjakoski, 2008; Sarjakoski & Sarjakoski, 2007; Scalable Vector Graphics, 2003), as in the case of visually impaired users.

Recent years have witnessed significant efforts on developing computer-based technologies for making maps accessible to people who are blind. The exploration and learning of a new environment by visually impaired users is a complex and difficult process, and requires the use of special information-technology aids. There are two types of aids: passive and active. Passive aids provide the user with information before his/her arrival to the environment. Examples of these include verbal descriptions, tactile maps, strip maps, and physical models (Herman et al., 1983; Rieser, 1989; Ungar et al., 1996; Espinosa & Ochaita, 1998). Active aids provide the user with information in situ, for example, Sonicguide (Warren & Strelow, 1985), Kaspa (Easton & Bentzen, 1999), Talking Signs, embedded sensors in the environment (Crandall et al., 1995), virtual sound display (Loomis et al., 1998; Loomis et al., 2005) and Personal Guidance System (PGS), based on satellite communication (Golledge et al., 1996; Golledge et al., 2004).

Jansson et al. (2005) studied the use of auditory and haptic feedback (VTPlayer) in map recognition and they stressed the big importance of border identification as well as the design of the haptic feedback. The University of Michigan provides the visually impaired students with a full tactile map of the University Campus (Disability INformation Resources). This specific tactile map, based on the Braille code, provides not only navigational assistance but also useful information concerning campus functionality like the courses program. Scalable Vector Graphics (SVG) maps (2003) have also been proposed.

Scalable Vector Graphics maps contain sound effects as also description tags and are based on SVG, which is a modularized XML-based language for describing two-dimensional vector and mixed vector/raster graphics. Wang et al. (2009) propose an automatic approach, complete with a prototype system, for supporting instant access to maps for local navigation by people with visual impairment. The approach first detects and segments texts from a map image and recreates the remaining graphical parts in a tactile form which can be reproduced immediately through a tactile printer. Then, it generates an SVG file, which integrates both text and graphical information. The tactile hardcopy and the SVG file together are used to provide a user with interactive access to the map image through a touchpad, resulting in a tactile-audio representation of the original input image. This supports real-time access to the map without tedious conversion by a sighted professional. Kostopoulos et al. (2007) proposed information extract from bitmapped maps through image processing and its representation using haptics and audio.

FROM HTML COMPONENTS TO HAPGETS

The proposed innovative interaction technique that enables haptic navigation on the web includes the transformation of each HTML component into a "hapget" (haptically-enhanced widget) (Kaklanis et al., 2008), a three dimensional widget with haptic feedback. The correspondence between the HTML components currently supported and their 3D equivalents (hapgets) is depicted on Figure 1. For each HTML component there are some predefined available choices for the corresponding hapget. It is obvious that the 3D shape of each hapget is very innovative and completely different from the 2D shape of the corresponding HTML component. The goal is to define some unique 3D objects that a visually impaired user would easily recognize using a haptic device (such as the PHANTOM[1]) even if the 3D representation has no similarities with the corresponding 2D representation. Each hapget contains a 3D representation (Figure 1) with haptic feedback, a description, an earcon, which is a short audio signal, and a haptic icon, which is a short haptic signal (Pasquero et al., 2006; Kaklanis et al., 2009). The haptic icon in conjunction with the earcon and the unique 3D shape of the hapget help the visually impaired user to identify the type (e.g. button, selection list, hyperlink, image, etc.) of the object that is "touched" using a haptic device. Each hapget has also concrete haptic characteristics such as: static friction, dynamic friction, stiffness, and some haptic effects (buzz effect, constraint effect, and inertia effect) that make the identification more easy and efficient.

A HAPTIC RENDERING ENGINE OF WEB PAGES

A rendering engine has been developed, in order to support the proposed interaction technique. The user can give a URL as input to the application, then the necessary transformations are executed and finally a 3D scene corresponding to the web page is created. The architecture of the rendering engine is presented in Figure 2.

As depicted in Figure 2, the rendering engine currently supports HTML components of eight different types (button, hyperlink, text, selection list, image, image with hyperlink, input text and checkbox). Each HTML component is transformed into the corresponding hapget containing a 3D representation with haptic feedback, a description, an earcon and a haptic icon. For hapgets representing images, (with or without hyperlink) there is also a 2D representation, which contains the original image. The application exploits the vi-

Figure 1. HTML components and their corresponding hapgets

HTML Component	Corresponding hapget (available choices)	
Hyperlink		
Image		
Image with hyperlink		
Text		
Selection list		
Input text		
Button		
Checkbox		

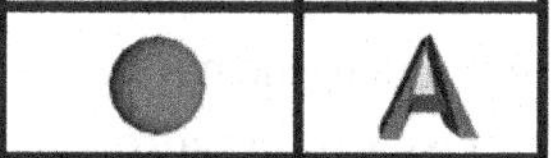

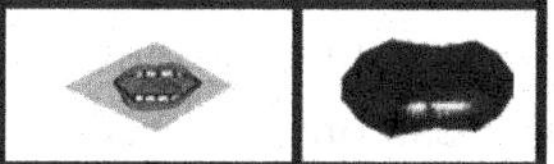

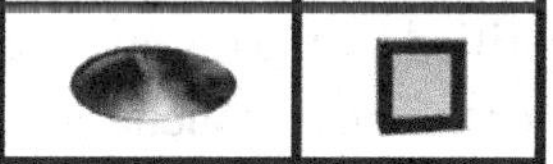

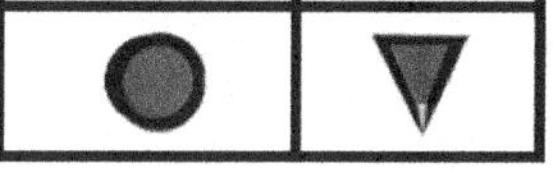

123

Figure 2. The architecture of the rendering engine

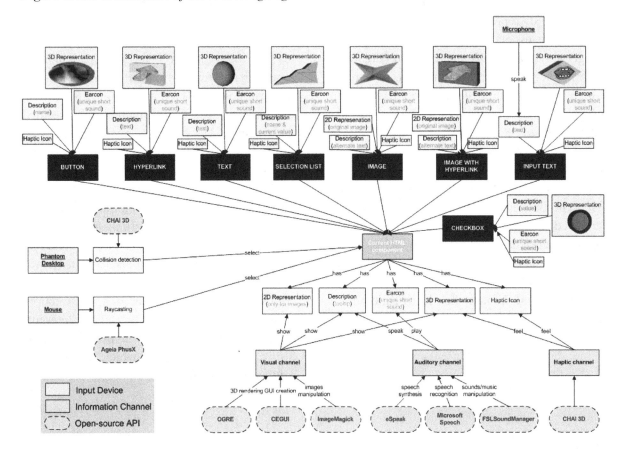

sual, the auditory as well as the haptic information channel.

The target group of users includes users with low vision as well as blind users. Thus, the representations of the components has to be meaningful for both categories. For instance, an image has no meaning for a blind person but the description of the image (alternate text) has. For this purpose, a speech synthesis engine is integrated to the haptic rendering engine so as to give visually impaired people the opportunity to hear what they cannot read. A speech-recognition engine, which offers the opportunity of inserting text without typing is also integrated. Additionally, earcons are used so as each widget can be identified by the unique short sound which is heard when the cursor touches one of the widget's surfaces.

The application has mouse support for low-sighted users and PHANTOM support for blind users. When the user navigates through the 3D scene using the mouse, the interaction with the hapgets is based on the raycasting technique (Figure 3).

According to the raycasting technique, the position of the cursor is calculated in each frame. Then, a ray on the z axis that intersects the specific point is calculated and the first 3D object that is being "hit" by the ray is considered as selected object.

When the PHANTOM is used for the interaction with the application, the selection of the hapgets is based on the collision detection technique (Figure 4).

According to the collision detection technique, possible collisions between the 3D cursor and the

Figure 3. Raycasting technique

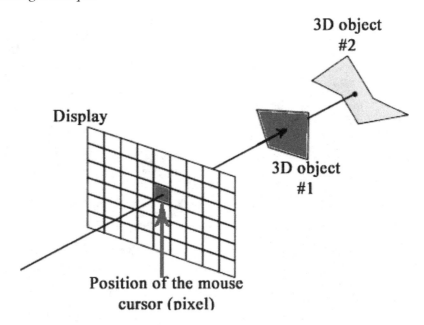

hapgets are being detected in each frame (Moustakas et al., 2007). If the cursor collides with a hapget, the hapget is considered as selected.

When the PHANTOM is in contact with a hapget, the user immediately hears the earcon that corresponds to the hapget. If user presses the LC-TRL button of the keyboard while the PHANTOM is in contact with an object, the object's description is heard via the speech synthesis engine.

Figure 5 illustrates a screenshot of the application and depicts the correspondence between the hapgets and the original HTML components, as they can be shown in a common web browser.

There is a set of options that the user can set according to specific needs/preferences. User can enable/disable the earcons and the haptic icons, exclude some component types from visual and haptic rendering, set the value of friction and stiffness for each hapget as well as change the size of the hapgets.

For a novice user it is recommended to use large hapgets, because as the size of the hapgets become larger, the identification of each hapget using the PHANTOM becomes easier/faster. The

negative point of having large hapgets is that the number of the hapgets contained in the 3D scene at a time becomes smaller and its consequence is the slower navigation in the web page. Figure 6 presents a test case where large hapgets have been chosen.

For every visited web site, a UsiXML document describing the corresponding 3D scene (including visual and haptic features, like hapgets' position) is automatically generated (Figure 7). UsiXML[2] is an XML-based language that describes multimodal user interfaces. The generated UsiXML document can be saved locally for further use. Additionally, a previously saved UsiXML file can be reloaded.

HAPTIC EXPLORATION OF 2D MAPS FOUND ON THE WEB

If an image included in a web page is identified as a map, a haptic-aural representation of the 2D map is automatically created. During this process, the road network structure, including street names,

Figure 4. Collision detection technique

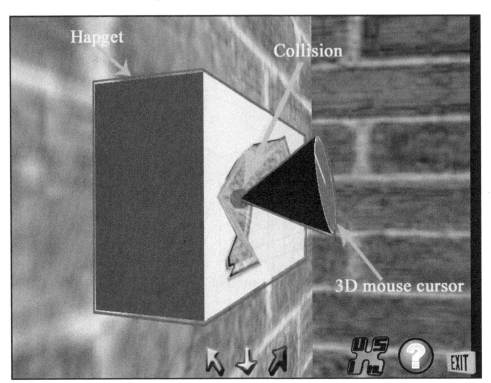

is recognized and a corresponding pseudo-3D representation is automatically created. Optical Character Recognition (OCR) as well as Text To Speech (TTS) mechanisms are being used in conjunction with the pseudo-3D representation for the multimodal map generation (Moustakas et al., 2007). For the efficiency of the multimodal map generation process there are some constraints that have to be followed concerning the color, the positioning, the resolution and some special symbols.

Figure 8 presents a test case where a visited web page includes a 2D map. In that case, the user can go into map exploration mode in order to haptically explore the map.

Prerequisites of the 2D Map

A number of map prerequisites that the map should meet have been carefully chosen in order to design a system that will not depend on the map provider. In particular:

Color constraints: Street names should be represented using a dark color in order to be discernible from the rest of the map and thus advancing the process of their recognition.

Positioning: Street names should be located inside the associated road so as to attain their correspondence.

Resolution: Map resolution should be adequate to utilize an OCR algorithm to retrieve street names.

Figure 5. Test case: "IGI Publishing: Call for Chapters" (http://old.igi-global.com/requests/details. asp?ID=752)

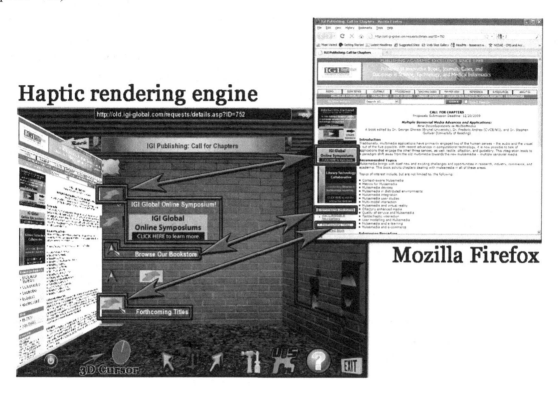

Figure 6. Large hapgets

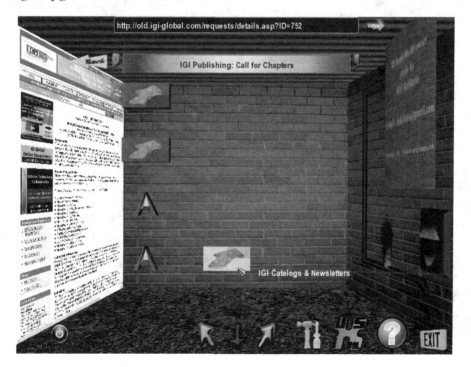

Map Image Analysis

The map image analysis includes the following steps:

- road names identification
  - An image containing only the road names is generated.
- road network structure identification
  - An image containing the graph of the road network structure is generated.
- 3D map model construction
  - The 3D map model is generated.
- road names transformation into speech
  - The road names are recognized by the OCR and the TTS module transforms them into speech.

In order to extract the road names, first of all, an erosion filter is applied to the primary image. The produced image is then subjected to thresholding dithering to two colours. Next, color inversion is applied. A region growing algorithm is applied in order to get the image segments containing the road names. A chromatic identity is given to each segment to enable the identification of each distinct road (Figure 9).

In order to find the relative angle of each road with respect to the X axis, dilation is initially applied in order to expand the road names and then the angle is calculated using linear Least Squares. By knowing the position of each image segment containing a road name in conjunction with the angle from the X axis and the chromatic identity of each road, the graph of the road network structure is generated.

For the estimation of the road network structure, the system initially discards all street names from the primary map and then connected operators (Salembier et al., 1998) are applied as illustrated in Figure 11.

Figure 7. Automatically generated UsiXML document describing the current state of the 3D scene

During the first step, the image g_0 is calculated according to the equation:

$$g_o = \delta_c(M) + T^{-1}[M] \tag{1}$$

where M is the primary map, $\delta_c(M)$ is the dilation of M and $T^{-1}[M]$ is the binary image of the street name's regions.

In the second step, the image g_k is calculated according to the equation:

$$g_k = \max(\varepsilon_c(g_{k-1}), M) \tag{2}$$

where $\varepsilon_c(g_{k-1})$ is the erosion of (g_{k-1}).

Next, the two sequential terms g_{k-1} and g_k are being examined. If

$$\beta = \frac{N_V}{RC} = \begin{cases} \geq Thr, \text{ end} \\ < Thr, \text{ proceed in step b} \end{cases} \tag{3}$$

where N_V is the amount of elements of set V,

$$V = \left\{ (x,y) \in g_k \mid g_{k(x,y)} = g_{k-1(x,y)} \right\} \tag{4}$$

R, C are the dimensions of the image and Thr is the relative threshold experimentally selected to be: Thr = 0.98.

The next step is the construction of the 3D map model. The 3D representation of the map is generated as a grooved line map (Moustakas et al., 2007) (Figure 10b). The grooved line map has been chosen since it is reported in the literature that such a structure is better perceived using a haptic device, when compared to a raised line map (Pun et al., 2007).

Finally, for the transformation of the road names into speech, an OCR[3] (Optical Character Recognition) as well as a TTS[4] (Text-to-Speech) module are being used (Moustakas et al., 2007). Figure 12 presents the procedure that is followed

Figure 8. Test case: "Canton Beach Holiday Park Caravan, Camping and Cabin Tourist Park Accommodation" (http://www.cantonbeachhp.com.au/contact_us.html)

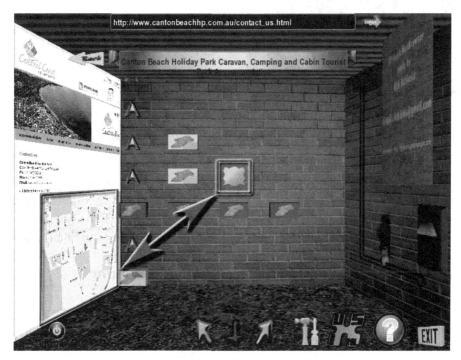

Figure 9. Road names identification

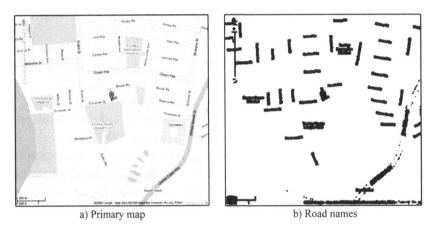

a) Primary map   b) Road names

Figure 10. Road network structure identification and 3D map model creation

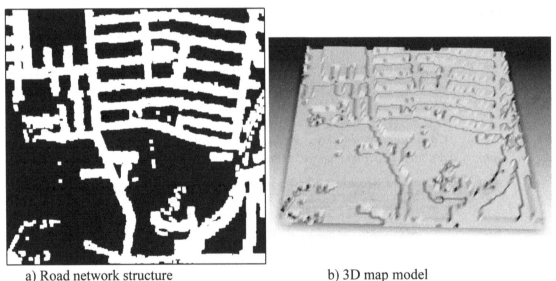

a) Road network structure   b) 3D map model

in order to extract the names of the roads and transform them into speech. First of all, the image that contains only the road names is generated. In step (b), the segment that contains the name of each road is recognized as well as the angle of the name from the X axis. In steps (c) and (d) the corresponding parts of the primary map image containing the road names are being cut. The segments are first converted into black and white images and then they are being rotated and scaled

in order to be used by the OCR (Optical Character Recognition) module.

The OCR module outputs the recognized text and passes it to the TTS (Text-to-Speech) module in order to be transformed into speech.

Haptic Rendering

Since the map environment is static, a force-field haptic rendering method is supported by the pro-

Figure 11. Anti-extensive connected operators block diagram (Kostopoulos et al., 2007)

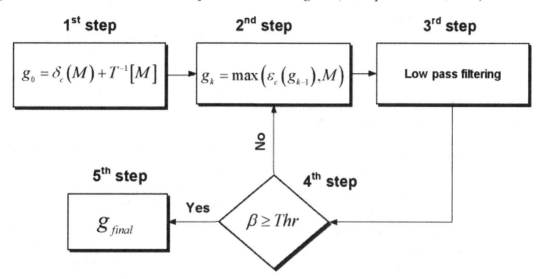

Figure 12. Road names transformation into speech

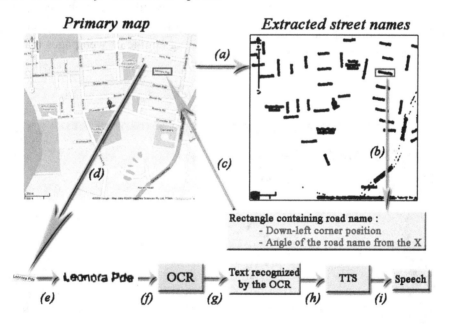

posed framework that generates a 3D force field from visual data (Moustakas et al., 2007). While the user is navigating in the virtual environment, the force value that corresponds to the user's current position is displayed through the haptic device. The typical spring-damper model (Burdea, 1996)

is used to calculate the force feedback's magnitude. In particular, for a point z that enters the surface, the magnitude of the applied force is $\|F\| = k \cdot d$ where k is the elasticity constant and d the distance of z from the surface obtained from the distance field D. Summarizing the final force feedback for a point $z \in \mathrm{R}^3$ can be calculated it as follows:

$$F_{haptic} = k \cdot D(x) \cdot F(x), \qquad (5)$$

where D(x) and F(x) are the value and the vector stored in the distance and force field, respectively.

Map Exploration Mode

When the user is in contact with a hapget whose alternative text or URL show that it is a map, the user can choose to step into map exploration mode.

In map exploration mode (Figure 13), the 3D model of the map is automatically created as previously explained. The original 2D map is visually rendered and the generated 3D model is visually and haptically rendered, in a way that maintains consistent matching between the positioning of the 2D image and the 3D model at X and Y axis. During the exploration of the multimodal map, audio messages inform the user about his/her position on the map (including street names, crossroads, etc.).

The haptic and audio feedback of the generated multimodal map offer passive aids to visually impaired users, providing them with information before their arrival to the real environment.

CONCLUSION AND FUTURE WORK

In the present chapter, an innovative interaction technique that enables haptic navigation through the web as well as haptic exploration of 2D maps found in web pages was presented. According to the proposed technique, each web page is transformed into an equivalent 3D scene and each 2D map found in a web page is transformed into a multimodal (haptic-aural) map. This offers great potential for the visually impaired users to have access to information that is totally inaccessible using the existing assistive technologies. A rendering engine of web pages that was developed

Figure 13. Multimodal map exploration

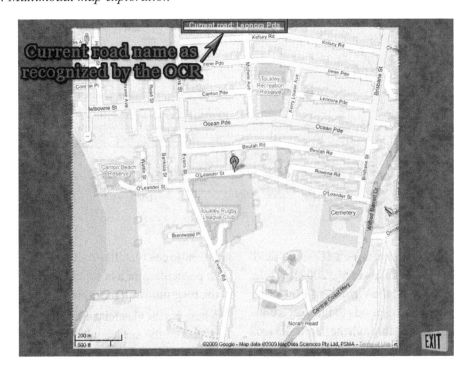

according to the proposed interaction technique was also presented.

Future extensions of the proposed framework may include support for more HTML components, Javascript, Java applets, Flash technologies, ActiveX components, files downloading/uploading, bookmarks, history and user profiling. Additionally, possible interconnection of the proposed rendering engine with some of the most known geographical information systems (GIS) (e.g. Google Maps, OpenStreetMap, etc.) will be examined.

REFERENCES

Amemiya, T., Ando, H., & Maeda, T. (2008). Lead-me interface for a pulling sensation from hand-held devices. *ACM Transactions on Applied Perception*, *5*(3), 1–17. doi:10.1145/1402236.1402239

Asakawa, C., Takagi, H., Ino, S., & Ifukube, T. (2002). *Auditory and Tactile Interfaces for Representing the Visual Effects on the Web. Proc. Assets, 65.-72.* ACM Press.

Asano, T., Ishibashi, Y., Minezawa, S., & Fujimoto, M. (2005). Surveys of exhibition planners and visitors about a distributed haptic museum. *Proceedings of the 2005 ACM SIGCHI International Conference on Advances in computer entertainment technology*. Valencia, Spain, ACM Press.

Avizzano, C., Marcheschi, S., Angerilli, M., Fontana, M., Bergamasco, M., Gutierrez, T., & Mannegeis, M. (2003). A multi-finger haptic interface for visually impaired people. *Robot and Human Interactive Communication, 2003. Proceedings. ROMAN, 2003*, 165–170.

Ayala, A. (2008). Immersion hits another milestone: 25 million mobile phones sold with touch feedback technology, *http://ir.immersion.com/releasedetail.cfm?ReleaseID=331864.*

Baccini, M., Rinaldi, L. A., Federighi, G., Vannucchi, L., Paci, M., & Masotti, G. (2006). Effectiveness of fingertip light contact in reducing postural sway in older people. *Age and Ageing*, afl072.

Brajnik, G. (2004). Achieving universal web access through specialized user interfaces. *In: Stephanidis, C. (ed.) Proceedings of 8th ERCIM UI4ALL'04 Workshop*, Vienna, Austria, 28–29 June.

Brewster, S. A. (2002). Visualization tools for blind people using multiple modalities. *Disability and Rehabilitation*, *24*, 613–621. doi:10.1080/09638280110111388

Burdea, G. C. (1996). *Force and Touch Feedback for Virtual Reality*. Wiley-Interscience.

Butler, M., & Neave, P. (2008). Object appreciation through haptic interaction, *In Hello! Where are you in the landscape of educational technology? Proceedings ascilite Melbourne 2008*, http://www.ascilite.org.au/ conferences/melbourne08/ procs/butler-m.pdf.

Carneiro, M. M., & Velho, L. (2004). *Assistive interfaces for the visually impaired using force feedback devices and distance transforms*. Info. Tech.and Disab.E J.

Colwell, C., Petrie, H., Kornbrot, D., Hardwick, A., & Furner, S. (1998). Haptic virtual reality for blind computer users. In *Assets '98: Proceedings of the third international ACM conference on Assistive technologies*. ACM Press, New York, NY, USA, 92–99.

Crandall, W., Bentzen, B. L., Myers, L., & Mitchell, P. (1995). Transit Accessibility Improvement Through Talking Signs Remote Infrared Signage, a Demonstration and Evaluation. *Washington, DC: Final report to US Department of Transportation, Federal Transit Administration and Project ACTION of the National Easter Seal Society*, 1-30. Disability INformation Resources (DINF). *http://www.dinf.ne.jp/doc/ english/Us Eu/conf/csun 98/*

Easton, R. D., & Bentzen, B. L. (1999). The effect of extended acoustic training on spatial updating in adults who are congenitally blind. *Journal of Visual Impairment & Blindness, 93*(7), 405–415.

Espinosa, M. A., & Ochaita, E. (1998). Using tactile maps to improve the practical spatial knowledge of adults who are blind. *Journal of Visual Impairment & Blindness, 92*(5), 338–345.

Faconti, G. P., Massink, M., Bordegoni, M., Angelis, F. D., & Booth, S. (2000). Haptic cues for image disambiguation. *Computer Graphics Forum, 19*, 3. doi:10.1111/1467-8659.00409

Gerber, E., & Kirchner, C. (2001). Who's surfing? Internet access and computer use by visually impaired youths and adults. *Journal of Visual Impairment & Blindness, 95*, 176–181.

Golledge, R. G., Klatzky, R. L., & Loomis, J. M. (1996). Cognitive mapping and wayfinding by adults without vision. In Portugali, J. (Ed.), *The Construction of Cognitive Maps* (pp. 215–246). Netherlands: Kluwer Academic Publishers. doi:10.1007/978-0-585-33485-1_10

Golledge, R. G., Marston, J. R., Loomis, J. M., & Klatzky, R. L. (2004). Stated preferences for components of a personal guidance system for nonvisual navigation. *Journal of Visual Impairment & Blindness, 98*(3), 135–147.

Scalable Vector Graphics (SVG) 1.1 (2003) *Specification W3C Recommendation.*

Grow, D. I., Verner, L. N., & Okamura, A. M. (2007). Educational Haptics. *AAAI 2007 Spring Symposia - Robots and Robot Venues*, Resources for AI Education.

Hackett, S., Parmanto, B., & Zeng, X. (2004). Accessibility of Internet web sites through time. *In: Proceedings of the Sixth International ACM Conference on Computers and Accessibility*, pp. 32–39. ACM Press, Atlanta, GA, USA.

Harder, A., & Michel, R. (2002). The Target-Route Map: Evaluating Its Usability for Visually Impaired Persons. *Journal of Visual Impairment & Blindness, 96*, 711.

Hardwick, A., Furner, S., & Rush, J. (1998). Tactile display of virtual reality from the World Wide Web - a potential access method for blind people. *Displays, 18*(3), 153–161. doi:10.1016/S0141-9382(98)00016-X

Hayward, v., Astley, O., Cruz-Hernandez, M., Grant, D., & Robles-De-La-Torre, G. (2004), Haptic interfaces and devices. *Sensor Review, 24*, 16-29.

Herman, J. F., Herman, T. G., & Chatman, S. P. (1983). Constructing cognitive maps from partial information: a demonstration study with congenitally blind subjects. *Journal of Visual Impairment & Blindness, 77*(5), 195–198.

Hoggan, E., Brewster, S. A., & Johnston, J. (2008). Investigating the effectiveness of tactile feedback for mobile touchscreens. *Proceeding of the twenty-sixth annual SIGCHI conference on Human factors in computing systems*, 1573-1582.

Iglesias, R., Casado, S., Gutierrez, T., Barbero, J., Avizzano, C., & Marcheschi, S. (2004). Computer graphics access for blind people through a haptic and audio virtual environment. *Haptic, Audio and Visual Environments and Their Applications, 2004. HAVE, 2004*, 13–18.

Jansson, G., Juhasz, I., & Cammilton, A. (2005). A virtual map read with a haptic mouse: Effects of some tactile and audio-tactile information options. *Tactile Graphics, 2005*, 49–50.

Jay, C., Stevens, R., Hubbold, R., & Glencross, M. (2008). Using haptic cues to aid non-visual structure recognition. *ACM Transactions on Applied Perception, 5*(2). doi:10.1145/1279920.1279922

Kaklanis, N., Gonzalez Calleros, J. M., Vanderdonckt, J., & Tzovaras, D. (2008). Hapgets, Towards Haptically-enhanced Widgets based on a User Interface Description Language. *Proc. of Multimodal interaction through haptic feedback (MITH) Workshop*, Naples, May 28-30.

Kaklanis, N., Tzovaras, D., & Moustakas, K. (2009). *Haptic navigation in the World Wide Web*. HCI International.

Karshmer, A., & Gillian, D. (2005). Math readers for blind students: errors, frustrations, and the need for a better technique. *Proceedings of the 2005 International Conference on Human-Computer Interaction (HCII)*.

Karshmer, A. I., & Bledsoe, C. (2002). Access to mathematics by blind students—introduction to the special thematic session. *International Conference on Computers Helping People with Special Needs (ICCHP)*, Linz, Austria.

Kawai, Y., & Tomita, F. (1996). Interactive tactile display system: a support system for the visually disabled to recognize 3D objects. *In Proceedings of the second annual ACM conference on Assistive technologies*, pages 45-50.

Kim, H. N. (2010). Usable Accessibility and Haptic User Interface Design Approach, *PhD Dissertation, Blacksburg, Virginia, http://scholar.lib.vt.edu/theses/* available/etd-04152010-092642/unrestricted/ HNKim-Dissertation.pdf.

Kortum, P. (2008). *HCI beyond the GUI: Design for haptic, speech, olfactory, and other nontraditional interfaces*. Burlington, MA: Morgan Kaufmann.

Kostopoulos, K., Moustakas, K., Tzovaras, D., & Nikolakis, G. Thillou, & C., Gosselin, B. (2007), Haptic Access To Conventional 2D Maps For The Visually Impaired. *Journal on Multimodal User Interfaces, Vol. 1, No. 2*.

Kurze, M. (1997). Interaktion Blinder mit virtuellen Welten auf der Basis von zweidimensionalen taktilen Darstellungen. *In Tagungsband Software-Ergonomie 97*.

Kurze, M. (1999). Methoden zur computergenerierten Darstellung raumlicher Gegenstande fur Blinde auf taktilen Medien. *PhD thesis, Department of mathematics and Computer Science, Freie UniversitÄat Berlin*.

Lahav, O., & Mioduser, D. (2000). Multisensory virtual environment for supporting blind persons acquisition of spatial cognitive mapping, orientation, and mobility skills. *Proceedings of the Third International Conference on Disability, Virtual Reality and Associated Technologies, ICDVRAT 2000*, pages 23-25.

Lahav, O., & Mioduser, D. (2008). Haptic-feedback support for cognitive mapping of unknown spaces by people who are blind. *International Journal of Human-Computer Studies, 66*, 23–35. doi:10.1016/j.ijhcs.2007.08.001

Lazar, J., Allen, A., Kleinman, J., & Malarkey, C. (2007). What Frustrates Screen Reader Users on the Web: A Study of 100 Blind Users. *International Journal of Human-Computer Interaction, 22*(3), 247–269. doi:10.1080/10447310709336964

Lazar, J., Beere, P., Greenidge, K., & Nagappa, Y. (2003). Web accessibility in the mid-Atlantic United States: a study of 50 home pages. *Univers. Access Inf. Soc., 2*(4), 1–11.

Liffick, B. W. (2003), A haptics experiment in assistive technology for undergraduate HCI students. *HCI International 2003*.

Loomis, J. M., Golledge, R. G., & Klatzky, R. L. (1998). Navigation system for the blind: auditory display modes and guidance. *Presence (Cambridge, Mass.), 7*, 193–203. doi:10.1162/105474698565677

Loomis, J. M., Marston, J. R., Golledge, R. G., & Klatzky, R. L. (2005). Personal guidance system for people with visual impairment: a comparison of spatial displays for route guidance. *Journal of Visual Impairment & Blindness, 99*(4), 219–232.

MacLean, K. E., Shaver, M. J., & Pai, D. K. (2002). Handheld Haptics: A USB Media Controller with Force Sensing. *Symp. On Haptic Interfaces for Virtual Environment and Teleoperator Systems, IEEE-VR.*

Magnusson, C., & Rassmus-Grohn, K. (2005). A Virtual Traffic Environment for People with Visual Impairments. *Visual Impairment Research, 7*(1), 1–12. doi:10.1080/13882350490907100

Magnusson, C., Rassmus-Grohn, K., Sjostrom, C., & Danielsson, H. (2002). Navigation and recognition in complex haptic virtual environments - reports from an extensive study with blind users. *Proceedings of Eurohaptics.*

Magnusson, C., Tan, C., & Yu, W. (2006). Haptic Access to 3D Objects on the Web. *Proc. Eurohaptics.* MapQuest: http://www.mapquest.com/

MapsG.http://maps.google.com/

Mcmullin, B. (2002). Users with disability need not apply? Web accessibility in Ireland. *First Monday, http://www.firstmonday.org* /issues/issue7_12/mcmullin/

Minogue, J., & Jones, M. G. (2006). Haptics in Education: Exploring an Untapped Sensory Modality. *Review of Educational Research, 76,* 317–348. doi:10.3102/00346543076003317

Morris, D. & Joshi, N. (2003). Alternative 'Vision': A Haptic and Auditory Assistive Device. *CHI 2003 Extended Abstracts.*

Moustakas, K., Nikolakis, G., Kostopoulos, K., Tzovaras, D., & Strintzis, M. G. (2007). Haptic Rendering of Visual Data for the Visually Impaired. *IEEE Multimedia Magazine, 14*(1), 62–72. doi:10.1109/MMUL.2007.10

Moustakas, K., Tzovaras, D., Dybkjaer, L., & Bernsen, N. O. (2009). *A Modality Replacement Framework for the Communication between Blind and Hearing Impaired People.* HCI International.

Moustakas, K., Tzovaras, D., & Strintzis, M. G. (2007). SQ-Map: Efficient Layered Collision Detection and Haptic Rendering. *IEEE Transactions on Visualization and Computer Graphics, 13*(1), 80–93. doi:10.1109/TVCG.2007.20

Murphy, E., Kuber, R., McAllister, G., Strain, P. & Yu, W. (2008). An Empirical Investigation into the Difficulties Experienced by Visually Impaired Internet Users. *Journal of Universal Access in the Information Society.*

Nikolakis, G., Moustakas, K., Tzovaras, D., & Strintzis, M. G. (2005). *Haptic Representation of Images for the Blind and the Visually Impaired.* Las Vegas: HCI International.

Nikolakis, G., Tsampoulatidis, I., Tzovaras, D., & Strintzis, G. (2004). Haptic Browser: A Haptic Environment to Access HTML pages. *SPECOM 2004.*

Nivala, A. M., Brewster, S. A., & Sarjakoski, L. T. (2008). Usability Evaluation of Web Mapping Sites. *The Cartographic Journal Use and Users Special Issue, 45*(2), 129–138.

Nivala, A. M., & Sarjakoski, L. T. (2003). Need for Context-Aware Topographic Maps in Mobile Devices. In Virrantaus, K., & Tveite, H. (Eds.), *ScanGIS'2003.* Espoo, Finland.

Nivala, A. M., Sarjakoski, L. T., Jakobsson, A., & Kaasinen, E. (2003). Usability Evaluation of Topographic Maps in Mobile Devices. *21st International Cartographic Conference,* Durban, South Africa.

Nivala, A. M., Sarjakoski, L. T., & Sarjakoski, T. (2007). Usability methods' familiarity among map application developers. *IJHCS, Int. J. Human-Computer Studies, Elsevier, 65*, 784–795. doi:10.1016/j.ijhcs.2007.04.002

O'Malley, M., & Hughes, S. (2003). Simplified Authoring of 3D Haptic Content for the World Wide Web. *Proceedings of 11th International Symposium on Haptic Interfaces for Virtual Environment and Teleoperator Systems*, pp. 428-429, Los Angeles, California, USA, 22-23 March 2003. OpenStreetMap: http://www.openstreetmap.org/

Paciello, M. (2000). *Web accessibility for people with disabilities*. Lawrence, KS: CMP Books.

Parente, P., & Bishop, G. (2003). *BATS: The Blind Audio Tactile Mapping System*. Savannah, GA: ACMSE.

Pasquero, J., Luk, J., Little, S., & MacLean, K. (2006). Perceptual Analysis of Haptic Icons: an Investigation into the Validity of Cluster Sorted MDS, *Proceedings of the Symposium on Haptic Interfaces for Virtual Environment and Teleoperator Systems*, p.67.

Petrie, H., Fisher, W., O'Neill, A., Fisher, W., & Di Segni, Y. (2001). Deliverable 2.1: Report on user requirements of mainstream readers and print disabled readers. *Available:http://www.multireader.org /workplan.htm*.

Petrie, H., Morley, S., Mcnally, P., O'Neill, A. M., & Majoe, D. (1997). Initial design and evaluation of an interface to hypermedia systems for blind users. *In: Bernstein, M., Carr, L., Osterbye, K. (eds.) Proceedings of the Eighth ACM Conference On Hypertext*, pp. 48–56. ACM Press, Southampton, UK, April 6–11.

Plimmer, B., Crossan, A., Brewster, S. A., & Blagojevic, R. (2008). Multimodal collaborative handwriting training for visually-impaired people. *Proceeding of the twenty-sixth annual SIGCHI conference on Human factors in computing systems*, 393-402.

Priplata, A. A., Niemi, J. B., Harry, J. D., Lipsitz, L. A., & Collins, J. J. (2009). Vibrating insoles and balance control in elderly people. *Lancet, 362*.

Proctor, R. W., & Vu, K. P. L. (2005). *Handbook of human factors in Web design*. London: Lawrence Erlbaum Associates.

Pun, T., Roth, P., Bologna, G., Moustakas, K., & Tzovaras, D. (2007). Image and video processing for visually handicapped people, *Eurasip International Journal on Image and Video Processing, volume 2007*, article ID 25214.

Ramloll, R., Yu, W., Brewster, S., Riedel, B., Burton, M., & Dimigen, G. (2000). Constructing sonified haptic line graphs for the blind student: First steps, *ACM conference on Assistive technologies*, (Arlington, USA).

Rieser, J. J. (1989). Access to knowledge of spatial structure at noval points of observation. *Journal of Experimental Psychology. Learning, Memory, and Cognition, 15*(6), 1157–1165. doi:10.1037/0278-7393.15.6.1157

Rotard, M., Knodler, S., & Ertl, T. (2005). A Tactile Web Browser for the Visually Disabled. *Proc Hypertext and Hypermedia*, ACM Press, 5-22.

Rotard, M., Taras, C., & Ertl, T. (2008). Tactile Web Browsing for Blind People. *In Multimedia Tools and Applications*, Springer, Vol. 37(1):53-69.

Roth, P., Petrucci, L., Assimacopoulos, A., & Pun, T. (2000). From dots to shapes: An auditory haptic game platform for teaching geometry to blind pupils. *ICCHP 2000, International Conference on Computer Helping People with Speical Needs, Karlsruhe, Germany,* 603-610.

Roth, P., Petrucci, L. S., Assimacopoulos, A., & Pun, T. (2000). Audio-Haptic Internet Browser And Associated Tools For Blind And Visually Impaired Computer Users. *In Workshop on Friendly Exchanging Through the Net,* 57-62.

Roth, P. & Pun, T. (2003). Design and Evaluation of a Multimodal System for the Non-Visual Exploration of Digital Pictures. *In proceedings of Interact '03.*

Salembier, P., Oliveras, A., & Garrido, L. (1998). Anti-extensive connected operators for image and sequence processing. *IEEE Transactions on Image Processing, 7,* 555–570. doi:10.1109/83.663500

Sallnas, E. L., Rassmus-Grohn, K., & Sjostrom, C. (2000). Supporting presence in collaborative environments by haptic force feedback. *ACM Transactions on Computer-Human Interaction, 7,* 461–476. doi:10.1145/365058.365086

Sanchez, J., & Lumbreras, M. (1999). Virtual environment interaction through 3D audio by blind children. *Journal of Cyberpsychology and Behavior, 2*(2), 101–111. doi:10.1089/cpb.1999.2.101

Sarjakoski, L. T., & Nivala, A. M. (2005). Adaptation to Context - A Way to Improve the Usability of Mobile Maps. In Meng, L., Zipf, A., & Reichenbacher, T. (Eds.), *Mapbased mobile services - Theories, Methods and Implementations* (pp. 107–123). Springer Berlin Heidelberg New York.

Sarjakoski, L. T., & Sarjakoski, T. (2008). *User Interfaces and Adaptive Maps. Encyclopedia of GIS* (pp. 1205–1212). Springer.

Sarjakoski, T., & Sarjakoski, L. T. (2007). A Real-Time Generalisation and Map Adaptation Approach for Location-Based Services. In Mackaness, W. A., Ruas, A., & Sarjakoski, L. T. (Eds.), *Generalisation of Geographic Information: Cartographic Modelling and Applications, Series of International Cartographic Association* (pp. 137–159). Elsevier.

Semwal, S. K., & Evans-Kamp, D. L. (2000). Virtual environments for visually impaired. *2nd International Conference on Virtual Worlds,* Paris, France.

Shim, H. M., Lee, E. H., Shim, J. H., Lee, S. M., & Hong, S. H. (2005). Implementation of an intelligent walking assistant robot for the elderly in outdoor environment. *Proceedings of the 2005 IEEE 9th International Conference on Rehabilitation Robotics June 28 - July 1, 2005, Chicago, IL.*

Sinks, S., & King, J. (1998). Adults with disabilities: perceived barriers that prevent Internet access. *In Proceedings of CSUN 1998 Conference,* Los Angeles, CA, USA, March 17–21.

Sjostrom, C. (2001). Designing haptic computer interfaces for blind people. *In Proceedings of the 3rd International Workshop on Website Evolution,* IEEE, 2001

Sjostrom, C. (2001). *Virtual haptic search tools - the white cane in a haptic computer interface.* Ljubljana, Slovenia: In AAATE.

Sjostrom, C., Danielsson, H., Magnusson, C., & Rassmus-Grohn, K. (2003). Phantom-based haptic line graphics for blind persons. *Visual Impairment Research, 5,* 13–32. doi:10.1076/vimr.5.1.13.15972

Sjotrom, C., & Rassmus-Grohn, K. (1999). The sense of touch provides new computer interaction techniques for disabled people. *Technology and Disability, 10*(1), 45–52.

Smith, C. M. (1997). Human factors in haptic interfaces. *Crossroads, 3,* 14. doi:10.1145/270974.270980

Stigmar, H. (2006). Amount of Information in Mobile Maps: A Study of User Preference. *Mapping and Image Science, No. 4,* pp. 68-74.

Tzovaras, D., Nikolakis, G., Fergadis, G., Malasiotis, S., & Stavrakis, M. (2004). Design and implementation of haptic virtual environments for the training of the visually impaired. *IEEE Transactions on Neural Systems and Rehabilitation Engineering, 12*(2), 266–278. doi:10.1109/ TNSRE.2004.828756

Ungar, S., Blades, M., & Spencer, S. (1996). The construction of cognitive maps by children with visual impairments. In Portugali, J. (Ed.), *The Construction of Cognitive Maps* (pp. 247–273). Netherlands: Kluwer Academic Publishers. doi:10.1007/978-0-585-33485-1_11

Urbano, J., Terashim, K., Miyosh, T., & Kitagawa, H. (2005). Collision avoidance in an omnidirectional wheelchair by using haptic feedback. *Proceedings of the 4th WSEAS International Conference on Signal Processing, Robotics and Automation, 18.*

Virginia Assistive Technology System (2004). *Assistive technology and aging: A handbook for Virginian's who are aging and their caregivers.*

Wang, Z., Li, B., Hedgpeth, T., & Haven, T. (2009). Instant Tactile-Audio Map: Enabling Access to Digital Maps for People with Visual Impairment. *International ACM Conference on Computers and Accessibility (SIGASSETS).*

Warren, D. H., & Strelow, E. R. (1985). Electronic Spatial Sensing for the Blind. *Martinus Nijhoff Publishers*, Massachusetts. Web Content Accessibility Guidelines (WCAG) 2.0: http://www.w3.org/TR/WCAG20/

Williamson, K., Wright, S., Schauder, D., & Bow, A. (2001). The Internet for the blind and visually impaired.*J. Comput. Mediat. Commun. [Online]. Available:http://jcmc.indiana.edu/vol7* /issue1/ williamson.html.

Yu, W., Ramloll, R., & Brewster, S. A. (2001). Haptic graphs for blind computer users. Paper presented at the Haptic Human-Computer Interaction. *First International Workshop. In: Brewster, S.A., Murray-Smith, R. (Eds.), Lecture Notes in Computer Science, vol. 2058*, Springer, Berlin, pp. 41–51.

Yu, W., Reid, D., & Brewster, S. A. (2002). Web-based Multi-modal Graphs for Visually Impaired People. *In Proceedings of CWUAAT'02*, 97-108.

Zajicek, M., Powell, C., & Reeves, C. (1998). A Web navigation tool for the blind. *Proceedings of the ACM Conference on Assistive Technology (ASSETS),* 204–206.

Zajicek, M., Powell, C., & Reeves, C. (1999). Web search and orientation with BrookesTalk, *In Proceedings of Tech. and Persons with Disabilities Conf.*

Zhao, H., Plaisant, C., Shneiderman, B., & Lazar, J. (2006). *A framework for auditory data exploration and evaluation with geo-referenced data sonification. HCIL Technical Report (HCIL-2005-28), Human-Computer Interaction Lab*. College Park, Maryland, U.S.A: University of Maryland.

ENDNOTES

[1] http://www.sensable.com/products-haptic-devices.htm

[2] http://usixml.developpement.defimedia.be/en/home.html?IDC=6

[3] The OCR that has been used is *tesseract v.2.04 (*http://code.google.com/p/tesseract-ocr*)*

[4] The TTS that has been used is *espeak v.1.42.04* (http://espeak.sourceforge.net/*)*

Chapter 7
Olfactory Display Using Solenoid Valves and Fluid Dynamics Simulation

Takamichi Nakamoto
Tokyo Institute of Technology, Japan

Hiroshi Ishida
Tokyo University of Agriculture and Technology, Japan

Haruka Matsukura
Tokyo University of Agriculture and Technology, Japan

ABSTRACT

Olfaction is now becoming available in Multiple Sensorial Media because of recent progress of an olfactory display. One of the important functions of the olfactory display is to blend multiple of odor components to create a variety of odors. We have developed the olfactory display to blend up to 32 odor components using solenoid valves. High -speed switching of a solenoid valve enables us to blend many odors instantaneously at any recipe even if the solenoid valve has only two states such as ON and OFF. Since it is compact and is easy to use, it has been so far used to demonstrate a movie, an animation and a game with scents. However, a contents developer must manually adjust its concentration sequence because the concentration varies from place to place. The manually determined concentration sequence is not accurate and, moreover, it takes much time to make the plausible concentration sequence manually. Thus, it is adequate to calculate the concentration sequence using CFD (Computational Fluid Dynamics) simulation in the virtual environment. Since the spread of odor in spatial domain is very complicated, the isotropic diffusion from the odor source is not valid. Since the simulated odor distribution resembles the distribution actually measured in the real room, CFD simulation enables us to reproduce the spatial variation in the odor intensity that the user would experience in the real world. Most of the users success- fully perceived the intended change in the odor intensity when they watched the scented movie, in which they approached an odor source hindered by an obstacle. Presentation of the spatial odor distribution to the users was tried, and encouraging results were obtained.

DOI: 10.4018/978-1-60960-821-7.ch007

INTRODUCTION

Since the technology of presenting visual and auditory information is matured, people then want to have haptic interface to obtain the feeling of touch. The haptic interface has been so far studied and it can be used to some extent in virtual reality. Thus, the next technology of presenting sensory information should be related to the olfaction.

Olfactory display is a gadget to present smells. Nowadays it is quite easy to deal with visual and auditory information in a computer. We can acquire much visual and auditory information through Internet. However, sensory information except these senses also gives us different sensation. For example, when we see delicious food on TV, its smell is indispensable for reproducing much reality.

Sensing is another important aspect to realize artificial sense in virtual reality. We have studied an odor sensing system using multiple sensors with different characteristics and pattern recognition technique (Nakamoto, and Moriizumi, 1988). Although there have been many reports about the artificial sensor called the electronic nose (Pearce et al., 2003; Persaud, and Dodd, 1982), it has been studied separately from the olfactory display.

Thus, we proposed an odor recorder, which reproduces smell as well as records it (Nakamoto et al., 2001; Nakamoto, 2005). The composition of several odor components is determined so that a sensor array output pattern of blended odor can be identical to that of the target odor in an odor recorder. It was successful to replicate several fruit flavors using this gadget (Somboon et al., 2007a). Moreover, we recently demonstrated the experiment on teleolfaction (Nakamoto et al., 2008a), where sensed smell is reproduced at the remote site. Although a broad variety of application is feasible, we focus on olfactory display in this study.

There have been several works on the olfactory display even if the number of reports related to olfactory display is small. An olfactometer has been used for many years to give a human

an olfactory stimulus so that human sense of smell or EEG (Electroencephalogram) induced by olfactory stimulus could be studied (Kendal-Reed et al., 1998). However, the olfactometer is large and complex. Although a commercially available diffuser is simple, the smell cannot be changed quickly because the cartridge should be exchanged (www.scentair.com). Although another PC-controlled scent diffuser that could present several smells was proposed, it has no blending function (Messager, 2002).

Although they are useful in certain situations, one of the most important functions of an olfactory display is to present a variety of smells. A variety of smells can be generated when the function of blending is introduced. An important point is, however, what kinds of odor components should be prepared for blending.

Buck and Axel reported the multigene family of G-protein-coupled ORs (olfactory receptors) in 1991 and, then, the molecular biology of olfaction rapidly progressed [11]. However, primary smells (Amoore, 1970) are not known, unlike the primary colors in vision. In this situation, a device for blending as many odor components as possible is indispensable to cover a wider range of smells.

Even if primary smells have so far not been found, it is still important to blend smells because the blending process is currently essential in creating new smells, particularly in the flavor and fragrance industry.

In addition to novel scent creation in the flavor and fragrance industry, a variety of olfactory-display applications are feasible, such as a smell-presenting device in, for example, an odor recorder, a movie with scents, games, exhibitions, on-line shopping, restaurants, educational tools, medical-diagnostic tools, museums and art. In particular, a product with scent indispensable for evaluating its quality should be presented using an olfactory display in various situations.

Recently, we exhibited a cooking game with scents at several places in collaboration with artists, and 300-400 people experienced this game

(Nakamoto et al., 2008b). In the cooking game, smells are essential to reproduce reality. People enjoyed the game using three senses, such as vision, hearing and olfaction in the virtual environment. Some of them said that they felt hungry after they had tried the game.

Olfactory information also contributes greatly to a sense of presence when it is presented synchronously with a movie. We have made a scented animation movie and a questionnaire survey revealed the contribution of smells to the sense of presence (Nakamoto and Yoshikawa, 2006). Since the intensity of the smell is different from place to place, a contents developer must manually adjust the concentration sequence according to animation scene. The manually determined concentration sequence is not accurate and, moreover, it takes much time to make the concentration sequence manually. Since the fluid dynamics governs odor flow (Nakamoto and Ishida, 2008), the fluid dynamics simulation is effective to determine odor concentration at each place in the virtual environment. Since the spread of odor in spatial domain is very complicated, the isotropic diffusion from the odor source is not valid. The smell distribution can be calculated using a computational fluid dynamics.

For example, even in a closed room with no active ventilation or air-conditioning, convective airflow in the order of several centimeters per second is generated due to the small temperature variations in the room. In the olfactory display systems described in (Ishida et al., 2008; Matsukura et al., 2009), the distribution of the smell in the convective airflow field in a closed room was obtained by computational fluid dynamic simulation. To let the user search for the source of the smell in this virtual environment, the intensity of the smell presented to the user was adjusted in accordance with the concentration of the smell vapor at the position of the user in the virtual room. In (Matsukura and Ishida, 2009; Matsukura, Ohno, and Ishida, 2010; Matsukura, Yoshida, Nakamoto, and Ishida, 2010), we tried

synchronized presentation of smell with airflow, and investigated the effects of airflow on our sensation of smells.

In this chapter, we first review the smell presentation device and then explain the olfactory display using solenoid valves. Latter part includes computational fluid dynamics and the actual experiment on olfactory display for perceiving spatial distribution of odor.

OVERVIEW OF SMELL PRESENTATION DEVICE

Specification Required for Olfactory Display

There are several aspects of olfactory display required for its specification as is tabulated in Table 1.

First, the number of smells to be generated is important. Although there has so far been no equipment to emit arbitrary smells, the range of smell can be extended if many odor components can be blended in an arbitrary composition.

Second, the function of the concentration adjustment is necessary. A wide dynamic range of odor intensity is better since human perception covers several order of concentration.

Third, the speed of odor variation in both intensity and quality should be taken into account. The speed of odor variation is required when

Table 1. Specification required for olfactory display.

No.	Item
1	Number of smells to be presented
2	Concentration adjustment (Dynamic range of odor intensity)
3	Speed of odor variation in quality and intensity
4	Direction to scented object (Localization of smell source)
5	Area of smell diffusion

smells are generated in the dynamical scene. Smell persistence should be considered from this aspect. Odor generation synchronous with breathing is related to this point.

Moreover, the direction to an odor source should be perceived when people localize the odor source in a virtual environment. Final point is the area of smell diffusion. It depends upon how many people simultaneously perceive the smell.

Research on Olfactory Display

Although there has not been many researchers related to olfactory display, several researchers in virtual reality started studying olfactory displays (Nakamoto, 2008).

Kaye (2004) constructed a device to present plural smells according to the state of the stock market using solenoid-activated perfume bottles. An atomizer is used to diffuse a smell into space. He also made scent reminder to remind a user's schedule.

The application of the olfactory display to the entertainment, which is known as Sensorama, was investigated even in 1962. Then, Mochizuki et al. (2004) made the game for taking an object to sniff its smell. Tominaga et al. (2001) also demonstrated the virtual space with smell. Thus, several attempts to apply the olfactory display to the entertainment have been so far performed.

Yamada et al. (2006) demonstrated an olfactory display for localizing a smell source in a virtual environment. His group developed a simple wearable olfactory display to present spatiality of odor in an outdoor environment. Since the user's position was obtained using RF ID tag space, the wearable olfactory display attached to the user emitted smell with its intensity according to the distance to a virtual odor source. Users can search for the odor source in a virtual environment to localize it.

Nakaizumi et al. (2006) proposed a projection-based olfactory display to deliver a smell to specified person without disturbing people around the user. The smell is delivered by carrying scented air within a vortex ring emitted from an air cannon. Although the original machine let users feel unnatural airflow, the improved one has two air cannons to emit two vortex rings simultaneously so that two rings can collide in front of their faces. They reported that this collision reduced this wind effect significantly.

Sato et al. (2009) studied the pulse ejection technique of scent to reduce the influence of smell persistence. They tried to minimize the quantity of odor substance to prevent the user from the adaptation so that dynamic scene related smell could be created. They also discussed about the smell presentation method synchronous with breath inspiration.

Several concepts of the olfactory display have been described by Davide et al. (2001). Their concept includes even odorant precursors, odorant formers and mixer before odorant delivery. They said that the introduction of odorant precursor, which produces odorants after a reaction, might make broad range of smell from a limited set of stored precursors. Since they only showed the concept, the actual example was not presented.

Another method to obtain the impressions of a variety of smells from a limited set of smells is to use cross modality between vision and olfaction (Nambu et al., 2010). People tend to feel not olfactory but visual stimulation as scents. Thus, it is somewhat possible to enlarge the range of smells. However, it cannot be used in case that the visual cue is not available and the smell much different from one of the representative ones cannot be expressed even if the visual cue is used.

A more realistic way to make broad range of smell is to blend multiple odor components. Although a set of primary smells has not been found as mentioned previously, it is certain that the new fragrance and flavor smells can be created by many ingredients. Thus, odor blending technique for olfactory display is presented in the next subsection.

Odor Blending Method

There are several methods to realize aroma blender. The principles of the olfactory display with the function of the blending aromas are shown in Figure 1 (a)-(c). First method is to use MFC (Mass Flow Controller)s. The mixture with any composition can be realized by adjusting the flow rates (Nakamoto et al., 1994). The MFC is a good equipment to control the flow rate precisely and electronically. Since MFC has feedback control loop by itself to keep the flow rate constant, a system designer can treat MFC as open-loop component. Although the MFC is typically controlled using an analog voltage, the recent model of MFC is equipped with a digital interface. Thus, the implementation of MFCs into a flow system is very easy. However, it is not suitable for realizing the blender with many components because of its cost and size. If a number of MFCs are integrated on a silicon chip using MEMS technology (Shoji and Esashi, 1994), more sophisticated olfactory displays might be realized.

The second one is an inkjet-based olfactory display. The inkjet devices individually controlled by a computer are used to blend aromas at any composition. The organic solvent free device should be used for the purpose of generating smell. When we use the inkjet device, not the vapor but the liquid droplet is spouted from its nozzle. Since the odorant with high odor intensity typically has high boiling point, it is difficult for it to evaporate completely in spite of the tiny droplet size. Thus, the heater or other vaporizer should be used to let it evaporate immediately and completely. In our case, the mesh heater was adopted. The combination of the inkjet device with the mesh heater enables the rapid concentration change of the odor with high odor intensity, which often remains inside the plumbing tubes in the MFCs system (Nakamoto et al., 2004).

An odorant with high odor intensity has typically low volatility and often causes the problem of smell persistence. Although an inkjet device is appropriate from that viewpoint, it is still questionable whether it is suitable for blending many odor components. It also needs skill to adjust the pressure at the nozzle to obtain the stable amount of liquid droplet.

The third one is the olfactory display made up of solenoid valves. The solenoid valve is originally a fluidic switching device and could not be used to express the fine difference of the concentration. However, it becomes possible to express the subtle concentration change by its high speed switching followed by a fluidic low pass filter. Our group applied delta-sigma modulation technique, 1-bit A/D conversion technique, to the switching of the solenoid valves (Yamanaka et al., 2002). Since the solenoid valve is cheap, robust and is easily controlled by a computer, it is not difficult to realize the olfactory display equipped with many components using the solenoid valves.

Another method is to use an autosampler (Somboon et al., 2007b). The commercially available autosampler for liquid chromatography can be modified to blend odorant liquids. Since it can accommodate a large number of odor components, an odor blender for up to 96 components was realized. However, the autosampler cannot achieve real-time blending.

Since selection method of odor components as well as hardwares to blend odor components is important, we briefly describe it next.

Selection of Odor Components

Selection of odor components is quite essential to realize an olfactory display to cover wide range of smells. Unlike the primary colors in vision, the primary smells have not been found. However, there has been the attempt to find it as we mentioned in Introduction.

However, it is not clear what kind of odor components should be prepared to cover a wide range of smells. Amoore proposed a set of the seven primary smells mainly based on molecular shape. However, these primary smells were insuf-

Figure 1. Odor bending technique in real time for olfactory display (a) MFC, (b) inkjet device, (c) solenoid valve

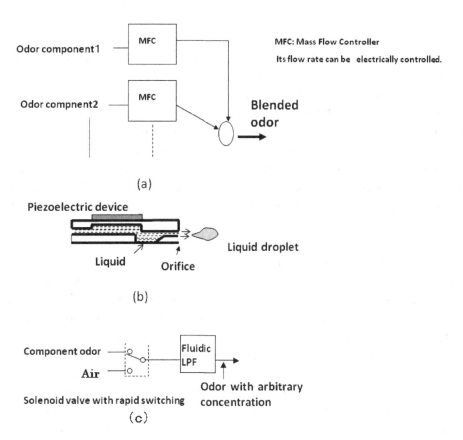

ficient to express a variety of smells. Buck and Axel reported a multigene family of olfactory receptors. Later, it was reported in the field of gene engineering that the number of receptor types was approximately 350 [3]. However, the 350 odor receptors have partially overlapping specificities. Thus, it might be possible to express smells using a smaller number of odor components.

Although a sensory test might be the best way to reveal an appropriate set of odor components, a huge amount of labor and time would be needed to obtain a reliable result. Thus, a database of mass spectrometry is focused on. A very large amount of mass spectrum data is available for investigating the odor components.

Once a large database of odors is available, a mathematical method of extracting the basis vec-

tors corresponding to odor components is required. Moreover, the basis vectors should be synthesized using the vectors of existing compounds. The NMF (nonnegative matrix factorization) method (Lee and Seung, 1999) was applied to extract basis vectors, and the nonnegative least-squares method was used to determine the mixture composition of the odor corresponding to the basis vectors.

Mass spectrometry is often used together with gas chromatography. However, it is also possible to classify smells only using mass spectra; this method is known as an MS-based electronic nose. A mass spectrometer without GC (gas chromatography) can be also used to quantify mixtures (Dittman et al., 1998; Mamun and Nakamoto, 2008). When an odorant molecule is injected, it is ionized and detected in the vacuum as a sequence of m/z (ratio of mass to charge) values.

When the EI (electronic ionization) method is used, the molecule is divided into multiple fragments. Thus, not a single peak but multiple peaks are observed even for a single compound. This fragmentation provides rich information about odor. The dimension of the data is typically a few hundreds.

Another feature of mass spectrometry is the applicability of the linear superposition theorem. Since this theorem is not valid for most of chemical sensors, this property of mass spectrometry greatly reduces the complexity of the analysis.

The feature extraction was performed using the NMF method. NMF can be used with the constraints that all the elements of data vectors are nonnegative and that the ratio of each odor component in the mixture is nonnegative. Furthermore, the detector output at each m/z should not be less than zero. Those constraints are important when the data obtained from the mass spectra are analyzed. Although principal component analysis is a well known feature extraction method (Dillon and Goldstein, 1984), it violates the constraints mentioned above. The nonnegativity constraints lead to a parts-based representation since they allow only additive, and not subtractive combinations. When NMF was applied to face images, several versions of mouths, noses and other facial features were extracted as basis images(Lee and Seung, 1999).

The simulation using NMF indicates that 30-50 odor components are required to approximate smells even if seven primary smells proposed by Amoore are insufficient (Nakamoto and Murakami, 2009). The experiment as well as simulation should be performed to pursue odor components.

In the next subsection, the olfactory display using multiple solenoid valves is explained in detail.

OLFACTORY DISPLAY USING MULTIPLE SOLENOID VALVES

We used solenoid valves for olfactory display because they are cheap and easy to handle. Since they are stable and relatively small, they are suitable for integration in order to realize an olfactory display with many odor components in spite of compact size.

The principle of olfactory display using solenoid valves is shown in Figure 1 (c) as mentioned above. Although a solenoid valve is a fluidic switching device with only two states, such as ON and OFF, high-speed switching enables any concentration. The frequency of the ON state corresponds to odor concentration. Switching noise does not appear at the outlet because of the fluidic LPF (low-pass filter). Since a solenoid valve is relatively cheap and small, it is easy to integrate many valves. Thus, it is possible to realize an olfactory display with many odor components. Some people are worried about wear of the valve due to the huge number of switchings. However, it is very robust and seldom breaks.

The entire structure of an earlier-version olfactory display is illustrated in Figure 2 (Yamanaka et al., 2003). It can blend up to 8 odor components using 16 three-way solenoid valves and 16 bottles comprising 8 for odor components and 8 empty bottles. An odorant liquid is put into the sample bottle and the vapor of the headspace over liquid surface is transported by carrier gas. Two paths are required: one for outputting smells and the other for bypath.

Flow path control at the outlet and at a sample bottle are shown in Figures 3 (a) and (b), respectively. Flow rate at an outlet can be kept constant even when the odor component is not connected to an outlet. The empty bottle is used for the path of air because the flow-path symmetry should be maintained to guarantee the same flow rate at each path.

Figure 2. Schematic diagram of earlier-version olfactory display using multiple solenoid valves

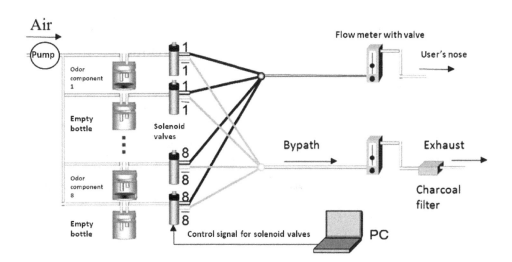

The flow rate at a sample bottle should also be kept constant because the concentration at the bottle depends upon its flow rate. The concentration at the sample bottle should be maintained because the concentration of each odor component set by a user is relative to the concentration at the sample bottle. The algorithm to control solenoid valves in the previous system is the delta-sigma modulation known as the 1-bit analog to digital conversion technique (Nordworthy et al., 1997).

In the previous olfactory display made up of solenoid valves, many empty bottles are required to maintain the symmetry of the flow system and the redundant space is required.

Moreover, the dynamic range of odor concentration decreases as the number of odor components increases. In the olfactory display in Figure 2, each odor component flows independently of others. Thus, the maximum concentration at the outlet is one-eighth of that at the sample bottle. The olfactory display was improved to extend the range of smells using more odor components while maintaining small size.

The improved olfactory display is shown in Figure 4 (Nakamoto and Minh, 2009). Thirty-two odor components can be equipped with this system. The number of odor components is four times greater than that of the previous one whereas its size is still compact. In the previous olfactory display, a pair of an odor component bottle and an empty bottle was used and the corresponding two solenoid valves worked complementarily. On the other hand, only one empty bottle is used to supply air to the outlet in the improved system. Other physical structure is similar to the previous one.

However, the control method of the solenoid valves is much different. The comparison of the improved method with the previous one is illustrated in Figure5.

In the previous method, the concentration of each odor component is independently controlled and thereafter all the components are blended. Although the concentration of each odor component is reliably controlled, one empty bottle is required for each odor component. Furthermore, the maximum concentration of each odor component decreases.

In the improved system, only one odor component is allowed to connect to the outlet at a certain time and the time division multiplexing technique is adopted to blend multiple odor components. The dead space of the tube and connector acts as a fluidic low-pass filter in the same manner as that in Figure 1(c). The concentration

Figure 3. Flow path control of conventional olfactory display, (a) at the outlet and (b) at a sample bottle

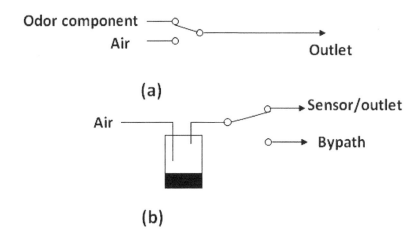

Figure 4. Schematic diagram of 32-component olfactory display using solenoid valves

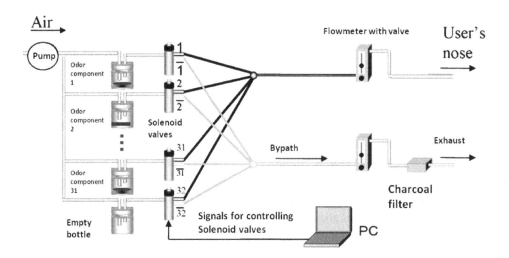

of each odor component corresponds to its duty cycle ratio. The repetition cycle here is 1s. As a result, the maximum odor concentration to be output reaches the concentration in each sample bottle and the problem of the dynamic range in the previous version was solved. Moreover, only one empty bottle is used when the air is flowed at the outlet. Thus, the number of empty bottles is considerably decreased.

In the improved system, only one sample bottle is connected to the outlet at a certain time and other sample bottles are connected to the bypath. Thus, the two flow paths are not symmetric and the flow rate at the bypath is much higher than that at the outlet.

The photo of olfactory display is shown in Figure 6. The size of the olfactory display is still compact although the number of odor components has been increased fourfold. Sample bottle No.1 is the closest to the outlet whereas Sample bottle No.32 (empty bottle) is the farthest from the outlet. Since the symmetry is lost in this structure, the flow

Figure 5. Comparison of improved method with previous one

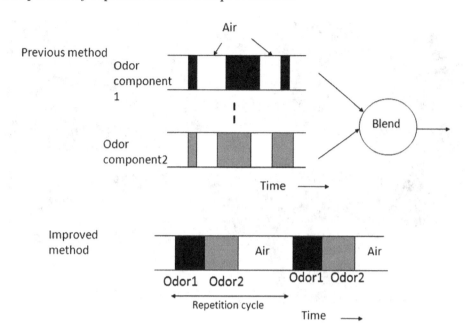

rate at each sample bottle is not always the same. However, this does not cause a problem because we can calibrate the system even in such a case.

Thirty-two solenoid valves are directly attached to the manifold without plumbing. Since the response speed of the solenoid valve is fast (nominal value:1ms), the accuracy of blending increases when the repetition cycle of odor presentation is fixed. Moreover, the noise sound generated due to switching is small.

The experiment on a single odor component was performed to check the behavior of the olfactory display. The relationship between a specified concentration and the sensor response is shown in Figure 7. The 20MHz AT-CUT QCM (Quartz Crystal Microbalance) coated with the sensing film (Apiezon L) was used to measure the relative concentration. The response of QCM sensor is in the form of a frequency shift from the air-level value and is proportional to the vapor concentration. The sample used here was 2-hexanone. It was found from the figure that the sensor response increased almost linearly with the vapor concentration relative to the concentration at the sample

bottle in terms of the unit [%RC]. Thus, it can be said that the vapor at the specified concentration can be generated using this olfactory display.

In 2008, more compact olfactory display shown in Figure 8 was developed. 13 odor components including the air bottle can be used in this system. The total system is compact enough to carry it by hand to the exhibition sites such as Tokyo big sight, Makuhari Messe etc, whereas we previously used a car for the transportation to the demo sites. This olfactory display includes a FPGA board where CPU core (NIOS, Altera) is implemented. Since the complicated timing control of all the solenoid valves is performed by the CPU core, a user of the olfactory display does not have to care about it. The host computer sends that CPU core in that olfactory display the relative concentration of each odor component every second via serial interface. The implementation of the olfactory display into a system became easier after the introduction of the FPGA board. Thus, several universities and companies have those olfactory displays to develop their own applications.

Figure 6. Photo of 32-component olfactory display

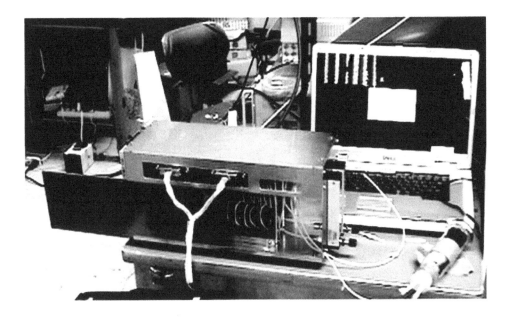

Figure 7. Sensor response to 2-hexanone at specified concentration

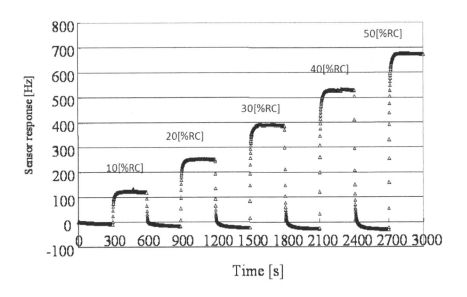

The latest-version olfactory display has the resolution of 0.2%, whereas the previous one's resolution is 1%. The minimum ON time of the solenoid valve was reduced from 10ms to 2ms, which is almost the limit.

Although it became easier to use the olfactory display, labour is somewhat required to exchange sample bottles when odor components are changed. An easier way, such as the use of cartridges, to handle odor components will be required in the near future.

Figure 8. Latest version of olfactory display using solenoid valves

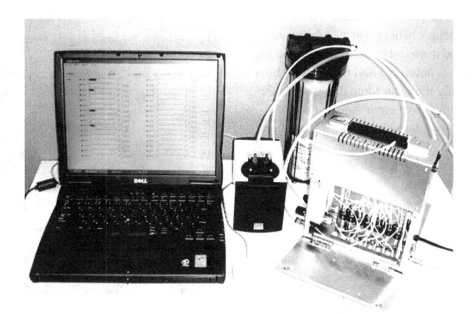

This olfactory display can be used in many applications. The application of fluid dynamics simulation to olfactory display will be presented in the next section.

APPLICATION OF FLUID DYNAMICS SIMULATION TO OLFACTORY DISPLAY

One of the main applications of olfactory displays is to add special effects to movies. Releasing smells relevant to specific scenes in the movies is effective in making those scenes particularly impressive (Nakamoto and Yoshikawa, 2006). To provide realistic olfactory experience to the users, the olfactory display device must be able to generate realistic smells with appropriate intensities in a timely manner. Suppose that you are watching a movie in which the main character is walking along a path to a flower garden. Releasing a sweet smell of roses would improve the sense of reality. However, the intensity of the released smell should be carefully adjusted. When the camera moves

along with the main character of the movie, you will feel like watching the scene from the position of the camera. The concentration of the rose smell released from the olfactory display should be low at the beginning to reproduce a faint scent drifting in the air. As the camera approaches the garden, the intensity of the smell should be gradually increased.

Only a handful of researchers have addressed the issue of determining the appropriate strength of the odor stimuli. The odor recorders reported in [4–6] uses the "electronic noses" consisting of several different gas sensors to discriminate among different odors and measure their intensities. The change in the odor intensity that you would feel in the real environment can thus be recorded by using the odor recorder together with a movie camera. However, this technique cannot be applied to science fiction movies or animations. In the effort to establish a method that enables automatic adjustment of the release rate of odors, we proposed to introduce computational fluid dynamics (CFD) simulation into olfactory display systems. There is a common misunderstanding on the dispersal of odor vapor. If you open a jar full of a stinky rotten food, how fast does the malodor spread in the room? Many people believe that the odor vapor is instantly spread in a room by molecular diffusion. However, this is not true. Fluid dynamic motion of air is actually the main force that spreads the odor vapor in the given environment.

Figure 9 shows the white smoke trailing from a cigarette. The distribution of the odor vapor released from its source is similar to the distribution of this cigarette smoke. The molecules of chemical substances contained in the odor vapor exhibit random Brownian motion, and therefore, are gradually transported from a region of high concentration to one of a lower concentration. Unless there is an obstacle or temperature gradation, the odor vapor diffuses isotropically in the environment. Therefore, in theory, a spherical odor distribution is generated from a point source of an odor. However, this happens only in the environment with no significant airflow. The diffusion of odor molecules into air is an extremely slow process. The diffusion length of a typical gas for an hour is only a few tens of centimeters (Ishida and Moriizumi, 2003). On the other hand, the airflow in the order of a few centimeters per second is almost always found even in closed indoor environments. Even though air conditioners and ventilators are turned off, slight temperature variations in the room induce airflow. The transport of the odor molecules by the resultant convective airflow field dominates the slow molecular diffusion. The streak of white smoke shown in Figure 9 first went up from the cigarette since the smoke had a higher temperature than that of the surrounding air. The smoke was then carried toward the left due to the airflow in the room. The smell of the cigarette smoke follows the almost same distribution as the smoke.

Another important aspect having a large impact on the odor dispersal in real environments is the turbulence of airflow. The airflow we encounter in our daily lives is almost always turbulent and contains a number of eddies with a variety of

Figure 9. Smoke from a cigarette

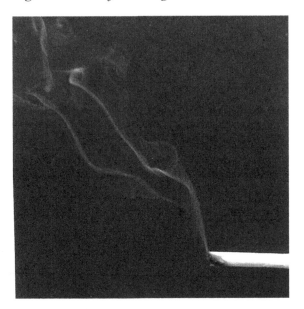

sizes. A streak of an odor vapor being carried by turbulent airflow is stretched and twisted by those eddies. Therefore, the aerial trail of the odor vapor extending from its source comes to have a patchy structure, just like the tangled filamentous structure of the cigarette smoke. The width of the trail thus becomes wider than that in a laminar flow. The trail also meanders randomly due to the large eddies contained in the turbulent flow. The intensities of the odors we perceive in real-life situations are, therefore, always fluctuating.

Since the distribution of the odor vapor is mainly determined by the airflow and its turbulent intensities, it is governed by the theories of fluid dynamics. Therefore, the fluid dynamic simulation is effective in predicting the odor distribution in an unknown environment. Consider the room shown in Figure 10, and suppose that a source of an odor vapor was placed near the window as shown in Figure 11. The coordinate system shown in Figure 11 is used in the following figures. We took ethanol gas as an example of the odorous vapor since its concentration can be easily measured using gas detectors and sensors. The room has a large window, and natural convection occurs due to the temperature difference between the window and the other part of the room. Figure 12 shows the airflow field measured in the wintertime. The airflow velocity at each location was measured using an ultrasonic anemometer (Model 81000, Young) assuming that the airflow field would stay the same throughout the measurement of the velocities at all locations. The instantaneous values of the airflow velocities were randomly fluctuated due to the turbulence of the airflow. Therefore, the airflow velocity averaged for three minutes at each location is shown in Figure 12. The outside temperature was lower than the temperature in the room. Therefore, the air near the window was cooled down, and was forced to descend along the window. As a result, a circulating airflow field was generated in the room.

Figure 13 shows the distribution of the ethanol gas in the room. Saturated ethanol vapor was generated using a bubbler, and was released at the rate of 200 ml/min from a nozzle placed on the floor. Eight metal-oxide semiconductor gas sensors (TGS2620, Figaro Engineering) were used to measure the concentration of the ethanol gas. The gas concentrations at eight locations were measured at a time, and the averages of the concentration values for one minute were calculated. The room was then completely ventilated, and

the same measurement was repeated at another eight locations. It is clearly seen in Figure 13 that the released ethanol gas was trailing to the right being carried by the convective airflow. The airflow velocity was only 15 cm/s and below the detection threshold of humans. Figure 13 shows that such weak airflow field still has a large impact on the dispersal of the gas/odor vapor.

The airflow field and the gas distribution in the room can be simulated in a computer by solving the Navier-Stokes equations simultaneously with the diffusion equation and the equation of the state of the ideal gas. Navier-Stokes equations are the basic equations defining the behavior of viscous heat-conducting fluid. They describe the conservation of the momentum, and are solved together with equations describing the conservation of the mass and the energy. The diffusion equation describes the molecular diffusion that makes a gas patch being carried by the airflow gradually grow over time. The ideal gas law is applied to determine the density of the air with a certain temperature and a pressure. However, to reproduce the behavior of turbulent airflow in the simulation is not a trivial task. The equations must be solved using an extremely fine grid and a small time step in order to fully resolve the motions of the smallest eddies in the turbulent flow. Gener-

Figure 10. Closed room with a large window

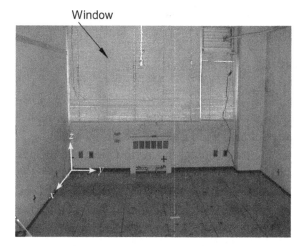

Figure 11. Model of the room shown in Figure 10 and the location of the gas source

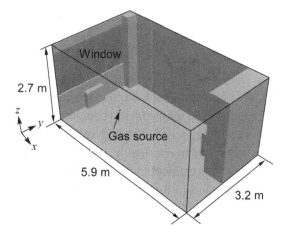

Figure 12. Airflow field measured using an ultrasonic anemometer on the vertical plane at the mid-width of the room. The maximum airflow velocity on this vertical plane was 15 cm/s and was found near the floor

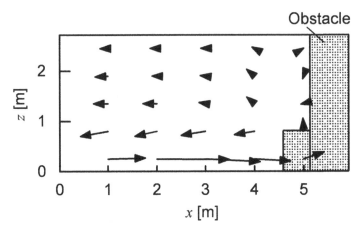

Figure 13. Distribution of the ethanol gas on the horizontal plane at 20 cm from the floor. The dots indicate the locations where the gas sensors were placed

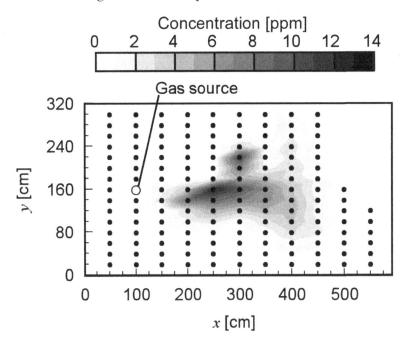

ally, the computational load for such calculation is too much even for the fastest computer at present. Therefore, various turbulent models are proposed to obtain reasonable calculation results with less computational load. The models describe the contribution of the small eddies to the main flow, and allow the calculation to be done with a coarser grid and a larger time step.

Figure 14 shows the airflow field and the gas concentration distribution reproduced in a CFD simulation. A commercial software package (CFD2000, Adaptive Research) was used for the CFD calculation. The room model shown in Figure

Figure 14. Result of CFD simulation. (a) Airflow field and gas distribution in the vertical plane at the mid-width of the room. The maximum airflow velocity on this plane was 11 cm/s. (b) Airflow field and gas distribution in the horizontal plane at 20 cm from the floor. The maximum airflow velocity on this plane was 10 cm/s.

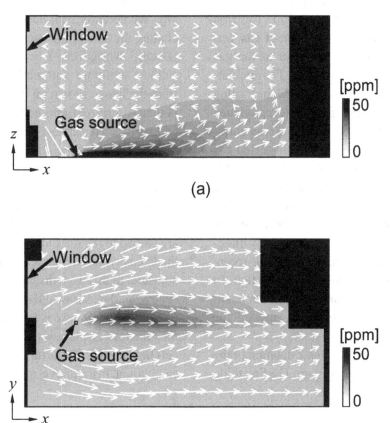

11 was discretized into $93 \times 75 \times 51$ cells. The cells near the floor were made small since that is the place where the turbulence is developed. The accuracy in the calculation of airflow velocity at such places has a significant impact on the result of the CFD simulation. The standard k-ε model was used, and the time step was set to 0.05 s. In this widely used method, only the time-averaged airflow velocity and the gas concentration are calculated. The model provides a reasonable calculation result even with a relatively coarse grid and a large time step by giving up the reproduction of high-frequency fluctuations of the airflow and gas concentration. To simulate the natural convection

that occurs in an un-air-conditioned room in the wintertime, the temperature of the window was set to 10°C while the initial temperature of all walls and the air inside the room was set to 15°C. The odor source was assumed to be a 5 cm × 5 cm region located one meter from the window. It was assumed that the saturated ethanol vapor was released at the rate of 200 ml/min. The molecular diffusion coefficient was set to 0.1 cm²/s, the value for the diffusion of ethanol into air. For simplicity, the other properties of the released gas, e.g., the density and the specific heat, were assumed to be the same as air. This simplification does not cause a significant discrepancy between the measured and simulated results since the gas concentration was low at most of locations in the room.

In the simulation, it was assumed that there was initially no movement in air. The development of the convective airflow field for 600 s was first calculated. The release of the odorant gas was then initiated, and the development of the gas distribution for 300 s was calculated. The circulating airflow field seen in Figure 12 and the trailing gas distribution shown in Figure 13 are reproduced well in Figure 14. The cross-sectional concentration profiles of the measured and simulated gas trails across the wind are compared in Figure 15. Although the perfect match was not attained between the simulated and real gas distributions, at least the qualitative nature, e.g., the distortion of the gas distribution toward the positive y direction due to the asymmetric shape of the room, was reproduced well in the CFD simulation. In Figure 15, both measured and simulated concentration profiles have longer tailing toward the positive y direction.

Figure 16 shows the schematic diagram of the proposed olfactory display system. The first thing

to do for adding olfactory stimuli to a specific scene in a movie or a game is to extract information on the scene and build its model of the CFD simulation. Currently, this process is done manually. We determine all necessary parameters including the size of the room and the initial temperature distribution. It would be interesting to achieve in future automatic model generation from the image shown on the screen. The model is then discretized into cells, and provided to a CFD solver. The airflow field in the environment and the spread of the odor molecules are calculated. The intensity of the odor presented to the user should be adjusted based on the three-dimensional position of the user in the virtual environment. The data obtained in the CFD simulation are passed to the olfactory display device so that the intensity of the released odor can be properly adjusted. In this way, the change in the odor concentration the user would experience at the position of the user's nose is faithfully reproduced in the olfactory display system. The biggest technical challenge here is the time required for the CFD calculation. In the above-mentioned example, the

Figure 15. Comparison between the cross-sectional concentration profiles of the measured and simulated gas trails across the airflow at 2 m downwind from the odor source. The dotted line shows the mid-width of the room.

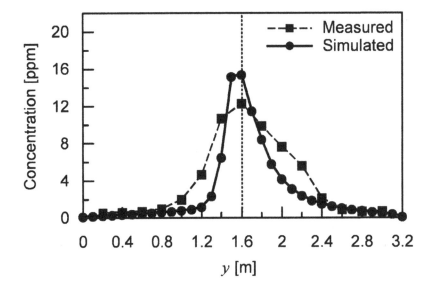

time required for the calculation of the development of the airflow field and the gas distribution for 300 s was 23.5 hours. The computational load is still large even for this simple environment, and real-time calculation is hard to achieve. However, once the heavy calculation is done off-line and the data is stored in the hard drive, the concentration values corresponding to the user's position can be quickly retrieved on the fly. Therefore, this technique can be even applied to interactive applications as long as the user's actions do not alter the airflow field and the gas distribution (Matsukura et al., 2009).

OLFACTORY DISPLAY FOR MAKING THE USER PERCEIVE SPATIAL ODOR DISTRIBUTION

The concept of the odor presentation based on CFD simulation was applied to the scenario shown in Figure 17. The room model is the same as that shown in Figure 11. However, it was assumed this time that a teapot containing peach-flavored tea was placed on the floor as an odor source. Moreover, a screen (180 cm in height, 90 cm in width, and 4 cm in depth) was placed downwind from the source to disturb the airflow field and the odor distribution. The user was assumed to be a small child walking slowly across the room. CFD

Figure 16. Introduction of CFD simulation into olfactory display system

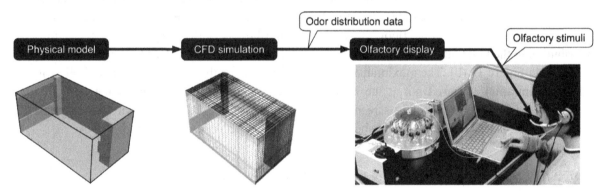

Figure 17. Scenario assumed to present spatial odor distribution using the olfactory display

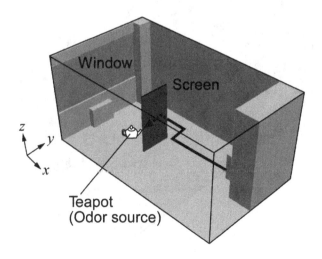

calculation was done in a similar way as described in the previous section. The concentration of the released odor was kept same as in the previous section, but the rate of release was changed to 500 ml/min. The user experiences the change in the odor intensity that the small child would experience in this virtual room. Figure 18 shows the mesh used for the CFD calculation.

The result of the CFD simulation is shown in Figure 19. The airflow field on the vertical plane shows that the circulating natural convection was again created in the room. The airflow near the left wall was pointing down because of the cold window. The airflow near the floor was pointing to the right, but this time, the airflow was deflected upward by the screen. The odor distribution corresponds well to the airflow field. The released odor was first carried to the right, and then, raised by the screen. The child was assumed to have a nose at 80 cm from the floor. The odor distribution in the horizontal plane at this height is shown in Figure 19 (b). The maximum of the odor concentration appeared not at the source location but at the upwind side of the screen since the source was placed not at the height shown in Figure 19 (b) but directly on the floor. It appears in the figure that most part of the odor flux was deflected upward at the screen, but some part was observed flowing to the downwind side of the screen.

To confirm the validity of the CFD simulation, the odor distribution was again measured in the real room. A screen made of Styrofoam was placed in the room as in the simulation. Saturated ethanol vapor was released at 500 ml/min from a nozzle, and the ethanol concentration was measured using the metal-oxide gas sensors at various locations in the room. The result is shown in Figure 20. Eight gas sensors were first placed on the upwind side (left) of the screen, and their responses were recorded. Their positions were then changed to the downwind side (right) of the screen, and the responses were recorded. The concentration values shown in Figure 20 were obtained by averaging the gas sensor responses for three minutes. The simulated odor distribution shown in Figure 19 (a) resembles the ethanol distribution in the real room. This result suggests that the qualitative nature of the odor dispersal was successfully reproduced in the simulations.

Figure 18. Computational grid used for CFD simulation

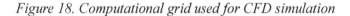
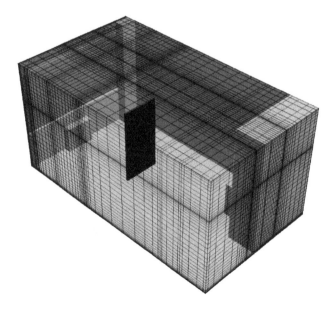

Figure 19. Result of CFD simulation for the room with a screen. (a) Airflow field and gas distribution in the vertical plane at the mid-width of the room. The maximum airflow velocity on this plane was 11 cm/s. (b) Airflow field and gas distribution in the horizontal plane at 80 cm from the floor. The maximum airflow velocity on this plane was 3 cm/s.

Figure 20. Distribution of ethanol vapor around the screen measured with gas sensors. The arrows schematically indicate the airflow directions, and the dots indicate the locations where the gas sensors were placed.

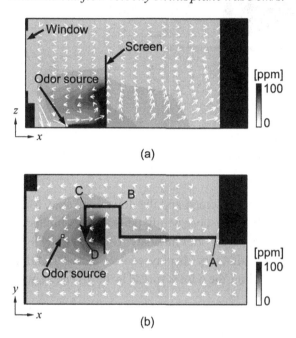

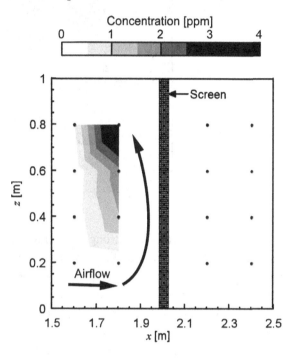

We first tested the path shown in Figure 19 (b). The small child was assumed to walk along the path at 10 cm/s. This situation corresponds to the scenario that you perceived the smell of the peach tea coming from somewhere and walked around the screen to check if there was a teapot behind the screen. Firstly, a movie clip was created assuming the small child walking along the path. The snapshots extracted from the movie clip are shown in Figure 21. The movie clip shows the image seen from the child's point of view. The values of odor concentration along the path were collected from the simulation result by extracting the data at the corresponding location and time. The collected data was passed to the eight-component olfactory display with solenoid valves. The variation in the odor concentration that the user would experience in a real-life situation was

thus reproduced using the olfactory display. Figure 22 shows the variation in the odor concentration presented to the user. To let the user experience large variation in the odor intensity, the concentration value was normalized to make the maximum concentration on the path to be 100%, i.e., the maximum odor concentration that can be generated with the eight-component olfactory display.

Five university students tried this odor presentation. A liquid sample of peach flavor was set in the olfactory display. The movie clip was shown on the computer screen, and the odor with appropriate concentration was released from a tube attached near the user's nose synchronously with the movie clip. After experiencing the odor presentation, we asked the student if they felt that the peach smell was emanating from the teapot. All students answered yes. Four out of the five

Figure 21. Snapshots extracted from the movie clip. A-D correspond to points A-D in Figure 19 (b), respectively

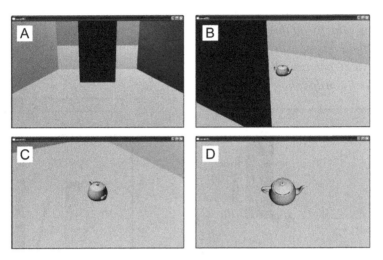

students told us that they felt stronger smell when the viewpoint of the movie clip approached the teapot. The rest told us that the strongest smell was felt when the teapot was first came in the field of view. Three out of five students told us that they felt that the spread of the smell was blocked by the screen since they perceived large variation in the odor intensity between the upwind side of the screen and the downwind side. Most of the users successfully perceived the intended change in the odor intensity. The proposed CFD-based olfactory display can let the users think about how the odor is spread in the given environment.

Figure 22. Variation in odor concentration observed on the path shown in Figure 19 (b). A-D correspond to points A-D in Figure 19 (b), respectively

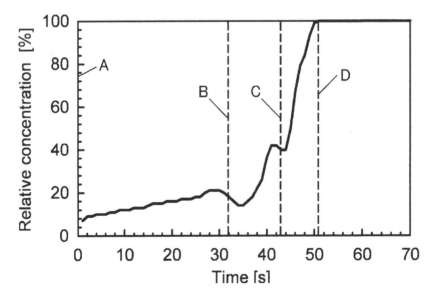

CONCLUDING REMARKS

We have reviewed the recent advancements in the olfactory display devices and the way of odor presentation. In order to reproduce variety of odors for movies and games, the olfactory display must be able to generate new odors by mixing some basic odor components. The olfactory display using solenoid valves are promising because of its ease in handling. The solenoid valves enable easy control on the mixing and dilution ratio of the odor components. The released odor can be immediately switched to different one. CFD simulation was introduced to reproduce the spatial variation in the odor intensity that the user would experience in the real world. Presentation of the spatial odor distribution to the users was tried, and encouraging results were obtained.

The research on olfactory displays started with the development of hardware devices for odor vapor generation. The research is now coming to a new stage where the odor vapor generators with additional functionalities and new ways of odor presentation are being proposed. We believe that those research efforts will further expand the application areas of olfactory displays.

REFERENCES

Amoore, J. E. (1970). *Molecular basis of odor.* New York: Charles C Thomas Publisher.

Buck, L., & Axel, R. (1991). A novel multigene family may encode odorant receptors: Molecular basis for odor recognition. *Cell, 65,* 175–187. doi:10.1016/0092-8674(91)90418-X

Davide, F., Holmberg, M., & Lundstorm, I. (2001). In Riva, G., Davide, F., & Press, I. O. S. (Eds.), *Virtual olfactory interfaces, electronic noses and olfactory displays, Communication through virtual technology: Community and technology in the Internet age* (pp. 193–220). Amsterdam.

Dillon, W. R., & Goldstein, M. (1984). *Multivariate analysis* (pp. 23–52). Wiley.

Dittman, B., Nitz, S., & Horner, G. (1998). A new chemical sensor on a mass spectrometric basis, Adv. Food Sci., (CMTL) 20, 115.

Ishida, H., Matsukura, H., Yoshida, H., & Nakamoto, T. (2008) Application of computational fluid dynamics simulation to olfactory display, *Proc. Int. Conf. Artificial Reality and Telexistence,* pp.285-288.

Ishida, H., & Moriizumi, T. (2003). *Machine olfaction for mobile robots, Handbook of machine Olfaction, T.C.Pearce, S.S.Schiffman, H.T.Nagle, and J.W* (pp. 399–417). Weinheim, Germany: Gardner, Eds., Wiley-VCH.

Kaye, J. J. (2004) Making scents, Interactions, Jan.+Feb.,2004, pp. 49-61.

Kendal-Reed, M., Walker, J. C., Morgan, W. T., LaMacchio, M., & Lutz, R. W. (1998). Human responses to propionic acid. I. *Quantification of within- and between-participant variation in perception by normosmics and anosmics. Chemical Senses,* 71–82. doi:10.1093/chemse/23.1.71

Lee, D. D., & Seung, H. S. (1999). Learning the parts of objects by non-negative matrix factorization. *Letters to Nature, 401*(21), 788–791.

Mamun, A., & Nakamoto, T. (2008). Recipe Estimation Using Mass Spectrometer and Large-scale Data. *IEE of Japan, 128-E,* 467–471. doi:10.1541/ieejsmas.128.467

Matsukura, H., & Ishida, H. (2009). Olfactory display: Fluid dynamics considerations for realistic odor presentation, In *Proc. Joint Virtual Reality Conference of EGVE - ICAT – EuroVR,* pp.61-64.

Matsukura, H., Ohno, A., & Ishida, H. (2010). On the effect of airflow on odor presentation, In *Proc. IEEE Virtual Reality,* pp.287-288.

Matsukura, H., Yoshida, H., Ishida, H., & Nakamoto, T. (2009) Interactive odor playback based on fluid dynamics simultation, In *Proc. IEEE Virtual Reality 2009*, pp.255-256.

Matsukura, H., Yoshida, H., Nakamoto, T., & Ishida, H. (2010). Synchronized presentation of odor with airflow using olfactory display. *Journal of Mechanical Science and Technology, 24*, 253–256. doi:10.1007/s12206-009-1178-6

Messager, J. (2002). *The diffusion of fragrances in a multimedia environment, 3rd Aroma Science Forum*, Sep 13 2002, Tokyo, pp. 2-7 (in Japanese).

Mochizuki, A., Amada, T., Sawa, S., Takeda, T., Motoyashiki, S., & Kohyama, K. (2004). *Fragra: A Visual-Olfactory VR Game*. ACM SIGGRAPH, Sketches.

Nakaizumi, F., Yanagida, Y., Noma, H., & Hosaka, K. (2006). *SpotScents: A novel method of natural scent delivery using multiple scent projectors*, Proc. IEEE Virtual Reality 2006, pp. 207-212.

Nakamoto, T. (2005). Odor recorder. *Sensor Letters, 3*, 136–150. doi:10.1166/sl.2005.018

Nakamoto, T. (Ed.). (2008). *Olfactory display, Fragrance Journal Ltd*, 2008 (in Japanese).

Nakamoto, T., & Ishida, H. (2008). Chemical sensing in spatial/temporal domains. *Chemical Reviews, 108*, 680–704. doi:10.1021/cr068117e

Nakamoto, T., & Minh, P. D. (2009). Improvement of olfactory display using solenoid valves, *Proc. IEEE Virtual Reality* 2009, pp.179-186.

Nakamoto, T., & Moriizumi, T. (1988) Odor sensor using quartz-resonator array and neural-network pattern recognition,In *Proc. IEEE Ultrason. Symp.*, pp.613-616.

Nakamoto, T., & Murakami, K. (2009) Selection method of odor components for olfactory display using mass spectrum database, In *Proc. IEEE Virtual Reality 2009*, pp. 159-162.

Nakamoto, T., Nakahira, Y., Hiramatsu, H., & Moriizumi, T. (2001). Odor recorder using active odor sensing system. *Sensors and Actuators. B, Chemical, 76*, 465–469. doi:10.1016/S0925-4005(01)00587-1

Nakamoto, T., Nimsuk, N., Wyszynski, B., Takushima, H., Kinoshita, M., & Cho, N. (2008). *Experiment on Teleolfaction Using Odor Sensing System and Olfactory Display Synchronous with Visual Information, ICAT* (International Conference on Artificial Reality and Telexistence), pp. 85-92.

Nakamoto, T., Otaguro, S., Kinoshita, M., Nagahama, M., Ohnishi, K., & Ishida, T. (2008). Cooking up an interactive olfactory game display. *IEEE Computer Graphics and Applications, 28*, 75–78. doi:10.1109/MCG.2008.3

Nakamoto, T., Takigawa, H., & Yamanaka, T. (2004). *Fundamental study of odor recorder using inkjet devices for low-volatile scents*, Trans. on IEICE, 2004. *E (Norwalk, Conn.), 87-C*, 2081–2086.

Nakamoto, T., Utsumi, S., Yamashita, N., & Moriizumi, T. (1994). Active gas sensing system using automatically controlled gas blender and numerical optimization technique. *Sensors and Actuators. B, Chemical, 20*, 131. doi:10.1016/0925-4005(93)01193-8

Nakamoto, T., & Yoshikawa, K. (2006). Movie with scents generated by olfactory display using solenoid valves, *IEICE, Vol. E (Norwalk, Conn.), 89-A*(11), 3327–3332.

Nambu, A., Narumi, T., Nishimura, K., Tanikawa, T., & Hirose, M. (2010) Visual-Olfactory Display Using Olfactory Sensory Map, *Proc. IEEE Virtual Reality* 2010, pp. 39-42.

Nordworthy, S. R., Scheier, R., & Temes, G. C. (1997). *Delta-sigma data converter* (pp. 206–222). IEEE Press.

Pearce, T. C., Schiffman, S. S., Nagle, H. T., & Gardner, J. W. (Eds.). (2003). *Handbook of machine olfaction*. New York: Wiley-VCH.

Persaud, K. C., & Dodd, G. (1982). Analysis of discrimination mechanisms in the mammalian olfactory system using a model nose. *Nature, 299*, 352. doi:10.1038/299352a0

Sato, J., Ohtsu, K., Bannai, Y., & Okada, K. (2009) Effective Presentation Technique of Scent Using Small Ejection Quantities of Odor, In *Proc. IEEE Virtual Reality* 2009, pp.151-158.

Shoji, S., & Esashi, M. (1994). J. Micromechanics. *Microengineering, 4*, 157. doi:10.1088/0960-1317/4/4/001

Somboon, P., Wyszynski, B., & Nakamoto, T. (2007a). Novel odor recorder for extending range of recordable odor. *Sensors and Actuators. B, Chemical, 121*, 583–589. doi:10.1016/j.snb.2006.04.105

Somboon, P., Wyszynski, B., & Nakamoto, T. (2007b). Realization of recording a wide range of odor by utilizing both of transient and steady-state sensor responses in recording process. *Sensors and Actuators. B, Chemical, 124*, 557–563. doi:10.1016/j.snb.2007.01.030

Tominaga, K., Honda, S., Ohsawa, T., Shigeno, H., Okada, K., & Matsushita, Y. (2001). *"Friend Park"—expression of the wind and the scent on virtual space* (pp. 507–515). Proc. Virtual Systems and Multimedia.

Yamada, T., Tanikawa, T., Hirota, K., & Hirose, M. (2006) Wearable olfactory display: Using odor in outdoor environment, *Proc. IEEE Virtual Reality 2006*, pp. 199-206.

Yamanaka, T., Matsumoto, R., & Nakamoto, T. (2002). Study of odor blender using solenoid valves controlled by delta-sigma modulation method. *Sensors and Actuators. B, Chemical, 87*, 457. doi:10.1016/S0925-4005(02)00300-3

Yamanaka, T., Matsumoto, R., & Nakamoto, T. (2003). Fundamental study of odor recorder for multi-component odor using recipe exploration based upon a singular value decomposition. *IEEE Sensors Journal, 3*, 468–474. doi:10.1109/JSEN.2003.815778

Section 4
MulSeMedia Applications

Chapter 8
Entertainment Media Arts with Multi–Sensory Interaction

Masataka Imura
Osaka University, Japan

Shunsuke Yoshimoto
Osaka University, Japan

ABSTRACT

In a field of application of virtual reality technologies, lots of multi-sensory entertainments have been developed. Researchers have been trying not only to develop the haptic, tactile, olfactory, and taste displays individually, but also to represent subtle sensations with combinations of multiple displays. In this chapter, we will introduce three entertainment applications which utilize multi-sensory stimulation for representing and improving the reality of virtual worlds. (1) Haptic Canvas: An entertainment system with dilatant fluid based haptic device, (2) Fragra: An entertainment system with a hand-mounted olfaction display, and (3) Invisible: An entertainment system that reproduce presence of virtual creatures by indirect information.

INTRODUCTION

Currently one of the largest entertainment field in which applications are interactive and utilize digital technologies is a video game industry. In the field of video game consoles, players receive a large part of feedback through visual and auditory senses (sometimes we have vibration of controllers, but it is auxiliary). In 2006, Nintendo's Wii introduced player's motion as an input method to gaming consoles. Sony's PlayStation 3 and Microsoft's Xbox360 have been following Wii and now they are ready to release motion input devices based on image processing. However, these new devices extend only input modality and the senses which are utilized as output from virtual worlds are still limited.

Virtual Reality (VR) technology is a collection of technologies that reproduce the essential part of the real world by stimulating users' senses appropriately. To reconstruct realistic virtual environment, VR technology must cover the wide-

DOI: 10.4018/978-1-60960-821-7.ch008

range fundamental technologies which include multi-sensory inputs and outputs. In a field of application of virtual reality technologies, lots of multi-sensory entertainments have been developed. Researchers have been trying not only to develop the haptic, tactile, olfactory and taste displays individually, but also to represent subtle sensations with combinations of multiple displays, for example, a sucking feeling (Hashimoto, 2005) or a creepy feeling (Sato, 2008).

In this chapter, we will introduce three entertainment applications which utilize multi-sensory stimulation for representing and improving the reality of virtual worlds.

- Haptic Canvas: An entertainment system with dilatant fluid based haptic device (Yoshimoto, 2010).
- Fragra: An entertainment system with a hand-mounted olfaction display (Mochizuki, 2004).
- Invisible: An entertainment system that represents existence of virtual creatures by indirect information (Nakano, 2006).

These applications were created by the students in (1) BioImaging Group (Oshiro Laboratory), Department of Mechanical Science and Bioengineering, Graduate School of Engineering Science, Osaka University, and (2, 3) Image Processing Laboratory, Graduate School of Information Science, Nara Institute of Science and Technology from 2003 to 2009. All of these applications were submitted to International collegiate Virtual Reality Contest (IVRC) which has been hosted by Virtual Reality Society of Japan from 1993. To know more about the IVRC, please visit their web site: http://ivrc.net.

HAPTIC CANVAS: DILATANT FLUID BASED HAPTIC DEVICE

Introduction

Painting visually attracts peoples. To add colorings on the canvas and to draw a picture are also the entertainments of visual sensation. Like painting, to draw haptic sensations on the canvas could be an entertainment. The purpose of this study is to realize "Haptic Canvas" on which users can paint and arrange haptic sensations like painting a picture on the canvas. Users blend and draw the haptic sensations, which we call "haptic colors", on the canvas with his hand directly touching virtual "haptic" paints, thus paint a haptic picture. Users intend to blend haptic colors to create a new sensation so that the picture can haptically attract peoples. While we need several paints to draw colorful pictures, users also need haptic paints, i.e., "haptic primary colors" to draw colorful haptic pictures. While we can create fascinating colors by blending paints, in case of haptic sensations, some paints could be attractive by themselves when we touch them.

The slurry made from water and starch - i.e., dilatant fluid, is one of the haptically fascinating substances and presents amusing but mysterious feelings like playing in the mud when you were in childhood. The distinct haptic sensation comes from the property of the fluid, "dilatancy", which means reversible change of state from liquid-like material to solid-like material according to an external force (Cates, 2005). The change in the state of the fluid is not only useful for building a soft and morphing robot (Mozeika, 2009) but also for building haptic devices. If we can mechanically control the state of the dilatant fluid, we can present wide range of haptic sensations because the change of the state of dilatants fluid from the liquid to the solid is drastically and even fast. As shown in Figure 1, the concept of Haptic

Canvas is based on both blending haptic colors like paintings and feeling haptic colors by using dilatant fluid.

The requirements of the system are both direct touch with the viscoelastic liquid to present haptic sensations and the control of the dramatic change in the state to present variable sensations. Previous haptic devices using other smart fluids (e.g. Electrorheological fluid or Magnetorheological fluid) are not sufficient for the former, while the tactile display using dilatant fluid controlled by vibrations (Saga, 2010) is not sufficient for the latter. We propose a new mechanism for haptic interaction by using jamming of the fluid caused by suction of water. Then we define haptic primary colors based on the sensations which can be presented by the proposed haptic device. This chapter mainly discusses how to present haptic primary colors by using dilatant fluid based haptic device and how users can interact with the haptic colors on "Haptic Canvas".

Dilatant Fluid Based Haptic Device

We propose sucking/ejecting and filtering functions which cause change in the state of the dilatant fluid. The device presents haptic sensation by the sucking the water through the filter which causes jamming of the particle. Jamming is the mechanism by which particulate material can make transition between a liquid-like and a solid-like state with external energy. We intentionally produce the jamming by using the sucking structure with filtration of the particle of the starch. Furthermore, we apply the function to the glove which enables users to make direct interaction with the viscoelastic liquid and to feel the dramatic change of the substance state in their hand by attaching the structure to the fingertip of the glove. Figure 2 illustrates the mechanism of presenting haptic sensation by using dilatant fluid. The haptic sensation will be presented as follows.

Figure 1. Artistic concept: Like blending paints to create a new color, users blend haptic primary colors to create a new haptic color. Each haptic primary color is presented by controlling dilatant fluid.

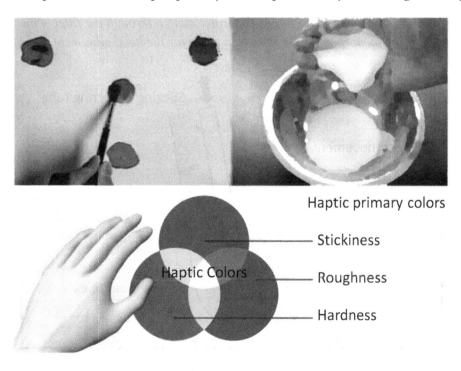

1. Users attach the sucking tube with the filter of the particle to their fingertip and put the finger into the dilatant fluid.
2. During suction, the particles are gathering around the filter, making the concentration of the slurry higher thus leading the jamming.
3. The friction between the accumulated particle around the fingertip and the bottom one is presented when the finger moves.

The proposed haptic device has four advantages. 1) The device enables users to touch directly with the dilatant fluid and to present distinct sensation of the viscoelastic fluid, like "sliminess" sensation so that exhibits the haptic entertainment. 2) The functional glove is small and light because of the simple structure consists of the tube and the filter. 3) The device can present large force because the force is presented according to user-intended hand movement (dilatant fluid works as a brake for the hand movement). 4) Some other sensory modalities can be presented by considering the structure. We can set both sucking pressure and duration to control the amount of the accumulated particles. The device can also eject the air through the filter so that vibrate the filter. We found that the sensations that the device can present are "stickiness", "hardness" and "roughness" sensations based on the preliminary qualitative analysis of the device. Each sensation is represented by setting the parameters as described below.

1. *Stickiness:* We define stickiness sensation as the sensation which comes from resisting force when trying to escape from the contacting objects. The finger will stick to the subsided particles at bottom of the pool during sucking the water with high pressure. We simply control the sensory intensity of stickiness with the sucking duration. Especially, we assume that the device can present various stickiness sensations according to the frequency of the sucking pressure.
2. *Hardness:* We define hardness sensation as resisting force when deforming an object. As the amount of the jammed particles becomes larger, the contact area between the jammed particles and the subsided particles becomes

Figure 2. The mechanism of presenting force: The water can go through the filter, while the particles jammed at the filter. The jammed particles work as a brake for the hand movement.

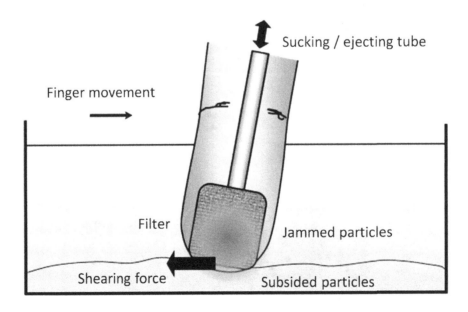

larger. Therefore, the shearing force between these particles becomes larger and makes users to feel touch sensation harder. This phenomenon occurs when the water is sucked with low pressure. The amount of jammed particles varies with sucking duration and the pressure. We vary the sucking duration to control the amount of the jammed particles, while keeping sucking pressure at low. We can present various hardness sensations according to the frequency of the sucking pressure.

3. *Roughness:* We define roughness sensation as the sensation which comes from the vibration during tactual exploration of a concave-convex shape of an object. The impression of the roughness is related to the spatial wavelength of the concave-convex shape of the object (Konyo, 2005). The frequency of the vibration at the fingertip is determined by the wavelength and the relative velocity of the hand. We adopt this model and introduce the intensity of roughness by using the ejecting duration and velocity of the hand. We can present various roughness sensations according to the frequency of the ejecting pressure.

Haptic Primary Colors

We define haptic primary colors as the sensations which can be presented by the proposed haptic device (i.e., stickiness, hardness and roughness). As we can create an arbitrary color from some primary colors, users can create a new haptic sensation by blending some defined haptic primary colors. Each haptic primary color has unique motional and haptic effect and is visualized in the same manner as ordinary colors. Users can feel a haptic sensation at his hand during touching haptic colors with the proposed haptic device.

To realize the concept of blending haptic colors, we need a model to create a new haptic sensation by using haptic primary colors. The relationship between the sensory modality and the activation of the device is designed as shown in Figure 3. Like the visual sensation, we assume that the mixture ratio of the haptic primary colors determines the haptic sensations **HC**. Namely, a haptic color is decided by three dimensional vector whose elements are intensities of the stickiness S, hardness H, and roughness R.

$$\mathbf{HC} = (S, H, R) \qquad (1)$$

Users feel the mixed haptic sensation when the three haptic sensations are presented nearby. Although the device can switch the presented a haptic primary color and control the sensory intensity at each finger, the device cannot present all haptic primary colors at the same time. Therefore, we assume that haptic colors can be blended and presented even when the three haptic primary colors are presented at different fingers. Users perceive a blended haptic color with their whole hand. Note that the device appropriately switches the haptic primary colors to prevent from each haptic sensation perceived independently.

Haptic Canvas System

Figure 4 illustrates the system overview. The system consists of positional sensing, visual and haptic calculation and presenting visual and haptic effects. The input of the system is user's hand position which is utilized for the next process, visual and haptic calculation. The system enables users to generate, blend, draw and erase the haptic colors projected on the shallow pool filled with the dilatant fluid. Users paint a haptic picture by locating the haptic colors on the arbitrary space on the canvas and enjoy feeling haptic sensation with the dilatant fluid based haptic device. We discuss each element and implementation of the system below.

Figure 3. The model of haptic colors: We can vary the haptic modality by controlling the pressure (suction or ejection). The sensory intensity of each haptic modality varies with the duration of the pulsed pressure.

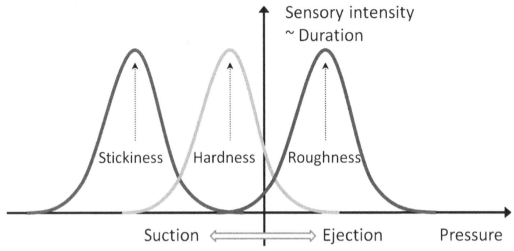

Positional Sensing

The positional data of the glove is required for visual and haptic calculation process. In this system, the important thing is that users can feel the integrated haptic sensation at the hand rather than perceive the shape of the objects with each finger. Therefore, we only need to sense the center of the hand. We install an infrared LED at middle finger of the haptic glove. The position of the infrared LED is measured by two infrared cameras, using triangulation method. We install the cameras above the canvas – two-dimensional virtual space, and ease the calibration thus enhances the accuracy of the sensing.

Visual and Haptic Effects

According to the positional data, the visual and haptic effects of the haptic colors are calculated. For the visualization of the haptic paints, we associate the haptic primary colors stickiness, hardness and roughness with light's primary colors red, green, blue and its intensity is also associated.

On the canvas, haptic paints are represented as the collection of particles. Each particle has one own haptic sensation and the density of particles which determines the sensory intensities affecting user's finger. We represent the haptic primary color with BOIDS model so that activates the haptic paints automatically and visually affects on the haptic sensations. A haptic color in the canvas corresponds to a BOID whose each particle represents a haptic paint. Considering the interaction, we define the four rules: generate, transfer, blend and erase as follows.

- A BOID is generated when the users touch the sources of the haptic paints (Generate).
- Users can move a BOID during putting their hand in the pool (Transfer).
- The particles of each BOID are combined when the users contact them each other (Blend).
- The particles of the BOID are disappeared when the users contact the erase tool with the BOID (Erase).

Figure 4. System overview: The system consists of a pool filled with dilatant fluid, a computer, two infrared cameras, a projector and the proposed haptic glove

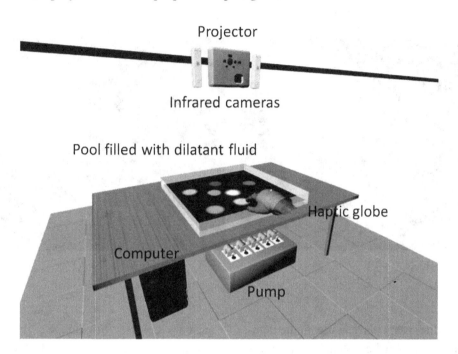

Furthermore, we empirically represent visual effect of haptic sensation by setting the parameters of the BOIDs. Then the haptic sensation is calculated based on the contacting information between the BOIDs and the position of the hand.

Haptic Presenting

The prototype of the haptic glove is shown in Figure 5. The requirements for the haptic device are functionality of representing haptic sensation and ease of wearing. In terms of functionality, the filter is attached to each finger of the glove and controls the dilatant fluid. The filter has the small holes which enable water to go through, while the insoluble particles cannot go through the filter. The suction or ejection of the water is achieved with a vacuum pump respectively and switched by an electromagnetic valve. The motor of the pump is controlled by PWM. We assumed that the duty rate of the voltage can be used for

controlling the pressure, while the period can be used for controlling the sensory intensity. The haptic glove is two-layer structure: disposable waterproof glove and removable functional glove.

Implementation

Figure 6 is the scene of the demonstration of "Haptic Canvas" system. Users enjoy the visual and haptic interaction of haptic colors projected on the canvas with the haptic glove. The haptic primary colors are generated by touching the sources of haptic sensation (haptic paints) placed on the canvas and utilized to blend the haptic colors. Users can move the produced haptic primary colors and blend them by visually contacting each other. The intensity of the light is directly presenting the intensity of the haptic sensations. Users paint a haptic picture by drawing haptic colors with feeling the haptic sensations.

Figure 5. Haptic glove: (a) The back of the developed haptic glove. For the positional sensing, an infrared LED is installed at the middle finger of the glove. (b) The front of the developed haptic glove. Four filters are attached to each finger.

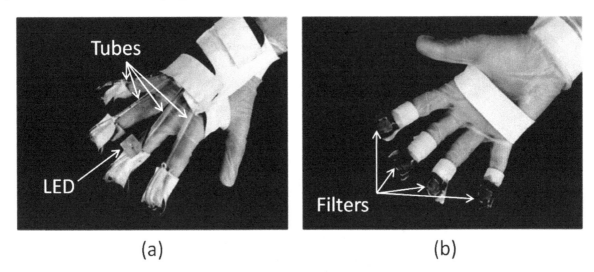

(a) (b)

Fifteen healthy users participated in the demonstration and evaluated the system from the view point of haptic entertainment. Lots of participants could discriminate the sensation among the haptic primary colors and gave high evaluation for the unique sensation presented by the proposed haptic device and the new interaction that is blending haptic sensation. They also pointed out that the drawbacks of the system are the poor usability of the haptic colors and the stability of the presented sensations. We should carry out the quantitative evaluation of the proposed haptic device in the future work.

Conclusion

The purpose of this study is to construct "Haptic Canvas" which enables users to paint haptic pictures by blending and drawing haptic sensation on the canvas. The concept is blending and painting haptic primary colors as an analogy of light's primary colors. Especially, we focused on the haptic entertainment of dilatant fluid, and developed the haptic glove which can present some haptic modality. We introduced three haptic

primary colors: "Stickiness", "Hardness", and "Roughness". The users could blend and draw haptic colors on the canvas and feel them. The haptic canvas system revealed that dilatant fluid based haptic device expands possibility of haptic entertainment.

FRAGRA: A VISUAL-OLFACTORY VR GAME

"Fragra" is a visual-olfactory VR game that enables players to explore the interactive relationship between olfaction and vision. For this purpose, when a virtual object is displayed by both visual and olfactory stimuli, "Fragra" does not always display fragrances that correspond to images. So observers must distinguish what each visual and olfactory information means and compare them.

Introduction

In our everyday life, we tend to disregard olfactory information except during mealtime, and sometimes even treat it as a primitive sense. But

Figure 6. Haptic Canvas: Red, green and blue correspond to stickiness, hardness and roughness respectively. When users touch the color, they can feel the haptic sensation varying with brightness value.

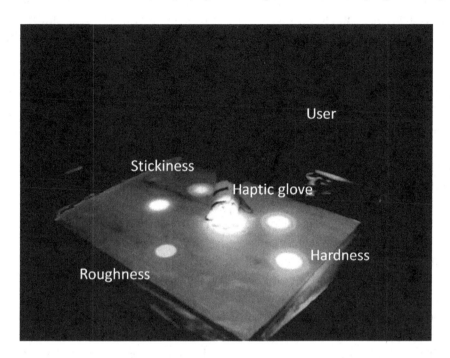

does anyone like the flowers without their scents? No, of course not. And although olfaction is generally less well understood than the other senses, it is well known that olfactory information affects memory and emotion deeply. Aromatherapy is a good example of an application of this fact. Furthermore, some researchers have reported that when a monkey smells a fruit's scent, not only the olfactory area of a brain but also the visual area becomes activated.

Therefore we think that the olfactory information is necessary for VR environment and the interaction between olfaction and vision is a domain that merits further exploration. Thus we developed a new visual-olfactory display device and a novel visual-olfactory game "Fragra" to enable us to experience this cross-modal interaction as an enlightening form of entertainment. If we can understand the relationship between olfaction and vision, our lives can be enhanced by presenting olfactory information simultaneously.

For example, cooking programs that enable us to smell the dishes on demand, or a new type of restaurant menu which we can see and also smell, will be realized.

Entertainment with Smells

Some trials have been made to display smells with movies to give a high realistic and immersive sensation to viewers. A comedy film "Polyester" (1981) provided a small card named "Odorama". On the card, there were 10 spots which are numbered from 1 to 10. Viewers scratched the corresponding spot when the number was shown on the screen. Then they can sniff the appropriate smell which matched the scene. In 2005, some movie theaters screened "Charlie and the Chocolate Factory" with the blowing fans which sent smell of chocolate (Aromatrix, Promotool Corp.).

Musicians introduce fragrance into their concerts. For example, Japanese pianist Yukie

Nishimura fills the concert hall with different fragrance according to locations.

In the applications of fragrances described above, smell is treated as a subordinate sense. Even if there is no fragrance, the entertainments work well.

In this section, we will describe the trial of development of entertainment application in which a fragrance plays an indispensable role.

Related Researches of Olfactory Displays

Heilig's sensorama (Heilig, 1992) was one of the earliest implementations of visual-olfactory entertainment, but it does not enable players to smell the scent of object interactively. To investigate the cross-modal interaction between olfaction and vision, to display visual and olfactory information simultaneously is required. Thus we developed a new visual-olfactory display device.

Some olfactory displays that use tubes to transfer scented air (Yamada, 2003) locate the end of the tube in front of the player's nose. Al-

though this arrangement is effective to display scents directly, some devices and tubes must be attached to a player's head and prevent a player's free movement. Therefore we attached the emitter of scented air on a hand.

One typical example of olfactory displays which achieve to be wireless and device-free on a head is "An Unencumbering Localized Olfactory Display" (Yanagida, 2004). This display utilizes air cannon to transfer the scented air, so there must be a certain time delay between emission and perception.

Hand-Mounted Olfactory Display

To represent several kinds of smells interactively, adaptation to a single kind of smell and mixture of several kinds of smell become serious problems. To avoid these problems, the olfactory display should limit the amount of ejected scent. We developed a hand-mounted olfactory display that utilizes the temporal improvement of capability of snuffing (Figure 7).

Figure 7. Hand-mounted olfactory display

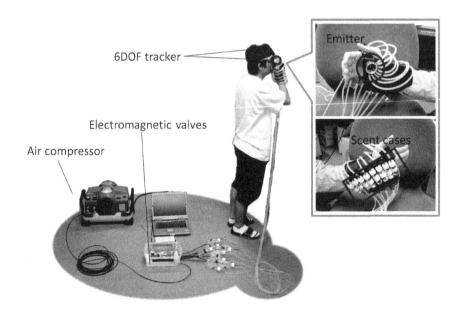

In the developed game "Fragra", a player grasps a virtual fruit and smells the fruit. The developed display recognizes the moment when the player starts sniffing of the fruit based on the distance between player's hand and nose. After the recognition of start of sniffing, the display ejects scented air from the emitter attached on a player's hand. For measurement of the distance between the hand and the nose, we use electro-magnetic 6 Degree-Of-Freedom tracking system Fastrak (Polhemus).

For displaying scent, we use the method of sending scented air to a player's nose. We use an air compressor to generate airflow. The airflow is divided and introduced individually into small cases which are filled with scent sources (perfumed silicate particles). Electromagnetic valves which are controlled from a computer select which scent is displayed to a player. The scent cases and emitter are attached on a player's hand. This arrangement enables the distance between the scent sources and the emitter to shorten so as to avoid attenuation of amount of scent.

Application

By using the developed olfactory display, we have implemented a visual-olfactory game "Fragra" that enables players to experience the cross-modal interaction between olfaction and vision (Figure 8).

In this game, players wear a head-mounted display and are shown a 3-dimensional virtual forest, in which stand mysterious trees that bear many kinds of food objects.

Players can pluck them from the trees by moving their hand. When they grasp one food object and move it in front of their own nose, they can smell a scent that is emitted from the hand-mounted olfactory display. The point of this game is that the scent may or may not correspond to the appearance. Sometimes the appearance and the scent are consistent, but sometimes they are not.

Players must distinguish between "honest" foods, which show exact scents corresponding to their appearance, and "deceiving" foods, which

present disparate scents. Through this task, players experience the cross-modal interaction between olfaction and vision by trying to sense olfactory and visual information independently, which is difficult to experience in the real world.

Exhibition

We exhibited this application in the following exhibitions: (1) International collegiate Virtual Reality Contest (IVRC) on July and September 2003 in Tokyo and Kakamigahara, Gifu, Japan. (2) Laval Virtual 2004 on May 2004 in Laval, France. Over 1000 people have experienced our game.

In our preliminary experiment, the percentage of questions answered correctly varied according to the combination of visual information and olfactory information. So there is a possibility that some foods' appearance might have stronger information than their scents, and vice versa.

INVISIBLE: THE SHADOW CHASER

"Invisible" is an interactive game which makes you feel the existence of unseen creatures through indirect information such as creatures' shadows, sounds, and weights. In this game, invisible goblins are running inside a playfield and you can only see their shadows. Two players form a team to find and capture these invisible goblins by special flashlight-like and vacuum-like devices. When the goblin is captured, the player feels a weight of the creature on the backpack.

Introduction

The main purpose of virtual reality technologies is to represent a virtual object to observers with reality. For this purpose, our sensory receptors should be stimulated in appropriate way. However, if the stimuli are inconsistent with our experience in the real world, we cannot construct a proper virtual image of the presented object.

Figure 8. Screenshot and playing scene of "Fragra"

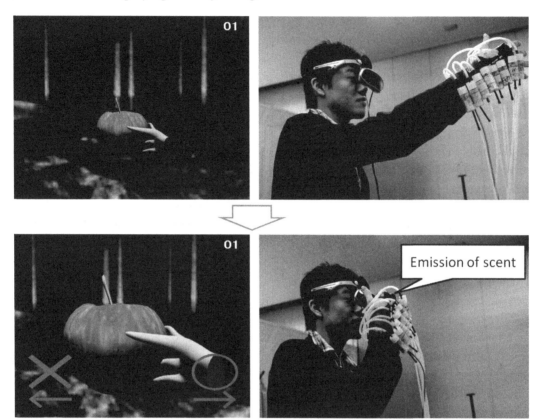

In this section, we divide information provided from VR system into two categories: direct and indirect. Direct information of virtual objects is defined as description of their appearances such as a stereoscopic image in the scene. Indirect information is defined as incidental information which they may cause in the environment around them, for example, shadows, sounds, and weights etc. While inconsistency of direct information is easily detected by players, indirect information is more ambiguous and causes less inconsistency. This project aims the representation of feeling that a user can feel the existence of unseen objects through their indirect information.

In this project, we produce the game "Invisible" (Figure 9). The setting of this game is like the movie "Ghostbusters". In this game, invisible goblins are running in the cubic game space and only their shadows can be seen on the floor when they are lit by a flashlight-like device. Also their footsteps can be heard when they are running. Players have to estimate their position from the shadows and sounds, and then catch them. Goblin's shadow is projected from projector. The position and shape of the shadow is calculated from position and orientation of the projector and goblins. When a player catch a goblin, the weight of the captured goblin is represented on a backpack by transportation of fluid (water) into the backpack.

Related Researches

There are some applications and works to generate feeling of existence of virtual objects in the field of entertainment.

Aoki's "Kobito -- Virtual Brownies --" is a work to realize haptic interaction with virtual creatures through real objects (Aoki, 2005). In their work,

Figure 9. Playing scene of "Invisible" and Devices

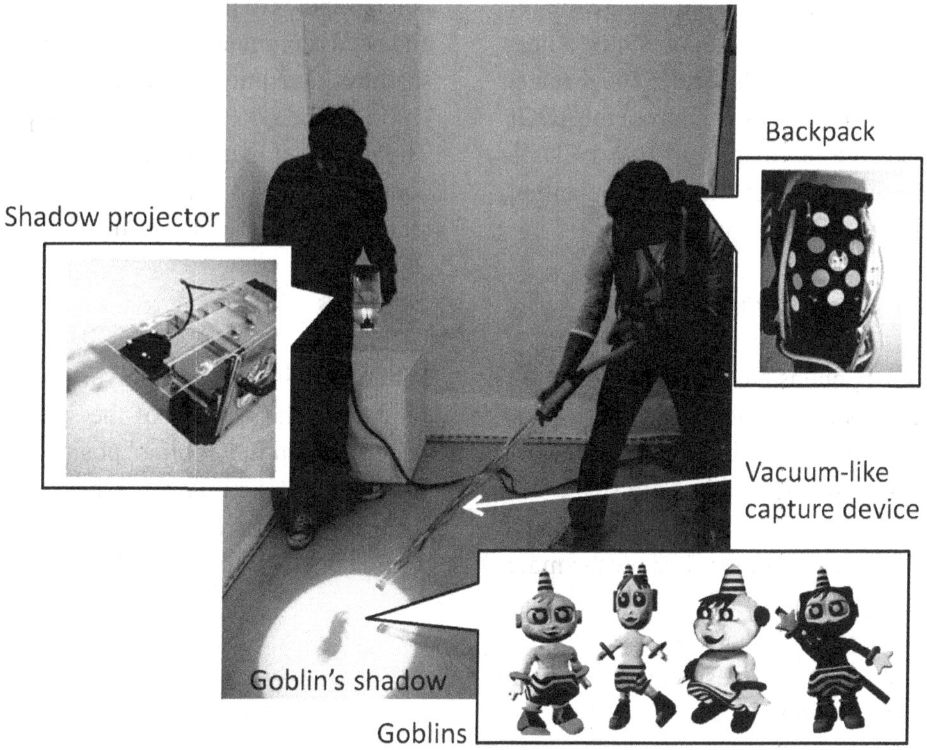

Shadow projector

Backpack

Vacuum-like capture device

Goblin's shadow

Goblins

real objects look like moving by themselves. However, through the monitor, we can see the virtual brownies pushing the real objects. In this work, the existence of virtual brownies is represented by the autonomous moving of real objects.

Narumi's "inter-glow" is a work to produce conversations of unseen family when users point their lamps at the table in a miniature living room (Narumi, 2007).

Shadows play an important role in this application. Some applications utilize shadows for displaying information (Cypher, 2006, Uchida, 2007). In this application, we utilize the causal relation that if there is a shadow, there should be an object which shuts out a light.

Components

The configuration of the system is shown in Fig. 14. In this application, one player uses a special flashlight-like device to project shadows of the invisible goblins. The other uses a special vacuum-like device to capture the invisible goblins.

Measurement of Position and Orientation of Devices

For natural projection of the shadow shapes, we need to obtain the 3D position and orientation of the projector in player's hands in real-time. Two infrared LEDs and a 3DOF angular sensor are attached on the projecting device. We realized high- speed positioning system by following simple method.

An infrared camera is installed at the ceiling and looking down vertically. From the image captured by the infrared camera, we can obtain two lines on which two infrared LEDs locate. The distance between two LEDs is known and from the 3DOF angular sensor the orientation of two LEDs is measured. Based on the distance and orientation, we can decide the position of two LEDs.

Projection of Shadow

The shadows of goblins are shown by projection of an image of spotlight from which the shape of goblins is removed. To make a shadow image, a viewpoint for rendering a silhouette shape of a goblin is set to the position of the projector in the real world. To render goblin's shadow, the material color of the 3D model of goblin is set black and the reflectivity is set none. Rendered image is used as a mask image so as to make an actual spotlight shape (Figure 10).

In general, generation of shadows in computer graphics requires 3D model of environment and needs computational power to apply popular shadow generation method such as a shadow volume method or a shadow mapping method. The proposed method has the advantage of low computational cost and high geometric consistency between the real world and virtual shadows.

Sounds

When goblins move, players can hear their footsteps. The volume of the speakers changes depending on the goblins' position on the floor. In addition, when players capture goblins, they hear goblins' scream and vacuuming sounds. These sounds give players better sense of reality.

Figure 10. Process of making spotlight image with the shadow of the invisible goblin

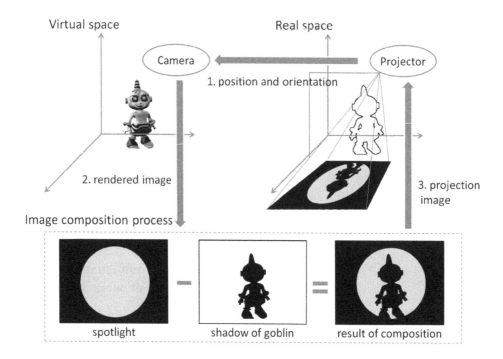

CAPTURE DEVICE: VIBRATION AND WEIGHT

Our work is an interactive game in which players capture goblins by a vacuum-like device, so the responses from the captured goblins are quite important issue. The player feels a sense of capturing through the vibration and a change of the weight of the backpack. A number of small vibrating motors are placed regularly in the hose of the device. When a player captures a goblin, these motors vibrate sequentially from the nozzle toward the handle. This movement of vibration represents the movement of captured goblins through the hose.

Then a large vibrating motor equipped at the backpack is used to present a sense that the captured goblin is struggling. At the same time, water is moved from a tank on the ground to another tank in the backpack. Thus, the player can feel increase of the weight by the captured goblins (Figure 11).

Exhibition

We showed this application in the following exhibitions: (1) International collegiate Virtual Reality Contest (IVRC) on August and October 2005 in Tokyo and Kakamigahara, Japan, (2) Laval Virtual 2006 on April 2006 in Laval, France, and (3) SIGGRAPH 2006 Emerging Technologies on July-August 2006 in Boston, USA.

To capture invisible goblins, two players should cooperate and exchange information about the location of goblins. This game design brings inartificial cooperation between players. Because two players are required to play this application, sometimes an instant pair was formed and two players' native languages were different. Even in such a case, two players enjoyed playing with communication by gestures and broken English.

From the aspect of multi-sensory entertainment, the existence of invisible goblins is shown in various forms in the capturing process: (1) shadow and sound before capturing, (2) vibration

Figure 11. Presentation method of weight by transferring water into backpack

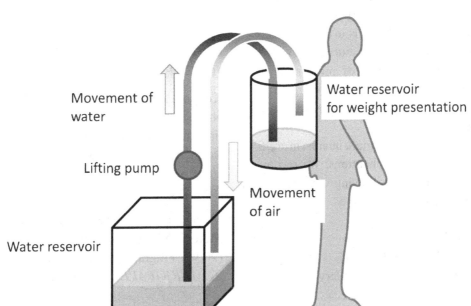

while capturing, and (3) weight after capturing. Especially, the presentation of existence of goblins after capturing is useful to make an impression that goblins are living creatures, not a mere objective of capturing like in usual video games.

Conclusion

The concept of this project is to give a presence of virtual object in a real space by representing only indirect information, such as sounds, shadows and weights. Based on this concept, we produced an interactive game "Invisible". Our game enabled users to feel the existence of virtual objects in a real space by representing only indirect information instead of direct information. Furthermore, we proposed a new system for presentation of weights of virtual objects by transportation of fluid.

CONCLUSION OF THIS CHAPTER

In this chapter, we introduced three multi-sensory entertainment systems utilizing virtual reality technology. Haptics, olfaction and indirect information, which play important roles in our applications, are not used widely in current video game system. We hope that our applications could show the possibilities of multi-sensory entertainment system to establish more realistic interaction between players and virtual worlds in the application.

For the readers who have more interest in multi sensory entertainment applications, we recommend to look over the following conferences, competitions and events:

- In United States:
  ○ ACM SIGGRAPH Emerging Technologies / Art Gallery
- In Europe:
  ○ Ars Electronica
  ○ Laval Virtual

- In Japan:
  ○ International collegiate Virtual Reality Contest (IVRC)
  ○ Interactive Tokyo
  ○ Japan Media Arts Festival

REFERENCES

Aoki, T., Matsushita, T., Iio, Y., Mitake, H., Toyama, T., Hasegawa, S., et al. Matumura, I. (2005). Kobito: virtual brownies. In *ACM SIGGRAPH 2005 Emerging Technologies* (Article No. 11).

Cates, M. E., Haw, M. D., & Holmes, C. B. (2005). Dilatancy, jamming, and the physics of granulation. *Journal of Physics Condensed Matter, 17*(24), S2517–S2531. doi:10.1088/0953-8984/17/24/010

Cypher, M. (2006). Biophilia. In *ACM SIGGRAPH 2006 Sketches* (Article No. 24).

Hashimoto, Y., Nagaya, N., Kojima, M., Ohtaki, J., Mitani, T., Yamamoto, A., et al. Inami, M. (2005). Straw-like user interface. In *ACM SIGGRAPH 2005 Emerging Technologies* (Article No. 20).

Heilig, M. L. (1992). El cine del futuro: the cinema of the future. *Presence (Cambridge, Mass.), 1*(3), 279–294.

Konyo, M., Tadokoro, S., Yoshida, A., & Saiwaki, N. (2005). A tactile synthesis method using multiple frequency vibrations for representing virtual touch. In *Proceedings of IEEE/RSJ International Conference on Intelligent Robots and Systems* (pp. 3965-3971).

Mochizuki, A., Amada, T., Sawa, S., Takeda, T., Motoyashiki, S., Kohyama, K., et al. Chihara, K. (2004). Fragra: a visual-olfactory VR game. In *ACM SIGGRAPH 2004 Sketches* (p. 123).

Mozeika, A., Steltz, E., & Jaeger, H. M. (2009). The first steps of a robot based on jamming skin enabled locomotion. In *Proceedings of IEEE/RSJ International Conference on Intelligent Robots and Systems* (pp. 408-409).

Nakano, Y., Ouwa, H., Kawashima, K., Komura, H., Sagano, M., Shirazawa, T., et al. Chihara, K. (2006). INVISIBLE: the shadow chaser. In *ACM SIGGRAPH 2006 Emerging Technologies* (Article No. 19).

Narumi, T., Hiyama, A., Tanikawa, T., & Hirose, M. (2007). Inter-glow. In *ACM SIGGRAPH 2007 Emerging Technologies* (Article No. 14).

Saga, S., & Deguchi, K. (2010). Dilatant fluid based tactile display -Basic concept. In *Proceedings of IEEE Haptics Symposium* (pp. 309-312).

Sato, K., Sato, Y., Sato, M., Fukushima, S., Okano, Y., Matsuo, K., et al. Kajimoto, H. (2008). Ants in the Pants. In *ACM SIGGRAPH 2008 New Tech Demos* (Article No. 3).

Uchida, Y., Naito, M., & Hirayama, S. (2007). "Kage no Sekai": interactive animation of shadow based on physical action. In *Proceedings of International Conference on Advances in Computer Entertainment Technology* (pp. 274-275).

Yamada, T., Yokoyama, S., Tanikawa, T., Hirota, K., & Hirose, M. (2006). Wearable olfactory display: Using odor in outdoor environment. In *Proceedings of IEEE Virtual Reality Conference* (pp. 199-206).

Yanagida, Y., Kawato, S., Noma, H., Tomono, A., & Tesutani, N. (2004). Projection based olfactory display with nose tracking. In *Proceedings of IEEE Virtual Reality* (pp. 43-50).

Yoshimoto, S., Hamada, Y., Tokui, T., Suetake, T., Imura, M., Kuroda, Y., & Oshiro, O. (2010). Haptic canvas: dilatant fluid based haptic interaction. In *ACM SIGGRAPH 2010 Emerging Technologies* (Article No. 13).

Chapter 9

Thinking Head MulSeMedia:
A Storytelling Environment for Embodied Language Learning

Tom A. F. Anderson
Flinders University of South Australia, Australia

Zhi-Hong Chen
National Central University, Taiwan

Yean-Fu Wen
National Chiayi University, Taiwan

Marissa Milne
Flinders University of South Australia, Australia

Adham Atyabi
Flinders University of South Australia, Australia

Kenneth Treharne
Flinders University of South Australia, Australia

Takeshi Matsumoto
Flinders University of South Australia, Australia

Xi-Bin Jia
Beijing University of Technology, China P.R.C

Martin Luerssen
Flinders University of South Australia, Australia

Trent Lewis
Flinders University of South Australia, Australia

Richard Leibbrandt
Flinders University of South Australia, Australia

David M. W. Powers
Flinders University of South Australia, Australia

ABSTRACT

With technological improvements and widespread computer usage, the need for user-friendly human-machine interfaces is steadily increasing. Computer graphics and audio provide a colourful world of visual and auditory experiences; nevertheless, tutoring systems have traditionally used keyboard and mouse almost exclusively, limiting significantly the input mechanisms available to content designers. Multisensory learning is beneficial for learning a new language (Birsh, 1999), and through increasing the affordances of interaction, learning scenarios can be significantly augmented.

DOI: 10.4018/978-1-60960-821-7.ch009

The Thinking Head is an embodied conversational agent that be used in intelligent tutoring systems as the representation of a teacher and tutor for one-on-one computer learning and teaching. Although there are many applications that benefit from an embodied conversational agent and there has been a push in our research community towards improving embodied conversational agents, our main area of research lies in the creation of applications for second language learning (as introduced in Powers, 2007; Powers et al., 2008). We have explored speech synthesis and speech recognition to permit users to interact with computer systems with their voices. To facilitate language learning through conversation, we have incorporated these auditory capabilities into the Thinking Head; additionally, we seek to create a bridge between the virtual and physical worlds through physical manipulation, achieved primarily through visual input recognition with affordable devices such as webcams.

The hybrid world provides a framework for the creation of lessons that teach and test knowledge in the second language. In one of our example grammar and vocabulary lessons, the Thinking Head instructs the student to move a tiger to a lake—a student moving the toy tiger in the real world effectively moves a virtual tiger in the virtual arena. This type of interaction is beneficial for computer-based language learning especially because we are able to see a student has successfully understood the directions if the tiger is moved to the vicinity of the virtual lake. Physical movement helps the learner to internalise the novel relationships in the second language. We also provide for additional forms of communication, including dialogue with an embodied conversational agent and writing stories using markers on a whiteboard. In summary, our system provides a natural interface with which to communicate with the hybrid-reality learning environment.

INTRODUCTION

In this chapter, we explore interactions with the Thinking Head computer interface arising from a fusion of inputs of voice, objects, and writing—without keyboard and mouse. The Thinking Head system for language learning teaches through stories; however, the Thinking Head is not just the storyteller, but rather the medium in which the storyteller and story exist, and through which a learner learns to tell the stories. A learner engages in the multisensory storytelling activity by interacting with physical props within a room to learn the stories.

A user manipulates real-world objects within the Thinking Head virtual arena. In our implementation, objects are most commonly small graspable things; however, our use of the term *object* applies more generally to refer to things of all sizes, persons, places, and ideas. Indeed, humans have given names to objects for thousands

of years, and the meanings of objects take form as the words we use as tools in communication. In SIMULA 67, arguably the first object-oriented computer programming language, objects were representations in a discrete event system (Dahl, 1968). As Lorenz (1993, p. 12) characterises objects in computer programming, "An object is anything that models 'things' in the real world. These 'things' may be physical entities such as cars, or events such as a concert, or abstractions such as a general-purpose account." Thus, for our purposes, an object is any natural thing or combination of things that can be quantified, described, or elaborated by man or machine.

Traditionally, computer multimedia applications consist of audio and video, while MulSeMedia, or multiple sensorial media, enhances the user interaction experience. The use of realia (physical props such as apples, hats, and magazines) adds to the language learning experience because realia engages the senses. Object recognition determines the identity, location, and movements of known physical objects, and classification heuristics categorise unknown objects. Those objects are rendered with respect to landmarks in the virtual world, creating a hybrid media experience that enhances class-based learning and provides a strong practical component that is easily accessible in the classroom or at home. Finally, writing practice reinforces the lessons and adds more latitude for expressing creativity.

The first question we need to address is how to promote modes of MulSeMedia learning beyond the standard keyboard and mouse interface. Although interactive systems challenge the brain, Crawford (2003) notes that the typical scenario for play with a computer works with most of the body immobile. The advantage of learning in a multisensory computer environment is that the user can retain the benefits of computer processing while interacting with tangible objects in the environment. The goal of language learning is to become functional in the real world. As it is impractical and expensive for many language learners to travel to the part of the world where people speak the target language, it is desirable to learn by oneself in an immersive and interactive environment.

Language is produced as a reflection of multisensory perceptions of the world around. As children, we naturally acquire language of our physical, social, and cultural environment, but as we grow older, the gaining of fluency in a new language takes a different route. Although some believe that it is more difficult for teens and adults to learn a language, Krashen (1987) argues that it is not that the older learners proceed more slowly, it is rather that the interactive and comprehensible nature of the environment of the younger learners favours their learning. It is common knowledge that adults simplify the complexity of the language when they speak with children. By gradually and incrementally increasing language complexity while maintaining comprehension, learners of all ages come to perceive language not simply as a logical collection of information but also as a system of understanding the world. We believe that when a learner engages in MulSeMedia experiences that are challenging yet stimulating, the language that is learned is grounded in experience, providing basic language skills that are later necessary to engage in reading.

There are substantial technical barriers to providing an interactive and adaptive language experience, difficulties which arise in the way that the computer perceives, represents, and portrays the world. For many years, the computer has been restricted to two-dimensional representations on flat screens. The computer, equipped with sensors, thereby has an agency that allows it to perceive meanings in the world, channelling the actions of the learner towards effective practices.

Furthermore, by perceiving learners and gaining a better model of the learner in three-dimensional spaces, we can gain a closer understanding of how the learner views the language as a mechanism of conveying understanding about the world. Through video, the computer can communicate with the learner, gently informing the learner that their actions have somehow inadequately achieved the goal communicated to them, or alternately, commending their satisfactory actions.

The computer has become a very large part of people's lives, and as such, it is necessary for a language learner to acquire the language corresponding to computer-based environments. Experience gained with the Thinking Head for learning natural languages extends to learning programming languages and the interfaces of computer systems. The interface that we are talking about has no keyboard or mouse, but it does include speech recognition and speech synthesis, and object and gesture recognition. Arguably, even speech recognition is multisensory, because the throat muscles move and the vocal chords produce sound, and the listener perceives feedback with multiple senses on multiple levels—directly as proprioception, and indirectly through other respondents.

It is theoretically possible to explicitly hard-wire the behaviour of the system in response to each change in relationship, but as the number of objects grows, the complexity of the system increases accordingly. Therefore, in order to reduce complexity it is desirable to pass many of the decisions about the intended result of user interactions to the system itself. In later sections, we will discuss the creation of a system to support interactive stories for the purposes of language learning.

THE STATE OF THE ART

A room-based system for second language learning is a system of interactive services that provides different outputs based on the locations and behaviours of people and objects. First, we review previous work on systems for interactive storytelling, including room-based systems, where embodied conversational agents portray the role of teacher, confidante, or storyteller. Then, we present factors involved in facilitating interaction with a computer system primarily through spoken language and movements of body and objects, including machine use and recognition of human language, speech synthesis and recognition, vision, wireless sensors, and machine learning. We provide a brief overview of second language learning for context, but then present a more in-depth research basis of our approach to language learning through stories. Subsequently, we present the literature on computer-based education with a focus on MulSeMedia and interactive education with embodied conversational agents.

Storytelling Platforms

It has traditionally been difficult to build an interactive story-based language learning computer system, which is essential to defining the space of a story environment that uses a tangible interface. More recently, however, a wide array of low-cost multiprocessors and sensors have become available, making the visions of dream-based research[1] increasingly possible.

One-to-one[2] technology-enhanced learning (i.e., each student has at least one computing device to help his/her learning) brings promising potentials for students, including active, productive, creative, and collaborative learning (Chan et al., 2005). When all students have a computing device that has wireless access to Internet resources and multiple sensors to identify tangible objects in a learning context, students can acquire relevant information and can even interact with different learning objects. Such technology support is crucial for some learning activities, especially for storytelling activity, because an enriched environment could facilitate students' productive thinking, creative ideas, and collaborative behaviours.

Storytelling platforms provide a composite and changing environment in which to act together with a computer (Crawford, 2004). In the Story-Rooms of Alborzi et al. (2000), it was reported that a multisensory environment for storytelling is intrinsically motivating. Ribiero et al. (2009) demonstrated that interaction with robots is a useful educational tool for arts and languages, and can be applied to storytelling. Their learners used robots as their characters in a drama, but rather than using a natural language interface, they scripted the interactions by using a visual programming language. Likewise, participatory design researchers Druin et al. (1999) demonstrated that children could successfully build personas for robots that could be a medium for storytelling.

Tangible Interfaces

Although computers and virtual reality offer many advantages, real-world tangible objects may be superior to them in certain ways. O'Malley and Fraser (2004) categorised tangibles for education into four main classes: (1) digitally augmented paper and books; (2) physical items used as interfaces to virtual worlds; (3) digitally enhanced tangibles (e.g. robots or other devices that interact with other tangibles); and (4) sensors, which gather information about the world. Our storytelling world incorporates all these types of tangibles.

Tangible interfaces compare favourably to virtual ones. Wooden blocks, which are moved by grasping, contrasted with virtual blocks that are moved by a computer mouse, were found to have distinct advantages for learning (Verhaegh, 2008). This phenomenon is attributable to the ease of manipulation of real-world objects, which can be moved into different arrangements more efficiently, with positive effects on learning. An implication of this is that the innate human ability to manipulate real-world objects can improve computer interfaces.

Yet real objects need not be without the advantage of computer processing. "A networked toy may provide aural, visual, motion, tactile and other feedback, and be able to sense speech, physical manipulation, and absolute and relative location." (Srivastava et al., 2001, p. 2) Such toys equipped with wireless sensors in a smart room for learning also offer significant capabilities for the lesson designer. Tangible interfaces, in the form of physical objects that are to be touched and moved, allow for tighter representational mappings between the objects and the meanings they represent (O'Malley & Fraser, 2004).

Research into multimodality finds implications for language learning. Audio-only learning is inferior to multimodal conditions in which language is visually grounded; not only in terms of the quality of machine learning of language, but also, for a computer system learning human language, the availability of more modalities of inputs offers more understanding (Roy, 1999). Computational models of language provide insight for improving the capabilities of computer systems, and furthermore also shed light on the abilities of humans to use language.

Handheld objects and devices offer an additional level to the hybrid reality. These location-aware objects represent many different things

for language learning—learners grasp and move them to reflect changes in the story, and these objects provide outputs such as haptic feedback or sound. Despite having relatively smaller screens than computers with situated LCD monitors, users perceive that handheld devices have a larger field of view and provide a natural interface that promotes proprioception and immersion (Hwang *et al.*, 2006).

Online and offline character recognition mechanisms allow users to write on real-world surfaces with everyday marking utensils, for example, by using a marker on a standard whiteboard. Handwriting recognition forms an important component in building human-machine interfaces (Plamondon, 2000), and the interactional aspect of real-time processing of handwriting offers a great deal to educational media designers. The accuracy of classification results increases as a result of tracking the position of the hand and movements of the pen as users write, but more significantly, this mechanism also provides the user with a natural language interface with which to communicate with the learning environment.

Embodied Conversational Agents

Embodied conversational agents are known by several names; depending on the domain, they may be referred to as intelligent, animated agents, as pedagogical agents or as educational agents (for a more in-depth discussion, see Veletsianos *et al.*, 2010). Embodied conversational agents are computer-generated animated characters that engage in multi-modal dialogue involving speech, intonation, and gestures. They are most commonly used in video games, but over the years, a number of such agents have been developed for a variety of applications in a broad array of disciplines. The trend in recent years has been towards increasing realism in terms of graphics and agent behaviour. Their inclusion in interactive systems makes user interactions with the computer more like interactions with a human.

Virtual agents can be used in the storytelling context in the roles such as the storyteller, characters in the story or the audience. Some embodied conversational agents are tailored for specific teaching tasks, e.g. Baldi (Massaro, 2004). Others like Greta (Poggi, 2005) take a more holistic approach. On the other hand, a pedagogical agent with only a single identity is constrained to that identity, which might not be advantageous among some target audiences. Our previous work was to create a platform for embodied conversational agents, specifically designed to portray multiple and varied personas (Luerssen & Lewis, 2010).

Embodied educational virtual characters have the capability to drive learning in terms of two factors: *learning motivation* and *learning experience* (Chen *et al.*, 2009). By involving the learners emotionally in the virtual characters, we maintain their attention and drive to succeed in the educational activity. And by improving the emotional ties of the learning experience, we enhance the learning opportunities based on relationships within the environment. As students build relationships with virtual characters, they increase their affinity for the domain subjects.

When humans interact, the participants modify their strategies based on the conversation. In embodied conversational agents, template matching is a common strategy, and audible or visual speech is generally processed to and from text-based expressions. Thus dialogue systems are natural language systems that represent dialogue and productions as text. The findings of Chu-Carroll (2000), who developed MIMIC, a dialogue manager with strategic generative mechanisms that adapted to the interaction, suggest that dialogue managers should determine when to take the initiative to better match the expectations of humans who interact with embodied conversational agents.

Second Language Learning

In early childhood, we acquired language through the activities of play with objects, not in deliberate efforts to transfer knowledge from one person to another but in symbolic activities with intentions to imitate basic events (Nelson, 1998). We can draw some useful analogies from the way that a child learns their mother tongue, but in the case of learning a second language, learners may be of any age. It is thus relevant to consider that the main purpose of learning a language is to gain a tool. The production and comprehension of the foreign language vocabulary in the context of sentences is thus a tool to receive and create the expression of thoughts of others. A word or phrase is a symbolic representation, "a close amalgam of thought and language that it is hard to tell whether it is a phenomenon of speech or a phenomenon of thought". (Vygotsky, 1964) Reality, generalized in a word, takes different meanings and associations according to the circumstances and the evolutions of the language. Thus, from our perspective, the learning of language is the learning of shared cultural meanings towards participating in that culture.

There are a number of popular approaches to language teaching, including: grammar-translation, the audio-lingual method, and the communicative approach, but these, as with most language learning methods, have little to do with physical action in the real world. Total Physical Response (often known as TPR) is a method that involves physical movement in the learning of a new language (Asher, 2000). In Total Physical Response, as in more traditional classrooms, a teacher leads the second language lesson, but unique to the Total Physical Response methodology, the teacher produces utterances that demand a physical response from the learners, many times involving the manipulation of objects. The involvement of the body in such kinaesthetic learning activates portions of the brain—in particular, the right hemisphere—which is considered to be under-stimulated in standard language learning through lectures and repetition. Through Total Physical Response, learners acquire a new language through whole-body interactions much faster rather than the rote learning and analysis of the logistics of language that is prevalent in many language lessons. In particular, we feel that the learners gain a shared cultural understanding of the components of language grounded in physical interactions.

Stories for Language Learning

Our current work centres on the telling of stories as a form of language learning. We seek to enhance language learning by incorporating the methodology of Teaching Proficiency through Reading and Storytelling (TPR Storytelling), which extends movement-based learning to the learning of language in stories (Ray & Seeley, 1997)[2]. The storytelling procedures elaborated in this chapter arise in TPR Storytelling, the cornerstone of our current efforts. A classroom teacher who adheres to the TPR Storytelling method engages learners in the stories through active responses and involves them directly—both as actors and as storytellers. Language learning through storytelling creates a social context that brings together the participants as a community that has certain stories in common (Brune, 2004). Allowing for sufficient questioning to tease out the finer details, the learners of a language taught through stories are learning as insiders. Furthermore, learners are using all their human senses and are therefore implicitly learning the language that conveys meaning about things perceived.

Stories have many of the essential elements required for successful language learning. Stories are handed down for generations because stories communicate something through language that echoes within our imaginations. It is through hearing stories that we come to understand the relationships between things in the words of another. Much of human cultural memory is stored in stories, and the language that facilitates the telling of stories is the heart of language. Knowing the basics of a language allows any learner to be able to learn more of the language through comprehensible stories (Krashen, 1987). To understand a story, it is necessary to understand how the relationships between things change over time. Stories communicate the changes in inter-relationships between elements over time, and when stories are interesting, those who receive the stories are motivated to listen.

There are many different kinds of stories. We describe these with words like comedy and tragedy—terms which describe the emotions evoked. The learner attaches meaning to an emotional context that is grounded in the experience. In a story, the intertwining of language learning and the content of the story rewards the learner, who understands the language because there is a story to understand. The learner understands why things happen, gaining insight into the important objects in the story.

TPR storytelling provides for scaffolding and expansion of language. The first time that the story is told, it is told in broad strokes, in generalities that the learner gradually recognises as the basic story; successively, as the learner becomes more able to understand the story, increased levels of details emerge. For example, a love story can be expressed in general terms as between a man and a woman, but attention is piqued by insider details. Questions are bound to arise when a storyteller reveals that the man is a 112-year-old man named Dave Armstrong who is a new resident of Manhattan. There is always more to any story than can be received on its first telling. Additionally, as details emerge, the audience begins to relate the objects with the cultural memory. When the audience find out that Dave has been in cryogenic sleep for 65 years, they will begin to draw analogy to stories or folktales – both Rumplestiltskin and Snow White depict the events that unfold for people who sleep for long periods.

To learn a new language, it is vitally important to learn a great deal, but it is also quite important to have something new to learn about. Television and movies are the media with the most familiarity in society today, but lessons delivered through the television are not successful for language learning, as it is not enough to just see and hear language learning media: you must be able to understand it (Krashen, 1987). We extend Krashen's argument, believing that it is just not sufficient to click a mouse to communicate to the system when you do not understand—you need to be able to talk with the storyteller, to ask and answer questions. Furthermore, the storyteller should be able to ask questions, and the system receives the answer by way of natural speech or physical movements. The people who learn in this way can apply the memorable experiences that they gain with the stories to interactions in the outside world; for example, when the learner gets the chance to interact with a native speaker, they will know how to ask for clarification because the computer system frequently asked for clarification in a real and friendly way.

The greatest stories transcend language barriers because of their themes and narratives, as in the mythology of Joseph Campbell's hero journey (Inchauste, 2010). A compelling story follows a storytelling arc, meaning that the events in the story build repeatedly towards a climax. A compelling story is one that influences our emotions, which arouses the curiosities. Therefore, to allow the curiosity to drive the language learning, we must also make the story change in a way that is adaptive to the learner. Using stories in language learning, when the learner comes to understand that certain ways of speaking are natural, we have succeeded to a certain degree. When we ask questions about the occurrences in a story, we have a shared space that contains a memory of things and events that have occurred.

Nonverbal Communication

Human communication is a means of expression and is more than just the words of the language; accordingly, interaction with an embodied conversational agent is not limited to communication with words. "Believable nonverbal behaviours for embodied conversational agents (ECA) can create a more immersive experience for users and improve the effectiveness of communication." (Lee & Marsella, 2006) To indicate the location of an object, a turn of the head or a move of the hand suffices better than a detailed explanation. Similarly, when a speaker increases the rapidity of their eye blinks, it signals that the speaker has an increased emotional attachment to the topic.

An embodied conversational agent can also employ nonverbal behaviours to deepen the experience of interaction and to improve the quality of communication. Many elements of nonverbal communications are culture-specific, thus of interest for language learning. An embodied conversation agent has many qualities that make it an ideal teacher for teaching language, including: it never tires of teaching the same thing repeatedly with multitudes of different students, and it can collect user data for grading the learning and for system evaluation. For an overview of expression and virtual characters, see Vinayagamoorthy *et al*. (2006).

Visual Speech Synthesis

Many streams of information are manifest in human perception of speech. The visible movements of the face of the speaker contribute a great deal to the comprehension of speech. Modelling correct pronunciation is more than just the correct modelling of acoustic phenomena. If a student is to learn to control the position of their mouth in a suitable fashion, it is also favourable to interact with a working example, for example a human teacher or a realistic virtual head, to provide a mechanism for learning to know how to produce a particular phoneme. Vision is an important part of the listening process (Kellerman, 1988), and particularly for language learners, this means that designers should provide ways to supplement audio with mouth movements, such as with a talking head (Massaro, 2004).

IMPLEMENTATION

The Thinking Head system is an extensible framework for interaction with a multimedia system. First, we present the implementation of the Thinking Head system for second language learning and the system architecture. We then describe the system's embodiment in terms of the perceptions of users of the language learning system. Subsequently, we recount the capabilities of the system to perceive and act in the world. Finally, we provide a sample language lesson to give readers a sample of the capabilities of the system.

Thinking Head

The Thinking Head is an animated head (see Figure 1) with several screens, cameras, and tangible objects—but conspicuously, there is no keyboard or mouse. The system perceives and interprets inputs primary from the visual and auditory domains captured by the respective sensors. It responds in accordance with the in-built dialogue manager, which defines the function of the Thinking Head as a Teaching Head that provides instruction and companionship, and which has been extended to present multimedia lessons that promote second language acquisition.

Although perception by the system is the main feature of this project, the appearance (or synthesis) of the system what users perceive most immediately. Since first impressions matter, we have implemented virtual characters that animate realistically and are visually appealing and likeable. The framework that drives the system provides both the external form (e.g. through monitors,

speakers and tangible objects) and a perceptive system that allows it to produce reactions to human stimuli that appear intelligent. It can be configured to specific language learning tasks and is interoperable with other subsystems, such as with vision processing and audio/visual speech synthesis. We use both pre-recorded audio, which allows for high quality pronunciation, and a text-to-speech engine, which allows the natural language production system to produce unique utterances. Additionally, the speaking voice synchronizes with lip movements of the Thinking Head.

In terms of outputs, the Thinking Head is in many ways like standard media, which is dependent on sight and sound. On the other hand, the Thinking Head provides for multiple modes of inputs and outputs to engage the senses of the language learner, particularly to situate the learning of the new language in vivid, multisensory experiences. We have a sound system to produce audio and a colour monitor for vision; many of the monitors we use are standard LCDs, but we also have implementations that use LCD projectors or 3D monitors. On the other hand, the fixed location of a standard computer monitor restricts interaction: in our implementation, a number of user-movable LCD screens provide output devices that can provide 3D information. Users of the system can manipulate these screens, which may be unattached or anchored, and the outputs of the system change in accordance with the changes in spatial locations and orientations.

Objects of interest, including the monitors and screens, are more than just display devices; they also provide affordances for interaction. The holding and moving of these objects is a form of input for the system, and the learner sees and touches these objects—and potentially smells or tastes them, in the case of fragrant objects or food, respectively. Additional output capabilities of objects of interest include localised sound production and haptic feedback, but the changes in outputs are not restricted. The environment—or

Figure 1. This representation of the Thinking Head, an embodied conversational agent, is used as a mediator for storytelling

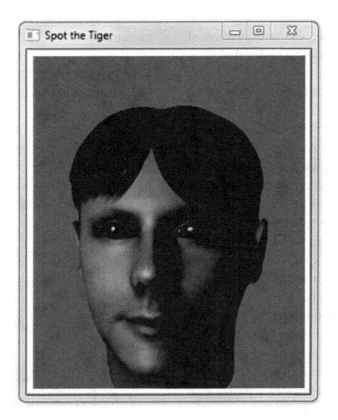

the objects of interest themselves—responds by providing contextualised output, which provides learners with feedback naturally grounded in the language system.

As a form of hybrid reality, many tangible objects in the learning space have correspondences in the virtual world. A child's toy held in the hand, merely a simple graspable object in the real world, becomes any object or objects in the virtual world, promoting multimodal channels for messages that expose spatial and relational meanings.

What Information Does the System Perceive?

The inputs to the system come from the environment of the learning space, which is comprised of objects, some movable and others fixed. In this context, the learner and the infrastructure are also elements of the environment. The system gathers information about the environment and the interactions with the environment through sensors in the room. Some of our cameras possess pan-tilt mechanisms; by way of moving the camera judiciously, the learning space system can fine-tune its survey of the visual field. The perceptive components of the system additionally observe the outputs that the system produces, allowing for improvements based on these observations.

The Thinking Head system can see and hear. Unlike traditional systems that simply forward or record video or voice data, the Thinking Head can analyse the data to perceive certain attributes and changes to the environment. The system is able to upload data from the learning space that it perceives to the Internet using web services.

This data would be stored securely to maintain the confidentiality of learner data. Future use of the data allows for fine-tuning of algorithms, inter-learner comparisons, and re-evaluation of results under new theoretical frameworks.

How are Objects Located and Tracked?

An important component of our language learning lessons is the use of tangible objects. It is through the interactions of learners with these objects that we are able to determine comprehension levels for the stories. We have investigated a number of different techniques to recognise and track the movements of objects. Our focus is on the tracking of objects with low cost webcams through primary geometric representation of objects detected through colour channels.

Each of the tangible objects used in the language lessons has a unique colour signature, determined based on hue and saturation, which enables the system to differentiate it from other objects. Analysis of the visual scene uses a database of object colour signatures. In Figure 2, for example, the low saturation of the hourglass (shown in Figure 1) is most prominent in the blue colour area. In Figure 4, on the other hand, the saturation of the pencil sharpener (shown in Figure 3) spread in the red hue is clearly distinct from that of the hourglass. The algorithm for object recognition enables real-time object recognition with low demands on processing (for more technical details, see Franzel & Newman, 2009).

Sensor data transmitted wirelessly improves the accuracy of object localisation beyond the visual recognition. For example, accelerometers that measure rotations in different axes provide some information about the movement of a tangible object in three-dimensional space. If the object moves through a position in which it is partially obscured, the sensor data contributes to the object localisation task through data fusion techniques. Other location data collected within the learning space include wireless TOA, audio

and vision processing by combining views of the scene from multiple cameras. Estimations of body positioning provide constraints on the possible movements.

What Does Location Information Provide?

The use of optimised algorithms such as these allow for real-time tracking and localisation, enabling us to create lessons that incorporate the movements of real-world objects. When learning one of our mini-stories, for example, a learner

Figure 2. An image of a pig

Figure 3. Hue-saturation fingerprint of the image in Figure 2

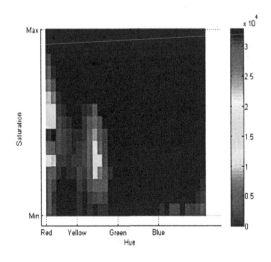

Figure 4. An image of a tiger

Figure 5. Hue-saturation fingerprint of the image in Figure4

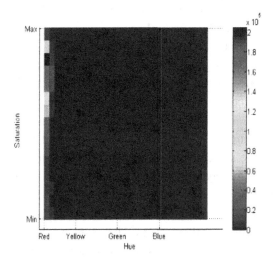

The system can locate the toy animal in regards to the other objects of interest, and when the learner makes a correct gesture with the objects, the system provides positive feedback. If the toy is moved into a particular location, feedback relates to the system of understanding that is be-ing constructed for that location: for example, (1) haptic feedback in the form of vibration; (2) a noticeable sound emerges; and (3) the visual appearance of the toy or its representation in the virtual environment becomes noticeably changed. This feedback, which varies from situation to situation and location to location, becomes part of the learner's understanding. What is on its face a lesson in human communication is indeed a shared perception of the infinite possibilities of human existence manifested as stories, and thus the language of communicating about events and situations is realised as a bridge between entities such as humans and machines.

In conjunction with object localisation is the expression of those locations in relation to other tangible and virtual objects and locations. Configurations of objects are determined through natural language training of the system. In creating a language-learning lesson, the lesson designer trains the system to recognize those locations of the tangible object that correspond to the relative phrases.

For example, take the phrase with the general meaning: "the animal is in the water". The lesson designer must indicate those configurations of objects that are in agreement with the phrase, and there are additionally innumerable variations of the phrase that are also synonymic or holonymic with the phrase, such as: "the creature is in the water", "the big animal has jumped in the lake", or even "the foamy seawater readily engulfs the eager tiger". The building blocks of speech (such as adjectives and adverbs) add richness to an interaction experience that conveys, through language, more fine-grained and deeper meaning. Conversely, lending such tools for expression to the lesson designer complicates the task of training the computer to identify agreement with a sentence that conveys meaning that corresponds to complex interrelationships between concrete objects and abstract concepts in space and time.

Additionally, the system must recognise when configurations agree. In our previous example, if the learner evidenced relationships between objects according to the sentence: "it went into and then out of the water", then it would not be construed as an acceptable understanding of that aspect of the multimedia lesson. The Thinking Head system provides feedback to the learner to reduce misunderstandings and to promote rapid comprehension and assimilation of ways of communicating.

Mini-Story

To provide the reader with a clear example that explicates language learning through MulSeMedia, we here elaborate the short mini-story lesson called Spot the Hungry Tiger. This mini-story teaches the new phrases and words: "loaf of bread", "very dirty", and "wash up". We have elected to use several real world objects for the lesson: A toy tiger, a plastic banana, a real loaf of bread, and a manipulable LCD screen. Although this story is short, it incorporates the storytelling

techniques of building toward a climax to maintain interest and promote emotional attachment with the movements of the story.

Initially, it is our assumption that the learner knows a fair number of the words in the story, but not all of them. The first part of the lesson is vocabulary acquisition exercises, conducted through images, question and answer, repetition drills and mnemonics. Learners can associate gestures with phrases as a physical mnemonic technique. For example, the learner enacts the phrase "wash up" by an imaginary opening of a faucet and rubbing hands under the stream of water. By the simple monitoring of changes in hand positions, the learner is quizzed on their learning of this hand movement, and research into Total Physical Response (as presented in the literature review) has demonstrated its effectiveness—learners are able to naturally associate the kinaesthetic mode of expression with the words and phrases (Asher, 2000). Once the learner is confident with the set of three or four words and phrases, a procedure that takes up to five minutes, they proceed to learn the story.

A brief version of the story is as follows: "Spot is a tiger. Spot goes to the market and eats a loaf of bread and six pieces of chocolate. The shopkeeper laughs because the chocolate makes Spot's face very dirty. Spot runs to the lake to wash up." This story, though short and simple, can be a memorable experience for a learner in the early stages of language acquisition. Although the story can be written as it was above, the focus is on the meanings and interrelationships, not on the sentences themselves. Therefore, as there are many possible ways to tell any story, there are also many versions of the story.

Through repeated retellings, the story becomes more elaborate in accordance with the comprehension of the learners. For example, at the beginning of the story, the learner discovers that the tiger is small and lives with his aunt. This morning, the small tiger woke up in his blue and yellow bedroom feeling extremely hungry. Later, learners discover that the market's name is Willie's Marvellous Grocery Store, and that Spot runs away to a unique location, perhaps the Rock of Gibraltar. Learners will not quickly forget these stories, in part because of their interesting and vivid details, nor will they forget many of the ways to describe the details. This is essential for language learning—the learner gradually builds a meaningful mental system of expression in the new language. Furthermore, as the system is adaptive, the learner adds some of the details in response to the system's questions. Giving the learner a voice in the process means that the learner feels a part of the process, and because the computer can store the details of learning in its persistent memory, subsequently these personalisations are incorporated into later language learning lessons.

Procedures of Telling the Stories

Vocabulary Learning

The learner first learns what the new phrases mean through a series of physical actions. This is where we need the MulSeMedia user interface. The learner moves the real objects around. When learners are learning the verb "laugh", the computer asks the learner to really laugh. This builds a strong association with the verb and a natural memory of it.

Comprehension Checks

As the computer tells the story, it performs comprehension checks throughout. This means that the animated teaching head can ask a question. For example, there are a number of ways that the system can ensure complete understanding at the part of the story where Spot eats the piece of bread. For example, in one part of the story it asks the comprehension check questions: "What was it that Spot ate a piece of" or "Is Spot a dog or is he a tiger?" If the learner does not give the right answer, then an inadequate level of language understanding is apparent. In order to facilitate

later retellings of the story, the system would then attempt to better acquaint the learner with the understanding of bread. For example, since a loaf of bread was prepared for the lesson, the learner can really take a bite of a piece of bread. By associating the taste of bread with the foreign language, we believe that the learner acquires the new word, grounded in experience.

As the computer tells the story, the learner acts it out, as shown in Figures 6 and 7. Figure 6 illustrates the learner, who is holding a toy tiger. The colour signature of the tiger, derived from the hue and saturation, determines the yellow bounding box. Figure 7 shows the tiger running away from the shopkeeper.

Retelling the Story

A significant goal of the TPR Storytelling system of instruction is to teach a learner to a point where they are able to produce unique utterances in the new language. In our view, language is a thought provoking and motivating tool. In addition to physical acting, the learner interacts with the learning space through speaking. Learners use multiple avenues to express the stories, including

Figure 6. The view of the tiger from the webcam. Note that the camera is looking from the front, so the virtual image seems reversed.

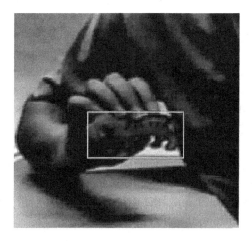

Figure 7. Spot the Tiger heads for the lake in the virtual world, movements controlled by the actions depicted in Figure 6

word webs, oral retellings, and reframing. Word webs provide a safe way for learners to reflect upon the interrelationships inherent to the story and the intrinsic relationships between characters and places. Word webs change over time to reflect the different parts of the story leading up to the climax. The learner tells the story in portions or in whole to the Thinking Head or to other learners. As stories naturally take place over time, reframing allows the learning of different verb tenses. Through repeated retellings of the story from the perspective of different characters in the story, learners acquire an understanding of the first person, second person and third person.

To act out the story, the learner uses a device with a small screen to tell the story. The learner holds the moveable device that represents the shopkeeper, who is the manager of the grocery store known as Marvellous Market. The learner sees three types of facial expression appear on the small movable screen, and by selecting the appropriate one, the grocer laughs heartily in response to the dirty face of the tiger.

Writing on the Whiteboard

Finally, to indicate their accomplishment learners write their versions of the story. Our system requires low-cost webcams, calibrated to acquire words written on a standard whiteboard using a marker, with both off-line and on-line writing recognition algorithms designed for this purpose (c.f. Gustainis, 2009; Sydlowski, 2009). The system records the writing of learners, and a natural language system could be used to recognise common errors made by second language learners.

Learners in the early stages of language acquisition may simply copy the majority of their ministory, while replacing key phrases with their own words. For example, a learner may write a story about a small white dog that goes to the market. This story is similar to the story "Spot the Thief" that was learned in the lesson, but allows the creative expression within a familiar framework. As learners become more confident in their language abilities, their stories in the new language become creations that are more individual.

DISCUSSION

Despite the advantages of new ways to interact with the computer, it is important to keep the educational goals in sight. Learning a new language is learning a view of the new language as a system that represents changing relationships within the real world. Accordingly, to provide learning experiences that are transferable, it is relevant to consider new ways of interacting with educational media, since learning improves, particularly when more senses are involved.

Not all learning must occur through the strict processes of formal schooling. As Papert (1980) suggests, microworlds serve as "incubators of knowledge". Learning the particular details of a language in the certain context of a specific story implies that learners are gaining their knowledge through direct experience. Learning the details of the story facilitates a natural acquisition of the language of the story, and provided that the designers choose the language that is frequently useful for conveying these stories, learners gain facility with the language of the stories and they also naturally gain the rudiments necessary for fluency in the language.

For efficient and natural teaching, we involve the learners physically. The physical response of a learner becomes an anchor on which the learner can hang more language. For example, we might ask a learner to associate a certain action with a word that they are learning. For example, if they are to remember the word "mobile phone", they would put their hand to their ear as though they were talking on the phone. When they respond with their body movements, what they are envisioning is a certain kind of object. This type of memory is much deeper than the simple memorization of how to spell the word phone. The learner can reach out to show that they know what the phone means, and the computer system can also know that the learner understands. In this manner, it is possible to hold the language learner accountable to internalise the language through the muscle movements.

Likewise, expansion of our system affords interaction with learners in other learning spaces. As learners improve their language skills, their lessons will include virtual tours of real locations in real-time or historical time, which allows for interaction with humans outside the learning spaces and with embodied conversational agents.

Challenges

As mentioned in the literature, some research explores giving learners the opportunity to create their own stories. A significant challenge that arises is that the space of understanding expands beyond the initial parameters. In the StoryRooms of Alborzi *et al.* (2009), for example, children would bring their own toys from home to augment the physical environment. In terms of implementations, the sensors of the room must have the capability to learn new objects without a great deal of effort on the part of the lesson designer. One might argue that the best way to design a lesson would be to teach a new story to the system, which would subsequently connect the details it learned from the story to the stories it had previously learned, interacting with objects, and asking questions of more knowledgeable experts to confirm its knowledge. In the same way that the system provides feedback to the learner to create a seamless experience for the learner, the lesson designer provides a story and sufficient feedback to create a suitable story environment in the system.

On the other hand, unforeseen circumstances of language arise when the system is to produce novel language and interactions between objects, even when it is in the framework of previously known stories. Adding to the challenge, learners that incorporate ideas from outside the framework of existing stories create unforseen situations that are difficult to test, and are therefore unknown until the problems have arisen. For example, plural nouns in English typically take an –s suffix. However, if a student wishes to have a story about four sheep, the system must be able to deal with this situation. We see this as one of the significant challenges to scalability of our system. Whether it is beneficial to give options to learners if the system occasionally produces incorrect language as a result is an unanswered research question for future research.

OUR RELATED WORK

Our work with the interactive Thinking Head and hybrid world harnesses the tactile aspect of handling real-world objects within three-dimensional virtual scenes. We seek to understand how modes of physical world kinaesthetic interactions can enhance human-machine interactions, and more specifically, how real-world experiences of users connect with gains in second language learning. This chapter reflects the work of the Flinders Artificial Intelligence and Language Technology Laboratory on the Thinking Head for language learning. We also collaborate with the Flinders University Medical Devices in addition to our work in autonomous robot teaming. In addition to the work presented in the current chapter for a MulSeMedia environment for storytelling, we here present a number of our related projects of interest to the field of MulSeMedia, as follows.

MANA for Memory Assistance

Recent projects include MANA, which is a Thinking Head embodied conversational agent reminder system in conjunction with Alzheimer's Association of South Australia. It is of particular interest to explore the use of multimodal interaction in cases where people are unable to use traditional input/output devices such as the keyboard or mouse, or may not have had sufficient exposure to the use of these devices, e.g. children, people with disabilities, and people with memory loss.

A recent initiative targeting this latter group is our MANA Calendar application, which gives a person with some form of memory impairment spoken reminders about the tasks and appoint-

ments, which they have scheduled for each day. No keyboard or mouse is used, and interaction is purely through spoken commands, and spoken acknowledgement of the spoken reminders. Currently, the system uses a face-finding algorithm to determine when the user is in the room; in future, we hope to extend the system's multisensory awareness of the situation in which the users find themselves, to allow safety-monitoring functions, smart advice-giving and even assistance in finding one's way through town. At the time of writing, trials are underway in conjunction with the Alzheimer's Association of South Australia, in which we are trialling the MANA system with patients in their homes.

AVAST for Autism

The AVAST project aims to investigate the potential for using autonomous virtual agents as social tutors for children with autism. Individuals with autism suffer from what are known as the 'triad' of impairments, including deficits in imaginative and conceptual skills, difficulties with social behaviours, and problems with language (both verbal and non-verbal) (DSM-IV-TR, 2000). We have developed a prototype software module that utilises the Thinking Head virtual agent technology. The lifelike appearance and ability to model realistic facial expressions makes the Thinking Head well suited to this application.

The modules developed for the preliminary investigation centred on interactions with virtual tutors to reduce difficulties children with autism often face: conversation skills and dealing with bullying. The evaluation component of the conversation skills lesson examined children's ability to recognize particular facial expressions and to choose appropriate social actions to take. For the dealing with bullying skills tutor, the focus was on participants' abilities to distinguish between friendly and bullying situations, and laughing with and laughing at someone. Following this, the tutor presented a simple and safe strategy for dealing with bullying situations. The ability of participants to distinguish between situations and their retention of the steps was tested. As presented in Milne *et al*. (2010), an average improvement of 54% was found between pre- and post-testing for the bullying skills tutor, and an average of 32% was found for the conversation tutor. Post-testing survey outcomes were very positive overall: every participant rated the virtual tutors as 'friendly', which indicates that the environment provides a non-judgemental learning tool. The positive feedback from the survey and the modest but significant improvements in test scores for both modules suggest that this approach to teaching social skills has much potential. Further research into this project is now underway; eventually, we hope to include provisions for tutoring based on the gestures and facial expressions of the learners.

Brain-Controlled Wheelchair

This project is aimed towards the design of a non-invasive (EEG-based) brain-controlled wheelchair for completely paralysed patients. The design includes a series of signal processing algorithms and an interface to a powered wheelchair. In addition, we have implemented a 3D virtual environment for training, evaluating and testing the system prior to establishing the wheelchair interface. Simulation of a virtual scenario replicating the real world also gives subjects a chance to become familiar with operating the device. Literature shows that effective feedback presentations in a virtual environment result in improved control in the real world. The more real and motivating this environment is, the better the improvement in control (Ron-Angevin & Diaz-Estrella, 2009), leading to the idea that a realism in the virtual wheelchair driving environment results in more realistic responses for the person driving a real wheelchair using brain signals.

Virtual simulation is an environment that allows the user to practice operating the controls before actually engaging the chair. A virtual world

is an appropriate first step to this in that using a first person game engine can give a reasonably realistic perspective whilst avoiding dangers to participants and dramatically simplifying the early stages of data collection for training and evaluation purposes. Therefore, asynchronous evaluation of the system after signal processing is necessary prior to establishing the wheelchair interface, predominantly as a safety measure. The simulated 3D environment created for the purpose of this project would improve subjects' response in controlling the wheelchair using thought. Moreover, this technique achieves significant reductions in the time necessary for subjects to learn to control a wheelchair. Eventually this simulated environment would make a more reliable experimental environment for evaluation of human factors.

Flinders Magician Autonomous Robot Team

The Flinders University of South Australia's robotic team 'Magician' is a semi-finalist in the Multi-Autonomous Ground-robotic International Challenge (MAGIC 2010), co-sponsored by the Australian Defence Science and Technology Organization (DSTO) and the U.S. Department of Defense. Two human operators supervise a swarm of robots tasked with counter-terrorist activities—but the operators do not engage in moment-to-moment control. The competition addresses various degrees of complexity including: i) heterogeneous, autonomous robots within an urban environment; ii) limited, unpredictable communications infrastructure; and iii) and degree of autonomy and associated impact on human situational awareness.

The Magician situational awareness system provides real-time display of events perceived and reported by each of twenty robots within the competition arena. In addition to the human-robot interface, we designed a simulator to examine the feasibility of various strategies prior to the competition. The simulator generates scenarios over a variety of environmental and behavioural parameters to assess competition strategies. By interconnecting the simulator with the graphical user interface, we have created a user interface with the simulated environment for operator training and for assessment of operator workload for diverse display configurations. As in the competition, operator-robot interactions receive penalties, so that we are motivated to minimize interaction time; a major focus has been on how to create perceptually salient and cognitively rich information displays through visual and aural modalities. Using a rich user-interface with simulation strategies allows us to address complexity prior to the actual event.

CONCLUSION

Our quick sweep through the larger picture of hybrid reality and our detailed focus on a language teaching application illustrates how the manipulation of tangible real-world objects, including toys and mini-screens, provides a powerful learning experience. Learners use our MulSeMedia system to ground their newly learned language skills in compelling stories that engage their senses and involve them in the retelling. Comprehension checks, expressed bimodally in natural language descriptions and in virtual reality as relationships between tangible objects and places, ensure maximum learning of subject matter.

A key to success is the telling of stories that are interesting and novel. Through sensors and appropriate questions, the system must be able to maintain the comprehension levels of the learner at high levels. In the future, media will improve along with advances in computer-related technologies and input and output devices, and accordingly, we expect to see an increase in development of tangible interfaces for computer-based story environments.

ACKNOWLEDGMENTS

We would like to thank the following for their review and insight: Fatemeh Khazar and Sean Fitzgibbon. Additional thanks to William Newman, Daniel Franzel, David Gustainis, and Adrian Sydlowski for their contributions in their Honours projects.

REFERENCES

Alborzi, H., Druin, A., Montemayor, J., Platner, M., Porteous, J., Sherman, L., et al. (2000). Designing StoryRooms: Interactive storytelling spaces for children. In Boyarski, D., & Kellogg, W. A. (Eds.) *Proceedings of the 3rd conference on designing interactive systems*, New York City, NY: ACM, 95-104.

Asher, J. (2000). *Learning another language through actions* (6th ed.). Los Gatos, CA: Sky Oaks Productions, Inc.

Birsh, J. R. (1999). *Multisensory teaching of basic language skills*. Baltimore, MD: P.H. Brookes Pub. Co.

Brune, M. K. (2004) *Total physical response storytelling: An analysis and application.* Thesis, University of Oregon.

Chan, T.-W., Roschelle, J., & Hsi, S., Kinshuk, Sharples, M., Brown, T., et al. (2006). One-to-one technology-enhanced learning: An opportunity for global research collaboration. *Research and Practice in Technology Enhanced Learning, 1*(1), 3–29. doi:10.1142/S1793206806000032

Chang, S.-B., Lin, C.-L., Ching, E., Cheng, H. N. H., Chang, B., & Chen, F.-C. (2007). EduBingo: Developing a content sample for the one-to-one classroom by the content-first design approach. *Journal of Educational Technology & Society, 12*(3), 343–353.

Chen, Z.-H., Anderson, T. A. F., Cheng, H. N. G., & Chan, T.-W. (2009). Character-Driven Learning: Facilitating Students' Learning by Educational Virtual Characters. In Kong, S.C., Ogata, H., Arnseth, H.C., Chan, C.K.K., Hirashima, T., Klett, F., Lee, J.H.M., Liu, C.C., Looi, C.K., Milrad, M., Mitrovic, A., Nakabayashi, K., Wong, S.L., Yang, S.J.H. (Eds.) *Proceedings of the 17th International Conference on Computers in Education,* Hong Kong: Asia-Pacific Society for Computers in Education.

Chu-Carroll, J. (2000). MIMIC: An adaptive mixed initiative spoken dialogue system for information queries. In *Proceedings of the Sixth Conference on Applied Natural Language Processing,* Seattle, WA: Association for Computational Linguistics, 97-104.

Crawford, C. (2003). *Chris Crawford on game design.* Berkeley, CA: New Riders Publishing.

Crawford, C. (2004). *Chris Crawford on interactive storytelling.* Berkeley, CA: New Riders Publishing.

Dahl, O.-J., Myhrhaug, B., & Nygaard, K. (1968). Some features of the SIMULA 67 language. In *Proceedings of the Second Conference on Applications of Simulations.* New York City, NY: Winter Simulation Conference, 29-31.

Druin, A., Montemayor, J., Hendler, J.A., McAlister, B., Boltman, A., Fiterman, E., Plaisant, A., Kruskal, A., Olsen, H., Revett, I., Schwenn, T.P., Sumida, L., Wagner, R. (1999). Designing PETS: A personal electronic teller of stories. *Computer Human Interaction,* 326-329.

DSM-IV-TR. *(2000). American Psychiatric Association: Diagnostic and Statistical Manual of Mental Disorders, Fourth Edition, 299.00 Autistic Disorder.* Washington, DC: American Psychiatric Association.

Franzel, D., & Newman, W. (2009) *Virtual world: Hybrid reality for computer learning and teaching.* Thesis: Flinders University of South Australia.

Gustainis, D. (2009). *Hybrid character recognition using a visual input.* Thesis: Flinders University of South Australia.

Hwang, J., Jung, J., & Kim, G. J. (2006). Handheld virtual reality: A feasibility study. In *Proceedings of the ACM symposium on Virtual reality software and technology,* New York City, NY: ACM, 356-363.

Inchauste, F. (2010). Better user experience with storytelling. *Smashing Magazine.* Retrieved March 25, 2010, from http://www.smashingmagazine.com /2010/01/29/better-user-experience-using-storytelling-part-one

Kellerman, S. (1988). Lip service: The contribution of the visual modality to speech perception and its relevance to the teaching and testing of foreign language listening comprehension. *Applied Linguistics, 11*(3), 272–280. doi:10.1093/applin/11.3.272

Krashen, S. D. (1987). *Principles and practice in second language acquisition.* New York City, NY: Prentice-Hall International.

Lee, J., & Marsella, S. (2006). Nonverbal behaviour generator for embodied conversational agents. In *Proceedings of the Sixth International Conference on Intelligent Virtual Agents,* Marina Del Rey, CA: IVA, 243-255.

Lorenz, M. (1993). *Object-oriented software development.* Englewood Cliffs, NJ: PTR Prentice Hall.

Luerssen, M. & Lewis, T. (2009). Head X: Tailorable Audiovisual Synthesis for ECAs. *Proceedings of HCSNet Summerfest 2009.*

Massaro, D. W. (2004). From multisensory integration to talking heads and language learning. In Calvert, G., Spence, C., & Stein, E. S. (Eds.), *Handbook of Multisensory Processes* (pp. 153–156). Cambridge, MA: MIT Press.

Milne, M., Leibbrandt, R., Lewis, T., Luerssen, M., & Powers, D. M. W. (2010). Development of a Virtual Agent Based Social Tutor for Children with Autism Spectrum Disorders. In *Proceedings of the 23rd International Joint Conference on Neural Networks*, in press

Nelson, K. (1998). *Language in cognitive development: The emergence of the mediated mind.* New York City, NY: Cambridge University Press.

O'Malley, C., & Fraser, D. S. (2004) *Literature review in learning with tangible technologies.* Bristol, UK: Futurelab, Report 12.

Papert, S. (1980). *Mindstorms: Children, computers, and powerful ideas.* New York City, NY: Basic Books, Inc.

Plamondon, R. (2000). On-line and offline handwriting recognition: A comprehensive survey. *IEEE Transactions on Pattern Analysis and Machine Intelligence, 22*(1), 63–84. doi:10.1109/34.824821

Poggi, I., Pelachaud, C., De Rosis, F., Carofiglio, V., & De Carolis, B. (2005). Building expression into virtual characters. In Stock, O., & Zancanaro, M. (Eds.), *Multimodal Intelligent Information Presentation* (pp. 3–25). Netherlands: Springer. doi:10.1007/1-4020-3051-7_1

Powers, D. M. (2007). A multimodal environment for immersive language learning - space, time, viewpoint and physics. In *Proc. Joint HCSNet-HxI Workshop on Human Issues in Interaction and Interactive Interfaces.* Sydney, Australia: HCSNet.

Powers, D. M. W., Leibbrandt, R., Pfitzner, D., Luerssen, M., Lewis, T., Abrahamyan, A., & Stevens, K. (2008). Language teaching in a mixed reality games environment. In F. Makedon, L. Baillie, G. Pantziou, and I. Magliogiannis (Eds.) *Proceedings of the 1ˢᵗ International Conference on Pervasive Technologies Related to Assistive Environments, PETRA '8,* Vol. 282. New York City, NY: ACM.

Ray, B., & Seely, C. (1997). *Fluency through TPR Storytelling: Achieving real language acquisition in school.* Berkeley: Command Performance Language Institute.

Ribiero, C. R., Costa, M. F. M., & Pereira-Coutinho, C. (2009). Robotics in child storytelling. In Costa, M.F.M. (*Eds.*) *Science for all, quest for excellence: Proceedings of the Sixth International Conference on Hands-on Science.* Ahmedabad, India, 198-205

Roy, D. (1999). *Learning words from sights and sounds: A computational model.* Dissertation, Massachusetts Institute of Technology.

Srivastava, M., Muntz, R., & Potkonjak, M. (2001). Smart Kindergarten: Sensor-based wireless networks for smart developmental problem-solving environments. In *Proceedings of the Seventh Annual International Conference on Mobile Computing and Networking*, Rome, Italy: MobiCom, 132-138.

Sydlowski, A. (2009). *Offline and online character recognition using a visual input.* Thesis: Flinders University of South Australia.

Veletsianos, G., Heller, R., Overmyer, S., & Procter, M. (2010). Conversational agents in virtual worlds: Bridging disciplines. *British Journal of Educational Technology, 41*(1), 123–140. doi:10.1111/j.1467-8535.2009.01027.x

Verhaegh, J., Fontijn, W., & Jacobs, A. (2008). On the benefits of tangible interfaces for educational games. *Proceedings of the Second IEEE International Conference on Digital Game and Intelligent Toy Enhanced Learning (DIGITEL)*, 141-145.

Vygotsky, L. (1964). *Thinking and Speaking* (Hanfmann, E., & Vakar, G., Trans.). Boston: The M.I.T. Press. (Original work published 1934)

Yilmaz, A., Javed, O., & Shah, M. (2006). Object tracking: A survey. *ACM Computing Surveys*, 13(4). *Article*, *13*, 1–45.

ENDNOTES

[1] Dream-based research is the pursuit of innovation and potentialities for some distant future, as defined in Chang et al. (2009).

[2] More information can be found in the G1:1 website (http://www.g1on1.org)

[3] Note that TPR Storytelling emerged as an evolution of Total Physical Response, though the acronym for TPR differs for each. Hereon in, we reference to TPR Storytelling in the sense of Teaching Proficiency through Reading and Storytelling as our primary language learning pedagogy.

Chapter 10
User Perception of Media Content Association in Olfaction-Enhanced Multimedia

George Ghinea
Brunel University, UK

Oluwakemi Ademoye
Brunel University, UK

ABSTRACT

Olfaction (smell) is one of our commonly used senses in everyday life. However, this is not the case in digital media, where it is an exception to the rule that usually only our auditory and visual senses are employed. In MulSeMedia, however, together with these traditional senses, we envisage that the olfactory will increasingly be employed, especially so with the increase in computing processing abilities and in the sophistication of olfactory devices employed. It is not surprising, however, that there are still many unanswered questions in the use of olfaction in MulSeMedia. Accordingly in this chapter we present the results of an empirical study which explored one such question, namely does the correct association of scent and content enhance the user experience of multimedia applications?'

INTRODUCTION

Olfaction-enhanced multimedia concerns itself with associating computer generated smell with other media to enrich the users' experience and perception of a multimedia presentation. In this way, olfactory media is already being used towards a variety of goals in multimedia applications.

However, in infotainment multimedia applications, it might be possible that users will just appreciate the novelty factor of integrating scents with multimedia applications, and that the actual scent being emitted might not be of importance. Moreover, it might also be that users would not mind what scent is being emitted as long as it is "close" to the one that matches their expectations.

DOI: 10.4018/978-1-60960-821-7.ch010

As a result, in this chapter, we aim to answer the following research question: *'does the correct association of scent and content enhance the user experience of multimedia applications?'*

Accordingly in this chapter, we present the results of an empirical study carried out to discover if the *correct* association of scent and content is important when augmenting multimedia applications with computer generated scent. The chapter is structured as follows: in "Experimental Methodology" we introduce the user to related scented media work, while "Results" and "Conclusion" present the details of our experimental methodology and the results of our experiment respectively.

SCENTED MULTIMEDIA

Scented Media in the Film Industry

The first recorded attempt of combining artificially generated smell with audiovisual content dates back to 1906 when an audience was sprayed with the scent of roses while watching the screening of the Rose Bowl football game (Longino in Kaye, 2001), however, there is no mention of what the audience reaction to this was. The next significant development in the use of scented media in the film industry happened in 1943 (Kiger and Smith, 2006; Smith and Kiger, 2006), when Hans Laube, who had earlier discovered a technique for removing odours from an enclosed place, such as an auditorium, was also able to reverse this process to release selected odours into similar places at specific times and durations. Using his newly discovered technology, and with the help of his colleague, Robert Barth, they produced a 35 minute 'smell-o-drama' movie called Mein Traum in which 35 different odours were released to accompany the drama presentation. However, the technology behind the production of the emitted smells enjoyed more success than the scented drama presentation itself, with the audience agreeing that while the smells emitted were promptly

released and subsequently removed, they smelled fake. Nonetheless, it was the success of Laube's technology for emitting smells that Michael Todd Jr was to rely on later in 1960 in his Smell-O-Vision Scent of Mystery film production (Kiger and Smith, 2006; Smith and Kiger, 2006).

In 1959, a year before the release of the aforementioned Michael Todd Jr's Smell-O-Vision Scent of Mystery film production, there was the AromaRama presentation, a documentary about Red China called Behind the Great Wall (ABC 1999; Kaye, 2001; Kiger and Smith 2006; Variety, 2001). Smells were emitted via the theatre's air-conditioning system to accompany the presentation of this documentary. Unfortunately, the producers had no way of knowing what a significant impact the characteristic nature of smell would have on their presentation, and they went all-out and had over 30 different smells released during the presentation. The reaction of the audience to this presentation is probably best described from the following extract from the review published back then by Time magazine (Kaye, 2001):

To begin with, most of the production's 31 odors will probably seem phoney, even to the average uneducated nose. A beautiful old pine grove in Peking, for instance, smells rather like a subway rest room on disinfectant day. Besides, the odors are strong enough to give a bloodhound a headache. What is more, the smells are not always removed as rapidly as the scene requires: at one point, the audience distinctly smells grass in the middle of the Gobi desert.

In the year following the AromaRama presentation, and hot on the heels of Laube's success with the technology used in the 'smell-o-drama' movie of 1943, there was another attempt at creating scented media for the film industry in a film production called Scent of Mystery (Kaye, 2001; Kiger and Smith, 2006; Smith and Kiger, 2006; Variety 2001). This film production was a murder mystery in which were synchronised with certain scenes of the film in order to scents aid in revealing the identity of the murderer. This time, the producers had done more research into the matter and of course had the added advantage of being able to refer to the AromaRama experience and of using technology that had proved reliable when it came to promptly releasing and subsequently removing smells. Thus, they went ahead and also released as many as 30 smells during the film, as after all, the technology had proven that it could cope with this (Kiger and Smith, 2006; Smith and Kiger, 2006). Unfortunately, despite the better preparation and the better technology, this scented media production also fared badly and the Smell-O-Vision Scent of Mystery drama continues to live in infamy to date (ABC 1999; Kaye, 2001; Kiger and Smith, 2006; Smith and Kiger, 2006; Variety 2001). The audience complained that the scents emitted reached them seconds too late, were too faint resulting in them sniffing repeatedly to catch whiffs of the emitted smells and were accompanied by a hissing sound which they found distracting and the following comment was published in the New York Times then about the experience (Kaye, 2001):

If there is anything of lasting value to be learned from Michael Todd's "Scent of Mystery" it is that motion pictures and synthetic smells do not mix.

After these well publicised failures with the use of smell in the film industry, the production of scented films disappeared for a while, and though there have been a few more attempts to create scented media experiences for users since then, the idea still has not quite caught on to date. Some of the more popular of these later attempts at creating scented film productions include Polyester by John Waters in 1981 and Love for Three Oranges by the English National Opera Company in 1989, which both made use of the popular scratch 'n' sniff cards similar to those used in advertising perfumes in magazines (Kaye, 2001). In these productions, at specific intervals during the films,

the audience had to scratch and sniff the smells on numbered cards they had been given prior to the start of the movie; *one can only imagine how distracting that must have been as this cannot exactly be described as being advanced technology.* More recently, in 2006, there was mention that audiences going to see the screening of the movie, The New World, in Japan will be treated to a scented movie experience (BBC, 2006; Heritage, 2006; NTT 2006). However, whilst there were several reports advertising the 'smellovision' experience to-be, it is not quite clear if this actually happened and if it did what the audience's reaction to it was, as follow-up reports appear to be non-existent. It would definitely have been interesting to see how much the technology had improved since those earlier not so successful attempts at creating scented film productions, as well as if users are now more receptive towards the idea of scented films.

The predominant cause of these failed attempts at creating notable scented film experiences for users was the failure of the technology. Hence, with computing technology already well underway by the 70s, and enjoying considerable success, research started to look at ways of using computing technology to control the emission of scents in order to create an olfaction-enhanced experience for users. In the next section, we take a look at some of these efforts.

Scented Media in Computing

The relative scarcity of commercially available olfactory data generating devices has certainly contributed to the slow progress of the use of olfaction in computing. However, a further hindrance stems from the fact that whilst it is usually easy to combine other data formats (e.g. sound and video) to produce a desired output mix, this is extremely difficult to do with olfactory data as a standard additive process or model for combining different scents does not exist. Consequently, more often than not smell generating devices are limited to producing the specific smells that have been loaded into their respective storage systems. Nonetheless, there has been some olfactory data usage in the computing field over the years, with a number of researchers building their own computer generating smell systems (Boyd Davis et al., 2006; Kaye, 2001) and others relying on the few that are commercially available. More recently, Nakamoto and his team (2005a,b) have developed a smell generating device which works by combining chemicals to produce the desired scents as and when required, but this device is also not yet commercially available and still under research development.

The areas of computing that have experienced significant usage of olfactory data over the years include virtual reality, multimodal displays and alerting systems, and media and entertainment systems. At the forefront are the research efforts of Kaye (2001, 2004), which focused extensively on the practicality of using computer generated smell in computing and creating an awareness of the issues, problems and limitations, associated with the use of olfactory data and particularly for scented media displays.

Olfaction in Virtual Reality Systems

In 1962, Morton Heilig created what is now popularly dubbed as the first virtual reality experience for users, even though digital computing and virtual reality systems did not exist then (see Dinh et al., 1999; Kaye, 2001). He created Sensorama, an arcade-style device, which took users on an immersive 3-D virtual reality bike ride experience through the streets of Brooklyn (Lefcowitz, 2003). Using motion and vibrations, sounds, fans and smells, Sensorama created a multi-sensory experience for users which simulated those sensations one is likely to experience on a motorbike ride through the streets of Brooklyn. These sensations included the bumpy feeling a rider may experience as he/she travels over cobblestones, as well as the sights, sounds and smells (the aroma of freshly

baked bread from the bakery, scents of hibiscus and jasmine from the flower gardens passed) that may be experienced as the rider continues on his journey.

Although VR systems are quite popular today, most still fall short of providing the kind of multi-sensory experience that Heilig's mechanical device did, as most of these systems still only engage our visual and audio senses, with a few more our tactile sense. Indeed, olfaction is still something of a rarity in these systems. One of the most notable virtual reality systems involving the use of olfaction reported since Heilig's invention is the fire-fighter virtual reality training system designed by Cater and his team in 1992 (Dinh et al., 1999). Here, the user wears a backpack mounted device, which emits a range of scents, including burning wood, grease and rubber, sulphur, oil and diesel exhaust, through an oxygen mask connected to the device, whilst immersed in the virtual reality environment. The essence in this case is to familiarise potential fire-fighters with those smells often associated with fires, as it is often thought and argued that it is easier to recognise smells already known by a person. Moreover, in a fire-fighter's profession, being able to easily detect the presence of such smells could well prove to be invaluable. Notable feedback from Cater's virtual reality training system, and another worthy contribution to the guidelines on the use of olfactory data, was that one has to be careful with the intensity of smells used in any experiments involving the use of olfactory data as users can suffer a variety of reactions from smells, ranging from headaches to allergic reactions and being physically sick.

Dinh et al (1999) report on an experimental study carried out which investigated the use of tactile, olfactory, and auditory sensory modalities with different levels of visual information on a user's sense of presence and on the user's memory of details of the virtual experience. Their study, motivated by a suggestion by Fontaine in (Dinh et al., 1999) that access to a broader range of sensory cues promotes a greater sense of presence, involved participants evaluating a virtual corporate office suite environment system that could also be potentially used by real estate brokers to show prospective tenants available properties. The olfactory cue used was the scent of coffee as the participant entered the reception area, and there was a coffee maker machine located in this room. The findings from their study showed that additional sensory input can increase both the sense of presence in a virtual environment and memory for the objects in the environment, with the sense of presence increased mostly by the addition of tactile and auditory cues. Olfactory cues produced a non-significant trend in the case of the effect on the sense of presence, but a significant main effect on memory. In comparison with the other sensory cues analysed in this study, however, the use of olfaction was restricted to the emission of just a single odour (scent) during the experiment as opposed to the multiple occurrences of the other sensory cues analysed.

Another reported study that investigates the use of olfaction in virtual reality environments is the study carried out by the Research in Augmented & Virtual Environment Systems (RAVES) project team at the Institute of Simulation & Training, University of Central Florida (Jones et al, 2004). The focus of this study was to test the impact of olfaction on a human operator's sense of immersion into a virtual environment. The experimental study involved participants playing a computer game in an immersive virtual experiment. The experimental conditions consisted of a control case where no scents were released whilst the participant played the game and two experimental cases, one involving concordant scents (i.e. emission of the scent of ocean mist as the player passed the ocean and a musty scent when the player was in the fort in the immersive environment) and the other a discordant scent (smell of maple syrup throughout the game). The results from their study showed that the addition of an olfactory component did not significantly enhance immersion into a simulated environment, that is, the experimental group did not differ significantly from the control or discordant groups in any analyses.

In (Tijou, Richard and Richard, 2006), a multi-modal virtual reality application that aims to investigate the effect of olfaction on learning, retention, and recall of complex 3D structures such as organic molecules in chemical structures is presented. The researchers of this study had also presented another virtual reality system, DIODE (Richard, Tijou, Richard and Ferrier, 2006; Tijou, Richard and Richard, 2006), that enables olfactory feedback in a virtual reality environment. In this system, the user navigates through the Vendôme Square in Paris and experiences the corresponding smell (scents of a Christmas, orange and rose tree) as he/she navigates through the 'olfactive spheres' in the virtual reality environment. More recently, the respective researchers have developed yet another virtual reality learning system called VIREPSE which provides both olfactory and haptic feedback (Richard, Tijou, Richard and Ferrier, 2006). However, they do not report on any detailed evaluation of either of these applications, but rather focus their research efforts on discussing the significance of developing such multi-modal VEs for education.

Olfaction in Multimodal Displays and Alerting Systems

Benefits of multi-modal systems include synergy, redundancy and an increased bandwidth of information transfer (Sarter, 2006). Most of the developments involving the use of olfactory data in multi-modal systems have, however, been where the addition of another modality has been used to provide redundancy, i.e. the use of several alternative modalities for processing and/or presenting the same information to users. One benefit of having such multi-modal information displays is to share attention and information processing demands between our different senses. As it is, our visual and auditory senses are already overburdened with the respective visual and auditory cues we are required to respond to in computer information systems. Thus applications used to gain the users attention, more popularly known as notification or alerting systems, represent one of the areas in which olfactory data output has been found quite beneficial.

To support his theories on symbolic olfactory displays, Kaye (2001, 2004) designed a number of notification and alerting prototypical applications that made use of olfactory data alarms. These include 'inStink', a simple application he built to demonstrate the viability of computer-generated smell. Its mode of operation was simple – when a particular spice was used from a spice rack, the corresponding smell of the spice was released by the simple olfactory device. Next came 'Scents and Dollars', an application that used computer-generated smells to notify observers of when the stock market went up or down; 'Smell Reminder', which allows users to use what he calls smicons) to create personal, notification alarms, and 'Honey, I'm home', an application shared between two people which ensures that out of sight, is not out of mind and where smicons are used to alert the other that you are thinking of him/her. Unfortunately, with the exception of general feedback from observers such as their disappointment with the quality of the scents generated by the device (smelt artificial), he does not report on any detailed evaluation of these applications.

Bodnar, Corbett and Nekrasovski (2004) also created a notification system that makes use of olfactory data. In their work, they conducted an experimental study to compare the effect the use of visual, audio or olfactory displays to deliver notifications had on a user's engagement of a cognitive task. Participants were given an arithmetic task to complete and at various intervals two types of notifications were triggered, one where the participants had to immediately stop what they were doing and record some data before returning to the completion of their task, and the other they were to ignore. With their experiment, they found that while olfactory notifications were the least effective in delivering notifications to end users, they had the advantage of producing the least disruptive effect on a user's engagement of a task. It is also worthy to note that they encountered most of the problems of using smell output as highlighted by Kaye in their experiment and had participants mostly commenting that some of the smells used were too similar to be distinguishable, lingering smells in the air made it difficult to detect the presence of new ones and the lack of experience of working with olfactory data impacted on their performance of the assigned task.

In the realm of multi-modal information processing, we mention the study carried out by Brewster, McGookin and Miller (2006). Here, they use olfactory data for multimedia content searching, browsing and retrieval, more specifically to aid in the search of digital photo collections. In their experiment, they compare the effects of using text-based tagging and smell-based tagging of digital photos by users to search and retrieve photos from a digital library. To achieve this, they developed an olfactory photo browsing and searching tool, which they called Olfoto. Smell and text tags from participants' description of photos (personal photographs of participants were used) were created and participants had to use these tags to put a tag on their photos. At a later date, participants then had to use the same tags to search and answer questions about the previously tagged photographs. The results of their experiment showed that although performance with the text-based tags was better, smell and its ability to trigger memories in individuals does have some potential for being used as a querying method for multimedia content searching.

Olfaction in Multimedia Entertainment Systems

Multimedia entertainment, such as computer games, is one area that is expected to benefit greatly from the addition of our other sensory cues which are currently virtually non-existent in such applications. It is expected that they will heighten the sense of presence and reality and hence impact positively on user experience, e.g. make it a more engaging experience for users. Below, we mention some media entertainment systems that involve the use of olfactory data in one way or another.

Fragra (Fraga, 2003; Mochizuki et al., 2004), a Visual-Olfactory virtual reality game that enables players to explore the interactive relationship between olfaction and vision, is one such application. The objective of the game is for the player to identify if the visual cues experienced correspond to the olfactory ones simultaneously. In the game, there is a mysterious tree which bears many kinds of foods. Players can catch these food items by moving their right hand and when they catch one of the items and move it in front of their nose, they smell something which does not necessarily correspond to the food item they are holding. Although they do not report on any detailed evaluation of their implemented game, they do report that in their preliminary experiment, the percentage of questions answered correctly varied according to the combination of visual information and olfactory information and conclude that there is a possibility that some foods' appearance might have stronger information than their scents, and vice versa. A similar interactive computer game, 'Cooking Game', has also been created by Nakamoto and his research team at the Tokyo Institute of Technology (Nakamoto 2005a,b).

More recently, Boyd Davis et al. (2006) used olfactory data to create an interactive digital olfactory game. In their work, they developed a suite of digital games in which they use olfactory data, 3 different scents, to engage users in game play and the users' sense of smell is the main skill needed to win the games. The findings from their work further confirm what previous researchers like Kaye (2001) have discovered about the use of olfactory data and set down guidelines for.

EXPERIMENTAL METHODOLOGY

Participants

A total of fifty participants, 21 males and 29 females between the ages of 18 and 38, from a wide variety of backgrounds, took part in the study. Potential participants were asked if they had undergone any smell recognition training, and if they responded in the affirmative, they were not allowed to participate in the experiment. Potential participants also suffering from colds, or any other conditions that might have impaired their sense of smell were also stopped from participating in the study, or asked to return at a later date when their sense of smell was no longer impaired if they so wished. Participants were not offered any incentives to take part in any of the investigative studies and they were also allowed to opt out of the experiment at any point in time during the course of the experiment. Once recruited and vetted, participants were randomly split into two groups, an experimental study group and a control study group, each made up of 25 participants.

Experimental Materials

We used the Vortex Active device to dispense olfactory data during our experiments. This is a line-of-sight device, which was mounted at an angle to and approximately half a metre from the participant's nose, and uses fans to disperse scents. As regards the scents themselves, it is advisable that familiar smells be used for experiments involving the use of olfactory data (Kaye, 2001). We finally opted for six smells which distinguish between the odour classes of flowery, foul, fruity, burnt, resinous and spicy. Six video clips, whose content respectively corresponded to the six scents, were used in our study:

- **Burnt** (Documentary on bush fires in Oklahoma)
- **Flowery** (News broadcast featuring perfume launch)
- **Foul** (Documentary about rotting fruits)
- **Fruity** (Cookery show on how to make a fruit cocktail)
- **Resinous** (Documentary on spring allergies & Cedar Wood)
- **Spicy** (Cookery show on how to make chicken curry).

Each clip was shown in a 240x180 window and was roughly 90s long, with the duration of the olfactory data lasting for about 30 seconds, in the middle third of the clip. The duration of 30s for the olfactory data was chosen since, as a result of odour adaptation, scents are generally recognisable in the ambient vicinity for a period of 30s (Washburn et al., 2003).

Experimental Procedure

The experimental procedure involved participants watching the set of six video clips augmented with computer generated scent. The olfactory data was varied for each of the six video clips watched so that participants got to watch each video clip with a different smell. After watching a particular olfaction-enhanced video clip, each user filled in his/her opinion in relation to the following two statements: *The smell heightened the sense of reality whilst watching the video clip*, and, *The smell was annoying*. For each question, the user could select one of five possible responses: *Strongly Disagree, Disagree, Neither Agree or Disagree, Agree, Strongly Agree*.

As mentioned above, participants were split into two study groups. In the experimental group, the twenty-five participants watched the olfaction-enhanced videos with semantically unrelated scent, while for the control study group, the participants watched all of the six olfaction-enhanced videos with the correctly associated scent (i.e. a scent that was semantically related to the audiovisual content of the watched video). Accordingly, the independent variable measured for this experiment was the type of olfactory media content associated with each of the video clips, which varied between semantically related and unrelated olfactory media content.

Table 1 shows how the mismatched olfactory data synchronised with the videos was distributed across participants in the experimental study, with subject case 1 applying to participants 1, 6, 11 and 16, subject case 2 to participants 2, 7, 12 and 17, and so on. The videos viewed by all of the participants in the control study group were synchronised with the correctly associated scent as shown in the table. The playback of the videos with each of the predefined associated scents was randomised in order to minimise order effects.

RESULTS

The results from the investigative study have been analysed using the repeated measures Analysis of Variance (ANOVA) test to show the influence of content, i.e. the six different video categories, and the influence of association between olfactory media and audiovisual content, i.e. differences between the two study groups, on the user-perceived experience.

Impact of Associating Smell with Content on the Perceived Sense of Reality of the Olfaction-Enhanced Multimedia

To measure the user-perceived experience of the sense of reality of the olfaction-enhanced multimedia video clips, we use participants' responses to the statement, '*The smell heightened the sense of reality whilst watching the video clip*'. Accordingly, we consider to what extent participants felt that the use of olfactory data heightened the sense of reality in the multimedia

Table 1. Summary breakdown of olfactory data associated with audiovisual content assigned to the different subject cases in the experimental and control group studies

Study Group	Subject Case	Burnt Video	Flowery Video	Fruity Video	Foul Video	Resinous Video	Spicy Video
Experiment Group	1	Curry	Burning Wood	Wall-flower	Straw-berry	Rubbish Acrid	Cedar Wood
	2	Cedar Wood	Curry	Burning Wood	Wall-flower	Straw-berry	Rubbish Acrid
	3	Rubbish Acrid	Cedar Wood	Curry	Burning Wood	Wall-flower	Straw-berry
	4	Straw-berry	Rubbish Acrid	Cedar Wood	Curry	Burning Wood	Wall-flower
	5	Wall-flower	Straw-berry	Rubbish Acrid	Cedar Wood	Curry	Burning Wood
Control Group	All	Burning Wood	Wall-flower	Straw-berry	Rubbish Acrid	Cedar Wood	Curry

Table 2. Influence of associating smell with content on the perceived sense of reality of the olfaction-enhanced clips

GLM Repeated Measures Test		F	Sig.
Within-Subjects Effects	Video	2.591	0.026
Within-Subjects Effects	Video * Association	2.420	0.036
Between-Subjects Effects	Association	30.195	0.000

video clips. The repeated measures ANOVA test (Table 2) revealed that both content (F=2.591, p=0.026) and the association between olfactory media and content (F=30.195, p=0.000) had a significant influence on participants' perception of the sense of reality of the multimedia video clips. Furthermore, the interaction between both factors was also statistically significant (F=2.420, p=0.036), which shows that there is a combined influence of content and smell association on the perceived sense of reality.

Table 3 and Figure 1 show the mean opinion values of participants' opinions obtained in the study. This confirms the possibility that some of, or even all, the mismatched scents used for the *Resinous* video clip created a greater perceived sense of reality than the scent we considered to

be the most appropriate to use for this video, i.e. *Cedar Wood*. Moreover, participants in the control study were also more neutral in their opinion that this scent heightened the sense of reality of this video clip. It is also possible that participants did not find the Cedar Wood scent as familiar as the other scents used in the experiment.

The mean opinion values, however, generally show that participants mostly did not think that the unrelated scents combined with the videos in the experimental study case heightened the sense of reality. These results further emphasise that the semantic relationship between olfactory media and other media content is important in olfaction-enhanced multimedia, as it has an impact on the perceived sense of reality in such environments.

Table 3. Mean opinion scores (MOS) reflecting participants' perception of the sense of reality of the olfaction-enhanced multimedia videos

Study Group	Burnt	Flowery	Fruity	Foul	Resinous	Spicy
Control	3.72	3.76	3.12	3.60	3.32	3.36
Experimental	1.88	2.56	1.76	2.40	3.52	1.80

Figure 1. Mean opinion scores (MOS) reflecting participants' perception of the sense of reality of the olfaction-enhanced multimedia videos

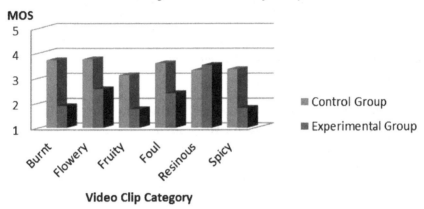

Perceived Acceptability of Associating Olfactory Media with Content

We consider the user acceptability of the olfactory media from the perspective of how annoying participants found the use of unrelated scents in the olfaction-enhanced video clips. Analysis is based on participants' responses to the questionnaire statement, '*The smell was annoying*'. The results from the repeated measures ANOVA test conducted are shown in Table 4.

The repeated measures ANOVA test results in Table 4 show the impact of using unrelated olfactory media on the subsequent level of annoyance as regards this media content in olfaction-enhanced multimedia clips. These results reveal that the association between olfaction and content did not have a significant impact on the perceived level of annoyance towards the olfactory media ($F=1.381$, $p=0.246$). Content, on the other hand, had a significant impact on the perceived level of annoyance towards the olfactory media used ($F=3.370$, $p=0.006$). Moreover, the results also showed that the influence of associating smell with content on the perceived level of annoyance towards the olfactory media depends on content ($F=4.873$, $p=0.000$). In Table 5 and Figure 2 we show the mean opinion score values obtained from our results to further highlight how annoying, or not, participants actually found the olfactory media used to enhance the video clips.

Table 4. Influence of associating smell with content on the perception of how annoying the olfactory media was

GLM Repeated Measures Test		F	Sig.
Within-Subjects Effects	Video	3.370	0.006
Within-Subjects Effects	Video * Association	4.873	0.000
Between-Subjects Effects	Association	1.381	0.246

Table 5. Mean opinion scores (MOS) reflecting participants' perception of how annoying the olfactory media associated with the videos was

Study Group	Burnt	Flowery	Fruity	Foul	Resinous	Spicy
Control	2.96	1.96	1.60	3.08	2.52	2.76
Experimental	2.72	2.08	3.20	2.32	2.96	3.00

Figure 2. Mean opinion scores (MOS) reflecting participants' perception of how annoying the olfactory media associated with the videos was

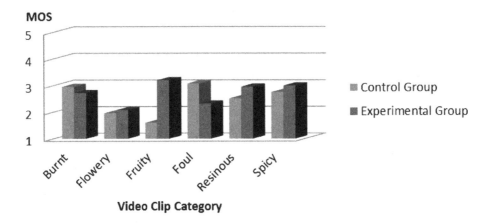

Participants in both study groups mostly had a neutral opinion or did not find the presence of the olfactory media annoying. However, in the case of the *Burnt* and *Foul* video clips, participants found the unrelated scents used in the experimental study cases less annoying than the related *Burning Wood* and *Rubbish Acrid* scents used respectively in the control study cases. This may be attributed to the fact that humans generally tend to have a more positive bias towards pleasant smells. Hence the likely reason for participants generally finding the unrelated smells used in the experimental study case less annoying, since they were more pleasant than the related smells chosen to accompany these particular clips. Moreover, the repeated measures ANOVA test has already shown that the combined effect of video content and scent association had a significant impact on the degree to which participants found the olfactory media annoying. As such, the combination of these less entertaining video clips and what can be termed as unpleasant smells had a more detrimental effect on the perceived level of annoyance towards the olfactory media.

CONCLUSION

The experiment reported in this chapter aimed to discover the effect the association between olfactory data and audiovisual content has on the user-perceived experience of olfaction-enhanced multimedia applications. In order to achieve this, we varied olfactory media content association by combining our video excerpts with semantically *related* and *unrelated* scents, and subsequently measured the impact this variation had on participants' perception of the olfaction-enhanced multimedia experience.

Results showed that there was a significant difference in opinions in respect of the ability of olfactory media to heighten the sense of reality. Interestingly, the use of unrelated scents was not found to significantly affect the degree to which participants found the olfactory media annoying. Thus, although participants noticed the semantically incorrect association between olfactory media content and video content, it did not result in a significantly more annoying experience than if 'semantically correct' smells had been used. This is a finding most probably due to humans' poor ability to discriminate between odours and further work is required to establish the spectrum of olfactory data to which it applies.

REFERENCES

BBC. (2006) *'Smellovision' for Japan cinema*, BBC. Available: http://news.bbc.co.uk/ 1/ hi/ entertainment/ 4903984.stm [Accessed: August 21, 2007].

Bodnar, A., Corbett, R., & Nekrasovski, D. (2004) "AROMA: Ambient awareness through olfaction in a messaging application: Does olfactory notification make 'scents'?", *ICMI'04 - Sixth International Conference on Multimodal Interfaces*, pp. 183.

Boyd Davis, S., Davies, G., Haddad, R., & Lai, M. (2006) "Smell Me: Engaging with an Interactive Olfactory Game", *Proceedings of the Human Factors and Ergonomics Society 25th Annual Meeting*, pp. 25-40, UK.

Brewster, S. A., McGookin, D. K., & Miller, C. A. (2006) "Olfoto: Designing a smell-based interaction", *CHI 2006: Conference on Human Factors in Computing Systems*, pp. 653.

Communications, N. T. T. (2006) *Movie Enhanced with Internet-based Fragrance System*. Available: http://www.in70mm.com/ news/ 2006/ new_ world/ index.htm [Accessed: August 21, 2007].

Dinh, H. Q., Walker, N., Hodges, L. F., Song, C., & Kobayashi, A. (1999) "Evaluating the importance of multi-sensory input on memory and the sense of presence in virtual environments", *Proceedings - Virtual Reality Annual International Symposium*, pp. 222-228.

Fragra - An Interactive Olfactory Game System, 2003, IVRC (Inter-collegiate Virtual Reality Contest) www.ivrc.net. Available: http://chihara. aist-nara.ac.jp/ ivrc2003/ index.html [Accessed: August 23, 2007].

Heritage, S. (2006) *The New Colin Farrell Movie Stinks In Japan*. Available: http://www.hecklerspray.com/ the-new-colin-farrell- movie-stinks-in-japan/ 20062756.php [Accessed: August 23, 2007].

Jones, L., Bowers, C. A., Washburn, D., Cortes, A., & Satya, R. V. (2004). The Effect of Olfaction on Immersion into Virtual Environments. In *Human Performance, Situation Awareness and Automation: Issues and Considerations for the 21st Century* (pp. 282–285). Lawrence Erlbaum Associates.

Kaye, J.J. (2004) "Making Scents: aromatic output for HCI", *interactions,* vol. 11, no. 1, pp. 48-61.

Kaye, J. N. (2001) *Symbolic Olfactory Display,* Master of Science edn, Massachusetts Institute of Technology, Massachusetts, U.S.A. Available: http://www.media.mit.edu/ ~jofish/ thesis/ [Accessed: September 11, 2005].

Kiger, P. J., & Smith, M. J. (2006) *Lesson #9 - Beware of Unproven Technologies The Lingering Reek of "Smell-O-Vision"*, HarperCollins. Available: http://www.in70mm.com/ news/ 2006/ oops/ index.htm [Accessed: August 21, 2007].

Lefcowitz, E. (2003) *Sensorama's Pre-Virtual Reality,* Available: http://www.retrofuture.com/ sensorama.html [Accessed: August 23, 2007].

Mochizuki, A., Amada, T., Sawa, S., Takeda, T., Motoyashiki, S., & Kohyama, K. (2004). Fragra: a visual-olfactory VR game. In *SIG-GRAPH '04: ACM SIGGRAPH 2004 Sketches* (p. 123). New York, NY, USA: ACM Press. doi:10.1145/1186223.1186377

Nakamoto, T. (2005a). Odor recorder. *Sensor Letters, 3*(2), 136–150. doi:10.1166/sl.2005.018

Nakamoto, T. (2005b). Record of dynamic changes of odors using an odor recorder. *Sensors and Materials, 17*(7), 365–383.

News, A. B. C. (1999). *Smell-O-Vision Coming to Internet Soon.* Available: http://www.temple. edu/ ispr/ examples/ ex99_10_20.html [Accessed: August 21, 2007].

Richard, E., Tijou, A., Richard, P., & Ferrier, J. (2006). Multi-modal virtual environments for education with haptic and olfactory feedback. *Virtual Reality (Waltham Cross), 10*(3-4), 207–225. doi:10.1007/s10055-006-0040-8

Sarter, N. B. (2006). Multimodal information presentation: Design guidance and research challenges. *International Journal of Industrial Ergonomics, 36*(5), 439–445. doi:10.1016/j. ergon.2006.01.007

Smith, M. J., & Kiger, P. J. (2006), *The Lingering Reek of Smell-O-Vision*, Los Angeles Times. Available: http://www.latimes.com/ features/ magazine/ west/ a-tm-oops6feb 05,1,2932206. story?coll =la-iraq- complete [Accessed: August 21, 2007].

Tijou, A., Richard, E., & Richard, P. (2006) "Using Olfactive Virtual Environments for Learning Organic Molecules", *1st International Conference on Technologies for E-Learning and Digital Entertainment, Edutainment 2006*, pp. 1223.

Variety staff (2001) *Variety review of "Scent of Mystery"*, Variety, Inc., Available: 16 [Accessed: August 21, 2007].

Washburn, D.A., Jones, L.M., Satya, R.V., Bowers, C.A. and Cortes, A. (2003) Olfactory Use in Virtual Environment Training, *Modelling and Simulation Magazine*, 2(3).

Chapter 11
Multimedia Sensory Cue Processing in the FIVIS Simulation Environment

Rainer Herpers
Hochschule Bonn-Rhein-Sieg, Germany; York University & University of New Brunswick, Canada

David Scherfgen
Hochschule Bonn-Rhein-Sieg, Germany

Michael Kutz
Hochschule Bonn-Rhein-Sieg, Germany

Jens Bongartz
RheinAhrCampus Fachhochschule Koblenz, Germany

Ulrich Hartmann
RheinAhrCampus Fachhochschule Koblenz, Germany

Oliver Schulzyk
RheinAhrCampus Fachhochschule Koblenz, Germany

Sandra Boronas
Hochschule Bonn-Rhein-Sieg, Germany

Timur Saitov
Hochschule Bonn-Rhein-Sieg, Germany

Holger Steiner
Hochschule Bonn-Rhein-Sieg & Institut Für Arbeitsschutz (IFA), Germany

Dietmar Reinert
Hochschule Bonn-Rhein-Sieg & Institut Für Arbeitsschutz (IFA), Germany

ABSTRACT

Virtual reality applications and related to this immersive environments provide an ideal test bed for the integration of multiple sensory cues. This is due to the goal of VR simulation environments to copy reality as good as possible and this again is due to the nature of human users who are relating their reactions and behavior on the evaluation of several sensory cues. Therefore, the integration of multimedia sensory cues is considered as an integral objective of any virtual reality application to allow addressing multiple sensors for human users. At Bonn-Rhein-Sieg University of Applied Sciences in Sankt Augustin, Germany, an immersive bicycle simulator called FIVISquare has been developed.

DOI: 10.4018/978-1-60960-821-7.ch011

The simulator features a bicycle equipped with steering and pedaling sensors, an electrical motor brake, an immersive panoramic back-projection-based visualization system, an optical tracking camera system. It can be applied jointly with a hydraulic motion platform.

The FIVIS simulator system addresses the classical visual and acoustical cues as well as vestibular and further physiological cues. Sensory feedback from skin, muscles, and joints are integrated within this virtual reality visualization environment. By doing this it allows for simulating otherwise dangerous traffic situations in a controlled laboratory environment. The system has been successfully applied for road safety education applications of school children. In further research studies it is applied to perform multimedia perception experiments. It has been shown, that visual cues dominate by far the perception of visual depth in the majority of applications but the quality of depth perception might depend on the availability of other sensory information. This however, needs to be investigated in more detail in the future.

INTRODUCTION

For almost all modern means of transportation (car, train, airplane) training simulators exist that provide realistic models of the vehicle's dynamics, interiors and the outer environment. They allow for complex and potentially dangerous situations to be simulated under defined and safe laboratory conditions. For many years, these simulators have been successfully applied for driver training and education, and as a consequence have contributed to the overall safety in the respective fields. In general, simulators allow for more cost-effective training in comparison to real vehicles, especially for expensive aircrafts. Sometimes, the vehicles being simulated do not even exist at that point in time.

Unfortunately, there is no such commonly available simulation system for bicycles, although the number of bicycle accidents in Germany has been increasing against the common trend (according to the Federal Statistical Office). Hence, the objective of the FIVIS project at the Bonn-Rhein-Sieg University of Applied Sciences is to develop a bicycle simulator that is embedded into an immersive visualization environment. The immersive visualization environment provides visual input cues also to peripheral areas of the visual field of the trainee. Visualizing three-dimensional content in such an environment allows spectators to become part of the computer-generated world

and experience depth and three-dimensional space almost like they are used to in the real world ((Herpers2008a) ((Herpers2008b) ((Herpers2009a). Moreover, the FIVIS environment is used for conducting perception research experiments within the context of multimedia sensory cue processing, all integrated in one coherent simulation framework.

In the FIVIS project, a real bicycle is equipped with sensors and actuators, which are connected to a simulation computer. It computes the bicycle dynamics, interactions with the virtual world and also graphically renders the three-dimensional immersive visualization of the environment. The computer-generated images are projected onto three seamlessly joined screens that surround the bicycle rider (see Figure 1), using back projection with mirrors to make the system more compact. The screens cover a wide range of the visual field and therefore allow for a high degree of immersion. Using an optical infrared tracking system, the rider's head and body parts are tracked in order to adjust the virtual camera view according to the most recent head position. Hand signs given by the rider are detected, evaluated, and might influence the further processing of the simulation. Optionally, the FIVIS simulation and visualization system can be extended by a hydraulic 6DOF motion platform ((Schulzyk2007), which allows for simulating several forces acting upon the bicycle (see Figure 2).

COMPUTATION OF THE BICYCLE SIMULATION AND ITS VISUALIZATION

The task of the simulation software is to perform the actual simulation of the virtual world. Therefore, a flexible simulation model for objects such as the bicycle, buildings, traffic lights and other road users has been developed. Additionally, the software has to read data from the bicycle's sensors and transfer it to the simulation model. Moreover, the immersive 3D visualization has to be computed in real-time.

Layered Simulation Model

In the developed simulation, all objects exist on three different abstraction layers: the physical, the logical and the control layer. The layered approach allows for the reuse of parts of objects and therefore makes the program more extensible and maintainable. As an example, the bicycle object itself will be discussed in further detail in the remainder, which is the most important object in our simulation, since it has to represent the bicycle in the virtual world.

On the physical layer, the bicycle consists of a collection of geometric shapes connected by joints. These geometric shapes are not visualized. They only serve as the physical representation of the bicycle. For example, the wheels are modeled by spheres. It needs to be noted that the physical representation does not have to correlate with the visual representation as it is most cases in the real world. The purpose of the definition joints between two physical bodies is to restrict the relative motion between the two. In the bicycle model, the wheels are fixed to the frame and can only rotate around one axis (see Figure 3). Without joints, the bicycle components would not be connected to each other and would fall apart. The visual representation, a textured 3D model, is also defined on this layer

Figure 1. The FIVIS bicycle simulator running a simulation of an urban environment for traffic training. Elementary school children were trained within this environment to get prepared for their bicycle driver's license examination

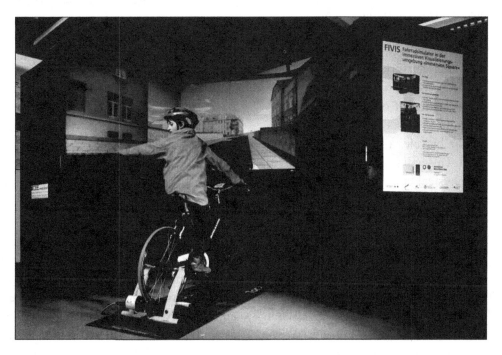

but does not need to match the physical properties of the physical representation in general.

The second layer is the logical layer. It introduces input parameters such as the desired steering angle or the target forward velocity of the bicycle. It is responsible for manipulating the physical representation of objects according to the input parameter values. For example, in order to accelerate the bicycle, a torque is applied to the back wheel. This will make the bicycle move forward. The physical or virtual source of input values is not yet defined at this simulation stage.

Finally, on the control layer, special controllers are assigned to the objects. A controller sets the input values of the logical object. For example, the hardware bicycle controller reads the current steering angle and back wheel velocity of the real bicycle and transfers these values to the virtual bicycle's input values. This enables the virtual

bicycle to show the same behavior one would expect from a real bicycle which is steered and paddled forward by a rider. Additional controllers exist that allow steering the bicycle applying other input devices such as mouse and keyboard or that can record and play back user input. For other road users, controllers can be specified that exploit artificial intelligence methods to control their behavior.

Rendering Procedure

The special screen setup (three angled screens) realized for the FIVIS visualization environment requires an adapted rendering procedure. The three screens are combined logically for the computation to a single virtual screen by a special piece of hardware. However, during rendering, this combined screen cannot simply be treated like a single traditional screen, since it is not planar in reality (the angle of the two side views with respect to the central one is 135°). Ignoring that aspect would result in a perspectively distorted image. Instead, one has to render each screen individually applying an individually adjusted viewing frustum. The difference becomes obvious when considering that a single planar screen can never cover a 180° horizontal field of view (no matter how close the observer is standing to the screen), while the screens in FIVIS surround the bicycle rider and therefore easily cover more than 180°. Figure 4 shows two renderings of the same scene, where the upper one has been rendered traditionally (treating all screens as a single flat screen), while the lower one appears perspectively correct to an observer sitting on the simulator's bicycle.

Audio

In order to increase the immersive effect of the simulation, a spatial audio component has been added. Spatial audio evaluates the relative position and velocity of the listener and sound sources, as well as properties of the environment. For ex-

Figure 3. The physical representation of the virtual bicycle shown with the physical representation of some buildings in the background. The bicycle consists of four rigid bodies (two wheels, main frame and handlebar) connected by joints that restrict their relative motion. The handlebar and the two wheels can rotate only around one axis

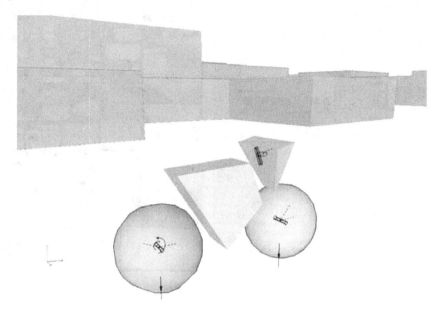

Figure 4. Screenshots of the visualization comparing the simple (top) and adapted (bottom) rendering approach. The top image is only a single rendering and can therefore never cover a horizontal field of view of 180°. The bottom image consists of three sub-images rendered individually using an adapted viewing frustum for the screen and stitched together seamlessly. The image covers more than 180° of the horizontal visual field. Note the differences in the perspective distortions in peripheral areas

Figure 5. A building's visual and physical representation and the texture that was created from a number of photographs. The texture also contains information about static lighting and shadows based on ambient occlusion

ample, the motor sound of a car appears to have a higher frequency when the car is approaching the observer, due to the Doppler Effect. Additionally, sound signals further away from the observer sound different than closer ones, since some frequencies get filtered more than others while the signal is transmitted through space. A convincing simulation of these effects contributes to the overall simulation quality and the degree of immersion. In the urban simulation scenario, various ambient sound effects have been recorded from the real city. Additionally, a headwind sound effect is modified in volume and frequency depending on the virtual bicycle's speed.

3D Content Representation

Parts of the city of Siegburg have been modeled in 3D. In order to make the scenery look realistic, photographs of the buildings were taken and used as textures for the models. Google Sketch Up was chosen as the modeling software, since it is well suited for efficiently modeling relatively simple

geometric shapes like houses. The models are exported to a different file format, including all the high-resolution photographs used as textures. In a final step, these textures are combined into one single texture data structure per building, which also includes static lighting and self-shadowing (hemisphere-based ambient occlusion; see figure 5). For this step, 3ds max is used. Using only one texture per building has shown a significant speed-up of the rendering process, since a greater amount of triangles can be rendered at once, without changing rendering parameters in-between. As an additional performance optimization, all building textures are compressed in GPU memory using the DXT1 image format. This reduces the image quality slightly, but also cuts the memory consumption to 1/8 compared to 32-bit RGBA. Hence, it is possible to keep huge amounts of texture data in memory at the same time.

An XML file describing the position, orientation, and additional properties of each object is also generated through a plug-in for Google Sketch Up. This means that the software serves both as a modeling program and a "world editor". However, in future, a dedicated content editor will be developed that allows placing objects in the virtual world and changing their properties.

Implementation Details

The core simulation software module is written in C++ in order to achieve optimal performance. It uses the open source graphics engine Ogre3D[1] for rendering, FMOD[2] for audio and NVIDIA PhysX[3] for the physics simulation. On the upper layer, simulation scenarios are implemented in the Python scripting language, which is generally more comfortable and easier to maintain than C++. However, computation is also slower than C++ code, but the performance-critical parts of the application are implemented on a lower level. The advantage of this two-level design is that the core modules can be reused easily in order to create different and independent simulation scenarios using an easy-to-learn programming language. Virtual worlds and objects are both represented using XML, in a both human- and machine-readable form. This makes it possible to perform quick adjustments just using a text editor.

APPLICATIONS

The FIVIS bicycle simulator has been successfully applied to the following scenarios: road safety education for children, as a controlled simulation environment for testing combined physical and psychological stress factors as well as for systematically investigating perception in virtual environments.

Road Safety Education Training Environment

Vehicle simulators usually serve the purpose of educating drivers or pilots in both handling the vehicle and reacting appropriately to common and extreme situations. The FIVIS bicycle simulator is different in one aspect: it is not designed for practicing the physical task of riding a bicycle (keeping it in balance, turning, braking) since it cannot simulate this part realistically enough. However, it can be used as a training device to practice the appropriate behavior to common and dangerous situations in a safe environment. This is of particular interest for the education of elementary school children as well as elderly people who are intended to ride their bicycles again after not having used it for many years.

However, in order to evaluate if and how the bicycle simulator can be used for practicing the behavior in (potentially dangerous) traffic situations, a research and evaluation studies have been conducted. Several school children of a close-by elementary school have been tested. For this purpose, a part of their hometown – the city of Siegburg – was carefully modeled in 3D. Each child was asked to virtually ride through the specified course twice. The results showed a clear improvement on the second run: the amount of mistakes was reduced significantly.

The next question of interest was, whether the children would be able to transfer these gained abilities on driving in real traffic conditions. Therefore, the training course was adjusted in cooperation with a local elementary school in Siegburg. The newly modeled course is an 1:1 copy of the one that the children have to complete in reality in order to pass the practical part of their bicycle driver's license examination. A cohort of sixteen children of the school mentioned above has then been selected to practice for their bicycle driver's license examination in the FIVIS bicycle simulator. The rest of their classmates (n=36) served as a control group as they did not get training in the simulator. The conditions for the virtual training were very close to reality: the children had to act and react as if they were riding in reality. For instance they had to wear a bicycle helmet and were required to give the correct hand signs and watch for other road users. The experiment was

Figure 6. Graphic chart of the percentage of mistakes made per child. One group of children was trained within the FIVIS-simulator (displayed in green), the control group was not (displayed in orange). The amount of mistakes they made is shown on the x-axis. The y-axis shows how many children per group made this amount of mistakes. Obviously, children trained on the FIVIS simulator showed in average a better performance as they made fewer mistakes than their not trained classmates

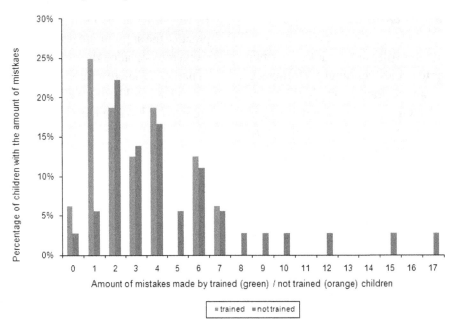

supervised by a traffic policeman who is assigned in traffic education in the community. Every child was asked first to perform a practice ride within the simulator to get used to the virtual environment. After this, they were told about eventual mistakes and they were given the chance to ask questions. Afterwards, they were asked to perform another ride on the same course, but this time their mistakes and behavior were recorded exactly as in the real examination. Feedback was provided so that they could correct their shown mistakes during a second ride. Few weeks later they had to practice their real examination in the reality. After all children passed their examination on the real roads, the results of the two cohorts were evaluated.

The evaluation showed that the children indeed were able to transfer successfully the experience they gained in the FIVIS simulator to the real world since they did fewer mistakes than the control group (see Figure 6). Children that were

trained in the FIVIS simulator (green colored bars in Figure 6) made 2.9 mistakes on average during the real bicycle driver's examination. Their overall performance turned out to be more homogeneous (standard deviation at 2.1) in comparison to untrained children (orange colored bars in Figure 6). Children of the control group made 4.9 mistakes on average (standard deviation of 3.8). This can be considered as a significant statistical effect based on a 10% percentile ($F=3.7$, $p=0.06$).

Testing Environment for Stress and Perception Research

In work safety research, an interesting question is how well humans can simultaneously handle physical and psychological stress conditions. This is considered as an important aspect for many occupations mainly found in the industrial area, as both physical and psychological stress might be a risk for the health of employees and result in high costs for health insurance companies. Researching the strain employees encounter during their work can help to prevent or reduce the strain, for example by modifying the working environment or tools, leading to safer working conditions for the employees and reduced costs for the insurance companies. Unfortunately, the assessment of psychological strain which is accompanied by physiological strain is not an easy task ((Steiner2009).

For a research project of the German Social Accident Insurance (Institute for Occupational Safety and Health), a method of assessing and distinguishing physical and psychological stress components experienced by employees directly at their workplaces was developed. For this purpose, the "CUELA Activity" measurement system, a light-weight sensor suit which uses accelerometers and gyroscopes to determine the current body posture and movement ((Weber2008), was extended by adding sensors for the acquisition of several physiological parameters. Theses parameters include the heart rate and its variability, muscle activity in the neck and shoulder region, respiration rate and the skin conductance. By feeding well-chosen machine learning algorithms with this combination of physiological and physical activity data, it is possible to draw conclusions about the (relative) amount and type of stress a subject experiences.

The FIVIS bicycle simulator was applied as an investigation environment to conduct several experiments in order to evaluate the developed measurement system under joint simulation conditions. The underlying idea was to apply physical as well as cognitive strain in parallel under controlled condition to subjects. In the simulation scenario designed for this purpose, the cyclist is asked to follow a particular course through a virtual environment defined by checkpoints that have to be reached within a limited amount of time. Since the given time to reach these checkpoints could be controlled dynamically this was meant to motivate

the subjects to adapt their physical performance to the required test condition. In other words this was designed as the physical strain condition. By controlling the resistance of the motor brake at the back wheel, the requested physical strain can be computationally manipulated even more. Psychological stress is generated by the time pressure and randomly appearing obstacles that have to be avoided. Within certain limits, both factors can be independently scaled on purpose. While performing the pre-defined task, the subject wears the measurement system on top of his clothing. The acquired data is transmitted to an attached laptop computer and stored for later off-line analysis. In addition, the experiments are videotaped with a digital camera.

For the experiments, a subject (male, 23) who already knew the FIVIS simulator environment was chosen. This way, additional stress that might be caused in a subject using the simulator for the first time (e.g. excitement or anxiety) could be avoided. In the first minutes of the measurement, the subject was sitting quietly on a chair. Afterwards, he started riding the bicycle until the end of the measurement.

After the measurement, the recorded data were analyzed using the software tool "WIDAAN". This software presents the recorded data graphically and synchronized to the video, as well as to apply a variety of filtering and analysis techniques (Figure 7). An exemplary selection of the results of the measurements is shown in the following figures: Figure 8 presents the acquired heart rate and heart rate variability data, while figure 9 shows the physical activity (i.e. intensity of body movement) over the time of the experiment.

As expected, the physical activity of the subject changed during the experiments due to different cycling speeds. It can be noticed that the heart rate was strongly correlated with the physical activity intensity (PAI) index. The heart rate variability was varying strongly during the resting phase. In contrast to this, it decreased significantly as soon as the subject began to cycle and

Figure 7. Data analysis software used in the stress generation scenario. The subject's physical and physiological parameters, which were recorded during the runtime of the experiment is visualized and analyzed in detail

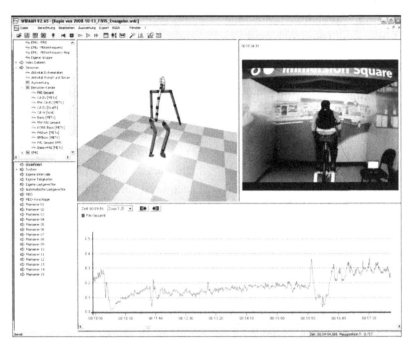

Figure 8. Heart rate and heart rate variability of the subject during the experiment

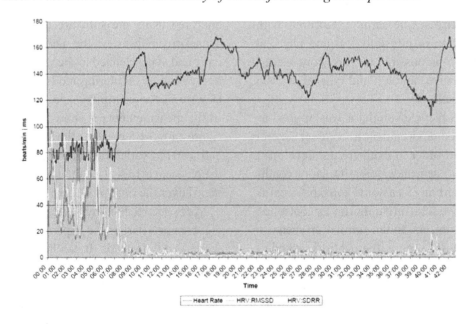

Figure 9. Physical activity of the subject during the experiment

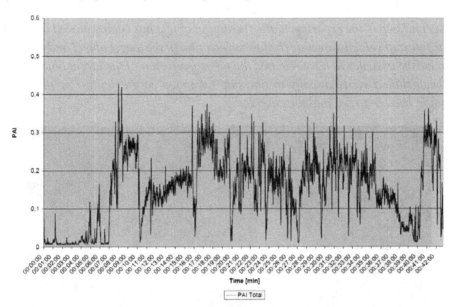

it remained constantly low until the end, except for a few short peaks, which are correlated to a decrease of the heart rate at the same time. During the cycling phase, the muscle activity (which is not shown in the figures) seemed to be correlated with the physical activity to a certain extent, too. The same applied to the results provided by the respiration sensor.

In order to evaluate the amount and the nature of the strain, the data recorded during the experiments has been fed into a machine learning algorithm. With the help of such algorithms, the data samples can be classified into specific, previously defined categories. A set of nine categories, covering different strain scenarios with all combinations of no, low and high psychological and physical strain, has been designed for this purpose. Respective training data has been generated by inducing each combination of strain. It has been shown that decision tree algorithms are best suited for this classification problem, as they were able to correctly classify up to 98% of the data samples acquired from the subject they had been trained on. This means that a very precise

detection and evaluation of psychological strain is possible even when physiological strain is applied simultaneously.

The FIVIS system proved to be suited for the induction of both psychological and physiological strain in a subject simultaneously, although the physical component seemed to be clearly superior to the psychological component during the performed experiments. This might be compensated by reducing the physical workload of the subject, for example by lowering the pedals resistance, or by changing the design of the experiments in a way that they induce a higher amount of psychological strain. This could be done either by choosing a subject with less experience in riding a bicycle in complex traffic situations, for example school children during road safety training, or by adding psychologically stressful tasks that have to be solved on top of riding a bicycle. Therefore, FIVIS promises to be very useful for the generation of training data for the classification algorithms on the one hand, as well as for testing and evaluating the developed measurement system on the other hand.

Figure 10. A perception experiment in the FIVIS visualization environment with a reduced visual field. The test subject is asked to memorize the visual observed depth of a target object placed in a virtual corridor. In a second step of the experiment after the target object has been removed the subject is moved virtually with a constant velocity towards the former position of the target object and the subject is asked to report when he/she assumes to have reached the former position of the target object. The focal point however has been shifted systematically to one side (changed eccentricities) so that only peripheral visual areas might be able to see into the corridor

Environment for Investigations on Human Perception

The ability to move within a three dimensional environment is one of the most important abilities of human beings as it allows us to view the world from different locations and orientations and to interact with things that are not directly surrounding us. The distance we travel is based on many different cues originating from many different senses, for instance proprioceptive and pressure information from the limbs, vestibular signals from the vestibular organs, optical flow information, air pressure changes and many more. Based on the patterns of the cues we perceive, which occur naturally in the real world, we estimate how far we have travelled. When building a virtual environment that is supposed to copy the real world, one therefore has to ensure to simulate these cues

appropriately. But which cues are the most important ones and how can they be simulated in such a way that allows for close-to-real perception? The FIVIS bicycle simulator has therefore been applied to investigate these important questions. In a first experiment, the impact of optical flow has been investigated (see Figure 10).

A flickering corridor has been generated that should give no other hints on the travelled distance than one can get from optical flow. The subject has to judge a passively travelled distance under changing eccentricities and different velocity conditions. The first results show that subjects tend to underestimate the distance and therefore press the stop button too early. Right now, more data need to be collected to evaluate these initial results. Further experiments regarding vision and sound as well as the combination of the two are planned.

SYSTEM SETUP

The FIVIS bicycle simulation system consists of a real/physical bicycle, sensors and actuators, the visualization environment and the simulation computer hardware. These will be described in more detail in the following sections.

Bicycle

The bicycle (physically present hardware) is a standard model with only a few modifications. The front wheel is detached and the fork is connected to a spring and a steering angle sensor. The spring exerts a torque to the handle bar so that it has a tendency to always return to its neutral position. When riding a real bicycle, this happens automatically due to its physical motion. Since the bicycle in the simulator is stationary, this effect has to be accounted for in another way. Finally, since the front wheel is missing, the corresponding brake has been removed.

Sensors and Actuators

Sensors provide the simulation system with the necessary data so that it can react to the user's actions. On the bike, there is a steering angle sensor, a velocity sensor at the back wheel and a cadence sensor that measures how fast the rider is pedaling.

The motion tracking system makes use of several infrared tracking cameras (OptiTrack system[4]) installed from a bird's perspective in front of the rider. Any objects that should be tracked (for example, a bicycle helmet / the head of the rider) are equipped with patterns of reflective markers. The tracking system can then determine these objects' position and orientation within the visualization environment. Knowing the user's head position relative to the screens, the 3D visualization can be adjusted in such a way that the screens act as a window into the virtual world. This improves the simulation's degree of immersion and also allows

the bicycle rider, for example, to lean to one side in order to check for opposing traffic behind an occluding object.

While sensors gather user input (steering, pedaling frequency) and send it to the simulation computer, actuators provide (physical) feedback to the bicycle rider. The bicycle's back wheel is connected to an electric motor brake. It can actively decelerate the back wheel in order to simulate ascents or to stop the wheel when the virtual bicycle hit an obstacle. On the other hand, the motor brake can also accelerate the back wheel for simulating rolling and downhill rides. When the bicycle is mounted on the 6DOF motion platform, it can also be moved and rotated. This allows for a more realistic simulation of ascents, descents, road surface properties and the physical forces involved in bicycle riding.

Visualization System

The visualization system used for FIVIS ("FIVISquare") is a further development of the Immersion Square technology also developed at the Bonn-Rhein-Sieg University of Applied Sciences ((Herpers2001, Hetmann2002, Herpers2005, Herpers2009b). It is based on three seamlessly joined angled back projection screens surrounding the bicycle rider, and three projectors that project images from the back side (see figure 11). Horizontally, the screens cover more than 180° of the bicycle rider's field of view. By using mirrors, the system is kept compact in size. Its modular setup allows it to be disassembled and assembled within a few hours.

Each projector has a native resolution of 1280×1024 pixels. The projectors are attached to a Matrox TripleHead2Go device[5], which combines up to three displays to create a single virtual display with a total resolution of 3840×1024 pixels (see Figure 12). It is directly connected to the output of the simulation computer's graphics card.

Figure 11. The partially assembled visualization system. The projectors and mirrors are visible

Figure 12. The TripleHead2Go device combines three displays to one single display. This enables the rendering of 3D graphics to all three screens at the same time without special graphics hardware that offers three video outputs

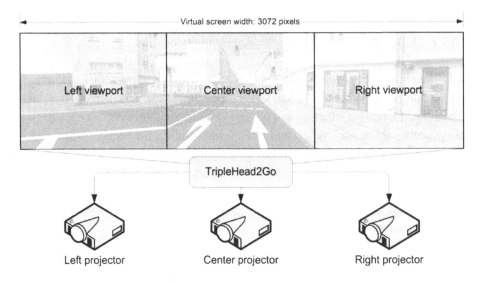

Simulation Computer

Most simulators require several computers for different tasks. However, FIVIS only requires a single standard PC. All computation is integrated with one PC hardware platform, which contrib-

utes to the low price of the overall system. The PC receives data from the sensors, controls the actuators, computes the simulation and renders the 3D visualization. It runs a Windows operating system and features an Intel Quadcore processor,

Figure 13. Sample representation of an urban street network overlaid with a directed graph to model the actual possible pathway of different road users (image source of Google maps)

4 GB of RAM and a Dual-GPU NVIDIA GeForce 295 GTX graphics card.

CONCLUSION AND FUTURE WORK

In our experiments, the simulation system has proven to be extensible (due to the use of the Python scripting language and XML) and well suited for road safety education as well as perception and stress research. The visualization system's projection screens occupy a high percentage of the rider's visual field, which, together with the adapted 3D rendering process, contributes to a high degree of immersion. This allows for compelling and realistic simulations. Using the controllable motor brake and the hydraulic motion platform, physical feedback can be given to the bicycle rider, and the optical tracking system can monitor the user's actions.

FIVIS is an ongoing research project that is well suited as a platform for several different research tasks investigating and exploring multimedia cues

to a wide variety of applications. In the following subsections, several extensions will be discussed, which are planned to be implemented in the future.

Traffic Simulation

In its current development state, the FIVIS simulation does not include fully autonomous artificial intelligence agents for controlling other road users. Cars just follow predefined tracks and stop if the bicycle rider is in their way. However, for more realistic and complex scenarios, this approach needs to be extended. Therefore, a traffic system based on a graph representation of the environment (see figure 13) and artificial intelligence supported behavior of other road users is planned to be developed. Some research work has already been done on that subject, including the simulation of different psychological characteristics of road users, with promising results (Kutz2008).

Fully Automatic Feedback

In road safety education scenarios, so far all actions performed by the subjects needed to be monitored and documented by a human supervisor. It seems like an interesting idea to provide support to the human supervisor by a computer-based one. Solutions for tracking the subject's head turns and hand signs have already been investigated. However, algorithms and models need to be developed to interpret the rider's actions within the context of the current traffic situation.

Training for Professional Bicyclists

Professional bicyclists use bicycle exercise machines for a part of their training. However, these machines usually don't provide compelling visual feedback. A trimmed-down version of the FIVIS bicycle simulator could be considered for this purpose. By simulating a landscape or race track including computer-generated opponents, the rider's motivation and performance could possibly be animated or manipulated. An interesting psychological question that could be investigated as well is how the relation between the physically expected bicycle velocity and the visually displayed velocity affects the athlete's behavior and performance. For example, when the virtual velocity is always lower than the expected velocity, may this take him to limits more effectively? In this case, immersive bicycle simulators might become the standard indoor training equipment for professional bicyclists in the future. A related question would be how does multimedia cues influence the performance of the physical exercise.

In conclusion, FIVIS offers an affordable immersive bicycle simulation system based on an immersive projection environment and a bicycle equipped with sensors and actuators. On top of the so called classical cues (visual and acoustical) it also addresses further physiological cues. More simulated conditions for instance as face wind will be integrated soon and will allow the stimulation of skin and olfactorial sensors. This will contribute to the overall performance of a virtual reality simulation environment which integrates different sets of multimedia cues. The FIVIS simulation system has already proven its effectiveness in several scientific tasks such as traffic education of children and in work-safety research. Additional applications will be explored in the future.

ACKNOWLEDGMENT

The authors gratefully acknowledge the financial support of the BMBF-FH[3] program "Angewandte Forschung an Hochschulen im Verbund mit der Wirtschaft"; project "FIVIS" grant: 1736A05 and the Alexander von Humboldt Foundation, Trans-Coop Program, project "Self-motion perception in virtual environments".

REFERENCES

Herpers, R. Heiden, W. Kutz, M. Scherfgen, D. Hartmann, U. Bongartz, J. Schulzyk, O. (2008). FIVIS Bicycle Simulator – An Immersive Game Platform for Physical Activities. International Conference on Future of Game Design and Technology, ACM FuturePlay 2008, 3.-5.11., pp. 244-249, 2008.

Herpers, R., Heiden, W., Kutz, M., & Scherfgen, D. (2009). *Immersion Square – A cost-effective multi-screen VR Visualisation Technology*, Electronic displays 2009 Conference, ED2009, 3.-4.03. 2009, WEKA Fachmedien GmbH (Ed.)

Herpers, R., Heiden, W., Kutz, M., Scherfgen, D., Hartmann, U., Bongartz, J., & Schulzyk, O. (2008). FIVIS – Bicycle Simulator in the Immersive Visualisation Environment "Immersion Square. In Zacharias, C. (Eds.), *Forschungsspitzen und Spitzenforschung* (pp. 61–68). Physica-Verlag.

Herpers, R., & Hetmann, F. (2001). *Dreiwandprojektionssystem*, Deutsches Patentamt, Az. 101 28 347.4.

Herpers, R., Hetmann, F., Hau, A., & Heiden, W. (2005). The Immersion Square – A mobile platform for immersive visualizations. In *Aktuelle Methoden der Laser und Medizinphysik, 2nd Remagener Physiktage* (pp. 43–48). Berlin: VDE Verlag.

Herpers, R., Scherfgen, D., Kutz, M., Hartmann, U., Schulzyk, O., Reinert, D., & Steiner, H. (2009). FIVIS – A Bicycle Simulation System, World Congress on Medical Physics and Biomedical Engineering (WC 2009), Munich, O. Dössel and W. Schlegel (Eds.), IFMBE Proceedings 25/IV, pp. 2132-2135, 2009.

Hetmann, F., Herpers, R., & Heiden, W. (2002). *The Immersion Square - Immersive VR with Standard Components. VEonPC02 Proceedings* (pp. 23–32). St. Petersburg: Protvino.

Kutz, M., & Herpers, R. (2008). Urban Traffic Simulation for Games. International Conference on Future of Game Design and Technology, ACM FuturePlay 2008, Toronto, 3.-5.11., pp. 181-185.

Schulzyk, O., Bongartz, J., Bildhauer, T., Hartmann, U., Herpers, R., Goebel, B., & Reinert, D. (2007). A bicycle simulator based on a motion platform in a virtual reality environment FIVIS project. In Buzug, H., Weber, B., & Kohl-Bareis, H. (Eds.), *Proceeding in Physics 114: Advances in Medical Engineering* (pp. 323–328). Berlin, New York: Springer-Verlag.

Steiner, H., Reinert, D., & Jung, N. (2009). Combined Measurement System for the Evaluation of Multi Causal Strain. In Karsh, B.-T. (Ed.), *Ergonomics and Health Aspects of Work with Computers*. Springer. doi:10.1007/978-3-642-02731-4_22

Weber, B., Hermanns, I., Ellegast, R. P., & Kleinert, J. (2008). Assessment of Physical Activity at Workplaces. In Bust, P. (Ed.), *Contemporary Ergonomics*. Taylor & Francis, Oxfordshire.

ENDNOTES

[1]   http://www.ogre3d.org/

[2]   http://www.fmod.org/

[3]   http://www.nvidia.com/object/nvidia_physx.html

[4]   http://www.naturalpoint.com/optitrack/

[5]   http://www.matrox.com/graphics/en/products/gxm/th2go/

Chapter 12
Cross-Modal Semantic-Associative Labelling, Indexing and Retrieval of Multimodal Data

Meng Zhu
University of Reading, UK

Atta Badii
University of Reading, UK

ABSTRACT

Digitalised multimedia information today is typically represented in different modalities and distributed through various channels. The use of such a huge amount of data is highly dependent on effective and efficient cross-modal labelling, indexing and retrieval of multimodal information. In this Chapter, we mainly focus on the combining of the primary and collateral modalities of the information resource in an intelligent and effective way in order to provide better multimodal information understanding, classification, labelling and retrieval. Image and text are the two modalities we mainly talk about here. A novel framework for semantic-based collaterally cued image labelling had been proposed and implemented, aiming to automatically assign linguistic keywords to regions of interest in an image. A visual vocabulary was constructed based on manually labelled image segments. We use Euclidean distance and Gaussian distribution to map the low-level region-based image features to the high-level visual concepts defined in the visual vocabulary. Both the collateral content and context knowledge were extracted from the collateral textual modality to bias the mapping process. A semantic-based high-level image feature vector model was constructed based on the labelling results, and the performance of image retrieval using this feature vector model appears to outperform both content-based and text-based approaches in terms of its capability for combining both perceptual and conceptual similarity of the image content.

DOI: 10.4018/978-1-60960-821-7.ch012

WHY IMAGE AND TEXT?

Digitised information nowadays is typically represented in multiple modalities and distributed through various information channels. Massive volumes of multimedia data are being generated every day due to the advances in digital media technologies. Efficient access to such an amount of multimedia content largely relies on effective and intelligent multi-modal indexing and retrieval techniques. The notion of multimodal implies the use of at least two human sensory or perceptual experiences for receiving different representations of the same information (Anastopoulou et al., 2001). According to the information need, a distinction can always be made between the primary and collateral information modalities. For instance, the primary information modality of an image retrieval system is of course the image content, while all the metadata in other modalities that explicitly or implicitly relate to the image content, e.g. collateral texts such as file name, captions, title, URL etc, could be considered as the collateral modality. Despite the rapid development in multi-sensory techniques, information in different modalities acquired though various sensors needs to be intelligently fused and integrated, so as to transform the raw sensory data into a semantically meaningful form. This will facilitate the paradigm shift away from the old multimedia towards the new MulSeMedia, i.e. multiple sensorial media.

As a result of the rapid advances in digital imaging technology, a massive number of annotated digital images are widespread all over the world. Typical examples include the online galleries (e.g. the National Gallery, London[1]), online news photo archives, as well as the commercial digital image libraries, such as the Corel Stock Photo Library which contains 60,000 annotated images. The most straightforward use of such collections is for the users to browse and search the images that match their needs. Therefore, there is a growing interest in user's search requirements which motivates research to increase the efficacy of indexing and re-

trieval of images. Google and Yahoo image search engines can easily gather more than one billion images from the WWW. It is worth mentioning that those images are normally accompanied by certain types of collateral text, such as captions, titles, news, URL, etc. It is this collateral textual information that is utilised for image indexation and retrieval, which is currently the dominant commercial solution. The annotated image collections can either be indexed and searched by text (i.e. annotation) (Lew, 2000), or by image content (i.e. visual features). The annotations, typically but not always, refer to the content of the image, and are usually neither fully specific nor comprehensive. For example, the annotations in the digital image gallery often include some content-independent information (Bimbo, 1999), such as artist's name, date, ownership, etc. For most annotated image collections, such as Corel Stock Photo Library and news photo archives, the annotations focus on describing specific content of the images, but cannot cover all of the information conveyed by the images. It is this collateral textual information that is utilised for image indexation and retrieval, which is currently the dominant commercial solution. However, the performance of such kinds of image search engines is limited by the subjectivity of the accompanied descriptive texts. Moreover, the text-based retrieval approach also suffers from inherent shortcomings such as, the use of synonyms and word sense ambiguity. Content-Based Image Retrieval (CBIR), which concentrates on exploiting computer vision and image processing methods to facilitate image indexing and retrieval, has become the dominant paradigm for image indexing and retrieval in research, development and application since the 1990s (Rui et al., 1998). This was proposed mainly due to the inadequacy of text in representing and modelling the perceptual information conveyed by the rich content of images. Well known CBIR systems that have been widely used include: Blobworld (Carson et al., 1999;2002), QBIC by IBM (Flickner, 1995), Virage (Gupta, A. and Jain,1997), MARS system

(Rui et al., 1997), VisualSEEk (Smith and Chang, 1997). Each of the above systems allows the user to query it using low-level visual features through either a weighted combination of visual features (e.g. colour, shape, texture, etc.) or an exemplar query image. Despite the significant achievements these researchers have made, it is widely acknowledged that strong retrieval performance can only be achieved on low-level visual features matching such as colour, texture, edge, etc. The research progress in CBIR is limited when matching the images content towards object-level semantics. This is to be expected, because it is always very difficult for computer vision approaches alone to identify visually similar but conceptually different objects. Hence, a "semantic gap" still exists between the low-level visual primitives and the high-level semantics conveyed by the same image content (Zhao and Grosky, 2002). In addition, some researchers who investigated the users' needs found that: i) users search both by types and identities of the entities in images, ii) users tend to request images both by the innate visual features and the concepts conveyed by the picture (Enser, 1993; Keister, 1994; Markkula and Sormunen, 2000; Markkula and Sormunen, 2000; Ornager, 1996). With this conclusion, clearly we can see that using text or image features alone cannot suffice for the users' requests.

Text and image are two distinct types of information from different modalities, as they represent and interpret the world in quite different ways. However, there are still some unbreakable, implicit connections between them. A text can be used to describe the content of an image, and an image may convey some semantics within the context of a text. The reason that we call them implicit connections is due to a gap between text and image information, which is usually referred to as the "semantic gap". "The semantic gap is the lack of coincidence between the information that one can extract from the visual data and the interpretation that the same data may have for a user in a given situation." (Smeulder et al., 2000).

Different people may describe the same image in various ways using different words for different purposes, each of which may be relevant to a particular idiosyncratic personal world-view or data-view. The textual description is almost always contextual, whereas the images may live by themselves. Moreover, the textual descriptions of images often remain at a higher level to depict the properties that are very difficult to infer by vision, such as the name of the person, disregarding the low-level visual features, for example the colour of the person's clothing, whereas, images can show things in detail that cannot (or are very difficult) to describe using language. The conclusion of the relationship between image and text is that they are very different but at same time complement each other.

We propose to use both the primary image and the collateral textual modalities in a complementary fashion to perform semantic-based image labelling, indexing and retrieval. Accordingly, a framework for semantic labelling of image content using multimodal cues was developed aiming at automatically tagging image regions with textual keywords. We have exploited the collateral knowledge to bias the mapping from low-level visual primitives to semantic-level visual concepts defined in a visual vocabulary. We have introduced a novel notion of "collateral context" represented as a matrix of the co-occurrence of the visual keywords. The mapping procedure is a collaborative scheme using statistical methods such as Gaussian distribution or Euclidean distance together with a collateral content and context driven inference mechanism. By using automatic labelling of image regions, the semantics is localised within the given image. We propose a high-level image feature vector model which combines multi-modal cues i.e. visual and textual cues for semantic-based image retrieval in order to bridge the so called "semantic gap". The construction of this novel multi-modally sourced image content descriptor is based on the automated image labelling framework that we refer to as the Collaterally Cued Labelling (CCL). Two different feature vector models are devised based on the CCL framework for clustering and retrieval purposes respectively. The effectiveness of the clustering and retrieval as supported by our proposed feature vector models is examined using Self Organising Maps (SOMs).

In "Multimodal and Multimedia Systems," we introduce some recent work related to this research. "A Semantically and Collaterally Cued Multi-modal Method for Image Labelling" provides the details of our proposed method for multimodal collaterally-cued semantic-based collateral image labelling. In "Semantic-Driven High-Level Image Feature Vector Model," we describe how our proposed high-level image content descriptors are built up based on the CCL labelling output. "Experimentation and Discussion" reports the experiments conducted and discusses the experimental results. Finally, "Conclusion and Future Work" concludes this research and points out the future working direction.

MULTIMODAL AND MULTIMEDIA SYSTEMS

As multimodal systems are mentioned more and more recently, there may be much confusion between the notion of multimodal and multimedia. In this section, we compare the concepts of multimodal and multimedia systems by reviewing different researcher's perspectives on this issue. The relationships between image and text information together with the user needs investigation are reported. Then, we concentrate on some recent effort in this area which is related to our work in terms of combining visual and textural modalities.

Differentiating Multimodal and Multimedia Systems

Anastopoulou et al. (2001) provided a short and essential review on the commonalities and dif-

ferences between the multimedia and multimodal system. They differentiated the notions of modality and media firstly as modality referring to the sensory or perceptual experience (e.g. visual, tactile, etc.), while medium is a means of conveying a representation (to a human), e.g. a diagram or a text. The concept of multimodality needs to be introduced here, it being based on the use of at least two sensory modalities by which humans receive information, e.g. tactile, visual, auditory, etc. (Baber and Mellor, 2001). They also pointed out that multimedia (or multiple representations) and multimodal systems share a common aim: the effective interaction with the user.

However, important differences between multimedia and multimodal systems have also been discussed by many researchers from different angles. Lee (1996) identified that multimedia systems deal with the presentation of information, while multimodal systems interpret and regenerate information presented in different media. According to Turk and Robertson (2001), the distinction between multimedia and multimodal user interfaces is based on the systems input and output capabilities. A multimedia user interface supports multiple outputs only whereas a multimodal user interface supports multiple input and output. Anastopoulou et al. (2001) also argued that in multimedia systems the user has to adapt to the perceptual capabilities of the system, while in multimodal systems the system adapts to the preferences and needs of the user. In this chapter, we adopt a more general definition of a multimodal system, in which the system takes two sensory modalities, i.e. visual and textual modalities, as input, and processes them in a complementary manner in order to better fulfil the user's perceptual and conceptual needs. According to the relevant literature and the research findings reported in this chapter, the combination of visual and textual modalities has proven to be effective for enhancing the understanding of the multi-sensory information through a gestalted sensory space comprising cross-model information correlation and integration, which could be implemented as a crucial layer for the system architecture of many MulSeMedia applications.

On Combining Visual and Textual Modalities

It has been widely argued that the low-level visual primitives exploited by CBIR systems are not sufficient for depicting distinctive semantic (object) level representations of the images. On the other hand, dominant commercial solutions such as Google and Yahoo image search engines which for indexation and retrieval take advantage of the collateral textual information co-occurring with the images, such as the title, caption, URL, etc, cannot always meet the user's perceptual needs and sometimes the retrieval results may be unpredictable due to the inconsistency between the collateral text and image content. Figure 1 shows the response of the Yahoo image search engine to the query: "bear in water". Meanwhile, the research regarding the user need for visual information retrieval systems has also been carried out. The literature on the request studies of users of image collections is much smaller than that on image retrieval. The most comprehensive user study is Enser's (1993) work, which is based

on 3000 requests received by the Hulton Deutsch Collection. Other research includes Keister(1994) who collected and studied the requests received by the National Library of Medicine, Ornager (1996) who interviewed archivists and observed journalists to clarify the needs of newspaper journalists, and Markkula and Sormunen (2000) who studied practice at a Finnish newspaper digital archive. Although the results of these user need studies are quite difficult to summarise as the studies varied from each other in the classification criteria for the requests, characteristics of the data collections studied, etc., two common grounds can be easily found among these studies: i) users search both by types and identities of the entities in images, ii) users request images both by the innate visual features of the picture itself and the concept or meaning conveyed by the picture. With this conclusion, clearly we can see that using text or image features alone cannot adequately support users' requests. Therefore, any attempt to combine both visual and textual cues for image representation and indexation should exploit the next generation of integrative multi-modal semantically-cued image retrieval approaches.

Mori et al. (1999) proposed a co-occurrence model, which formulated the co-occurrency relationships between keywords and sub-blocks of

Figure 1. Yahoo's retrieval result in response to the query of "bear in water"

images. Duygulu et al. (2002) improved the Mori et al. (1999) co-occurrence model by incorporating the machine translational model of Brown et al. (1993), which assumes image annotation can be considered as a task of translating blobs to a vocabulary of keywords. Barnard and Forsyth (2001) and Barnard et al. (2003) proposed a statistical model for organising image collections into a hierarchical tree structure, which integrates semantic information provided by associated text and perceptual information provided by image features. The model is also a clustering model, which maps documents into clusters and models the joint distribution of document and features. The data is modelled as being generated through the nodes of the hierarchical tree, with a path from a leaf to the root corresponding to a cluster. Each document is modelled by a sum of the clusters, weighted by the probability that the document is in that cluster. The authors also pointed out that the use of a hierarchical model, which imposes coarse to fine on the image classification can facilitate large image database browsing. Also, they believe that such a tree structure is part of the semantics. Hence, they propose that a hierarchical system is better at capturing semantics than a flat one. A highlight of their system is that the nodes of the tree structure generate both image segments by Gaussian distribution and words by multimodal distribution. The integration of and the correspondence learnt between textual and visual features at a blob/keyword level within the model makes the two modalities mutually underpin each other to perform more semantic and accurate classification and retrieval. Some novel applications of multimodal information processing can benefit from this research, including, cross-modal information retrieval, automatic image annotation and illustration.

One of the earliest attempts for bridging the so called "semantic gap" is to extract high-level visual semantics from low-level image content. Typical examples include: the discrimination between 'indoor' and 'outdoor' scenes (Paek et al., 1999; Szummer and Picard, 1998), 'city' vs. 'landscape' (Gorkani, and Picard, 1994), 'natural' vs. 'manmade' (Bradshaw, 2000), etc. Paek et al. (1999) present an integration framework for combing the image classifiers which are based on information from different modalities, i.e. images and associated textual descriptions. Among the early research on indoor and outdoor image classification, Paek et al.'s work is distinctive because instead of purely or mainly using low-level visual features to infer semantic-level features, they attempted to integrate both linguistic and visual-based approaches for the content labelling and classification of indoor/outdoor photographs in the domain of terrorism. On the text side, they use the text accompanying an image in a novel TF*IDF vector-based approach for classification. TF*IDF is short for Term Frequency Inversed Document Frequency. The higher TF*IDF value will be assigned to the key-terms that appear in certain documents much more often than in other documents. Hence, these key-terms with high TF*IDF can be considered as the most significant and representative keywords in the document. Both the TF*IDF scores for each document and class TF*IDF for all documents associated with indoor or outdoor images are computed and then aggregated by computing the dot product between the two TF*IDF scores. On the image side, they present a novel OF*IIF (Object Frequency Inverse Image Frequency) vector-based approach for classification (Paek et al., 1999). Feature vectors extracted from sub-blocks of each image are then clustered. Different visual objects are associated with the corresponding cluster centroids. Having TF*IDF scores for each image caption and OF*IIF scores for each image, they aggregate them by simply adding the two scores together as the classification score to indoor and outdoor categories. By integrating the two classifiers, the classification accuracy exceeded the performance of each classifier alone. They also challenged Szummer and Picard's research by arguing that despite the high classification accuracy (90.3%)

their system achieved for the Kodak consumer photographs, the accuracy becomes significantly lower at 74.7% on the set of terrorist news images that they worked with where Paek et al.'s system improved the accuracy by approximately 12% over the former to 86%.

Li and Wang (2003) created a system for automatic linguistic indexing of pictures using a statistical modelling approach. The two-dimensional multi-resolution hidden Markov model is used for profiling categories of images, each corresponding to a concept. There are three major components within their system, the feature extraction process, the multi-resolution statistical modelling process, and the statistical linguistic indexing process. Block-based features of the training images are characterised using wavelet transforms at several resolutions. They relate a concept with a certain category of images which do not have to be visually similar. A manually prepared short but informative description is also assigned to each concept. In such a way, a dictionary of concepts, which was subsequently used as the linguistic indexing source, was built up. The system automatically indexes images by firstly extracting multi-resolution block-based features by the same approach used to extract features for the training images, then selecting top k categories with the highest log likelihood of the given image to the category, and finally determining a small subset of key terms from the vocabulary of those selected categories stored in the concept dictionary as indexing terms. Li and Wang (2003) also mentioned Barnard et al.'s (2003) system and argued that one major limitation of their system is that the model relies on semantically meaningful segmentation, which is unavailable for most of the image database, and automatic segmentation is still an open issue in computer vision. In contrast, a highlight of Li and Wang's system is that the model does not rely on any image segmentations. Moreover, the block-based multi-resolution feature model they constructed using wavelet, implied the spatial

relationship among image pixels within and across resolutions. Such a spatial relationship is taken into consideration with probabilistic likelihood as a universal measure.

Zhou and Huang (2002) explored how keywords and low-level content features can be unified for image retrieval. They proposed a seamless joint querying and relevance feedback scheme based on the combination of both visual features and keywords incorporating keyword similarities which is underpinned by an algorithm for learning of the word similarity matrix. The learning had been carried out in conjunction with the user interaction, i.e. word association via relevance feedback. The learned word similarity matrix was used for the thesaurus construction, because they argued that although keywords have more direct mapping towards high-level semantics than low-level visual features, the mapping is therefore not one-to-one due to the context-dependent interpretation of and/ or the use of synonyms. By using the thesaurus, they avoid the inconsistencies caused by image annotations from different users at different times according to different preferences, etc. They used a semantic network for grouping the keywords in a meaningful way, and weights in the semantic network were dynamically updated via user relevance feedback during the retrieval process. Also, they used what they called a soft vector representation indicating the probability of the appearance of the keyword in a given image, which gives more flexibility for feature matching. They pointed out further research in this area should focus on intermediate features, semantics-guided segmentation and spatial relationship modelling, and the use of machine learning techniques to unify low-level features and keywords.

Cascia et al. (1999) and Westerveld (2000) chose on-line newspaper archives with photos as their testing dataset to combine the visual cues from low-level visual features and textural cues from the collateral texts. They also used a similar approach in latent semantic indexing for textual feature representation. Both of the two research works compared their proposed multimodal methods with other traditional methods developed based on single modality, such as CBIR. The experimental results showed that the combined feature vector model enhanced by LSI outperformed the content-based approach for Cascia et al. (1999) and both the content and context (text) based approach for Westerveld (2000).

Srihari is one of pioneer researchers in the area of combining visual and linguistic modalities for image understanding and object recognition (Srihari 1995a,1995b). Srihari and Zhang (2000) developed a semi-automated image annotation system called 'Show&Tell', which is capable of generating object-oriented conceptual level labels for the region of interest within the images in order to build recognition. Human intervention is required from domain experts to give spoken descriptions to the regions. The constraint spatial relationships between objects were inserted in a constraint graph-based representation of the scene. Speech recognition and natural language processing techniques were exploited in order to map the low-level image content to the high-level semantic interpretation.

Another system also developed by Srihari and Burhans (1994) focused on face recognition for identifying human faces in newspaper photographs accompanying collateral textual information. In this work they defined the notion of visual semantics as the technique for systematically extracting picture-specific information from collateral texts. They also argued that general-purpose vision without a priori knowledge remains a very difficult task at best. Researchers are looking for external knowledge whenever it is possible to enhance to performance of the vision based systems. Such knowledge can be easily found within the collateral text accompanying the visual content. They also constructed a visual hierarchical structure in terms of visual super-concepts which reflect low-level content-based properties and links (visual-is-a, visual-part-of) defined from the existing Word-Net. A highlight of this work is the integration of

visual hierarchy into a semantic lexicon in order to generate visual constraints, which made the application a knowledge-based vision system.

Athansiadis et al. (2007) proposed a framework for simultaneous image segmentation and object labelling. The work focused on semantic analysis of images, which contributes to knowledge-assisted multimedia analysis and bridging the semantic gap. Traditionally the possible semantic labels, formally represented as fuzzy sets, facilitate the decision making on handling image regions instead of visual features. Two well known image segmentation algorithms, i.e. watershed and recursive shortest spanning tree, were modified in order to stress the proposed method's independence of a specific image segmentation approach. Meanwhile, a visual context representation and analysis approach, blending global knowledge in interpreting each object locally, had been developed. Fuzzy algebra and ontological taxonomic knowledge representation had been combined in order to formulate the visual contextual information. The contextual knowledge had been utilised for re-adjusting the labelling results taken from semantic region growing, by means of fine-tuning membership degrees of detected concepts.

Zhang and Izquierdo (2007) proposed a novel method for object-based image retrieval, which is designed to adaptively and efficiently locate salient blocks in images. Semantically meaningful objects in images were represented using salient blocks and subsequently labelled via object-oriented annotation. An algorithm had been developed for adaptively locating the most suitable blocks representing the query concept or object of interest in images. Associations between low-level patterns and semantic concepts are modelled by an optimised concept-specific multi-descriptor space, based on which a fitting block is selected. Relevance feedback had been seamlessly integrated into the retrieval process.

Promising experimental results had been indicated throughout the literature in this innovative research area. The combination of the two modalities had been conducted in various ways, e.g. complementary or competitive etc. These studies have largely motivated our research in combining both visual and textual cues in semantic-driven visual content labelling and high-level image feature vector model construction.

A SEMANTICALLY AND COLLATERALLY CUED MULTIMODAL METHOD FOR IMAGE LABELLING

We propose a novel method of multimodal semantic-based collateral image labelling, aiming to automatically assign textual keywords to image regions. A visual vocabulary comprising 236 visual concepts was constructed based on 3748 manually annotated image segments. The collateral knowledge extracted from the collateral textual modality of the image content was exploited as a bias to the mapping from the low-level region-based visual features to high-level visual concepts defined in the visual vocabulary. Two different types of collateral knowledge can be identified, namely collateral content and collateral context. A conditional probabilistic co-occurrence matrix representing the conditional co-occurrency of the visual keywords was created to represent the collateral contextual knowledge. A collaborative mapping scheme was devised by using statistical methods such as Gaussian distribution or Euclidean distance together with a collateral content and context driven inference mechanism.

System Architecture

The proposed system architecture for collateral image labelling aims to assign textual keywords to regions of interest for a given image automatically. The typical system output would be image regions associated with a set of keywords that depict the semantics of the visual content to which they are related. Such an application would help close the semantic gap, and by localising the semantics to image regions, more accurate and sensible visual content recognition and understanding will be enabled.

Figure 2 illustrates the architecture of the proposed framework and the typical system workflow. Four key components can be identified, namely image segmentation and region-based low-level visual feature extraction, collateral knowledge base, a visual vocabulary and a collaborative mapping procedure. The raw image data will firstly be segmented into a number of regions and then low-level visual features, such as colour, edge, shape, texture, will be extracted from each segment. Using the region-based feature vectors, we map those low-level visual features to the visual concepts defined in the visual vocabulary with the help of the external knowledge extracted from the collateral content and context. In the following sections, we will introduce each individual component in detail.

Extracting Visual Features from Image Regions

We used the normalised cut (Jianbo and Jitendra, 2000) method to segment images into a number of regions. The reason for choosing this method for image segmentation is that it outputs image segments with no overlaps and salient regions. One aspect worth mentioning here is that the segmentation is based on the grouping of visual similarity of pixels without any concern about the semantics of the object. Hence, for example, a semantic visual object may be segmented into different parts due to the perceptual variety of the object surface.

A 54-dimensional feature vector, comprising colour, edge, shape and texture features, is created for each segment. Twenty one colour features of the image are extracted using the intensity histogram. Nineteen edge features, are extracted by applying an edge filter and the water-filling algorithm (Zhou and Huang, 2000) on the binary

Figure 2. An overview of the proposed system architecture for collateral image labelling

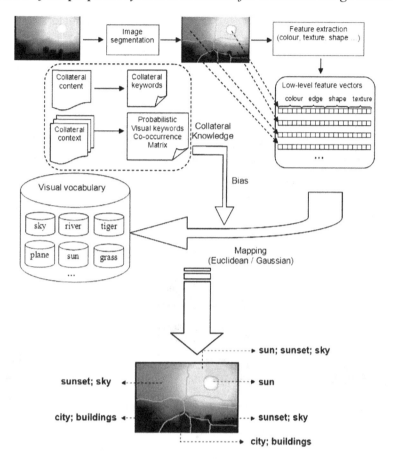

edge image. A statistical texture analysis method proposed by Haralick et al. (1973), the Grey Level Co-occurrence Matrices, was used to extract six texture features from every segment. Finally, eight features related to shape were extracted using Matlab-based functions for extracting the statistics of image regions. We have constructed the final feature vector by sequentially assembling all the four kinds of features together.

Constructing a Visual Vocabulary

The visual vocabulary developed in our system is a set of clusters of region-based visual feature vectors labelled by textual keywords (see Figure 3).

The construction of the visual vocabulary is based on a dataset provided by Barnard et al.

(2003), which consists of 3478 manually annotated image regions segmented from 454 Corel images. The image segments were annotated by Duygulu with a controlled vocabulary which is a subset of the terms that had been used for annotating the Corel images. An image segment may be annotated using single or multiple keywords. Figure 4 shows an example of such annotations.

There are two basic approaches for clustering the region-based visual feature vectors. One is to use statistical clustering methods, such as K-means or Hierarchical clustering, to classify the visual feature vectors into a number of clusters and manually label those clusters using keywords. The drawback of this method is that sometimes it would group together some segments which are visually very similar but conceptually very dif-

Figure 3. A visual vocabulary consists of 236 visual concepts

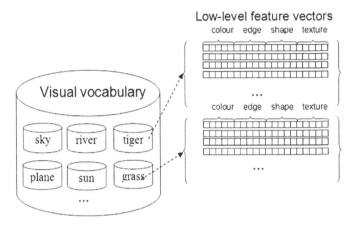

Figure 4. An example of blob-based manual annotation

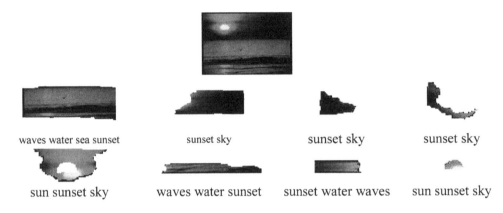

ferent. In other words, this method does not overcome the limitation of content-based image feature classification. Since we had this dataset of manually labelled image segments, we decided to use another approach to cluster those segments, which is a simple process of grouping the segments labelled by the same keyword together. Finally, 236 visual concepts were extracted to constitute the vocabulary. However, since the segments may be labelled by multiple keywords, there would be overlaps among the clusters.

Constructing a Collateral Knowledge Base

There are two kinds of collateral knowledge within the knowledge base, i.e. collateral content and collateral context.

Collateral Content

The collateral content refers to the knowledge that can be extracted directly from the collateral modality, in our case the collateral keywords accompanying the images. As mentioned above, such a kind of collateral textual information becomes easier and easier to acquire due to the multimodal nature of the modern digitised information dis-

Table 1. Conditional probabilistic co-occurrence matrix of visual keywords

	K1	*K2*	*K3*	...	*Kn*
K1		P(K2 | K1)	P(K3 | K1)	...	P(Kn | K1)
K2	P(K1 | K2)		P(K3 | K2)	...	P(Kn | K2)
K3	P(K1 | K3)	P(K2 | K3)		...	P(Kn | K3)
...	...	...	...	...	...
Kn	P(K1 | Kn)	P(K2 | Kn)	P(K3 | Kn)	...	

semination. Moreover there are many different sources where the collateral keywords can be extracted, such as captions, titles, URL, etc. Such keywords are expected to depict the subject or concepts conveyed by the image content.

Collateral Context

Collateral context is another new concept that we introduced in this research, which refers to the contextual knowledge, representing the relationships between the visual concepts. We use a conditional probabilistic co-occurrence matrix which represents the co-occurrency relationships between the visual concepts defined in the visual vocabulary. A 236×236 matrix is created based on the annotations of the image segments (see Table 1).

Each element of the matrix can be formally defined as follows:

$$P\left(K_j \big| K_i\right) = \frac{P\left(K_i, K_j\right)}{P\left(K_i\right)} \quad \left(i \neq j\right) \qquad (1)$$

The relationships could be considered as bi-directional, because the value of each element is calculated based on the conditional probability of the co-occurrency between two visual keywords. The relationships appear to be reasonable in many cases (see Figure 5). For instance, the relationship between sky and clouds showing that clouds have a bigger co-occurrence probability against sky than the other way round. This appears to be reasonable, because clouds must appear in the sky while there may be a lot of other things appearing in the sky.

By exploiting this co-occurrence matrix, we believe that this is a novel way of bridging the gap between the computer generated image segmentation and the semantic visual object. Image segmentation unaided by other domain information is still not fully resolved and remains as an open issue with no dominant solution. So far, even the most state-of-the-art image segmentation techniques have failed to generate perfect assigned segmentation which can separate whole objects from each other. Normally, image segments either contain a part of an object or several parts of different objects which are occluded by each other. For instance, it is very common to find segments containing a wing of an airplane with the background of sky. With our co-occurrence matrix, if the segments can be firstly recognised as a wing then the system will most probably provide other labels such as plane, jet, sky, etc. according to the conditional probability between the visual keyword 'wing' and the others.

Collaboratively Mapping Towards Visual Concepts

Having constructed the visual vocabulary and collateral knowledge base, it is now time to map the low-level visual feature vectors of the image segments to the visual keywords. We used two methods to do the mapping, namely Euclidean distance and Gaussian distribution.

Figure 5. A graph representation of the visual keyword co-occurrence matrix

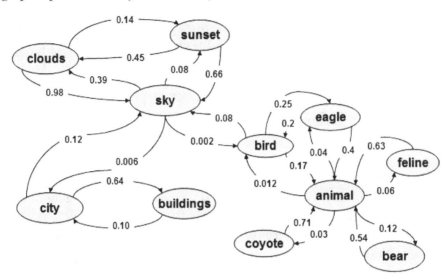

For the Euclidean distance method, we calculate the distance between the segment features and the centroids of each cluster within the visual vocabulary (see equation 2).

$$D = \sqrt{\sum_{i=1}^{n} \left(x_i - c_i \right)^2} \qquad (2)$$

x is the segment's feature vector and c is the mean vector of the visual feature cluster. For the Gaussian distribution method, we calculate the probability between the segment's feature vector and visual feature clusters, which can be defined as follows:

$$P = \frac{1}{\sqrt{2\pi\sigma^2}} \exp\left(\frac{-\left(x - a\right)^2}{2\sigma^2} \right) \qquad (3)$$

Where a and σ are the mean vector and standard deviation of the cluster respectively.

However, a method only based on the shortest Euclidean distance and highest Gaussian probability cannot always provide accurate labels.

This is the reason why we introduce the collateral knowledge to bias the mapping procedure. Again, the two different knowledge bases of collateral content and collateral context were used as the bias.

For the collateral content based labelling, the process is quite straightforward. Instead of finding the shortest Euclidean distance or highest Gaussian probability against all the clusters within the visual vocabulary, we just find the best matching visual keywords which appear as collateral keywords. See equation 4 and 5.

Euclidean Distance: $Min\left(\sqrt{\left\| \vec{f} - \vec{u} \right\|^2} \right) \qquad (4)$

Gaussian Distribution

$$Max\left(\frac{1}{\sqrt{2\pi\sigma^2}} \exp\left(\frac{-\left(\vec{f} - \vec{u}\right)^2}{2\sigma^2} \right) \right) \qquad (5)$$

Where f is the blob feature vector; $\vec{u}$ and σ are the mean vector and standard deviation of selected *clusters* which can be defined as:

$clusters \in \{k \mid k \in collateral\_keyword\} \cap \{k \mid k \in visual\_vocabulary\}$

For the collateral context based labelling, we use a thresholding mechanism to combine both visual similarity between the feature and visual keywords of the segment and co-occurrence probability between the collateral content based label and the rest of the visual keywords within the visual vocabulary. See equations 6 and 7. The determination of Threshold T is based on experiment and can be adjusted according to the different needs. For example, the lower the value is the more context related labels you get, however the relevance of the label may decrease accordingly. In contrast, greater value leads to more relevant but a lesser number of labels.

Euclidean Distance:

$$\left(Min\left(\sqrt{\left\| \vec{f} - \vec{u}_{kn} \right\|^2} \right) \middle/ \sqrt{\left\| \vec{f} - \vec{u}_{km} \right\|^2} \right) \times P\left(K_m \middle| K_n \right) \geq Threshold$$

(6)

Gaussian Distribution

$$\left(\frac{1}{\sqrt{2\pi\sigma^2}} \exp\left(\frac{-\left(\vec{f} - \vec{u}_{km} \right)^2}{2\sigma^2} \right) \right) \times P\left(K_m \mid K_n \right) \geq Threshold$$

(7)

Where
$$kn \in \left\{ k; k \in col\_kw \right\} \cap \left\{ k; k \in vis\_voc \right\}$$

$$km \in \left\{ k; k \in vis\_voc \right\}$$

Figure 6 shows an example of the collateral labelling results.

SEMANTIC-DRIVEN HIGH-LEVEL IMAGE FEATURE VECTOR MODEL

Based on the region-based labels generated using the Collaterally Cued Labelling Framework, i.e. the CCL Framework, we construct a novel homogenous semantic-level image feature vector model.

Thus the new feature vector model combines both the visual features of the image content and the textual features of its collateral text. Two different kinds of feature vectors are created for retrieval and classification purposes respectively.

As indicated the in the Table below, a typical result of the labelling is a set of keywords associated with each segment (see Figure 2). Based on such linguistic labels, we can calculate the weight of each term on the basis of the frequency of its appearance in the labels of all the segments. Therefore, it is expected that the weights should reflect the proportion of the occurrence of the visual object within the whole scene. For the example shown in Figure 2, we can generate the proportions of the key terms as below (see table 2):

A 236-dimensional feature vector, where each dimension represents a visual keyword in the vocabulary, can be created based on those proportions. Each element of the vector can be defined as:

$$w_i = \frac{f_i}{N} \qquad i \in \left[1, 236 \right]$$

(8)

Where the f_i refers to the total number of keywords that are automatically assigned to the image. N refers to the total number of keywords that are automatically assigned to the image.

Another feature vector model can be applied in a similar way. However instead of defining each visual keyword as a dimension, this time we group

Table 2. Proportions of each visual object within the scene

Key term	Proportion
sunset	*3/12 = 25%*
sky	*3/12 = 25%*
sun	*2/12 = 17%*
city	*2/12 = 17%*
buildings	*2/12 = 17%*

Figure 6. An example of collateral labelling results

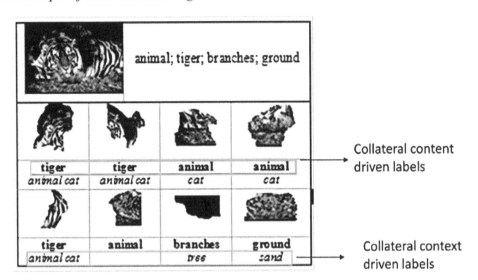

Table 3. An example of exponential partition based feature vector

	Category 1				Category 2				...
	Part. 1	**Part. 2**	**Part. 3**	**Part. 4**	**Part. 1**	**Part. 2**	**Part. 3**	**Part. 4**	**...**
No. of Words	$3^0=1$	$3^1=3$	$3^2=9$	$3^3=27$	$3^0=1$	$3^1=3$	$3^2=9$	$3^3=27$	...
Proportion of Words in Partition	3/5	1/5	0	0	0	0	1/5	0	...
Weight value	0.6	0.06	0	0	0	0	0.02	0	...

the keywords into exponential partitions using a function described in equation 9, according to the *tf*×*idf* values for the key terms for each category.

$$f(x) = a^x \qquad x \in \{0, 1, 2, 3, .., n\} \qquad (9)$$

Where *a* is a statistic parameter which can be specified accordingly.

The aim of developing such kind of feature vector model is to give more weight to the most important keywords for each category. Accordingly the value of the element of the feature vector will be the quotient of the keyword proportion divided by the number of keywords within the exponential partition.

Table 3 shows an example of an exponential partition based high-level image feature vector, where the value of each element of the vector can be formally defined as follows:

$$\frac{\sum w_i}{a^x} \qquad (10)$$

Where w_i is the proportion of the keyword calculated using equation 8. $\sum w_i$ is the sum of proportion values of labels appearing in the corresponding group and a^x is number of keywords in the exponential partition of each pre-defined category. The number of the categories depends on how the training datasets are organised and classified.

The range of x should be adjusted according to how many key terms appeared in each category.

We believe that this feature vector model can facilitate the classification, because more weight is given to the most significant and representative key terms for each category which is encoded at the beginning while assigning less weight to the keywords which are located towards the end of each partition.

EXPERIMENTATION AND DISCUSSION

All the experiments which were carried out were based on the Corel dataset which contains more than 600 CDs, each of which has 100 photos grouped as one theme. An interesting aspect of the collection is that each image has been annotated with two kinds of annotation, one is the caption, which describes the subject of the whole image in free text, i.e. thematically contextualises the image, and, the other is keywords which depict the key objects contained within the image. In our experiments, we took advantage of the given keywords as the collateral textual cues to the image tagging. Those keywords can be considered for being extracted from the collateral text information of the image using natural language processing or keyword extraction techniques. We selected 30 categories of Corel images as our experimental dataset.

Collaterally Cued Image Labelling

The 3000 Corel images were firstly segmented into 27953 regions of interest. The segments for each image were sorted in the descending order of the size (or area), and we selected the top 10 segments, if the image was segmented into more than 10 regions, as the most significant visual objects in the image to label. We carried out two experiments to label the 3000 Corel images using the two different mapping methods, namely

Euclidean distance and Gaussian distribution. However, as there is no benchmarking dataset for evaluating such an application. We could not carry out any direct evaluation on the performance of the region-based image labelling. Figure 7 shows an example output of the labelling system using the Gaussian distribution method. The keywords in Bold are the labels assigned to the region based on the collateral content, namely the Corel keywords. The keywords in Italic are the labels given based on the visual keywords co-occurrence matrix arising from equation 7.

Semantic-Based Image Classification, Indexing and Retrieval

As there is no way to examine the performance of the proposed region-based image labelling model directly we determined to evaluate this method by encoding the labelling results into feature vectors, and examine the effectiveness of the classification and retrieval on the basis of those feature vectors.

Two different kinds of feature vectors, as proposed in "Semantic-driven High-level Image Feature Vector Model," were generated for all the 3000 Corel images. One was the 236-dimensional feature vector, whereby the value of each dimension is determined by the weights (calculated using equation 8) of the visual keywords defined in the visual vocabulary. The other one is the feature vectors based on the exponential partitioning of the keywords in each category. In our case, we divided the keywords into 4 groups by applying the function $f(x) = 3^x$ where $x \in \{0, 1, 2, 3\}$ according to the $tf \times idf$ values of each keyword of the category (See Table 4). Therefore, there were 120 (4 × 30) dimensions in this feature vector. Because we also used different methods for the mapping from the region-based low-level feature vectors to the visual keywords, i.e. Euclidean distance and Gaussian distribution, we finally generated 4 sets of feature vectors for each of the

Figure 7. Image labelling result using Gaussian distribution

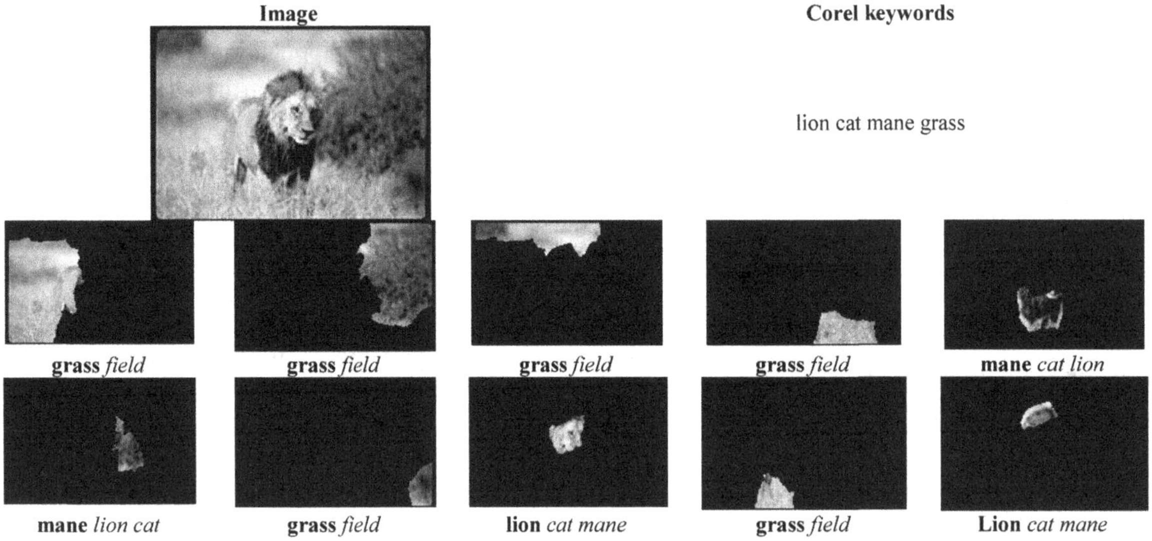

Table 4. Exponential partitioning of the Corel keywords

Partition	Sunsets & Sunrises	Bear	...
$3^0=1$	sun	bear	...
$3^1=3$	clouds	polar	...
	sea	black	...
	city	tundra	...
$3^2=9$	waves	snow	...
	bay	ice	...
	sky	river	...
	lake	bears	...
	boat	grass	...
	mountain	beach	...
	boats	water	...
	hills	forest	...
	birds	head	...
$3^3=27$	...	...	...

tracted 3000 image feature vectors based on the visual content of the image and text feature vectors based on the Corel keywords. For the visual feature vector, we constructed a 46-dimensional feature vector which consisted of colour, edge and texture features for each image. For the textual feature vector, we selected the top 15 keywords with the highest $tf \times idf$ values in each category. Then we merged the duplicate keywords, and finally built up a 333-dimensional text feature vector model. The value of each element is the occurrence of the keywords.

We created four 30 × 30 SOMs (i.e. Self Organising Maps) in order to learn to classify the four kinds of feature vectors, i.e. Euclidean 120D, Gaussian 120D, Visual 46D, and Textual 333D. We summarise all the feature vectors we extracted from the 3000 Corel images in the following table (Table 5).

We divided the 3000 Corel images into training and test sets with a ratio of 1:9. Ten images were randomly selected from each category making a total number of 300 test images, and the rest, 2700 images, as a training set. Each one of the four SOMs was trained with the 2700 feature vectors extracted from the training images using

3000 Corel images, namely Euclidean 236D and 120D, Gaussian 236D and 120D.

In order to compare the performance of the proposed feature vector model with the traditional feature extraction methods, we also ex-

Table 5. Feature vectors generated from 3000 Corel images using 6 methods

Method	Dimensionality	Short name
Euclidean distance	236D	Euclidean 236D
Euclidean distance with exponential partitioning	120D	Euclidean 120D
Gaussian distribution	236D	Gaussian 236D
Gaussian distribution with exponential partitioning	120D	Gaussian 120D
Visual features	46D	Visual 46D
Textual features	333D	Textual 333D

the four methods for 100 epochs. Then, we tested the trained network using the 300 test feature vectors. Four confusion matrices were created based on the test result. Figure 8 indicates the SOM classification accuracy using the four different kinds of feature vectors. The Euclidean 120D shows the best average accuracy at 71% followed by the Gaussian 120D at 70%. Also, the performance of the Euclidean 120D and Gaussian 120D appeared to be more stable than the Textual 333D and Visual 46D.

The trained SOMs were also used to perform the image retrieval on the four different kinds of feature vectors. The SOM-based retrieval is based on the principle that advocates the retrieval of the selection of candidate matched items from the training repository with respect to their activation values to the Best Matching Unit (BMU) of the

test input. The Euclidean 120D and Gaussian 120D outperformed both the textual and visual feature vectors for the top five retrieved items, and significantly increased the precision over the alternative of purely using content-based image feature vectors (see Figure 9).

Our other image retrieval experiment deployed all six different feature vector models, i.e. Euclidean 120D, Euclidean 236D, Gaussian 120D, Gaussian 236D, visual 46D and textual 333D, using cosine distance matching. Despite the fact that Textual 333D provided the best precision in results this time, it has been proved that for 12 categories, at least one of our proposed feature vector models outperforms the traditional textual and visual feature vector models.

However, the statistical calculations alone are sometimes not enough for the evaluation. We believe that one of the advantages of our proposed semantic-based high-level image feature vector models is that they can combine both the visual and conceptual similarity of the image. Take the retrieval results showed in Figure 10 as an example; although Textual 333D achieved the best statistical results, it cannot meet the user's perceptual needs for the objects of interest. Moreover, the word 'animal' for instance misleads the system to retrieve any image whose annotation contains this word. However, by using our proposed high-level image feature vector model the objects of interest can be successfully identified e.g. bear

Figure 8. SOM classification accuracy using four kinds of feature vectors

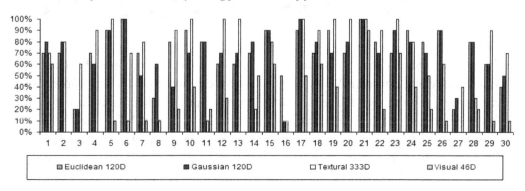

251

Figure 9. Precisions of the SOM-based image retrieval using four different feature vector sets

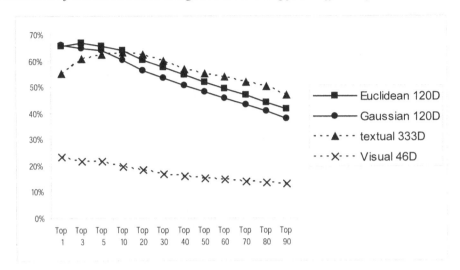

Figure 10. An example of retrieval results using six different kinds of feature vectors

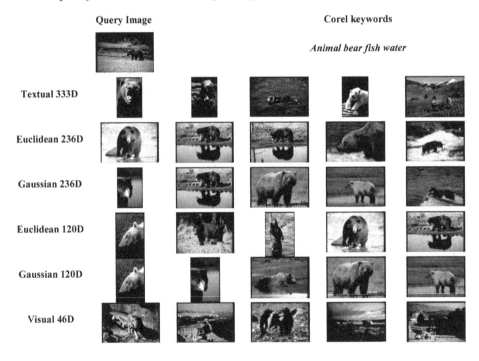

and water in this case, and we can retrieve images that are both visually and conceptually similar to the query images, even though the retrieved images were categorised into different classes by the annotator compared to that of the query image. This is also consistent with the empirical observation that sometimes the statistical calculations, e.g. precision/accuracy, appear to be lower for the proposed features than for the textual features. Also, recall the retrieval results of the Yahoo image search engine in response to the query "bear in water" - this is a good example for demonstrating the shortcomings of purely using collateral textual information for image indexation and retrieval due to the subjectivity of the textual annotations. Hence, we believe that in realistic scenarios, where the collateral text may contain a lot of noise or may prove to be too subjective, the advantage of the proposed high-level image feature vector model will become more obvious due to its ability of visually re-confirming that the concept does indeed exist in the images.

Semantic Tagging on Film Post-Production Industry Outtake Material

The proposed method of the collaterally-cued visual content labelling framework had been further extended and adapted accordingly to automatically annotate the video clips produced in the film post-production industry, whereby both the proposed method extensibility, in terms of moving from image to video annotation, and the adaptability on domain specific applications had been examined. The proposed collaterally-cued visual content labelling framework had been tai-

lored, extended and tested on the special effects video data produced in the film post-production industry which were provided by some of the major film post-production companies in the UK. The automatic video labelling framework for the film post-production industry, aims at automatically assigning semantic keywords to objects of interest appearing in the video segment. The framework had been implemented to label the raw video data in a fully automated manner. The typical user of the system is the video content library manager who will be enabled to use the system to facilitate the labelling and indexing of the video data. With this function, all the objects of interest including moving and still foreground objects will be labelled with linguistic keywords.

In order to comprehensively evaluate the performance of the automatic video labelling framework, we conducted a number of system tests based on different experimental setups. The training and test dataset were manually selected based on 3 different ratios, i.e. 9:1, 7:3, and 5:5. For each experimental setup we examined the labelling accuracy for each one of the 31 semantic

Table 6. Semantic categories of the film post-production industry special effect video data

1_1	blood and gore; blood;	7_3	misc; washing line;
1_2	blood and gore; gore;	7_4	misc; welding;
2_1	bullet hits; sparks;	8	muzzle flash;
2_2	bullet hits; turf hits;	9	sparks;
3	crowds figures;	10_1	water; bilge pumps;
4_1	explosions fire smoke; explosion;	10_2	water; boat wakes;
4_2	explosions fire smoke; fire;	10_3	water; bubbles;
4_3	explosions fire smoke; fire burst;	10_4	water; cascading water;
4_4	explosions fire smoke; flak;	10_5	water; drips;
4_5	explosions fire smoke; sheet fire;	10_6	water; interesting water surfaces;
4_6	explosions fire smoke; smoke;	10_7	water; rain;
4_7	explosions fire smoke; steam;	10_8	water; rivulets;
5	falling paper;	10_9	water; splashes;
6	lens flares;	10_10	water; spray;
7_1	misc; car crash;	11_1	weather; clouds;
7_2	misc; poo;	11_2	weather; snow;

categories listed in Table 6. A total number of 453 shots were selected from the film post-production special effects dataset as our experimental corpus.

Table 7 shows the labelling accuracy delivered by the automatic video labelling framework, including both content- and context-related labels,

based on the training/test ratio of 9:1, 7:3 and 5:5, respectively. Among the three different experimental setups, 7:3 achieved the best performance with an average accuracy of 80% followed by 75% for 5:5 and 66% for 9:1; many other catego-

Table 7. Automatic Video Labelling accuracy based on the train/test ratio of 9:1, 7:3 and 5:5

Class ID	9:1	7:3	5:5	Class ID	9:1	7:3	5:5
1.1	75%	94%	83%	7.4	100%	100%	100%
1.2	0%	100%	100%	8	0%	100%	100%
2.1	75%	100%	100%	9	0%	25%	40%
3	100%	100%	100%	10.1	100%	100%	100%
4.1	100%	92%	75%	10.1	100%	100%	80%
4.2	100%	100%	90%	10.2	100%	67%	50%
4.3	100%	0%	100%	10.3	0%	0%	0%
4.4	100%	100%	100%	10.4	0%	0%	50%
4.5	100%	100%	100%	10.5	100%	100%	50%
4.6	86%	90%	90%	10.6	0%	50%	67%
4.7	100%	100%	100%	10.7	0%	75%	71%
5	100%	100%	100%	10.8	0%	100%	0%
6	100%	86%	83%	10.9	0%	100%	60%
7.1	0%	0%	0%	11.1	100%	100%	100%
7.2	100%	89%	86%	11.2	100%	100%	50%
7.3	100%	100%	100%	Average	66%	80%	75%

Figure 11. Exemplar automatic labelling result for special effect video shots

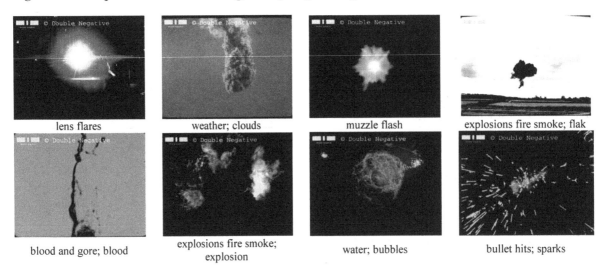

lens flares

weather; clouds

muzzle flash

explosions fire smoke; flak

blood and gore; blood

explosions fire smoke; explosion

water; bubbles

bullet hits; sparks

ries achieved a very high labelling accuracy percentage; some achieving 100% accuracy.

Figure 11 shows some typical examples of the labelling results on the special effect video shots. The images are the key frames of each video shot.

CONCLUSION AND FUTURE WORK

The research on traditional multimedia systems and the future MulSeMedia systems, i.e. multiple sensorial media, is motivated by the twin obectives of both achieving advanced sensory and distribution techniques, as well as, more importantly, the fusion, integration and understanding of such multi-sensory information. In this way such research attempts to bridge two kinds of gaps: **i)** the communication gap between different sensorial modalities in the MulSeMedia system, and, **ii)** the semantic gap between the multimodal data generated by MulSeMedia system as well as the semantic interpretation of such data. This work has contributed towards the closing of these two gaps; by proposing, developing and evaluating a novel framework for semantically labelling image regions through using multimodal information cues in a cooperative and complementary fashion. We have introduced the use of collateral content-and-context-based knowledge in image labelling applications. Accordingly a collaborative mapping scheme has been devised to combine statistical methods and a collateral knowledge based inference mechanism. We have proposed a semantically empowered intermediate image content descriptor model underpinned by a Collaterally Cued Labelling (CCL) Framework. We have validated our method by examining the classification and retrieval effectiveness of a semantic-level visual descriptor, developed based on the labelling results. The test results using four different kinds of high level image feature vector models were compared with the results obtainable using traditional text-based and content-based image feature models. This showed that the former consistently

yields a better performance than the latter in terms of satisfying both the perceptual and conceptual needs of the user. We also explored the use of CCL in realistic retrieval scenarios i.e. those pertaining to the film post-production industry which could be another challenging proving ground.

REFERENCES

Anastopoulou, S., Baber, C., & Sharples, M. (2001) "Multimedia and multimodal systems: commonalities and differences". Proc. of the 5th Human Centred Technology Postgraduate Workshop, University of Sussex.

Athanasisadis, T., Mylonas, P., Avrithis, Y., Kollias, S. (2007) "Semantic image segmentation and object labelling", IEEE Trans. On Circuits and systems for video technology, vol. 17, no, 3, pp 298-312.

Baber, C., & Mellor, B. (2001). Using critical path analysis to model multimodal human-computer interaction. *International Journal of Human-Computer Studies*, *54*, 613–636. doi:10.1006/ijhc.2000.0452

Barnard, K., Duygulu, P., de Freitas, N., Forsyth, D., Blei, D., & Jordan, M. I. (2003). Matching Words and Pictures. *Journal of Machine Learning Research*, *3*, 1107–1135. doi:10.1162/153244303322533214

Barnard, K., & Forsyth, D. (2001) "Learning the Semantics of Words and Pictures". Proceedings of Int. Conf. on Computer Vision, pp. II: 408-415.

Bimbo, A. D. (1999). *Visual Information Retrieval*. San Francisco, California, USA: Morgan Kaufmann Publishers, Inc.

Bradshaw, B. (2000) "Semantic based image retrieval: a probabilistic approach", Proc. of the eighth ACM Int. conf. on Multimedia, pp: 167 - 176.

Brown, P. Pietra, S.D. Pietra, V. D. and Mercer, R. (1993) "The mathematics of statistical machine translation: Parameter estimation". In Computational Linguistics, vol. 19, no. 2, pp.263-311.

Carson, C., Belongie, S., Greenspan, H., & Malik, J. (2002). Blobworld: Image Segmentation Using Expectation-Maximization and Its Application to Image Querying. *IEEE Transactions on Pattern Analysis and Machine Intelligence, 24*(8), 1026–1038. doi:10.1109/TPAMI.2002.1023800

Carson, C., Thomas, M., & Belongie, S. Hellerstein J. M., Malik J., (1999) "Blobworld: A System for Region-Based Image Indexing and Retrieval". In Proc. of the Third Int. conf. on Visual Information Systems, pp. 509-516.

Cascia, M. L., Sethi, S., & Sclaroff, S. (1998) "Combining Textual and Visual Cues for Content-Based Image Retrieval on the World Wide Web". Proceedings of IEEE Workshop on Content-Based Access of Image and Video Libraries.

Duygulu, P. Barnard, K. Freitas, N. and Forsyth, D. (2002) "Object recognition as machine translation: Learning a lexicon for a fixed image vocabulary". In 7th European Conf. on Computer Vision, pages 97-112.

Enser, P. G. (1993). Query analysis in a visual information retrieval context. *Journal of Document and Text Management, 1*, 25–52.

Flickner, M., Sawhney, H., Niblack, W., Ashley, J., Huang, Q., Dom, B., Gorkani, M., Hafine, J., Lee,D. Petkovic, D., Steele, D. and Yanker, P. (1995) "Query by image and video content: The QBIC system", IEEE Computer.

Gorkani, M. M., & Picard, R. W. (1994) "Texture orientation for sorting photos 'at a glance'", In proc. of the IEEE Int. Conf. on Pattern Recognition.

Gupta, A., & Jain, R. (1997). Visual information retrieval. *Communications of the ACM, 40*(5), 71–79. doi:10.1145/253769.253798

Haralick, R. M., Shanmugam, K., & Dinstein, I. (1973). "Texture features for image classification", IEEE Trans. On Sys, Man, and Cyb. *SMC, 3*(6), 610–621.

Jianbo, S., & Jitendra, M. (2000). Normalized Cuts and Image Segmentation. *IEEE Transactions on Pattern Analysis and Machine Intelligence, 22*(8).

Keister, L. H. (1994). *"User types and queries: impact on image access systems", Challenges in indexing electronic text and images.* Learned Information.

Lee, J. (1996). *Introduction. "Intelligence and Multimodality in Multimedia Interfaces: Research and Applications". J. e. Lee.* Menlo Park, CA: AAAI Press.

Lew, M. S. (2000). Next-generation web searches for visual content. *IEEE Computer., 33*, 46–53.

Li, J., & Wang, J. Z. (2003). Automatic linguistic indexing of pictures by a statistical modelling approach. *IEEE Transactions on Pattern Analysis and Machine Intelligence, 25*(9), 1075–1088. doi:10.1109/TPAMI.2003.1227984

Markkula, M., & Sormunen, E. (2000). End-user searching challenges indexing practices in the digital newspaper photo archive. *Information Retrieval, 1*, 259–285. doi:10.1023/A:1009995816485

Mori, Y. Takahashi, H. and Oka, R. (1999) "Image-to-word transformation based on dividing and vector quantizing images with words". In MISRM'99 First Int. Workshop on Multimedia Intelligent Storage and Retrieval Management.

Ornager, S. (1996). View a picture: Theoretical image analysis and empirical user studies on indexing and retrieval. *Swedish Library Research, 2*(3), 31–41.

Paek, S., Sable, C. L., Hatzivassiloglou, V., Jaimes, A., Schiffman, B. H., Chang, S.-F., & McKeown, K. R. (1999) "Integration of visual and text based approaches for the content labelling and classification of Photographs", ACM SIGIR'99 Workshop on Multimedia Indexing and Retrieval, Berkeley, CA.

Rui, Y., Huang, T., Mehrotra, S., & Ortega, M. (1997) "A relevance feedback architecture in content-based multimedia information retrieval systems", In Proc of IEEE Workshop on Content-based Access of Image and Video Libraries.

Rui, Y., Huang, T. S., & Chang, S. F. (1998). *Image Retrieval: current techniques, promising directions and open issues*. Dept. of ECE & Bechman Institute University of Illinois at Urbana-Champaign Urbana, Dept. of EE & New Media Technology Centre Columbia University New York.

Smeulder, A. W. M., Worring, M., Anntini, S., Gupta, A., & Jain, R. (2000). Content-Based Image Retrieval at the End of the Early Years. *IEEE Transactions on Pattern Analysis and Machine Intelligence, 22*(12), 1349–1380. doi:10.1109/34.895972

Smith, J., & Chang, S. (1997). *Intelligent multimedia information Retrieval, Chapter Query by colour regions using the VisualSEEk content-based visual query system* (pp. 23–41). AAAI Press.

Srihari, R., & Zhang, Z. (2000). Show&Tell: A Semi-Automated Image Annotation System. *IEEE MultiMedia, 7*(3), 61–71. doi:10.1109/93.879769

Srihari R.K. (1995a) "Use of Collateral Text in Understanding Photos". Artificial Intelligence Review, special issue on Integrating Language and Vision, vol. 8, pp. 409--430.

Srihari, R.K. (1995b) "Computational Models for Integrating Linguistic and Visual Information: A Survey". Artificial Intelligence Review, special issue on Integrating Language and Vision, vol. 8, pp. 349--369.

Srihari, R. K., & Burhans, D. T. (1994) "Visual semantics: Extracting visual information from text accompanying pictures". In Proceedings of AAAI-94, pages793-798, Seattle.

Szummer, M., & Picard, R. W. (1998) "Indoor-outdoor image classification". In IEEE Int. Workshop on Content-based Access of Image and Video Databases.

Turk, M., & Robertson, G. (2001). Perceptual User Interfaces. *Communications of the ACM, 43*(3), 33–34.

Westerveld, T. (2000). *Image Retrieval: Content versus Context* (pp. 276–284). Proceedings of Content-Based Multimedia Information Access.

Zhang, Q., & Izquierdo, E. (2007). Adaptive salient block-based image retrieval in multi-feature space. *Signal Processing Image Communication, 22*, 591–603. doi:10.1016/j.image.2007.05.005

Zhao, R., & Grosky, W. I. (2002). Bridging the semantic gap in image retrieval. In Shih, T. K. (Ed.), *Distributed Multimedia Databases: Techniques and Applications* (pp. 14–36). Hershey, PA: Idea Group Publishing Series. IGI Publishing.

Zhou, X. S., & Huang, S. T. (2000) "Image Retrieval: Feature Primitives, Feature Representation, and Relevance Feedback". IEEE Workshop on Content-based Access of Image and Video Libraries (CBAIVL-2000), in conjunction with IEEE CVPR-2000, pp. 10-13.

Zhou, X. S., & Huang, S. T. (2002). Unifying Keywords and Visual Contents in Image Retrieval. *IEEE Transactions on Multimedia, 9*(2), 23–33. doi:10.1109/93.998050

ENDNOTE

[1]   http://www.nationalgallery.org.uk/

Chapter 13
The MultiPlasticity of New Media

Gianluca Mura
Politecnico di Milano, Italy

ABSTRACT

Interaction systems with the user need complex and suitable conceptual and multisensorial new media definition. This study analyzes social and conceptual evolutions of digital media and proposes an interactive mixed-space media model which communicates the information contents and enhances the user experience between interactive space of physical objects and online virtual space. Its feedback gives information through user performance among its multisensorial interfaces. The research widens previous research publications, and gives precisely a definition of a fuzzy logic cognitive and emotional perception level to the metaplastic multimedia model. It augments the interaction quality within its conceptual media space through an action-making loop and gives as a result new contents of information within its metaplastic metaspace configurations.

INTRODUCTION

From the Sixties of the last century, the technological advances of traditional communication media as film,images,music,spoken and written language have improved their properties of powerful interactivity with the user. They allow the possibility of open access to their contents through different computer and internet communication technologies. They have become a new, distinguished subject that could be defined as New Media. The increased communication between people all over the world has determined the globalization phenomena of the digital "democratization" through the creation,publication, distribution and consumption of media content for everyone as one of the most important aspect of the new media.

DOI: 10.4018/978-1-60960-821-7.ch013

They mainly allows people to express themselves with different kind of user-generated content through websites,blogs,videoclips,pictures and other digital media. These self-defined networks establish online globalised societies that transcend geographical boundaries, eliminating often social restrictions. Howard Rheingold(2000) describes this social phenomena driven by digital technology with the term of "Virtual Communities".People learn to use "words on screens to exchange pleasantries and argue,engage in intellectual discourse,conduct commerce,make plans ,brainstorm,gossip,feud,fall in love,create a little high art and a lot of idle talk" (Rheingold cited in Slevin 2000:91).These studies suggested that the technology drives the process of globalization through a multiplicity of processes by which it is funded,researched and produced within a feedback loop of transformation by users that guide their future development.

INTERACTIVITY OF NEW MEDIA

Interactivity has become the main aspect for new media since their rapid evolving processes of digitalization and media convergence on the web. The notion of interactivity briefly means the possibility of real time interaction with digital media. The new media with technology convergence change the model of mass communication into new ways for people to interact and communicate with one another. The digital innovations of Internet have made possible the shifting to the new media model of communication from the traditional "one-to-many" mass communication to the wide range of possibilities of a "many-to-many" web communication.Vin Crosbie(2002) describes three communication media types: the Interpersonal media as "one to one",Mass media as "one to many" and New Media as Individuation Media or "many to many". The conversational dynamics of communication mediated forms can be considered as a central point in understanding

new media. Different media types possess various degree of interactivity, but some forms of digital and converged media are not interactive at all. For example, digital television uses the most recent technologies to increase the number and the quality of the channels and the offered services, but it does not transform the user's experience of television within a more fully interactive dimension.

Instead, Virtual Realities as extension of the world we live in actually appears the best possible digital conceptualization in terms of interactive new media environment.

THE VIRTUAL MEDIUM

At the beginning of the 21st century, Manovich(2001) declared that the first decades of the last century, the Early Age of Machines, have been more relevant to New Media culture than any other time period. "The earlier plastic art movements characterized the conceptual and structural basis of the virtual media with the spatial and kinetic methodologies activated by the user during its interaction processes"(Mura,2010). Manovich utilizes the term Meta-Media to describe contemporary works that coincides with a postmodernism's "ready-made" design concept of making new artefact from reinterpreting old artefacts. This New media Avant-Garde "is about new ways of accessing and manipulating information"(Manovich,2001) (e.g. hypermedia,databases,search engines etc.). Meta-media is an example of how quantity can change into quality as in new media technology and manipulation techniques can "recode modernist aesthetics into a very different postmodern aesthetics"(Manovich,2001).

Lev Manovich stated,according to Ted Nelson(1965) and Marshall McLuhan(1964) that the new relationship between form and content in the development of new technologies and new media are focused on social and cultural collaboration across interactive media to software development methodologies. Laurel(1990) explicitly discussed

Human-Computer Interaction and Interface Design research fields, emphasizing the importance of natural experience of ours' interaction with technological media. She describes a medium in terms of Mimesis, imitation or representation of the sensible world aspects, especially human actions in literature and art, as relations between user and technology from acting to gaming. The Engagement, emotional state described by Laurel, serves as a critical factor in personal relations. Aesthetics of participation found its new redefinition within actual digital technologies. Technological progresses have conducted to the creation of the first interactive media for Internet with reintroducing and extending on the web experiences based on relations between digital artwork, audiences and authors. Digital creative process (and resulting processes) becomes the outcomes of complex collaborations among different co-authors from various levels, and matter of research in interdisciplinary areas.

Interactive media contain dialogs with their spectators that are more than simply observers, they have an acting function. The interactive media is created with two actors. The first actor that originates or defines programming rules for (user's)spectator's conditions and the second actor-spectator that introduces the progress of artwork with the goal of acting its potentiality, differently from the traditional spectator(user) that has no possibility of interaction.

The media-art-work is therefore, constituted of two different semiotic objects: the actor that is the computer program and the other object, the spectator(user) with the role of co-authoring or co-acting.

The *Plasticity*, in digital media terms, is a characteristic defined by the user's activities that within its own interaction process can create,modify and perform every form and content of the newer digital media. The increased plasticity of the post Web 2.0 digital media include the social dimension as another level of potentiality to extend human communicative and creative possibility for the new virtual communities.

The term *Metaplasticity* is defined within the neuroscience or in an algorithmic sense of plasticity which are different point of view from a definition that would be given in the Metaplastic discipline.

Digital Metaplasticity is the specific transdisciplinary research area that includes Art,Design, Architecture, Cybernetics, Cognitive Psychology, Artificial Intelligence and Computer Sciences. From a point of view technical-scientific studies, it describes plastic qualities of digital media high configurations and its conceptual expressions through the applications of abstract art languages and methodologies to computational symbolic systems (new media).

Metaplastic discipline defines proper goals and characteristics with derivation from its originary disciplines as (Mura,2010):

- *Interdisciplinarity* of existing relations between Art, Design, Science and Technology;
- *Dematerialization* of artworks and its processes from their disciplines;
- *Hybridization* between Aesthetics and Technology(called hybridization type1) becomes re-definition of sensible forms production practices;it becomes in socialization through artworks and in different levels of interaction modalities: between artwork, author and spectator(called hybridization type 3) and between society,science and technology (called hybridization type 2);
- *Interactivity* as a fundamental paradigm of dynamic relations occurred among author,spectator and artwork;
- *Synaesthetic immersivity* of spectator through his sensorial and psychological involvement coordinated in the interactive representation;

- *Communication of Wisdom* as a cultural goal to be obtained through the creation of new metaplastic media.

THE METAPLASTIC MEDIA

The *Metaplastic Media,*one of discipline's objectives follows and extends the previous definition (Mura,2010), within its own aesthetic and semantic codes, it defines a new culture of the representation. *Multiplasticity* extends the metaplastic qualities to the multi-sensorial and multi-directional communications properties of the metaplastic media. Interaction processes defined with metaplastic codes, trace their own behaviors and multiplastic qualities. The users within their social networks, become informational nodes within their own individual web networks,website or web-blog.

Metaplastic languages or codes are methodologies based on abstract art languages rules applied to digital symbolic systems needed for the construction of Metaplastic media and their other Entities. The Ontology of the metaplastic media, includes the extended explanation of the notions and the relations below (Mura,2010):

- *Metaplastic Entities* are complex objects of any present and future typology, which directly act and interact within the applied metaplastic metalanguage rule configurations;
- *Metaplastic Virtual Worlds* are digital spaces typology of Metaplastic Entities;
- *Metaplastic Metaspace (Figure 1)* is a conceptual cyberspace composed by a single Metaplastic Entity(digital device) or a network of Entities (virtual worlds). The dynamic relations between each network nodes and the user establish the metaspace meaning representation through its shapes and behaviors. The Metaspace acquires knowledge during its processes from every element. At the same time, some part of the ontological knowledge base is shared between the entities. The structures of elements are described in term of group and individual roles hierarchy. Every virtual world (node) has its own web address(URL) and a hyperlink network that refers to other virtual worlds (subnodes) connected to the previous one and all between each other.

"The visual language is made of related meaning and events dynamics within the metaspace. The movement is determined from the qualitative relations and quantitative elements between the environment, its own network nodes and the user. These dynamic relations establish the equilibrium of the virtual space determining the meaning representation through its shapes and spatial relations"(Mura,2007).

The Metaplastic Metaspace is espressed through the following formulation as:

Metaplastic Metaspace (FSM) ={ Σ, Q, δ, s, F }

Where:

- FSM, fuzzy state machine, a finite state machine with logic fuzzy;
- the fuzzy rules are the metaplastic composition design criteria;
- Σ is a set of input events (Events) and output(Actions) of the system;
- The virtual user, entity subclass, is represented by his extended sensorial state values that the system output generates within the interaction processes;
- Q is a finite set of States, including the initial state; example:initial state,optimal state, excellent state,final state;
- δ are the functions of the Transition states. The function assumes the actual state from an input event and gives a new output value to the next state. Some states can be designated to be final states.
- s is a state that initializes the system;

Figure 1. Ontology of the Metaplastic Media. ©2010 Gianluca Mura

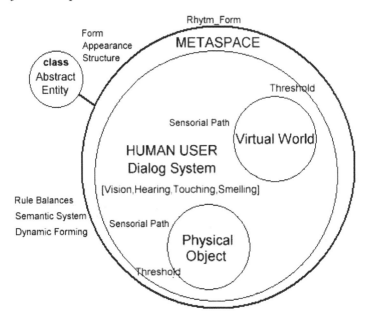

- F is the set of final states.

More specific definition (in Mura,2007):

- *Abstract figures* Composed Elements.
- *Alphabet* Set of symbols (Figures). •
- *Visual Syntax* The composition equilibrium Syntax
- *Semantics* Dynamic opposition Semantics.
- *Composition criteria* Quality and relations of the environment.

METASPACE DYNAMIC RULES

The Metaplastic Metaspace, follows the previous explanations:

"It is driven by abstract art rule relations that transform sequences of user's sensory inputs, which produce feedback and send them as a response to the output of the environment to generate complex forms, movements and behaviors". The sensorial result is a fuzzy truth value that activates the decision making process of the metaspace itself

and its own sub-spaces. "The user during his own visit experience, differs his emotional states with the environment, which change from "Sensing" to "Feeling" through recursive cycles of feedback. The transitions of sensorial states are activated by proximity to the objects"(Mura,2007).

The activation level of the system is calculated by the following general rule:

$MS_i^{new}=f(Proximity_i(MSstate_i(Entity_k state_i)))+MS_i^{old};$

Proximity $f(Px)=f(User.position - Threshold);$

Dialogue State changes:if Px>0 Then MS=Vs. rules[Sensing interactions];

if Px=0 then MS=Vs.rules [Feeling interactions];

if Px<0 Then MS=Vs.rules [Acting interactions].

where: MS=metaplastic metaspace; f=trigger function; i,j =state; k= item shown.

Dynamic syntax = Σ_i (fSenses(weight)*f(interp (Entity $_k$ state$_i$, Entity $_{k+1}$ state$_i$));

In this way, It assigns meaning through movement codification of figures in the "Red and Black" semantic space (Mura,2007).

Semantic meaning[i] = Σ_i (f Senses(weight)*f(interp(RB weight $_k$, RB weight $_{k+1}$)).

The whole system processes are defined by: MS$_{ij}$^{new} = f(semantic$_i$ (syntax$_j$(Δproximity$_{ij}$)))+MS$_{ij}$^{old}.

HUMAN INTERACTION WITH REAL AND VIRTUAL OBJECT-SPACES

The Metaplastic Metaspace interactive media is a vision of interaction and network technology. Multiplasticity's multi-sensorial and multi-directional communications properties are driven by their own dialog system. The system includes the whole body interaction through the production of multisensorial feedback within both the metaplastic virtual spaces(see paragraph "The Web Metaspace") and physical interactive devices (see paragraph "The Picubino Open System"). The human haptic interaction in the shared virtual space produces the sensation of tele-presence within the system while the mediated physical feedbacks with the objects enforce the feeling of extended body senses.

PRESENCE IN VIRTUAL MEDIA

The concept of Presence is relevant for designing and evaluating the metaplastic virtual media.

This concept has been introduced by Marvin Minsky (1980) with his referring to teleoperat-

ing systems on remote manipulation of objects. It is the key for understanding virtual reality's experience, but it isn't the only parameter. The user's emotions are essential for understanding how humans interpret virtual worlds and how to obtain important implications for conceptual understanding of virtual experience (Hang,1999).

The process of adaptation to artificial environments provides us with knowledge of biological features, creation of interaction,building artifacts, behavioral rules and development of new culture. The virtual environment dynamics, as it has been previously described, realize the expressions of human psychology, with this statement:"Psychology is the physics of virtual reality"(Woolley,,1993,p.21).

This psychological human state is generally defined as a user's subjective sensation of "being there", a part of the scene developed by the medium (Barfield W.,1995). Moreover, Virtual Reality is defined within ours individual consciousness; in fact it's related to various factors needed for the creation of a sense of presence, which differs in every individual. Perceptual states are influenced with different contents of mediated environment,its entities' types and interactions levels. We need other concepts for giving a definition to every characteristic of this phenomenology. Multimedia artist Michael Naimark defines these characteristics as "realness" and "interactivity". Brenda Laurel(1990) and Rheingold(1991) made similar distinctions. TeleGarden(1995) installation made by Ken Goldberg and exposed at Linz's Center Ars Electronica, explores the theme of telepresence with connecting the spectator's real space with installation's remote space.

The connected "Inter-nauts" interact with plants in a garden and they could see the consequences of their action in real time. There are many studies that try to define individual factors which contribute to a forming of perceptions, experienced in the virtual environment. Most of the researches are related to a sense of presence or self-consciousness of being in a virtual environment. It becomes a place where mediated communication happens. Discussions and trials searched for elements from natural environments which should be reproduced or modeled to facilitate our consciousness of "Being Present"(Lombard&Ditton,1997). The advances in scientific areas dedicated to mediated experiences are closely related to the technological improvements and to the Human Computer Interface developments. Steuer(1995) with the definition of Vividness and Interactivity indicated them as the basic elements which contribute to the immersion level in a CMC communication channel(Computer Mediated Communication). The parameters of mediated experience compose the structure of the Virtual Medium. Virtual Environment in its general composition function could be defined with its peculiar characteristics, which differs from other media, like Communication Systems. Communication systems are composed with a group of functions that are identified with a main interface, communication channels and organization infrastructures. McLuhan(1964) clearly defines that this is a prototype of Communication System and the physical world is his content. "All Media are human sensorial extensions"(McLuhan,1964).Researchers of Virtual Reality have proceeded into developing new sensorial extensions and their interfaces. Confronting Virtual Reality developments with other communication media like Television,Computers and Telephone, VR emerges as a relevant Metamedium (Kay&Goldberg,1997). "It isn't only a technology but it is a destination" (Biocca,1995). The final goal is, in fact, making a "full immersion of the human sensorimotor channels into a vivid *experience*"(Biocca,1995). Sensorial immersion in simulated worlds excludes the user from real world with inducing psychological phenomena of disembodiment. This phenomenology announces the possibility of freeing the body and becoming another living being: a Cyborg. The concept of Cyborg,of extended body and post humanity

are frequently used in Digital Art. Stelarc is a performance artist that made numerous artworks which propose different systems of prostheses-interfaces which unify humans to machines as Exoskeleton(1998). In this ideal system, human body is immersed in the communication process with Information. Other media also include us in their environment: radio and television stimulate our imagination and observation, but they don't immerse our senses inside their environments.

The user's immersive experience is produced by the Metaplastic Metaspace simultaneously in three ways: the absorption of the input device into the user's body image, the integration of the screen interface into the user's extended body boundaries, and the activation of surrounding space through multisensory and haptic feedback.

THE DIALOGUE SYSTEM INTERACTIVE PROCESS

The latest development in psychological fields introduces many structural models of human behavior applied also in cybernetics. "However, there are still remarkable difficulties in the research and complete understanding of the human brain's functioning complexity. In lack of certainty in matter,there are several hypotheses of systemic models. Some of these models were introduced for their importance regarding this chapter. They are: homeostatic system model (John H.Milsum,1966); Human Systems interacting in social systems (A.Kuhn, 1974); Human Behavior determination model (Miller, J.G., 1978); Emotional Cognitive Structural system for productive or creative thought(Gray,2007). From comparative studies of several listed models, a famous psychologist and neurophysiologist Charles A.Fink(1979) has elaborated a successful experimental model applied to the artificial environment. The inadequacy of mathematical models for the description of objects and immaterial processes, has motivated the development of this dynamic model in analogy to the methodologies used in economic systems. The results of these analyses concur to compose, on reasonable bases, the models for human behavior. The dynamic system developed by Fink from 1975 to 1999, becomes important for cognitive models, because it describes the human being as a whole made of different stimuli. Analyses and decision-making are divided in subprocesses, structures or interconnections, with complex cycles of feedback, and a set of possible responses"(Mura,2007). The decision on a specific methodology in order "to convert" human sensorial system and the virtual reality is of fundamental importance for metaplastic theory. It has been developed a suitable cognitive system, called Dialogue System (Mura,2007). Some essential definitions are brought back for clarity:

- *Dialogue System*: dynamic system for the interpretation of sensorial interaction processes between human and machine;
- *Extended Senses*: sensorial motor channels of transmission;
- *Sense Threshold*: synthetic responsive membrane for the interpretation of sensorial interaction processes between users and the system;

Within the human-machine interaction processes, human emotional states (objective tasks, worlds, cognitive awareness, emotional awareness, physiological awareness) are induced by the artificial context ("Sensing"), becomes analyzed by the system("Thinking") through the sequence of feedback stimulus-to-decision making-to-response.

Every stage of the process is compared with previous experiences. The importance of the response is analyzed and if judged positively,it produces a consequent action. In the opposite case,results are stored in the system and made available for successive appraisals.The final phase is produced from a human action towards the environment ("Acting") that at the same time induces in itself the emotional consciousness ("Feeling").

The Metaplastic Metaspace, a metaplastic media, includes the Multiplasticity multi-sensorial and multi-directional communication properties within its own interaction processes through the dialog system. The sensorial results coincide with the composition of a human behavior model developed from cybernetic studies (Carver,1998,reprinted). Certain qualities of feeling, may be linked to other qualities of imagination and, as result, the system gives a high-level human feedback quality of synaesthetic perceptions which creates a sensorial path. The intensity of a feeling state may be linked to the brightness of a figure; the color may influence the level of feeling; some kind of movements may "feel" with the interactor. The quality of the synaesthetic effects depends on fuzzy functions connections or overlaps of our sensorial systems. In traditional psychophysics, the term "fuzzy function" was defined as:

"Any modeling involving a representational system and either an input channel or an output channel in which the input or output channel involved is a different modality from the representational system which it is being used" (Grinder,1975).

In this way, fuzzy functions are typically characterized by terms such as see-feel or hear-feel circuits. In the extended Dialog System this concerns mean a particular application of the fuzzy-state machine.

THE PICUBINO OPEN SYSTEM

The Metaplastic Metaspace FSM(fuzzy logic state machine) system could be implemented within a hardware and software open-source creative system for coded artifacts named PICUBINO©.

PICUBINO© is a development system and the resulting coded object is both, dedicated to the creation of interactive devices through its specific programming and visual assembling language.

It is used as a tool to experiment physical interactions within the Metaplastic Metaspace virtual environment. The extension of the user's body senses occurs within the integration of input devices to the user's hands or arms or elsewhere. The body movements simultaneously involve both main and peripheral zones of the body and include interactive activities within the device.

The effect of whole-body is introduced for explaining the user's emotional interaction level. This is important because it is used as a trigger for switching to any programmed type of interaction. Another theoretical layer is necessary to be introduced, for explaining the user's emotional interaction level. About the emotional transition within the Dialog System(Mura,2009), it would be reused some important notions referring on three main factors such as sign value,intensity and duration:

- *Sense weight sign.* We can find two phases in our activities during the interaction with the object giving as signal result the sign + and – respectively.
- *Emotional intensity.* Emotional process is affected by the intensity of input signal and the intensity can be drawn on the sense weight values with + and -.
- *Emotional duration.* The signal varies and is evoked depending on the duration of the interaction process with the objects. The user's internal emotional state variation is supposed to be caused by input signal and included into a fuzzy inference mechanism. The user's emotional level is evaluated through a simple system composed within five fuzzy inference rules shown below (Table 1). The related five Sense's defuzzified values can be used as an expression of the user's stimulation and its new emotional state caused by external environmental inputs and output system

values. The emotional evaluation interactive process is defined with the following expression:

- ◦ Rule 1: if sign value - and intensity -100 then w = 0.00 [Relaxed emotional state];
- ◦ Rule 2: if sign value +/- and intensity 0 then w = 0.20 [Mildly interested emotional state];
- ◦ Rule 3: if sign value + and intensity 50 then w = 0.50 [Interested emotional state];
- ◦ Rule 4: if sign value + and intensity 100 then w = 0.75 [Involved emotional state];
- ◦ Rule 5: if sign value + and intensity 150 then w = 0.85 [High involved emotional state].

FSM $Act_i = 1 - f(interp(S_i(w)vision, S_i(w) hearing, S_i(w) touch, S_i(w) body movement)_t$;

where: Act = Interaction state graduation; S = Senses function; t=action time; interp=interpolation function; w = Emotional state weight [0..1]; i = dialogue state.

The resulting w value from the previous function is used to obtain final Act state graduation for different output channels interaction processes results (vision,hearing,body,touch).

The Picubino includes the Metaplastic fuzzy state machine into its processes within its various steps regulated by previously established conditions. Its interactive steps are controlled with the predefined visual system of the metaplastic coded signs. Every interactive step value is read from the system as a call to an interactive routine which corresponds to the current dialog state.

The machine runs until the user ends its interactive processes with leaving the Sensing state of the system. The following schema and figure (Table 2 and Figure 2) visually explain an example of the Picubino Metaplastic device system application.

Table 1. FSM interaction process description ©2010 Gianluca Mura

FSM Interaction process							
	Sensing			Feeling		Acting	
Vision	Eye tracking off haptic vision off	Various interaction steps [0..1]	Eye tracking off haptic vision on	Various interaction steps [0..1]	Eye tracking on haptic vision on	Various interaction steps [0..1]
Hearing	Hearing on		Hearing on		Hearing on	
Touch	Activation off		Activation on		Activation on	
Body Movement	Body position Gestures		Body position Gestures		Body position Activation on	

Figure 2. The Picubino open device system. ©2010 Gianluca Mura

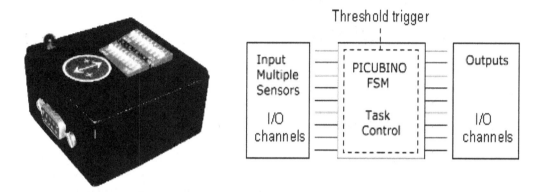

THE WEB METASPACE

The user's pointing and clicking action through traditional hypertext browsers is the dominant navigation paradigm for the World Wide Web. The Web is so interconnected that clicking one's way can also be very disorienting for the user to establish a mental model of its structure and its own navigation path. The one-dimension history lists are a common navigational aid.

The navigation list provides a way of thinking about the documents only at a time, but it doesn't offer any help to understand the connection between them. Traditional web browser limits the user's knowledge of a document seen in its connections only in one-way modality without showing their incoming links. Moving up to three dimensions allow us to see both multiple documents and the links between them. In this way, we can explore a

huge section of the Web through the Metaplastic abstract Metaspace representation.

"The Metaplastic Metaspace shows its own dynamic semantics through the visual formalization of the rings structure (the complete metalanguage ring structure is visualized in the figure above on the left bottom) which are linked between them, compose the grammatical rules of the visual language. The groups of rings define the signs of the language set, the selected token and the relations among them. The settings vary with rotations of their axes. Different rings structure configuration define new kind of metaplastic visual language"(Mura, 2007).

The following formulation and schema (Figure 3) describe the FSM dynamic interactions processes performed between the User and the

Table 2.Picubino FSM engine schema. ©2010 Gianluca Mura

Picubino Metaplastic device engine		
Act state	**Input transition state**	**Output transition state**
Sensing Task	If Proximity(Sensing)>0 Then FSM Routine1	Goto Feeling Task
Feeling Task	If Proximity(Feeling)=0 Then FSM Routine2	Goto Acting state
Acting Task	If w value>0 and w value<0.3 Then FSM Routine3 else If w value>0.3 and w value<0.6 Then FSM Routine4 else If w value>0.6 and w value<1.0 Then FSM Routine5	Goto Sensing state or Exit

Figure 3.The Metaplastic Metaspace system. ©2010 Gianluca Mura

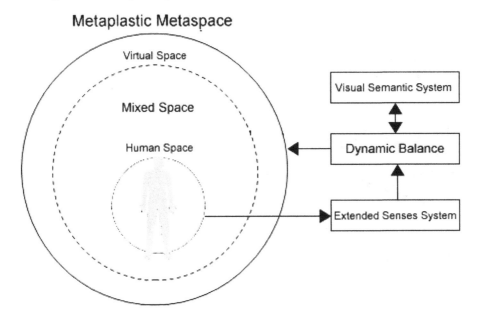

Metaspace environment and how its own complex Rhytm Form is computated:

Metaspace dynamic Rhytm Form $= \Sigma_i$ (f Act $_i$ *f(interp(Entity$_k$ state$_i$, Entity$_{k+1}$ state$_i$))$_t$;where: Act = Interaction state graduation; i = dialogue state; t = action time; interp=interpolation function; Entity state = Metaspace Entity state.

NETWORK SYSTEM ARCHITECTURE

The system implementation requires a client/server network architecture because it has additional advantages of providing simpler connections modalities with the users and the best world state storing information capabilities. These factors are very important for the target applications in the middle/large scale platform systems. To avoid a lack of connectivity and to enhance the performance of the system, it is opportune to adopt a multi-server architecture instead of the single-server architecture. The server has a database containing the user's networks and every other proper entities' state and characteristics. Entities send their messages to the server regarding their state evaluation during the Dialog function. The server computes every network's interaction state and decide what message should be sent and to which entity. This process continues from and to every connected server in the network. The network system cooperates online for simultaneous and distributed execution of each of its own virtual space_node between the client browser and the server through various plugged software components. The graphic engine of every system server provides a virtual space to the client and connects it to the network. It contains a 3D software platform which includes many 3d data format (basically VRML and other object data files), suitable for the main operating systems (Windows, Linux, Java). The software engine is based on a specific graphic library that guides the system capabilities to draw the virtual space contents in real-time mode. The scene control acts with script module routines, which uses low-level functions of the system to combine properly virtual space elements with the user inputs.

CONCLUSION

This chapter demonstrates the implementation of user's surrounding space that is produced as a response to the interactive mixed spaces between local space and the screen-world. The integrated Metaplastic Metaspace multi-sensory environment is composed by the user's physical gestures. The visual and auditory feedbacks contribute to a user's sense of "flow" that is immersed in an activity which leads to an altered perception of time and the exclusion of peripheral surroundings and events. The embodied interaction can increase the potential for immersion in several inter-related modalities. The interactive body as an input device becomes an extension of the body in action and it is absorbed into the body image of the user. At the same time, the user's body represented on the screen, establishes a sense of presence in the Metaspace screen-space and bridges the intermediate space between the body action and the action on the screen. The embodied interaction increase immersion and presence in a virtual environment and its internal activities. The system operates with two levels of interaction and gives a contribution to the experience of online communication with the inhabitants of its internal world as well as with a user in a distant site. It enables aspects of telepresence. It means that the user is able to both affect and observe an event's occurrence at a remote site in real time. We achieve the sense of "being there" through the presence in a virtual environment that is suspended between separated sites. It allows users, through its embodied interaction, to experience the sense of socially "being there" with someone else within the new typology of the Metaplastic Metaspace Cyberspace (Figure 4).

Figure 4. Metaplastic Cyberspace configurations.© 2010 Gianluca Mura

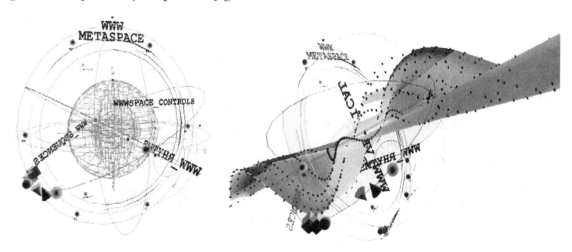

REFERENCES

Artsmachine Media Lab. (2010), from http://www.artsmachine.com

Ashby, R. (1956). *Introduction to Cybernetics*. London, England: Chapman&Hall.

Barfield, W., Zelter, D., Sheridan, T. B., & Slater, M. (1995). Presence and Performance within Virtual Environments. In Barfield, W., & Furness, T. A. (Eds.), *Virtual Environments and advanced interface design*. Oxford, England: Oxford University Press.

Benedict, M. (Ed.). (1991). *Cyberspace First Step*. Cambridge, MA, USA: MIT Press.

Biocca, F., & Levy, M. R. (1995). *Communication in the age of virtual reality*. Hillsdale, NJ, USA: Lawrence Erlbaum associates.

Bush, V., (1945) *As We May Think*, v.176, 1, p.101-108,USA:Atlantic Monthly

Carver, C. S., & Scheier, M. (1998). *On the self-regulation of behavior*. London: Cambridge University Press.

Castells, M. (1996). Rise of the Network Society, The Information Age:Economy [Massachusetts,Blackwell Publishing]. *Society and Culture, 1*.

Coates, G. (1992). *A virtual Show. A multimedia performance work, San Francisco, CA, USA: Couchot, E., Hillaire, N. (1991) L'Art Numerique*. Paris, France: Ed. Flammarion.

Crosbie, V. (2002), What is New Media? Retrieved from http://www.sociology.org.uk/_as4mm3a.doc

Feldman, T. (1997). *An Introduction to Digital Media*. London: Routledge. doi:10.4324/9780203398401

Fink, C. A. (1979). *Searching for the most powerful behavioral theory:the whole of the Behavior Systems Research Institute and the Behavioral Model Analysis Center*. Falls Church, Va: Fink.

Flew, T. (2002). *New Media:An Introduction*. UK: Oxford University Press.

Grau, O. (2003). *Virtual Art*. Cambridge, MA, USA: MIT Press.

Gray, W. D. (Ed.). (2007). *Integrated Models of Cognitive Systems*. USA: Oxford University Press.

Grinder, J., & Bandler, R. (1975). *The Structure of Magic II: A Book About Communication and Change*. Palo Alto, CA: Science & Behavior Books.

Hang, H. P., & Alessi, N. E. (1999). *Presence as an Emotional Experience in Medicine meet Virtual Reality. The Convergence of Physical and Information Technologies options for a new era in HealthCare* (pp. 148–153). Amsterdam: IOS Press.

Holmes (2005), "Telecommunity" in Communication Theory:Media,Technology and Society,Cambridge: Polity

Holtzman, S. R. (1995). *Digital Mantras*. Cambridge, MA, USA: MIT Press.

Kosko,B., *Il Fuzzy pensiero*,trad.it, Milano,Italy: Baldini&Castoldi

Laurel, B. (1990). *The Art of Human-Computer Interface Design*. Reading, Massachusetts, USA: Addison-Wesley.

Lévy, P. (1997) *Qu'est-ce que le virtuel? Il Virtuale, it.translation*, Milano,Italy: Raffaello Cortina Editore, Lévy, P., (1992) *Le tecnologie dell'intelligenza*, trad. it, Ed.A/Traverso

Manovich, L. (2001). *The Language of New Media*. Cambridge: MIT Press.

McLuhan, M. (1964). *Understanding Media:The extension of Man*. Toronto: McGraw Hill.

Mura, G. (2005) *Virtual Space Model for Industrial Design,*Unpublished doctoral dissertation, Politecnico di Milano University, Italy

Mura, G. (2006) Conceptual artwork model for virtual environments in *JCIS journal*(ISSN 1553-9105),Vol.3, n.2, pp.461-465, BinaryInfoPress

Mura, G. (2006). *The red and black semantics:a fuzzy language in Visual Computer, n.23* (pp. 359–368). Berlin, Germany: Springer.

Mura, G. (2007) The Metaplastic Virtual Space in Wyeld, T.G., Kenderdine,S.,Docherty,M.(Eds) *Virtual Systems and Multimedia* (pp. 166-178), Berlin,Germany: Springer

Mura, G. (2008) The meta-plastic cyberspace:a network of semantic virtual worlds in *ICIWI 2008* WWW/Internet International Conference, Freiburg, IADIS

Mura, G. (2008) The Metaplastic Constructor in *CAC 2 Computer Art*, Paris: ed. Europia

Mura, G. (2009). *Cyberworld Cybernetic Art Model for Shared Communications in Cyber-Worlds 2009, Bradford University.* UK: IEEE.

Mura, G. (Ed.). (2010). *Metaplasticity in Virtual Worlds:Aesthetics and Semantics Concepts.* USA: IGI-Global Publishing. doi:10.4018/978-1-60960-077-8

Nelson, T. H. (1965). *A File Structure for the Complex, The Changing and the Indeterminate.* New York, Cambridge, MA,USA: MIT Press.

Newman, W., & Sproul, R. F. (1987). *Computer Graphics principles.* New York, USA: McGraw Hill.

Parker, S. P. (Ed.). (2002). *McGraw-Hill Dictionary of Scientific & Technical Terms.* New York, NJ, USA: McGraw-Hill.

Perrot, X., & Mura, G. (2005) VR Workshop 2005 "Virtuality in Arts and Design" Virtual Exhibition Projects, Archives&Museum Informatics, from http://www.archimuse.com/ publishing/ichim_05.html

Picubino system, from http://www.picubino.com

Popper, K. R., & Eccles, J. C. (1977). *The self and its brain.* New York, USA: Springer International.

Rafaeli, S. (1988), Interactivity:from new media to communication,Beverly Hills,CA

Rheingold, H. (1991). *Virtual Reality.* London, UK: Secker&Warburg Limited.

Steuer, J. (1992). Defining Virtual Reality:dimensions determining Telepresence. *The Journal of Communication,* 42.

Sutherland, I. (1965) *The ultimate Display,* Paper presented at the IFIP Congress,*65, 506-508,* Information Processing

Valéry, P. (1928). La Conquete de l'ubiquite. In *De La Musique avant toute chose.* Paris: Editions du Tambourinaire.

Wiener, N. (1948). *Cybernetics or Control and Communication in the Animal and the Machine.* New York, Cambridge, MA,USA: MIT Press.

Wiener, N. (1988). *The Human Use of Human Beings:Cybernetics and Society.* Cambridge, MA, USA: Da Capo Press.

Williams, R. (1974). *Television:Technology and Cultural Form.* London: Routledge. doi:10.4324/9780203426647

Woolley, B. (1993). *Virtual Worlds.* Oxford, England: Blackwell Publishers.

Young, P. T. (1967) Affective Arousal. *American psychologist,* n.22, pp.32-40

Zadeh, L. (1969). *Biological application of the theory of fuzzy sets and systems in the proceedings of an international symposium on BioCybernetics of the central nervous system* (pp. 199–206). Boston: Little Brown.

Compilation of References

Ackerl, K., Atzmueller, M., & Grammer, K. (2002). The scent of fear. *Neuroendocrinology Letters*, *23*, 79–84.

Alais, D., & Burr, D. (2004). The ventriloquist effect results from near-optimal bimodal integration. *Current Biology*, *14*, 257–262.

Alborzi, H., Druin, A., Montemayor, J., Platner, M., Porteous, J., Sherman, L., et al. (2000). Designing StoryRooms: Interactive storytelling spaces for children. In Boyarski, D., & Kellogg, W. A. (Eds.) *Proceedings of the 3rd conference on designing interactive systems*, New York City, NY: ACM, 95-104.

Aldrich, C. (2009). *Learning Online with Games, Simulations, and Virtual Worlds: Strategies for Online Instruction*. San Francisco: Jossey-Bass.

Alexander S (1998) Blind Programmers Face An Uncertain Future. ComputerWorld.

Allport, G. W. (1937). *Personality: A psychological interpretation*. New York: Holt & Co.

Alostath, J. (2006). "Culture-Centred Design: Integrating Culture into Human-Computer Interaction," Doctoral Thesis, The University of York, UK.

Alostath, J., & Wright, P. (2005). "Integrating Cultural Models into Human-Interaction Design," Conference on Information Technology in Asia (CITA2005), Kuching, Sarawak, Malaysia.

Amemiya, T., Ando, H., & Maeda, T. (2008). Lead-me interface for a pulling sensation from hand-held devices. *ACM Transactions on Applied Perception*, *5*(3), 1–17. doi:10.1145/1402236.1402239

Amoore, J. E. (1970). *Molecular basis of odor*. New York: Charles C Thomas Publisher.

Anastopoulou, S., Baber, C., & Sharples, M. (2001) "Multimedia and multimodal systems: commonalities and differences". Proc. of the 5th Human Centred Technology Postgraduate Workshop, University of Sussex.

Aoki, T., Matsushita, T., Iio, Y., Mitake, H., Toyama, T., Hasegawa, S., et al. Matumura, I. (2005). Kobito: virtual brownies. In *ACM SIGGRAPH 2005 Emerging Technologies* (Article No. 11).

Arangarasan, R., & Gadh, R. (2000, 10-13 September). *Geometric modeling and collaborative design in a multimodal multi-sensory virtual environment*. Paper presented at the DETC'00 ASME Design Engineering Technical Conference, Baltimore, Maryland.

Armel, K. C., & Ramachandran, V. S. (2003). Projecting sensations to external objects: Evidence from skin conductance response. *Proceedings. Biological Sciences*, *270*, 1499–1506. doi:10.1098/rspb.2003.2364

AromaJet. (2000). AromJet.com Retrieved 3 March, 2010, from http://www.aromajet.com

Artsmachine Media Lab. (2010), from http://www.artsmachine.com

Asakawa, C., Takagi, H., Ino, S., & Ifukube, T. (2002). *Auditory and Tactile Interfaces for Representing the Visual Effects on the Web. Proc. Assets, 65.-72.* ACM Press.

Asano, T., Ishibashi, Y., Minezawa, S., & Fujimoto, M. (2005). Surveys of exhibition planners and visitors about a distributed haptic museum. *Proceedings of the 2005 ACM SIGCHI International Conference on Advances in computer entertainment technology*. Valencia, Spain, ACM Press.

Ashby, R. (1956). *Introduction to Cybernetics*. London, England: Chapman&Hall.

Asher, J. (2000). *Learning another language through actions* (6th ed.). Los Gatos, CA: Sky Oaks Productions, Inc.

Aspell, J. E., Lenggenhager, B., & Blanke, O. (2009). Keeping in touch with one's self: Multisensory mechanisms of self-consciousness. *PLoS ONE*, *4*(8), e6488. doi:10.1371/journal.pone.0006488

Asthmeir, P., Feiger, W., & Muller, S. (1993). Virtual design: a generic VR system for industrial applications. *Computer Graphics*, *17*, 671–677. doi:10.1016/0097-8493(93)90116-Q

Atanassova-Shopova, K. S., & Boycheva, I. (1973). On certain neurotropic effects of lavender essential oil. *Bulletin of the Institute of Physiology*, *XV*, 149–156.

Athanasisadis, T., Mylonas, P., Avrithis, Y., Kollias, S. (2007) "Semantic image segmentation and object labelling", IEEE Trans. On Circuits and systems for video technology, vol. 17, no, 3, pp 298-312.

Aubrey, J. B., & Dobbs, A. R. (1990). Age and sex differences in the mental realignment of maps. *Experimental Aging Research*, *16*(3), 133–139. doi:10.1080/07340669008251540

Auvray, M., Myin, E., & Spence, C. (2010). The sensory-discriminative and affective-motivational processing of pain. *Neuroscience and Biobehavioral Reviews*, *34*, 214–223. doi:10.1016/j.neubiorev.2008.07.008

Avizzano, C., Marcheschi, S., Angerilli, M., Fontana, M., Bergamasco, M., Gutierrez, T., & Mannegeis, M. (2003). A multi-finger haptic interface for visually impaired people. *Robot and Human Interactive Communication, 2003. Proceedings. ROMAN, 2003*, 165–170.

Ayala, A. (2008). Immersion hits another milestone: 25 million mobile phones sold with touch feedback technology, *http://ir.immersion.com/* releasedetail.cfm?ReleaseID=331864.

Baber, C., & Mellor, B. (2001). Using critical path analysis to model multimodal human-computer interaction. *International Journal of Human-Computer Studies*, *54*, 613–636. doi:10.1006/ijhc.2000.0452

Baccini, M., Rinaldi, L. A., Federighi, G., Vannucchi, L., Paci, M., & Masotti, G. (2006). Effectiveness of fingertip light contact in reducing postural sway in older people. *Age and Ageing*, afl072.

Bakker, N. H., Werkhoven, P. J., & Passenier, P. O. (1999). The Effects of Proprioceptive and Visual Feedback on Geographical Orientation in Virtual Environments. *Presence (Cambridge, Mass.)*, *8*(1), 36–53. doi:10.1162/105474699566035

Bangay, S., & Preston, L. (1998). An investigation into factors influencing immersion in interactive virtual environments. *Studies in Health Technology and Informatics*, *58*, 43–51.

Baram, Y., & Miller, A. (2006). Virtual reality cues for improvement of gait in patients with multiple sclerosis. *Neurology*, *66*, 178–181. doi:10.1212/01.wnl.0000194255.82542.6b

Barber, W., & Badre, A. N. (1998). Culturability: The merging of culture and usability. In 4th Conference on Human Factors and the Web: Baskin, Ridge, New Jersey.

Bardot, I., Bochereau, L., Bourgine, P., Heyd, B., Hossenlopp, J., Martin, N., et al. (1992). Cuisiner artificiel: Un automate pour la formulation sensorielle de produits alimentaires [Artificial oven: A robot for synthesizing the smells of food]. *Proceedings of the Interface to Real and Virtual Worlds Conference*, 451-461.

Barfield, W., & Danas, E. (1996). Comments on the use of olfactory displays for virtual environments. *Presence (Cambridge, Mass.)*, *5*, 109–121.

Barfield, W., Zelter, D., Sheridan, T. B., & Slater, M. (1995). Presence and Performance within Virtual Environments. In Barfield, W., & Furness, T. A. (Eds.), *Virtual Environments and advanced interface design*. Oxford, England: Oxford University Press.

Barfield, W., & Weghorst, S. (1993). The sense of presence within virtual environments: A conceptual framework. In Salvendy, G., & Smith, M. (Eds.), *Human computer interaction: Hardware and software interfaces* (pp. 699–704). Amsterdam: Elsevier.

Barnard, K., Duygulu, P., de Freitas, N., Forsyth, D., Blei, D., & Jordan, M. I. (2003). Matching Words and Pictures. *Journal of Machine Learning Research*, *3*, 1107–1135. doi:10.1162/153244303322533214

Barnard, K., & Forsyth, D. (2001) "Learning the Semantics of Words and Pictures". Proceedings of Int. Conf. on Computer Vision, pp. II: 408-415.

Barnett, K. (1972). A theoretical construct of the concepts of touch as they relate to nursing. *Nursing Research, 21*, 102–110.

Baron, R. A. (1997). Of cookies, coffee, and kindness: Pleasant odors and the tendency to help strangers in a shopping mall. *Aroma-Chology Review, 6*, 3–11.

Basdogan, C., & Srinivasan, M. A. (2002). Haptic rendering in virtual environments. In Stanney, K. M. (Ed.), *Handbook of virtual environments: design, implementation, and applications* (pp. 117–134). Mahwah: Lawrence Erlbaum Associates.

Bason, P. T., & Cellar, B. G. (1972). Control of the heart rate by external stimuli. *Nature, 4*, 279–280. doi:10.1038/238279a0

Bax D D (July 1982) Computer Programmer Aptitude Test for the Totally Blind. Journal of Rehabilitation 48/3/ pp. 65-68

BBC. (2006) *'Smellovision' for Japan cinema*, BBC. Available: http://news.bbc.co.uk/ 1/ hi/ entertainment/ 4903984.stm [Accessed: August 21, 2007].

Begel, A., Garcia, D. D., & Wolfman, S. A. (2004). Kinesthetic Learning in the Classroom. *ACM SIGSCE Bulletin, 36*(1), 183–184. doi:10.1145/1028174.971367

Bellik, Y. (2001). "Technical Requirements for a Successful Multimodal Interaction", International Workshop on Information Presentation and Natural Multimodal Dialogue, Verona, Italy.

Benedict, M. (Ed.). (1991). *Cyberspace First Step*. Cambridge, MA, USA: MIT Press.

Benoit, C., Martin, J. C., Pelachaud, C., Schomaker, L., & Suhm, B. (2000). "Audio-Visual and Multimodal Speech Systems". Handbook of Standards and Resources for Spoken Language Systems - Supplement Volume. D. Gibbon (Ed.). 1-95.

Bensafi, M. (2004). Sniffing human sex-steroid derived compounds modulates mood, memory and autonomic nervous system function in specific behavioral contexts. *Behavioural Brain Research, 152*, 11–22.

Bergamesco, M., Frisoli, A., & Barbagli, F. (2002). *Haptics technologies and cultural heritage application.* Paper presented at the Computer Animation Conference.

Berkeley, G. (1732). *An essay towards a new theory of vision* (4th Ed.). http://psychclassics.yorku.ca/ Berkeley/ vision.htm

Berkelman, P. J., & Hollis, R. L. (1997). Dynamic performance of a hemispherical magnetic levitation haptic interface device. In *SPIE International Symposium on Intelligent Systems and Intelligent Manufacturing, SPIE Proc. Vol. 3602*, Greensburgh PA, September 1997.

Berkelman, P., & Dzadovsky, M. (2009). Extending the motion ranges of magnetic levitation for haptic interaction. World Haptics 2009 - *Third Joint EuroHaptics conference and Symposium on Haptic Interfaces for Virtual Environment and Teleoperator Systems*, 2009 (pp. 517-522).

Bernhardt, J. (1987). Sensory capabilities of the fetus. *MCN. The American Journal of Maternal Child Nursing, 12*, 44–46. doi:10.1097/00005721-198701000-00014

Bessou, P., Burgess, P. R., Perl, E. R., & Taylor, C. B. (1971). Dynamic properties of mechanoreceptors with unmyelinated (C) fibers. *Journal of Neurophysiology, 34*, 116–131.

Bimbo, A. D. (1999). *Visual Information Retrieval*. San Francisco, California, USA: Morgan Kaufmann Publishers, Inc.

Biocca, F., & Choi, J. K. Y. (2001). Visual Touch in Virtual Environments: An Exploratory Study of Presence, Multimodal Interfaces, and Cross-Modal Sensory Illusions. *Presence (Cambridge, Mass.), 10*(3), 247–265. doi:10.1162/105474601300343595

Biocca, F., & Levy, M. R. (1995). *Communication in the age of virtual reality*. Hillsdale, NJ, USA: Lawrence Erlbaum associates.

Birsh, J. R. (1999). *Multisensory teaching of basic language skills*. Baltimore, MD: P.H. Brookes Pub. Co.

Blade, R. A., & Padgett, M. L. (2002). Virtual Environments Standards and Terminology. In Stanney, K. M. (Ed.), *Handbook of Virtual Environments: Design, Implementation, and Applications* (pp. 15–27). New Jersey: Erlbaum Associates.

Blascovich, J., Loomis, J. M., Beall, A. C., Swinth, K. R., Hoyt, C. L., & Bailenson, J. N. (2002). Immersive Virtual Environment Technology as a Methodological Tool for Social Psychology. *Psychological Inquiry, 13*(2), 103–124. doi:10.1207/S15327965PLI1302_01

Bocconi, S., Dini, S., Ferlino, L., Martinoli, C., & Ott, M. (2007). ICT educational tools and visually impaired students: Different answers to different accessibility needs. In Stephanidis, C. (Ed.), *Universal access in human computer interaction: Applications and services* (pp. 491–500). Heidelberg: Springer. doi:10.1007/978-3-540-73283-9_55

Bodker, K., & Pederson, J. (1991). Workplace cultures: Looking at artifacts, symbols, and practices. In: Greenbaum, J., Kyng. M. (eds): Design at work: Cooperative Design of Computer Systems. Lawrence Erlbaum, Hillsdale, NJ.

Bodnar, A., Corbett, R., & Nekrasovski, D. (2004) "AROMA: Ambient awareness through olfaction in a messaging application: Does olfactory notification make 'scents'?", *ICMI'04 - Sixth International Conference on Multimodal Interfaces*, pp. 183.

Bolt, R. A. (1980). Put-that-there: voice and gesture at the graphics interface. *Computer Graphics, 14*(3), 262–270. doi:10.1145/965105.807503

Bonk, C. J., & Zhang, K. (2006). Introducing the R2D2 Model: Online Learning for the Diverse Learners of the World. *Distance Education, 27*(2), 249–264. doi:10.1080/01587910600789670

Bonzi, L. (1959). *Writer*. USA: Behind the Great Wall.

Booth K. Fisher B. Page S. Ware C. & Widen S. (2000). *Wayfinding in a virtual environment*. Graphics Interface.

Borgman, C. L. (1986). The User's Mental Model of an Information Retrieval System: an Experiment on a Prototype Online Catalog. *International Journal of Man-Machine Studies, 24*, 47–64. doi:10.1016/S0020-7373(86)80039-6

Boulos, M. N. K., Hetherington, L., & Wheeler, S. (2007). Second Life: an overview of the potential of 3-D virtual worlds in medical and health education. *Health Information and Libraries Journal, 24*(4), 233–245. doi:10.1111/j.1471-1842.2007.00733.x

Bourges-Waldegg, P., & Scrivener, S. A. R. (1998). Meaning, the central issue in cross-cultural HCI design. *Interacting with Computers, 9*(3), 287–309. doi:10.1016/S0953-5438(97)00032-5

Boyd Davis, S., Davies, G., Haddad, R., & Lai, M. (2006) "Smell Me: Engaging with an Interactive Olfactory Game", *Proceedings of the Human Factors and Ergonomics Society 25th Annual Meeting*, pp. 25-40, UK.

Bradshaw, B. (2000) "Semantic based image retrieval: a probabilistic approach", Proc. of the eighth ACM Int. conf. on Multimedia, pp: 167 - 176.

Brajnik, G. (2004). Achieving universal web access through specialized user interfaces. *In: Stephanidis, C. (ed.) Proceedings of 8th ERCIM UI4ALL'04 Workshop*, Vienna, Austria, 28–29 June.

Brand, P., & Ebner, M. A. (1969). Pressure sensitive devices for denervated hands and feet: A preliminary communication. *Journal of Bone and Joint Surgery, 51*, 109–116.

Brand, P., & Yancey, P. (1993). *Pain: The gift nobody wants*. New York: Harper Collins.

Brewer, W. F. (2000). *Bartlett's concept of the schema and its impact on theories of knowledge representation in contemporary cognitive psychology*. In Saito (Ed.), Bartlett, culture and cognition, 69-89, Psychology Press

Brewer, W. F., & Nakamura, G. V. (1984). *The nature and functions of schemas*. Handbook of social cognition, 1, 119-160.

Brewster, S. A. (2002). Visualization tools for blind people using multiple modalities. *Disability and Rehabilitation, 24*, 613–621. doi:10.1080/09638280110111388

Brewster, S. A., McGookin, D. K., & Miller, C. A. (2006) "Olfoto: Designing a smell-based interaction", *CHI 2006: Conference on Human Factors in Computing Systems*, pp. 653.

Brindza, J., & Szweda, J. (2008). *Wiimote interactions for freshman engineering education*. Notre Dame, Indiana: NetScale Laboratory.

Brooks, F. P. Jr, Ming, O.-Y., Batter, J. J., & Kilpatrick, P. J. (1990). Project GROPE: Haptic displays for scientific visualization. *Computer Graphics*, *24*, 177–185. doi:10.1145/97880.97899

Brown, P. Pietra, S.D. Pietra, V. D. and Mercer, R. (1993) "The mathematics of statistical machine translation: Parameter estimation". In Computational Linguistics, vol. 19, no. 2, pp.263-311.

Brune, M. K. (2004) *Total physical response storytelling: An analysis and application.* Thesis, University of Oregon.

Bryden, S. M., & Tapley, M. P. (1977). An investigation of sex differences in spatial ability: mental rotation of three-dimensional objects. *Canadian Journal of Psychology*, *31*(3), 122–130. doi:10.1037/h0081655

Buck, L., & Axel, R. (1991). A novel multigene family may encode odorant receptors: Molecular basis for odor recognition. *Cell*, *65*, 175–187. doi:10.1016/0092-8674(91)90418-X

Burdea, G., & Coiffet, P. (1994). *Virtual reality technology*. New York: Wiley.

Burdea, G. C. (1996). *Force and touch feedback for virtual reality*. New York: John Wiley & Sons.

Bush, V., (1945) *As We May Think*, v.176, 1, p.101-108,USA:Atlantic Monthly

Butler, M., & Neave, P. (2008). Object appreciation through haptic interaction, *In Hello! Where are you in the landscape of educational technology? Proceedings ascilite Melbourne 2008,* http://www.ascilite.org.au/conferences/melbourne08/ procs/butler-m.pdf.

Cain, W. S., & Turk, A. (1985). Smell of danger: An analysis of LP-gas odorization. *American Industrial Hygiene Association Journal*, *46*, 115–126. doi:10.1080/15298668591394527

Calvert, G. A., Spence, C., & Stein, B. E. (Eds.). (2004). *The handbook of multisensory processes*. Cambridge, MA: MIT Press.

Cameron, J. (Writer) (2009). Avatar [Film]. In J. Cameron & J. Landau (Producer). USA: 20th Century Fox.

Cardiff, J. (Writer) (1960). Scent of Mystery [Film]. In M. Todd, Jr (Producer). USA.

Carlin, A. S., Hoffman, H. G., & Weghorst, S. (1997). Virtual reality and tactile augmentation in the treatment of spider phobia: A case report. *Behaviour Research and Therapy*, *35*, 153–158. doi:10.1016/S0005-7967(96)00085-X

Carneiro, M. M., & Velho, L. (2004). *Assistive interfaces for the visually impaired using force feedback devices and distance transforms*. Info.Tech.and Disab.E J.

Carson, C., Belongie, S., Greenspan, H., & Malik, J. (2002). Blobworld: Image Segmentation Using Expectation-Maximization and Its Application to Image Querying. *IEEE Transactions on Pattern Analysis and Machine Intelligence*, *24*(8), 1026–1038. doi:10.1109/TPAMI.2002.1023800

Carson, C., Thomas, M., & Belongie, S. Hellerstein J. M., Malik J., (1999) "Blobworld: A System for Region-Based Image Indexing and Retrieval". In Proc. of the Third Int. conf. on Visual Information Systems, pp. 509-516.

Carver, C. S., & Scheier, M. (1998). *On the self-regulation of behavior*. London: Cambridge University Press.

Caschera, M. C., Ferri, F., & Grifoni, P. (2007b). An Approach for Managing Ambiguities in Multimodal Interaction. OTM 2007 Ws, Part I, LNCS 4805. *Springer-Verlag Berlin Heidelberg, 2007*, 387–397.

Caschera M. C., Ferri F., Grifoni P. (2007): Multimodal interaction systems: information and time features, International Journal of Web and Grid Services (IJWGS), Vol. 3 - Issue 1, pp 82-99.

Caschera, M. C., Ferri, F., & Grifoni, P. (2008). Ambiguity detection in multimodal systems. Proceedings of the working conference on Advanced visual interfaces. Pp.331-334.

Cascia, M. L., Sethi, S., & Sclaroff, S. (1998) "Combining Textual and Visual Cues for Content-Based Image Retrieval on the World Wide Web". Proceedings of IEEE Workshop on Content-Based Access of Image and Video Libraries.

Cassell, J. (1998). *A Framework for Gesture Generation and Interpretation, Computer Vision in Human Machine Interaction* (Cipolla, R., & Pentlan, A., Eds.). New York, USA: Cambridge University Press.

Castells, M. (1996). Rise of the Network Society, The Information Age:Economy [Massachusetts,Blackwell Publishing]. *Society and Culture, 1*.

Castle, W. (Writer) (1959). The Tingler [Film]. USA: Columbia Pictures.

Castranova, E. (2001). *Virtual Worlds: A First-Hand Account of Market and Society on the Cyberian Frontier*. Center for Economic Studies & Ifo Institute for Economic Research.

Cater, J. P. (1992). The noses have it! *Presence (Cambridge, Mass.), 1*, 493–494.

Cates, M. E., Haw, M. D., & Holmes, C. B. (2005). Dilatancy, jamming, and the physics of granulation. *Journal of Physics Condensed Matter, 17*(24), S2517–S2531. doi:10.1088/0953-8984/17/24/010

Chalmers, A., Debattista, K., Mastroropoulou, G., & dos Santos, L. P. (2007). There-Reality: Selective Rendering in High Fidelity Virtual Environments. *The International Journal of Virtual Reality, 6*(1), 1–10.

Chalmers, A., Debattista, K., & Ramic-Brkic, B. (2009). Towards high-fidelity multi-sensory virtual environments. *The Visual Computer, 25*(12), 1101–1108. doi:10.1007/s00371-009-0389-2

Chalmers, A., & Zányi, E. (2009). *Real Virtuality: emerging technology for virtually recreating reality* (pp. 1–20). BECTA.

Chan, T.-W., Roschelle, J., & Hsi, S., Kinshuk, Sharples, M., Brown, T., et al. (2006). One-to-one technology-enhanced learning:An opportunity for global research collaboration. *Research and Practice in Technology Enhanced Learning, 1*(1), 3–29. doi:10.1142/S1793206806000032

Chandler P., & Sweller J. (1996) *Cognitive Load While Learning to Use a Computer Program*. Applied Cognitive Psychology.

Chang, S.-B., Lin, C.-L., Ching, E., Cheng, H. N. H., Chang, B., & Chen, F.-C. (2007). EduBingo: Developing a content sample for the one-to-one classroom by the content-first design approach. *Journal of Educational Technology & Society, 12*(3), 343–353.

Chen, D., Katdare, A., & Lucas, N. (2006). Chemosignals of fear enhance cognitive performance in humans. *Chemical Senses, 31*, 415–423. doi:10.1093/chemse/bjj046

Chen, S. Y., & Macredie, R. D. (2001). Cognitive styles and hypermedia navigation: Development of a learning model. *Journal of the American Society for Information Science and Technology, 53*(1), 315. doi:10.1002/1532-2890(2000)9999:9999<::AID-ASI1074>3.0.CO;2-2

Chen, S. Y., Magoulas, G. D., & Dimakopoulos, D. (2005). A Flexible Interface Design for Web Directories to Accommodate Different Cognitive Styles. *Journal of the American Society for Information Science and Technology, 56*(1), 70–83. doi:10.1002/asi.20103

Chen, Z.-H., Anderson, T. A. F., Cheng, H. N. G., & Chan, T.-W. (2009). Character-Driven Learning: Facilitating Students' Learning by Educational Virtual Characters. In Kong, S.C., Ogata, H., Arnseth, H.C., Chan, C.K.K., Hirashima, T., Klett, F., Lee, J.H.M., Liu, C.C., Looi, C.K., Milrad, M., Mitrovic, A., Nakabayashi, K., Wong, S.L., Yang, S.J.H. (Eds.) *Proceedings of the 17th International Conference on Computers in Education,* Hong Kong: Asia-Pacific Society for Computers in Education.

Chu-Carroll, J. (2000). MIMIC:An adaptive mixed initiative spoken dialogue system for information queries. In *Proceedings of the Sixth Conference on Applied Natural Language Processing*, Seattle, WA: Association for Computational Linguistics, 97-104.

Clark, S. A., & Wong, B. L. W. (2000). *QTVR Support for Teaching Operative Procedures in Dentistry*. People and Computer XIV. Usability or Else! Proceedings of HCL 2000, London.

Coates, G. (1992). *A virtual Show. A multimedia performance work, San Francisco, CA, USA: Couchot, E., Hillaire, N. (1991) L'Art Numerique*. Paris, France: Ed. Flammarion.

Cobb S.U.G. & D'Cruz, M. D. (1994). *First UK national survey on industrial application of virtual reality*. VR News, 3.

Cockburn, A., & McKenzie, B. (2002). Evaluating the effectiveness of spatial memory in 2D and 3D physical and virtual environments. *CHI 2002, April 20-25.* Minneapolis, Minnesota, USA.

Cohen, R., & Schuepfer, T. (1980). The representation of landmarks and routes. *Child Development, 51*, 1065–1071. doi:10.2307/1129545

Cohen, P. R., Johnston, M., McGee, D., Oviatt, S., Pittman, J., Smith, I., et al. (1997). "QuickSet: Multimodal interaction for distributed applications". Fifth ACM International Multimedia Conference, ACM Press/Addison-Wesley 31-40.

Colgate, J., Stanley, M., & Brown, J. (1995). Issues in the haptic display of tool use. *International Conference on Intelligent Robots and Systems*, Pittsburgh, August 1995.

Colwell, C., Petrie, H., Kornbrot, D., Hardwick, A., & Furner, S. (1998). Haptic virtual reality for blind computer users. In *Assets '98: Proceedings of the third international ACM conference on Assistive technologies.* ACM Press, New York, NY, USA, 92–99.

Communications, N. T. T. (2006) *Movie Enhanced with Internet-based Fragrance System.* Available: http://www.in70mm.com/ news/ 2006/ new_world/ index.htm [Accessed: August 21, 2007].

Cooper. G. (2004). *Research into Cognitive Load.* Theory and Instructional Design at UNSW.

Craig, A. D. (2002). How do you feel? Interoception: The sense of the physiological condition of the body. *Nature Reviews. Neuroscience, 3*, 655–666.

Crandall, W., Bentzen, B. L., Myers, L., & Mitchell, P. (1995). Transit Accessibility Improvement Through Talking Signs Remote Infrared Signage, a Demonstration and Evaluation. *Washington, DC: Final report to US Department of Transportation, Federal Transit Administration and Project ACTION of the National Easter Seal Society,* 1-30. Disability INformation Resources (DINF). *http://www.dinf.ne.jp/doc/* english/Us Eu/conf/csun 98/

Crawford, C. (2003). *Chris Crawford on game design.* Berkeley, CA: New Riders Publishing.

Crawford, C. (2004). *Chris Crawford on interactive storytelling.* Berkeley, CA: New Riders Publishing.

Creighton, I., & Ho-Stuart, C. (2004). *A sense of touch in online sculpting.* Paper presented at the 2nd international conference on Computer graphics and interactive techniques in Australasia and South East Asia Singapore.

Crook, T. H., Young, J. R., & Larrabee, G. J. (1993). The influence of age, gender and cues on computer-simulated topographic memory. *Developmental Neuropsychology, 9*, 41–53. doi:10.1080/87565649309540543

Crosbie, V. (2002), What is New Media? Retrieved from http://www.sociology.org.uk/ as4mm3a.doc

Crusco, A. H., & Wetzel, C. G. (1984). The Midas touch: The effects of interpersonal touch on restaurant tipping. *Personality and Social Psychology Bulletin, 10*, 512–517. doi:10.1177/0146167284104003

Cypher, M. (2006). Biophilia. In *ACM SIGGRAPH 2006 Sketches* (Article No. 24).

D'Ulizia, A. (2009). *Exploring Multimodal Input Fusion Strategies. In the Handbook of Research on Multimodal Human Computer Interaction and Pervasive Services: Evolutionary Techniques for Improving Accessibility* (pp. 34–57). IGI Publishing.

D'Ulizia A., Ferri F., Grifoni P. (2010). Generating Multimodal Grammars for Multimodal Dialogue Processing. *IEEE Transactions on Systems, Man, and Cybernetics - Part A: Systems and Humans.* (in press, forthcoming in the Volume 40, Issue 4, July 2010).

Dahl, O.-J., Myhrhaug, B., & Nygaard, K. (1968). Some features of the SIMULA 67 language. In *Proceedings of the Second Conference on Applications of Simulations.* New York City, NY: Winter Simulation Conference, 29-31.

Damasio, A. R. (1994). *Descartes' error: Emotion, reason, and the human brain.* New York: Putnam Publishing.

Darken, R. P., Allard, T., & Achille, L. B. (1998). Spatial Orientation and Wayfinding in Large-Scale Virtual Spaces: An Introduction. *Presence (Cambridge, Mass.), 7*(2), 101–107. doi:10.1162/105474698565604

Darken, R. P., Allard, T., & Achille, L. B. (1999). Spatial Orientation and Wayfinding in Large Scale Virtual Spaces II. *Presence (Cambridge, Mass.), 8*(6).

Darken, R. P., & Banker, W. P. (1998). Navigating in Natural Environments: A Virtual Environment Training Transfer Study. *Proceedings of VRAIS, 98*, 12–19.

Darken, R. P., & Peterson, B. (2001). *Spatial Orientation, Wayfinding, and Representation. Handbook of Virtual Environment Technology* (Stanney, K., Ed.).

Darken, R. P., & Sibert, J. L. (1996). Wayfinding strategies and behaviours in large virtual worlds. *Proceedings of ACM CHI96*, 142-149.

Darken, R. P., Cockayne, W. R., & Carmein, D. (1997). *The Omni-Directional Treadmill: A Locomotion Devic for Virtual Worlds.* Paper presented at the UIST '97, Banff, Canada.

Darroch, I., Goodman, J., Brewster, S., & Gray, P. (2005) The Effect of Age and Font Size on Reading Text on Handheld Computers. In *Proceedings of IFIP INTERACT05: Human-Computer Interaction* pp. 253-266.

Darwin, C. (1872). *The expression of the emotions in man and animals.* London: Murray. doi:10.1037/10001-000

Davide, F., Holmberg, M., & Lundström, I. (2001). Virtual olfactory interfaces: Electronic noses and olfactory displays. In *Communications through virtual technology: Identity community and technology in the internet age* (pp. 193–220). Amsterdam: IOS Press.

Davide, F., Holmberg, M., & Lundstorm, I. (2001). In Riva, G., Davide, F., & Press, I. O. S. (Eds.), *Virtual olfactory interfaces, electronic noses and olfactory displays, Communication through virtual technology: Community and technology in the Internet age* (pp. 193–220). Amsterdam.

Davis, E. T., Scott, K., Pair, J., Hodges, L. F., & Oliverio, J. (1999). *Can audio enhance visual perception and performance in a virtual environment.* Paper presented at the Human Factors and Ergonomics Society 43rd Annual Meeting

De Laine, M. (2000). *Fieldwork, Participation and Practice: Ethics and dilemmas in qualitative research.* London: Sage.

De Thomas, M. T. (1971). Touch power and the screen of loneliness. *Perspectives in Psychiatric Care, 9*, 112–118. doi:10.1111/j.1744-6163.1971.tb01082.x

Dede, C. (1995). The Evolution of Constructivist Learning Environments: Immersion in Distributed, Virtual Worlds. *Educational Technology, 35*(5), 46–52.

Dede, C. (2009). Immersive Interfaces for Engagement and Learning. *Science, 323*(5910), 66–69. doi:10.1126/science.1167311

Dede, C., Salzman, M. C., Loftin, R. B., & Sprague, D. (1999). Multisensory Immersion as a Modeling Environment for Learning Complex Scientific Concepts. In Roberts, N., & Feurzeig, W. (Eds.), *Modeling and Simulation in science and mathematics education.* New York: Springer.

Del Galdo, E. (1990). Internationalization and translation: some guidelines for the design of human-computer interfaces. In Factors, E. A. I. H., & Series, E. (Eds.), *Designing User interfaces For international Use, J. Nielsen (Vol. 13*, pp. 1–10). Essex: Elsevier Science Publishers Ltd.

Demattè, M. L., Österbauer, R., & Spence, C. (2007). Olfactory cues modulate judgments of facial attractiveness. *Chemical Senses, 32*, 603–610. doi:10.1093/chemse/bjm030

Deneve, S., & Pouget, A. (2004). Bayesian multisensory integration and cross-modal spatial links. *Journal of Physiology, Paris, 98*, 249–258. doi:10.1016/j.jphysparis.2004.03.011

Dennett, D. C. (1991). *Consciousness explained.* Boston: Little & Brown.

Denzin, N. K., & Lincoln, Y. S. (Eds.). (2005). *The SAGE Handbook of Qualitative Research.* Thousand Oaks, California: Sage.

Desor, J., & Beauchamp, G. (1974). The human capacity to transmit olfactory information. *Perception & Psychophysics, 16*, 551–556. doi:10.3758/BF03198586

Dettori, A., Avizzano, C. A., Marcheschi, S., Angerilli, M., Bergamasco, M., Loscos, C., et al. (2003). *Art Touch with CREATE haptic interface.* Paper presented at the ICAR 2003: The 11th International Conference on Advanced Robotics.

Dillon, W. R., & Goldstein, M. (1984). *Multivariate analysis* (pp. 23–52). Wiley.

Dinh, H. Q., Walker, N., Hodges, L. F., Song, C., & Kobayashi, A. (1999). Evaluating the importance of multi-sensory input on memory and the sense of presence in virtual environments. *Proceedings of IEEE Virtual Reality Conference 1999*, Houston, TX, 13-17 March (pp. 222-228).

Dittman, B., Nitz, S., & Horner, G. (1998). A new chemical sensor on a mass spectrometric basis, Adv. Food Sci., (CMTL) 20, 115.

Dix, A., Finlay, J., Abowd, G., & Beale, R. (1993). *Human computer interaction*. New York: Prentice Hall.

Douglas G (2002) ICT, Education and Visual Impairment. British Journal of Educational Technology 32/3/ pp. 353-364

Driver, J. (1996). Enhancement of selective listening by illusory mislocation of speech sounds due to lip-reading. *Nature, 381*, 66–68. doi:10.1038/381066a0

Druin, A., Montemayor, J., Hendler, J.A., McAlister, B., Boltman, A., Fiterman, E., Plaisant, A., Kruskal, A., Olsen, H., Revett, I., Schwenn, T.P., Sumida, L., Wagner, R. (1999). Designing PETS: A personal electronic teller of stories. *Computer Human Interaction*, 326-329.

DSM-IV-TR. *(2000). American Psychiatric Association: Diagnostic and Statistical Manual of Mental Disorders, Fourth Edition, 299.00 Autistic Disorder.* Washington, DC: American Psychiatric Association.

Duridanov, L., & Simoff, S. (2007). 'Inner Listening' as a Basic Principle for Developing Immersive Virtual Worlds. *Online - Heidelberg Journal of Religions on the Internet, 2*(3).

Durie, B. (2005). Future sense. *New Scientist, 2484,* 33–36.

Duygulu, P. Barnard, K. Freitas, N. and Forsyth, D. (2002) "Object recognition as machine translation: Learning a lexicon for a fixed image vocabulary". In 7th European Conf. on Computer Vision, pages 97-112.

Easton, R. D., & Bentzen, B. L. (1999). The effect of extended acoustic training on spatial updating in adults who are congenitally blind. *Journal of Visual Impairment & Blindness, 93*(7), 405–415.

Eberts, R. E. (1994). *User interface design*. Englewood Cliffs, NJ: Prentice Hall.

Efron, D. (1941). *Gesture and environment*. New York: King's Crown Press.

Egsegian, R., Pittman, K., Farmer, K., & Zobel, R. (1993). Practical applications of virtual reality to firefighter training. In *Proceedings of the 1993 Simulations Multiconference on the International Emergency Management and Engineering Conference* (pp. 155–160). San Diego, CA: Society of Computer Simulation

Ehrsson, H. H. (2007). The experimental induction of out-of-body experiences. *Science, 317,* 1048. doi:10.1126/science.1142175

Ein-Dor, P., & Segev, E. (1990). End-user computing: A crosscultural study. Proc. of the Twenty-Third Annual Hawaii International Conference on System Sciences 1990, Vol. 4, IEEE, 240-250.

Ekman, P., & Friesen, W. (1969). The repertoire of nonverbal behavioral categories -- origins, usage, and coding. *Semiotica, 1*, 49–98.

Elger, G., & Furugren, B. (1998) SmartBo: An ICT and computer-based demonstration home for disabled people. Paper presented at TIDE 98 Conference, Tokyo, Japan, August 1998

Enser, P. G. (1993). Query analysis in a visual information retrieval context. *Journal of Document and Text Management, 1*, 25–52.

Erceau, D., & Guéguen, N. (2007). Tactile contact and evaluation of the toucher. *The Journal of Social Psychology, 147*, 441–444. doi:10.3200/SOCP.147.4.441-444

Eriksson, Y. (1998). Tactile Pictures: Pictorial Representations for the Blind 1784-1940. Göteborg: Göteborg University Press Estivill-Castro V & Seymon S (2007) Mobile Robots for an E-mail Interface for People Who are Blind. In Bredenfeld, A., Jacoff, A., Noda, I., & Takahashi, Y. (Eds.), *RoboCup 2006: Robot Soccer World Cup X* (pp. 338–346). Heidelberg: Springer.

Ernst, M. O., & Banks, M. S. (2002). Humans integrate visual and haptic information in a statistically optimal fashion. *Nature, 415*, 429–433. doi:10.1038/415429a

Ernst, M. O., & Bülthoff, H. H. (2004). Merging the senses into a robust percept. *Trends in Cognitive Sciences, 8*, 162–169. doi:10.1016/j.tics.2004.02.002

Espinosa, M. A., & Ochaita, E. (1998). Using tactile maps to improve the practical spatial knowledge of adults who are blind. *Journal of Visual Impairment & Blindness, 92*(5), 338–345.

Esselman, P. C., Thombs, B. D., Magyar-Russell, G., & Fauerbach, J. A. (2006). Burn rehabilitation: State of the science. *American Journal of Physical Medicine & Rehabilitation, 85*, 383–413. doi:10.1097/01.phm.0000202095.51037.a3

Faconti, G. P., Massink, M., Bordegoni, M., Angelis, F. D., & Booth, S. (2000). Haptic cues for image disambiguation. *Computer Graphics Forum, 19*, 3. doi:10.1111/1467-8659.00409

Fassbender, E., & Richards, D. (2008). *Using a Dance Pad to Navigate through the Virtual Heritage Environment of Macquarie Lighthouse, Sydney Virtual Systems and Multimedia* (pp. 1–12). Berlin: Springer.

Faure, C., & Julia, L. (1993). "Interaction homme-machine par la parole et le geste pour l'édition de Documents: TAPAGE ". International Conference on Interfaces to Real and Virtual Worlds, 171-180.

Feldman, A., & Acredolo, L. P. (1979). The effect of active versus passive exploration on memory for spatial location in children. *Child Development, 50*, 698–704. doi:10.2307/1128935

Feldman, T. (1997). *An Introduction to Digital Media.* London: Routledge. doi:10.4324/9780203398401

Felleman, D. J., & Van Essen, D. C. (1991). Distributed hierarchical processing in primate cerebral cortex. *Cerebral Cortex, 1*, 1–47. doi:10.1093/cercor/1.1.1-a

Field, T. (2001). *Touch.* Cambridge, MA: MIT Press.

Filpus, P. (2008) Computer Programmer and Analyst. Downloaded from http://www.afb.org/Section.asp? SectionID=7&TopicID=267&SubTopicID=83&DocumentID=3179, on the 12ᵗʰ December 2008)

Fink, C. A. (1979). *Searching for the most powerful behavioral theory:the whole of the Behavior Systems Research Institute and the Behavioral Model Analysis Center.* Falls Church, Va: Fink.

Fisher, S. S. (1991). Virtual Environments, Personal Simulation & Telepresence. In Helsel, S., & Roth, J. (Eds.), *Virtual Reality: Theory, Practice and Promise.* Westport: Meckler Publishing.

Fitzgerald, W. (2004). Models for cross cultural communications for cross-cultural website design. NRC/ERB-1108. April 6, 2004. 11 pages. NRC Publication Number: NRC 46563.

Fitzpatrick, L. (2009). *The Art of Avatar.* New York: Abrams.

Fleming, N., & Baume, D. (2006). Learning Styles Again: VARKing up the Right Tree! *Educational Developments, 7*(4), 4–7.

Flew, T. (2002). *New Media:An Introduction.* UK: Oxford University Press.

Flickner, M., Sawhney, H., Niblack, W., Ashley, J., Huang, Q., Dom, B., Gorkani, M., Hafine, J., Lee,D. Petkovic, D., Steele, D. and Yanker, P. (1995) "Query by image and video content: The QBIC system", IEEE Computer.

Foley, W. (1995). *Anthropological Linguistics.* Blackwell Publishers Ltd.

Ford, N., & Chen, S. Y. (2001). Matching/mismatching revisited: An empirical study of learning and teaching styles. *British Journal of Educational Technology, 32*(1), 5–22. doi:10.1111/1467-8535.00173

Ford, G., & Kotzé, P. (2005). Designing usable interfaces with cultural dimensions. In Costabile, M. F., & Paternó, F. (Eds.), *Lecture Notes in Computer Science LNCS 3585, Human-Computer Interaction - INTERACT 2005* (pp. 713–726). Berlin: Springer.

Foreman, N., Stanton, D., Wilson, P., & Duffy, H. (2003). Spatial Knowledge of a Real School Environment Acquired From Virtual or Physical Models by Able Bodied Children and Children With Physical Disabilities. *Journal of Experimental Psychology, 9*(2), 67–74.

Fragra - An Interactive Olfactory Game System, 2003, IVRC (Inter-collegiate Virtual Reality Contest) www.ivrc.net. Available: http://chihara.aist-nara.ac.jp/ ivrc2003/index.html [Accessed: August 23, 2007].

Fraguas, R., Marci, C., Fava, M., Iosifescua, D. V., Bankier, B., Loh, R., & Dougherty, D. D. (2007). Autonomic reactivity to induced emotion as potential predictor of response to antidepressant treatment. *Psychiatry Research, 151*, 169–172. doi:10.1016/j.psychres.2006.08.008

Franceschi, K. G., Lee, R. M., & Hinds, D. (2008). *Engaging E-Learning in Virtual Worlds: Supporting Group Collaboration.* Paper presented at the 41st Hawaii International Conference on System Sciences.

Franqueiro, K. G., & Siegfried, R. M. (2006) Designing a Scripting Language to Help the Blind Program Visually. Proceedings of the 8ᵗʰ International ACM SIGACCESS Conference on Computers and Accessibility, Portland, Oregon, October 2006

Franzel, D., & Newman, W. (2009) *Virtual world: Hybrid reality for computer learning and teaching.* Thesis: Flinders University of South Australia.

Gallace, A., & Spence, C. (2008). The cognitive and neural correlates of "tactile consciousness": A multisensory perspective. *Consciousness and Cognition, 17*, 370–407. doi:10.1016/j.concog.2007.01.005

Gallace, A., & Spence, C. (2009). The cognitive and neural correlates of tactile memory. *Psychological Bulletin, 135*, 380–406. doi:10.1037/a0015325

Gallace, A., & Spence, C. (2010). The science of interpersonal touch: An overview. *Neuroscience and Biobehavioral Reviews, 34*, 246–259. doi:10.1016/j.neubiorev.2008.10.004

Gallace, A., & Spence, C. (in press). Do Gestalt grouping principles influence tactile perception? *Psychological Bulletin.*

Gallace, A., Tan, H. Z., & Spence, C. (2006a). Numerosity judgments in tactile perception. *Perception, 35*, 247–266. doi:10.1068/p5380

Gallace, A., Tan, H. Z., & Spence, C. (2006b). The failure to detect tactile change: A tactile analogue of visual change blindness. *Psychonomic Bulletin & Review, 13*, 300–303. doi:10.3758/BF03193847

Gallace, A., Tan, H. Z., & Spence, C. (2007). The body surface as a communication system: The state of art after 50 years of research. *Presence (Cambridge, Mass.), 16*, 655–676. doi:10.1162/pres.16.6.655

Gallace, A., Tan, H. Z., & Spence, C. (2008). Can tactile stimuli be subitized? An unresolved controversy within the literature on numerosity judgments. *Perception, 37*, 782–800. doi:10.1068/p5767

Gallagher, B., Connolly, N., & Lyne, S. (2005) Equal Access to Technology Training (EATT): Improving computer literacy of people with vision impairments aged over 35. International Congress Series Vol. 1282 / pp. 846-850

Gallistel, C. R. (1990). *The organisation of learning.* Cambridge M.A. The MIT Press.

Gerber, E., & Kirchner, C. (2001). Who's surfing? Internet access and computer use by visually impaired youths and adults. *Journal of Visual Impairment & Blindness, 95*, 176–181.

Ghazanfar, A. A., & Schroeder, C. E. (2006). Is neocortex essentially multisensory? *Trends in Cognitive Sciences, 10*, 278–285. doi:10.1016/j.tics.2006.04.008

Gilbert, A. (2008). *What the nose knows: The science of scent in everyday life.* New York: Crown Publishers.

Gildea, R A J. (1970) Guidelines for Training Blind Computer Programmers. New Outlook for the Blind 64/9/pp. 297-300

Gillner, S., & Mallot, H. A. (1998). Navigation and acquisition of spatial knowledge in a virtual maze. *Journal of Cognitive Neuroscience, 10*, 445–463. doi:10.1162/089892998562861

Goerger, S. Darken R. Boyd M. Gagnon T. Liles S. Sullivan J. & Lawson J.P (1998). Spatial Knowledge Acquisition from Maps and Virtual Environments in Complex Architectural Spaces. In *Proceedings of the 16th Applied Behavioral Sciences Symposium,* 2223, April, U.S. Air Force Academy. Colorado Springs, 610.

Goldmeier, S. (2009a). Virtual Worlds: Seven failed virtual reality technologies.

Golledge, R. G., Dougherty, V., & Bell, S. (1995). Acquiring Spatial Knowledge: Survey versus Route Based Knowledge. *Unfamiliar Environments Reginald Annals of the Association of American Geographers, 85*(1), 13158.

Golledge, R. G., Marston, J. R., Loomis, J. M., & Klatzky, R. L. (2004). Stated preferences for components of a personal guidance system for nonvisual navigation. *Journal of Visual Impairment & Blindness, 98*(3), 135–147.

Golledge, R. G., Klatzky, R. L., & Loomis, J. M. (1996). Cognitive mapping and wayfinding by adults without vision. In Portugali, J. (Ed.), *The Construction of Cognitive Maps* (pp. 215–246). Netherlands: Kluwer Academic Publishers. doi:10.1007/978-0-585-33485-1_10

Gomez, L. M. Egan D.E. & Bowers C. (1986). Learning to use a text editor: Some learner characteristics that predict success. *HumanComputer Interaction, 2*, 1–23.

Goodenough, D. (1976). The role of individual differences in field dependence as a factor in learning and memory. *Psychological Bulletin, 83*, 675–694. doi:10.1037/0033-2909.83.4.675

Gori, M., Del Viva, M., Sandini, G., & Burr, D. C. (2008). Young children do not integrate visual and haptic form information. *Current Biology, 18*, 694–698. doi:10.1016/j.cub.2008.04.036

Gorkani, M. M., & Picard, R. W. (1994) "Texture orientation for sorting photos 'at a glance'", In proc. of the IEEE Int. Conf. on Pattern Recognition.

Gottlieb, G. (1971). Ontogenesis of sensory function in birds and mammals. In E. Tobach, L. R., Aronson, & E. F. Shaw (Eds.), *The biopsychology of development* (pp. 67-128). New York: Academic Press.

Grau, O. (2003). *Virtual Art*. Cambridge, MA, USA: MIT Press.

Gray, M. A., Harrison, N. A., Wiens, S., & Critchley, H. D. (2007). Modulation of emotional appraisal by false physiological feedback during fMRI. *PLoS ONE, 2*(6), e546. doi:10.1371/journal.pone.0000546

Gray, W. D. (Ed.). (2007). *Integrated Models of Cognitive Systems*. USA: Oxford University Press.

Gregory, R. L. (1966). *Eye and brain: The psychology of seeing*. New York: McGraw-Hill.

Gregory, R. L. (1967). Origin of eyes and brains. *Nature, 213*, 369–372. doi:10.1038/213369a0

Griffin, C. (1985). Qualitative Methods and Cultural Analysis: Young women and the transition from school to un/employment. In Burgess, R. (Ed.), *Field methods in the study of education*. London: Falmer Press.

Grinder, J., & Bandler, R. (1975). *The Structure of Magic II: A Book About Communication and Change*. Palo Alto, CA: Science & Behavior Books.

Grow, D. I., Verner, L. N., & Okamura, A. M. (2007). Educational Haptics. *AAAI 2007 Spring Symposia - Robots and Robot Venues*, Resources for AI Education.

Guilford, J. P., & Zimmerman, W. S. (1948). The Guilford Zimmerman Aptitude Survey. *The Journal of Applied Psychology, 32*, 24–34. doi:10.1037/h0063610

Gupta, A., & Jain, R. (1997). Visual information retrieval. *Communications of the ACM, 40*(5), 71–79. doi:10.1145/253769.253798

Gustafson-Pearce O, Billett E & Cecelja F (2007) Comparison Between Audio and Tactile systems for Delivering Simple Navigational Information to Visually Impaired Pedestrians. British Journal of Visual Impairment 25/3/pp.255-265

Gustainis, D. (2009). *Hybrid character recognition using a visual input*. Thesis: Flinders University of South Australia.

Gustavsson, M. (1999). *Designing a multimodal system for a culturally diverse user group*. www.ida.liu.se/~ssomc/papers/Gustavsson.pdf

Haans, A., IJsselsteijn, W. A., Graus, M. P., & Salminen, J. A. (2008). The virtual Midas touch: Helping behavior after a mediated social touch. In *Extended Abstracts of CHI 2008* (pp. 3507–3512). New York: ACM Press.

Hackett, S., Parmanto, B., & Zeng, X. (2004). Accessibility of Internet web sites through time. *In: Proceedings of the Sixth International ACM Conference on Computers and Accessibility*, pp. 32–39. ACM Press, Atlanta, GA, USA.

Haden, R. (2005). Taste in an age of convenience. In Korsmeyer, C. (Ed.), *The taste culture reader: Experiencing food and drink* (pp. 344–358). Oxford: Berg.

Hall, E., & Hall, M. R. (1990). *Understanding Cultural Differences*. Yarmouth, Maine: Intercultural Press.

Hancock, P. A., Oron-Gilad, T., & Szalma, J. L. (2007). Elaborations of the multiple-resource theory of attention. In Kramer, A. F., Wiegmann, D. A., & Kirlik, A. (Eds.), *Attention: From theory to practice* (pp. 45–56). Oxford: Oxford University Press.

Hang, H. P., & Alessi, N. E. (1999). *Presence as an Emotional Experience in Medicine meet Virtual Reality. The Convergence of Physical and Information Technologies options for a new era in HealthCare* (pp. 148–153). Amsterdam: IOS Press.

Haralick, R. M., Shanmugam, K., & Dinstein, I. (1973). "Texture features for image classification", IEEE Trans. On Sys, Man, and Cyb. *SMC, 3*(6), 610–621.

Harder, A., & Michel, R. (2002). The Target-Route Map: Evaluating Its Usability for Visually Impaired Persons. *Journal of Visual Impairment & Blindness, 96*, 711.

Hardwick, A., Furner, S., & Rush, J. (1998). Tactile display of virtual reality from the World Wide Web - a potential access method for blind people. *Displays, 18*(3), 153–161. doi:10.1016/S0141-9382(98)00016-X

Harper, M. P., & Shriberg, E. (2004). Multimodal model integration for sentence unit detection. *ICMI, 2004*, 121–128. doi:10.1145/1027933.1027955

Harris, R. W. (1979) Aesthetic Development of Visually Impaired Children: A Curriculum Model for Grades Kindergarten Thru Six. Unpublished Ed.D. thesis, Indiana University, Bloomington.

Hasher, L., & Zacks, R. T. (1979). Automatic and effortful processes in memory. *Journal of Experimental Psychology, 108*, 356–388.

Hashimoto, Y., Nagaya, N., Kojima, M., Miyajima, S., Ohtaki, J., & Yamamoto, A. (2007). Straw-like user interface: Virtual experience of the sensation of drinking using a straw. [Los Alamitos, CA: IEEE Computer Society.]. *Proceedings World Haptics, 2007*, 557–558.

Hashimoto, Y., Inami, M., & Kajimoto, H. (2008). Straw-like user interface (II): A new method of presenting auditory sensations for a more natural experience. In M. Ferre (Ed.), *Eurohaptics 2008, LNCS, 5024*, 484-493. Berlin: Springer-Verlag.

Hashimoto, Y., Nagaya, N., Kojima, M., Ohtaki, J., Mitani, T., Yamamoto, A., et al. Inami, M. (2005). Straw-like user interface. In *ACM SIGGRAPH 2005 Emerging Technologies* (Article No. 20).

Hayhoe, S. (2008a). *God, Money & Politics: English attitudes to blindness and touch, from Enlightenment to integration*. Charlotte, North Carolina: Information Age Publishing.

Hayhoe, S. (2008b). *Arts, Culture and Blindness: Studies of blind students in the visual arts*. Youngstown, New York: Teneo Press.

Hayhoe, S. (2003). The Development of the Research of the Psychology of Visual Impairment in the Visual Arts. In Axel, E., & Levent, N. (Eds.), *Art Beyond Sight* (pp. 84–95). New York: The American Foundation for the Blind.

Hayhoe, S. (1995) The Art Education of Blind Adults. Unpublished MEd by research thesis, Leicester University, British Isles

Hayhoe, S. (2000a) The Effects of Late Arts Education on Adults with Early Visual Disabilities. Educational Research & Evaluation 6/3/ pp. 229-249

Hayhoe, S. (2000b) The Cultural Subjectivity of Research Ethics. Paper presented at the 6th Discussion Group Conference, Keele University, British Isles, November 2000

Hayhoe, S. (2002) The Experience of Children with Visual Impairments in Visual Arts Education. Paper presented at the International Conference on the Politics of Childhood, Hull University, 10th September 2002

Hayhoe, S. (2005) An Examination of Social and Cultural Factors Affecting Art Education in English Schools for the Blind. Unpublished doctoral thesis, Birmingham University, England

Hayhoe, S., & Rajab, A. (2000) Ethical Considerations of Conducting Ethnographic Research in Visually Impaired Communities. Paper presented at The European Conference on Educational Research 2000, Edinburgh University, September 2000

Hayward, v., Astley, O., Cruz-Hernandez, M., Grant, D., & Robles-De-La-Torre, G. (2004), Haptic interfaces and devices. *Sensor Review, 24*, 16-29.

Hegarty, M., & Waller, D. (2004). A dissociation between mental rotation and perspective-taking spatial abilities. *Intelligence*, *32*, 175–191. doi:10.1016/j.intell.2003.12.001

Heilig, M. L. (1992). El cine del futuro: The cinema of the future. *Presence (Cambridge, Mass.)*, *1*, 279–294.

Heilig, M. (1962). *Sensorama stimulator*. U.S. Patent #3,050,870.

Heller, M. A. (2000). *Touch, Representation and Blindness*. Oxford: Oxford University Press.

Hendrix, C., & Barfield, W. (1996). The sense of presence with auditory virtual environments. *Presence (Cambridge, Mass.)*, *5*, 290–301.

Henricson, M., Berglund, A.-L., Määttä, S., Ekman, R., & Segesten, K. (2008). The outcome of tactile touch on oxytocin in intensive care patients: A randomised controlled trial. *Journal of Clinical Nursing*, *17*, 2624–2633. doi:10.1111/j.1365-2702.2008.02324.x

Heritage, S. (2006) *The New Colin Farrell Movie Stinks In Japan*. Available: http://www.hecklerspray.com/ the-new-colin-farrell-movie-stinks-in-japan/20062756.php [Accessed: August 23, 2007].

Herman, J. F., Herman, T. G., & Chatman, S. P. (1983). Constructing cognitive maps from partial information: a demonstration study with congenitally blind subjects. *Journal of Visual Impairment & Blindness*, *77*(5), 195–198.

Herpers, R., Hetmann, F., Hau, A., & Heiden, W. (2005). The Immersion Square – A mobile platform for immersive visualizations. In *Aktuelle Methoden der Laser und Medizinphysik, 2nd Remagener Physiktage* (pp. 43–48). Berlin: VDE Verlag.

Herpers, R., Heiden, W., Kutz, M., Scherfgen, D., Hartmann, U., Bongartz, J., & Schulzyk, O. (2008). FIVIS – Bicycle Simulator in the Immersive Visualisation Environment "Immersion Square. In Zacharias, C. (Eds.), *Forschungsspitzen und Spitzenforschung* (pp. 61–68). Physica-Verlag.

Herpers, R. Heiden, W. Kutz, M. Scherfgen, D. Hartmann, U. Bongartz, J. Schulzyk, O. (2008). FIVIS Bicycle Simulator – An Immersive Game Platform for Physical Activities. International Conference on Future of Game Design and Technology, ACM FuturePlay 2008, 3.-5.11., pp. 244-249, 2008.

Herpers, R., & Hetmann, F. (2001). D*reiwandprojektionssystem*, Deutsches Patentamt, Az. 101 28 347.4.

Herpers, R., Heiden, W., Kutz, M., & Scherfgen, D. (2009). *Immersion Square – A cost-effective multi-screen VR Visualisation Technology*, Electronic displays 2009 Conference, ED2009, 3.-4.03. 2009, WEKA Fachmedien GmbH (Ed.)

Herpers, R., Scherfgen, D., Kutz, M., Hartmann, U., Schulzyk, O., Reinert, D., & Steiner, H. (2009). FIVIS – A Bicycle Simulation System, World Congress on Medical Physics and Biomedical Engineering (WC 2009), Munich, O. Dössel and W. Schlegel (Eds.), IFMBE Proceedings 25/IV, pp. 2132-2135, 2009.

Hertenstein, M. J., Keltner, D., App, B., Bulleit, B. A., & Jaskolka, A. R. (2006). Touch communicates distinct emotions. *Emotion (Washington, D.C.)*, *6*, 528–533. doi:10.1037/1528-3542.6.3.528

Hetmann, F., Herpers, R., & Heiden, W. (2002). *The Immersion Square - Immersive VR with Standard Components. VEonPC02 Proceedings* (pp. 23–32). St. Petersburg: Protvino.

Hinrichs, E., & Polanyi, L. (1986). Pointing the way: A unified treatment of referential gesture in interactive contexts. In A. Farley, P. Farley & K.E. McCullough (Eds.), Proceedings of the Parasession of the Chicago Linguistics Society Annual Meetings (Pragmatics and Grammatical Theory). Chicago: Chicago Linguistics Society.

Ho, C., Reed, N. J., & Spence, C. (2006). Assessing the effectiveness of "intuitive" vibrotactile warning signals in preventing front-to-rear-end collisions in a driving simulator. *Accident; Analysis and Prevention*, *38*, 989–997. doi:10.1016/j.aap.2006.04.002

Ho, C., & Spence, C. (2005). Olfactory facilitation of dual-task performance. *Neuroscience Letters*, *389*, 35–40. doi:10.1016/j.neulet.2005.07.003

Hoffman, H. G., Hollander, A., Schroder, K., Rousseau, S., & Furness, T. I. (1998). Physically touching and tasting virtual objects enhances the realism of virtual experiences. *Journal of Virtual Reality*, *3*, 226–234. doi:10.1007/BF01408703

Hofstede, G. (1991). *Cultures and Organizations: Software of the Mind*. New York, New York: McGraw-Hill.

Hofstede, G. (2001). *Culture's consequences II: Comparing values, behaviors, institutions & organizations across nations*. Beverly Hills, CA: Sage.

Hoggan, E., Brewster, S. A., & Johnston, J. (2008). Investigating the effectiveness of tactile feedback for mobile touchscreens. *Proceeding of the twenty-sixth annual SIGCHI conference on Human factors in computing systems*, 1573-1582.

Holmes (2005), "Telecommunity" in Communication Theory: Media, Technology and Society, Cambridge: Polity

Holmes, N. P., & Spence, C. (2006). Beyond the body schema: Visual, prosthetic, and technological contributions to bodily perception and awareness. In Knoblich, G., Thornton, I. M., Grosjean, M., & Shiffrar, M. (Eds.), *Human body perception from the inside out* (pp. 15–64). Oxford: Oxford University Press.

Holtzman, S. R. (1995). *Digital Mantras*. Cambridge, MA, USA: MIT Press.

Howard, I. P., & Templeton, W. B. (1966). *Human spatial orientation*. New York: Wiley.

Hu, W., Lu, J., Zhang, L., Wu, W., Nie, H., & Zhu, Y. (2006). A preliminary report of penile transplantation. *European Urology*, *51*, 1146–1147.

Hunt, E. & Waller, D. (1999). *Orientation and wayfinding: A review*. ONR Technical Report.

Hwang, J., Jung, J., & Kim, G. J. (2006). Hand-held virtual reality: A feasibility study. In *Proceedings of the ACM symposium on Virtual reality software and technology*, New York City, NY: ACM, 356-363.

Iggo, A. (1977). Cutaneous and subcutaneous sense organs. *British Medical Bulletin*, *33*, 97–102.

Iglesias, R., Casado, S., Gutierrez, T., Barbero, J., Avizzano, C., & Marcheschi, S. (2004). Computer graphics access for blind people through a haptic and audio virtual environment. *Haptic, Audio and Visual Environments and Their Applications, 2004. HAVE, 2004*, 13–18.

Inchauste, F. (2010). Better user experience with storytelling. *Smashing Magazine*. Retrieved March 25, 2010, from http://www.smashingmagazine.com /2010/01/29/better-user-experience-using-storytelling-part-one

Insko, B. E. (2001). *Passive Haptics Significantly Enhances Virtual Environments.* Chapel Hill: University of North Carolina.

Ishida, H., & Moriizumi, T. (2003). *Machine olfaction for mobile robots, Handbook of machine Olfaction, T.C. Pearce, S.S. Schiffman, H.T. Nagle, and J.W* (pp. 399–417). Weinheim, Germany: Gardner, Eds., Wiley-VCH.

Ishida, H., Matsukura, H., Yoshida, H., & Nakamoto, T. (2008) Application of computational fluid dynamics simulation to olfactory display, *Proc. Int. Conf. Artificial Reality and Telexistence*, pp.285-288.

Iwata, H. (2008). Design issues in haptic devices. In Lin, M. C., & Otaduy, M. A. (Eds.), *Haptic rendering: Foundations, algorithms, and applications* (pp. 53–66). Wellesley, MA: AK Peters. doi:10.1201/b10636-5

Iwata, H., & Fujii, T. (1996). *Virtual perambulator: A novel interface device for locomotion in virtual environment*. Paper presented at the Virtual Reality Annual International Symposium (VRAIS 96).

Iwata, H., Yano, H., Uemura, T., & Moriya, T. (2003). *Food Simulator*. Paper presented at the International Conference on Artificial Reality and Telexistence 2003.

Jacob, S., Kinnunen, L. H., Metz, J., Cooper, M., & McClintock, M. K. (2001). Sustained human chemosignal unconsciously alters brain function. *Neuroreport*, *12*, 2391–2394. doi:10.1097/00001756-200108080-00021

Jacob, S., & McClintock, M. K. (2000). Psychological state and mood effects of steroidal chemosignals in women and men. *Hormones and Behavior*, *37*, 57–78. doi:10.1006/hbeh.1999.1559

Jansson, G., Juhasz, I., & Cammilton, A. (2005). A virtual map read with a haptic mouse: Effects of some tactile and audio-tactile information options. *Tactile Graphics, 2005,* 49–50.

Jay, C., Stevens, R., Hubbold, R., & Glencross, M. (2008). Using haptic cues to aid non-visual structure recognition. *ACM Transactions on Applied Perception, 5*(2). doi:10.1145/1279920.1279922

Jianbo, S., & Jitendra, M. (2000). Normalized Cuts and Image Segmentation. *IEEE Transactions on Pattern Analysis and Machine Intelligence, 22*(8).

Jochim, S. (2006). CTS: A Motion Company Retrieved 2 March, 2010, from http://customtheatersolutions.biz

Johnston, M., Cohen, P. R., McGee, D., Oviatt, S. H., Pittman, J. A., & Smith, I. (1997). "Unification-based multimodal integration". 35th Annual Meeting of the Association for Computational Linguistics, Madrid, Spain, 281-288.

Jones, C. (2005). Who are you? Theorising from the Experience of Working Through an Avatar. *E-learning, 2*(4), 414–425. doi:10.2304/elea.2005.2.4.414

Jones, L., Bowers, C. A., Washburn, D., Cortes, A., & Satya, R. V. (2004). The Effect of Olfaction on Immersion into Virtual Environments. In *Human Performance, Situation Awareness and Automation: Issues and Considerations for the 21st Century* (pp. 282–285). Lawrence Erlbaum Associates.

Jones R (2004) Comparison of the Use of the Internet by Partially-Sighted and Blind Pupils Placed in a Special School Environment. British Journal of Visual Impairment 22/2/pp. 55-58

Kaklanis, N., Tzovaras, D., & Moustakas, K. (2009). *Haptic navigation in the World Wide Web*. HCI International.

Kaklanis, N., Gonzalez Calleros, J. M., Vanderdonckt, J., & Tzovaras, D. (2008). Hapgets, Towards Haptically-enhanced Widgets based on a User Interface Description Language. *Proc. of Multimodal interaction through haptic feedback (MITH) Workshop*, Naples, May 28-30.

Karshmer, A. I., & Bledsoe, C. (2002). Access to mathematics by blind students—introduction to the special thematic session. *International Conference on Computers Helping People with Special Needs (ICCHP)*, Linz, Austria.

Karshmer, A., & Gillian, D. (2005). Math readers for blind students: errors, frustrations, and the need for a better technique. *Proceedings of the 2005 International Conference on Human-Computer Interaction (HCII).*

Katz, D., & Krueger, L. E. (1989). *The world of touch.* Hillsdale, NJ: L. Erlbaum Associates.

Katz, D. (1946). *How Do Blind People Draw?* Stockholm: Stockholm Kooperitava Bokfoerlag.

Kawai, Y., & Tomita, F. (1996). Interactive tactile display system: a support system for the visually disabled to recognize 3D objects. *In Proceedings of the second annual ACM conference on Assistive technologies*, pages 45-50.

Kaye, J. J. (2004). Making Scents: aromatic output for HCI. *Interaction, 11*(1), 48–61. doi:10.1145/962342.964333

Kaye, J. J. (2004) Making scents, Interactions, Jan.+Feb.,2004, pp. 49-61.

Kaye, J. N. (2001) *Symbolic Olfactory Display*, Master of Science edn, Massachusetts Institute of Technology, Massachusetts, U.S.A. Available: http://www.media.mit.edu/ ~jofish/ thesis/ [Accessed: September 11, 2005].

Keister, L. H. (1994). *"User types and queries: impact on image access systems", Challenges in indexing electronic text and images.* Learned Information.

Keller, P., Kouzes, R., Kangas, L., & Hashem, S. (1995). Transmission of olfactory information in telemedicine. In K. Morgan, R. Satava, H. Sieburg, R. Matteus, & J. Christensen (Eds.), *Interactive technology and the new paradigm for healthcare* (pp. 168-172). Amserdam: IOS.

Kellerman, S. (1988). Lip service: The contribution of the visual modality to speech perception and its relevance to the teaching and testing of foreign language listening comprehension. *Applied Linguistics, 11*(3), 272–280. doi:10.1093/applin/11.3.272

Kendal-Reed, M., Walker, J. C., Morgan, W. T., LaMacchio, M., & Lutz, R. W. (1998). Human responses to propionic acid. I. *Quantification of within- and between-participant variation in perception by normosmics and anosmics. Chemical Senses*, 71–82. doi:10.1093/chemse/23.1.71

Kennedy, J. (1993). *Drawing and the Blind*. New Haven, Connecticut: Yale University Press.

Kennedy, J. M. (1983) What Can We Learn About Pictures from the Blind? American Scientist 71/pp. 19-26

Kennedy, J. M. (1997) How the Blind Draw. Scientific American, 276/1/pp. 60-65

Kennedy, J. M., & Merkas, C. (2000) Depictions of Motion Devised by a Blind Person. Psychonomic Bulletin and Review 7/pp. 700-706

Kiger, P. J., & Smith, M. J. (2006) *Lesson #9 - Beware of Unproven Technologies The Lingering Reek of "Smell-O-Vision"*, HarperCollins. Available: http://www.in70mm.com/ news/ 2006/ oops/ index.htm [Accessed: August 21, 2007].

Kim, H. N. (2010). Usable Accessibility and Haptic User Interface Design Approach, *PhD Dissertation, Blacksburg, Virginia,http://scholar.lib.vt.edu/theses/* available/etd-04152010-092642/unrestricted/ HNKim-Dissertation.pdf.

Kirasic, K. C. (2000). Age differences in adults' spatial abilities, learning environmental layout, and wayfinding behavior. *Spatial Cognition and Computation, 2*, 117–134. doi:10.1023/A:1011445624332

Klatzky, R. L., Loomis, J. M., Beall, A. C., Chance, S. S., & Golledge, R. G. (1998). Spatial updating of self-position and orientation during real, imagined, and virtual locomotion. *Psychological Science, 9*(4), 293–298. doi:10.1111/1467-9280.00058

Knill, D. C., & Richards, W. (1996). *Perception as Bayesian inference*. Cambridge, MA: Cambridge University Press.

Koh, G., Wiegand, T. E., Garnett, R., Durlach, N., & Cunningham, B. S. (1999). Use of Virtual Environments for Acquiring Configurational Knowledge about Specific Real World Spaces. *Preliminary Experiment, 8*(6), 632–656.

Kole, A., Snel, J., & Lorist, M. M. (1998). Caffeine, morning-evening type and coffee odour: Attention, memory search and visual event related potentials. In Snel, J., & Lorist, M. M. (Eds.), *Nicotine, caffeine and social drinking: Behaviour and brain function* (pp. 201–214). Amsterdam: Harwood Academic.

Konyo, M., Tadokoro, S., Yoshida, A., & Saiwaki, N. (2005). A tactile synthesis method using multiple frequency vibrations for representing virtual touch. In *Proceedings of IEEE/RSJ International Conference on Intelligent Robots and Systems* (pp. 3965-3971).

Kortum, P. (2008). *HCI beyond the GUI: Design for haptic, speech, olfactory, and other nontraditional interfaces*. Burlington, MA: Morgan Kaufmann.

Kosko, B., *Il Fuzzy pensiero*, trad.it, Milano, Italy: Baldini&Castoldi

Kostopoulos, K., Moustakas, K., Tzovaras, D., & Nikolakis, G. Thillou, & C., Gosselin, B. (2007), Haptic Access To Conventional 2D Maps For The Visually Impaired. *Journal on Multimodal User Interfaces, Vol. 1, No. 2*.

Kotian, H. P. (2008) India's First Blind Computer Programmer. Downloaded from http://www.esight.org/view.cfm?id=0&room=n&x=65, on the 12th December 2008)

Krashen, S. D. (1987). *Principles and practice in second language acquisition*. New York City, NY: Prentice-Hall International.

Kuipers, B. J. (1975). A frame for frames: Representing knowledge for recognition. In Bobrow, D. G., & Collins, A. (Eds.), *Representation and understanding: Studies in cognitive science*. New York: Academic Press.

Kurze, M. (1997). Interaktion Blinder mit virtuellen Welten auf der Basis von zweidimensionalen taktilen Darstellungen. *In Tagungsband Software-Ergonomie 97*.

Kurze, M. (1999). Methoden zur computergenerierten Darstellung raumlicher Gegenstande fur Blinde auf taktilen Medien. *PhD thesis, Department of mathematics and Computer Science, Freie UniversitÄat Berlin*.

Kutz, M., & Herpers, R. (2008). Urban Traffic Simulation for Games. International Conference on Future of Game Design and Technology, ACM FuturePlay 2008, Toronto, 3.-5.11., pp. 181-185.

Kyritsis M., Gulliver S., (2009). *Guilford Zimmerman Orientation Survey: A Validation*, ICICS 2009.

Lahav, O., & Mioduser, D. (2008). Haptic-feedback support for cognitive mapping of unknown spaces by people who are blind. *International Journal of Human-Computer Studies, 66*, 23–35. doi:10.1016/j.ijhcs.2007.08.001

Lahav, O., & Mioduser, D. (2000). Multisensory virtual environment for supporting blind persons acquisition of spatial cognitive mapping, orientation, and mobility skills. *Proceedings of the Third International Conference on Disability, Virtual Reality and Associated Technologies, ICDVRAT 2000*, pages 23-25.

Lampinen, J., Copeland, S., & Neuschatz, J. (2001). Recollections of things schematic: rooms schemas revisited. *Cognition, 27*, 1211–1222.

Laurel, B. (1995). Virtual reality. *Scientific American, 273*(3), 90.

Laurel, B. (1990). *The Art of Human-Computer Interface Design*. Reading, Massachusetts, USA: Addison-Wesley.

Lavie, N. (2005). Distracted and confused?: Selective attention under load. *Trends in Cognitive Sciences, 9*, 75–82. doi:10.1016/j.tics.2004.12.004

Lawrence, G. H. (1986). Using computers for treatment of psychological problems. *Computers in Human Behavior, 2*(2), 43–62. doi:10.1016/0747-5632(86)90021-X

Lazar, J., Allen, A., Kleinman, J., & Malarkey, C. (2007). What Frustrates Screen Reader Users on the Web: A Study of 100 Blind Users. *International Journal of Human-Computer Interaction, 22*(3), 247–269. doi:10.1080/10447310709336964

Lazar, J., Beere, P., Greenidge, K., & Nagappa, Y. (2003). Web accessibility in the mid-Atlantic United States: a study of 50 home pages. *Univers. Access Inf. Soc., 2*(4), 1–11.

Lee, J.-H., & Spence, C. (2009). Feeling what you hear: Task-irrelevant sounds modulates tactile perception delivered via a touch screen. *Journal of Multisensory User Interfaces, 2*, 145–156. doi:10.1007/s12193-009-0014-8

Lee, D. D., & Seung, H. S. (1999). Learning the parts of objects by non-negative matrix factorization. *Letters to Nature, 401*(21), 788–791.

Lee, J. (1996). *Introduction. "Intelligence and Multimodality in Multimedia Interfaces: Research and Applications". J. e. Lee*. Menlo Park, CA: AAAI Press.

Lee, Y. S. (2005). The Impact of ICT on Library Services for the Visually Impaired. In Fox, E. A., Neuhold, E., Premsmit, P., & Wuwongse, V. (Eds.), *Digital Libraries: Implementing strategies and sharing experiences* (pp. 44–51). Heidelberg: Springer. doi:10.1007/11599517_6

Lee, C. H., & Liu, A. Del_Castillo, S., Bowyer, M., Alverson, D. C., Muniz, G., et al. (2007). Towards an Immersive Virtual Environment for Medical Team Training. In J. D. Westwood, R. S. Haluck, H. M. Hoffman, G. T. Mogel, R. Phillips, R. A. Robb & K. G. Vosburgh (Eds.), *Medicine Meets Virtual Reality 15: in vivo, in vitro, in silico: Designing the Next in Medicine* (Vol. 125, pp. 274-279). Amsterdam: IOS Press.

Lee, J., & Marsella, S. (2006). Nonverbal behaviour generator for embodied conversational agents. In *Proceedings of the Sixth International Conference on Intelligent Virtual Agents*, Marina Del Rey, CA: IVA, 243-255.

Lee, J.-H., & Spence, C. (2008). Assessing the benefits of multimodal feedback on dual-task performance under demanding conditions. In *Proceedings of the 22nd British Computer Society Human-Computer Interaction Group Annual Conference* (pp. 185-192). Liverpool John Moores University, UK, 1-5 September 2008. British Computer Society.

Lee, J.-H., Poliakoff, E., & Spence, C. (2009). The effect of multimodal feedback presented via a touch screen on the performance of older adults. In M. E. Altinsoy, U. Jekosch, & S. Brewster (Eds.), *Lecture Notes in Computer Science (LNCS), 5763*, 128-135.

Lefcowitz, E. (2003) *Sensorama's Pre-Virtual Reality*, Available: http://www.retrofuture.com/ sensorama.html [Accessed: August 23, 2007].

Lehrner, J., Eckersberger, C., Walla, P., Pötsch, G., & Deecke, L. (2000). Ambient odor of orange in a dental office reduces anxiety and improves mood in female patients. *Physiology & Behavior, 71*, 83–86. doi:10.1016/S0031-9384(00)00308-5

Lenggenhager, B., Tadi, T., Metzinger, T., & Blanke, O. (2007). Video ergo sum: Manipulating bodily self-consciousness. *Science, 317*, 1096–1099. doi:10.1126/science.1143439

Levin, D. T., & Simons, D. J. (1997). Failure to detect changes to attended objects in motion pictures. *Psychonomic Bulletin & Review, 4*, 501–506. doi:10.3758/BF03214339

Lévy, P. (1997) *Qu'est-ce que le virtuel? Il Virtuale, it.translation,* Milano,Italy: Raffaello Cortina Editore, Lévy, P., (1992) *Le tecnologie dell'intelligenza,* trad. it, Ed.A/Traverso

Lew, M. S. (2000). Next-generation web searches for visual content. *IEEE Computer., 33*, 46–53.

Li, W., Moallem, I., Paller, K. A., & Gottfried, J. A. (2007). Subliminal smells can guide social preferences. *Psychological Science, 18*, 1044–1049. doi:10.1111/j.1467-9280.2007.02023.x

Li, J., & Wang, J. Z. (2003). Automatic linguistic indexing of pictures by a statistical modelling approach. *IEEE Transactions on Pattern Analysis and Machine Intelligence, 25*(9), 1075–1088. doi:10.1109/TPAMI.2003.1227984

Liffick, B. W. (2003), A haptics experiment in assistive technology for undergraduate HCI students. *HCI International 2003.*

Lin, M.-Y. (2009). United States Patent No. FreshPatents. com: USPTO.

Liu, Y., & Ginther, D. (1999). Cognitive Styles and Distance Education. *Online Journal of Distance Learning Administration, 2*(3).

Loftin, R. B. (2003). Multisensory perception: Beyond the visual in visualization. *Computing in Science & Engineering, 5*(4), 56–58. doi:10.1109/MCISE.2003.1208644

Löken, L. S., Wessberg, J., Morrison, I., McGlone, F., & Olausson, H. (2009). Coding of pleasant touch by unmyelinated afferents in humans. *Nature Neuroscience, 12*, 547–548. doi:10.1038/nn.2312

Loomis, J. M., Fujita, N., Da Silva, J., & Fukusima, S. S. (1992). Visual Space Perception and Visually Directed Action. *Journal of Experimental Psychology. Human Perception and Performance, 18*(4), 906–921. doi:10.1037/0096-1523.18.4.906

Loomis, J. M., Golledge, R. G., & Klatzky, R. L. (1998). Navigation system for the blind: auditory display modes and guidance. *Presence (Cambridge, Mass.), 7*, 193–203. doi:10.1162/105474698565677

Loomis, J. R., Marston, J. R., Golledge, R. G., & Klatzky, R. L. (2005). Personal guidance system for people with visual impairment: a comparison of spatial displays for route guidance. *Journal of Visual Impairment & Blindness, 99*(4), 219–232.

Lorenz, M. (1993). *Object-oriented software development.* Englewood Cliffs, NJ: PTR Prentice Hall.

Löwenfeld, V. (1959). *The Nature of Creative Activity.* London: Routledge and Kegan Paul.

Löwenfeld, V., & Munz, L. (1934). *Sculpture for the Blind.* Vienna: R M Rohrer.

Lowenfeld, B. (1981) Effects of Blindness on the Cognitive Functioning of Children. In Berthold Lowenfeld on Blindness and Blind People: Selected papers. New York: American Federation for the Blind

Luerssen, M. & Lewis, T. (2009). Head X: Tailorable Audiovisual Synthesis for ECAs. *Proceedings of HCSNet Summerfest 2009.*

Luursema, J.-M., Verwey, W. B., Kommers, P. A. M., & Annema, J.-H. (2008). The role of stereopsis in virtual anatomical learning. *Interacting with Computers, 20*(4-5), 455–460. doi:10.1016/j.intcom.2008.04.003

Luursema, J.-M., Verwey, W. B., Kommers, P. A. M., Geelkerken, R. H., & Vos, H. J. (2006). Optimizing conditions for computer-assisted anatomical learning. *Interacting with Computers, 18*, 1123–1138. doi:10.1016/j.intcom.2006.01.005

Lynn, R. (2004). Ins and outs of teledildonics. *Wired.* September 24, 2004. Downloaded 20-03-2010.

MacLean, K. E., Shaver, M. J., & Pai, D. K. (2002). Handheld Haptics: A USB Media Controller with Force Sensing. *Symp. On Haptic Interfaces for Virtual Environment and Teleoperator Systems, IEEE-VR.*

Magnusson, C., & Rassmus-Grohn, K. (2005). A Virtual Traffic Environment for People with Visual Impairments. *Visual Impairment Research, 7*(1), 1–12. doi:10.1080/13882350490907100

Magnusson, C., Rassmus-Grohn, K., Sjostrom, C., & Danielsson, H. (2002). Navigation and recognition in complex haptic virtual environments - reports from an extensive study with blind users. *Proceedings of Eurohaptics.*

Magnusson, C., Tan, C., & Yu, W. (2006). Haptic Access to 3D Objects on the Web. *Proc. Eurohaptics.* MapQuest: http://www.mapquest.com/

Maguire, E. A., Burgess, N., & O'Keefe, J. (1999). Human spatial navigation: cognitive maps, sexual dimorphism, and neural substrates. *Current Opinion in Neurobiology, 9*, 171–177. doi:10.1016/S0959-4388(99)80023-3

Maguire, E. A., Frackowiak, R. S. J., & Frith, C. D. (1996). Recalling Routes around London: Activation of the Right Hippocampus in Taxi Drivers. *The Journal of Neuroscience, 17*(18), 7103–7110.

Maguire, E. A., Gadian, D. G., & Johnsrude, I. S. Good C.D. Ashburner, J. Frackowiak R.S.J., & Frith C.D. (2000). Navigationrelated structural change in the hippocampi of taxi drivers. *Proceedings of the national academy of science* (USA), 97(8)

Makin, T. R., Holmes, N. P., & Ehrsson, H. H. (2008). On the other hand: Dummy hands and peripersonal space. *Behavioural Brain Research, 191*, 1–10. doi:10.1016/j.bbr.2008.02.041

Mamun, A., & Nakamoto, T. (2008). Recipe Estimation Using Mass Spectrometer and Large-scale Data. *IEE of Japan, 128-E*, 467–471. doi:10.1541/ieejsmas.128.467

Manchón, P., Pérez, G., & Amores, G. (2006). *Multimodal Fusion: A New Hybrid Strategy for Dialogue Systems.* In Proceedings of Eighth International Conference on Multimodal Interfaces (ICMI 2006), Banff, Alberta, Canada. ACM: New York, pp. 357-363.

Mania K. Robinson A. & Brandt K.R. (2005). The effect of memory schemas on object recognition in virtual environments. *Presence: Teleoperators and Virtual Environments archive, 14*(5), 606 – 615

Manovich, L. (2001). *The Language of New Media.* Cambridge: MIT Press.

Marescaux, J., Leroy, J., Gagner, M., Rubino, F., Mutter, D., & Vix, M. (2001). Transatlantic robot-assisted telesurgery. *Nature, 413*, 379–380. doi:10.1038/35096636

Markkula, M., & Sormunen, E. (2000). End-user searching challenges indexing practices in the digital newspaper photo archive. *Information Retrieval, 1*, 259–285. doi:10.1023/A:1009995816485

Marsh, T. Smith S. (2001). *Guiding user navigation in virtual environments using awareness of virtual off-screen space.* User Guidance in Virtual Environments: Proceedings of the Workshop on Guiding Users through Interactive Experiences- Usability Centered Design and Evaluation of Virtual 3D Environments. Volker Paelke, Sabine Volbracht(Editors). pg 149-154, Shaker Verlag, Aachen, Germany

Martin, R. L., McAnally, K. I., & Senova, M. A. (2001). Free-field equivalent localization of virtual audio. *Journal of the Audio Engineering Society. Audio Engineering Society, 49*, 14–22.

Martin, J. C. (1997) "Toward Intelligent Cooperation Between Modalities: The Example of a System Enabling Multimodal Interaction with a Map". Proceedings of International Joint Conference on Artificial Intelligence (IJCAI'97) Workshop on "Intelligent Multimodal Systems." Nagoya, Japan.

Massaro, D. W. (2004). From multisensory integration to talking heads and language learning. In Calvert, G., Spence, C., & Stein, E. S. (Eds.), *Handbook of Multisensory Processes* (pp. 153–156). Cambridge, MA: MIT Press.

Mathews, M. H. (1992). *Making Sense of Place: Children's Understanding of Large Scale Environments.* Hertfordshire, England: Harvester Wheatsheaf.

Matsukura, H., Yoshida, H., Nakamoto, T., & Ishida, H. (2010). Synchronized presentation of odor with airflow using olfactory display. *Journal of Mechanical Science and Technology*, 24, 253–256. doi:10.1007/s12206-009-1178-6

Matsukura, H., & Ishida, H. (2009). Olfactory display: Fluid dynamics considerations for realistic odor presentation, In *Proc. Joint Virtual Reality Conference of EGVE - ICAT* – EuroVR, pp.61-64.

Matsukura, H., Ohno, A., & Ishida, H. (2010). On the effect of airflow on odor presentation, In *Proc. IEEE Virtual Reality*, pp.287-288.

Matsukura, H., Yoshida, H., Ishida, H., & Nakamoto, T. (2009) Interactive odor playback based on fluid dynamics simultation, In *Proc. IEEE Virtual Reality 2009*, pp.255-256.

McClintock, M. K. (1971). Menstrual synchrony and suppression. *Nature*, 229, 244–245. doi:10.1038/229244a0

McLuhan, M. (1964). *Understanding Media: The extension of Man*. Toronto: McGraw Hill.

McMahan, A. (2003). Immersion, Engagement, and Presence: A Method for Analyzing 3-D Video games. In Wolf, M. J. P., & Perron, B. (Eds.), *The Video Game Theory Reader* (pp. 67–86). New York: Routledge.

Mcmullin, B. (2002). Users with disability need not apply? Web accessibility in Ireland. *First Monday, http://www.firstmonday.org* /issues/issue7_12/mcmullin/

Meehan, M., Insko, B., Whitton, M., & Brooks, F. (2001). *Objective measures of presence in virtual environments*, Presence 2001, 4th International Workshop, May 21-23, http://www.temple.edu/presence2001 / conf-format&schd.htm, paper can be found on http:/ / www. cs. unc.edu/-meehan/presence2000 /MeehanPresence2000.htm

Mehrabian, A. (1967). Attitudes inferred from nonimmediacy of verbal communication. *Journal of Verbal Learning and Verbal Behavior*, 6, 294–295. doi:10.1016/ S0022-5371(67)80113-0

Meredith, M. (2001). Human vomeronasal organ function: A critical review of best and worst cases. *Chemical Senses*, 26, 433–445. doi:10.1093/chemse/26.4.433

Messager, J. (2002). *The diffusion of fragrances in a multimedia environment, 3rd Aroma Science Forum*, Sep 13 2002, Tokyo, pp. 2-7 (in Japanese).

Messick, S. (1976). *Individuality in learning*. San Francisco: Jossey-Bass.

Messick, S. (1994). The Matter of Style: Manifestations of Personality in Cognition. Learning, and Teaching. *Educational Psychologist*, 29(3), 121–136. doi:10.1207/ s15326985ep2903_2

Meulenkamp, W. (n.d.). Osmooze Perfume Distribution Solution Retrieved 3 March, 2010, from http://www.osmooze.com

Miller, G. A. (1956). The magical number seven, plus or minus two: Some limits on our capacity for processing information. *Psychological Review*, 63, 81–97. doi:10.1037/h0043158

Milne, M., Leibbrandt, R., Lewis, T., Luerssen, M., & Powers, D. M. W. (2010). Development of a Virtual Agent Based Social Tutor for Children with Autism Spectrum Disorders. In *Proceedings of the 23rd International Joint Conference on Neural Networks*, in press

Mine, M. R. (1995). *Virtual Environment Interaction Techniques*. Chapel Hill: University of North Carolina.

Mine, M. R. (1997). *Exploiting Proprioception in Virtual-Environment Interaction*. Chapel Hill: University of North Carolina.

Mine, M. R., Brooks, F. P., Jr., & Sequin, C. H. (1997). *Moving objects in space: exploiting proprioception in virtual-environment interaction*. Paper presented at the 24th Annual International Conference on Computer Graphics and Interactive Techniques, Los Angeles.

Minogue, J., & Jones, M. G. (2006). Haptics in Education: Exploring an Untapped Sensory Modality. *Review of Educational Research*, 76, 317–348. doi:10.3102/00346543076003317

Mochizuki, A., Amada, T., Sawa, S., Takeda, T., Motoyashiki, S., & Kohyama, K. (2004). *Fragra: A Visual-Olfactory VR Game*. ACM SIGGRAPH, Sketches.

Moffat, S. D., Hampson, E., & Hatzipantelis, M. (1998). Navigation in a "virtual" maze: sex differences and correlation with psychometric measures of spatial ability in humans. *Evolution and Human Behavior*, *19*, 73–78. doi:10.1016/S1090-5138(97)00104-9

Montagu, A. (1971). *Touching: The human significance of the skin*. New York: Columbia University Press.

Montello, D. R. (2005) Navigation. In P. Shah & A. Miyake (Eds.), *The Cambridge Handbook of Visuospatial Thinking*. Cambridge University Press, 257-294.

Moore, K., Wiederhold, B. K., Wiederhold, M. D., & Riva, G. (2002). Panic and Agoraphobia in a Virtual World. *Cyberpsychology & Behavior*, *5*(3), 197–202. doi:10.1089/109493102760147178

Morhenn, V. B., Park, J. W., Piper, E., & Zak, P. J. (2008). Monetary sacrifice among strangers is mediated by endogenous oxytocin release after physical contact. *Evolution and Human Behavior*, *29*, 375–383. doi:10.1016/j.evolhumbehav.2008.04.004

Mori, Y. Takahashi, H. and Oka, R. (1999) "Image-to-word transformation based on dividing and vector quantizing images with words". In MISRM'99 First Int. Workshop on Multimedia Intelligent Storage and Retrieval Management.

Morie, J. F., Iyer, K., Valanejad, K., Sadek, R., Miraglia, D., Milam, D., et al. (2003). *Sensory design for virtual environments*. SIGGRAPH 2003 Sketch, July, 2003; www.ict.usc.edu/publications /SensDesign4VE.pdf

Morris, D. & Joshi, N. (2003). Alternative 'Vision': A Haptic and Auditory Assistive Device. *CHI 2003 Extended Abstracts.*

Morrot, G., Brochet, F., & Dubourdieu, D. (2001). The color of odors. *Brain and Language*, *79*, 309–320. doi:10.1006/brln.2001.2493

Moseley, G. L., Gallace, A., & Spence, C. (2008). Is mirror therapy all it is cracked up to be? Current evidence and future directions. *Pain*, *138*, 7–10. doi:10.1016/j.pain.2008.06.026

Moseley, G. L., Gallace, A., & Spence, C. (in press). Bodily illusion in health and disease: physiological and clinical perspectives and the concept of a cortical body matrix. *Neuroscience and Biobehavioral Reviews.*

Moseley, G. L., Olthof, N., Venema, A., Don, S., Wijers, M., Gallace, A., & Spence, C. (2008). Psychologically induced cooling of a specific body part caused by the illusory ownership of an artificial counterpart. *Proceedings of the National Academy of Sciences of the United States of America*, *105*, 13168–13172. doi:10.1073/pnas.0803768105

Moustakas, K., Nikolakis, G., Kostopoulos, K., Tzovaras, D., & Strintzis, M. G. (2007). Haptic Rendering of Visual Data for the Visually Impaired. *IEEE Multimedia Magazine*, *14*(1), 62–72. doi:10.1109/MMUL.2007.10

Moustakas, K., Tzovaras, D., Dybkjaer, L., & Bernsen, N. O. (2009). *A Modality Replacement Framework for the Communication between Blind and Hearing Impaired People*. HCI International.

Moustakas, K., Tzovaras, D., & Strintzis, M. G. (2007). SQ-Map: Efficient Layered Collision Detection and Haptic Rendering. *IEEE Transactions on Visualization and Computer Graphics*, *13*(1), 80–93. doi:10.1109/TVCG.2007.20

Mozeika, A., Steltz, E., & Jaeger, H. M. (2009). The first steps of a robot based on jamming skin enabled locomotion. In *Proceedings of IEEE/RSJ International Conference on Intelligent Robots and Systems* (pp. 408-409).

Mura, G. (2006). *The red and black semantics: a fuzzy language in Visual Computer, n.23* (pp. 359–368). Berlin, Germany: Springer.

Mura, G. (2009). *Cyberworld Cybernetic Art Model for Shared Communications in CyberWorlds 2009, Bradford University*. UK: IEEE.

Mura, G. (Ed.). (2010). *Metaplasticity in Virtual Worlds: Aesthetics and Semantics Concepts*. USA: IGI-Global Publishing. doi:10.4018/978-1-60960-077-8

Mura, G. (2005) *Virtual Space Model for Industrial Design,* Unpublished doctoral dissertation, Politecnico di Milano University, Italy

Mura, G. (2006) Conceptual artwork model for virtual environments in *JCIS journal* (ISSN 1553-9105), Vol.3, n.2, pp.461-465, BinaryInfoPress

Mura, G. (2007) The Metaplastic Virtual Space in Wyeld, T.G., Kenderdine, S., Docherty, M. (Eds) *Virtual Systems and Multimedia* (pp. 166-178), Berlin, Germany: Springer

Mura, G. (2008) The meta-plastic cyberspace:a network of semantic virtual worlds in *ICIWI 2008* WWW/Internet International Conference, Freiburg, IADIS

Mura, G. (2008) The Metaplastic Constructor in *CAC 2 Computer Art*, Paris: ed. Europia

Murphy, E., Kuber, R., McAllister, G., Strain, P. & Yu, W. (2008). An Empirical Investigation into the Difficulties Experienced by Visually Impaired Internet Users. *Journal of Universal Access in the Information Society*.

Murray, C. D., Patchick, E., Pettifer, S., Caillette, F., & Howard, T. (2006). Immersive virtual reality as a rehabilitative technology for phantom limb experience. *Cyberpsychology & Behavior*, *9*, 167–170. doi:10.1089/cpb.2006.9.167

Murray, C. D., Pettifer, S., Howard, T., Patchick, E., Caillette, F., Kulkarni, J., & Bamford, C. (2007). The treatment of phantom limb pain using immersive virtual reality: Three case studies. *Disability and Rehabilitation*, *29*, 1465–1469. doi:10.1080/09638280601107385

Nakaizumi, F., Yanagida, Y., Noma, H., & Hosaka, K. (2006). *SpotScents: A novel method of natural scent delivery using multiple scent projectors*, Proc. IEEE Virtual Reality 2006, pp. 207-212.

Nakamoto, T. (2005). Odor recorder. *Sensor Letters*, *3*, 136–150. doi:10.1166/sl.2005.018

Nakamoto, T., & Ishida, H. (2008). Chemical sensing in spatial/temporal domains. *Chemical Reviews*, *108*, 680–704. doi:10.1021/cr068117e

Nakamoto, T., Nakahira, Y., Hiramatsu, H., & Moriizumi, T. (2001). Odor recorder using active odor sensing system. *Sensors and Actuators. B, Chemical*, *76*, 465–469. doi:10.1016/S0925-4005(01)00587-1

Nakamoto, T., Otaguro, S., Kinoshita, M., Nagahama, M., Ohnishi, K., & Ishida, T. (2008). Cooking up an interactive olfactory game display. *IEEE Computer Graphics and Applications*, *28*, 75–78. doi:10.1109/MCG.2008.3

Nakamoto, T., Takigawa, H., & Yamanaka, T. (2004). *Fundamental study of odor recorder using inkjet devices for low-volatile scents*, Trans. on IEICE, 2004. *E (Norwalk, Conn.)*, *87-C*, 2081–2086.

Nakamoto, T., Utsumi, S., Yamashita, N., & Moriizumi, T. (1994). Active gas sensing system using automatically controlled gas blender and numerical optimization technique. *Sensors and Actuators. B, Chemical*, *20*, 131. doi:10.1016/0925-4005(93)01193-8

Nakamoto, T., & Yoshikawa, K. (2006). Movie with scents generated by olfactory display using solenoid valves, *IEICE, Vol. E (Norwalk, Conn.)*, *89-A*(11), 3327–3332.

Nakamoto, T. (2005b). Record of dynamic changes of odors using an odor recorder. *Sensors and Materials*, *17*(7), 365–383.

Nakamoto, T. (Ed.). (2008). *Olfactory display, Fragrance Journal Ltd*, 2008 (in Japanese).

Nakamoto, T., & Minh, P. D. (2009). Improvement of olfactory display using solenoid valves, *Proc. IEEE Virtual Reality* 2009, pp.179-186.

Nakamoto, T., & Moriizumi, T. (1988) Odor sensor using quartz-resonator array and neural-network pattern recognition, In *Proc. IEEE Ultrason. Symp.*, pp.613-616.

Nakamoto, T., & Murakami, K. (2009) Selection method of odor components for olfactory display using mass spectrum database, In *Proc. IEEE Virtual Reality 2009*, pp. 159-162.

Nakamoto, T., Nimsuk, N., Wyszynski, B., Takushima, H., Kinoshita, M., & Cho, N. (2008). *Experiment on Teleolfaction Using Odor Sensing System and Olfactory Display Synchronous with Visual Information, ICAT* (International Conference on Artificial Reality and Tel-existence), pp. 85-92.

Nakano, Y., Ouwa, H., Kawashima, K., Komura, H., Sagano, M., Shirazawa, T., et al. Chihara, K. (2006). INVISIBLE: the shadow chaser. In *ACM SIGGRAPH 2006 Emerging Technologies* (Article No. 19).

Nambu, A., Narumi, T., Nishimura, K., Tanikawa, T., & Hirose, M. (2010) Visual-Olfactory Display Using Olfactory Sensory Map, *Proc. IEEE Virtual Reality* 2010, pp. 39-42.

Narumi, T., Hiyama, A., Tanikawa, T., & Hirose, M. (2007). Inter-glow. In *ACM SIGGRAPH 2007 Emerging Technologies* (Article No. 14).

Navarre, D., Palanque, P., Bastide, R., Schyn, A., Winckler, M., Nedel, L. P., et al. (2005). *A Formal Description of Multimodal Interaction Techniques for Immersive Virtual Reality Applications*. Paper presented at the Tenth IFIP TC13 International Conference on Human-Computer Interaction.

Nelson, T. (1974). *Computer lib/dream machines*. Self-published.

Nelson, K. (1998). *Language in cognitive development: The emergence of the mediated mind*. New York City, NY: Cambridge University Press.

Nelson, T. H. (1965). *A File Structure for the Complex, The Changing and the Indeterminate*. New York, Cambridge, MA, USA: MIT Press.

Newman, W., & Sproul, R. F. (1987). *Computer Graphics principles*. New York, USA: McGraw Hill.

News, A. B. C. (1999). *Smell-O-Vision Coming to Internet Soon*. Available: http://www.temple.edu/ ispr/ examples/ ex99_10_20.html [Accessed: August 21, 2007].

Niederhoffer, K. G., & Pennebaker, J. W. (2002). Linguistic style matching in social interaction. *Journal of Language and Social Psychology*, *21*, 337–360. doi:10.1177/026192702237953

Nigay, L., & Coutaz, J. (1995). "A generic platform for addressing the multimodal challenge". International Conference on Computer-Human Interaction, ACM Press, 98-105.

Nikolakis, G., Moustakas, K., Tzovaras, D., & Strintzis, M. G. (2005). *Haptic Representation of Images for the Blind and the Visually Impaired*. Las Vegas: HCI International.

Nikolakis, G., Tsampoulatidis, I., Tzovaras, D., & Strintzis, G. (2004). Haptic Browser: A Haptic Environment to Access HTML pages. *SPECOM 2004*.

Nivala, A. M., Brewster, S. A., & Sarjakoski, L. T. (2008). Usability Evaluation of Web Mapping Sites. *The Cartographic Journal. Use and Users Special Issue*, *45*(2), 129–138.

Nivala, A. M., Sarjakoski, L. T., & Sarjakoski, T. (2007). Usability methods' familiarity among map application developers. *IJHCS, Int. J. Human-Computer Studies, Elsevier*, *65*, 784–795. doi:10.1016/j.ijhcs.2007.04.002

Nivala, A. M., & Sarjakoski, L. T. (2003). Need for Context-Aware Topographic Maps in Mobile Devices. In Virrantaus, K., & Tveite, H. (Eds.), *ScanGIS'2003*. Espoo, Finland.

Nivala, A. M., Sarjakoski, L. T., Jakobsson, A., & Kaasinen, E. (2003). Usability Evaluation of Topographic Maps in Mobile Devices. *21st International Cartographic Conference*, Durban, South Africa.

Nordworthy, S. R., Scheier, R., & Temes, G. C. (1997). *Delta-sigma data converter* (pp. 206–222). IEEE Press.

Nowak, K. L., & Biocca, F. (2004). The Effect of the Agency and Anthropomorphism on Users' Sense of Telepresence, Copresence, and Social Presence in Virtual Environments. *Presence (Cambridge, Mass.)*, *12*(5), 481–494. doi:10.1162/105474603322761289

O'Malley, C., & Fraser, D. S. (2004) *Literature review in learning with tangible technologies*. Bristol, UK: Futurelab, Report 12.

O'Malley, M., & Hughes, S. (2003). Simplified Authoring of 3D Haptic Content for the World Wide Web. *Proceedings of 11th International Symposium on Haptic Interfaces for Virtual Environment and Teleoperator Systems*, pp. 428-429, Los Angeles, California, USA, 22-23 March 2003. OpenStreetMap: http://www.openstreetmap.org/

Olausson, H. (2008). Functional role of unmyelinated tactile afferents in human hairy skin: Sympathetic response and perceptual localization. *Experimental Brain Research*, *184*, 135–140. doi:10.1007/s00221-007-1175-x

Onyesolu, M. O. (2009). Virtual reality laboratories: An ideal solution to the problems facing laboratory setup and management. In *Proceedings of the World Congress on Engineering and Computer Science*. San Francisco, CA, USA, 20-22 October, 2009.

O'Regan, J. K. (1992). Solving the "real" mysteries of visual perception: The world as an outside memory. *Canadian Journal of Psychology*, *46*, 461–488. doi:10.1037/h0084327

Ornager, S. (1996). View a picture: Theoretical image analysis and empirical user studies on indexing and retrieval. *Swedish Library Research*, *2*(3), 31–41.

Orne, M. T. (1962). On the social psychology of the psychological experiment: With particular reference to demand characteristics and their implications. *The American Psychologist, 17*, 776–783. doi:10.1037/h0043424

Paciello, M. (2000). *Web accessibility for people with disabilities*. Lawrence, KS: CMP Books.

Paek, S., Sable, C. L., Hatzivassiloglou, V., Jaimes, A., Schiffman, B. H., Chang, S.-F., & McKeown, K. R. (1999) "Integration of visual and text based approaches for the content labelling and classification of Photographs", ACM SIGIR'99 Workshop on Multimedia Indexing and Retrieval, Berkeley, CA.

Papert, S. (1980). *Mindstorms: Children, computers, and powerful ideas*. New York City, NY: Basic Books, Inc.

Parente, P., & Bishop, G. (2003). *BATS: The Blind Audio Tactile Mapping System*. Savannah, GA: ACMSE.

Parente, P. (2004) Audio Enriched Links: Web page previews for blind users. Proceedings of the 6th international ACM SIGACCESS conference on Computers and accessibility 2004, Atlanta, GA, USA October 2004 pp. 2-8

Parker, S. P. (Ed.). (2002). *McGraw-Hill Dictionary of Scientific & Technical Terms*. New York, NJ, USA: McGraw-Hill.

Parks, J. R. (2006, September). Hold on to your CTS. *A2Z Magazine, September*.

Pask, G. (1979). *Final report of S.S.R.C. Research programme HR 2708*. Richmond (Surrey): System Research Ltd.

Pasquero, J., Luk, J., Little, S., & MacLean, K. (2006). Perceptual Analysis of Haptic Icons: an Investigation into the Validity of Cluster Sorted MDS, *Proceedings of the Symposium on Haptic Interfaces for Virtual Environment and Teleoperator Systems*, p.67.

Pass, F., & Renkl A. Sweller, J. (2003). Cognitive Load Theory and Instructional Design: Recent Developments. *Educational Psychologist, 38*(1), 1–4. doi:10.1207/S15326985EP3801_1

Paulson, W. R. (1987). *Enlightenment, Romanticism and the Blind in France*. Princeton, NJ: Princeton University Press.

Pearce, T. C., Schiffman, S. S., Nagle, H. T., & Gardner, J. W. (Eds.). (2003). *Handbook of machine olfaction*. New York: Wiley-VCH.

Pearson, E., & Bailey, C. (2007). *Evaluating the potential of the Nintendo Wii to support disabled students in education*. Paper presented at the ICT: providing choices for learners and learning. ascilite. from http://www.ascilite.org.au/ conferences/singapore07/procs/ pearson-poster.pdf

Peck, J., & Childers, T. L. (2003a). Individual differences in haptic information processing: The "Need for Touch" scale. *The Journal of Consumer Research, 30*, 430–442. doi:10.1086/378619

Pelagatti, G., Negri, M., Belussi, A., & Migliorini, S. (2009). From the conceptual design of spatial constraints to their implementation in real systems. In *Proceedings of the 17th ACM SIGSPATIAL international Conference on Advances in Geographic information Systems* (Seattle, Washington, November 04 - 06, 2009). GIS '09. ACM, New York, NY, 448-451.

PERCO. (2002). The Museum of Pure Form Retrieved 6th June, 2009, from http://www.pureform.org

Perrot, X., & Mura, G. (2005) VR Workshop 2005 "Virtuality in Arts and Design" Virtual Exhibition Projects, Archives&Museum Informatics, from http://www.archimuse.com/ publishing/ ichim_05.html

Persaud, K. C., & Dodd, G. (1982). Analysis of discrimination mechanisms in the mammalian olfactory system using a model nose. *Nature, 299*, 352. doi:10.1038/299352a0

Pesce, M. (2010, 21 February). Keep doing that and you'll go blind. Weblog posted to http://www.abc.net.au/unleashed/ stories/s2813511.htm.

Petersen, A. C., & Linn, M. A. (1985). Emergence and characterization of sex differences in spatial ability. *Child Development, 56*, 1479–1498. doi:10.2307/1130467

Petkova, V. I., & Ehrsson, H. H. (2008). If I were you: Perceptual illusion of body swapping. *PLoS ONE, 3*(12), e3832. doi:10.1371/journal.pone.0003832

Petrie, H., Fisher, W., O'Neill, A., Fisher, W., & Di Segni, Y. (2001). Deliverable 2.1: Report on user requirements of mainstream readers and print disabled readers. *Available: http://www.multireader.org* /workplan.htm.

Petrie, H., Morley, S., Mcnally, P., O'Neill, A. M., & Majoe, D. (1997). Initial design and evaluation of an interface to hypermedia systems for blind users. *In: Bernstein, M., Carr, L., Osterbye, K. (eds.) Proceedings of the Eighth ACM Conference On Hypertext*, pp. 48–56. ACM Press, Southampton, UK, April 6–11.

Piaget, J. (1999). The Stages of the Intellectual Development of the Child. In Slater, A., & Muir, D. (Eds.), *The Blackwell Reader in Developmental Psychology* (pp. 35–42). Oxford: Blackwell Publishing.

Picubino system, from http://www.picubino.com

Pine, D. S., Grun, J., Maguire, E. A., Burgess, N., Zarahn, E., & Koda, V. (2002). Neurodevelopmental Aspects of Spatial Navigation: A Virtual Reality fMRI Study. *NeuroImage, 15*, 396–406. doi:10.1006/nimg.2001.0988

Plamondon, R. (2000). On-line and offline handwriting recognition: A comprehensive survey. *IEEE Transactions on Pattern Analysis and Machine Intelligence, 22*(1), 63–84. doi:10.1109/34.824821

Plimmer, B., Crossan, A., Brewster, S. A., & Blagojevic, R. (2008). Multimodal collaborative handwriting training for visually-impaired people. *Proceeding of the twenty-sixth annual SIGCHI conference on Human factors in computing systems*, 393-402.

Poggi, I., Pelachaud, C., De Rosis, F., Carofiglio, V., & De Carolis, B. (2005). Building expression into virtual characters. In Stock, O., & Zancanaro, M. (Eds.), *Multimodal Intelligent Information Presentation* (pp. 3–25). Netherlands: Springer. doi:10.1007/1-4020-3051-7_1

Popper, K. R., & Eccles, J. C. (1977). *The self and its brain*. New York, USA: Springer International.

Posner, M. I., Nissen, M. J., & Klein, R. M. (1976). Visual dominance: An information-processing account of its origins and significance. *Psychological Review, 83*, 157–171. doi:10.1037/0033-295X.83.2.157

Powers, D. M. (2007). A multimodal environment for immersive language learning - space, time, viewpoint and physics. In *Proc. Joint HCSNet-HxI Workshop on Human Issues in Interaction and Interactive Interfaces*. Sydney, Australia: HCSNet.

Powers, D. M. W., Leibbrandt, R., Pfitzner, D., Luerssen, M., Lewis, T., Abrahamyan, A., & Stevens, K. (2008). Language teaching in a mixed reality games environment. In F. Makedon, L. Baillie, G. Pantziou, and I. Magliogiannis (Eds.) *Proceedings of the 1st International Conference on Pervasive Technologies Related to Assistive Environments, PETRA '8*, Vol. 282. New York City, NY: ACM.

Priplata, A. A., Niemi, J. B., Harry, J. D., Lipsitz, L. A., & Collins, J. J. (2009). Vibrating insoles and balance control in elderly people. *Lancet, 362*.

Proctor, R. W., & Vu, K. P. L. (2005). *Handbook of human factors in Web design*. London: Lawrence Erlbaum Associates.

Pun, T., Roth, P., Bologna, G., Moustakas, K., & Tzovaras, D. (2007). Image and video processing for visually handicapped people, *Eurasip International Journal on Image and Video Processing, volume 2007*, article ID 25214.

Questler, H. (1956). Studies of human channel capacity. In Cherry, C. (Ed.), *Information theory: Papers read at a symposium on 'information theory' held at the Royal Institution, London, September 12th to 16th 1955* (pp. 361–371). London: Butterworths Scientific Publications.

Rafaeli, S. (1988), Interactivity:from new media to communication,Beverly Hills,CA

Ramloll, R., Yu, W., Brewster, S., Riedel, B., Burton, M., & Dimigen, G. (2000). Constructing sonified haptic line graphs for the blind student: First steps, *ACM conference on Assistive technologies*, (Arlington, USA).

Raudenbush, B., Corley, N., & Eppich, W. (2001). Enhancing athletic performance through the administration of peppermint odor. *Journal of Sport & Exercise Psychology, 23*, 156–160.

Ray, B., & Seely, C. (1997). *Fluency through TPR Storytelling: Achieving real language acquisition in school*. Berkeley: Command Performance Language Institute.

Reeves, B., & Nass, C. (2002). *The Media Equation: How People Treat Computers, Television, and New Media Like Real People and Places*. Stanford: CSLI Publications.

Rheingold, H. (1991). *Virtual Reality*. London, UK: Secker&Warburg Limited.

Ribiero, C. R., Costa, M. F. M., & Pereira-Coutinho, C. (2009). Robotics in child storytelling. In Costa, M.F.M. (*Eds.*) *Science for all, quest for excellence: Proceedings of the Sixth International Conference on Hands-on Science.* Ahmedabad, India, 198-205

Riccobono M A (2004) A Brighter Future for Blind Children. Braille Monitor, February 2004

Richard, E., Tijou, A., Richard, P., & Ferrier, J.-L. (2006). Multi-modal virtual environments for education with haptic and olfactory feedback. *Virtual Reality (Waltham Cross), 10*(3/4), 207–225. doi:10.1007/s10055-006-0040-8

Riding, R. J. (1991). *Cognitive styles analysis.* Birmingham, UK: Learning and Training Technology.

Riding, R. J., & Grimley, M. (1999). Cognitive Style, Gender and Learning from Multi-media. *British Journal of Educational Technology, 30*(1), 43–56. doi:10.1111/1467-8535.00089

Rieser, J. J. (1989). Access to knowledge of spatial structure at noval points of observation. *Journal of Experimental Psychology. Learning, Memory, and Cognition, 15*(6), 1157–1165. doi:10.1037/0278-7393.15.6.1157

Riva, G., & Gambrini, L. (2000). Virtual reality in telemedicine. *Telemedicine Journal, 6*, 327–340. doi:10.1089/153056200750040183

Robertson, I. T. (1985). Human information processing strategies and style. *Behaviour & Information Technology, 4*(1), 19–29. doi:10.1080/01449298508901784

Robertson, G. G., Czerwinski, M., Larson, K., Robbins, D., Thiel, D., & Van Dantzich, M. (1998). Data mountain: using spatial memory for document management. *Proceedings of UIST '98, 11th Annual Symposium on User Interface Software and Technology, 153,* 162.

Robertson, G., Czerwinski, M., & van Dantzich, M. (1997). *Immersion in Desktop Virtual Reality.* Paper presented at the 10th annual ACM symposium on User interface software and technology Banff, Alberta.

Robertson, J., de Quincey, A., Stapleford, T., & Wiggins, G. (1998). *Real-Time Music Generation for a Virtual Environment.* Paper presented at the ECAI98 workshop on AI/Alife and Entertainment.

Robinett, W. (1992). Comments on "A nose gesture interface device: Extending virtual realities". *Presence (Cambridge, Mass.), 1,* 493.

Robson, C. (2002). *Real World Research: A resource for social scientists and practioner-researchers.* Oxford: Blackwell Publishing.

Rotard, M., Knodler, S., & Ertl, T. (2005). A Tactile Web Browser for the Visually Disabled. *Proc Hypertext and Hypermedia*, ACM Press, 5-22.

Rotard, M., Taras, C., & Ertl, T. (2008). Tactile Web Browsing for Blind People. *In Multimedia Tools and Applications*, Springer, Vol. 37(1):53-69.

Roth, P. & Pun, T. (2003). Design and Evaluation of a Multimodal System for the Non-Visual Exploration of Digital Pictures. *In proceedings of Interact '03.*

Roth, P., Petrucci, L., Assimacopoulos, A., & Pun, T. (2000). From dots to shapes: An auditory haptic game platform for teaching geometry to blind pupils. *ICCHP 2000, International Conference on Computer Helping People with Speical Needs, Karlsruhe, Germany,* 603-610.

Roth, P., Petrucci, L. S., Assimacopoulos, A., & Pun, T. (2000). Audio-Haptic Internet Browser And Associated Tools For Blind And Visually Impaired Computer Users. *In Workshop on Friendly Exchanging Through the Net,* 57-62.

Rothbaum, B. O., Hodges, L. F., Kooper, R., Opdyke, D., Williford, J., & North, M. M. (1995). Effectiveness of virtual reality graded exposure in the treatment of acrophobia. *The American Journal of Psychiatry, 152,* 626–628.

Roy, D. (1999). *Learning words from sights and sounds: A computational model.* Dissertation, Massachusetts Institute of Technology.

Ruddle, R. A., & Péruch, P. (2004). Effects of proprioceptive feedback and environmental characteristics on spatial learning in virtual environments. *International Journal of Human-Computer Studies, 60,* 299–326. doi:10.1016/j.ijhcs.2003.10.001

Rui, Y., Huang, T. S., & Chang, S. F. (1998). *Image Retrieval: current techniques, promising directions and open issues.* Dept. of ECE & Bechman Institute University of Illinois at Urbana-Champaign Urbana, Dept. of EE & New Media Technology Centre Columbia University New York.

Rui, Y., Huang, T., Mehrotra, S., & Ortega, M. (1997) "A relevance feedback architecture in content-based multimedia information retrieval systems", In Proc of IEEE Workshop on Content-based Access of Image and Video Libraries.

Sadowski, W., & Stanney, K. (2002). Presence in Virtual Environments. In Stanney, K. M. (Ed.), *Handbook of Virtual Environments: Design, implementation, and applications* (pp. 791–806). Mahwah: Lawrence Erlbaum Associates Publishers.

Saga, S., & Deguchi, K. (2010). Dilatant fluid based tactile display -Basic concept. In *Proceedings of IEEE Haptics Symposium* (pp. 309-312).

Salembier, P., Oliveras, A., & Garrido, L. (1998). Anti-extensive connected operators for image and sequence processing. *IEEE Transactions on Image Processing, 7*, 555–570. doi:10.1109/83.663500

Sallnas, E., Rassmus-Grohn, K., & Sjostrom, C. (2000). *Supporting presence in collaborative environments by haptic force feedback. ACM Transactions on Computer-Human Interaction (TOCHI)*. New York: ACM Press.

Salmon, G. (2009). The future for (second) life and learning. *British Journal of Educational Technology, 40*(3), 526–538. doi:10.1111/j.1467-8535.2009.00967.x

Salthouse, T., Donald, K., & Saults, S. (1990). Age, Self Assessed Health Status and Cognition. *Journal of Gerontology, 45*(4), 156–160.

Sanchez, J., & Lumbreras, M. (1999). Virtual environment interaction through 3D audio by blind children. *Journal of Cyberpsychology and Behavior, 2*(2), 101–111. doi:10.1089/cpb.1999.2.101

Sanders, R. L., & McKeown, L. (2008). Promoting Reflection through Action Learning in a 3D Virtual World. *International Journal of Social Sciences, 2*(1), 50–55.

Sandstrome, N. J., Kaufman, J., & Huettel, S. A. (1998). Males and females use different distal cues in a virtual environment navigation task. *Brain Research. Cognitive Brain Research, 6*, 351–360. doi:10.1016/S0926-6410(98)00002-0

Sarjakoski, L. T., & Sarjakoski, T. (2008). *User Interfaces and Adaptive Maps. Encyclopedia of GIS* (pp. 1205–1212). Springer.

Sarjakoski, T., & Sarjakoski, L. T. (2007). A Real-Time Generalisation and Map Adaptation Approach for Location-Based Services. In Mackaness, W. A., Ruas, A., & Sarjakoski, L. T. (Eds.), *Generalisation of Geographic Information: Cartographic Modelling and Applications, Series of International Cartographic Association* (pp. 137–159). Elsevier.

Sarjakoski, L. T., & Nivala, A. M. (2005). Adaptation to Context - A Way to Improve the Usability of Mobile Maps. In Meng, L., Zipf, A., & Reichenbacher, T. (Eds.), *Mapbased mobile services - Theories, Methods and Implementations* (pp. 107–123). Springer Berlin Heidelberg New York.

Sarter, N. B. (2006). Multimodal information presentation: Design guidance and research challenges. *International Journal of Industrial Ergonomics, 36*(5), 439–445. doi:10.1016/j.ergon.2006.01.007

Sathian, K. (2005). Visual cortical activity during tactile perception in the sighted and the visually deprived. *Developmental Psychobiology, 46*, 279–286. doi:10.1002/dev.20056

Sato, J., Ohtsu, K., Bannai, Y., & Okada, K. (2009) Effective Presentation Technique of Scent Using Small Ejection Quantities of Odor, In *Proc. IEEE Virtual Reality 2009*, pp.151-158.

Sato, K., Sato, Y., Sato, M., Fukushima, S., Okano, Y., Matsuo, K., et al. Kajimoto, H. (2008). Ants in the Pants. In *ACM SIGGRAPH 2008 New Tech Demos* (Article No. 3).

Scalable Vector Graphics (SVG) 1.1 (2003) *Specification W3C Recommendation*.

Schaefer, M., Heinze, H.-J., & Rotte, M. (2009). My third arm: Shifts in topography of the somatosensory homunculus predict feeling of an artificial supernumerary arm. *Human Brain Mapping, 30*, 1413–1420. doi:10.1002/hbm.20609

Schlosser, A. E. (2003). Experiencing Products in the Virtual World: The Role of Goal and Imagery in Influencing Attitudes versus Purchase Intentions. *The Journal of Consumer Research, 30*(2), 184–198. doi:10.1086/376807

Schmeck R.R (1988). Learning strategies and learning styles Plenum Press.

Schroeder, C. E., & Foxe, J. (2005). Multisensory contributions to low-level, "unisensory" processing. *Current Opinion in Neurobiology, 15*, 454–458. doi:10.1016/j.conb.2005.06.008

Schuemie, M. J., van der Straaten, P., Krijin, M., & Mast, C. (2001). Research on presence in virtual reality: A survey. *Journal of Cyber Psychology and Behavior, 4*(2), 183–202.

Schuemie, M. J., Van der Straaten, P., Krijn, M., & Van der Mast, C. A. P. G. (2001). Research on Presence in Virtual Reality: A Survey. *Cyberpsychology & Behavior, 4*(2), 183–201. doi:10.1089/109493101300117884

Schulzyk, O., Bongartz, J., Bildhauer, T., Hartmann, U., Herpers, R., Goebel, B., & Reinert, D. (2007). A bicycle simulator based on a motion platform in a virtual reality environment FIVIS project. In Buzug, H., Weber, B., & Kohl-Bareis, H. (Eds.), *Proceeding in Physics 114: Advances in Medical Engineering* (pp. 323–328). Berlin, New York: Springer-Verlag.

Semwal, S. K., & Evans-Kamp, D. L. (2000). Virtual environments for visually impaired. *2nd International Conference on Virtual Worlds*, Paris, France.

Sereno, M. I., Dale, A. M., Reppas, J. B., Kwong, K. K., Belliveau, J. W., & Brady, T. J. (1995). Borders of multiple visual areas in humans revealed by functional magnetic resonance imaging. *Science, 268*, 889–893. doi:10.1126/science.7754376

Shen, S., Woolley, M., & Prior, S. (2006, July). Towards culture-centred design. *Interacting with Computers, 18*(Issue 4), 820–852. doi:10.1016/j.intcom.2005.11.014

Shim, H. M., Lee, E. H., Shim, J. H., Lee, S. M., & Hong, S. H. (2005). Implementation of an intelligent walking assistant robot for the elderly in outdoor environment. *Proceedings of the 2005 IEEE 9th International Conference on Rehabilitation Robotics June 28 - July 1, 2005, Chicago, IL.*

Shoji, S., & Esashi, M. (1994). J. Micromechanics. *Microengineering, 4*, 157. doi:10.1088/0960-1317/4/4/001

Siegel, A. W., & White, S. H. (1975). The Development of Spatial Representation of Large- Scale Environments. In Reese, H. W. (Ed.), *Advances in Child Development and Behavior*. New York: Academic Press.

Siegfried, R. M. (2002) A Scripting Language to Help the Blind Program Visually. ACM SIGPLAN Notices 37/2/ pp. 53 – 56

Siegfried, R. M. (2006) Visual Programming and the Blind. ACM CIGCSE Bulletin 38/1/pp. 275-278

Silverman, D. R., & Spiker, V. A. (1997), *Ancient wisdom—future technology. Proceedings of the Human Factor and Ergonomics Society*, 41st Annual Meeting Albuquerque, New Mexico.

Sinks, S., & King, J. (1998). Adults with disabilities: perceived barriers that prevent Internet access. *In Proceedings of CSUN 1998 Conference*, Los Angeles, CA, USA, March 17–21.

Sivak, M. (1996). The information that drivers use: Is it indeed 90% visual? *Perception, 25*, 1081–1089. doi:10.1068/p251081

Sjostrom, C. (2001). *Virtual haptic search tools - the white cane in a haptic computer interface*. Ljubljana, Slovenia: In AAATE.

Sjostrom, C., Danielsson, H., Magnusson, C., & Rassmus-Grohn, K. (2003). Phantom-based haptic line graphics for blind persons. *Visual Impairment Research, 5*, 13–32. doi:10.1076/vimr.5.1.13.15972

Sjostrom, C. (2001). Designing haptic computer interfaces for blind people. *In Proceedings of the 3rd International Workshop on Website Evolution,* IEEE, 2001

Sjotrom, C., & Rassmus-Grohn, K. (1999). The sense of touch provides new computer interaction techniques for disabled people. *Technology and Disability, 10*(1), 45–52.

Slater, M. (2002). Presence and the sixth sense. *Presence (Cambridge, Mass.), 11*, 435–439. doi:10.1162/105474602760204327

Slater, M. (2004). How colourful was your day? Why questionnaires cannot assess presence in virtual environments. *Presence (Cambridge, Mass.), 13*, 484–493. doi:10.1162/1054746041944849

Slater, M., Perez-Marcos, D., Ehrsson, H. H., & Sanchez-Vives, M. V. (2009). Inducing illusory ownership of a virtual body. *Frontiers in Neuroscience, 3*(2), 214–220. doi:10.3389/neuro.01.029.2009

Slater, M., & Wilbur, S. (1997). A framework for immersive virtual environments (FIVE): Speculations on the role of presence in virtual environments. *Presence (Cambridge, Mass.)*, *6*, 603–616.

Slater, M., Usoh, M., & Steed, A. (1994). Depth of Presence in Immersive Virtual Environments. *Presence (Cambridge, Mass.)*, *3*(2), 130–144.

Slater, M., & Usoh, M. (1994). Body-Centred Interaction in Virtual Environments. In Thalmann, N. M., & Thalmann, D. (Eds.), *Artificial Life and Virtual Reality* (pp. 125–147). John Wiley and Sons.

Smeulder, A. W. M., Worring, M., Anntini, S., Gupta, A., & Jain, R. (2000). Content-Based Image Retrieval at the End of the Early Years. *IEEE Transactions on Pattern Analysis and Machine Intelligence*, *22*(12), 1349–1380. doi:10.1109/34.895972

Smith, M. L., & Milner, B. (1981). The role of the right hippocampus in the recall of spatial location. *Neuropsychologia*, *19*, 781–793. doi:10.1016/0028-3932(81)90090-7

Smith, R. M. (1984). *Learning how to learn*. Milton Keynes: Open University.

Smith, A., Dunckley, L., French, T., Minocha, S., & Chang, Y. (2004). A process model for developing usable cross-cultural websites. *Interacting with Computers*, *16*(1), 69–91. doi:10.1016/j.intcom.2003.11.005

Smith, C. M. (1997). Human factors in haptic interfaces. *Crossroads*, *3*, 14. doi:10.1145/270974.270980

Smith, J., & Chang, S. (1997). *Intelligent multimedia information Retrieval, Chapter Query by colour regions using the VisualSEEk content-based visual query system* (pp. 23–41). AAAI Press.

Smith, M. J., & Kiger, P. J. (2006), *The Lingering Reek of Smell-O-Vision*, Los Angeles Times. Available: http://www.latimes.com/ features/ magazine/ west/ a-tm-oops6feb 05,1,2932206. story?coll =la-iraq- complete [Accessed: August 21, 2007].

Somboon, P., Wyszynski, B., & Nakamoto, T. (2007a). Novel odor recorder for extending range of recordable odor. *Sensors and Actuators. B, Chemical*, *121*, 583–589. doi:10.1016/j.snb.2006.04.105

Somboon, P., Wyszynski, B., & Nakamoto, T. (2007b). Realization of recording a wide range of odor by utilizing both of transient and steady-state sensor responses in recording process. *Sensors and Actuators. B, Chemical*, *124*, 557–563. doi:10.1016/j.snb.2007.01.030

Spence, C. (2002). *The ICI report on the secret of the senses*. London: The Communication Group.

Spence, C. (2003). A new multisensory approach to health and well-being. *Essence*, *2*, 16–22.

Spence, C. (2011b). Mouth-watering: The influence of environmental and cognitive factors on salivation and gustatory/flavour perception. *Journal of Texture Studies*, *42*, 157–171. doi:10.1111/j.1745-4603.2011.00299.x

Spence, C., Bentley, D. E., Phillips, N., McGlone, F. P., & Jones, A. K. P. (2002). Selective attention to pain: A psychophysical investigation. *Experimental Brain Research*, *145*, 395–402. doi:10.1007/s00221-002-1133-6

Spence, C., & Driver, J. (1997). Cross-modal links in attention between audition, vision, and touch: Implications for interface design. *International Journal of Cognitive Ergonomics*, *1*, 351–373.

Spence, C., & Driver, J. (Eds.). (2004). *Crossmodal space and crossmodal attention*. Oxford, UK: Oxford University Press.

Spence, C., & Gallace, A. (2007). Recent developments in the study of tactile attention. *Canadian Journal of Experimental Psychology*, *61*, 196–207. doi:10.1037/cjep2007021

Spence, C., & Gallace, A. (2011). Multisensory design: Reaching out to touch the consumer. *Psychology and Marketing*, *28*, 267–308. doi:10.1002/mar.20392

Spence, C., Kettenmann, B., Kobal, G., & McGlone, F. P. (2000). Selective attention to the chemosensory modality. *Perception & Psychophysics*, *62*, 1265–1271. doi:10.3758/BF03212128

Spence, C., Levitan, C., Shankar, M. U., & Zampini, M. (2010). Does food color influence taste and flavor perception in humans? *Chemosensory Perception*, *3*, 68–84. doi:10.1007/s12078-010-9067-z

Spence, C., & Gallace, A. (2008). Making sense of touch. In Chatterjee, H. (Ed.), *Touch in museums: Policy and practice in object handling* (pp. 21–40). Oxford: Berg Publications.

Spence, C., Sanabria, D., & Soto-Faraco, S. (2007). Intersensory Gestalten and crossmodal scene perception. In Noguchi, K. (Ed.), *Psychology of beauty and Kansei: New horizons of Gestalt perception* (pp. 519–579). Tokyo: Fuzanbo International.

Spence, C. (2011a). Sound design: How understanding the brain of the consumer can enhance auditory and multisensory product/brand development. In K. Bronner, R. Hirt, & C. Ringe (Eds.), *Audio Branding Congress Proceedings 2010* (pp. 35-49). Baden-Baden, Germany: Nomos Verlag.

Spence, C., & Ho, C. (2008). Crossmodal information processing in driving. In C. Castro & L. Hartley (Eds.), *Human factors of visual performance in driving* (pp. 187-200). Boca Raton, Fl: CRC Press.

Sproull, L., & Kiesler, S. B. (1986). Reducing social context cues: Electronic mail in organizational communication. *Management Science, 32*, 1492–1512. doi:10.1287/mnsc.32.11.1492

Sreedharan, S., Zurita, E. S., & Plimmer, B. (2007). *3D Input for 3D Worlds*. Paper presented at the OzCHI Conference.

Srihari, R., & Zhang, Z. (2000). Show&Tell: A Semi-Automated Image Annotation System. *IEEE MultiMedia, 7*(3), 61–71. doi:10.1109/93.879769

Srihari R.K. (1995a) "Use of Collateral Text in Understanding Photos". Artificial Intelligence Review, special issue on Integrating Language and Vision, vol. 8, pp. 409--430.

Srihari, R. K., & Burhans, D. T. (1994) "Visual semantics: Extracting visual information from text accompanying pictures". In Proceedings of AAAI-94, pages793-798, Seattle.

Srihari, R.K. (1995b) "Computational Models for Integrating Linguistic and Visual Information: A Survey". Artificial Intelligence Review, special issue on Integrating Language and Vision, vol. 8, pp. 349--369.

Srivastava, M., Muntz, R., & Potkonjak, M. (2001). Smart Kindergarten: Sensor-based wireless networks for smart developmental problem-solving environments. In *Proceedings of the Seventh Annual International Conference on Mobile Computing and Networking*, Rome, Italy: MobiCom, 132-138.

Standley, J. M. (1991). The effect of vibrotactile and auditory stimuli on perception of comfort, heart rate, and peripheral finger temperature. *Journal of Music Therapy, 28*, 120–134.

Stankiewicz, B. J., & Kalia, A. (2004). Acquisition and Retention of Structural versus Object Landmark Knowledge When Navigating through a Large-Scale Space. *Journal of Experimental Psychology. Human Perception and Performance, 33*(2), 378–390. doi:10.1037/0096-1523.33.2.378

Stanney, K., & Salvendy, G. (1998). Aftereffects and Sense of Presence in Virtual Environments: Formulation of a Research and Development Agenda. *International Journal of Human-Computer Interaction, 10*(2), 135–187. doi:10.1207/s15327590ijhc1002_3

Stanney, K. M., & Salvendy, G. (1995). Information visualization; assisting low spatial individuals with information access tasks through the use of visual mediators. *Ergonomics, 38*(6), 1184–1198. doi:10.1080/00140139508925181

Stein, B. E., & Meredith, M. A. (1993). *The merging of the senses*. Cambridge, MA: MIT Press.

Stein, B. E., & Stanford, T. R. (2008). Multisensory integration: Current issues from the perspective of the single neuron. *Nature Reviews. Neuroscience, 9*, 255–267. doi:10.1038/nrn2331

Steiner, H., Reinert, D., & Jung, N. (2009). Combined Measurement System for the Evaluation of Multi Causal Strain. In Karsh, B.-T. (Ed.), *Ergonomics and Health Aspects of Work with Computers*. Springer. doi:10.1007/978-3-642-02731-4_22

Steingarten, J. (2002). *It must've been something I ate*. New York: Knopf.

Stern, K., & McClintock, M. K. (1998). Regulation of ovulation by human pheromones. *Nature, 392*, 177–179. doi:10.1038/32408

Steuer, J. (1992). Defining Virtual Reality:dimensions determining Telepresence. *The Journal of Communication*, 42.

Stigmar, H. (2006). Amount of Information in Mobile Maps: A Study of User Preference. *Mapping and Image Science, No. 4*, pp. 68-74.

Stivers, T. Enfield, N.J. Levinson, S.C. (2007). Person reference in interaction: Linguistic, cultural and social perspectives. Language, culture and cognition. Publisher: Cambridge: Cambridge University Press. pp.1-20.

Strickland, D., Hodges, L., North, M., & Weghorst, S. (1997). Overcoming phobias by virtual reality exposure. *Communications of the ACM, 40*, 34–39. doi:10.1145/257874.257881

Sullivan J (2009) Braille Becomes Electric: The trials and triumphs of Braille translation software. Journal of Visual Impairment & Blindness. 103/7/ pp. 389-391

Sun, H.-J., Campos, J. L., & Chan, G. S. W. (2004). Multisensory integration in the estimation of relative path length. *Experimental Brain Research, 154*(2), 246–254. doi:10.1007/s00221-003-1652-9

Sur, M., & Leamey, C. A. (2001). Development and plasticity of cortical areas and networks. *Nature Reviews. Neuroscience, 2*, 251–262. doi:10.1038/35067562

Sutherland, I. (1965) *The ultimate Display,* Paper presented at the IFIP Congress, *65, 506-508,* Information Processing

Sydlowski, A. (2009). *Offline and online character recognition using a visual input.* Thesis: Flinders University of South Australia.

Szummer, M., & Picard, R. W. (1998) "Indoor-outdoor image classification". In IEEE Int. Workshop on Content-based Access of Image and Video Databases.

Tashner, J. H., Riedl, R. E., & Bronack, S. C. (2005, January 2005). *Virtual Worlds: Further Development of Web-Based Teaching.* Paper presented at the Hawaii International Conference on Education, Honolulu, Hawaii.

Tavakoli, M., & Howe, R. D. (2008). Haptic implications of tool flexibility in surgical teleoperation (pp. 377-378). *2008 Symposium on Haptic Interfaces for Virtual Environment and Teleoperator Systems.*

Taylor, J. L., & McCloskey, D. I. (1991). Illusions of head and visual target displacement induced by vibration of neck muscles. *Brain, 114*, 755–759. doi:10.1093/brain/114.2.755

Thorndyke, P. (1980). *Performance models for spatial and locational cognition (R2676ONR).* Washington, D.C.: The Rand Corporation.

Thorndyke, P., & Hayes-Roth, B. (1982). Differences in spatial knowledge acquired from maps and navigation. *Cognitive Psychology, 14*, 560–589. doi:10.1016/0010-0285(82)90019-6

Tijou, A., Richard, E., & Richard, P. (2006) "Using Olfactive Virtual Environments for Learning Organic Molecules", *1st International Conference on Technologies for E-Learning and Digital Entertainment, Edutainment 2006*, pp. 1223.

Tominaga, K., Honda, S., Ohsawa, T., Shigeno, H., Okada, K., & Matsushita, Y. (2001). *"Friend Park"—expression of the wind and the scent on virtual space* (pp. 507–515). Proc. Virtual Systems and Multimedia.

Trantakis, C., Bootz, F., Strauss, G., Nowatius, E., Lindner, D., & Cakmak, H. (2003). Virtual endoscopy with force feedback – a new system for neurosurgical training. *International Congress Series, 1256*, 782–787. doi:10.1016/S0531-5131(03)00292-9

Trompenaars, F. (1993). *Riding the Waves of Culture: Understanding the Cultural Diversity in Business.* London: Nicholas Brealey.

Turk, M., & Robertson, G. (2001). Perceptual User Interfaces. *Communications of the ACM, 43*(3), 33–34.

Tzovaras, D., Nikolakis, G., Fergadis, G., Malasiotis, S., & Stavrakis, M. (2004). Design and implementation of haptic virtual environments for the training of the visually impaired. *IEEE Transactions on Neural Systems and Rehabilitation Engineering, 12*(2), 266–278. doi:10.1109/TNSRE.2004.828756

Uchida, Y., Naito, M., & Hirayama, S. (2007). "Kage no Sekai": interactive animation of shadow based on physical action. In *Proceedings of International Conference on Advances in Computer Entertainment Technology* (pp. 274-275).

Ungar, S., Blades, M., & Spencer, S. (1996). The construction of cognitive maps by children with visual impairments. In Portugali, J. (Ed.), *The Construction of Cognitive Maps* (pp. 247–273). Netherlands: Kluwer Academic Publishers. doi:10.1007/978-0-585-33485-1_11

Urbano, J., Terashim, K., Miyosh, T., & Kitagawa, H. (2005). Collision avoidance in an omni-directional wheelchair by using haptic feedback. *Proceedings of the 4th WSEAS International Conference on Signal Processing, Robotics and Automation, 18.*

Valéry, P. (1928). La Conquete de l'ubiquite. In *De La Musique avant toute chose*. Paris: Editions du Tambourinaire.

Vallbo, A. B., Olsson, K. A., Westberg, K.-G., & Clark, F. J. (1984). Microstimulation of single tactile afferents from the human hand: Sensory attributes related to unit type and properties of receptive fields. *Brain, 107,* 727–749. doi:10.1093/brain/107.3.727

Vallns, S. (1966). Cognitive effects of false heart-rate feedback. *Journal of Personality and Social Psychology, 4,* 400–408. doi:10.1037/h0023791

Variety staff (2001) *Variety review of "Scent of Mystery"*, Variety, Inc., Available: 16 [Accessed: August 21, 2007].

Vaspori, T., & Arato, A. (1994) Ten Years of Computer Use by Visually Impaired People in Hungary. Information Technology & Disabilities 1/3/---. Downloaded from http://people.rit.edu/easi/itd /itdv01n3/arato.htm on the 12th December 2008

Västfjäll, D. (2006). *Affecting emotional experience with auditory-vibrotactile heartbeat false feedback.* Poster presented at the 7th Annual Meeting of the International Multisensory Research Forum. Trinity College, Dublin, 18-21 June.

Vatakis, A., & Spence, C. (2010). Audiovisual temporal integration for complex speech, object-action, animal call, and musical stimuli. In Naumer, M. J., & Kaiser, J. (Eds.), *Multisensory object perception in the primate brain* (pp. 95–121). New York: Springer. doi:10.1007/978-1-4419-5615-6_7

Veletsianos, G., Heller, R., Overmyer, S., & Procter, M. (2010). Conversational agents in virtual worlds: Bridging disciplines. *British Journal of Educational Technology, 41*(1), 123–140. doi:10.1111/j.1467-8535.2009.01027.x

Verhaegh, J., Fontijn, W., & Jacobs, A. (2008). On the benefits of tangible interfaces for educational games. *Proceedings of the Second IEEE International Conference on Digital Game and Intelligent Toy Enhanced Learning (DIGITEL)*, 141-145.

Vicente, K. J., Hayes, B. C., & Williges, R. C. (1987). Assaying and isolating individual differences in searching a hierarchical file system. *Human Factors, 29*(3), 349–359.

Vila, J. Beccue B. Anandikar S. (2002). The Gender Factor in Virtual Reality Navigation and Wayfinding. *Proceedings of the 36th Hawaii International Conference on System Sciences* (HICSS'03).

Vinayagamoorthy, V., Brogni, A., Gillies, M., Slater, M., & Steed, A. (2004). *An investigation of presence response across variations in visual realism*. Paper presented at the 7th Annual International Presence Workshop.

Vinson, N. G. (1999) *Design Guidelines for Landmarks to Support Navigation in Virtual Environments*. Proceedings of CHI '99, Pittsburgh, PA.

Virginia Assistive Technology System (2004). *Assistive technology and aging: A handbook for Virginian's who are aging and their caregivers.*

Vlahos, J. (2006). The smell of war. *Polar Science, 8,* 72–95.

Vo, M. T., & Waibel, A. (1997). "Modeling and interpreting multimodal inputs: A semantic integration Approach". Technical Report CMU-CS-97-192, Carnegie Mellon University.

Vo, M. T., & Wood, C. (1996). "Building an application framework for speech and pen input integration in multimodal learning interfaces". International Conference on Acoustics, Speech and Signal Processing, IEEE Computer Society, 3545-3548.

Vygotsky, L. (1964). *Thinking and Speaking* (Hanfmann, E., & Vakar, G., Trans.). Boston: The M.I.T. Press. (Original work published 1934)

W3C (2003) NOTE 8 January 2003, "Multimodal Interaction Requirements", http://www.w3.org/TR/2003/NOTE-mmi-reqs-20030108/.

Waller, D., Hunt, E., & Knapp, D. (1998). The transfer of spatial knowledge in virtual environment training. *Presence (Cambridge, Mass.)*, *7*, 129–143. doi:10.1162/105474698565631

Waller, D., Knapp, D., & Hunt, E. (2001). Spatial Representations of Virtual Mazes: The Role of Visual Fidelity and Individual Differences. Human Factors. *The Journal of the Human Factors and Ergonomics Society*, *43*(1), 147–158. doi:10.1518/001872001775992561

Wang, Z., Li, B., Hedgpeth, T., & Haven, T. (2009). Instant Tactile-Audio Map: Enabling Access to Digital Maps for People with Visual Impairment. *International ACM Conference on Computers and Accessibility (SIGASSETS)*.

Warren, D. H., & Strelow, E. R. (1985). Electronic Spatial Sensing for the Blind. *Martinus Nijhoff Publishers*, Massachusetts. Web Content Accessibility Guidelines (WCAG) 2.0: http://www.w3.org/TR/WCAG20/

Washburn, D., & Jones, L. M. (2004). Could olfactory displays improve data visualization? *Computing in Science & Engineering*, *6*(6), 80–83. doi:10.1109/MCSE.2004.66

Washburn, D. A., & Jones, L. M. (2004). Could olfactory displays improve data visualization? *Computing in Science & Engineering*, *6*(6), 80–83. doi:10.1109/MCSE.2004.66

Washburn, D.A., Jones, L.M., Satya, R.V., Bowers, C.A. and Cortes, A. (2003) Olfactory Use in Virtual Environment Training, *Modelling and Simulation Magazine*, *2*(3).

Waters, J. (Writer) (1981). Polyester [Film]. USA: New Line Cinema.

Weber, B., Hermanns, I., Ellegast, R. P., & Kleinert, J. (2008). Assessment of Physical Activity at Workplaces. In Bust, P. (Ed.), *Contemporary Ergonomics*. Taylor & Francis, Oxfordshire.

Weinstein, S. (1968). Intensive and extensive aspects of tactile sensitivity as a function of body part, sex, and laterality. In Kenshalo, D. R. (Ed.), *The skin senses* (pp. 195–222). Springfield, Ill.: Thomas.

Westerveld, T. (2000). *Image Retrieval: Content versus Context* (pp. 276–284). Proceedings of Content-Based Multimedia Information Access.

Wickens, C. D. (2008). Multiple resources and mental workload. *Human Factors*, *50*, 449–454. doi:10.1518/001872008X288394

Wickens, C. D., Olmos, O., Chudy, A., & Davenport, C. (1997). *Aviation display support for situation awareness. University of Illinois Institute of Aviation Technical Report (ARL-97-10/LOGICON-97-2)*. Savoy, IL: Aviation Research Laboratory.

Wickens, C. D. (1980). The structure of attentional resources. In Nickerson, R. S. (Ed.), *Attention and performance* (*Vol. 8*, pp. 239–257). Hillsdale, NJ: Erlbaum.

Wickens, C. D. (1984). Processing resources in attention. In Parasuraman, R., & Davies, D. R. (Eds.), *Varieties of attention* (pp. 63–102). San Diego, CA: Academic Press.

Wiener, N. (1948). *Cybernetics or Control and Communication in the Animal and the Machine*. New York, Cambridge, MA,USA: MIT Press.

Wiener, N. (1988). *The Human Use of Human Beings:Cybernetics and Society*. Cambridge, MA, USA: Da Capo Press.

Wilkniss, S. M., Jones, M., Korel, D., Gold, P., & Manning, C. (1997). A ge related differences in an ecologically based study of route learning. *Psychology and Aging*, *12*(2), 372–375. doi:10.1037/0882-7974.12.2.372

Williams, L. E., & Bargh, J. A. (2008). Experiencing physical warmth promotes interpersonal warmth. *Science*, *322*, 606–607. doi:10.1126/science.1162548

Williams, R. (1974). *Television:Technology and Cultural Form*. London: Routledge. doi:10.4324/9780203426647

Williamson, K., Wright, S., Schauder, D., & Bow, A. (2001). The Internet for the blind and visually impaired. *J. Comput. Mediat. Commun. [Online]. Available:http://jcmc.indiana.edu/vol7* /issue1/williamson.html.

Willis, C. M., Church, S. M., & Guest, C. M. (2004). Olfactory detection of human bladder cancer by dogs: Proof of principle study. *British Medical Journal*, *329*, 712–715. doi:10.1136/bmj.329.7468.712

Wilson, P. N., Foreman, N., & Tlauka, M. (1997). Transfer of spatial information from a virtual to a real environment. *Human Factors*, *39*(4), 526–531. doi:10.1518/001872097778667988

Witkin, H. A., Moore, C. A., Goodenough, D. R., & Cox, P. W. (1977). Field dependent and field independent cognitive styles and their educational implications. *Review of Educational Research, 47*, 1–64.

Witkin, H. A. Oltman P.K. Raskin E. & Karp S.A. (1971). *A manual for the group embedded figures test*. Palo Alto, CA: Consulting Psychologists Press.

Witmer, B. G., & Singer, M. J. (1998). Measuring Presence in Virtual Environments: A Presence Questionnaire. *Presence (Cambridge, Mass.), 7*(3), 225–240. doi:10.1162/105474698565686

Witmer, B. G., Bailey, J. H., Knerr, B. W., & Parsons, K. C. (1996). Virtual spaces and real world places: transfer of route knowledge. *International Journal of Human-Computer Studies, 45*(4), 413–428. doi:10.1006/ijhc.1996.0060

Witmer B.G. Bailey J.H. & Knerr B.W. (1995), *Training Dismounted Soldiers in Virtual Environments: Route Learning and Transfer*. U.S. Army Research Institute for the Behavioral and Social Sciences

Wong, F., Nagarajan, R., & Yaacob, S. (2003) Application of Stereovision in a Navigation Aid for Blind People. Proceedings of the 2003 Joint Conference on Information, Communications and Signal Processing 2003, and the Fourth Pacific Rim Conference on Multimedia

Woolley, B. (1993). *Virtual Worlds*. Oxford, England: Blackwell Publishers.

Yamada, T., Tanikawa, T., Hirota, K., & Hirose, M. (2006) Wearable olfactory display: Using odor in outdoor environment, *Proc. IEEE Virtual Reality 2006*, pp. 199-206.

Yamada, T., Yokoyama, S., Tanikawa, T., Hirota, K., & Hirose, M. (2006). Wearable olfactory display: Using odor in outdoor environment. In *Proceedings of IEEE Virtual Reality Conference* (pp. 199-206).

Yamanaka, T., Matsumoto, R., & Nakamoto, T. (2002). Study of odor blender using solenoid valves controlled by delta-sigma modulation method. *Sensors and Actuators. B, Chemical, 87*, 457. doi:10.1016/S0925-4005(02)00300-3

Yamanaka, T., Matsumoto, R., & Nakamoto, T. (2003). Fundamental study of odor recorder for multi-component odor using recipe exploration based upon a singular value decomposition. *IEEE Sensors Journal, 3*, 468–474. doi:10.1109/JSEN.2003.815778

Yanagida, Y., Kawato, S., Noma, H., & Tetsutani, N. (2004). Personal olfactory display with nose tracking. *Proceedings of IEEE Virtual Reality Conference* (pp. 43-50). IEEE CS Press.

Yanagida, Y., Kawato, S., Noma, H., Tomono, A., & Tesutani, N. (2004). Projection based olfactory display with nose tracking. In *Proceedings of IEEE Virtual Reality* (pp. 43-50).

Yannier, N., Basdogan, C., Tasiran, S., & Sen, O. L. (2008). Using haptics to convey cause-and-effect relations in climate visualization. *IEEE Transactions on Haptics, 1*, 130–141. doi:10.1109/TOH.2008.16

Yilmaz, A., Javed, O., & Shah, M. (2006). Object tracking: A survey. *ACM Computing Surveys, 13*(4). *Article, 13*, 1–45.

Yoshimoto, S., Hamada, Y., Tokui, T., Suetake, T., Imura, M., Kuroda, Y., & Oshiro, O. (2010). Haptic canvas: dilatant fluid based haptic interaction. In *ACM SIGGRAPH 2010 Emerging Technologies* (Article No. 13).

Young, P.T. (1967) Affective Arousal in *American psychologist*, n.22, pp.32-40

Yu, W., Ramloll, R., & Brewster, S. A. (2001). Haptic graphs for blind computer users. Paper presented at the Haptic Human-Computer Interaction. *First International Workshop. In: Brewster, S.A., Murray-Smith, R. (Eds.), Lecture Notes in Computer Science, vol. 2058*, Springer, Berlin, pp. 41–51.

Yu, W., Reid, D., & Brewster, S. A. (2002). Web-based Multi-modal Graphs for Visually Impaired People. *In Proceedings of CWUAAT'02*, 97-108.

Zadeh, L. (1969). *Biological application of the theory of fuzzy sets and systems in the proceedings of an international symposium on BioCybernetics of the central nervous system* (pp. 199–206). Boston: Little Brown.

Zajicek, M., Powell, C., & Reeves, C. (1998). A Web navigation tool for the blind. *Proceedings of the ACM Conference on Assistive Technology (ASSETS)*, 204–206.

Zajicek, M., Powell, C., & Reeves, C. (1999). Web search and orientation with BrookesTalk, *In Proceedings of Tech. and Persons with Disabilities Conf.*

Zampini, M., & Spence, C. (2004). The role of auditory cues in modulating the perceived crispness and staleness of potato chips. *Journal of Sensory Science, 19*, 347–363. doi:10.1111/j.1745-459x.2004.080403.x

Zhang, Q., & Izquierdo, E. (2007). Adaptive salient block-based image retrieval in multi-feature space. *Signal Processing Image Communication, 22*, 591–603. doi:10.1016/j.image.2007.05.005

Zhao, H., Plaisant, C., Shneiderman, B., & Lazar, J. (2006). *A framework for auditory data exploration and evaluation with geo-referenced data sonification. HCIL Technical Report (HCIL-2005-28), Human-Computer Interaction Lab*. College Park, Maryland, U.S.A: University of Maryland.

Zhao, R., & Grosky, W. I. (2002). Bridging the semantic gap in image retrieval. In Shih, T. K. (Ed.), *Distributed Multimedia Databases: Techniques and Applications* (pp. 14–36). Hershey, PA: Idea Group Publishing Series. IGI Publishing.

Zhou, W., & Chen, D. (2008). Encoding human sexual chemosensory cues in the orbitofrontal and fusiform cortices. *The Journal of Neuroscience, 28*, 14416–14421. doi:10.1523/JNEUROSCI.3148-08.2008

Zhou, X. S., & Huang, S. T. (2002). Unifying Keywords and Visual Contents in Image Retrieval. *IEEE Transactions on Multimedia, 9*(2), 23–33. doi:10.1109/93.998050

Zhou, X. S., & Huang, S. T. (2000) "Image Retrieval: Feature Primitives, Feature Representation, and Relevance Feedback". IEEE Workshop on Content-based Access of Image and Video Libraries (CBAIVL-2000), in conjunction with IEEE CVPR-2000, pp. 10-13.

Zhu, Q., Xiang, K., & Hu, S. (2007). *Design an Immersive Interactive Museum in Second Life*. Paper presented at the Second Workshop on Digital Media and its Application in Museum & Heritage.

Zimler J and Keenan J M (1983) Imagery in the Congenitally Blind: How Visual are Visual Images? Journal of Experimental Psychology: Learning, Memory, and Cognition. 9 / p. 269-282.

Zimmerman, M. (1989). The nervous system in the context of information theory. In R. F. Schmidt & G. Thews, *Human physiology* (2nd complete Ed.) (pp. 166-173). Berlin: Springer-Verlag.

Zybura, M., & Eskeland, G. A. (1999). *Olfaction for Virtual Reality*. University of Washington.

About the Contributors

George Ghinea received the B.Sc. and B.Sc. (Hons) degrees in Computer Science and Mathematics, in 1993 and 1994, respectively, and the M.Sc. degree in Computer Science, in 1996, from the University of the Witwatersrand, Johannesburg, South Africa; he then received the Ph.D. degree in Computer Science from the University of Reading, United Kingdom, in 2000. He is a Reader in the School of Information Systems, Computing and Mathematics at Brunel University, United Kingdom. Dr Ghinea has over 100 refereed publications and currently leads a team of 8 research students in his fields of interest, which span perceptual multimedia, semantic media management, human computer interaction, and network security. He has co-edited three books including Digital Multimedia Perception and Design for IGI.

Stephen Gulliver received a BEng. (Hons) degree in Microelectronics, an MSc. degree (Distributed Information Systems) and a PhD in 1999, 2001, and 2004 respectively. Stephen worked within the Human Factors Integration Defence Technology Centre (HFI DTC), before getting a job as a lecturer at Brunel University (2005-2008). Now, as a lecturer within the Informatics Research Centre (IRC), a core part of Henley Business School (Reading University), his personal research relates to the area of user and pervasive Informatics. Dr. Gulliver has published in a number of related fields, including: multimedia and information assimilation, usability, key performance indicators and user acceptance. Dr Gulliver supervises research relating to topics including: VR information acquisition, extensible modelling frameworks, CRM and ERP acceptance, intelligent building systems, eye-tracking technologies and multimedia content personalisation.

Frederic Andres has been an Associate Professor in the Digital Content and Media Sciences Research Division at the National Institute of Informatics (NII) since 2000 and at The Graduate University for Advanced Studies since 2002. He received his Ph.D. from University of PARIS VI and his Doctor Habilitate (specialization: information engine) from University of Nantes, in 1993 and 2000 respectively. For more than 10 years Dr. Andres has been pursuing basic and applied research in semantic management, semantic digital library, knowledge clustering and Topic Maps. Since 2003, Dr. Andres continues to develop and to refine innovative learning based on procedural memory and related to semantic and pedagogy/didactic enrichment. His research interests include digital ecosystem, semantic digital Library, image learning ontology, immersive knowledge, and MulSeMedia. He has published more than 100 scientific papers and he produced various patents on Cost Evaluation and Modeling. In the past 5 years, he has been participating in innovative digital ecosystem projects in Luxembourg (CVCE), France (Bourgogne University), Thailand (KU, NECTEC), India (Bishop Heber College(Autonomous) and Nepal. He is project leader of the Geomedia project and Myscoper project. Dr. Frederic Andres is a senior member of ACM, a member of IEEE, of the IEEE Technical Committee on Semantic Computing and IPSJ. He is also observer in ISO SC29/WG11/MPEG and SC34/W3 on Topic Maps working groups.

* * *

Oluwakemi Ademoye received a B.Sc. degree in Computer Science, in 1996, from the University of Benin, Nigeria; she then received a M.Sc. degree in Distributed Information Systems, and a Ph.D. degree in Information Systems & Computing, from Brunel University, United Kingdom, in 2002 and 2008 respectively. Her field of research interest is focused on olfactory enhanced media and its use in virtual and augmented reality environments.

Tom Adam Frederic Anderson received a B.S. degree in Applied Mathematics and Cognitive Science from the University of California at Los Angeles, US, and a M.S. degree from the Graduate Institute of Network Learning Technology at National Central University, Taiwan, R.O.C. in July 2009. He is currently a PhD candidate in computer science at the Flinders University of South Australia. His research interests include artificial intelligence, communication, localization and networks. He is a student member of IEEE and ACM, and a Microsoft Student Partner.

Adham Atyabi received a B.Sc in Computer Engineering from Azad University of Mashad-Iran in 2002. He received his M.Sc by research from the faculty of Computer Science and Information Technology at Multimedia University in Malaysia in 2009. Currently, he is studying his PhD under Prof. Powers supervision at the School of Computer Science, Engineering and Mathematics, Flinders University and he is also a member of the Flinders University robotics team called Magician. He is a student member of IEEE and ACM, and is a PhD representative of the Australian Computing Society. His research interests include brain-computer interfaces, evolutionary algorithms, swarm technology and robotics.

Atta Badii, holds a professorial research leader position as the founding director of the Intelligent Media Systems and Services Research Laboratories (IMSS, www.imss.reading.ac.uk). Atta has maintained a strong *multi-disciplinary* academic and industrial research track record in Distributed Intelligent Systems (Assistive Technologies) as underpinned by dynamic personalised and context-aware information retrieval and mobile media distribution, pattern recognition, data intelligence, secure and trust-based *Internet of People, Things and Services* (IoPTS), semantic workflow modelling, interactive systems and secure middleware technologies for semantic interoperability of sensor networks. His work on semantic-cognitive architectures has contributed to advances in secure service-oriented interactive systems design as crucial to the vision of Ambient Intelligence and Pervasive Cooperativity of the future *Trustworthy IoPTS*. To contribute to such a vision, Atta's work has included frameworks for multi-modal interactivity control, semantic services matchmaking, digital media adaptation, workflow integration, context–aware security policy management, dynamic usability and behaviour modelling. . He has served as the scientific and technical leader and/or expert advisor of several large collaborative projects at both UK and international level. He has served on various scientific journals editorial boards and specialist conference programme committees; and is the invited chair of International Specialist Interest Groups and European Networks of Excellence.

Maria Chiara Caschera received her degree in Computer Science Engineering from the University of Rome 'La Sapienza', and the PhD in Computer Science from the 'Roma Tre' University sponsored by the MultiMedia & Modal Laboratory (M3L) of the National Research Council of Italy. She is now researcher at CNR-IRPPS (National Research Council, Institute Of Research On Population And Social Policies). She is mainly interested in Human-Computer Interaction, Multimodal Interaction, Visual Languages, Visual Interfaces and Sketch-based Interfaces and Social Network Visualization.

Zhi-Hong Chen received a PhD from the Department of Computer Science and Information Engineering at National Central University, Taiwan, R.O.C. He is currently a post-doctoral researcher in the Graduate Institute of Network Learning Technology at National Central University. His research interests include game based learning, virtual animal companions and technology enhanced learning.

Helen Farley is a lecturer in virtual worlds at the Australian Digital Futures Institute (ADFI) at the University of Southern Queensland, and a lecturer in higher education within the Teaching and Educational Development Institute (TEDI) at the University of Queensland. Helen was an early pioneer in the use of Second Life in the Australian university context. Her build, UQ Religion Bazaar, attracted numerous accolades and widespread media attention. Helen's current research focuses on immersion in 3D virtual environments, authentic movement in virtual environments and the educational affordances of the Nintendo Wii. She in demand as a facilitator for workshops about technology-enriched learning spaces, incorporating elearning into the curriculum and teaching in virtual worlds.

Fernando Ferri received the degrees in Electronics Engineering in 1990 and the PhD in Medical Informatics in 1993 from the University of Rome "La Sapienza". He is currently senior researcher at the National Research Council of Italy. From 1993 to 2000 he was professor of "Sistemi di Elaborazione" at the University of Macerata. From 1996 to 2001 he was researcher at the National Research Council of Italy. He is the author of more than 150 papers in international journals, books and conferences. He has been responsible of several projects funded by Italian Ministry of University and Research and European Commission. His main methodological areas of interest are: Human-Computer Interaction, Visual Languages, Visual Interfaces, Sketch-based Interfaces, and Multimodal Interfaces and languages, Data and knowledge bases, Geographic Information Systems, Web technologies, Social Networks and Risk governance.

Patrizia Grifoni received the MS degree in Electronics Engineering in 1990. From 1994 to 2000 she was professor of "Elaborazione digitale delle immagini" at the University of Macerata. She is currently researcher at the National Research Council of Italy (2001-2007). She is the author of more than 110 papers in international journals, books and conferences. She has been responsible of several projects funded by Italian and International Institutions. Her scientific interests have evolved from Query Languages for statistical and Geographic Databases to the focal topics related to Human-Computer Interaction, Multimodal Interaction and languages, Visual Languages, Visual Interfaces, Sketch-based Interfaces, Web technologies, social networks and Risk governance.

Ulrich Hartmann studied physics in Heidelberg and Göttingen. The main focus of his studies was on medical physics. After having received his diploma in 1995 he started his PhD in Leipzig at the

Max-Planck-Institute for Cognitive Neuroscience working in the field of finite element modelling for neurological problems. In 1998 he took the position as a research staff member at the NEC Research Labs. Here, he continued his work on finite element models in medicine. In 2001 he became professor of medical engineering at the University of Applied Sciences Koblenz where he is responsible for the biomechanics and the VR laboratories.

Simon Hayhoe is founding editor of the website blindnessandarts.com and is a researcher of blindness, technology and visual culture. In addition Simon has taught ICT, design and computing, and published a number of monographs on this topic, including God Money & Politics and Arts Culture & Blindness. In intervening years, he has also researched educational attainment at the universities of London and Toronto. Simon is currently involved in philosophical and social research as a visiting academic at the London Scool of Economics, and consultation in the field of arts and blindness for Art Beyond Sight (New York) and the Beyond Sight Foundation (Mumbai). He also writes on this subject as an honorary school teacher visitor at Pembroke College, Cambridge University.

Rainer Herpers is working since 1999 at the Department of Computer Science of Bonn-Rhine-Sieg University of Applied Sciences. He also is adjunct professor at two Canadian universities, since 2001 at York University in Toronto and since 2002 at the University of New Brunswick in Fredericton. He graduated at RWTH Aachen University in 1991 and did his PhD in 1997 at the Faculty of Engineering of Kiel University. During 1998 and 1999 he worked as a scientific co-worker at York University in Toronto. His research focuses are Image Processing, Computer Graphics and Computer Vision as well as Medical Computer Science and Health Telematics.

Masataka Imura received B.S. and M.S. in physics from Kyoto University, Japan, in 1996 and 1998, respectively. He then received M.E. and Ph.D. in information science from Nara Institute of Science and Technology, Japan, in 2000 and 2001, respectively. He is currently an associate professor at Osaka University, working in the fields of virtual reality, computer graphics, and biomedical engineering.

Hiroshi Ishida was born in Morgantown, WV, in 1970. He received M.E. and Ph.D. degrees in electrical and electronic engineering from the Tokyo Institute of Technology, Tokyo, Japan, in 1994 and 1997, respectively. From 1997 to 2004, he was a research associate of the Tokyo Institute of Technology. From 1998 to 2000, he visited the School of Chemistry and Biochemistry, Georgia Institute of Technology, Atlanta, GA, as a postdoctoral fellow. In 2004, he joined the Department of Mechanical Systems Engineering at the Tokyo University of Agriculture and Technology, Tokyo, Japan, where he is currently an associate professor. In 2007, he was a visiting researcher in the AASS Research Centre, Örebro University, Sweden. His research interests are in mobile robot olfaction and olfactory displays.

Xi-Bin Jia received a doctoral degree in applied computer technology from Beijing University of Technology (BJUT), P.R.C., in 2006. She is a member of the Beijing Key Laboratory of Multimedia and Intelligent Software Technology and an associate professor at the College of Computer Science at BJUT. She was Visiting Scholar at Flinders University Artificial Intelligence Laboratories in 2009. She is an IEEE member. Her research interests include visual speech processing, expression perception and video analysis.

Nikolaos Kaklanis is a PhD candidate at the University of Surrey, UK. He received the Diploma degree in Information and Communication Systems Engineering from the University of the Aegean, Greece in 2005 and the MSc in Advanced Communication Systems from the Aristotle University of Thessaloniki, Greece in 2008. His main research interests include 3D virtual environments, assistive technologies, data mining, haptic and multimodal user interfaces. His involvement in these research areas has led to his participation in the authoring of 6 papers in international conferences. He is a contributor in the development of UsiXML. He is also a member of the Technical Chamber of Greece.

Michael Kutz studied Computer Science at Bonn-Rhine-Sieg University of Applied Science. During 2006 and 2009 he worked as a scientific co-worker in the local Department of Computer Science in the context of the FIVIS project as a developer of the simulation software, in particular of the traffic simulation sub system. He received the degree Master of Science from the Bonn- Rhine-Sieg University of Applied Sciences in 2009. In his studies he focused mainly on software engineering, multi media, artificial intelligence and usability. Since 2009 he works as a software developer in an Open Source Software Company.

Markos Kyritsis graduated with a BSc (Hons) in Computer Science in 2002. He successfully completed a part-time PhD in 2009, which focused on Virtual Reality Training. Despite spending his time working as a developer for a variety of I.T. companies, he has published widely in the area of Spatial Knowledge Acquisition. His research interests include: Virtual Reality information acquisition and training, interaction on small hand-held devices, and gaming (especially 3D games).

Richard Leibbrandt earned his doctoral degree in computer science from Flinders University of South Australia. He has a background in Cognitive Psychology and Computer Science, and has several research publications in the fields of Embodied Conversational Agents and Language Development. His other interests include natural language processing, and mathematical treatments of psychological similarity.

Trent W. Lewis is a cognitive scientist who has broad interests in human and machine learning. He completed a PhD in the area of audio-visual speech processing, which explored techniques for fusing data from acoustic and visual input. He is currently a postdoctoral research fellow on the ARC/NHMRC Special Research Initiative the Thinking Head Project at the Artificial Intelligence Laboratories, Flinders University, investigating perceptual interfaces and learning behavior of anthropomorphic virtual agents.

Martin Holger Luerssen received a B.Sc. (Hons) degree in Cognitive Science and a Ph.D. in Evolutionary Computation from the Flinders University of South Australia in 2006. He is presently employed as a postdoctoral research fellow on the Thinking Head project, a Special Research Initiative by the Australian government that targets the development of intelligent Embodied Conversational Agents (ECAs). Martin's research interests include nature-inspired computing and effective audiovisual embodiment. He is an IEEE member.

Haruka Matsukura was born in Tochigi, Japan, in 1987. She received B.E. and M.E. degrees in mechanical systems engineering from the Tokyo University of Agriculture and Technology in 2009 and

2010, respectively. She is currently a Research Fellow of the Japan Society for the Promotion of Science, and pursuing her Ph.D. degree in mechanical systems engineering. Her research interest is in olfactory display systems and their applications.

Takeshi Matsumoto was awarded a PhD by the School of Computer Science, Engineering and Mathematics, Flinders University of South Australia, in 2010, for his research on Intelligent Systems and Artificial Intelligence. His research interests include epigenetic robotics, scene modelling, and ontology.

Marissa Milne received a combined B.Ed/B.Sc in Computer Science from Flinders University of South Australia, where she is currently undertaking a PhD. Her research interests include artificial intelligence, human-computer interfaces, embodied conversational agents as virtual tutors and human and computer learning. She is a student member of IEEE and ACM.

Konstantinos Moustakas received the Diploma degree and the PhD in electrical and computer engineering from the Aristotle University of Thessaloniki, Greece, in 2003 and 2007 respectively. He has been a teaching assistant in the same department (2004-2007) and a visiting lecturer during 2008-2009. He served as a research associate in the Informatics and Telematics Institute Centre for Research and Technology Hellas, Thessaloniki (2003-2007), where he is currently a post-doctoral research fellow. His main research interests include virtual reality, 3D content-based search, collision detection, haptics, deformable object modeling and simulation and stereoscopic image processing. During the latest years, he has been the (co)author of more than 60 papers in refereed journals, edited books, and international conferences. He serves as a regular reviewer for several technical journals. He has been also involved in nine research projects funded by the EC and the Greek secretariat of Research and Technology. He is a member of the IEEE, the IEEE Computer Society and the Technical Chamber of Greece.

Gianluca Mura is a transdisciplinary media researcher, architect, designer and artist. Researcher at the Politecnico di Milano University and Universidade Catolica Portuguesa, Porto, he holds a Phd in Industrial Design and Multimedia Communication from the Politecnico di Milano University. His research area is within interrelations among Design, Architecture, Art, Science, Technology. Founder and Editor of the International Scientific Journal of Art, Culture and Design Technologies(IJACDT), he is a member of several International Scientific Committees: Cae Computational Aesthetics, Artech, Cyberworlds, Webstudies, IEEE Italian Committee, Mimos(Italian Movement on Modeling and Simulation).He organized the International Workshop "Virtuality in Arts and Design" between Politecnico di Milano and Ecole du Louvre, Paris with the High Patronage of Italian Ministry of Foreign Affairs,Rome, Italy. His recent digital artwork "The Metaplastic Constructor" has been exhibited on the Museum of Modern Art of Toluca, Mexico and into the Rhizome Artbase digital art collection. He is doing research, publishes artworks and actively participates in numerous international meetings on digital culture.

Takamichi Nakamoto received his B.Eng. and M.Eng. degrees from the Tokyo Institute of Technology in 1982 and 1984, respectively. In 1991, he earned his PhD degree in the Electrical and Electronic Engineering from the same institution. He worked for Hitachi in the area of VLSI design automation from 1984 to 1987. In 1987, he joined the Tokyo Institute of Technology as a research associate. He has been an Associate Professor at the Department of Electrical and Electronics Engineering, Tokyo Institute of Technology since 1993. From 1996 to 1997, he was a visiting scientist at the Pacific Northwest Laboratories, Richland, WA, USA. His research interests cover chemical sensing system, acoustic wave sensor, olfaction in virtual reality and LSI design.

Mary Kim Ngo is a second year Ph. D student in the Crossmodal Research Laboratory in the Department of Experimental Psychology at Oxford University. Her research focuses on the effects of multisensory spatial and temporal cuing on visual perception and target identification. Specifically, she is interested in the application of auditory and tactile cues as warning signals for assisting in collision avoidance and traffic management systems in the automotive and aviation industries. Mary is a recipient of the Clarendon Fund Scholarship from the University of Oxford.

David M. W. Powers is a specialist in unsupervised learning and signal processing, with a focus on biologically plausible acquisition and modeling of natural language and grounded ontology. He took his PhD in this area from the University of New South Wales in 1989, and is the author of a monograph, some edited works, and 200 papers in the fields of artificial intelligence, cognitive science and distributed processing. Currently, Professor Powers is Director of the Artificial Intelligence and Language Technology Laboratories at the Flinders University of South Australia.

David Scherfgen is a scientific co-worker in the Department of Computer Science at the Bonn-Rhine-Sieg University of Applied Sciences in Sankt Augustin. He started working in the FIVIS project as a student assistant in 2007 and continued his work in the project after receiving the Bachelor degree in 2008 as a scientific co-worker during his Master studies. He contributed physics systems and implemented the visualisation in the system. His primary fields of interest are computer graphics and game development. He has developed a number of freeware computer games and published a book on the topic.

Oliver Schulzyk studied physical education at the DSHS in Cologne, and then continued his studies at the RheinAhrCampus Remagen and obtained a diploma in Applied Physics. He was then working on the realisation of a bicycle simulator and was holding classes in informatics at the same university. Now he´s working in Neuchâtel, Switzerland and does After Sales Service on Sun Simulators.

Charles Spence is the head of the Crossmodal Research Laboratory at the Department of Experimental Psychology, Oxford University (http://www.psy.ox.ac.uk/xmodal/default.htm). He is interested in how people perceive the world around them. In particular, how our brains manage to process the information from each of our different senses (such as smell, taste, sight, hearing, and touch) to form the extraordinarily rich multisensory experiences that fill our daily lives. His research focuses on how a better understanding of the human mind will lead to the better design of multisensory foods, products, interfaces, and environments in the future. His research calls for a radical new way of examining and understanding the senses that has major implications for the way in which we design everything from household products to mobile phones, and from the food we eat to the places in which we work and live. He is currently working on problems associated with the design of foods that maximally stimulate the senses with a number of the world's foremost food providers. Charles has acted as a consultant for a number of multinational companies advising on various aspects of multisensory design, packaging, branding, and atmospherics over the past decade, including Unilever, Procter & Gamble, ICI, McDonalds,

Starbucks, Quest, Firmenich, Britvic, Neurosense, Baiersdorf, Starbucks, Mother, JCPR, Thorntons, The Communications Group, and The Fat Duck restaurant. Charles has published more than 350 articles in top-flight scientific journals over the last decade. Charles has been awarded the 10th Experimental Psychology Society Prize, the British Psychology Society: Cognitive Section Award, the Paul Bertelson Award, recognizing him as the young European Cognitive Psychologist of the Year, and, most recently, the prestigious Friedrich Wilhelm Bessel Research Award from the Alexander von Humboldt Foundation in Germany.

Caroline Steel is a lecturer in Higher Education (eLearning) at the Teaching and Educational Development Institute (TEDI) at The University of Queensland, Australia. She is also Vice President of the Australasian Society for Computers in Learning in Tertiary Education (ascilite) – see www.ascilite.org. Caroline's research is focused on the integration of current and emerging learning technologies primarily in university education. She is particularly interested in the role of teacher beliefs, affordance theories and learning design in relation to university learning and teaching in virtual (LMS, Virtual worlds, 3D, Web 2.0 and beyond) and physical learning spaces and through mobile technologies and personalised learning environments. Caroline has been working with Dr Helen Farley to investigate the potential and application of immersion in MulSeMedia Virtual Reality in universities in Australia, Asia, the UK, USA and Europe.

Kenneth Treharne received his B.Sc in is a PhD candidate at Flinders University of South Australia. He is a researcher in the Flinders Artificial Intelligence Laboratories. His research interests include human factors, human-computer interaction, and interface development.

Dimitrios Tzovaras received the Diploma degree in electrical engineering and the Ph.D. degree in 2-D and 3-D image compression from Aristotle University of Thessaloniki, Thessaloniki, Greece, in 1992 and 1997, respectively. He is a Senior Researcher in the Informatics and Telematics Institute of Thessaloniki. Prior to his current position, he was a Senior Researcher on 3-D imaging at the Aristotle University of Thessaloniki. His main research interests include virtual reality, assistive technologies, 3-D data processing, medical image communication, 3-D motion estimation, and stereo and multiview image sequence coding. His involvement with those research areas has led to the coauthoring of more than 50 papers in refereed journals and more than 100 papers in international conferences. He has served as a regular reviewer for a number of international journals and conferences. Since 1992, he has been involved in more than 40 projects in Greece, funded by the EC, and the Greek Secretariat of Research and Technology. Dr. Tzovaras is a member of the Technical Chamber of Greece.

Arianna D'Ulizia received the M.S. degree in computer science engineering from the University of Rome 'La Sapienza', Rome, Italy, in 2005 and the Ph.D. degree in computer science and automation from the University 'Roma Tre', Rome, in 2009. She is currently a Researcher with the Institute of Research on Population and Social Policies, National Research Council of Italy, Rome. She is the author of more than 30 papers in international journal, conferences and books. She is mainly interested in human-computer interaction, multimodal interaction, visual languages, geographical query languages, risk governance, and knowledge management in virtual communities.

Yean-Fu Wen received an M.S. degree from the Department of Information Management, National Taiwan University of Science Technology, Taiwan, R.O.C., in 1998. He earned his doctoral degree from the Department of Information Management, National Taiwan University in 2007. In 2008 he joined the Department of Management Information Systems, National Chiayi University, Taiwan, R.O.C., as an assistant professor. His research interests include network planning and management, performance optimization, and cross-layer technology in next-generation wireless networks. He is a member of IEEE.

Shunsuke Yoshimoto received the B.S. degree in Osaka University, Japan, in 2009. He then received M.S. degree in biomedical engineering from Osaka University in 2010. His research covers several haptic and tactile topics and applications.

Meng Zhu received his BSc degree in computer science from Dalian Polytechnic University China in 2003. He subsequently took the Masters degree course on Internet Computing at the University of Surrey, UK and was awarded the MSc degree in 2004. In 2006, He joined Intelligent Media Systems and Services (IMSS) Research Centre at University of Reading UK as a Research Assistant where he conducted his PhD studies in the area of multi-modal multimedia indexing and retrieval. His research interests focus on collateral semantics-based modelling and metadata enhancements to support enhanced retrieval efficiency in large multimedia repositories, and computer vision, particularly biologically inspired methodologies, etc. His work has been published in learned journals and invited book chapters.

Index